MUSIC
IN
AMERICAN LIFE

MUSIC IN AMERICAN LIFE

An Encyclopedia of the Songs, Styles, Stars, and Stories That Shaped Our Culture

Volume 1
A–C

Jacqueline Edmondson, Editor

AN IMPRINT OF ABC-CLIO, LLC
Santa Barbara, California • Denver, Colorado • Oxford, England

Library of Congress Cataloging-in-Publication Data

Music in American life : an encyclopedia of the songs, styles, stars, and stories that shaped our culture / Jacqueline Edmondson, editor.
volumes cm.
Includes bibliographical references and index.
ISBN 978-0-313-39347-1 (hardcover : alk. paper) — ISBN 978-0-313-39348-8 (ebook)
1. Music—United States—Encyclopedias. 2. Music—United States—Bio-bibliography.
I. Edmondson, Jacqueline, 1967– editor.
ML101.U6M87 2013
780.973'03—dc23 2012049968

ISBN: 978-0-313-39347-1
EISBN: 978-0-313-39348-8

17 16 15 14 13 1 2 3 4 5

This book is also available on the World Wide Web as an eBook.
Visit www.abc-clio.com for details.

Greenwood
An Imprint of ABC-CLIO, LLC

ABC-CLIO, LLC
130 Cremona Drive, P.O. Box 1911
Santa Barbara, California 93116-1911

This book is printed on acid-free paper ♾
Manufactured in the United States of America

Contents

Alphabetical List of Entries

Volume 2

Volume 3

Volume 4

Guide to Related Topics

In the following lists the main entries in this book are arranged under broad topics.

Art

Album Art
Artist Musicians
Rock Concert Posters
Sheet Music Covers

Dance

Dance Instruction and Music
Electronic Dance Music and Youth Culture
Powwow Music and Dance
Proms and High School Dances

Education

Conservatories and Music Schools
Dance Instruction and Music
Education and Music
Ethnomusicology
Music Teachers
Musicology

Ethnic, Regional, and Special Interest

African American Influences on American Music
African American Women's Influences on American Music
Asian American Music
Barrio Rhythm
Border Music
Cajun and Creole Music
Conjunto
Deaf Music Culture
Disabilities and Music
Dixieland Jazz
Hawaiian Music
Jamaican Music in America
Jewish American Music and Musicians
Latin Music in America
Lesbian, Gay, Bisexual, and Transgender Artists
Mardi Gras Music
Middle Eastern Music in America
Musical Preferences, Cultural Identities, and Demographics
Native American Music
Powwow Music and Dance
Rockabilly
Route 66 Cities, Neighborhoods, and Music Culture
Russian Music in America
Salsa
Slave Songs
Southern Rock
Steel-Band Music
Taiko Drumming in America
Tejano Music
Waila
World Music
Zydeco

Events

Hurricane Katrina and Music
Mardi Gras Music
September 11th Commemorations

Holidays

Christmas Music, Contemporary
Halloween and Horror Recordings

Electronica
European Music in America
Fight Songs
Film Music
Folk Music
Free Jazz
Funk and Postpsychedelic Funk
Fusion
Garage Bands
Glam Rock
Gothic Rock
Grunge
Halloween and Horror Recordings
Hawaiian Music
Hip-Hop
Honky-Tonk Music
Idioms in American Music
Improvisation
Indie Rock
Industrial Music
Jam Bands
Jamaican Music in America
Jazz
Jazz, Women in
Latin Music in America
Lounge Music
Marching Bands
Metal
Middle Eastern Music in America
Military Bands and Songs
Minimalism
Motown
Musical Theater
Muzak
Native American Music
New Age Music
New Wave
Opera in America
Polka
Pop Music
Powwow Music and Dance
Prison Music
Progressive Rock
Psychedelic Music
Punk Rock
R&B
Ragtime
Rap and Rappers
Rock Musicals
Rock 'n' Roll (Rock)
Rock 'n' Roll (Rock), Women In
Rockabilly
Roots Music
Russian Music in America
Sacred Music
Salsa
Shaker Songs
Shape Note Singing
Ska
Slave Songs
Soap Opera Music
Soul
Southern Rock
Steel-Band Music
Studio Musicians
Super Bowl Half-Time Shows
Surf Music
Swing Music
Taiko Drumming in America
Tejano Music
Tribute Bands
Twee Pop
Vaudeville and Burlesque
Waila
Western Films and Music
World Music
Zydeco

Musical Groups

Aerosmith
Allman Brothers
B-52s, The
Beach Boys, The
Blues Brothers, The
Crosby, Stills & Nash
Dave Matthews Band
Dixie Chicks
Doors, The
Eagles
Fleetwood Mac
Four Seasons, The
Grateful Dead
Green Day
Haley, Bill, and His Comets
Indigo Girls
Jefferson Airplane
KISS
Lynyrd Skynyrd
Mamas and the Papas, The
Martha and the Vandellas
Metallica
Mormon Tabernacle Choir
New York Dolls
Nirvana
Parliament and Funkadelic
Pearl Jam
Peter, Paul and Mary
R.E.M.

Rage Against the Machine
Ramones
Red Hot Chili Peppers
Rock Bottom Remainders
Supremes, The
Talking Heads
Velvet Underground, The
Violent Femmes

Orchestras, Bands, and Choirs

Choruses, Men's
Choruses, Women's
Community Bands
Marching Bands
Military Bands and Songs
Mormon Tabernacle Choir
Orchestras
Orchestras, Pit

Organizations

American Federation of Musicians
Musical Societies
National Music Organizations
Philadelphia Folklore Project, The
Recording Industry Association of America
Young Concert Artists, Inc.

People

Adams, John Coolidge
Amos, Tori
Armstrong, Louis
Astaire, Fred
Autry, Gene
Badu, Erykah
Baez, Joan
Basie, William "Count"
Benatar, Pat
Benson, George
Berlin, Irving
Bernstein, Leonard
Berry, Chuck
Beyoncé
Brooks, Garth
Brown, James
Browne, Jackson
Buffet, Jimmy
Cage, John
Carey, Mariah
Carter Family, The
Cash, Johnny
Chapin, Harry
Charles, Ray
Checker, Chubby
Cher
Cline, Patsy
Clinton, George
Cobain, Kurt
Cole, Nat King
Coltrane, John
Combs, Sean
Cooper, Alice
Copland, Aaron
Cotten, Elizabeth "Libba"
Croce, Jim
Crosby, Bing
Crow, Sheryl
Davis, Gary (Reverend)
Davis, Miles
Denver, John
Diamond, Neil
Diddley, Bo
Domino, Fats
Dorsey, Jimmy, and Dorsey, Tommy
Dylan, Bob
Elfman, Danny
Ellington, Duke
Fitzgerald, Ella
Fleck, Bela
Foster, Stephen Collins
Franklin, Aretha
Garcia, Jerry
Garfunkel, Art
Garland, Judy
Gaye, Marvin
Gershwin, George
Gershwin, Ira
Gillespie, Dizzy
Glass, Philip
Goodman, Benny
Grandmaster Flash
Guthrie Family
Guy, Buddy
Hancock, Herbie
Hendrix, Jimi
Hill, Lauryn
Holiday, Billie
Holly, Buddy
Hooker, John Lee
Hurt, Mississippi John
Hynde, Chrissie
Ives, Charles
Jackson Family
Jackson, Michael
James, Etta
Jay-Z
Jefferson, Blind Lemon
Jett, Joan
Jewel
Joel, Billy
Johnson, Robert

Phenomena and Trends

Audiences
Awards and Prizes for Music
B-Side, The
Boy Bands
Brothers in Music
Children's Musical Lives
Clothing Styles and Musicians
Collaborations in Music
Commercial Successes in Music
Concerts for Social Causes
Controversies in Music
Counterculture in American Music
Cover Songs
Crossovers
Deadheads
Death and Violence in American Music
Disabilities and Music
Drugs and Music
Electronic Dance Music and Youth Culture
Environmental Activism in Music
Environmental Changes and Music
Expatriate Musicians in the United States
Family Values in Music
Fanzines
Fictional Composers
Food and Music
Fools and Foolish Behavior in Song
Gender and the Music Industry
Generation Gaps in Music
Groupies
Hip-Hop Nation
Historically Informed Performance
House, Edward James "Son," Jr.
Impossible Music Sessions, The
Karaoke
Language of Music in Everyday Life, The
Lesbian, Gay, Bisexual, and Transgender Artists
Life Stories of Musicians
Little Red Songbook
Mathematics in American Music
Murders and Murderers
Music Magazines and Journalism
Music Making at Home
Music Patrons and Supporters
Music Therapy
Musical Preferences, Cultural Identities, and Demographics
Musicians as Actors
National Identity in Music
Nonsense Lyrics
Notorious Musicians
Obesity in Song
One-Hit Wonders
Opening Tracks
Patriotic Music
Performance Artists
Professional Music Making
Psychology of Music
Remixes
Roadies
Rock Concert Posters
Rock 'n' Roll Record, First
Route 66 Cities, Neighborhoods, and Music Culture
School, Songs About
Second-Generation Musicians
Senior Citizens and Music
Sex and Sexuality in the Music Industry
Sheet Music Covers
Siblings in American Music
Silence in Music
Sisters in Music
Social Causes of Musicians
Soldiers and Military Personnel
Songsters
Sports and Music
Street Performing in America
Teen and Youth Heavy Hitters
Torture and Punishment through Music
Toys and Music
27 Club
Unusual Techniques and Uses of Musical Instruments
U.S. Presidents as Musicians
Voice Changes and Singing
War and Music

Places.
See Venues and Places

Recording and Records
Analog vs. Digital Recording
Animated Sound
B-Side, The
Christmas Music, Contemporary
Digital Music
Distortion and Feedback
Opening Tracks
Record Collecting
Recording Industry
Recording Industry Association of America
Studio Musicians
Vinyl Records
Walls of Sound

Religious and Spiritual Expression
African American Gospel Music
African American Influences on American Music
African American Spiritual Music
Alaskan Native Music

Social Causes and Protests

Technology

Venues and Places

Women

Preface

Music permeates life in the United States, and Americans of all ages spend a great deal of their daily lives surrounded by and engaged with it in both public and private places. Music is piped continually through sound systems in public spaces and incorporated into activities ranging from sporting events to political campaigns, shopping, religious observances, and the Occupy Wall Street movement. YouTube, iTunes, Pandora radio, and a multitude of computer and smartphone apps allow immediate and ongoing access to countless songs, videos, concerts, and artists. This was not always the case; just over a hundred years ago, people had to rely primarily on live performances to hear music. But advances in technology during the past century have allowed music to become integral to every aspect of life, from playlists new mothers assemble to help them through childbirth to songs and tributes that are part of memorial and funeral services. Distinct music is played during holidays and special occasions, reflecting a range of traditions in the United States. Music is closely linked to friendships, love affairs, memories, and identities. The intent of these volumes is to capture some of the many ways that music affects life and culture in the United States, as well as the ways American culture in all its complexities influences music.

About This Book

Music in American Life: The Songs, Styles, Stars, and Stories That Shaped Our Culture is a four-volume encyclopedia intended for high school and undergraduate students, music students, musicians, and general readers who have an interest in music and its connections to American culture. The entries cover a wide range of high-interest topics and artists, extending readers' understanding of and appreciation for the significant role music has played in American life. These volumes contextualize and explain the varieties and influences of music, taking our current knowledge and often tracing the topics or people historically to consider why and how they came to be as we presently find them.

The topics and resources in these volumes include singers, composers, lyricists, songs, musical genres, cultures, places, instruments, technologies, music in films and on television, cultural periods, uniquely American music ("bubblegum rock," garage bands, gospel, *Little Red Song Book,* the Mormon Tabernacle Choir), magazines and Web sites, and much more. One goal is to make explicit the extent to which music is an integral aspect of American culture, contributing to the ways in which Americans mediate and understand the world. These volumes will provoke readers to think about music and its influences in new and different ways, examine commonplace assumptions about music, and provide rich and accurate information.

These four volumes include more than five hundred alphabetically arranged entries, ranging from five hundred to six thousand words in length. These essays were written by more than 280 musicians, scholars, critics, and industry experts from the United States, Canada, Australia, and the United Kingdom, who offer a range of perspectives and insights. Entries are clear and concise, and many include sidebars for additional information.

Not every artist, band, or topic can be included as a main entry, but across the volumes readers will find a very comprehensive treatment of American music and musicians in many forms and contexts. Entries are cross-referenced to help readers navigate to more information, and an extensive index is included at the end of the set.

Special Features

It is hoped that this reference work will support student research not only by presenting valuable information about a wide range of topics related to American music and culture, but also by providing suggestions for further resources at the ends of all entries. A timeline in volume 1 is a concise guide to music in American culture, from pre-Columbian times to the present. A selected general bibliography at the end of the final volume provides further recommended reading, and a discography of select collected works, arranged by broad genre, lists some of the best recordings for readers to sample the artists and music profiled in this encyclopedia. A list of authoritative Web sites related to music also directs users to additional rich sources of information for further research.

Acknowledgments

I wish to thank Peter Buckland for his work as a research assistant and author on this project. Peter brought sharp insight, critique, and creativity to the project as it took shape. He was especially helpful in making sure metal music was visible throughout.

Anne Thompson was a wonderful editor and resource as we worked through various stages of this project.

I also wish to thank my sons, Jacob and Luke, and my husband Michael, for their ongoing support of my work, and their willingness to discuss this project and provide candid responses.

Introduction

American music is intertwined with music from around the world, so it is neither possible nor desirable to draw firm lines around what "American music" is. It has been said that jazz is distinctly American, yet it has been influenced by music from all parts of the world. Musicians who relocated to the United States, whether escaping from war and persecution or attempting to advance their careers, have also had a profound impact on American music and culture, bringing with them the influences of their home countries and cultures. Composers like Aaron Copland (1900–1990) tried to create a distinctly American music, yet his work was influenced by his studies with Nadia Boulanger in Paris; travels to work with composer Carlos Chávez in Mexico and to Africa and Europe; and interests in jazz, minimalism, and other forms of music. American music is not created and does not exist in isolation from other parts of the world.

Music in the United States reflects the complex and diverse social identities found in the country. Various genres, musical instruments, and approaches to performance reflect the varieties of socioeconomic, ethnic, racial, gender, generational, religious, and sexual orientations found in communities across the United States. Increasingly, barriers between what used to be considered high culture (classical music, orchestral performances, opera, etc.) and low culture (rock 'n' roll, blues, soul, etc.) are breaking down and merging, creating exciting possibilities and opportunities for diverse musical engagements. There are rich examples of this. The minimalist American composer Steve Reich (1936–) reimagined songs by the English rock band Radiohead (1985–present) into classical pieces that premiered at the Royal Festival Hall in London. On August 1, 2008, which would have been Jerry Garcia's sixty-sixth birthday, the Baltimore Symphony Orchestra played a concert of Grateful Dead music in tribute to the band. American banjo player Béla Fleck (1958–) performs music by Johann Sebastian Bach at concerts, as well as jazz, pop, country, and other genres.

Racial, social, sexual, and gender boundaries can be broken down by music. Elvis Presley (1935–1977) brought the sound of African American singers like Big Mamma Thornton (1926–1984) to broader audiences. Dick Clark's television show *American Bandstand* (shown from 1952 to 1989) featured African American artists and integrated audiences from the time of some of its earliest shows in the 1950s. In other performances, Billie Holiday's (1915–1959) rendition of "Strange Fruit" and Marvin Gaye's (1939–1984) "What's Going On" exposed racism and violence. Artists such as Lou Reed (1942–), Madonna (1958–), Prince (1958–), and Lady Gaga (1986–) challenge commonly accepted norms about sexuality and gender. Deaf culture has its own music and performers.

Although music used to be easily identifiable by decade, increasingly artists are incorporating sounds and styles from previous decades in their music, blurring time and place. British singer Adele's (1988–) music makes gestures toward American soul singer Etta James (1938–2012) and British artist Dusty Springfield (1939–1999), with her mixture of rhythm and blues and soul. Groups like the Black Eyed Peas (1992–present) and LMFAO (2006–present) have songs that evoke 1990s club music, rife with pounding beats and techno-pop sounds. Lady Gaga draws on 1980s sounds. The clear epoch-defining genres that existed in the past, like the distinctness of psychedelic music (1960s), disco (1970s), new wave (1980s), and grunge (1990s), no longer exist. Instead, artists blur genres and bend formerly accepted rules, drawing on the past to bring its sounds to contemporary technologies and audiences.

Music is not just for entertainment. It is used to improve health, sell commercial products ranging from cola to cars, and provide a sound track to the historical timelines of our lives. New age music is noted for its relaxing effects and opportunities to explore mind–body connections. The song "I'd Like to Teach the World to Sing" is associated with Coca-Cola products, and Audi used Woody Guthrie's "Take Me Riding in the Car" in one of its commercials. The rock band Collective Soul's "The World I Know" played on the radio in the days after the attacks on September 11, 2001, with clips of news coverage of the events layered over the music. Crosby, Stills, Nash, and Young's "Ohio" captures the events of the Kent State shootings on May 4, 1970, and Buffalo Springfield's "For What It's Worth," often associated with the Vietnam War, was written about the Sunset Strip riots in California in 1966.

The United States has the largest music industry in the world. From recording studios to radio stations, music televisions, magazines, concert venues, and community orchestras, it encompasses a wide range of outlets with total revenues exceeding $40 billion worldwide. The majority of the world's recording companies, represented by the Recording Industry Association of America (RIAA), are located in the United States, and musicians such as Australian country artist Keith Urban (1967–) relocate to the United States to take advantage of the extensive recording industry and opportunities to tour in large concert venues.

Billboard magazine (and Web site) charts rank music, and the evolution of the charts over the years reflects changes in the industry. Within a few years of its founding in 1894, the magazine was publishing information about live performance shows, including minstrels and vaudeville. The magazine began to cover radio in the 1920s. Its first music hit parade was printed in January 1936, and in July 1940 the first music popularity chart was published. Beginning in 1970, the radio show *American Top 40* aired the top songs from the *Billboard* charts. When the charts were first established, there was one top 100 list indicating a song's popularity based on jukebox play, radio play, and best-selling records. Over the years, the lists expanded to reflect a variety of genres: bluegrass, Christmas music, Christian rock, classical, country, dance, electronic, jazz, Latin, pop, rap, R&B, and rock. *Billboard* also includes charts for comedy albums, best hits (or catalog) albums, and ringtones for phones.

Cities across the United States are known for distinct music cultures. New Orleans has the Creole and Cajun sounds of its past brought together with the jazz of street musicians and the zydeco played in clubs in the French Quarter. Chicago has its distinct blues sound, derived from the Mississippi Delta and played originally on the acoustic guitar and harmonica. New York City was known for its major punk scene in the 1970s, with the New York Dolls (1971–1976, 2004–present), Patti Smith (1946–), and clubs like CBGB. Detroit was home to Motown Records, which launched the careers of some of the most popular recording acts in the world. It has been known as a hotbed for R&B and soul music. The Paisley Underground, an early alternative rock movement, was unique to Los Angeles in the 1980s, and the world knew Seattle as the home of grunge in the 1990s. Rap sprang from the inner cities of Los Angeles and New York, while Nashville became home to country music.

Many young people dream of "making it" as musicians, and popular television shows like *American Idol* fuel these hopes as viewers watch people go from relative obscurity to national headlines and recording contracts. More than ten thousand people may show up in cities where auditions for the show are held, hoping to land a spot. Singers such as Kelly Clarkson (1982–), Carrie Underwood (1983–), and Fantasia Barrino (1984–) all had their start on *American Idol.*

Music is generative and creative, but that does not always mean that new forms or styles need to be made. Some musicians study and preserve the music of the past, an endeavor that requires careful research and creativity. Musicologists and ethnomusicologists play a vital role in understanding and preserving the music of our past. Charles Seeger (1886–1979), Ruth Seeger (1901–1953), Mike Seeger (1933–2009), John Lomax (1867–1948), Alan Lomax (1915–2002), and others played a critical role in preserving American folk and Old Time music and traditions, sometimes evoking controversy. Other musicologists, like Anthony Seeger, have traveled abroad to understand the musical traditions of indigenous peoples, bringing new lenses and perspectives to understandings of music and culture.

The emphasis of these volumes is on the first decades of the twenty-first century, but linkages to the past are essential and are carefully made to provide a context for current uses and forms of music. Musicians create music, but they do so based on the influences of artists who preceded them. For example, roots music (the music that might be most simply described as homegrown in the cultures of the United States) is performed regularly by contemporary artists like Jewel (1974–), Ricky Skaggs (1954–), and Allison Krauss (1971–), and the sound track of the 2000 film *O Brother, Where Art Thou* is completely roots music. This genre has important historical connections to

American musicians of the past like Lead Belly (1888–1949), Burl Ives (1909–1995), Bill Monroe (1911–1996), and Mike Seeger (1933–2009), not to mention the many amateur musicians Seeger recorded in rural communities.

These volumes address both the commonplace and unique aspects of music in American life, demonstrating the symbiotic relationships between music and musicians and American culture. Music is a profound and enriching aspect of American life.

Timeline of Music in American Life

Pre-1500 Native American nations across the continent incorporate music into their customs and dances, using percussion, flute, copper and clay bells, and vocals.

mid-1500s Missionaries teach plainsong and Catholic liturgies to Native Americans.

1620 The Pilgrims arrive in Massachusetts, introducing a sacred song tradition.

1640 *The Bay Psalm Book* is published. It is the first printed book in the British colony and demonstrates the importance of religious music to the settlers.

1653 The earliest known military band in the New World is formed in New Hampshire.

1700 Spiritual songs (spirituals) are sung by enslaved people.

mid-1700s "Yankee Doodle" is a popular song among British soldiers. "Johnny's Gone for a Soldier" is adapted from an Irish folk tune and becomes popular during the Revolutionary War.

1814 Francis Scott Key writes the poem "The Defense of Fort McHenry." The next year he puts it to music and publishes it as "The Star Spangled Banner."

1842 The New York Philharmonic Society is founded.

1851 Stephen Foster writes "Old Folks at Home."

1854 John Philip Sousa, "The March King," is born.

1861 Julia Ward Howe writes the poem "Battle Hymn of the Republic."

1878 The New York Symphony Orchestra is founded.

1880 Gussie Lord Davis has his first hit, "We Sat Beneath the Maple on the Hill." He is later the first African American to be successful on Tin Pan Alley.

1881 The Boston Symphony Orchestra is founded by Henry Lee Higginson.

1882 The Fisk University Jubilee Singers become the first African American group to be invited to perform at the White House.

The autoharp is patented in the United States.

1883 The Metropolitan Opera House opens in New York City.

F. L. Ritter publishes *Music in America,* the first comprehensive music history of the United States.

1884 Julia Ettie Crane opens the first normal school to prepare music teachers, in Potsdam, New York.

1887 The Dawes Act establishes the Native American Reservation system. Native American customs, including traditional music and dance, are negatively affected.

The gramophone is invented by Emile Berliner.

1888 The American Folklore Society is formed.

1890 The Tin Pan Alley neighborhood begins to form.

The Native American Ghost Dance is banned after the Wounded Knee massacre.

1891 Carnegie Hall opens in New York City.

The Chicago Symphony Orchestra forms.

1895 The American Federation of Musicians is founded.

1897 John Philip Sousa composes "Stars and Stripes Forever."

1898 Puerto Rico becomes part of the United States.

The first coin-operated player piano is introduced by Wurlitzer.

1899 Ragtime is popularized by Scott Joplin, Joseph Lamb, and James Scott. Joplin's "Maple Leaf Rag" becomes a sheet music best seller.

1900 Symphony Hall is built in Boston.

Country and western music becomes popular in the southeastern United States and the Midwest.

Jazz develops in New Orleans.

Phonographs and gramophones become popular in homes across the United States.

Vaudeville begins to take shape.

Amy Cheney Beach becomes the first woman to perform her own work as a soloist, playing her piano concerto with the Boston Symphony Orchestra.

1901 Charles Albert Tindley, a pivotal figure in African American gospel music, publishes a collection of original songs.

1902 Ma Rainey incorporates blues into her minstrel shows.

1904 George M. Cohan writes *Little Johnny Jones,* one of the earliest examples of American musical theater.

Orchestra Hall is built in Chicago.

1906 Hawaiian music is first recorded by the Victrola Company and afterward becomes popular throughout the United States.

The first PhD in music is granted by Harvard University.

1907 Ziegfeld Follies is launched.

The first collection of cowboy music, *Songs of Cowboys* by N. Howard "Jack" Thorp, is published.

The University of Illinois Marching Illini provide the first half-time show by a marching band during a college football game.

1909 The Copyright Act is passed.

1911 Irving Berlin composes "Alexander's Ragtime Band."

The U.S. Army's bandmaster school is founded in New York.

1912 William Christopher Handy publishes *Memphis Blues.* He later is known as the Father of Blues.

1913 The American Society of Composers, Authors and Publishers (ASCAP) is formed.

1915 Alan Lomax is born. He later develops the Library of Congress's archive on folk music with his father, John Lomax.

1916 Charles Albert Tindley releases *New Songs of Paradise.* He is the first black gospel composer to be published.

1920s Blues becomes popular with singers like Ma Rainey and Bessie Smith.

Tin Pan Alley is the center for popular music in the United States.

Jazz is popular in Chicago, where Louis Armstrong and Jelly Roll Morton perform. Duke Ellington and his orchestra popularize jazz in New York.

Radio stations open across the country.

1920 Mamie Smith records "Crazy Blues," the first song recorded by an African American woman.

1924 Juilliard School opens in New York.

George Gershwin composes *Rhapsody in Blue* and the folk opera *Porgy and Bess.*

Serge Koussevitzky becomes conductor of the Boston Symphony Orchestra.

1925 The *Grand Ole Opry* airs as a Saturday night radio show in Nashville, Tennessee.

Blind Lemon Jefferson records more than eighty blues tunes in a four-year period, popularizing country blues.

Paul Robeson makes his concert debut at Greenwich Village. His was the first program that consisted entirely of "Negro spirituals."

1926 NBC is created.

Louis Armstrong releases "Heebie Jeebies," one of the earliest examples of scat.

1927 Jerome Kern and Oscar Hammerstein create *Show Boat,* the first popular musical comedy.

Duke Ellington's radio show, aired from the Cotton Club in New York City, gains a national following.

The Carter family is recorded in Bristol, Tennessee.

The Federal Radio Commission is formed.

Jerome Kern's musical *Show Boat* is a huge success.

1928 Russian pianist Vladimir Horowitz gives his debut performance at Carnegie Hall. He later becomes a U.S. citizen.

1930s Swing becomes popular.

Early Delta blues is defined by Charley Patton and Son House.

1930 Cornell University creates the first chair of musicology at an American university.

1931 George Gershwin and Ira Gershwin's *Of Thee I Sing* is performed, a popular musical theater political satire, the first of its kind.

The first National Folk Festival is organized by Sarah Gertrude Knott. It later becomes the longest running festival of its kind.

Duke Ellington writes "It Don't Mean a Thing If It Ain't Got That Swing," introducing the term *swing* into everyday language.

1932 Aaron Copland visits Mexico City, where he is inspired to write a major orchestral work, *El Salón México.*

1933 Johnny Mercer has his first hit, "Lazy Bones."

Fred Astaire begins to work with Ginger Rogers.

1934 John Lomax discovers Lead Belly and records his music.

Ella Fitzgerald makes her singing debut at the Apollo Theater in Harlem on November 21.

The Hammond organ is invented by Laurens Hammond.

1935 The Federal Music Project is established.

George Gershwin's *Porgy and Bess* premieres on Broadway.

1936 Count Basie's orchestra has a national following.

The electric guitar debuts as T-Bone Walker experiments with the instrument.

1937 Woody Guthrie hosts *Here Comes Woody and Lefty Lou* for KFVD in Los Angeles.

1938 Bill Monroe makes first appearance on radio in Nashville, Tennessee.

Ella Fitzgerald has her first major hit with the song "A-Tisket, A-Tasket."

1939 Jukeboxes are in operation across the country.

The movie *The Wizard of Oz* is released.

The *Grande Ole Opry* show is broadcast on NBC radio.

1940s Dizzy Gillespie helps to popularize bebop with his innovative trumpet playing.

1940 The Disney animated film *Fantasia* stars conductor Leopold Stokowski and the Philadelphia Orchestra.

1941 FM radio begins in Nashville, Tennessee. The city is emerging as a center for country music recording.

The Almanac Singers, the first urban folk-singing group, is formed, with Pete Seeger, Woody Guthrie, Millard Lampell, and Lee Elhardt Hays as members.

King Biscuit Time, one of the most influential blues radio programs, is broadcast from KFFA in Helena, Arkansas.

Bing Crosby sings Irving Berlin's "White Christmas." It becomes the biggest song of his career.

1942 Bandleader Glenn Miller is awarded a gold record for his million-selling hit "Chattanooga Choo Choo."

1943 John Lee Hooker begins to perform in Detroit at Brown's Bar.

1944 *Billboard* launches its music charts.

1945 *Oklahoma!* is the first musical to also be a major recording hit. By 1949 it is the first LP to sell a million copies.

The Berklee College of Music is founded.

1946 *Annie Get Your Gun,* an Irving Berlin musical, is a huge success.

1947 Singer Mahalia Jackson helps to popularize gospel music and inaugurate the golden age of gospel.

The Audio Engineering Society is formed to support the recording and audio-science professions.

1948 The long-playing vinyl record is introduced by Columbia Records.

Fender Broadcaster is the first commercially produced electric guitar.

1949 Hank Williams makes his debut on the *Grand Ole Opry.*

RCA introduces the 45-rpm record.

1950s Fats Domino and Nat King Cole top the charts with their respective hits.

1950 *Sing Out!,* a magazine for folk music fans, is published.

1951 Muddy Waters begins to assemble the greatest collection of electric blues recordings.

1952 Kitty Wells scores the first number one hit for a solo female country artist with “It Wasn’t God Who Made Honky Tonk Angels.”

Sam Phillips begins Sun Records, where he later records music by artists including B. B. King, Johnny Cash, Jerry Lee Lewis, and Elvis Presley.

John Cage releases “Imaginary Landscape No. 5,” the first tape composition by an American composer, and *4'33",* which consists entirely of silence.

1954 Bill Haley and the Comets have a hit with “Rock Around the Clock.”

1955 Chuck Berry’s “Maybellene” is the first of his many hits.

Elvis Presley is on his way to becoming the first rock star.

Little Richard records “Tutti Frutti,” which influences Otis Redding, James Brown, and The Beatles.

1956 *The Wizard of Oz* is shown on television for the first time.

Elvis Presley performs on *The Ed Sullivan Show.*

My Fair Lady begins a record six-year run on Broadway.

1957 *American Bandstand* debuts to a national television audience. Jackie Wilson is one of the show’s first African American performers.

West Side Story, with music by Leonard Bernstein and lyrics by Stephen Sondheim, opens.

1958 The Country Music Association is established.

Billboard begins its Hot 100 chart.

Mike Seeger cofounds the New Lost City Ramblers.

1959 The first Grammy Award for music is presented.

The Motown record company is founded in Detroit by Berry Gordy.

Buddy Holly is killed in a plane crash in Iowa, along with Richie Valens and the Big Bopper.

Sam Cooke signs with RCA Records, where he will have number one hits that include “Chain Gang,” and “Twisting the Night Away.”

1960s The Vietnam War and the civil rights movement provoke and inspire musicians to create music that addresses social unrest. The folk movement and counterculture and psychedelic music are popular.

1960 Elvis Presley is discharged from the U.S. Army.

1961 Patsy Cline is popular, with hits like “Crazy” and “I Fall to Pieces.”

Aretha Franklin releases her first album, *Aretha: With the Ray Bryant Combo.*

1962 The folk group Peter, Paul and Mary release their debut album.

1963 Philips introduces the audiocassette.

1964 The Beatles become popular in the United States, and Beatlemania sweeps across the country.

Bob Dylan releases *The Times They Are A-Changin’,* his first album of entirely original songs.

1965 The Grateful Dead and Jefferson Airplane play their first shows. Psychedelic rock becomes popular.

Loretta Lynn is among the most popular female country singers.

James Brown’s song “Papa’s Got a Brand New Bag” paves the way for funk.

Bob Dylan plays an electric guitar at the Newport Folk Festival.

1966 Otis Redding releases *Complete and Unbelievable: The Otis Redding Dictionary of Soul,* a gospel-oriented soul album that is later listed 250 among *Rolling Stone*’s five hundred greatest albums of all time.

The Beatles give their last live concert performance at Shea Stadium.

Ford Motors includes 8-track tape players in its new cars.

The Doors record "Light My Fire." The song is edited to three minutes for radio play, but many stations air the 7:05 minute version from the album.

1967 Janis Joplin, the Grateful Dead, Jimi Hendrix, and other counterculture bands perform at the Monterey Pop Festival.

Dolly Parton begins to sing on the *Porter Wagner Show.*

Rolling Stone magazine is founded.

1968 The International Polka Association is founded.

Steppenwolf's "Born to Be Wild" contains the phrase "heavy metal."

1969 The Woodstock Music and Arts Fair is attended by thousands of fans.

Maxine Feldman releases the first lesbian-oriented popular song, "Angry Athis."

The Songwriter's Hall of Fame is founded.

1970 Black Sabbath releases its debut studio album, and heavy metal grows in popularity.

Miles Davis releases *Bitches Brew,* a major influence on the jazz-rock genre and funk musicians.

Digital synthesizers are created.

The Beatles break up.

1971 The rock opera *Jesus Christ Superstar* appears on Broadway.

Quadrophonic recording is introduced.

Marvin Gaye releases *What's Going On?* It becomes the best-selling Motown album.

Jim Morrison dies in Paris.

1972 David Bowie performs across the United States in his Ziggy Stardust tour.

Carole King receives four Grammy awards for her album *Tapestry.*

The film *The Harder They Come* helps to popularize reggae in the United States.

1973 Marvin Hamlisch wins an Oscar for his music in the motion picture *The Sting.*

The film *American Graffiti* is released.

DJ Kool Herc begins to provide music for parties, which develops into hip-hop.

1974 Gloria Gaynor's song "Never Can Say Goodbye" hits the charts as disco becomes popular.

1975 The videocassette recorder (VCR) is introduced, allowing people to watch movies and concerts at home.

The Sex Pistols forms in London.

Bruce Springsteen releases *Born to Run.*

John Williams writes the musical score for the movie *Jaws.*

Patti Smith releases *Horses,* the first punk album from the New York scene.

Radio stations refuse to play "The Pill" by country singer Loretta Lynn because it references birth control.

1976 Philip Glass writes the opera *Einstein on the Beach.*

The B-52s forms in Athens, Georgia.

The U.S. bicentennial renews interest in traditional American and patriotic music.

1977 Elvis Presley dies.

The movie *Saturday Night Fever* popularizes disco.

1978 The Sony Walkman is introduced.

Soul Train airs on national television.

1979 The Sugarhill Gang releases "Rapper's Delight," launching rap music.

The film version of the rock musical *Hair* is released.

1980 The rock group R.E.M forms in Athens, Georgia.

John Lennon is murdered in New York City.

1981 Music television (MTV) debuts.

Alabama is the top vocal group of the year.

Metallica forms and goes on to sell more than one hundred million albums worldwide.

1982 Michael Jackson releases *Thriller.* It is among the best-selling albums of all time. The music video becomes a major hit.

1983 Compact discs become popular.

The movie *The Big Chill* makes it popular to use preexisting songs in film.

1984 Madonna releases her album *Like a Virgin.*

The International Bluegrass Music Association is founded.

Run-D.M.C.'s debut album goes gold, the first for hip-hop.

1985 Gloria Estefan and the Miami Sound Machine release *Primitive Love.*

Tipper Gore forms the Parents' Music Resource Center. Senate hearings engage questions of censorship, with testimony from John Denver, Frank Zappa, and Dee Snider.

"We Are the World," a charity single, is released and later sells more than ten million copies.

VH-1: Video Hits One is launched.

The first Farm Aid benefit concert is held to raise money for family farmers in the United States.

1986 Paul Simon releases *Graceland,* featuring African performers.

The *New Grove Dictionary of American Music* is published.

1987 John Adams's *Nixon in China* premieres.

The movie *Dirty Dancing* is popular.

1988 The *Phantom of the Opera* opens on Broadway.

1989 2 Live Crew's album *Nasty as They Wanna Be* is accused of obscenity.

Cher makes a comeback with the video for her hit single "If I Could Turn Back Time," recorded on the USS *Missouri,* causing controversy by wearing a fishnet stocking and revealing black bathing suit.

1990s Grunge rock becomes popular as Seattle bands like Nirvana and Pearl Jam gain national audiences.

East Coast–West Coast hip-hop rivalries emerge, with the Notorious B.I.G. and Tupac Shakur as focal points.

Dubstep, electronic dance music, emerges in the late 1990s.

1990 Rock the Vote is founded.

1991 Riot Grrrls, an underground female punk band, emerges.

1992 The House of Blues restaurant opens in Boston.

Branford Marsalis becomes bandleader for *The Tonight Show.*

Presidential candidate Bill Clinton plays the saxophone on the *Arsenio Hall Show.*

1993 Basketball player Shaquille O'Neal releases his debut album.

Whitney Houston's hit "I Will Always Love You" becomes the longest-running number one single of all time.

Guns n' Roses plays its final show.

Nirvana performs on MTV's *Unplugged.*

1994 Kurt Cobain commits suicide.

Lisa Marie Presley and Michael Jackson marry.

The band Marilyn Manson releases its debut album.

Green Day releases *Dookie,* launching a punk revival.

Woodstock '94, also called Mudstock, commemorates the twenty-fifth anniversary of the original music festival.

1995 The Rock and Roll Hall of Fame opens in Cleveland, Ohio.

Jerry Garcia of the Grateful Dead dies.

Popular Tejano singer Selena is murdered.

1996 Rapper Tupac Shakur, one of the best-selling artists of his time, is murdered in Las Vegas.

Country music stars Faith Hill and Tim McGraw marry.

1997 DVDs are released.

MP3 players are mass marketed.

Auto-tuning is developed to disguise off-key inaccuracies in vocal tracks. It emerges in the mainstream in 2009.

Rapper Notorious B.I.G. is murdered in Los Angeles.

Garth Brooks's free concert in Central Park draws the largest audience ever to attend a concert at that site. Also recorded for HBO, the program has more than fourteen million television viewers.

Lilith Fair, led by Sarah McLachlan, begins touring during the summer to raise money for women's charities. It features female solo artists and female-led bands.

1999 Woodstock '99 commemorates the thirtieth anniversary of the original festival. It ends in 3 deaths and 120 arrests.

Pop singer Ricky Martin gives a widely acclaimed performance at the Grammy Awards, introducing him to mainstream American audiences.

Britney Spears releases her debut album *. . . Baby One More Time.* It sells twenty-six million copies.

2000s The Internet transforms music.

2000 The movie *O Brother, Where Art Thou?* creates interest in roots music.

Napster, an Internet-based file-sharing service, is convicted of violating copyright law by allowing people to share music files without paying for them.

Santana wins eight Grammys in one night for *Supernatural,* tying Michael Jackson's 1984 record.

Christina Aguilera is recognized as Best New Artist at the Grammys.

2001 The September 11th attacks are followed by a number of music events to raise money for victims and their families, including the television show *America: A Tribute to Heroes.*

The war in Afghanistan begins.

Apple launches the iPod, a portable media player.

Rival boy bands the Backstreet Boys and 'N SYNC perform onstage together at the American Music Awards.

Former Beatle George Harrison dies of lung cancer in Los Angeles.

2002 *American Idol* airs on Fox Television.

The rock band U2 plays the Super Bowl half-time show as a tribute to the victims of the September 11th attacks.

2003 Apple Inc. introduces the online music store iTunes, allowing paying customers to download songs.

U.S. forces invade Iraq. Musicians like Dixie Chicks singer Natalie Maines speak out against the war.

Paul McCartney performs in Moscow at Red Square.

2004 Fourteen-year-old Taylor Swift moves to Nashville to pursue a career in country music. She goes on to win six Grammy Awards and sell more than twenty million albums in the first eight years of her career.

Usher releases *Confessions,* the first R&B album to sell over a million copies in one week.

Luciano Pavarotti gives his last opera performance at the Met in New York City.

2005 Hurricane Katrina devastates the Gulf Coast region of the United States, hitting New Orleans particularly hard. Musicians record charity songs to raise money for the city and its recovery. Harry Connick Jr. and Branford Marsalis create Musicians' Village, for musicians who have lost their homes.

Guitar Hero, a series of interactive music video games, is released.

The jukebox musical *Jersey Boys,* featuring the music of Frankie Valli and the Four Seasons, debuts on Broadway.

YouTube is founded, providing viewers access to music concerts, videos, and a range of performances by professional and amateur musicians.

Fortune magazine estimates that mobile ringtones have generated more than $2 billion in sales worldwide.

2006 Madonna launches her Confessions tour, the highest-grossing tour by a female artist.

Aerosmith's Steven Tyler and Joe Perry perform with the Boston Pops Orchestra.

Patti Smith performs the final show at the CBGB Club in New York before it closes due to a rent dispute.

The country group Lady Antebellum forms.

2007 The film *I'm Not There* uses nontraditional narrative techniques to tell the life of Bob Dylan.

Singer Celine Dion concludes her five-year performance engagement at Caesars Palace in Las Vegas.

2008 Canadian singer Justin Bieber is discovered on YouTube. "Bieber fever" begins.

Lady Gaga releases her debut album *The Fame.* Her worldwide Monster Ball Tour follows in 2009.

2009 Michael Jackson dies.

Singer Beyoncé is named Artist of the Decade by *The Observer.* She is one of the top-earning artists of all time.

President Barack Obama's inauguration event includes the We Are One concert at the Lincoln Memorial; Aretha Franklin singing "My Country 'Tis of Thee"; violinist Itzhak Perlman and cellist Yo-Yo Ma performing an original piece by John Williams; and Beyoncé singing "At Last" at one of the balls.

The Lamb of God album *Wrath* debuts at number two on the *Billboard* 200, making it the highest-charting extreme metal album.

Pete Seeger's ninetieth birthday is celebrated with a concert at Madison Square Garden.

2010 The Hope for Haiti telethon raises money for earthquake victims. Dave Matthews, Sheryl Crow, and Jay-Z are among the musicians involved in the benefit. The live album is released by preorder on iTunes and sets a record as the biggest one-day preorder.

Katy Perry's "California Gurls" tops the U.S. charts.

Rihanna launches her Last Girl on Earth tour.

2011 The alternative rock band Live re-forms.

R.E.M. disbands.

2012 The music world loses Whitney Houston, Etta James, Earl Scruggs, Dick Clark, Dave Brubeck, and Donna Summer.

British singer Adele, twenty-three years old at the time, wins six Grammy Awards for her second album, *21.* The album becomes the longest-running number one album by a female artist in *Billboard* history.

A hologram of the late rapper Tupac Shakur performs his songs "Hail Mary" and "2 of Amerikaz Most Wanted" onstage with Snoop Dogg at the Coachella Music Festival.

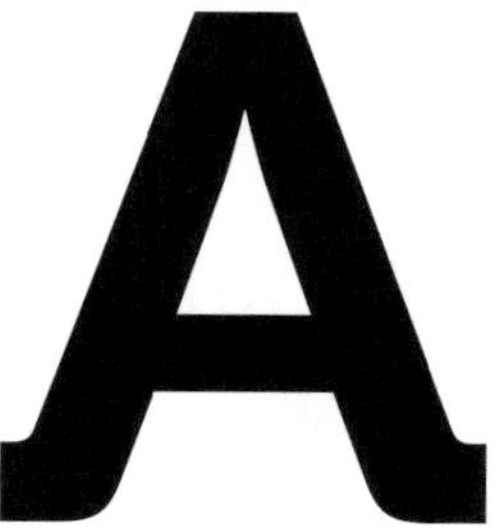

A Cappella

"*A cappella*" is Italian for "in the manner of the chapel." The term originally indicated a style of vocal music sung in church during the Renaissance. Today a cappella means "singing without accompaniment" in a more general sense, indicating any vocal music that is performed without instruments.

In the nineteenth century church musicians in Europe favored the style of music written in the 1500s, which was heavily polyphonic (it had multiple melodies happening at the same time). When instruments were used to accompany the singers, they read from the same musical score as the singers and played the same notes. So when musicians three centuries later looked at the scores, it appeared that these pieces were meant to be sung without instrumental accompaniment. This is how a cappella came to mean what it does today.

A cappella singing was an important feature of Native American music, especially before the arrival of Europeans. When settlers from the Old World arrived in North America, they brought their styles of a cappella singing with them, especially in religious contexts. In Protestant churches of the American colonies, psalms were often sung a cappella, as it was believed that the simplicity of unaccompanied singing was preferable to elaborate (and to some distracting) instrumental music. Besides, few churches had organs or other instruments to accompany the religious service or the money to support professional musicians to play them.

In the seventeenth century church leaders would sing a line from a hymn or psalm a cappella, and then the congregation would sing it back. This process was known as "lining out" and was useful because worshippers did not need to know how to read music. By the early eighteenth century, however, lining out was largely replaced by "regular singing," in which some worshippers read from printed books with musical scores. These singers often met outside of the church service in "singing schools" to practice their songs and improve their musical abilities.

In the early nineteenth century some musicians began experimenting with other ways to write down a cappella music that did not require singers to be able to read musical staff notation. One of the popular methods was "shape-note singing," in which pitches were represented with different shapes (triangle, circle, square, and diamond). "Sacred harp" is a tradition of a cappella singing based on this method. It was particularly popular in the South and Midwest during the nineteenth century, and it continues to be sung today.

By the nineteenth century a cappella singing was also found in choral societies that were not connected with a church. For example, the Handel and Haydn Society of Boston was founded in 1815, and its repertory included a cappella songs in addition to others accompanied by instruments. Soon other cities had similar societies, including New York, Philadelphia, Chicago, and others in the Midwest. These societies were significant because unlike many earlier traditions, to their members, choral singing was more of a secular activity than a sacred or religious one.

Although students at American colleges and universities were singing as early as colonial times, a cappella ensembles were frequently organized on college campuses in the nineteenth century. At Yale University, for example, informal singing groups were formed within each class. The first official college glee club was established at Harvard University in 1858. That club and the others that followed were usually directed entirely by students; faculty generally did not become involved until closer to the turn of the twentieth century. College glee clubs sang a mix of European art music, folk music, and popular tunes.

At the end of the nineteenth and into the twentieth centuries, another a cappella tradition became increasingly popular: "barbershop." Drawing on earlier white and black traditions of close harmony, this style of singing was originally highly improvisatory. Barbershop quartets, in which four people would sing a cappella, often performed popular songs from the first few decades of the twentieth century. Barbershop continues to be popular today, with both men's and women's quartets as well as larger choruses of singers in cities and towns throughout the country. It was among the first kinds of music to be recorded, because early recording equipment tended to reproduce voices better than many instruments. Musically, barbershop songs often lack a steady tempo, as singers slow down and let their chords "ring" as they sing nostalgically about love and camaraderie.

Popular music continued to be sung a cappella throughout the twentieth century. When jazz music developed in the first half of the century, vocal groups formed in addition to bands. For example, the Mills Brothers was a highly successful group of four brothers from Ohio who performed and recorded many jazz songs without instrumental accompaniment from the 1920s through the 1960s. During the 1950s and 1960s vocal groups sang a style of popular music called "doo-wop." Although many of the most popular doo-wop recordings include instruments, most groups sang a cappella in four- or five-part harmony in live performances. "In the Still of the Nite" (1956), by the Five Satins, remains a popular doo-wop song.

The late twentieth century also had some popular a cappella hits, including "Boy from New York City" (1982), by the vocal jazz group The Manhattan Transfer; "The Longest Time" (1983), by singer-songwriter Billy Joel; "Don't Worry, Be Happy" (1988), by vocal stylist Bobby McFerrin; and "It's So Hard to Say Goodbye to Yesterday" (1991), by the vocal group Boyz II Men. In the 1980s and 1990s there was a significant increase in the number of college and university singing groups. Rather than singing original works, these groups took popular songs—most of which included instruments—and performed them a cappella, using their voices to imitate the sounds of the guitars, drums, and other instruments.

See also: Joel, Billy; Musical Societies; Native American Music

Further Reading

Averill, Gage. 2003. *Four Parts, No Waiting: A Social History of American Barbershop Harmony.* New York: Oxford University Press.

Buechner, Alan Clark. 2003. *Yankee Singing Schools and the Golden Age of Choral Music in New England, 1760–1800.* Boston: Boston University.

Crawford, Richard. 2001. *America's Musical Life: A History.* New York: W.W. Norton.

Duchan, Joshua S. 2007. "Powerful Voices: Performance and Interaction in Contemporary Collegiate A Cappella." PhD diss., University of Michigan.

Joshua S. Duchan

Accordion

The accordion, which was nearly obsolete a few decades ago, is making a comeback in the United States as popular musicians and bands, including Bruce Springsteen, Sheryl Crow, Nirvana, the Dixie Chicks, and R.E.M., incorporate the unique sound into their music. The accordion is a free-reed instrument; its sound is produced when air pressure causes small steel reeds to vibrate within its body. Wind is produced by the opening and closing of bellows by the player's left hand, and air is allowed to flow to the various reeds by valves that open when keys or buttons are pressed by the player's fingers. The accordion's nearest taxonomical relatives are other instruments in the free-reed family, such as the harmonica or mouth organ, the concertina, the bandoneón, and the harmonium or reed organ.

One of the first free-reed instruments, the sheng, appeared in China probably around the seventh century BC or earlier. This mouth-blown instrument became an integral part of the orchestra of the imperial Chinese court and opera. Sometime during the late eighteenth century shengs began arriving in Europe, and instrument builders began creating new instruments utilizing free reeds, most notably the harmonica (a mouth-blown instrument) and the harmonium (a foot-pumped instrument with a keyboard).

The free reeds were unique and highly regarded because they were expressive. Their dynamics could be increased or decreased by increasing or decreasing the pressure of the air flowing through the reeds, unlike the flue or reed pipes in an organ, whose dynamics remain constant regardless of wind pressure. This may be one reason why the European free-reed instruments were invented and developed during this era, the age of romanticism, when expression was highly prized in music.

Probably in the 1810s or 1820s, an inventive European instrument builder connected two harmonicas with a bellows, and the first accordion was born. It was first patented in 1829 by Cyrill Demian (1772–1847), a piano and organ builder in Vienna, and was called "accordion" because the buttons of the left-hand manual produced both bass notes and preset chords (triads). The accordion spread quickly throughout the world, propelled by the creation of a new dance, the polka, which debuted about the same time.

European immigrants began bringing the accordion to the United States in the 1830s. By 1843 it had become so popular that one American music publisher began publishing method books and songbooks for the instrument.

From its beginnings the accordion has been a favorite instrument of the working-class people, not the wealthy. It was fairly easy to learn, it was not terribly expensive, and the performer could play a melody in the right-hand manual and accompany himself or herself with bass and chord buttons in the left-hand manual, thereby effectively creating a one-person "oompah" band.

The first accordions were single-action instruments; one pitch sounded on the press and another pitch on the draw, like a harmonica. Today these instruments are called "diatonic" button-accordions because they usually play in only one key. In 1852 Philippe Joseph Bouton of Paris attached an organ keyboard to an accordion and made the instrument double-action; the same pitches sounded both on the press and the draw. Today this is known as a "piano-accordion." The piano-accordion became popular by the end of the nineteenth century, especially in Italy.

At this time Americans were only familiar with the single-action diatonic button-accordions, which they could purchase by mail order from the Sears, Roebuck and Company catalog. In 1910, however, one young, handsome, and talented Italian accordionist, Guido Deiro (1886–1950), introduced the new "piano-accordion" to thousands of Americans during his performances on the vaudeville stage. Deiro was a sensation and quickly rose to stardom as a vaudeville headliner, the final act in the show. No one could top him.

Audiences were fascinated by this new "accordeon," the piano-accordion, and they began purchasing Deiro's Edison sound cylinders and Columbia records. Soon people began buying accordions and accordion music, and the "golden age of the accordion" (1910–1960) had arrived. Accordionists became a regular feature at social events such as parties and wedding receptions. They performed on and off vaudeville, and some even played with dance bands, jazz bands, and big bands. The accordion was a regular fixture on the radio. Charles Magnante (1905–1986) became known as the greatest American accordionist through his popular radio and concert appearances, his accordion master classes, and his dozens of sound records.

Accordion studios popped up throughout the United States, and hundreds of thousands of children took accordion lessons. Accordion music publishers were established to capitalize on this new craze, and accordion factories appeared in cities such as San Francisco, Chicago, and New York to produce instruments for all these new students. When customers walked into a music store, they saw hundreds of accordions on shelves along the walls. Accordionists played the popular music of the day: waltzes, rags, marches, mazurkas, polkas, tangos, fox trots, popular standards, and novelties. Many specialized in ethnic music, some specialized in jazz, and some of the more virtuosic performers played light classical music at their concerts, such as the famous opera overture "William Tell" by Rossini.

The accordion was rarely seen or heard in serious classical music concerts. A handful of composers, such as Tchaikovsky, Umberto Giordano, Charles Ives, Alban Berg, Paul Hindemith, and some others occasionally used the instrument in their compositions, usually to produce a comic, pastoral, or folk effect.

In the mid-twentieth century, a new type of accordion appeared that was more attractive to classical performers and composers: the free-bass accordion. This accordion was more versatile, especially in classical music, because the chord buttons in the left-hand manual were replaced by buttons that produced single notes, thereby allowing the performer to play polyphonic and contrapuntal works. This instrument has become popular in Europe, but in the United States it is virtually unknown.

Despite the accordion's enormous popularity, its golden age was not destined to last forever. During the late 1950s a new style of music appeared on the scene, rock 'n' roll, which sounded the death knell for many professional accordionists, teachers, and music publishers. Young people, fueled by the "generation gap," rebelled against the values of their parents. They adopted rock music and rejected the music of their elders, especially the light and cheerful champagne music epitomized by the popular television bandleader Lawrence Welk (1903–1992).

In the minds of young people the accordion was stigmatized; it was considered old-fashioned and "square." Youngsters abandoned the accordion in favor of the electric guitar, electric piano, and electronic organ. The instrument became the butt of many jokes. Gradually accordions disappeared entirely from music stores, and today the instrument has become something of a rarity in mainstream music circles.

Recently, however, it seems the accordion may be making a comeback. World music, such as Cajun, zydeco, and the Tex-Mex music of the southern United

Bandleader Lawrence Welk arrives at Idlewild Airport aboard an American Airlines nonstop flagship with his favorite instrument, ready to pour out some music, May 29, 1956. (AP Photo)

States, often includes an accordion. This type of music is becoming increasingly popular. Certainly the "golden age of the accordion" ended over fifty years ago, but today a handful of professional American accordionists manage to eke out a living by playing this instrument.

See also: Big Band Music; Cajun and Creole Music; Crow, Sheryl; Dixie Chicks; Ives, Charles; Jazz; Nirvana; R.E.M.; Rock 'n' Roll; Springsteen, Bruce; Vaudeville and Burlesque; World Music; Zydeco

Further Reading

Doktorski, Henry. 2001. "The Classical Squeezebox." *Musical Performance* 3, nos. 2–4: 12–13.

Doktorski, Henry. 2005. *The Brothers Deiro and Their Accordions.* Oakdale, PA: Classical Free-Reed, Inc.

Doktorski, Henry. 2006. "Interview with Fredrik Dillner—The Owner of What May Be the World's Oldest Accordion—Probably Built in 1816 or Earlier." The Classical Free-Reed, Inc. http://www.ksanti.net/free-reed/essays/dillner_interview.html.

Doktorski, Henry. 2007. "Deiro: The Original Master of the Piano-Accordion." CD booklet notes for *Guido Deiro: Complete Recorded Works,* vol. 1. Champaign, IL: Archeophone Records.

Flynn, Davison, and Chavez. 1992. *The Golden Age of the Accordion.* New York: Flynn Publications.

Muir, Peter C. 2001. "Looks Like a Cash Register and Sounds Worse: The Deiro Brothers and the Rise of the Piano-Accordion in American Culture 1908–1930." *The Free-Reed Journal* 3: 61.

Wagner, Christoph. 1995. "A Brief History of How the Accordion Changed the World." CD booklet notes for *Planet Squeezebox.* Roslyn, New York: Ellipsis Arts.

Henry Doktorski

Actors as Composers, Songwriters, or Performers

There is a long history of television and film stars making music as part of their careers. From the "singing cowboys" of early Western films, to the Disney "teen idols" of today, many actors have incorporated music into their lives and careers in some fashion. In some cases their music making is directly associated with their work as actors, but in other instances it is entirely separate. Whatever the case, it is certain that the impact of actors who also "do" music should not be underestimated. Some actors compose music for orchestras, some for use in films. There are actors who write and perform their own songs, either in a band or as solo artists. And there are actors who simply have a music career on the side in addition to their work on-screen. In many cases their impact on popular culture as musicians matches or exceeds the impact they make as actors. Indeed, when actors are also successful musicians, their fans can enjoy their talents in many different ways, be it at the cinema, on the living room television, or on the car radio.

Actors as Composers

Very few actors actually compose concert music of any kind as their means of expression. The training in musical notation and theory needed to do this is simply not something most actors have. Sir Anthony Hopkins (1937–) and Dudley Moore (1935–2002) are notable exceptions. Hopkins, the Oscar-winning star best known for playing Hannibal Lecter in *Silence of the Lambs* (1991), has recently written several pieces for orchestra, including "And the Waltz Goes On" for world-famous violinist Andre Rieu (1949–), who premiered the piece in Austria, where the waltz originated. Hopkins has also written other concert pieces and music for a couple of his films, including *Slipstream* and *August.*

Dudley Moore, who starred in the original *Arthur* (1981), turned to music at an early age because problems with his legs and feet left him unable to participate in sports. He became an accomplished pianist and began writing his own music. He composed music for several of his films and was also known for performing parodies of famous tunes (especially well-known classical pieces) at his live performances. In the early 1990s he did a series of programs designed to teach young audiences about classical music. He brought together young musicians from all over the world and invited very famous conductors to lead them. The rehearsals were filmed, edited, and then narrated by Moore himself. The result was a wonderful TV series called *Orchestra!,* which features conductor Sir Georg Solti (1912–1997), and *Concerto!,* with Michael Tilson Thomas (1944–) conducting. In addition to this work, Moore had numerous albums to his credit, most of which featured him playing jazz piano.

Few actors have been as active musically as Clint Eastwood (1930–). Although he is known primarily as the man who portrayed the outlaw Josey Wales and the cop Dirty Harry, or as the Oscar-winning director of *Million Dollar Baby* (2004), Eastwood's fans know that he also composed the music for many of his films, including *Mystic River, Grace Is Gone, Changeling,* and *Gran Torino* (a film for which he sings in a raspy voice at the beginning of the original theme song, which he wrote). Eastwood's musical roots are in jazz—he is a jazz pianist himself—so many of these films feature that element of his talent. He also expressed that interest through his directing, with such films as *Bird,* a biopic of jazz legend Charlie Parker (1920–1955), and a documentary on Johnny Mercer (1909–1976). In recognition of his musical accomplishments, both in directing and composing, the Berklee College of Music awarded him an honorary doctorate of music (Berklee College of Music 2007). He is also a board member of the Monterey Jazz Festival. Eastwood's legacy has been cemented and cuts across many generations. In 1997 a documentary called *Eastwood After Hours* was filmed; it features performances of his music at Carnegie Hall by several big names in jazz, including Joshua Redman (1969–) and others. He is also immortalized in a song called "Clint Eastwood" by Gorillaz and by a reggae artist who has taken his name.

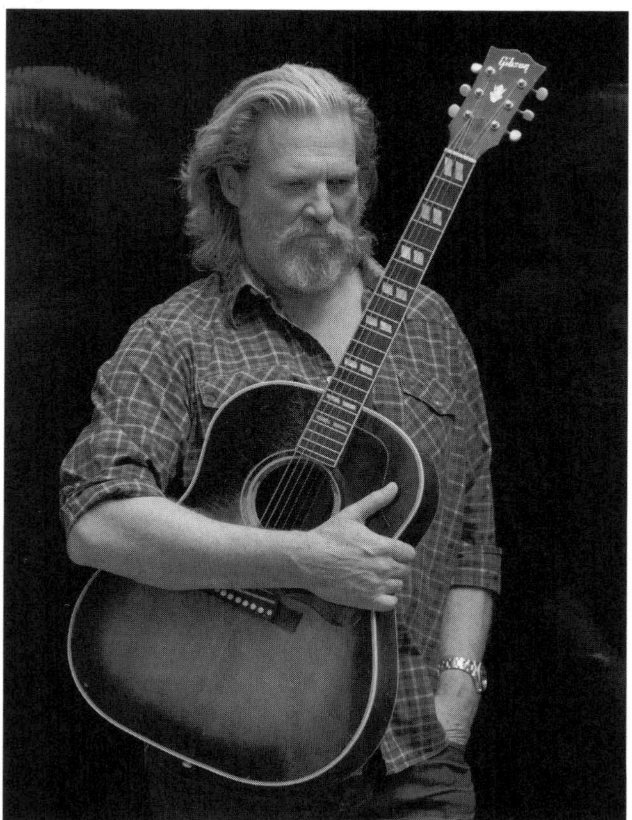

Actor and musician Jeff Bridges, who was releasing a self-titled album, poses for a portrait in Beverly Hills, August 4, 2011. (AP Photo/Jason Redmond)

Actors as Songwriters

Many actors have tried their hand at writing songs. Often they seek out the help of more established musicians, people who have made their living by songwriting. This is a significant point, because most true songwriters—such as Bob Dylan (1941–), Paul Simon (1941–), Jackson Browne (1948–)—tend to work on their own, seeking periods of seclusion in which they can develop their ideas. But with actors, this desire is replaced with a bit of insecurity that sends them looking for a collaborator with experience in the field. It is often not clear exactly what type of help they get. Do the actors just write the lyrics, with the professional musician actually creating the music? Or does the professional musician simply give general advice? Take Johnny Depp (1963–), for example. Depp has a strong musical background and sat in with the rock group Oasis (1991–2009), where he played guitar. Depp even has a couple of acoustic guitar tracks on the *Chocolat* (2000) sound track. But when it comes to writing songs, he turned to Steven Tyler (1948–)—lead singer of Aerosmith (1970–present)—for collaboration. In May 2011 Depp revealed that he was writing a song with Tyler.

Another example is Jeff Bridges (1949–), who has portrayed musicians in a couple of films. He won the Oscar for his portrayal of a drunken country singer named Bad Blake in *Crazy Heart* (2009), a role he almost turned down because of the high standard he had set for himself in his earlier work in *The Fabulous Baker Boys.* What convinced him to take the *Heart* role was that his longtime friend and record producer-songwriter T-Bone Burnett (1948–) signed on to help with the film. Bridges's long friendship with Burnett led to an album and performing in such famous venues as Austin City Limits (Brown 2010). But even on this solo album, Bridges only wrote a few of the songs entirely on his own. In most cases the songwriting was a collaboration of several people, including people whom Burnett had brought in to work with Bridges. This is certainly not to diminish the talent Bridges has for music; he is clearly a strong performer and writes touching and honest music. But it is only with guidance from professionals around him that he finds the strength and confidence to put his work out there.

Jamie Foxx (1967–) provides another recent example. Foxx, who portrayed Ray Charles (1930–2004) in *Ray* (2004), has several albums to his credit. His first album, *Peep This,* was released in 1994, when Foxx was still a star on the hit TV show *In Living Color.* All of the album's thirteen tracks were either written or cowritten by Foxx and are in the R&B style, with lots of similarities to R&B from the 1980s. In his second release, *Unpredictable* (2005), Foxx teamed up with several big-name musicians, including Ludacris (1977–), Snoop Dogg (1971–), Mary J. Blige (1971–), and Kanye West (1977–). Having just starred in *Ray,* Foxx was at that point a major star, with access to the top people in the business. All of this star power catapulted *Unpredictable* to number one on the *Billboard* top 200, making Foxx only the fourth artist ever to win an Oscar for acting and have a number one album. The other three are Frank Sinatra (1915–1998), Bing Crosby (1903–1977), and Barbra Streisand (1942–). For these three, their acting and musical careers are almost inseparable. Streisand also won an Oscar for songwriting "Evergreen," the love theme from *A Star Is Born* (1976).

There are plenty of examples of actors writing songs without the aid of more famous musicians. Jennifer Love-Hewitt (1979–) was a child television star on *Party of Five* (1994–2000). When she signed up with the television show, she also signed with Atlantic Records and has written lyrics for three albums' worth of material. When she became a film star in the *I Know What You Did Last Summer* movies, she penned "How Do I Deal," which became her biggest hit, topping out at number fifty-nine on the singles chart. Robert Downey Jr. (1965–), star of the *Ironman* films, has sung on several sound tracks and has a CD called *The Futurist,* for which he wrote several songs. Milla Jovovich (1975–), best known for her role in *The Fifth Element,* is definitely involved in creating the material for her band Plastic Has Memory. Joey Lawrence (1976–), who played Joey Russo on *Blossom,* wrote the hit single "Nothing My Love Can't Fix." Persia White (1972–) played Lynn Searcy on the CW sitcom *Girlfriends* and wrote the lyrics for and performed "Choices," a song featured on the show. White was also in XE03, an industrial band, and has released a solo album called *Mecca* (2009), for which she wrote and produced much of the material. And the list goes on: Kevin Bacon (1958–), Scarlett Johansson (1984–), Billy Bob Thornton (1955–), Patrick Swayze (1952–2009), Keith Carradine (1949–), David Hasselhoff (1952–), and Steven Seagal (1952–) are all well-known actors who have written songs and performed them in bands or as solo artists (Mapes and Comer 2011).

Actors as Performers

For many actors, whatever careers they may have as singer-songwriter are the direct result of characters they have portrayed on the big screen or on television. This is especially true when they are part of a variety show, where singing and dancing are part of the gig. In these cases, the distinction between the various performance types becomes blurred. The Disney Corporation has been launching careers like this for young performers for a long time. Some of the most recent examples are Hilary Duff (1987–), who was first famous on TV as Lizzie McGuire before launching a singing career. Miley Cyrus (1992–) followed closely, as Hannah Montana. These two have been among the most successful of many "teen idol" stars, with movies, TV shows, record deals, and merchandise all built around the same product. Selena Gomez (1992–), who played Alex Russo on *Wizards of Waverly Place,* is the lead singer of a band and has done music for some of her films. Demi Lovato (1992–), from the *Camp Rock* movies, along with the Jonas Brothers (active 2005–present), have had successful music careers. Ashley Tisdale (1985–), from *The Suite Life of Zack and Cody* and other shows and films, used her exposure to land a record deal and record an album. Raven Symone (1985–), from *That's So Raven,* had her career launched by Disney as well.

There are still others who take their fictional characters with them for musical careers of one kind or another. The Monkees (active 1966–1971) were actors who had a television series as an imaginary band and then went on to perform as musicians. *Star Trek* fans might be interested to follow up on an album called *Spaced Out: The Best of Leonard Nimoy and William Shatner.* This compilation draws from the many albums released by these actors in the late 1960s. Nimoy (1931–) especially channels his character, Mr. Spock, in a tune called "Highly Illogical," an oft-heard quote from the show. Shatner (1931–) does mostly spoken renditions of popular songs ("Mr. Tambourine Man" being the most famous), but we always know he is portraying Captain Kirk.

Spinal Tap (1964–1982; fictional), is a parody of a rock group, formed by Christopher Guest (1948–), Michael McKean (1947–), and Harry Shearer (1943–) for a "mockumentary" called *This Is Spinal Tap* (1984), a movie that told the story of a (fictional) heavy metal band. But after the movie's release, the actors who played the band members actually went on tour and released albums. When summarizing accounts of this band, one must include both fictional albums (i.e., those mentioned only in the movie) and actual albums (of which there are three). All the music for the band was written and performed by the three actors.

Spinal Tap actually had its roots in the late-night variety show *Saturday Night Live,* which has been a consistent source of actors who ultimately cross over into music. In most cases, the musical career is spillover from a skit on the show. Often, however, actors eventually break free from associations with the show and do music on their own. Steve Martin (1945–) is an excellent example. Known mostly as a comedian and actor, Martin has always used music as part of his show. And while not actually a cast member of *SNL,* Martin was a frequent guest in the 1970s. He performed his song "King Tut" on the show. Since then Martin has continued playing banjo, and recently he has toured with a bluegrass group. Perhaps the best known musical group spawned by *SNL* is the Blues Brothers (active 1978–1982, 1988–present). Dan Aykroyd (1952–) and John Belushi (1949–1982) portrayed them on the show, but then also released an album and eventually a movie.

Saturday Night Live also produced several comedians who went on to release solo albums. For example, Eddie Murphy (1961–) had a recurring character called Buckwheat. On an early comedy album, Murphy included a song in which Buckwheat converses with 1980s workout guru Richard Simmons. Though not a serious musical piece, it was an early glimpse of Murphy's desire to sing. He later collaborated with funk singer Rick James (1948–2004) to produce "Party All the Time" (1985), a pop song included on one of his albums of pure music. Adam Sandler (1966–) and Jimmy Fallon (1974–) provide further examples of comedians from *SNL* who include comedic songwriting on their comedy albums. A more recent example is Donald Glover (1983–), who plays Troy on *Community.* Glover started out primarily in comedy, writing sketches for *30 Rock* and doing stand-up. Once he had established himself on *Community,* he launched his hip-hop career under the name Childish Gambino. It seems that, for many comics, the path to a musical career must first pass through television, where their images can reach a wider audience.

Clearly there are many, many actors who pursue musical careers in one fashion or another. But why do these artists, who for the most part are already very successful in their acting careers, feel the need to establish a musical career as well? Shouldn't they "save [themselves] the potential embarrassment and stick to what [they] know [they're] good at?" (Overdeep 2011). For some it makes sense financially to strike while the "teen-idol" iron is hottest. In these cases, the singing is simply an extension of their jobs as actors. And with large companies running TV stations, movie production facilities, radio stations, and record labels, all under one roof, it becomes clear that they want to get as much bang for their buck as they can from each artist. Based on this "synergy," they can sell basically the same product to the same consumer many times over: watch the TV show, buy the album, buy the T-shirt, see the movie, buy the movie sound track, see the live concert performance, buy the DVD, and so forth (Moore 2001). They often create "teen idols." There are even cases of a band being formed on television, as in *Making the Band.* On this program, "record deals were the reward for success on TV" (Stahl 2002). To be sure, record executives have known since the 1950s that an appearance on television was sure to boost record sales (Forman 2002). So in this sense, image certainly has become a major factor in the music industry, thanks in no small part to actors who sing.

But for other actors, the reasons are more complex. Many actors have been talented musically their entire lives. Often this leads them to seek out acting roles that allow them to sing. This was certainly the case for Jeff Bridges and Jamie Foxx. There are many more examples, including Joaquin Phoenix (1974–), Gwyneth Paltrow (1972–), and others. Their singing roles in films reveal to their fans their hidden talent, which they can then go on to explore. But in general, it seems most actors simply enjoy performing and are drawn to music; they have rock 'n' roll fantasies, like many others

In fact, in some cases actors feel they need to explain their desire to pursue music. Perhaps Russell Crowe (1964–) put it best: "A lot of people just simply don't understand why I'm in a band in the first place. They think it's got something to do with the desire to be even more famous, or it's ego-driven and I think it's a really good idea that people should look at me. I just happen to write songs, and I've been doing it for most of my life." In reference to what it is about music that draws him, he states that "when you've felt the power of the unit as you become more comfortable with the material, then it's a very addictive thing, and it's something . . . I can't easily turn away from" (O'Keefe 2002).

Crowe's words help us understand why music is such a powerful draw to famous stars like him. It is not difficult to imagine that actors, while certainly using expression to play their parts in a film or show, might feel a bit like pawns, helping a director or producer or screenwriter realize his or her vision. But when a person can write a song and then perform that song, perhaps the level of personal expression becomes that much greater. Then if that song can be performed for a live audience—another element of music that actors do not often experience—it may well become "addictive" and worth whatever risk is involved in attempting to cross over into another means of expression. In any case, it is certain that these multitalented artists, through the music they make, the awards they have won, and the revenue they have generated, have in many ways helped shape the musical landscape as we know it today.

See also: Aerosmith; Blues Brothers; Browne, Jackson; Charles, Ray; Comedy and Satire in American Music; Crosby, Bing; Disney Music; Dylan, Bob; Film Music; Jazz; Parker, Charlie; *Saturday Night Live*; Simon, Paul; Sinatra, Frank; Streisand, Barbra; Teen and Youth Heavy Hitters; West, Kanye

Further Reading

Berklee College of Music. 2007. http://www.berklee.edu/news/2007/09/0924.html.

Brown, Lane. 2010. "Bad to the Bone: The Longtime Friendship Behind the Rusty Twang of *Crazy Heart.*" January. http://nymag.com/movies/features/63008/.

Eels, Josh. 2011. "Comedy's New Wave: Donald Glover, the Triple Threat." *Rolling Stone,* September 15, 4.

Forman, Murray. 2002. "'One Night on TV Is Worth Weeks at the Paramount': Musicians and Opportunity in Early Television, 1948–55." *Popular Music* 21, no. 3: 249–276.

Green, Douglas B. 2002. *Singing in the Saddle: The History of the Singing Cowboy.* Nashville, TN: The Country Music Foundation Press and Vanderbilt University Press.

Mapes, Jillian, and M. Tye Comer. 2011. "25 Awesome Movie Stars Turned Musicians." February 25. http://www.billboard.com/#/news/25–awesome-movie-stars-turned-musicians-1005049932.story.

Moore, Catherine. 2001. "A Picture Is Worth 1000 CDs: Can the Music Industry Survive as a Stand-alone Business?" *American Music* 22, no. 1: 176–186.

O'Keefe, Eric. 2002. "Russell Crowe." *Cowboys and Indians.* http://www.murphsplace.com/crowe/cowboys.html.

Overdeep, Meghan. 2011. "On Singers Who Act and Actors Who Sing, Inspired by Justin Timberlake." July 21. http://www.huffingtonpost.com/meghan-overdeep/justin-timberlake-movie_b_904085.html.

Stahl, Matthew. 2002. "Authentic Boy Bands on TV? Performers and Impresarios in *The Monkees* and *Making the Band.*" *Popular Music* 21, no. 3: 307–329.

Don Traut

Adams, John Coolidge (1947–)

John Coolidge Adams is one of the most influential and innovative American composers of his generation. He is described as a bold musical voice who does not shy away from taking on controversial and sensitive contemporary issues. Orchestras all over the world regularly perform his works.

Adams was born and raised in New England. He became interested in music in the third grade when his father taught him to play the clarinet, and his third-grade teacher took advantage of the fact that it was the bicentennial of Mozart's birth to read his class a biography about Mozart. The book, along with the classical music his teacher played in class, had a huge effect on Adams, and he soon made his first attempts at writing music.

In 1957 Adams's father purchased a 33rpm record player for Christmas. Adams later recalled that no other event in his childhood had changed his life so abruptly as this. He began to spend all his free time listening to recordings by composers and musicians that spanned the centuries from Mozart, Bach, and Beethoven to Duke Ellington and Benny Goodman. By the time he was thirteen years of age, Adams was determined to become a composer.

During his years at Harvard University, Adams explored innovations in sound and harmonies, including those made by popular bands like The Beatles and The Beach Boys. As a student, he conducted the Bach Society Orchestra and played clarinet with the Boston Symphony Orchestra. Adams studied with Leon Kirchner and Roger Sessions. In 1969 he read John Cage's book *Silence,* which had a huge impact on him, particularly Cage's ideas about change and uncertainty and his challenges to questions about what music was.

After graduating from Harvard, Adams moved to California. He taught at the San Francisco Conservatory of Music for twelve years. During this time he wrote several important pieces, including *American Standard,* which explored the American-ness of his background through humor and nostalgia.

Although his original work has spanned the many genres of classical music, Adams is perhaps best known for his operas, which have been controversial at times for his use of minimalist elements, particularly in his earlier music, as well as for his experiments with electronic technology. He remains open to artistic experiences and continues to create music that has connections to the past and present, yet pushes into new and innovative futures.

In 2002 Adams composed *On the Transmigration of Souls* as a memorial to the victims of the September 11, 2001, attacks on the World Trade Center for a commemoration held on the first anniversary of the tragedy.

He was at first reluctant to accept the commission, thinking it would be impossible to create a musical expression about this terrible event, and he felt conflicted over his own feelings about the attacks and his sense of civic duty. The twenty-five-minute piece was premiered by the New York Philharmonic Orchestra on September 19, 2002. Adams received the 2003 Pulitzer Prize for Music for this piece, and Best Classical Recording, Best Orchestral Performance, and Best Classical Contemporary Composition Grammy Awards.

The following composers influenced Adams's work:

Charles Ives
Aaron Copland
Duke Ellington
Conlon Nancarrow

Among his best-known works are the following:

Shaker Loops (1978)
Harmonielehre (1985)
Short Ride in a Fast Machine (1986)
Nixon in China (1987)
The Death of Klinghoffer (1991)
On the Transmigration of Souls (2001)
Dharma at Big Sur (2003)
Doctor Atomic (2007)
City Noir (2009)

See also: Cage, John; September 11th Commemorations

Official Web Site: http://www.earbox.com/

Further Reading

Adams, John. C. 2008 *Hallelujah Junction.* New York: Farrar, Straus & Giroux.

May, Thomas. 2006. *The John Adams Reader: Essential Writings on an American Composer.* Pompton Plains, NJ: Amadeus Press.

Jacqueline Edmondson

Aerosmith (Active 1970–Present)

Known as the "Bad Boys of Boston" and "America's greatest rock 'n' roll band," Aerosmith has left an indelible mark on American music and culture. With its blues-rock sound and raw energy, the group has appealed to audiences for more than forty years. Aerosmith is considered to be one of the best-selling American bands of all time, with more than 150 million albums sold. The band holds the record for the most gold and multiplatinum albums of any American band and has had twenty-one top 40 hits. In 2001 Aerosmith was inducted into the Rock and Roll Hall of Fame, the only band to receive this honor while simultaneously having a song active on the top *Billboard* charts ("Jaded").

Aerosmith started when Joe Perry (1950–) and Tom Hamilton (1951–) had a free-form blues band called the Jam Band. They performed at a venue in Sunapee, New Hampshire, where Steven Tyler (1948–; born Steven Tallarico) heard them play. Tyler and his childhood friend, guitarist Ray Tabano (1946–), had a band called the Chain Reaction (originally The Strangeurs) and dreams of being famous rock stars. Tyler, who loved Jam Band's sound, proposed they form one band, and everyone agreed. Drummer Joey Kramer (1950–), a student at Berklee College of Music, left school to join them. Their first gig was at Nipmuc Regional High School in Mendon, Massachusetts, in 1970. In 1971 Brad Whitford (1952–) replaced Ray Tabano as guitarist for the band.

Aerosmith signed with Columbia Records in 1972. The band's first album, *Aerosmith* (1973), reflected the blues-rock sound that became their signature. *Get Your Wings* (1974) followed, but it was *Toys in the Attic* (1975) that put the band on the international stage. Both *Toys in the Attic* and *Rocks* (1976) are on the *Rolling Stones* 500 Greatest Albums of All Time list.

Aerosmith developed a strong fan base, known as the Blue Army, primarily because they tended to be long-haired boys clad in denim. As the band's popularity grew

Aerosmith Studio Albums

Aerosmith. Columbia Records, 1973.
Get Your Wings. Columbia Records, 1974.
Toys in the Attic. Columbia Records, 1975.
Rocks. Columbia Records, 1976.
Draw the Line. Columbia Records, 1977.
Night in the Ruts. Columbia Records, 1979.
Rock in a Hard Place. Columbia Records, 1982.
Done with Mirrors. Geffen Records, 1985.
Permanent Vacation. Geffen Records, 1987.
Pump. Geffen Records, 1989.
Get a Grip. Geffen Records, 1993.
Nine Lives. Columbia Records, 1997.
Just Push Play. Columbia Records, 2001.
Honkin' on Bob. Columbia Records, 2004.
Music from Another Dimension! Columbia Records, 2012.

Aerosmith performs at New York's Radio City Music Hall during the 11th Annual MTV Video Music Awards, on September 8, 1994. Pictured from the left are: Joey Kramer, drums; Joe Perry, guitar; Steven Tyler, vocals; and Brad Whitford, guitar. (AP Photo/Bebeto Matthews)

and its touring and recording schedules intensified, problems surfaced. Tyler and Perry became known as the "Toxic Twins" because of their drug use both on and off stage. In 1979 Perry left Aerosmith, replaced first by Richard Supa and then by Jimmy Crespo (1954–), to form the Joe Perry Project. In 1981 Whitford left to tour with Joe Perry and was replaced by Rick Dufay (1952–). The band's popularity waned during this time. On February 14, 1984, Perry and Whitford attended an Aerosmith concert and soon after rejoined the band, launching a reunion tour called "Back in the Saddle."

The band's comeback in the late 1980s is considered to be one of the most remarkable in music history. The members went through drug rehabilitation programs and over the next two decades situated themselves firmly in American pop and music culture with appearances on MTV (including the famous "Walk This Way" video with hip-hop group Run-D.M.C., active 1981–2002), *Saturday Night Live,* film and television, and video game music. They toured in places as diverse as Abu Dhabi, Japan, and Latin America. *Permanent Vacation* (1987) was the band's first best-selling album in more than a decade, with three singles reaching the top 10 of the *Billboard* charts ("Dude Looks Like a Lady," "Ragdoll," and "Angel"). *Pump* (1989) soon followed, selling over seven million copies and resulting in three more top 10 singles: "Love in an Elevator," "What It Takes," and "Janie's Got a Gun," which also won Aerosmith its first Grammy. *Get a Grip* (1993) debuted at number one and enjoyed great success on the radio and MTV (including a video for the song "Crazy" that featured Tyler's daughter Liv).

Aerosmith has a firm place in the history of American music and culture. From a clothing line inspired by Steven Tyler's gypsy style of dress, including scarves that are integral to his wardrobe and onstage performances, to *Guitar Hero* and ongoing touring and recording, Aerosmith's influence and popularity persist with new generations of music fans.

Steven Tyler served as a judge on *American Idol* for two seasons beginning in 2010. In 2012 he announced that he would not return to the show because he would be touring with Aerosmith to promote a new album, *Music from Another Dimension!* (2012).

See also: Blues; Clothing Styles and Musicians; Hip-Hop; Music Television; Rock 'n' Roll (Rock); *Saturday Night Live*; Super Bowl Half-Time Shows

Official Web Site: http://www.aerosmith.com

Further Reading

Davis, Stephen. 1997. *Walk This Way: The Autobiography of Aerosmith.* New York: HarperCollins.

Huxley, Martin. 1995. *Aerosmith: The Fall and the Rise of Rock's Greatest Band.* New York: St. Martin's Press.

Tyler, Stephen. 2011. *Does the Noise in My Head Bother You? A Rock 'n' Roll Memoir*. New York: Ecco.

Jacqueline Edmondson

Affrilachian Music

Appalachia is generally conceived of as the contiguous mountainous area of the southern Appalachian Mountain range in eastern North America. "Affrilachian," a term coined by poet Frank X. Walker, refers to African Americans who reside in this region.

The area was first defined as a distinct cultural region in the latter half of the nineteenth century by missionaries and writers of fiction from outside the region. They created the misconception that Appalachia was an isolated and culturally archaic area inhabited by a "racially pure" (Euro-American) people whose culture was similar to that of Elizabethan England. Folk song collectors such as Cecil Sharp wrote about the racially and culturally pure mountaineers, and Dorothy Scarborough wrote about the absence of African Americans in the mountains, the mountaineers' distaste for them, and the "nordic" racial traits of the Appalachian people. Recognizing this as an unconscionable misrepresentation, anthropologist Patricia Beaver observed that Appalachia's history had been "white-washed and homogenized," and Fayetta Allen addressed the Affrilachians' "invisibility."

Affrilachians' invisibility applied not only to their presence in the mountains but also to their musical influence on white mountain music. British folk song collector Cecil Sharp failed to realize that the vocal peculiarity that distinguished Appalachian singing from that of English folksinging was African derived: "They have one vocal peculiarity . . . the habit of dwelling arbitrarily upon certain notes of the melody, generally the weakest accents. This practice, which is almost universal, by disguising the rhythm and breaking up the monotonous regularity of the phrases produces an effect of improvisation and freedom from rule which is very pleasing."

With this context in mind, it is not surprising that Affrilachian music has been invisible. Yet some of the greatest and most influential artists in American music have been Affrilachian. The first serious attempt to document this music came only in the twenty-first century with the three special issues of the *Black Music Research Journal* devoted to the "African-American Music of Appalachia" (2003/2004). The journal brought together for the first time scholarly articles covering diverse aspects of Affrilachian music: jazz, blues, R&B, African and European musical cross-fertilization in Appalachia, and the African origin of the banjo, that quintessential white Appalachian musical instrument, along with an extensive bibliography and a directory of Affrilachian musicians both living and now deceased.

Appalachia is ecologically and topographically the most diverse area in North America, with more plant species and a dazzling variety of microclimates and ecological niches. Not surprisingly, the variety of people and cultural practices reflects this natural diversity.

The diversity and many varieties of Affrilachian music also contribute to its invisibility. Logically, one would expect that the higher the percentage of African Americans in a region's population, the more likely a distinct African American musical style would develop. This is the case with the Mississippi Delta or the Piedmont blues, which can be described and a stylistic complex articulated. In Appalachia, an area in which African Americans represent a smaller proportion of the population and in which they are widely scattered, traditionally living in small, isolated communities, descriptions of coherent region-wide African American musical styles are not possible. Affrilachia ranges from urban centers, such as Birmingham, Alabama; Chattanooga, Tennessee; and Roanoke, Virginia, to small towns and farmsteads across the region, to the coalfields of Kentucky and West Virginia. Barry Lee Pearson observed that Affrilachian music is composed of a "musical Kaleidoscope rather than a single thread."

Pearson identified and describes four Appalachian blues styles: vaudeville blues, piano blues and boogie woogie, string band blues, and guitar and harmonica-based down-home blues. He also described their regional, and especially with vaudeville blues and Birmingham-based piano blues, national impacts. Affrilachian vaudeville or "classic blues" include such outstanding and influential figures as Bessie Smith, Ida Cox, Lucille Bogan, and Clara Smith. (Poet doris davenport, in her analysis of Cox's lyrics, identifies a distinctive "Appalachian Ballad Blues.") Nationally significant Affrilachian piano innovators include Birmingham-based Walter Roland, Robert McCoy, the boogie woogie stylings of Clarence "Pinetop" Smith (1904–1929), and Tennessee's Clarence "Cripple" Lofton, all of whom were born in the early twentieth or late nineteenth centuries. String band blues is represented by recording artists such as the Birmingham Jug Band and the trio of Howard Armstrong, Carl Martin, and Roland Martin, whom the record company dubbed the "Tennessee Chocolate Drops." World famous artists, including the guitarists Reverend Gary Davis (South Carolina), Walter "Brownie" McGhee (Tennessee), Josh White (South Carolina), and John Jackson (Virginia), and the harmonica player Walter "Jaybird" Coleman (Alabama), represent Pearson's fourth category of Affrilachian blues.

Jazz musicians and educators Todd Wright and John Higby conclude that there is not *an* Appalachian jazz, but several Appalachian jazz styles, found primarily in urban "pockets": Pittsburgh and the upper Ohio River watershed (including Earl "Fatha" Hines, Errol Garner, Ahmad Jamal, Art Blakey, Roy Eldridge, Billy Eckstine, and Kenny Clarke); Chattanooga/Knoxville/Birmingham (including Lovie Austin, Jimmy Blanton, Erskine Hawkins, Yusef Lateef, Lucky Millinder, and Sun Ra); and "the corridor of cities along I-85 and I-40 in the Carolinas" (Cat Anderson, Arthur and Red Prysock, and Alvin Jolly).

American gospel group the Dixie Hummingbirds singing around a CBS microphone. Included in the group are Ira Tucker, James Walker, Beachy Thompson, William Bobo and James Klavis, ca. 1955. (Frank Driggs Collection/ Getty Images)

Likewise, R&B in Appalachia is a diverse lot. Jerry Zolten traces the influence of African American gospel music, Affrilachian blues, Affrilachian vaudeville blues, and such early R&B stars as Granville "Sticks" McGhee (brother to Brownie McGhee) on the development of Affrilachian soul music. Affrilachian soul includes Alabama's Percy Sledge, Jimmy Hughes, Candi Station, Arthur Alexander, and Eddie Kendricks; North Carolina's Nina Simone and Roberta Flack; Tennessee's Lattimore; South Carolina's Peabo Bryson and Kip Anderson; Virginia's Carl Anderson and producer Creed Taylor; West Virginia's Bill Withers and Johnny Johnson (a pianist who had earlier helped shape the sound of Chuck Berry's rock 'n' roll); Georgia's Hamilton Bohannon and the Toccoa sound of Bobby Byrd and James Brown; Pittsburgh's rich and varied R&B scene; and Appalachia Kentucky radio station WMMT's combination of old-time white fiddle and banjo music with Affrilachian hip-hop. Zolten concludes that the whole history of R&B grew with important influences from Appalachia's African American community, "in contemporary Appalachia it would seem that these possibilities are still literally in the air."

Affrilachian gospel has had a profound influence on African American music. The great Dixie Hummingbirds from Greenville, South Carolina, were an influence on both gospel and secular music (such as that of James Brown). The Birmingham, Alabama, quartet tradition of the Famous Blue Jay Singers, Sterling Jubilees, Birmingham Jubilee Singers, Four Eagles, and more recently the Birmingham Sunlights have set the standard, influencing gospel quartet singing nationwide and, in addition, have influenced many crossover pop groups, including The Ink Spots and The Platters. Other outstanding Affrilachian quartets include Spartanburg, South Carolina's Sensational Nightingales and West Virginia–based Swan Silvertones. Affrilachian gospel was not just quartet singing, but rather a variety of performers, from Georgia's sanctified singer-guitarist Sister O. M. Terrell, to Birmingham's star Dorothy Love Coates, to South Carolina's famous guitar player and powerful singer, the Reverend Gary Davis.

Musicians from Affrilachia were important for their work not only in those musical genres traditionally associated with African America, but also in pop music, including such diverse artists as Georgia's Roland Hayes, Virginia's Basin Street Boys, and West Virginia's Maceo Pinkard, composer of such classics as "Sweet Georgia Brown" and "Them There Eyes." Country and western music is represented by Affrilachians such as Leslie Riddle, who taught A. P. Carter of The Carter Family many songs and who influenced Mother Maybelle Carter's guitar playing, and Georgia's Boyd Singleton, who taught medicine show performer–country and western singer Ramblin' Tommy Scott how to play guitar. Affrilachian musicians, including Josh White, Gary Davis, Etta Baker, and Brownie McGhee, among others, were lionized by and influential upon the folk revivals of the mid-twentieth century.

Music scholar Tony Russell observed in 1970 that due to "racial antipathy," white–black musical "interaction was more fertile in areas where blacks were scattered." Paul Oliver suggested that in those areas most peripheral to African American musical innovation and black population concentration—Appalachia is a periphery and the Mississippi Delta a center of black population concentration and musical innovation—would be more likely to have a more traditional African American music least affected by innovation. This is the case in Appalachia, where white music owed a great debt to the music of Affrilachia and vice versa. Thus Affrilachian music tends to be both more traditional and multicultural (as early as 1936, Alain Locke commented on the mountains' "parallel Negro versions of hill ballads") than the black music of the Delta. If we accept Russell and Oliver's arguments, then Affrilachian music on the peripheries of Appalachia and closer to areas of greater black population (western South Carolina, northeast Georgia, Birmingham and the Mississippi Hill Country) should be more innovative in terms of a distinctive black music than that in the region's interior.

Historian Sterling Stuckey wrote "that the oneness of black culture in the twentieth century abounds" and observed that the spread of southern black music and musicians to the north continued to influence new trends in African American music. The same can be claimed for the less African, more multicultural music of Affrilachia; its impact on the entire landscape of African diaspora music continues to be profound.

See also: Banjo; Blues; Carter Family, The; Davis, Gary (Reverend); Jazz; R&B

Further Reading

Hay, Fred J., ed. 2003–2004. "African-American Music from Appalachia." *Black Music Research Journal* 23, nos. 2/3; 24, no 1: 1–19. (All sources cited in this entry can be found in this article.)

Locke, Alain. 1937. *The Negro and His Music.* Bronze Booklet no. 2.Washington, DC: Associates in Negro Education.

Fred J. Hay

African American Gospel Music

African Americans have provided significant contributions to the cultural heritage of the United States. The visual art, poetry, dance, stories, and music of African Americans are rich chronicles of historical, social, economic, and aesthetic events that have framed the march toward freedom since the period of slavery. African American gospel music in particular has had broad influence on American culture, as singers like Whitney Houston (1963–2012), Aretha Franklin (1942–), Sam Cooke (1931–1964), Ray Charles (1930–2004), James Brown (1933–2006), and Marvin Gaye (1939–1984) transformed the gospel music of their youth for audiences around the world, bringing its influences to soul, R&B, rock, and popular music.

At the end of the nineteenth century there was a huge migration of blacks from the rural South to the North and West to pursue jobs. Many urban areas, such as Chicago, St. Louis, Kansas City, Los Angeles, Detroit, and New York City, provided opportunities in their communities for new churches, community-based organizations, lodges, and schools to develop. The Urban League (1910) and the National Association for the Advancement of Colored People (1909) were organized during this transition period in America to formally address the social, economic, and political needs of an emerging black community. The music that framed worship services in Baptist, Catholic, Pentecostal, Methodist, and other denominations drew from the sounds of hymns, spirituals, and gospel music of the day.

Black gospel music is among the genres of contemporary black culture that has contributed greatly to the culture and music of the United States and the world.

What Is Gospel Music?

Many understand gospel music to be a vocal/choral style performed in churches of a variety of denominations within the African American community. Texts may be based on stories from the Bible, revival or Sunday school hymns, African American spirituals, or freely composed pieces that express aspects of one's faith journey. The musical accompaniment may be as simple as a piano, harmonica, guitar, or organ, or the songs may simply be sung without instrumental support. In the end, it is the feeling that the performer brings to the act of sharing the "good news" from his or her walk with God that provides the congregation or concert audience with an opportunity to experience the emotional, spiritual, and musical release that frames much of what one considers traditional and contemporary gospel music.

Musicians

Thomas A. Dorsey (1899–1993) began his professional career as a blues pianist in Georgia before making the transition to Chicago, Illinois. A series of life-changing personal events forced Dorsey to consider his involvement with secular music. He composed "Precious Lord, Take My Hand" (1931) and championed the musical development of other gospel artists based in Chicago, in particular Roberta Martin (1907–1969), Sallie Martin (1895–1988), and Mahalia Jackson (1911–1972).

Influential African American Gospel Artists, Composers, and Arrangers

Shirley M. K. Berkeley (b. 1929)	Glenn Burleigh (1949–2007)	Rev. John P. Kee (b. 1962)
Shirley Caesar (b. 1938)	Walter Hawkins (1949–2010)	Kurt Carr (b. 1964)
Andraé Crouch (b. 1942)	Raymond Wise (b. 1961)	Smokie Norful (b. 1975)
Richard Smallwood (b. 1948)	Donald Lawrence (b. 1961)	

Dorsey organized the National Convention of Gospel Choirs and Singers in 1933. During his career as composer, performer, music publisher, and organizer, Dorsey helped to make gospel music for choirs in black American churches standard musical fare on Sunday morning. His compositions may be found in publications such as *The New National Baptist Hymnal* (1977) and the *African American Heritage Hymnal* (2001).

Reverend James Cleveland (1931–1991) was celebrated as the "Crown Prince of Gospel Music." Pianist, composer, singer, and founder of the Gospel Music Workshop of America (1968), Cleveland was born in Chicago, and his early music experiences at the Pilgrim Baptist Church where Thomas Dorsey was director of music brought him into close contact with many people who would ultimately provide inspiration and mentoring for his career in music and ministry. Cleveland inspired generations of singers and choirs through his work with Albertina Walker (1929–2010) and the Caravans; Roberta Martin; Delores Barrett Campbell (1926–2011); the James Cleveland Singers; Billy Preston (1946–2006); the Southern California Community Choir; the Voices of Tabernacle (Detroit, Michigan); the Angelic Choir (First Baptist Church, Nutley, New Jersey); and their pastor, Rev. Lawrence Roberts (1931–2007). In 1963 the musical collaboration with Cleveland and the Angelic Choir combined in the release of "Peace Be Still." Released by Savoy Records, this album sold over one million copies.

Cleveland organized the Gospel Music Workshop of America in 1968. The first convention of this international organization was held in Detroit at the King Solomon Temple. The organization now involves divisions for youth/children, women, men, ushers, religious announcers, quartets, and the massed choir, as well as the Academic Division, which provides classes and workshops in a wide range of topics for persons seeking instruction in or information on gospel music.

Dr. Margaret Douroux (1941–), daughter of Rev. Earl Pleasant, is a composer, pianist, singer, conductor, and scholar. Her significant contribution to the field of gospel music as composer has resulted in hundreds of published traditional gospel selections, including "Give Me a Clean Heart," "If It Had Not Been for The Lord on My Side," "Trees," "Mercy That Suits My Case," and "I Will Heal Your Land." She founded the Heritage Music Foundation (1985) for the preservation, promotion, performance, and study of black gospel music. She is minister of music at Pleasant Grove Baptist Church in Los Angeles, California, and a member of the Academic Division of the Gospel Music Workshop of America.

Three individuals' contributions as scholars or performers have positively enhanced the place of gospel music within academic and other institutional settings. Dr. Pearl Williams Jones (1931–1991) was a pianist, singer, composer, and teacher. Her articles on black gospel music may be found in the journal *Ethnomusicology.* A native of Washington, D.C., Jones's father and mother founded the Bible Way Church of Jesus Christ. She was a faculty member at the University of the District of Columbia, where she administered an undergraduate degree program in gospel music studies.

Dr. Horace Clarence Boyer (1935–2009) was a native of Winter Park, Florida, and along with his brother, James, performed as the Boyer Brothers, sharing their unique and creative arrangements of traditional gospel music and spirituals. Horace Boyer was also a prolific scholar who wrote articles on African American gospel music for the Music Educators National Conference (MENC), *Black Perspectives in Music,* and *The New Grove Dictionary of American Music.* Boyer was an amazing and inspiring pianist, vocalist, and composer.

Bernice Johnson Reagon (1942–), a native of Georgia, is the daughter of a pastor. She participated in the civil rights movement as a member of the Student Non-Violent Coordinating Committee, where she was a member of the SNCC Singers. Reagon's work in African American music emerged through her role as a curator at the Smithsonian Institution's Museum of American History. Of equal significance was her role as founder of the female a cappella group Sweet Honey in the Rock, which specializes in many genres of African/African American vocal music, as evidenced by their extensive concert performances and recording projects since 1973.

Timeline of Events, Trends, and Organizations in Gospel Music from 1960 to the Present

1960s Traditional gospel music, spirituals, hymns, and anthems are the basic repertoire performed by choirs in African American churches.

TV Gospel Time, a national syndicated show of gospel music artists, begins broadcasting.

Members of the all-female vocal group Sweet Honey in the Rock, founded in 1973 at the Washington, D.C., Black Repertory Theater Company. Pictured from the left are Ysaye Maria Barnwell, Nitanju Bolade-Casel, Shirley Childress Johnson, Carol Lynn Maillard, Aisha Kahlil, and Bernice Johnson Reagon in foreground, 1994. (Michael A. Smith/Time Life Pictures/Getty Images)

The first gospel choirs are organized on college campuses and at urban high schools across the United States. These ensembles are often led by students.

Community-based ensembles such as the Thompson Community Choir (Chicago), State Choir of Southwest Michigan C.O.G.I.C (Church of God in Christ), Voices of Hope (Los Angeles), and Utterbach Concert Ensemble (New York, N.Y.) are recognized through their recording projects and performances in churches and concert halls across the country.

Edwin Hawkins and Betty Watson organize the Northern California Youth Choir for the annual convention of the C.O.G.I.C. "O Happy Day" is presented to the world at this conference and receives national and international recognition.

Recordings by many gospel artists and choirs are distributed locally and through regional and national tours. Savoy Records is a primary distributor of recordings for artists, including Rev. James Cleveland, Albertina Walker, Dorothy Love Coates, The Davis Sisters, Alex Bradford, Mattie Moss Clark, Inez Andrews, and others.

1970s Traditional gospel, contemporary gospel, concert spirituals, hymns, and anthems are the basic repertoire performed by choirs in African American churches and community-based ensembles.

The New National Baptist Hymnal is published in 1978 and begins the transformation process for congregational singing, blending traditional gospel selections with traditional hymns. Other denominations in the black church also edit new hymnal editions.

Musical leadership of gospel choirs in academic institutions is provided by professional music educators and students. Gospel choirs in historically black colleges and universities are highly visible ensembles at campus events honoring the legacy of Martin Luther King Jr. and Black History Month.

Broadway welcomes shows such as *Purlie* and *Don't Bother Me, I Can't Cope,* which use a variety of musical styles, including traditional gospel.

Edwin Hawkins and Walter Hawkins organize the first Music, Arts and Love Fellowship Conference in 1979, bringing together gospel artists, composers, event presenters, pastors, and choirs from across the country.

Mar-Vel Music Publishing company is a primary distributor of traditional gospel, hymn settings for choirs, and anthems by African American composers. Roland Carter, CEO, is also director of choral activities at Hampton University and is pivotal in maintaining high print standards for this industry.

1980s Traditional gospel, contemporary gospel, gospel hip-hop, urban gospel, gospel rap, praise/worship choruses, concert spirituals, hymns, and anthems are the basic repertoire performed by choirs in African American churches and community-based ensembles. Many youth and young adult choirs begin to specialize in contemporary gospel idioms that involve choreography.

Business organizations such as Kentucky Fried Chicken, McDonald's, and Pathmark Supermarkets sponsor local, regional, and national competitions for gospel choirs in cities such as Philadelphia, Pennsylvania; Washington, D.C.; Chicago; New York; and Los Angeles.

The Gospel Music Workshop of America requires composers and arrangers submitting compositions for the National Massed Choir to no longer use manuscript scores. The New Music Seminar at GMWA is initiated as an additional venue for the presentation of traditional and contemporary gospel selections.

Composers Robert Ray ("Gospel Mass") and Glenn Burleigh ("Born to Die") create multi-movement works for choir, soloists, and orchestra that achieve recognition within the black church community and beyond.

Bobby Jones Gospel premieres on Black Entertainment Television (BET) in 1980. This program is nationally syndicated and helps to promote the careers of gospel artists Yolanda Adams, Kirk Franklin, and others.

A new trend for performing artists is to release a "songbook folio" along with their new recording projects. This gives choral conductors and musicians access to the scores. It also improves the quality of the accompaniment to support soloists, choirs, and congregations in performing music of the day.

1990s Compact disc, MIDI, DVD, and other electronic technologies positively transform the transmission process for live, recorded, and print music. Performance tracks are in greater use by vocal soloists, liturgical dance ensembles, and choirs emphasizing all aspects of urban and contemporary gospel.

The emphasis on getting gospel music distributed beyond American culture increases as a result of global travel by gospel artists and choirs, especially to Africa, the Pacific Rim, and Europe.

A trend emerges in the repertoire performed by high school and college or university and festival choirs, wherein the concert spiritual that traditionally closed a formal concert is replaced by a contemporary or traditional gospel selection. This trend may be documented by reviewing programs from choirs performing at state, regional, and national conventions of the Music Educators National Conference (MENC) and the American Choral Directors Association (ACDA).

Praise and worship choruses, hymns, and traditional spirituals provide the basis for most congregational singing in black churches. Some churches use video projection screens rather than hymnals in the pew to provide visual support for congregational singing. Electronic keyboards, guitars, percussion, and various wind instruments form the core of the instrumental accompaniment for congregational and ensemble performance. Emphasis on the use of acoustic keyboard instruments (grand piano, pipe organ) diminishes due to budget cuts, lack of maintenance, and changing trends in the music industry.

African American conductors in college and university institutions bridge the leadership gap in providing experiences for singers in traditional choirs and gospel choirs. Such institutions include University of Massachusetts, Florida State, Penn State, University of Arkansas, University of Illinois, Ohio State, Morgan State, University of California Northridge, Westminster Choir College, and others.

2000s Composers such as Moses Hogan, Roland Carter, Glenn Burleigh, Raymond Wise, Richard Smallwood, Kirk Franklin, Kurt Carr, Fred Hammond, Keith Hampton, Rosephanye Powell, Robert Morris, Nathan Carter, Rollo Dilworth, Joseph Joubert, Margaret Douroux, Rev. John P. Kee, V. Michael McKay, Stanley Spottswood, Jeffrey Ames, and Andre Thomas are the brightest and best contributors to the entire soundscape of African American choral music. The range of choral styles represented within this group of innovative artists is unlimited. Their ability to put in the musical score all of the performance practice requirements necessary to ensure high-caliber performances by choirs and ensembles of gospel and spiritual choral music is commendable.

Choral arrangements for child, youth, high school, female, male, church, college and university, and community choirs by music publishers such as Hal Leonard, GIA, Alliance, Heritage, earthsongs, and Boosey and Hawkes recognize the significant economic potential for African American sacred music.

Ntimemusic, based in Charlotte, North Carolina, has become a premier publisher of contemporary and traditional gospel music. Its inventory includes CDs, DVDs, sheet music, and instructional materials for gospel music. The company also provides an important download and music transcription service for composers and artists.

YouTube Music has transformed access to music performances from around the world. The archival capacity to upload historical and current performances of music from the African American community, as well as other musical entities, is unlimited.

See also: African American Influences on American Music; African American Spiritual Music; Brown, James; Charles, Ray; Dorsey, Jimmy, and Tommy Dorsey; Franklin, Aretha; Gaye, Marvin; Houston, Whitney; Sacred Music

Further Reading

Darden, Robert. 2005. *People Get Ready! A New History of Black Gospel Music.* New York: Continuum.

Heilbut, Anthony. 1997. *The Gospel Sound: Good News and Bad Times—25th Anniversary Edition.* New York: Proscenium Publishers.

Walker, Wyatt Tee. 1982. *Somebody's Calling My Name: Black Sacred Music and Social Change.* Valley Forge, PA: Judson Press.

Anthony T. Leach

African American Influences on American Music

Understanding how African American musical forms influence American music requires making a distinction that may betray the complex, historical evolution of American music. To be sure, many do not see a difference between African American music and American music. African American musical practices and traditions are considered to be under the cultural and nationalistic umbrella of American music because of the peculiar, historical circumstances that formed America's indigenous music. Styles of improvised music, for example, were pioneered by African American musicians. These styles and performance practices are usually referred to by the limiting moniker "jazz." Jazz is often referred to as "America's classical music," which not only represents a conservative view of a living, vibrant musical form that has continually changed American music, but possibly obscures the peculiar, marginalized African American cultural history that spawned this internationally beloved world music. Talking about Black musical influences requires a brief historical context that may illuminate this complex history.

Collision of Music Cultures/Origin of Influences

African American influences on American music resulted from the transatlantic slave trade (also referred to as The Middle Passage), which transported enslaved Africans on sea journeys for the purpose of building wealth in the New World. The subsequent adaptation and transformation of Euro-American music cultures by enslaved Africans was one of the unpredictable results of violent encounters that dehumanized enslaved Africans in horrific ways. In the midst of tragedy and violence, adaptation and transformation through syncretism was necessary. *Syncretism* is the combining of at least two different religions, cultures, philosophies, and worldviews and is often the result of colonialism. Distinct characteristics of African and European musical cultures predated the fusion of these musical worldviews into dynamic American musical forms.

The conflation of Euro-American and African musical practices resulted from exposure and adaptation of Africans to the melodies, rhythms, harmonies, and compositional structures of Euro-American music. Gaining aural exposure to those musical ideas, enslaved Africans incorporated and then transformed those ideas into their own musical styles, which reflected their social and musical priorities. Yet Sterling Stuckey (1987) teaches us that "the Ring Shout," the African American counterclockwise religious dance ceremony (still practiced today by the Gullah Geechee in Georgia) was the primary source of African values and communal inspiration for African American musical forms. This process of adaptation and musical transformation, which has happened throughout the history of American music, continues to shape American musical practices today. Before discussing specific influences, we briefly review how European musical culture differs from African music culture.

Divergent Musical Cultures and Practices

European and African musical traditions developed in divergent ways based on different cultures. Culture is a very complex thing to define. According to critical musicologist Christopher Small, "culture is a set of attitudes,

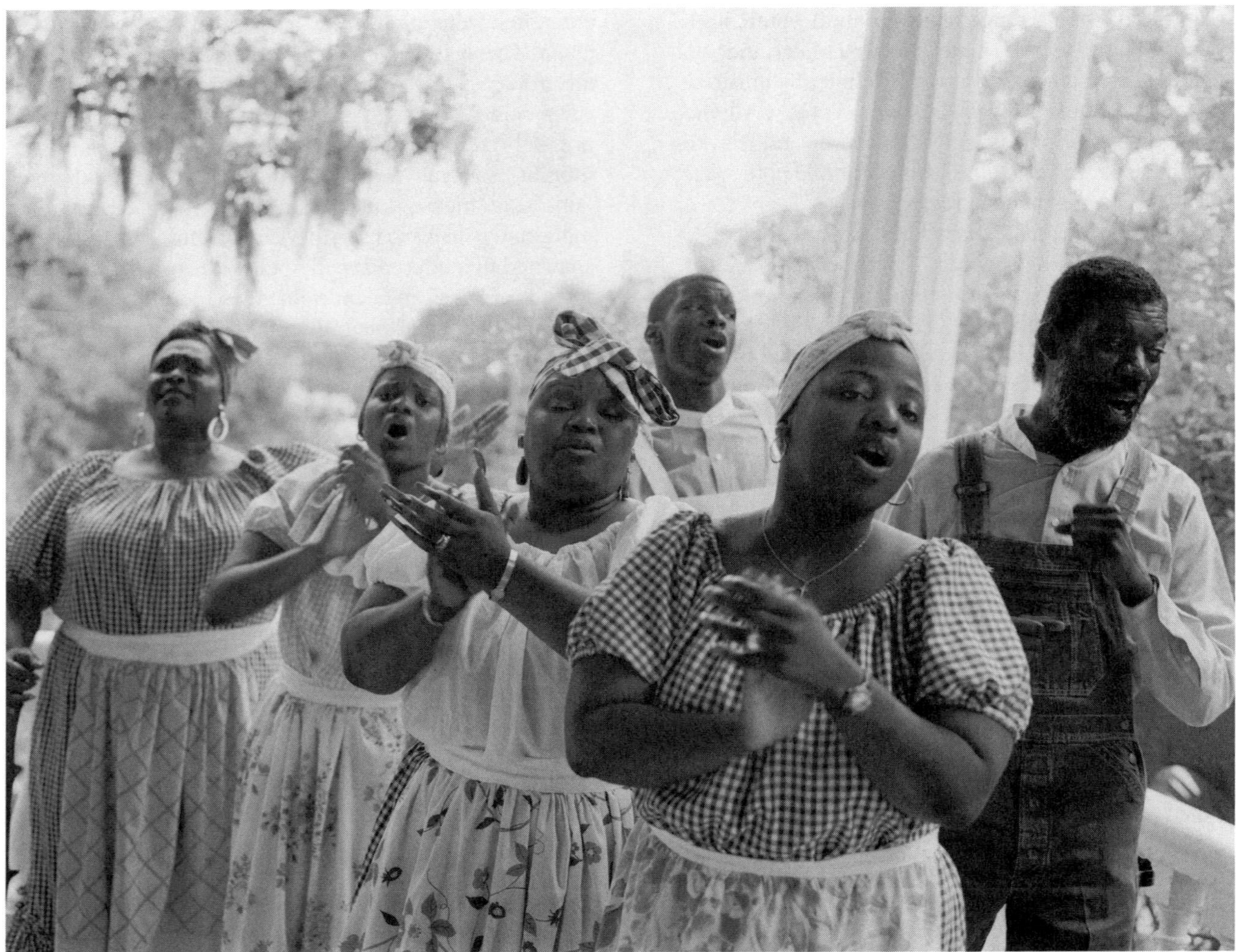

Gullah gospel singers perform in Beaufort, South Carolina. (Cathrine Wessel/Corbis)

assumptions and values by means of which a person or a group of people is able to find meaning in, or give meaning to, not only the objects and events of the environment but also to inner experiences, and to construct from them a consistent and usable picture of the world and of relationships within it. In this sense every single human being is cultured, since it is by means of the choices governed by culture that he or she is able to find some order in the seemingly limitless variety of experience" (1998, 120).

The precolonial differences between African and European approaches to music can be understood within this context. Musical cultures were constructed from an inner and social understanding of the world. For example, the European music tradition historically requires a distinction between musicians and audience/listeners (this distinction is symbolized by the stage that separates the artists and the laypeople), whereas the communal nature of African music making has no such distinction. Though professional African musicians are accorded a special place in society, the entire community is invited to participate in the music making process.

Music is not accorded a separate space in daily African life, but rather is the life-affirming thread that is woven through the most mundane activities and the most sacred rituals. Music, a word that does not exist in many African tribes, is not considered to be a sound track or accompaniment to daily life, but is instinctively understood to be the very nexus of African life.

The European musical tradition is largely characterized by the tradition of performing compositions as accurately as possible according to rigid historical performance practice requirements. Musicianship is judged by how well the performer repeats the song in the same way. For example, performing a Mozart symphony as closely to the performance practices of Mozart's era is a cultural expectation. Classical musicians of our time must rely on the score, or the written notes or notation of the composition, which includes notes on dynamics, phrasing, tempo, etc., to approximate the sound of an eighteenth-century Mozart composition. Euro-American tradition is the only one in which musical notation, or the art of transcribing notes onto paper, becomes the inspiration for musical creativity (Small 1998, 43). The identity and integrity of the Euro-American tradition of music is thought to survive through this practice. In stark contrast, African American musicians inherited a creative process informed by a tradition based on thinking of music as a process that continually develops. Space for constant musical evolution is the result of no fixed form of musical composition. African "compositions" and repertoire are not considered too important to be modified or changed. Historically, Africans discarded compositions that outlived their social purpose or function. Music was partially or completely discarded or referenced in new music. This is a stark contrast to the traditional and widespread Euro-American practice of adhering to strict performance traditions.

Alternate Takes

Several alternate takes or alternate performances of jazz musical compositions on popular 1960s Blue Note recordings illustrate how African American musicians have thought of creating music as a process. Jazz musicians often recorded a song more than once, because they wanted to try different arrangements, correct mistakes, or just have an alternate take. Realizing jazz compositions through improvisation is an example of African American musicians seeing performance as a continually evolving process instead of a musical object bound by rigid rules. Both "sampling" and covering earlier periods of Black music provide countless examples of how this process takes place. "Sampling" refers to the practice of using technology to take certain aspects of a musical composition from an earlier recording, such as a drum beat, guitar riff, or melody fragment (to cite just a few possibilities) and reorchestrate them into a new composition. "Covering" a song, in African American musical practices, refers to performing an older music composition with a new arrangement. Who wants to hear musicians fail at approximating an original version of a fantastic song? The covering of earlier Black music, such as The Brother Johnson's 1970s' classic *Strawberry Letter 23* by R&B singer Akon (1973–) on *Q: Soul Bossa Nostra,* is another example of how music evolves through a process of alteration and expansion. Sampling is brilliantly represented by how a portion of George Clinton's (1941–) *Parliament* song "Swing Down, Sweet Chariot" is used by rapper-producer-record executive Dr. Dre (1965–) in his song "Let Me Ride."

Dispersion of Musical Africanisms

The inner structures and philosophies of Black music can be taught and learned by nonblacks (Gilroy 1993). Certainly the innovations of Black musicians have been adopted by countless nonblack performers throughout the world. Moreover, African musical influences are not confined to American cultures, but have circulated throughout the Black diaspora. For example, Afrobeat inventor and Nigerian musician Fela Anikulapo-Kuti's style (1938–1997) was influenced by the Black nationalism message embedded in the grooves, horn arrangements, and compositional style of funk pioneer James Brown (1933–2006), but Brown was also influenced by the Afrobeat grooves of Fela (Veal 2000).

The inner structures and philosophies of Black music can be taught and learned by nonblacks. Certainly the innovations of Black musicians have been co-opted by countless nonblack performers throughout the world.

African musical retentions that have survived have been the basis for innovations in contemporary African American music. These retentions are not static and are revealed in multiple hybrid musical styles that are linked to the broader undercurrent and encompassing network of African retentions. African retentions influence the wider performance practices in every musical genre.

African Retentions in Sound, Delivery, and Style

Africanisms have been described by ethnomusicologist Portia Maultsby (1989) as a core group of conceptual approaches that shape modern-day African American music and consequently, American music. For example, music is communal and participatory. Second, innovative musical ideas are connected to old African music traditions. Third, concepts of what music should sound like and how it should be interpreted all come from an African frame of reference that has been retained in a collective African consciousness and cultural memory.

Maultsby identifies three areas of aesthetic significance in the Black musical tradition: the timbre, the sound quality or texture of instrumental performance; the delivery of the performance, which has to do with understanding of the pitch text and time in vocal performance; and the style delivery, which is how Black musicians embody their art through their bodily expressions.

The timbre of the iconic blues-laced trumpet sound of jazz musician Miles Davis (1926–1991) illustrates how markedly different concepts of timbre in traditional Western European art music are from those in African American art music. Davis's understanding of sound is situated within the context of his evolving experience as a Black male musician in America. A classical trumpet concerto sound requires a different approach to sound texture that bespeaks different musico-cultural priorities. Davis's sound, which has circulated around the globe in popular recordings such as "Kind of Blue," has influenced many American musicians and musicians all over the world, who have attempted to re-create his beautiful, ghostly sound on their own instruments.

African cultural retentions of mechanics and delivery are illustrated in the singing style of African American jazz vocalist Billie Holiday (1915–1959), which has been a performative model for many vocalists. Born out of the tapestry of the blues, Holiday's vocal innovations, which include brilliant manipulations of pitch linked to her iconic timbre and her conception of rhythm that defies common time and allows her to illuminate lyrics of well-worn torch songs, are all African American attributes that continue to impact American popular song. Frank Sinatra (1915–1998) (the Elvis of early twentieth-century American popular song), Joni Mitchell (1943–), and Madeleine Peyroux (1974–) are just a few examples of performers influenced by Holiday's innovations.

Impact on American Popular Music

We came over here and it was the same: nobody was listening to rock and roll or to Black music in America. We were coming to the land of its origin but nobody wanted to know about it.

—John Lennon

The Beatles' member John Lennon's (1940–1980) comments about resistance to Black musical culture portray the shunning of African American music culture by the dominant white culture, which associated blues-oriented music with Black depravity, and by many middle-class Blacks, who sought to avoid the stigma of a music associated with promiscuity, drugs, and itinerancy. Yet Lennon's valuable outsider narrative does not tell the entire story. Many African Americans embraced their music, transforming American popular culture in the process.

African Americans have long had an impact on American popular music. Tin Pan Alley songs, the popular songs of the 1920s and 1930s, were transformed into vehicles for jazz improvisation. Tin Pan Alley is a name given to a district in New York City where famous songwriters and music publishers were based. American composers Duke Ellington (1899–1974), George (1898–1937) and Ira Gershwin (1896–1983), and Richard Rodgers (1902–1979) are just a few of those associated with Tin Pan Alley. African American jazz musicians transformed these early twentieth-century popular songs by recording them at different tempos, with modernized harmonies and cutting edge arrangements that set the musical framework for highlighting their mastery of improvisation.

Transforming the harmony and rhythms of original versions of American popular songs into more harmonically and rhythmically sophisticated compositions is just one thing African American musicians brought to American popular song. Twentieth-century American pianist-composer Thelonious Sphere Monk (1917–1982) was a master of deconstructing melodies, harmonies, and rhythms of well-known popular songs and making a standard American popular song into a work that seemed as though it was written by his own hand. Monks's recording of Duke Ellington (1899–1974) compositions is an example of how an African American musician can transform well-known repertoire into something with a unique musical signature.

African American vocalist Aretha Franklin (1942–) and her band (*Live at the Fillmore*) transformed the Crosby, Stills & Nash (active 1968–1970, 1973–1974, 1977–present) hit "Love the One You're With," a folk song–style paean to bachelorhood that itself was influenced by African American gospel music, into an up-tempo, gospel, and R&B form with complex horn arrangements.

"Eleanor Rigby," a composition by The Beatles, whose harmonies are held together by a tight, unrelenting, and sometimes staccato string arrangement, is transformed by Franklin and her band into a two-chord gospel riff that is often heard in American Pentecostal, and Baptist Black churches. A song about loneliness, it is infused with the communal Black church experience represented in Franklin's transformative performance.

Elvis Presley (1935–1977) represents the complex conflation of black and white musical cultures that interrupts any clear definition of American musical culture. A committed disciple of Black music styles, Presley, who fused sounds of Black R&B with country music to create rockabilly, symbolizes the circulatory powers of Black music to transform and uplift a poor boy from Tupelo, Mississippi, into an international icon who had a major impact on American musical culture. A twentieth-century iconic conduit for representing through performance once-marginalized Black musical styles, Elvis distributed the bittersweet but benign pathogen of Black musical ideas that has spread across the global cultural topography, changing the musical cultures of other nations.

Many critics shunned Elvis, a white male, for what they viewed as his performances of fetishized Black male heterosexuality. Yet despite the vast, racist historical literature and caricatures about Black promiscuity, no race is inherently more sexual than another race, and the performance of sexuality is not uniform. Moreover, the embodiment of Black musical culture by nonblack artists is not the equivalent of understanding the deep, complex cultural values that make African American music so powerful. Historian and cultural critic Daphne Brooks's (2008) criticism of singer Amy Winehouse (1983–2011) for using the sound of racial uplift of Black artists from Motown to portray and celebrate debauchery in her lyrics and music videos reminds us that understanding how one sees oneself in the world of blues directs musical and life choices.

Social Progress and the Blues

Representations of independence, freedom, and sexuality in music can be traced to the work of early African American female blues singers who have influenced the performance practices of artists of both genders. Since the limited emancipation of enslaved African Americans in the late nineteenth century, the blues as an African American musical form has been a vehicle for challenging social norms and living a creative life (Davis 1998, 74).

Whereas male blues singers led itinerant lifestyles for the purpose of finding employment and enjoying new-found freedom, African American women were expected to focus on domestic duties, which ultimately denied them opportunities of travel. Yet blues singers such as Gertrude "Ma" Rainey (1886–1939) and Bessie Smith (1894–1937) defied social conventions and expectations as they led lives of rare, Black female autonomy.

The complex representations of cosmopolitanism; bold, unapologetic sexuality; and feminism that are found in the work of Beyoncé (1981–), Madonna (1958–), Katy Perry (1984); who boldly "kissed a girl and liked it"), Joni Mitchell (1943–; who sings eloquently of her life on the road in her album *Hejira*), and Lady Gaga (1986–), just to mention a few, can be traced to the work of defying social constructs by blues women. Moreover, African American female blues singers created unprecedented space for diverse and complex expression by both female and male artists. Even the random physical contortions of Rolling Stones lead vocalist Mick Jagger (1943–) benefited from the strength, courage, and boldness of pioneering women blues singers who set high standards for the music industry. The musical style and fame of singer Janis Joplin (1943–1970) were made possible by the work of Willie Mae "Big Mama" Thornton (1926–1984), who evoked the sacred ring shout in every note she sang.

African American Musicians' Use of Technology and Their Influence on American Music

African American influence on American music is not a one-way street. Blacks have historically incorporated musical cultures and environmental sounds around them. Whether it be the incorporation of the sound of train locomotion in traditional, jazz swing patterns; the dissonant harmonies of whistle sounds in innumerable blues songs, such as "Midnight Train to Georgia," performed by Gladys Knight & the Pips (active 1953–1989); or even the sound tracks in shopping malls, African American musicians have absorbed sounds and re-created them from their various non-monolithic musical perspectives and environments. Lipsitz (2007), citing John Swed, points out that nearly all of the familiar elements in electronic music are variations of African American acoustic instrumental performance. Wah-wah pedals replicated the sound of plunger mutes. Reverb, distortion, and multitonal effects originated in buzz tones and split tones. Phrasing and delay are forms of call and response. The art of feedback in the work of vocalist-guitarist Jimmy Hendrix (1942–1970) stems from the same genetic code that redefined and refined distortion techniques into beautiful human expression.

Many musical sounds upon which African American musicians have based their innovations were themselves influenced by African American music. The music of bands Radiohead (UK; active 1985–present) and singer-composer Björk (Iceland; 1965–), both of which have been influenced by the musical innovations of African American improvised music, have been performed by modern jazz stars such as saxophonist-composer Greg Osby (1960–) and pianist-composer Jason Moran (1975–). Detroit Techno is another example of how African American musicians have incorporated sounds into their creative practice.

Founders of Detroit techno Derrick May (1963–) and Juan Atkins (1962–) were exposed to the techno electronic art rock music of Kraftwerk (active 1970–present) and the Euro disco productions of Giorgio Moroder (1940–) in suburban shopping malls. Historian and cultural critic George Lipsitz draws a brilliant parallel by pointing out that in the same way blues musicians used technology available to them to combine industrial sounds with the sonic effects of acoustic instruments, May, Atkins, and many other Detroit techno musicians made "recombinant" art out of sounds they processed from their environment. Detroit techno sounds are peculiar to the soundscape of the deterioration of Detroit.

Rapper-singer and producer T-Pain (1985–) has used a pitch correction software plug-in called Autotune to create his own trademark vocal sound in hits like "Chopped and Screwed" and "Can't Believe It." His unique Autotune sound has gained a wide audience, as evidenced by the "I Am T-Pain" app (application) that was created for nonmusicians who wish to live vicariously through T-Pain by approximating his sound. T-Pain's work with Autotune is also an extension of Black innovations on acoustic instruments.

African American Influence on American Concert Music

George Gershwin's folk opera *Porgy and Bess* (1935) illustrates African American influence on American concert music. Many of the songs from his opera were based on Black musical forms. "Summertime," the most famous one, is based on the standard or codified blues form. The codification of a musical form is the process of making a complex, endlessly varied musical form, such as the blues, into a standard form, such as the "12 bar blues."

Although many academically trained American "concert music" composers have rightly looked to European composers for their compositional inspiration, Gershwin adopted the African American musical influences around him to create a distinct "American" opera. His work has

Kneeling on his crippled legs, Porgy, played by Sidney Poitier, urges Bess (Dorothy Dandridge, center) to join Maria (Pearl Bailey) at the picnic which was to change their lives, in this scene from the movie version of *Porgy and Bess*, November 17, 1958. (AP Photo)

inspired other American composers to draw from the rich well of African American music. Many of these American composers are African American women and men.

African American musicians have composed in every prominent musical form we know, despite being mostly celebrated for innovations in jazz and various forms of popular or "vernacular" music. They have had an impact on and transformed various European musical forms such as symphonies and operas.

The opera *X, The Life and Times of Malcolm X* (1985), by composer-pianist Anthony Davis (1951–) is based on his knowledge of avant-garde European music as well as the influences of legendary twentieth-century improvisers and composers such as Charles Mingus (1922–1979), Thelonious Monk (1917–1982), and Miles Davis (1926–1991). Davis's writing for voices; his use of rhythm, texture, and phrasing; and the inclusion of a "jazz" rhythm section in the orchestra all come from his grounding in the blues tradition. To be sure, Anthony Davis's fusing of Black music styles with European music forms is not a new phenomenon. Several Black composers, such as Scott Joplin (1867–1917; *Treemonisha*), antedate his work. However, his influence resides in how he has used the opera format to construct a musical narrative that relies heavily on the unfixed vocabulary of the blues.

See also: African American Women's Influence on American Music; Art Music; Avant-garde in American Music, The; Beyoncé; Blues; Brown, James; Crosby, Stills & Nash; Davis, Miles; Distortion and Feedback; Electronic and Computer Music; Ellington, Duke; Folk Music; Franklin, Aretha; Gershwin, George; Gershwin, Ira; Hancock, Herbie; Hendrix, Jimi; Hip-Hop; Holiday, Billie; Improvisation; Jazz; Joplin, Janice; Lady Gaga; Madonna; Mitchell, Joni; Monk, Thelonious; Opera in America; Presley, Elvis; R&B; Rap and Rappers; Rock 'n' Roll (Rock); Rockabilly; Smith, Bessie; Soul; Thornton, Willlie Mae; Tin Pan Alley

Further Reading

Baraka, Amiri. 1963. *Blues People: Negro Music in White America.* New York: W. Morrow.

Brooks, Daphne. 2008. "Amy Winehouse and the (Black) Art of Appropriation." *The Nation,* September 29. http://www.thenation.com/article/amy-winehouse-and-black-art-appropriation (accessed February 3, 2013).

Davis, Angela Y. 1998. *Blues Legacies and Black Feminism: Gertrude "Ma" Rainey, Bessie Smith, and Billie Holiday.* New York: Pantheon Books.

Gilroy, Paul. 1993. *The Black Atlantic: Modernity and Double Consciousness.* Cambridge, MA: Harvard University Press.

Lennon, John, and Jann Wenner. 1971. *Lennon Remembers.* [1st ed.] San Francisco: Straight Arrow Books.

Lipsitz, George. 2007. *Footsteps in the Dark: The Hidden Histories of Popular Music.* Minneapolis: University of Minnesota Press.

Maultsby, Portia K. 1989. "Africanisms in African American Music." In *Africanisms in American Culture,* edited by Joseph E. Holloway, 185–210. Bloomington: Indiana University Press.

Monson, Ingrid T. 1996. *Saying Something: Jazz Improvisation and Interaction.* Chicago: University of Chicago Press.

Rose, Tricia.1994. *Black Noise: Rap Music and Black Culture in Contemporary America.* Hanover, NH: University Press of New England.

Small, Christopher. 1998. *Music of the Common Tongue: Survival and Celebration in African American Music.* Hanover, NH: University Press of New England.

Stuckey, Sterling. 1987. *Slave Culture: Nationalist Theory and the Foundations of Black America.* New York: Oxford University Press.

Veal, Michael E. 2000. *Fela: The Life & Times of an African Musical Icon.* Philadelphia: Temple University Press.

james gordon williams

African American Spiritual Music

The spiritual song in African American culture remains at the core of musical expression for people of color as they struggle to find meaning, purpose, vision, and hope within current society. Many conditions that have framed the journey of African Americans from the period of slavery to the present day have morphed into the sophisticated language of political correctness, racial profiling, economic poverty, and social injustice. The musical trends in African American culture often provide a current response to the conditions in which people of color find themselves as they try to define their identity, spiritual focus, and appropriate artistic response to a quickly changing world.

The function of the spiritual remains much the same today as it was two hundred years ago. It is the folk music of a people who are singing about their hope for a better life. Congregational songs in many African American churches are often based on familiar hymns, praise songs, and traditional gospel music from the latter years of the twentieth century, but the spiritual, with its message of hope, salvation, and trust in God, remains at the core of inspiring music that soloists, institutional choirs, community-based choirs, and churches perform, often because of the familiar lyrics and melodies that anchor emotional and intellectual responses in a worship or concert setting.

Moses G. Hogan (1957–2003) had a profound influence on the preservation and presentation of the African American spiritual century. This native of New Orleans, Louisiana, tapped into his musical routes and emerging musical genius and created compelling choral arrangements that were performed by his ensemble, the Moses Hogan Chorale and ultimately the Moses Hogan Singers, and countless choirs across the United States, which commissioned Hogan to complete new projects. Three significant components contributed to Hogan's success with the spiritual: affiliation with the Hal Leonard Corporation and Oxford Music Publishing as primary distributors of his compositions; performance opportunities with the American Choral Directors Association; and creation of a multitalented choral organization that not only performed at the highest musical standard, but also recorded this music and made this product available to others around the world.

High school, collegiate, professional, and community choirs continue to seek creative arrangements of the African American spiritual for inclusion in concerts for the public. Various organizations are highly visible in the performance of the spiritual: American Spiritual Ensemble, Harlem Spiritual Ensemble, Vocal Essence, Chanticleer, Heritage Signature Chorale, Clayton White Singers, Morgan State University Choir, Hampton University Choir, Morehouse College Glee Club, Essence of Joy, Essence of Joy Alumni Singers, Chicago Community Chorus, Pittsburgh Gospel Choir, R. Nathaniel Dett Chorale, Noah Ryder Chorale, Fisk Jubilee Singers, and Howard University Concert Choir. In some scenarios the traditional concert closer has been the spiritual, while traditional gospel music is also making its way forward in the mainstream of repertoires performed by festival choirs.

In 1995 the Celebration of African-American Spirituals began at the Pennsylvania State University with a

African American Spiritual Music: Film, Video, and Audio Recordings

Chanticleer. *How Sweet the Sound.* [New York]: Warner Classics R2 60309, 2004.

Dawson, William Levi. *Concerts from the American Choral Directors Association National Convention, March 13–16, 1991, Phoenix, AZ: The Choral Heritage of William Dawson.* Glassboro State College Chamber Choir, Eugene Thamon Simpson, director; Jackson State University Chorale, Robert L. Morris, director; Morris Brown College Concert Choir, Glynn E. Halsey, director. Greene, IA: Comprehensive Sound Services, 1991.

DePaur, Leonard, and Mari Evans. *The Long Road to Freedom: An Anthology of Black Music.* [New York]: Buddha Records; distributed by BMG, 2001.

Gospels and Spirituals: The Gold Collection, 40 Classic Performances. RETRO, 1999.

A Home in That Rock: A Collection of Spirituals and Songs of Faith. Moses Hogan Singers; Moses Hogan Choral Series 2002 Double-CD Set by Moses Hogan, Various, and The Moses Hogan Singers & Chorale. 2002.

Moses Hogan Conducts Our Choral Heritage Series, Volume 1: I Can Tell the World. Moses Hogan and The Moses Hogan Chorale.

Peace. Love. Joy: An Essence of Joy Choral Soundscape 2003–2011. Anthony T. Leach, artistic director. 2012.

Philogene, Ruby, and the London Adventist Chorale. *Steal Away: Spirituals & Gospel Songs.* EMI Classics, 1997.

Ride the Chariot! A Pilgrimage to the Heart of the Spiritual. The Chamber Singers of Haverford and Bryn Mawr Colleges; Thomas Lloyd, director, 1998–2002.

Ross, John Andrew. *Comin' Up Shouting! Gospel Music & Spirituals.* Revels Records CD1097, 1997.

Spirituals. Barbara Conrad, Mezzo-Soprano; The Convent Avenue Concert Choir; The New England Symphonic Ensemble, Gregory Hopkins, conductor. Naxos 8.553036, 1994.

Spirituals: Give Me Jesus. Barbara Hendricks and the Mose Hogan Chorale, 1999.

Spirituals in Concert. Kathleen Battle, Jessye Norman; James Levine, conductor. Deutsche Grammophon 429790-2, 1991.

"Swing Low, Sweet Chariot." The American Spiritual Ensemble, 2011.

Wade in the Water, volumes 1–4. Smithsonian Folkways series. 1994.

Wise, Raymond, and The Raise Chorale. *21 Spirituals for the 21st Century.* Raise Records RA-11CD, 2005.

Witness: What a Mighty God—Spirituals and Gospels for Chorus. Vocal Essence Vocal Ensemble and Singers; Phillip Brunelle, conductor. 2004.

single choral event presented by Essence of Joy, a choir in the Penn State School of Music. Over the years this event has grown into an extended weekend occasion, with guest soloists, lecturers, choirs, and artists. In 2003 the choir commissioned several African American composers-arrangers to complete compositions that were then premiered by the choir. Composers included Glenn Burleigh, Moses Hogan, Roland Carter, Rosephanye Powell, Robert L. Morris, Keith Hampton, and Marvin Curtis. In 2009 the title of the festival was changed to provide more inclusive performance opportunities for instrumentalists and opera and keyboard artists. The Celebration of African American Music Festival is presented in February in honor of Black History Month. Recordings and video projects serve as a chronicle of performing artists, ensembles, and lecturers who have participated since 1996.

The spiritual is alive and well and remains a vibrant and vital musical offering by many composer-arrangers, performers, and scholars who are committed to preserving its heritage and legacy within American culture.

See also: African American Influences on American Music; Sacred Music; Slave Songs

Further Reading

Caldwell, Hansonia L. 2001. *African American Music, Spirituals: An Introduction to the Fundamental Folk Music of Black Americans.* 2nd ed. Culver City, CA: Ikoro Communications.

Lowell, John. 1986. *Black Song: The Forge and the Flame: The Story of How the Afro-American Spiritual Was Hammered Out.* New York: Macmillan.

Southern, Eileen, and Josephine Wright. 1990. *African-American Traditions in Song, Sermon, Tale and Dance, 1600–1920: An Annotated Bibliography of Literature, Collections, and Artworks.* Westport, CT: Greenwood Press.

Trice, Patricia Johnson. 1998. *Choral Arrangements of the African-American Spirituals: Historical Overview and Annotated Listings.* Westport, CT: Greenwood Press.

Anthony T. Leach

Selected Web Documents

Burnett, Lawrence E. 2008. "Spirituals, Hymns, and Gospel Music." http://apps.carleton.edu/events/spirituals/bios/.

"Explorations: Spirituals." 2011. Digital History. http://www.digitalhistory.uh.edu/learning_history/spirituals/spirituals_menu.cfm.

"Negro Spirituals." n.d. Spiritual Workshop. http://www.negrospirituals.com/.

Norfolk [Virginia] Public Library. 2012. "Reading List about Spirituals for 'Black Pearl Sings,' a Play Performed by the Virginia Stage Company." http://www.npl.lib.va.us/BlackPearlbibliography2012.pdf.

Pershey, Monica Gordon. 2000. "African American Spiritual Music: A Historical Perspective." *The Dragon Lode* 18, no. 2. http://www.reading.ccsu.edu/TheDragonLode/DLVol182Sp2000/DLVol182Sp2000%2024–29.pdf.

"Research Guide: Early African American Spirituals." 2011. In *Studying America: Exploring the Cultures of the United States.* http://www.studyingamerica.com/2011/10/research-guide-early-african-american-spirituals.html.

"Songs of Freedom." 2004. Owen Sound's Black History. http://www.osblackhistory.com/songs.php.

"Spirituals." 2010. Edsitement. National Endowment for the Humanities. http://edsitement.neh.gov/lesson-plan/spirituals#sect-introduction.

"Sweet Chariot: The Story of the Spirituals." 2004. Spirituals Project of the University of Denver. http://ctl.du.edu/spirituals/Religion/otanes.cfm.

African American Women's Influence on American Music

African American women's contributions to music are vast and varied. Their artistic endeavors can be heard in virtually every genre and style of music; their biographies could well narrate a history of the United States and its culture. Their musical creations can be heard in the voices of Janis Joplin and the playing of Louis Armstrong. African American women's musical legacies helped to bridge and break racial divides, create dominant marketing strategies for African American and broadly popular music, and negotiate new conceptions of femininity and sexuality that often contradict patriarchal, heterocentric norms. Far from being just influential musicians, these women influenced popular conceptions of race and femininity due to their high visibility in American popular culture.

Blues and Jazz

African American women's contributions are particularly strong in blues and jazz. Early blues history, which often intersects with early jazz history, is rife with strong African American female vocalists. The black blues queens of the 1920s were grounded in the vaudeville scene; women like Mamie Smith, Bessie Smith, and Ma Rainey broke boundaries and made history. Mamie Smith (1883–1946) was the first African American to be marketed specifically to a black audience, and her 1920s hit "Crazy Blues" is often cited in both blues and jazz histories as the start of a major trend in the recording and marketing of African American musicians. Gertrude "Ma" Rainey (1886–1939), also known as the "Mother of the Blues," is one of two women frequently portrayed as singularly important in the history of early blues recordings, the other being Bessie Smith. A popular artist on the TOBA (Theater Owning Booking Association) circuit, a group of Southern theater venues catering to black audiences, she most famously toured with the Rabbit Foot Minstrels. Her strong vocal style and repertoire influenced later musicians across racial boundaries, and she served as a mentor for the immortal Bessie Smith. Bessie Smith (1894–1937), known as the "Empress of the Blues," continues to be one of the most influential African American female musicians. Mentoring with "Ma" Rainey on the vaudeville circuit during the 1910s, she recorded *Downhearted Blues* in 1923, to great popular success. In addition to her large number of recordings, she also appeared in films, such as *St. Louis Blues* in 1929. Her voice reaches out and speaks to us through musicians like Janis Joplin and Mary J. Blige. Great black female vocalists can also be found in the jazz canon. Women like Billie Holiday (born Eleanora Fagan; 1915–1959), known for her lighter vocal style, and Ella Fitzgerald (1917–1996), known for her large range and vocal agility, are continually credited for being instrumental to the history of jazz.

In addition to these incredible vocalists, there is a largely unsung legacy of female jazz and blues instrumentalists and composers. Foremost among these women was Mary Lou Williams (1910–1981). Although the legacy of black female jazz instrumentalists is wide and varied, Williams swing piano style is often the only one mentioned with any regularity. She was also a much-lauded composer and arranger, contributing music to the bands of prominent jazz men Duke Ellington and Louis Armstrong. Just as influential were the all-girl bands of the 1930s, such as the Harlem Playgirls, who

Clara Ward Singers, about 1970. (Michael Ochs Archives/Getty Images)

are often forgotten actors in African American women's jazz history.

Although the biographies of these women are an important part of the larger narrative of American music, their influence stretches far beyond the realms of popular music. Mamie Smith paved the way for the commercial success of other African American recording artists and in the process changed the landscape of American popular music and culture. Bessie Smith and "Ma" Rainey were popular performers, but their music did more than entertain; songs like Rainey's "Prove It on Me Blues" frankly discussed lesbianism, and Bessie's "Pickpocket Blues" asserted women's sexual independence. Their voices, early in feminist and queer history in the United States, provided popular models of dissidence in a culture built primarily on compulsive heterosexuality and male domination of women.

Gospel

Much of African American women's musical influence can be seen in the arena of sacred music like gospel. In fact, many of the most popular and legendary performers of gospel music have been and continue to be African American women. Rosetta Tharpe (1915–1973), gospel singer, guitarist, and member of the sanctified church, pushed boundaries by taking sacred music out of the church and into the recording studio. Her releases of "Rock Me" and "This Train" were widely acclaimed both in and out of the church. Clara Ward (1924–1973) was a gospel singer and pianist who toured domestically and internationally, and along with the Clara Ward Singers and composer W. H. Brewster became one of the first financially successful gospel performers. Mahalia Jackson (1911–1972), inspired by the voices of Mamie Smith, "Ma" Rainey, and Bessie Smith, was the first gospel singer to sell one million records, with *Move on Up a Little Higher* in 1947. Jackson also became the face of gospel music during the 1950s, when she appeared regularly on her own and other television shows in the Chicago area. Her recording deal with Columbia records and the subsequent musical changes she made highlight the difficulty African American musicians found when trying to cross over to popular white markets. Singer Faye Adams (1925–), with her 1953 hit *Shake a Hand,* helped dissolve traditional boundaries between gospel and the secular realm of R&B. Adams's shift would mirror and help to dictate the move toward secularization that took place in the genre of gospel as a whole.

Soul and R&B

Any discussion surrounding African American women's contributions to American culture would be incomplete without the mention of soul and R&B divas. Willie Mae "Big Mama" Thornton (1926–1984) stands somewhere between blues and R&B in the pantheon of great African American women musicians. A singer and an instrumentalist, her recordings directly influenced Elvis Presley's recording of "Hound Dog." Her 1953 version topped the R&B charts in 1955, hitting its height before Presley recorded his version in 1956. Her 1967 hit "Ball and Chain" subsequently became a hit in 1969 for white blues singer Janis Joplin. Etta James's (1938–2012) legacy can be seen in recent films like 2008's *Cadillac Records,* featuring Beyoncé Knowles portraying the living legend. James's most popular hit, "At Last," recorded in 1961, is an essential track of not only the soul music canon, but American popular music as a whole. Aretha Franklin (1942–), dubbed the "Queen of Soul" and often described as a counterpart to Etta James, is perhaps the best known of these women. Recording her first album of gospel songs at the age of fourteen, she went on to record the R&B standards "Respect," "Chain of Fools," and "(You Make Me Feel Like) A Natural Woman"; she was the first woman to be inducted into the Rock and Roll Hall of Fame, in 1987. The girl groups of Motown have also been incredibly influential on the American musical landscape. Groups like The Temptations and The Supremes have been immortalized in popular American culture and music. The popularity of these groups, especially The Supremes, led to the 1981 Broadway musical *Dreamgirls,* which won six Tony Awards and propelled Jennifer Holliday to national acclaim. The 2006 film version, nominated for a record-breaking eight Oscars, won Jennifer Hudson an award for best supporting actress.

Hip-Hop

In contrast to the high visibility of women in gospel music is the marginalization of women as musicians in hip-hop. Many critics and feminist scholars have attacked the genre for lyrics that often emphasize misogyny, violence, and homophobia. Acknowledging the problematic space hip-hop sometimes occupies, it is interesting to examine how African American women have brilliantly negotiated and transcended these tricky gender roles even though the genre often presents them as objects of male desire and domination. Artists like MC Lyte and Salt-n-Pepa, who became popular in the 1980s mainstream musical culture, attack the genre's lyrical and visual domination of women (Rose 1994, 155). Queen Latifah's 1989 debut album *All Hail the Queen* presented a strong woman's voice influenced by a mixture of African diasporic musics. Missy Elliot also adds her voice to the list of strong black women's voices critiquing male dominance in the genre. Other artists like Lil' Kim and Foxy Brown have chosen to appeal to gender roles and use the appeal of their sexuality as part of their branding.

Art Music

African American women's contributions to art music have almost universally been overlooked. Until recently the history of Western art music has largely been written through the biographies of white men. Scholar Josephine Wright (1984) traces the participation of African American women in art music to around 1850. The earliest black women in the art music tradition were classically trained vocalists like Sissieretta Jones (1869–1933), who performed in both high culture and popular venues and eventually toured as a vaudeville star. African American women like Florence Beatrice Smith Price (1887–1953), the first to achieve national renown as a composer of symphonies, were responsible for large masterworks of modern art music. Eva Jessye (1895–1992), a composer in her own right, served as the choral director for George Gershwin's 1935 production of *Porgy and Bess.* Composer Evelyn Pittman (1910–1992), whose operas have been performed domestically and abroad, studied with one of the foremost composition teachers in modern history, Nadia Boulanger. Modern composers like Nkeiru Okoye (1972–) have been trained in some of the most prestigious conservatories and been honored by organizations such as ASCAP. Okoye's works, like *The Genesis* and *RUTH,* incorporate elements of popular and West

African traditional music. These women are only the proverbial tip of the iceberg of African American women in Western art music, yet their participation in the unfolding history of the genre is largely ignored. African American women performers and composers of classical music brought conceptions of blackness to audiences not familiar with the popular music discussed previously.

Music at the Intersections of Race and Gender

Feminist and queer musicology have recently focused heavily on how the intersections of race and gender affect African American women's musical performances and how those performances in turn affect the life and culture of Americans at large. Contemporary scholarship argues that race and gender are interconnected lenses through which individuals filter their experiences; as such, studies of African American women's music combine tools from both gender-feminist theory as well as race theory. Until recently the contributions of African American women and their music have been but a footnote in historical surveys, but musicologists and historians are including these women's histories and music in their works. Most discussions of African American women musicians' influence focus strictly on popular music and the aural influences, but even more important is how these women's negotiations of race, gender, and sexuality have informed national and international societal dialogues. Blues women like Bessie Smith and "Ma" Rainey contributed early models for the negotiation of gender and sexuality. Mamie Smith provided a model for marketing African American musicians to black audiences. The women of gospel have influenced and provided a window into the secularization of American popular culture, while the women of hip-hop are perfect examples of the myriad of ways black women negotiate the intersections of racism and sexism. African American women in Western art music have served as witnesses to the frequent intersection of race and gender as methods of exclusion in the canon. These women are more than just the sound track of American musical culture; their lives and work stand as representatives of the intersections of race and gender in American culture.

See also: African American Influences on American Music; Armstrong, Louis; Art Music; Beyoncé; Blues; Ellington, Duke; Fitzgerald, Ella; Franklin, Aretha; Gershwin, George; James, Etta; Jazz; Joplin, Janis; Hip-Hop; Holiday, Billie; Motown; Presley, Elvis; Queen Latifah; R&B; Rainey, Gertrude "Ma"; Smith, Bessie; Smith, Mamie; Soul; Supremes, The; Tharpe, Rosetta; Thornton, Willie Mae; Vaudeville and Burlesque

Further Reading

Hayes, Eileen M., and Linda F. Williams. 2007. *Black Women and Music: More Than the Blues.* Urbana: University of Illinois Press.

Davis, Angela Y. 1998. *Blues Legacies and Black Feminism: Gertrude "Ma" Rainey, Bessie Smith, and Billie Holliday.* New York: Pantheon Books.

Rose, Tricia. 1994. *Black Noise.* Hannover, N.H.: University Press of New England.

Wald, Elijah. 2004. *Escaping the Delta: Robert Johnson and the Invention of the Blues.* New York: Amistad.

Wright, Josephine. 1984. "Black Women and Classical Music." *Women's Studies Quarterly* 12, no. 3 (Fall): 18–21.

Lauren E. Joiner

Alaskan Native Music

With more than twenty indigenous languages, traditional Alaskan native musical cultures are quite varied. There are seven distinctive stylistic music areas: Yup'ik/Cup'ik, Inupiat, Siberian Yupik, the Unangan/Unangas, Sugpiaq, Athabascans, and Tlingit/Haida/Tsimshian. The impact of colonialism, widespread epidemics, and Christian missionization caused an immense loss of dances and songs. Revitalization gradually began in the 1960s. Today many festivals, including the Alaska Federation of Natives' annual Quyana Night, the World Eskimo/Indian Olympics Celebration, the Alaska Native Arts Festival, the Athabascan Fiddle Festival, the Messenger Feast or Kivgik in Bethel, the Yup'ik cultural celebration Cama-i, and the Hooper Bay Masked Dance Festival celebrate these expressions.

The drum is the main indigenous musical instrument. The Yup'ik *cauyaq* is a handheld, round or somewhat pear-shaped instrument with a membrane stretched over a bentwood frame. Fastened to the frame are a handle made of wood, ivory, reindeer, or caribou horn and a crossbar. Seal, walrus stomach, or walrus heart once formed the membrane, but today a substitute of synthetic nylon often suffices. The width varies from one to two feet across. The drum of the Inupiat, Siberian Yupik, and Sugpiaq is similar but without the crossbar. The crossbarless drum is used by the Unangan/Unangas, who also use a handheld drum, held at the back by lacing, similar to those used by Athabascans and Northwest Coast groups.

Yup'ik/Cup'ik

The Yup'ik drummer strikes the drumhead with a long, slender, carved wooden beater (*mumeq*). When using their large drum, three feet wide or more and with a handle four to five feet in length, two musicians hold the instrument while a third beats it. Traditionally these instruments were used for twenty-one cyclic ceremonials, each with its required music.

Cup'ik drummer, Nunivak Island, about 1930. (Library of Congress)

The melody sung by the musicians in unison can have an undulating shape of about an octave. Usually five or six pitches occur. The tonal center often will be a pitch at around the midpoint of the range. In performance the melody is repeated four times, with a drum beat interlude between the repetitions. The drum patterns are specific from one melody to another, but there is usually one section of the melody for which there is a steady one-beat pattern. Each song lasts approximately six minutes. First the song leader softly sings the song while tapping the rim of the drum as the performers move to the performance area. Then the formal presentation of the song commences with the chorus (*agnera*), then goes on to verse one (*apalluan ciuqlia*), the chorus, the voiceless section of a specific drum pattern (*cauyarialngua*), the chorus, verse two (*apalluan kinguqlia*), the voiceless section, the chorus, the voiceless section, an encore of the chorus at a faster tempo (*pamyua*), and the voiceless section. There are usually one to five drummers and ten or more dancers in a performance.

When dances accompany the song, the dancing movement occurs in the upper body. The male dancers sit on their knees. Each male hand holds a dance fan of two circular hoops of bent wood with duck feathers. The female dancers with elaborate headdresses stand, only gently bending their knees with the beat of the drum. Their fans are a solid circle, woven from grass with the long hairs of the caribou's beard attached.

The specific choreography for a dance comes from the text of the song in common dances (*ciuqitet*). The drum leader begins, setting the pulse. Gradually the leader increases the tempo. The dancers move only in the verses. A special kind of dance movement ends each verse and may consist of imitating an animal, shooting a duck, etc. As the verses continue, this concluding movement becomes more exaggerated.

An important occasion is the *Nakaciuryaraq* or annual Bladder Feast, a ceremony to honor and release the spirits of the mammals back to their world. It originally involved the wearing of elaborate masks, but Moravian missionaries banned their use. Today masks are rarely found in these performances. *Kevgiq* or Messenger Festival is an invitational event to exchange dances, music, and gifts. It also includes ancient motion dances belonging to certain families, but composition of new songs occurs for this ceremony. For example, when a child is initiated into the dance group and recognized, a song is composed with three verses to represent the father, mother, and child. The many different types of dances, each with their particular songs, include child's first, fast standing, slow mourning, common, family motion, invitational community, purification, mask, teasing, and healing for the ill.

Inupiat

At winter ceremonials, the Inupiat perform songs referring to the history of a family; the hunting skills of an ancestor; the gathering of berries or greens by the women; the hunting of seal, walrus, or whale; or the adventures of characters like Raven. A special category, sung by cross-cousins, is known as "teasing" songs.

The drum leader begins the song and establishes the tempo. Each of the five to twenty drummers holds a single-headed, handheld frame drum with handle. The beater, about three feet in length, only strikes the frame, not the membrane. For certain ceremonials such as the Wolf Dance and Inviting-In Feast, a large, suspended wooden box drum, some three to four feet in height, is used.

The undulating melody of the song normally has a narrow range of around a fifth and can use four or five different pitches within that range. On King and Diomede Islands, the Inupiat melodies can have wide leaps of a fifth and even an octave. One of the lower pitches generally repeats several times at the beginning and end of the melody. The structure consists of a chorus, verse one, chorus, and verse two, and may be repeated two or three times. A complete song lasts around four minutes. The beat of the drum is steady in the chorus, but it has a particular pattern corresponding to the movements of the dancers in the verses.

Both male and female dancers stand during the performance, and all wear gloves. The women use their arms and upper bodies, moving with their feet close together. The men use similar movements but in a more energetic manner, while stamping one foot to the beat of the drum. Some dances require the use of half masks, or full ones with the images of ravens, walrus, seal, bear, or another animal on them. Today only the King Island Inupiat Dancers continue to use masks and use drums made with the lining of walrus stomach.

Siberian Yupik of St. Lawrence Island

Also striking their Inupiat-like drum on the frame, Siberian Yupik use melodies of a narrow range and smaller intervals than those found in Western music. Consequently their musical expressions sound strikingly different from others in Alaska. The length of the songs is similar to that of the Inupiat. Men and women sing the melody an octave apart. The usual song structure consists of chorus, verse, chorus, verse, chorus. A steady pulse pattern appears in the chorus, while a specific drum beat pattern, unique to each song, happens in the verse.

The male dancers stand while performing and wear gloves. In the past they often used masks. A striking difference in the dance choreography is the lack of symmetry. In Yup'ik and Inupiat choreographies, a motion done on the right side will be repeated on the left side, or vice versa. In all three cultures, though, the beat of the drum emphasizes the movements used.

Unangan/Unangas (Eastern/Attuan or Aleut and Western Atkan)

The greatest cultural loss occurred in the Aleutian and Kodiak Islands, because colonialism was in effect there the longest. In the twenty-first century a vibrant revitalization is taking place as previously unknown resources for music and dance become known. Because no dances remained in oral memory in the area, the Atka Dancers from Commander Islands received their repertoire from a Russian woman of Kamchatka, Katiya, who taught them Koryak songs and dances and made their regalia.

When an Inupiat-type drum is used, the male and female drummers may move at times with the dancers and vigorously raise and lower the drum, hitting it either on the frame or directly on the membrane. With the handleless and wider frame type, the performer uses a padded stick to either strike the drum on the side or periodically hit the membrane. Different types of beats occur, usually directly related to the dance movements.

The song has a melody that is undulating in nature and within a relatively narrow range. Most songs are sung in unison or an octave apart. Occasionally the melody is presented in parallel thirds by the voices.

Dance choreographies vary considerably depending on the song and the occasion. In some dances the dancers remain relatively stationary, perhaps standing in a circle, but using much upper body movement. In other cases the dancers move in a clockwise circle, making gestures with their arms. Some dances have the participants using extensive dance space. Often the dancers will have fan-like objects in their hands to add to the movement.

Sugpiaq (Koniag or Alutiiq of Kodiak Island)

The renaissance of traditional culture is largely based on the programs of the Alutiiq Museum in Kodiak. Participants learn about their traditional music, which consisted of a cycle of dance performances in the communal *qasgit*.

Accompanied by Inupiat-like drums, dancers performed movements somewhat analogous to Yup'ik dance.

Often masks would be destroyed after use. The dancers could carry a puffin beak rattle of several concentric wooden hoops with clusters of puffin beaks attached.

Athabascans

Because traditionally the Athabascans hunted and gathered in small, family-based groups, most larger gatherings involving music and dance took place in winter. These annual Gathering-Up festivals happened when the host invited neighboring groups for feasting, dancing, and singing. Sometimes called a Messenger Feast, it would require the creation of new songs for the guests. Often held to honor a deceased family member, gifts would be distributed in his or her memory.

Variants seen at gatherings were the masks and puppets used by the Deg Hit'an or the Stickdance *Hi'o* ceremony, commonly used to honor a deceased person. For the latter, a pole would be selected and danced around the community, then traditionally fourteen songs had to be sung perfectly. After the feasting and dancing the pole would be broken up and the pieces thrown into the river.

When different groups met for a gathering, the initial greeting dance would consist of parallel lines, often arranged by gender. Dances could be done by individuals or by groups of men or women. Most commonly both genders would participate, either facing the center of the room or by moving clockwise, taking small steps, forward or sidewise. Normally there was little gestural movement of the upper body by the dancers.

The songs sung by the male singers-drummers came from song makers who often attributed their inspiration to the songs of birds. An occasional meaningful word occurred, but most of the text consisted of vocables. The performers, though, would be aware of additional meanings surrounding the songs and their creation. Singing in unison the generally downward melodic line using Western chordlike pitches, the men repeated the melody an indefinite number of times until the leader suggested the next song. Meanwhile, each singer beat his handheld, single-headed drum, usually in a steady one-beat pattern with a slender, wooden beater.

The Hudson Bay Company opened Fort Yukon in 1847, and soon Athabascans became entranced with the sounds of the fiddler playing Western European dance tunes. Although some other Alaskan groups such as the Yup'ik readily adopted the fiddle, Gwich'in fiddlers have been dominant over the past 150 years. As a result, a night of dancing may include Athabascan traditional dances and/or English or Scottish formation dances.

Tlingit, Haida, and Tsimshian

Among the Tlingit at ceremonial gatherings, a clan group of one of the moieties—Raven and Eagle, or among Northern Tlingit, Crow and Wolf—would sing four of their songs; then the other moiety's group would sing four songs. Today, with members from various clans and other heritages in the same dancing group, this alternation is not followed. However, acknowledgment of the composer of the song, the obtaining of the right to sing the song, and the song's background are given before its performance.

These cultures have distinctive, elaborate masks that serve three functions: 1) to transform an individual into a supernatural being, 2) for dramatization of a clan's history, and 3) for conflict resolution. Trading and giving songs (*gunana*) as well as other gifts (masks, rattles, etc.) commonly occurs among these cultures.

Spirit or *Yek* songs are performed with elaborate carved and painted hats. A blanket is held before the body of the dancer so that only the hat appears to be dancing. There are many songs referring to Raven, and these are often very humorous. All of these cultures have their own songs concerning myths, for ceremonial usage such as raising totem poles, as well as songs for personal use, such as lullabies and accompanying various labors.

To accompany the songs, a handheld, single-headed drum painted with the clan crest of the owner is beaten with a padded beater. For some ceremonial songs, a box drum may be used, and carved wooden rattles, some with attached puffin beaks or deer hooves, may be used by dancers. Usually there are one or two drummers and a song leader in the performance. The song leader carries a decorated paddle or carved baton to conduct the drummer's beats.

Men and women, proudly wearing their regalia, sing the melody an octave apart. Sometimes strong voices also sing the melody a third lower, while others sing a third higher, making four different parallel lines of the melody at once. The range of the melody is usually less than an octave and uses relatively small steps. The rhythmic patterns used by the drums emphasize the movement of the dancers.

Tlingit songs, whether ceremonial or nonceremonial, consist of an introduction of vocables, a refrain that is repeated, a first stanza, two repetitions of the refrain, and the second stanza. A third stanza may be present. The texts can be highly metaphorical. For some songs such as love songs, the repetition is preceded with a refrain of vocables, *aya ha he ani 'aye*. Certain songs of joy, commonly used at gatherings, have an accompaniment of clapping with hands.

Although performances of traditional music or dance unique to each Alaskan area abound, many indigenous persons also perform other types of music. Missionization brought various types of church music, which the indigenous peoples absorbed and continue to perform today. Many became proficient on instruments such as organs, accordions, fiddles, and guitars. Among the Unangans and Sugpiaq by 1915, these instruments and a phonograph were common. Today indigenous Alaskan musicians cover the latest hits from the popular, country, rock, and rap genres and might take part in the rare pow-wow that occurs in the state.

See also: Ceremonial Music; Dance Instruction and Music

Further Reading

Alaskan Orthodox Texts. n.d. "Audio Resources." http://www.asna.ca/alaska/ (accessed June 8, 2011).

Alutiiq Museum. n.d. "Alutiit Cauyait." http://alutiiqmuseum.org/exhibits/electronic-exhibits/271–alutiit-cauyait-alutiiq-peoples-music (accessed June 8, 2011).

Coray, Craig. 2009. "Artifacts in Sound: A Century of Field Recordings of Alaska Natives." In *The Alaska Native Reader: History, Culture, Politics,* edited by Maria Shaa Tláa Williams, 94–305. Durham/London: Duke University Press.

Elder, Sarah, and Leonard Kamerling. 1988/2008. *Uksuum Cauyai: The Drums of Winter.* Watertown, MA: Documentary Educational Resources. DVD.

John, Theresa Arevgaq. 2010. "Yuraryararput kangiit-llu: Our Ways of Dance and Their Meanings." PhD diss., University of Alaska, Fairbanks.

Krejci, Paul R. 2010. "Skin Drums, Squeeze Boxes, Fiddles and Phonographs: Musical Interactions in the Western Arctic, Late 18th Through Early 20th Centuries." PhD diss., University of Alaska, Fairbanks.

Mishler, Craig. 1993. *The Crooked Stovepipe: Athapaskan Fiddle Music and Square Dancing in Northeast Alaska and Northwest Canada.* Urbana/Chicago: University of Illinois Press.

Williams, Maria Del Pilar. 1996. "Alaska Native Music and Dance: The Spirit of Survival." PhD diss., University of California.

Worl, Rosita. 2008. *Celebration: Tlingit, Haida, Tsimshian Dancing on the Land.* Juneau, AK: Sealaska Heritage Institute/University of Washington Press.

Elaine Keillor

Album Art

Album art comprises the front and back album covers and any additional visual material included with the packaging of vinyl records and later compact discs. In its early stages, an album's packaging existed simply out of necessity and consisted of plain brown paper or a cardboard sleeve, with circular cutouts in the center to allow the record's label to be visible. Today's art is much more complex, as it continues to evolve along with the music industry into the digital world. Album art can be created by the musician, by a musician associated with the band, by the studio's in-house design team, or by an outside artist or designer.

The album cover is a component of the overall packaging of an album. The initial purpose of an album packaging is to protect the vinyl record from damage, especially scratches. In the case of vinyl records with cardboard sleeves, these packages are prone to wear and tear, although wear and tear does often take place to some degree on covers contained within the plastic cases of CDs. To improve the appearance and durability of album covers, a variety of treatments have been utilized, such as clear plastic wrap. In addition, many products are available for the storage of vinyl albums.

The surface of a vinyl record is readily damaged, so aside from the outer cardboard sleeve, which could scratch the record, there is usually an inner protective cover to protect against dust and handling. The inner sleeve is either thin white paper, plain or printed with information on other recordings available from the same company, or a paper sleeve supporting a thin plastic bag. These quite often have a circular cutout so that the record label can be read without directly handling the record, as the previous brown paper wrappers had been. However, when the inner sleeve is printed with lyrics, which has been quite common, then there is usually no hole.

Alex Steinweiss (1977–2011) is credited with replacing the brown paper wrapper with eye-catching graphics. In 1940 Columbia Records listened to its new art director and replaced paper bag covers with his designs. Within months its record sales increased eightfold. His covers for Columbia, combining bold typography with modern, elegant illustrations, took the industry by storm and revolutionized the way records were sold. Over three decades, Steinweiss made thousands of original artworks for classical, jazz, and popular record covers for Columbia, Decca, London, and Everest, as well as logos, labels, and advertising material, even creating his own typeface, known as the Steinweiss Scrawl.

Because of Steinweiss's work, the cover became an important part of the culture of music at the time. Under the influence of designers like Bob Cato (1923–1999), who at various stages in his long music career was vice president of creative services at both Columbia Records and United Artists, album covers became renowned for being a marketing tool and an expression of artistic intent. The Band's (active 1964 (1964)–1976, 1983–1999) 1970 release *Stage Fright* with Norman Seeff's (1939–) photograph as a poster insert is an early example; the poster quickly became a collector's item.

Besides the practicalities of identifying specific records, album covers serve the purpose of advertising the musical contents, through the use of graphic design, photography, or illustration. An album cover normally has the artist's name, sometimes in logo form, and the

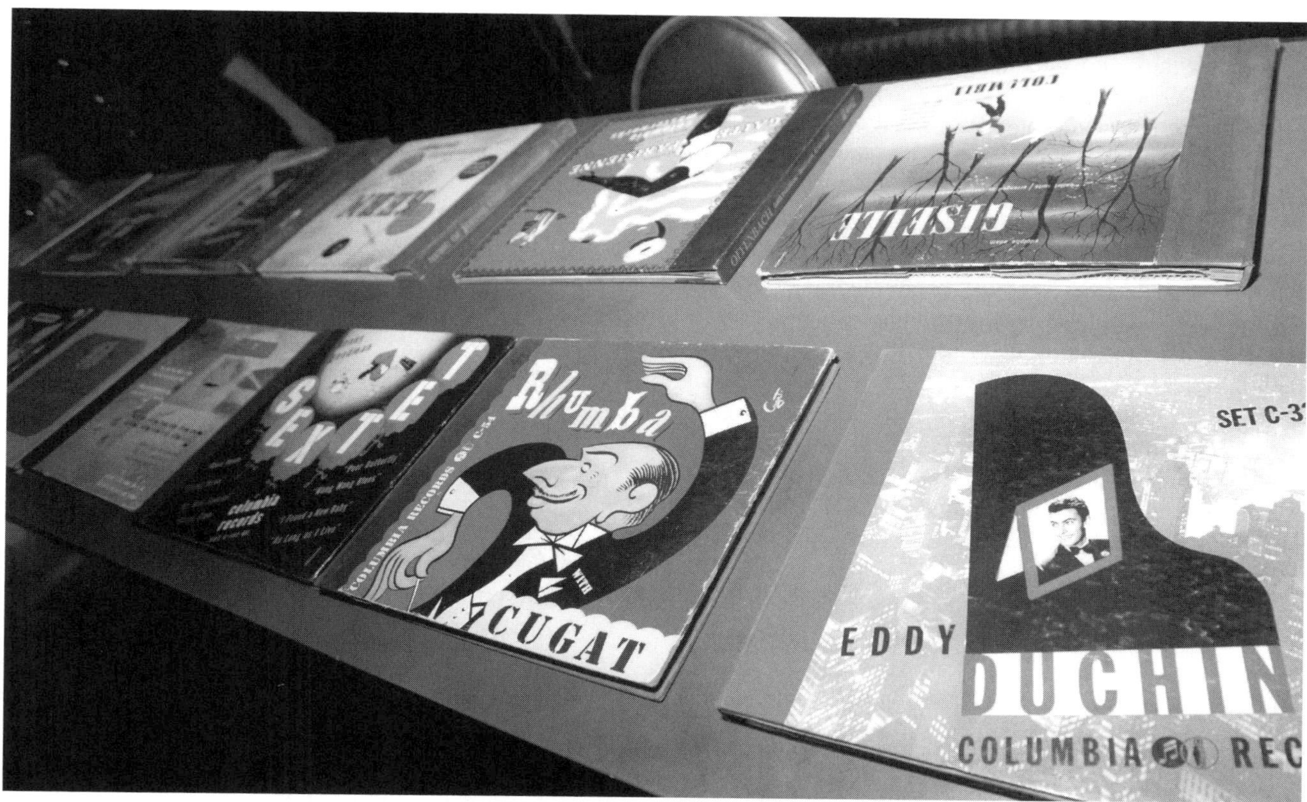

Album covers designed by Alex Steinweiss. (Paul Redmond/WireImage)

album title. Occasionally, though more common on historical vinyl records, the cover may include a reference number, the record label's branding, and possibly a track listing. Other information is seldom included on the cover and is usually contained on the rear or interior of the packaging, such as a track listing together with a more detailed list of those involved in making the record, band members, guest performers, engineers, and the producer. On the spine of the package the artist, title, and reference number are usually repeated so that albums can be identified while tightly packed on a shelf.

Gatefold covers, a folded double cover, and inserts made the album cover a desirable artifact in its own right. By increasing the packaging format, album covers expanded from simple packaging gimmicks to a more complex artistic statement. Some album cover designers and artists embraced the expanded format and created imagery and stories that filled every inch. The move to the small CD format (less than one-quarter the size of a record) eliminated that impact, although attempts have been made to create a more desirable packaging for the CD format. An example is Tori Amos's (1963–) *Abnormally Attracted to Sin,* which was initially intended to be an audiovisual project in which the music and photographs and accompanying videos worked together to present and develop the story of the album.

The importance of cover design was such that some artists specialized or gained fame through their work, notably the British design team Hipgnosis, through their work on Pink Floyd (1965–1996) albums, among others; English artist Roger Dean (1944–), famous for his Yes (1968–1981, 1983–2004, 2008–present) and Greenslade (1972–present) covers; and American artist Cal Schenkel for Captain Beefheart's (1941–2010) *Trout Mask Replica* and Frank Zappa's (1940–1993) *We're Only in It for the Money.* Schenkel (1947–) met Zappa in New York City in 1967 and quickly became his primary visual collaborator. Appreciated for his naïve and unfinished, folklike, surrealistic art, he captured the ironic nature of Zappa's music and worked with him, and later musicians represented by Zappa's agent, until the mid-1970s, before returning to the East Coast to focus on his art outside the music industry.

Eye-catching album covers have not just become visual markers for an album, but are also associated with the band as an icon. Stanley Mouse (1940–) and Alton Kelley (1940–2008) created a design for the Grateful Dead's (active 1965–1995) 1971 self-titled live album, using the image of a skeleton with a crown of roses based on a nineteenth-century illustration, which later evolved into one of the symbols of the Californian band. Mouse and Kelley became the band's preferred artists, creating the first eight album covers and many concert posters for the band. In addition, Mouse and Kelley created the wings and beetles used on Journey's (active 1973–1987, 1995–present) album covers. Derek Riggs (1958–) created heavy metal's most popular icon, Iron Maiden's (active 1975–present) "Eddie," who appears on nearly all its album and single covers. These examples illustrate icons derived from album covers.

With the increasing popularity of digital music downloading and the inflating cost of conducting business, the purpose and prevalence of the album cover are evolving. While the music industry attempts to keep up with technological and cultural shifts, the role that packaging will play in consumer music sales in the near future is uncertain, although its role is certainly changing, and digital forms of packaging will continue to surface, which to some degree take the place of physical packaging. Both MP3 and WMA music files can contain images embedded into the digital album. One digital solution is the iTunes LP format for interactive album artwork, introduced by Apple in September 2009, although most artists have not embraced this new format.

The artistic style of the album cover has morphed over time as the music industry itself has grown and expanded. As the audience for albums shifted, so did the imagery. With the growth of the youth culture in the 1950s and the proliferation of popular music, album covers shifted from ambiguous imagery of jazz and classical recordings to the familiar faces of the musicians, influenced by the growth of the movie and later television industries. The more the popular music market grew, the more the influence and demands of the musicians grew as well, enough to attract the interest of pop artists like Andy Warhol (1928–1987). Warhol designed many album covers, including the iconic banana album cover for The Velvet Underground (active 1964–1973, 1990, 1992–1994, 1996) and Nico's (1938–1998) self-titled 1967 album. By the end of the 1960s both record companies and musicians came to place value on eye-catching and elaborate packages, tempered to some extent by the paper shortage in 1973. Movies, fashion photography, modern art, fantasy, and science fiction appear together in unexpected combinations, further encouraging high standards of professionalism and specialization by younger designers.

In addition to images of the musicians, album covers exhibit a variety of themes, including death, drugs, ego, escape, identity, politics, and sex. As many of these themes lace through the music industry as a whole, the visual representative of the music itself follows. Bruce Springsteen's (1949–) 1984 album *Born in the USA* is a prime example of the politics theme. While the musician is present on the cover, attention is drawn to the red-and-white-striped background. Though nothing implicitly states that the background of the photograph by Annie Leibovitz (1949–) is the American flag, it is recognized as such because of the album title. This album, along with its iconic album cover, launched Springsteen's career into superstardom.

Although album covers were initially created to protect fragile vinyl records from damage, they became not only marketing tools but identifying icons for many musicians. Steinweiss gifted the music industry with one of its greatest and subtlest marketing and identity tools.

See also: Amos, Tori; Grateful Dead; Springsteen, Bruce; Vinyl Records; Zappa, Frank

Further Reading

Draper, Jason. 2008. *Brief History of Album Covers.* London: Flame Tree Publishing.

Morgan, Johnny, and Ben Wardle. 2010. *The Art of the LP: Classic Album Covers 1955–1995.* New York: Sterling.

Reagan, Kevin, and Steven Heller. 2011. *Alex Steinweiss: The Inventor of the Modern Album Cover.* Los Angeles: Taschen.

Thorgerson, Storm, and Aubrey Powell. 1999. *100 Best Album Covers.* London: DK Publishing.

Thorgerson, Storm, and Roger Dean. 1977. *Album Cover Album.* Surrey, UK: Dragon's World Ltd.

Wax Poetics. 2009. *Cover Story: Album Cover Art.* Brooklyn, NY: Wax Poetics Books.

Danielle Lewis

Allman Brothers (1969–1976, 1978–1982, 1989–present)

One of the most enduringly popular groups of the late 1960s, the Allman Brothers Band defined some of the best elements of rock music of the decade that followed, across several genres—blues-rock, hard rock, folk-rock, jazz-rock, and southern rock. Since their beginnings in the late 1960s, they have continued to perform through the present.

Guitarist Duane Allman (1946–1971) and singer-keyboard player Gregg Allman (1947–) were both lovers of American soul and British invasion rock, and they had freely mixed these influences in their early work, picking up what they needed from the sounds of The Beatles and The Rolling Stones and, later, Cream. They had been in several unsuccessful groups before it all came together in early 1969, when Duane Allman, by now a busy session musician, organized the band that would bear the siblings' name, consisting of himself, Dickey Betts (guitar), Berry Oakley (bass), Butch Trucks

The Allman Brothers Band performs in front of a television audience, 1972. Pictured from the left are Chuck Leavell, keys; Jamoie Johanson, drums; Dickey Betts, lead and slide guitar; Berry Oakley, bass; Butch Trucks, drums and percussion. (AP Photo)

(drums), Jamoie Johanson (drums), and Gregg (vocals, organ). By November they had cut their self-titled debut album and were starting to build a cult following, sufficient to get them booked at the Fillmore East for the first time the following February. And with the release of their second album, *Idlewild South,* in September 1970, their sound solidified around a mix of blues, soul, and hard rock spiced with elements of jazz and even classical, all played at a virtuoso level rivaling the best progressive rock bands of the era.

With the July 1971 release of their third album, *At Fillmore East*—a soaring, spellbinding double LP—their reputation was made. High school kids now raved about the Allmans the way they did about Eric Clapton and Jimi Hendrix. The future seemed to hold nothing but promise until October 29, 1971, when Duane was killed in a motorcycle accident. In a year that had already seen the loss of Jim Morrison, Jimi Hendrix, and Janis Joplin, his death was still a shock to the vast majority of fans who had only just discovered him. That might have been the end of the line, except that the Allmans had talent that was as wide as it was deep; with Dickey Betts taking over all of the guitar chores, and with some surviving live tapes to fill out their work-in-progress album *Eat a Peach* (released in April 1972), they not only survived, but bridged the huge gap left by Duane's death. Tragedy still stalked the band: that fall, bassist Berry Oakley died in a motorcycle accident. Their next album, *Brothers and Sisters,* issued in September 1973, proved that they could carry on and evolve. A relaxed country sound now shared space with the blues, jazz, and R&B influences, and they could fill arenas holding hundreds of thousands. In the decades since then, their reputation has risen and fallen, members coming and going in the process, but their tours and concerts remain legendary even in the twenty-first century.

See also: Hendrix, Jimi; Joplin, Janis; Morrison, Jim

Further Reading

Freeman, Scott. 1996. *Midnight Riders: The Story of the Allman Brothers Band.* Boston: Little, Brown.

Perkins, Willie. 2005. *No Saints, No Saviors: My Years with the Allman Brothers Band.* Macon, GA: Mercer University Press.

Poe, Randy. *Skydog: The Duane Allman Story.* 2006. San Francisco: Backbeat.

Bruce Eder

American Federation of Musicians (AFM)

The American Federation of Musicians of the United States and Canada (est. 1896) is a union representing the largest number of musicians in the world. Through the organization, musicians are connected to locals with the mission to live and work in dignity, to have fulfilling work and be compensated fairly, to have a meaningful voice in decisions that affect musicians, to have the opportunity to develop talents and skills, to have a collective voice and power that will be realized in a democratic and progressive union, and to oppose the forces of exploitation through union solidarity.

The AFM had its roots in the mutual aid societies of the mid-1800s, in which people joined together to help one another through financial difficulties and illness. Delegates from these early societies were invited by Samuel Gompers, president of the American Federal of Labor, to organize and charter a musician's trade union. Initially the organization had three thousand members, but today it serves approximately ninety thousand members. From its earliest days the union set wage scales, engaged in debates over copyright, and attempted to protect the rights of and provide financial support and relief to professional musicians.

In one of its more controversial moves, the AFM worked in conjunction with Immigration and Naturalization Services and the Department of Labor in 1964 in an attempt to ban The Beatles (active 1960–1970) from performing a second tour in the United States. Part of the rationale for this attempted ban was an agreement between the AFM and its British counterpart that musicians of high cultural value could move freely between the two countries. Rock music was not considered to be of high cultural value at the time, and then-AFM president Herbert Kenin and others believed that The Beatles had no special talent that American musicians didn't have. When Beatles fans learned of these plans, they waged a letter-writing campaign to political leaders and others, and the tour proceeded (although the AFM did prevent Capitol Records from making a live recording of The Beatles' performance in Carnegie Hall during the tour); however, other British bands such as The Kinks (active 1964–1996) and The Fortunes (active 1963–present) were less successful, as the AFM claimed to be protecting American musicians from losing work as British rock bands became increasingly popular in the United States.

Over the years the AFM has been actively involved in advocating for professional musicians as advances in technology have threatened to limit performance opportunities for artists and engendered controversies over performance rights. The development of phonograph records allowed people to enjoy music at home rather than listening to live musicians in music halls. "Canned music" in films eliminated the need for live musicians in movie theaters. Virtual orchestras in Broadway productions in the 2000s threatened the livelihood of pit orchestra musicians. Some of the AFM's responses to these challenges have been controversial. From 1942 to 1944, the organization banned members from commercially recording music (called the Petrillo Ban, after then-president James Petrillo) in an effort to pressure recording companies to provide better royalty payments to musicians. The AFM attempted a second ban in 1948. Radio stations were limited in what they could play for audiences, because no new music was recorded, and the early days of bebop are lost because the music was not recorded.

The AFM has also tried to help musicians and their families in times of need. In 1912 the organization made financial donations to widows and orphans of musicians who died on the *Titanic.* In the aftermath of Hurricane Katrina, the AFM created the Musicians Disaster Relief Fund for musicians affected by the devastation of the Gulf Coast.

See also: Bop and Hard Bop; Broadway; Hurricane Katrina and Music

Official Web Site: http://www.afm.org/

Further Reading

Pinta, Emil R. 2010. "Efforts by Record Ccompanies, the American Federation of Musicians and Truman's Cabinet to Resolve the 1948 Recording Ban." *ARSC Journal* 41, n. 1: 24–41.

Roberts, Michael. 2010. "A Working-class Hero Is Something to Be: The American Musicians' Union's Attempt to Ban the Beatles, 1963." *Popular Music* 29, no. 1: 1–16.

Seltzer, George. 1989. *Music Matters: The Performer and the American Federation of Musicians.* Metuchen, NJ: Scarecrow Press.

Jacqueline Edmondson

American Foreign Policy and Music

The April 13, 1970, release of Black Sabbath's (active 1969–2006) eponymous debut album signaled the dawn of the heavy metal era. The methodical, dirgelike instrumentation of guitarist Tony Iommi (1948–), bassist Terrence "Geezer" Butler (1949–), and drummer Bill Ward (1948–) provided an ideal sonic backdrop for vocalist

Globalization of Heavy Metal: A Sample Discography

Anthrax. "Antisocial," *State of Euphoria*. Island Records, 422-842 363-2, 1988 (orig. Trust. *Repression*. Sony Records 473573, 1980).

Aria. С Кем Ты? *(Who Are You With?)*. Self-published, 1986.

Gordi. Краљица смрти (*Queen of Death)*. Jugoton Records, 1982.

Helloween. *Walls of Jericho*. Noise Records 74024, 1986.

Kat. *Metal and Hell*. Anti-Goth Records 076, 1985.

V8. *Luchando Por El Metal (Fight for the Metal)*. Umbral Records 13002, 1983.

Voivod. *War and Pain*. Metal Blade Records 14049, 1984.

Ozzy Osbourne's (1948–) plaintive and mournful wail. Musically and lyrically, *Black Sabbath* reflects both the band's roots in the industrial city of Birmingham, England, and the uncertain spirit of the time in which it was recorded. While heavy metal has experienced a thematic diaspora since 1970, *Black Sabbath* has remained one of the genre's most influential recordings. Beginning with *Black Sabbath*'s bleak worldview, the genre has been notable for its rich use of dystopian themes and dark hyperbole. This imagery was particularly evident in early 1980s heavy metal, as increasingly vivid depictions of war and inhumanity became a point of focus for emerging acts in the genre. In turn, this focus provided heavy metal a common currency and allowed for its popular growth. Heavy metal's second generation is linked to the paradigm shift in American foreign policy during Ronald Reagan's first presidential term.

On the surface, the claim that Ronald Reagan influenced heavy metal's reinvention seems farfetched. The juxtaposition of Reagan, a relic of Hollywood's bygone studio-system era, with the seemingly antithetical tenets of heavy metal is, at the very least, a curious one. However, a closer examination shows a marked overlap between heavy metal and Reagan's early foreign policy.

This entry begins with a brief synopsis of foreign policy crises in Iran and Afghanistan during the final year of Jimmy Carter's presidency and their role in Ronald Reagan's victory in the 1980 presidential election. This is followed by an examination of the increasingly hard line of Reagan's foreign policy during his first term, focusing on his use of confrontational rhetoric toward the Soviet Union and staggering increases in defense spending. The consequences of this militaristic approach on heavy metal's thematic and lyrical evolution are examined through an analysis of the music of two of the era's most successful acts, Metallica (active 1981–present) and Iron Maiden (active 1975–present), demonstrating the influence of Reagan's increasingly antagonistic foreign policy on heavy metal's thematic and lyrical evolution. The entry concludes that the era's music may be seen as a transnational response to and rejection of Reagan's foreign policy and examines the legacy of apocalyptic imagery on post–Cold War era heavy metal.

Twin crises in Iran and Afghanistan in 1979 challenged the idea of American geopolitical primacy and contributed to Reagan's victory in the 1980 presidential election. On November 4, 1979, the American embassy in Teheran, Iran, was overrun and occupied by anti-American Islamic radicals. The embassy takeover threatened to destabilize the global security structure crafted by Richard Nixon that contributed to American foreign policy during the 1970s. Under the Nixon doctrine, regional allies such as Iran enjoyed military and economic aid from the United States in exchange for serving as American partners in regional security (see Maley 2002 and Kinzer 2003 for a comprehensive account of postwar Iranian–American relations). More immediately, fifty-two Americans were taken hostage during the siege. Carter's inability to secure the hostages' release was marked by a failed rescue attempt that left eight American soldiers dead on April 24, 1980, and caused significant damage to his reelection hopes; ultimately, the hostages were not released until January 20, 1981, Reagan's inauguration day.

Soviet–American relations also experienced a significant deterioration during this period, culminating with the American response to the December 27, 1979, Soviet invasion of Afghanistan. The relationship between the superpowers, which was already strained due to Carter's public criticism of the Soviet Union's human rights record, was further damaged when Carter characterized the invasion as the "greatest threat to peace since the Second World War" on January 8, 1980 (McCrisken 2004, 81). Carter's denunciation was underscored by his instructions to the Senate to shelve ratification of the second Strategic Arms Limitation Treaty and his decision to boycott the 1980 Olympic Games, which were to be held in Moscow. However, Carter's actions failed to secure a Soviet exit from Afghanistan, which, combined with the Iranian crisis, fueled the image of the president as an inept, powerless leader. Carter's inability to shed this negative image contributed to Reagan's victory in 1980.

Musical Examinations of Cold War Legacies

Pain of Salvation. *One Hour by the Concrete Lake.* SPV Records 08531342, 1999.

Savatage. *Dead Winter Dead.* Atlantic Records 82850, 1995.

Both releases are notable for their examination of Cold War legacies. *Dead Winter Dead* is a rock opera centered around the dissolution of Yugoslavia and the Bosnian War, while *One Hour by the Concrete Lake* focuses on the Cold War's environmental impacts, notably on Russia's Lake Karachy, which contains enough nuclear waste to create a lethal dose of radiation after one hour of exposure. Thomas B. Cochran, Robert Standish Norris, and Kristen Suokko, *Radioactive Contamination at Chelyabinsk-65, Russia* (Washington, DC: Natural Resources Defense Council, 1993).

Reagan's turn toward a more militaristic foreign policy was immediately apparent, as evidenced by a string of antagonistic statements that demonized the Soviet Union. In his January 20, 1981, inaugural address, Reagan issued a thinly veiled threat to Moscow, defiantly stating: "Our reluctance for conflict should not be misjudged as a failure of will. When action is required to preserve our national security, we will act. We will maintain sufficient strength to prevail if need be, knowing that if we do so we have the best chance of never having to use that strength." Reagan's forceful proclamation was not an anomaly; his characterization of the Soviet Union as an "evil empire" that would be relegated to "the ash heap of history" further illustrated the administration's hardening line. In contrast, Reagan spared no effort to beatify what he perceived to be inviolate American ideals and values. As historian George Herring notes in his landmark *From Colony to Superpower: U.S. Foreign Relations since 1776,* Reagan "accepted . . . the myth of American exceptionalism and repeatedly evoked John Winthrop's imagery of a 'city on a hill,' which he usually embellished by adding the adjective 'shining'" (2008, 64). Herring concludes that Reagan's enthusiastic belligerence may be seen as a smokescreen to mask his absence of foreign policy experience prior to assuming the presidency.

In addition, Reagan's determination to aggressively counter threats to American interests led to unprecedented administrative fiscal profligacy. Between 1981 and 1985, defense spending totaled $1 trillion, 30 percent of the federal budget. The administration's blank check proliferation hastened the development of nuclear weapons technology, along with the tanks, submarines, and aircraft needed to deploy them. This excessive spending was underscored by a string of covert and overt military engagements during Reagan's first term, including the shooting down of two Libyan Su-22 jets on August 19, 1981, by a pair of American F-14 fighters over the Gulf of Sidra; American involvement in the funding and training of anti-Marxist forces in El Salvador and Nicaragua; and the deployment of U.S. Marines to the small island nation of Grenada in 1983. In addition, on September 1, 1983, the Soviets shot down Korean Airlines (KAL) flight 007 over the Kamchatka peninsula, and NATO engaged in an overly realistic simulation of a European nuclear first strike, known as Able Archer, two months after the KAL 007 incident, bringing Soviet–American relations to a dangerous nadir.

Reagan's foreign policy was serendipitous for heavy metal. For a new generation of musicians living, as Black Sabbath sang a decade earlier, "in the shadow of atomic fear" (*Master of Reality,* 1971) the Reagan administration's belligerence and prevailing global insecurity were reflected in the names of emerging heavy metal acts and their songbooks. Names of emerging acts like Slayer (active 1981–present), Warlord (active 1981–1986, 2002), and Megadeth (active 1983–2002, 2004–present) reflected the increased tension of the times. The origin of the Megadeth name is especially notable: founding vocalist and guitarist Dave Mustaine (1961–) named the band after an impassioned statement from California senator Alan Cranston in which Cranston referred to the superpowers' nuclear stockpiles as "the arsenal of megadeath." Musically, the synthesis of punk rock's speed and inherently confrontational nature with the traditional bleak outlook of heavy metal's roots created an entirely new sound, with songs such as Metallica's "Seek and Destroy," Anthrax's (active 1981–present) "Aftershock," and Exodus's (active 1980–1993, 1997–1998, 2001–present) "And Then There Were None" becoming early staples of the genre, while also reflecting the growing adversarial sensibility within the White House at the time.

Lyrically, the looming nuclear threat offered a common focus for heavy metal, while simultaneously illustrating the genre's evolution. Broader themes of war and inhumanity had been the defining characteristic of early metal anthems, including Deep Purple's (active 1968–1976, 1984–present) "Child in Time," Thin Lizzy's (active 1969–1984, 1996–2001, 2004–present) "Fight or Fall,"

Resources Featuring New Interpretations of the Cold War

Gripentrog, John. "The Transnational Pastime: Baseball and American Perceptions of Japan in the 1930s." *Diplomatic History* 34:2 (April 2010): 247–273.

Manela, Erez. "A Pox on Your Narrative: Writing Disease Control into Cold War History." *Diplomatic History* 34:2 (April 2010): 299–323.

May, Elaine Tyler. *Homeward Bound: American Families in the Cold War Era.* New York: Basic Books, 1988.

McKevitt, Andrew. "'You Are Not Alone!': Anime and the Globalizing of America." *Diplomatic History* 34:5 (November 2010): 893–921.

Schwoch, James. *Global TV: New Media and the Cold War, 1946–69.* Chicago: University of Chicago Press, 2009.

and Black Sabbath's "Into the Void." The abstract allusions to a world in turmoil in "Into the Void" were typical of the genre's first generation, with references to "freedom from the final suicide."

In contrast, Reagan's revitalized arms race and bellicose rhetoric pushed heavy metal to evolve past abstract symbolism and placed a more refined point on its overarching themes. Two bands, San Francisco's Metallica and London's Iron Maiden, offer prime examples of this lyrical evolution. Metallica became a rising force in the heavy metal world in 1983. Its unique musical blend of speed, technical precision, and raw aggression turned the band into an underground phenomenon after the release of its debut album, *Kill 'Em All,* in July of that year. Songs like "The Four Horsemen," a contemporary version of the apocalyptic biblical tale, and "No Remorse," with its repeated refrain of "war without end," presented listeners with stark visions of an imminent, bleak dystopia. *Kill 'Em All* was followed by the July 1984 release of *Ride the Lightning,* which cemented Metallica's position at the forefront of American heavy metal. Featuring a rich tapestry of themes ranging from tales of pestilence inspired by the Old Testament's depiction of Egypt in "Creeping Death" to a tribute to Ernest Hemingway in "For Whom the Bell Tolls," the album opens with a vision of nuclear apocalypse in the song "Fight Fire with Fire." Vocalist James Hetfield's unpolished, staccato delivery keeps a metronomic narrative over a manic progression of guitar chords and pounding drums, leading to "The gods are laughing, so take your last breath." Lyrically, "Fight Fire with Fire" may be contextualized as a reaction to an increasingly unstable global nuclear structure. Its invocation of an imminent nuclear end-of-days reflects the trough in Soviet–American relations brought on, in part, by the KAL 007 and Able Archer 83 incidents. Although Metallica would revisit the topic of war's barbarism in future releases, "Fight Fire with Fire" represents a significant milestone in the band's evolution.

If Metallica was poised to conquer the heavy metal mountain in 1984, Iron Maiden was comfortably atop the summit. The band's *Powerslave* album drew from a rich wellspring of lyrical and thematic inspiration to craft an eclectic collection of songs that examined the Battle of Britain in "Aces High," used G. K. Chesterton's hymn "O God of Earth and Altar" as the basis of the song "Revelations," and perhaps most famously, gave a heavy metal slant to Samuel Taylor Coleridge's "Rime of the Ancient Mariner." In addition to these classic additions to the Iron Maiden songbook, "Two Minutes to Midnight" presented a dark commentary on the era's political and nuclear instability.

Drawing inspiration from the *Bulletin of Atomic Scientists*' Doomsday Clock, a theoretical construct in which "midnight" on the clock represents the outbreak of nuclear war, the song gives voice to the clock's movement to three minutes to midnight in January 1984. Backed by driving guitars, Bruce Dickinson's operatic vocals crackle like gunfire as he delivers a grim assessment of the impending doom, including such lines as "As the madmen play on words and make us all dance to their song." Like Metallica, while Iron Maiden's discography is rich in songs that address warfare and global discord, notably including "The Evil That Men Do" and "Afraid to Shoot Strangers," "Two Minutes to Midnight" stands as a uniquely vivid time capsule of one of the Cold War's lowest moments.

For heavy metal, the nuclear threat was the culmination of a steady evolution of the genre's lyrical and thematic focus. The dark hyperbole used to inspire the genre's second generation came to be used as a vehicle for presenting a cautionary tale that warned of the consequences inherent in an expansion of Reagan's policies. However, nuclear doomsday prophecies were not linked to the restrictions of record sales or geography. While Metallica and Iron Maiden thrilled stadia of fans around the globe, the landscape of the genre's second and third divisions was also rife with interpretations on the topic. Voivod's (active 1982–present) "Nuclear War,"

Queensrÿche's (active 1981–present) "En Force," and Corrosion of Conformity's (active 1982–1987, 1989–2006, 2010–present) "Poison Planet" each added a strand to the growing thread of nuclear consciousness within the genre. Similarly, heavy metal's global growth during this period allows for it to be seen as a transnational cultural text. The genre's growing popular wave reached both familiar and heretofore remote outposts, spawning a rich mixture of acts that experienced varying degrees of notoriety. The cult followings of Canada's Voivod, France's Trust (active 1977–1985, 1988, 1996–2000, 2006), and West Germany's Helloween (active 1984–present) satiated heavy metal fans in the traditional North American and Western European markets, while relatively anonymous acts such as the Soviet Union's Aria (active 1985–present), Argentina's V8 (active 1979–1987), Yugoslavia's Gordi (1977–1984), and Poland's Kat (active 1979–1987, 1990–1999, 2002–present) blazed the genre's trail in the sonic wilderness. This cross-pollination of culture and geography created an impressive and intricately woven musical tapestry, as evidenced by New York's Anthrax drawing on Trust's socialist predilections in recording a version of the latter's minor hit "Antisocial," while V8's criticism of Latin and South America's repressive dictatorships introduced socially conscious, aggressive music to a previously alien audience (see first sidebar).

The end of Reagan's first term was marked by a public backlash against his confrontational policies. A March 1983 Gallup poll showed higher support among the public for increases in education, Social Security, and welfare spending than on national defense, and a *New York Times*/CBS News poll conducted a month later found 64 percent of respondents in favor of a mutual Soviet–American nuclear freeze. The rising public antinuclear sentiment contributed to Reagan adopting a more flexible outlook on Soviet–American relations and nuclear disarmament, a position that was aided by Mikhail Gorbachev's 1985 election as Soviet General Secretary. By 1986 Reagan was applauding Gorbachev's plea for both sides to look past the perceived failures of that fall's Reykjavik summit toward a lasting peace. The following year's Intermediate Range Nuclear Forces Treaty signaled a new spirit of cooperation between Washington and its adversaries in the "evil empire," buoyed by the growing personal relationship between Reagan and Gorbachev. Meanwhile, Gorbachev's domestic reforms allowed the Soviet Union to back away from an economic model burdened by unsustainable military spending and introduced a greater focus on human rights and liberties that set into motion both the eventual dissolution of the USSR and the peaceful end of the Cold War itself by 1991.

For heavy metal, the Cold War's final years were also transitional. The drastically watered-down sound of acts like Mötley Crüe (active 1981–present) and Bon Jovi (active 1983–present) gained mainstream popularity and shifted the genre's focus to a more commercial and radio-friendly sound by the end of the decade. While a critical eye toward global politics remained a distinguishing characteristic of Queensryche's *Operation: Mindcrime,* Corrosion of Conformity's *Technocracy,* Megadeth's *Rust in Peace,* and Sacred Reich's (active 1985–2000, 2007–present) *The American Way,* the glut of softer-edged bands in the limelight drove these releases to the mainstream periphery. The rise of alternative and "grunge" rock in the 1990s drove the now traditional themes and presentation of heavy metal further underground and into obscurity. However, releases like Savatage's (active 1978–2002) *Dead Winter Dead,* Shadow Gallery's (active 1985–present) *Tyranny,* and Pain of Salvation's (active 1984–present) *One Hour by the Concrete Lake* are examples of heavy metal's reflection on the legacy of the post–Cold War world (see second sidebar). In addition, the overarching themes and lyrical content of Iced Earth's (active 1984–present) *The Glorious Burden,* Nevermore's (active 1991–present) *This Godless Endeavor,* and Iron Maiden's *A Matter of Life and Death* reflect the destabilization of global security and world peace triggered by the September 11, 2001, terrorist attacks on the United States and the ensuing American invasions of Afghanistan and Iraq.

Ultimately, it is no coincidence that heavy metal was at its most relevant when the Cold War was at its nadir. The genre's trademark gloom and despair was a perfect fit for an era of addled superpower relations and nuclear uncertainty. The general global turn toward confrontation and uncertainty at the end of the 1970s was an ideal breeding ground for an art form born from the dismal, dead end futures faced by the members of Black Sabbath in their native Birmingham a decade earlier. Left without citation, proclamations of evil empires, historically unprecedented menace, and impending Armageddon seem equally at home within the context of either a Reagan speech or a Slayer song. In this sense, the link between these two supremely incongruous commodities may be regarded as not only natural, but inevitable. The use of heavy metal as an academic lens for foreign relations history is an uncharted area of scholarship. However, it can—and should—be welcomed into the growing use of nontraditional methods of historical scholarship within the diplomatic history field. The rich wellspring of perspectives and sources found in examinations of sports, medicine, gender roles, television, and cartoons suggests that there is room at the table for heavy metal as a historical tool and presents fertile ground to be mined for new interpretations of the Cold War (see third sidebar).

See also: Grunge; Metallica; Punk Rock; War and Music

Further Reading

Christie, Ian. 2003. *The Sound of the Beast: The Complete Headbanging History of Heavy Metal.* New York: HarperCollins.

Dallin, Alexander. 1985. *Black Box: KAL 007 and the Superpowers.* Berkeley: University of California Press.

Fischer, Beth. 1997. *The Reagan Reversal: Foreign Policy and the End of the Cold War.* Columbia: University of Missouri Press.

Herring, George. 2008. *From Colony to Superpower: U.S. Foreign Relations Since 1776.* New York: Oxford University Press.

Kinzer, Stephen. 2003. *All The Shah's Men: An American Coup and the Roots of Middle East Terror.* Hoboken, NJ: John Wiley and Sons.

Maley, William. 2002. *The Afghanistan Wars.* Gordonsville, VA: Palgrave Macmillan.

Manchanda, Arnav. 2009. "When Truth Is Stranger Than Fiction: The Able Archer Incident." *Cold War History* 9, no. 1 (February): 111–133.

McCrisken, Trevor. 2004. *American Exceptionalism and the Legacy of Vietnam: U.S. Policy since 1974.* Gordonsville, VA: Palgrave Macmillan.

Wall, Mick. 1998. *Run to the Hills: The Official Biography of Iron Maiden.* London: Sanctuary Publishing.

Walser, Robert.1993. *Running with the Devil: Power, Gender, and Madness in Heavy Metal Music.* Middletown, CT: Wesleyan University Press.

Michael Cangemi

Amos, Tori (1963–)

Pianist, singer-songwriter, and composer Tori Amos has twelve studio albums and eight Grammy nominations to her credit, with nearly twenty million albums sold worldwide. Amos helped to reshape the image of piano in alternative music, turning it into a rock instrument and an essential part of her performances. She has said that the piano is where she chronicles everything, and it is integral to her life. Amos's music is known for its passion and power, and she writes songs by listening to other people's stories and watching her audiences react to her music. She is listed among VH1s top 100 women in rock and in 1996 was named one of *People* magazine's fifty most beautiful people.

Tori Amos was born Myra Ella Amos in Newton, North Carolina, the youngest of three children born to Edison and Mary Ellen Amos. Her paternal grandparents were Scotch Irish, and her maternal grandparents were Eastern Cherokee. Her grandfather had perfect pitch, and he sang to her and told her stories when she was a child. Amos's father was a minister in the Methodist church, and she grew up with a mixture of Cherokee spirituality and Christian influences. She adopted the name Tori at the suggestion of a friend's boyfriend.

Tori Amos in concert during the American Doll Posse World Tour, 2007. (Stefan Dumitru/Dreamstime.com)

Amos claims she always remembers playing the piano, and she considered it to be her best friend in the world. She began playing shortly after her family moved to Baltimore when she was two years of age, and she composed her first original music within the next three years. She was the youngest student ever to attend the Peabody Conservatory of Johns Hopkins University in Baltimore, enrolling as a piano student when she was five years old. Amos remained at Peabody until she was eleven, leaving primarily because she realized that she did not want to be a classical concert pianist and instead was more interested in popular music and composition. She loved John Lennon and Paul McCartney's work and enjoyed music by Led Zeppelin (active 1968–1980) and other popular artists. Amos won the Montgomery Teen Talent Competition when she was twelve years of age with one of her original songs, and with her father's encouragement she began performing in local lounges. Here she found strong support from the gay community who frequented the clubs where she played. A friend, Steve Himmelfarb, a recording engineer in California, encouraged Amos to move to Los Angeles to pursue her music career.

Y Kant Tori Read, her first album, recorded with her band of the same name, was a failure. Amos persevered and began her solo career with the release of her second album, *Little Earthquakes* (1992), which reached fifty-four on the *Billboard* 200. Her next album, *Under the Pink* (1993), had more favorable reviews and debuted at number one on the UK charts. Amos went on to push boundaries and cross genres in her composition and recordings, creating theme albums and songs that dealt with sometimes difficult and complex issues. *Night of Hunters* (2011) involved variations on a theme that pays tribute to Bach, Chopin, Debussy, Granados, Satie, and Schubert. She described the process for creating this album as frustrating until she worked out Schubert's "Star Whisperer," after which it became a love affair with the composers. The album tells the story of a couple who face a transformational night, and it includes her young daughter Natashya's voice, the first time the two recorded together.

A victim of sexual assault, Amos founded the non-profit organization Rape Abuse and Incest National Network (RAINN), a hotline that connects callers with their local rape crisis centers. She has worked to break down the silence around sexual assault issues through her music and activism.

See also: Rock 'n' Roll (Rock), Women In; Women in American Music

Official Web Site: http://www.toriamos.com

Further Reading

Amos, Tori, and Ann Powers. 2005. *Piece by Piece.* New York: Broadway Publisher.

Brown, Jake. 2011. *Tori Amos: In the Studio.* Toronto: ECW Press.

Rogers, Kalen. 1994. *Tori Amos: All These Years.* New York: Omnibus Press.

Jacqueline Edmondson

Analog vs. Digital Recording

The underlying reality of digital audio is mathematics, whereas the underlying reality of analog audio is physics
(Hugill 2012).

Today's music and sound production involves a complex hybrid of analog and digital technologies. Understanding the origins, the modes of convergence, the differences, and the specificities of these two domains is instrumental to developing and supporting rich interactions with music as a practitioner, composer, instrumentalist, producer, and even listener.

This combination of abstract representation, as in digital technologies and composing music, and very concrete transposition of physical phenomena, as in analog technologies and performing music, is certainly one of the most exciting characteristics of music as a human undertaking. From the invention of the earliest musical instruments to the Pythagorean research on the correspondences of variations of pitch to mathematical relationships between the length or size of sound-producing objects, the history of music and sound production is exemplary of this dual tendency to harmoniously combine digital and analog systems.

Analog Recording

The first attempts to record acoustic information date from the late nineteenth century and relied on the perfection and accuracy of the scientific description of auditory phenomena as wave generation, propagation, and reception.

Analog recording involves continuously translating the variations of air pressure, the sound waves caused by a vibrating object, into variations of another mechanical (shape or position), optical (intensity or position), or electrical (intensity or voltage) variable. The main characteristics of the analog translation are the strict preservation of a continuous time and the contiguity of the translating device, the transducer, with the actual phenomenon: analog recording is always a process synchronous, contemporaneous, and copresent with the acoustic phenomenon.

In the case of the earliest analog recording device, the Phonautograph, invented by Edouard-Léon Scott de Martinville in 1857, the sound waves were converted in mechanical deformations of an elastic membrane obstructing the small end of a funnel-shaped horn. A stylus attached to this membrane transmits and inscribes these deformations as a line on the moving surface of a sheet of paper coated with lampblack. Even though this rudimentary device did not support the reproduction of the recorded sound because of the fragility of the support, it is the archetype of all succeeding analog record technologies based on *tracing* or *drawing* the sound wave: cylinders, discs, and films.

Some of the limitations of these systems are directly dictated by the physical properties of the various components of the recording device: elasticity and mass of the membrane, sharpness, mass and size of the stylus, and plasticity of the medium. Some other limitations are dictated by the dynamic behavior of the mechanical apparatus and the nonlinear responses of its components to the mechanical excitation of the sound waves: resonance frequencies of the horn, membrane, and stylus tend to amplify bands of frequencies, thus leading to poor reproduction of the sound. Improvements in the strictly mechanical recording system consisting of better couplings of the various pieces used to maximize the transmission of mechanical energy are limited by the amount of initial energy conveyed by the sound waves and by the physicality of these components.

The next radical change in analog recording technology was the use of a nonmaterial element, that is, electricity, as a carrier or medium for the translation of sound waves. The microphone is the device that performs such translation. The modulated electric current output by the microphone can be used to drive an electromagnetic motor to inscribe the modulation in the groove of a disc, to modulate the intensity of a beam of light projected on a film, or to vary the magnetic field of an electromagnet.

Even though the transduction from mechanical to electrical energy allows for complex processing of the audio signal (i.e., amplification, filtering), the quality of analog recording remains intimately related to the necessary proximity and belonging of the transducer and the acoustic phenomenon to the same environment. The membrane of a microphone has to respond directly to sound waves producing mechanical impulses with wavelengths ranging from 50 feet to roughly 1 inch, and with pressure levels ranging from 0.00002 Pascals to 20 Pascals.

Digital Recording

Digital recording in general can be best described as the arbitrary transformation of a flow of information into a series of symbols. Such a transformation is performed by traditional musical notation, where the acoustic flow of sounds is transformed into a series of discrete symbols that represent only certain characteristics of the sounds (i.e., frequency, intensity, duration, and pitch). This transformation is established according to the preliminary definition of the granularity of the series and the density of the measuring scales. The definition of the granularity identifies segments of the flow of information that can be individualized and extracted out of the flow; these are the musical notes. The definition of the density of the measuring scales identifies the number of degrees used to accurately represent the meaningful variations of the characteristics of the units; these are the twelve degrees of the musical scale and the eight values of duration and intensity.

These two operations are referred to as sampling and quantizing in digital systems. In the audio domain, the process of digitizing is applied to electrical information analogically generated by a microphone and representing variations of air pressure over time.

The first operation, sampling, involves the transformation of the continuous time signal (i.e., the electrical flow output by the microphone) in a discrete series of grains of information, or samples. Each sample, taken at a regular time interval, records the intensity of the electrical current at this moment.

The number of samples influences the accuracy of the representation of the flow, and the "Shannon-Nyquist" theorem states that this sampling frequency or sampling rate (the number of samples per second) has to be at least double the bandwidth of the original signal. Because the human hearing system perceives frequencies up to 20,000 Hz, the necessary bandwidth for accurate representation of auditory perception is 20,000 Hz. Therefore, the sampling frequency has to be at least equal to 40,000 Hz.

If the signal to be sampled contains frequencies above the half of the sampling frequency, a special type of interference occurs, named *aliasing,* causing these high frequencies to be folded back onto the lower region of the spectrum, generating unwanted noise. To avoid this phenomenon, the incoming signal has to be processed with an analog low-pass filter cutting off all frequencies above the sampling frequency. This indispensable preparation of the signal points to another dependency of digital recording on analog technology. Most of the quality of an analog to digital converter depends on the quality of its analog filter.

The sampling rate used for digital audio disc, for example, is 44,100 Hz. In theory this value allows the representation of signals with a maximum frequency of 22,050 Hz and implies the use of an analog filter cutting all frequencies above this value and leaving the rest of the spectrum untouched, which is unachievable in the analog domain. The most common solution to this problem involves sampling the signal to a frequency way above the half of the necessary bandwidth, thus leaving room for an analog processing that does affect the useful part of the bandwidth. Today a sampling frequency of 96,000 Hz is commonly used to perform the initial acquisition of the analog signal, and then this digital signal is digitally filtered and resampled to bring its sampling frequency down to the standard value of 44,100 Hz.

The second operation in the process of digital representation is quantizing, projecting the measured values of each sample onto a discrete set of predefined values. When measuring the intensity of the electric current on any given sample, the value can vary continuously between the two extremities of the minimum and maximum. Whereas the number of possible values for each sample is infinite in the analog system, it is strictly finite in the digital system. Each measured value is rounded to the nearest discrete integer value available in the quantized system.

The most extreme quantization to be applied would only use two values, one (1) for the maximum of intensity and zero (0) for the minimum. Any given signal varying continuously between these two values would be represented through such quantization as a series of steps of various lengths. This quantization is said to use 1 binary digit, allowing for the encoding of the two values, 0 and 1. The relationship between the number of bits used to quantize analog values and the number of discrete values provided by the system is:

$$V = 2^n$$

where V is the number of discrete values and n the number of bits.

Quantization influences the accuracy of the represented information by influencing the signal-to-noise ratio of the signal. Noise is the result of the approximations made to convert the analog values into discrete values. The greater the number of discrete values, the smaller the difference between the "true" value and the discrete value and the smaller the amount of noise added to the signal. It is important to notice that the quality of an audio signal is exponentially proportional to the bit-depth used. In an 8-bit system, the number of discrete values is 256; in a 16-bit system, this number is 256 times greater

Digital Audio Disc technology uses a 16-bit quantizing system providing 65,536 values to record the variations of amplitude in the audio signal. This system offers a signal-to-noise ratio of 96 dB or a theoretical dynamic range of 96 dB, which is by far superior to what is allowed by the best analog recorder. However, a great difference exists between the analog and digital processes in handling signals at the two extremities of the range.

In the analog domain, when a signal reaches the lower end of the dynamic range, it progressively blends with the noise, to fade out and disappear in a manner very similar to the disappearance of a sound moving away from the listener. Such a progressive curve does not exist in the digital domain, where there is a clear-cut threshold between the quietest signal and the total absence of signal. A way to alleviate this issue of a constant and strict delineation is to add noise to the incoming signal to randomly distribute over time the crossing of this boundary line. This process is called *dithering*.

At the upper limit of the range, for the higher values and the values above the maximum admittance of the system, analog and digital processes diverge in a very significant way. In analog processing, a loud signal exceeding the dynamic capacity of the system will be progressively altered, with the result that extra power is sent to the output of system and generation of high harmonics. This type of analog distortion is proportional to the signal and preserves most of the qualities of the original signal; in fact, this effect is sometimes sought, as in the case of overdrive effects in electric guitar amplifiers that add overtones and warmth to the original sound. In a digital system, the maximum input is an absolute threshold set as a discrete value beyond which the intensity of the signal is simply rounded to this set value, resulting in a harsh-sounding effect. The only way to minimize the chances of clipping digital audio signal is to increase the bit depth; the available dynamic range is increased by 3 dB for each added bit. It is more and more common today to use 24 bit for audio signal, resulting in a 144 dB dynamic range.

Although it is certain that analog technologies will not be used anymore for inscription and storage of audio information, the combination of analog and digital technologies is definitely the most accurate mode of production of digital recordings of music. The lowering of the cost of digital storage and bandwidth allows the use of higher values in sampling and quantizing that can overcome most of the downsides of digitizing. The most important and crucial steps of audio recording remain the acquisition and restitution of audio information performed by the microphone and the loudspeaker.

See also: Mathematics and Music; Music Machines; Technology and Music

Further Reading

Hugill, Andrew. 2012. *The Digital Musician.* New York: Routledge.

Millard, Andre. 1995. *America on Record, a History of Recorded Sound.* New York: Cambridge University Press.

Milner, Greg. 2009. *Perfecting Sound Forever, an Aural History of Recorded Music.* New York: Faber & Faber.

Watkinson, John. 2001. *The Art of Digital Audio.* Woburn, MA: Focal Press.

Frank Dufour

Animated Sound

Most of the general public has spent thousands of hours experiencing cinema animation and is well acquainted with its many variations and subcategories, ranging from hand-drawn TV cartoons and claymation to 3D digital movies and video games. Yet there is an extraordinary kind of animation called "animated sound," which remains relatively unknown, a striking oversight considering its profound contribution to the fields of art, music, and entertainment. What is animated sound; when did it originate; and how has its remarkable legacy influenced the development of motion pictures, television, and electronic media?

Long before hip-hop began to use breakaway audio effects, such as "scratching" records and "one-shot" digital sampling in the 1990s, a succession of musically minded artists and animators investigated fresh approaches to the production of sound that were also highly unorthodox. Their innovative audio experiments, which began with the use of elementary electronic sound technology, opened up an entirely new direction in the emerging field of motion pictures. As early as 1922, and before the invention of the sound film, visionary Bauhaus artist and teacher Lazlo Moholy-Nagy began exploring the idea of "sound writing," a technique that consisted of manually scratching various kinds of graphic figures into a wax phonograph record. He theorized that this visual approach to generating sound could be an effective means of bypassing musicians and conventional instruments to deliver new, unfamiliar auditory experiences direct from the mind of the composer. It was in a sense an alchemistical concept, a theoretical strategy for transforming abstract shapes, symbols, and other types of graphic forms into an entirely new acoustical spectrum.

When the motion picture sound projector was introduced in the late 1920s, Moholy-Nagy finally had at his disposal a suitable instrument to demonstrate his theories. In 1933 he made *Sound ABC,* a 35mm film onto which he recorded, frame by frame, letters of the alphabet, fingerprints, profiles, and all kinds of signs and symbols. Each of the visual forms on his optical sound track, when run through a motion picture sound projector, was converted into a distinct audio result via the projector's photoelectric cell. In other words, the sound produced by Moholy-Nagy's film originated directly from a graphic source rather than from live audio sources, such as music and speech, which had to be recorded and then encoded onto the film. His newly devised sound technique closely resembled single-frame animation and would later be dubbed "animated sound" by Canadian film animator Norman McLaren. To complete his experiment, Moholy-Nagy rephotographed his sound track images onto the picture area of the film so that they could be projected and viewed along with the audio. In this dual cinematic presentation both sound and image were simultaneously generated from the same graphic images and patterns. This relatively simple film, which Moholy-Nagy (1965) termed "a lighthearted experiment," effectively demonstrated his acoustic theory and suggested a new and graphically unified approach to structuring the sound film.

In a parallel development beginning in 1930, several Russians at the Scientific Experimental Film Institute in Leningrad were also producing animated sound, or what they termed "ornamental animation in sound." From a historical perspective it should be noted that these works produced with animated sound were among the first forms of electronic music, an audio technology that was to shape a wide range of musical genres, from classical computer works of the 1950s and 1960s to contemporary types of popular music like glitch, techno, and electronica. There were other electronic devices developed during the early 1930s, but editing was problematic, and audio recording tape, naturally, was not available until much later. Animated sound, on the other hand, could be made and edited frame by frame and precisely synchronized to film imagery. The early research projects by Moholy-Nagy and others, particularly the animated sound works of Rudolph Pfenniger in Germany and A. M. Avzaamov, N. Y. Zhelinsky and N. V. Voinov in Russia, were shown throughout Europe, and both filmmakers and musicians immediately recognized their artistic implications.

About the same time Moholy-Nagy made *Sound ABC,* German animator Oskar Fischinger was also experimenting with synthetic sound on film. Fischinger's approach to the medium, however, was quite different from the theoretical exercises of Moholy-Nagy. Working with a holistic concept of film animation, Fischinger was attempting to create a new audiovisual language by using abstract animation as a vehicle of expression. Since the late 1920s he had been making animated films in which gracefully moving visual patterns were tightly synchronized with classical music recorded onto discs. This pioneering audiovisual approach had immense implications and was clearly a precursor and significant influence on modern music videos and the production techniques of MTV. Fischinger's basic aim was to artistically interrelate the sensory modes of sight and sound into a totally synthetic film experience. This holistic concept of cinema led him to experiment with the process of creating both sound and imagery from abstract animated graphic patterns.

His first sound studies were concerned with converting the characteristic elements of sound into a vocabulary of geometric shapes, in effect a form of "opto-acoustic notation." These shapes were drawn on paper scrolls and photographed frame by frame onto the sound track. He quickly developed this technique and was able to produce a wide range of sounds and complicated musical effects. Fischinger also tried drawing different kinds of symbolic designs and ornamental configurations that produced unusual or amusical sounds. This aspect of his research predates electronic and concrete music by many years, and its artistic implications were almost immediately recognized by composers Edgar Varèse and John Cage, both of whom were interested in expanding the boundaries of modern music. World War II interrupted

Fischinger's sound research, and his experiments were never fully developed into a cohesive artistic form that could be employed in his animated films. However, the sound experiments of Fischinger, along with the work of Moholy-Nagy and others, were publicized widely in Europe and England and helped prepare the groundwork for new holistic animated works that were to follow a few years later.

During the late 1930s, for example, Norman McLaren, at the National Film Board of Canada, began to use the principles established by these early experimenters and was the first to create a significant body of artistic work employing synthetic sound techniques (Dobson 1998; Valliere 1982). In his early films, such as *Allegro* and the brilliantly conceived *Dots* and *Loops,* McLaren drew both sounds and images directly onto film celluloid without the intervention of a camera or audio recording equipment. With this totally graphic approach to sound and image, McLaren created beautiful and refreshing animated films by delineating colorful abstract designs and a whole range of delightful auditory effects. Later, using a technique similar to Oskar Fischinger's he began to draw and index graphic patterns or waveforms, which were then photographed onto a sound track one frame at a time. With this photographic technique McLaren could create and control a wider range of synthetic effects, including chords, counterpoint, and harmony. This form of animated sound, which he occasionally combined with conventional musical instruments, is demonstrated in films such as *Now Is the Time, A Phantasy,* and *Neighbours,* for which he received an Oscar in 1953.

In 1941 John Whitney, a filmmaker and technical innovator, and his brother, James Whitney, a painter, began working with yet another form of synthetic sound on film. The purpose of their experiments was to develop a unified bisensory relationship between music and film. The Whitneys, however, felt that music produced by conventional instruments, because of their past associations and traditions, would be inappropriate for the abstract kinetic imagery of their films. They wanted something new and original, a fresh sonic construct that would meld with their technology-driven visual approach. Therefore, to create a different kind of audio that would directly relate to the quality and character of their elegant, animated visual patterns, they designed and built a highly specialized sound-producing apparatus (Whitney 1980).

As a result of their mechanical approach to sound as well as image, their early films were totally machine-realized art forms. Their graphic designs, which consisted of hard-edged geometric shapes, were manipulated by virtue of an optical printer, pantograph, and color filters. Multiple exposures, magnifications, reductions, and inversions enabled them to create an astounding variety of visual compositions in time and space. Their sound, which was produced with their specially designed infrasonic instrument, consisted of a series of pendulums that created light patterns directly on a sound track of normal specifications. The instrument did not produce an audible sound, but instead made an optical sound track from purely visual sources. Their sound track, which was a graphic record of oscillating light waves, was entirely synthetic and abstract, as was their imagery. Together the Whitneys demonstrated that the apparently cold world of machines could be effectively channeled to meet human and aesthetic needs. These early films, made in 1944–1945 and termed "exercises," were not only important artistic accomplishments, but also helped bridge the gap between film animation and the advanced forms of imaging technology, such as video and computer works, that were to emerge in the latter half of the twentieth century.

During the late 1970s and early 1980s Barry Spinello, a young animator working in the tradition of Norman McLaren, produced a series of abstract films using a new vocabulary of graphic techniques. To create his synthetic sounds and images Spinello, in addition to drawing and painting directly onto clear 16mm film celluloid, created patterns by using a variety of self-adhesive material, such as zip-a-tone shading sheets and press-apply lettering. These techniques were combined and used both on the sound track and in the picture area to create geometric patterns and musical effects, both of which undergo complex evolutionary changes. His overall intention was to shape and compress the tremendous kinetic energy of handmade images and sounds into a harmonious audiovisual unit. Two examples of this unique approach to animation are *Six Loop-Painting* and *Soundtrack.* During some of the more frenetic moments of these abstract films, sight and sound relationships change twenty-four times a second, and the visual patterns on the screen are frequently the same patterns that are creating the audio. As a result, this audiovisual form of animation supersedes synchronization and becomes a conceptually unified approach to filmmaking that stresses the synthesis and interdependence of sight and sound.

Over the years a number of beautiful and exhilarating animated films have been created with various forms of synthetic sound production. These works have not only contributed to the technical and artistic development of cinema animation, but have provided superb models for the production of other audiovisual genres, such as music videos, feature motion pictures, and assorted forms of visual music. MTV, for example, has mined the work of Fischinger, McLaren, the Whitneys, and other experimental animators who aspired to create multisensory and synchronized film experiences. Although most experimental animated films remain obscure to a mass audience, they are much admired and often emulated by the producers of music videos. Motion picture production, particularly the musical, has also been affected significantly. For instance, it is well documented by film historians that Walt Disney's *Fantasia,* an ambitious cinematic endeavor that combined classical music and animated vignettes, was influenced by the pioneering work of Oskar Fischinger. In a different adaptation of animated sound, with perhaps a whimsical nod to Norman McLaren, a contemporary pop music group in Germany called Ovals painted small images on the underside of CDs, thus creating skips and discordant musical effects. Clearly, synthetic sound and holistic film animation have been an influential force that manifested itself in many ways throughout the twentieth century.

The future of animated sound is difficult to predict, but in light of the digital revolution, it is reasonable to expect that there will be dramatic changes as well as a continuation of artistic activity. A new generation of computer wizards has begun to explore—through the use of emerging technologies, science, and cyberspace—a broad array of advanced visual and sonic modes. Since the 1990s an entirely new level of experimental imaging and audio possibilities has emerged, ushering in a growing gamut of surprisingly powerful and expressive procedures. Although animated sound has long been considered a technique that consists of individual images and sounds recorded frame by frame onto motion picture film, new digital possibilities have significantly expanded the definition of this venerable procedure. The unit of composition, for example, is no longer the single frame, but rather the pixel and digital data. These fast-moving developments have not only extended the range of holistic audiovisual expression, but could conceivably transform the way we think about animated sound as well as the art and entertainment environment that lies ahead.

See also: Cage, John; Digital Music; Hip-Hop

Further Reading

Alten, Stanley. 2010. *Audio in Media.* 9th ed. Boston: Wadsworth Press.

Beauchamp, Robin. 2005. *Designing Sound for Animation.* Oxford: Focal Press.

Bendazzi, Giannalberto. 1996. *Cartoons: One Hundred Years of Cinema Animation.* London: John Libbey & Company Ltd. in Association with Indiana University Press.

Brougher, Kerry, Olivia Mattis, Jeremy Strict, Ari Wiseman, and Judith Zilczer. 2005. *Visual Music: Synaesthesia in Art and Music Since 1900.* London: Thames and Hudson.

Curtis, David. 1971. *Experimental Cinema, A Fifty-Year Evolution.* New York: Universe Books.

Dobson, Terence. 1998. *The Film Work of Norman McLaren.* London: John Libbey & Company Ltd. in Association with Indiana University Press.

Furniss, Maureen. 1998. *Art in Motion: Animation Aesthetics.* London: John Libbey & Company Ltd. in Association with Indiana University Press.

Kahn, Douglas, and Gregory Whitehead, eds. 1994. *Wireless Imagination: Sound, Radio and the Avant-garde.* Cambridge, MA: MIT Press.

Kostelanetz, Richard. 1970. *Moholy-Nagy.* New York: Praeger Publishers.

Laybourne, Kit. 1998. *The Animation Book.* New York: Three Rivers Press.

Le Grice, Malcolm. 1977. *Abstract Film and Beyond.* Cambridge, MA: MIT Press.

Moholy-Nagy, Lazlo. 1965. *Vision in Motion.* Chicago: Hillison and Etten.

Moritz, William. 2004. *Optical Poetry.* London: John Libbey & Company Ltd. in Association with Indiana University Press.

Russett, Robert, and Cecile Starr. 1988. *Experimental Animation: Origins of a New Art.* New York: Da Capo Press.

Valliere, T. Richard. 1982. *Norman McLaren: Manipulator of Movement.* An Ontario Film Institute Book. Newark: University of Delaware Press.

Whitney, John. 1980. *Digital Harmony, On the Complementarity of Music and Visual Art.* Peterborough, NH: Byte Books/McGraw-Hill.

Youngblood, Gene. 1970. *Expanded Cinema.* New York: Dutton.

Robert Russett

Antiestablishment Themes in American Songs

"Yankee Doodle Dandy," "Follow the Drinking Gourd," and "John Henry" are all familiar songs, at least 150 years old, and still resonate in the American consciousness and in the American spirit of protest. "Yankee Doodle Dandy," originally a British song mocking Americans, was reworded into a pro-American anthem to rally the revolutionary militia. "Follow the Drinking Gourd" not only provided inspiration for a slave's escape, but also mapped out the route through its lyrics, and "John Henry," recorded more than two hundred times, sounds a cry for workers in jeopardy of losing jobs to technology.

Antiestablishment songs or protest songs focus on topical subjects and challenge traditional, governmental, corporate, and mainstream positions and mores,

Antiestablishment Songs

"Liar! Killer! Turncoat! Thief! Criminal with protection of the law" begins Anti-Flag's (1988–1989, 1993–present) opening salvo aimed at President Bush on *The Terror State*, the band's 2003 CD. It's a rousing punk anthem, but not simple ranting and sloganeering. The CD's accompanying twenty-four-page booklet explains the chant with footnotes referencing the *New York Times* and *Washington Post*. On *For Blood and Empire* (2006), the band samples Rep. Jim McDermott (D-WA), with whom they worked on the depleted uranium campaign. Formed in 1988, Anti-Flag combines fiery punk rock, scorching guitar riffs, and angry politics. Leader Justin Sane (1973–) explains, "I think having the ability to point out the injustice in your society and your country as well as see the things that are great about it is . . . what really makes a patriot. With that definition of a patriot, I consider myself a patriot."

Peter Buckland

providing a voice for the oppressed, the marginalized, and the underdog. Singers and songwriters of antiestablishment music generally consider themselves patriots who seek to inspire and mobilize others to defend and uphold America's basic principles "of life, liberty, and the pursuit of happiness." In the folk music tradition, protest songwriters will frequently write new lyrics to familiar melodies, a practice that emphasizes the message and makes the song easier for listeners to learn.

Although antiestablishment music concerns a wide range of topics, this entry considers its dominant themes since the twentieth century, specifically labor, civil rights, and war. The focus here is on the lyrics, but recognizes that just as countercultural can be a performer's gestures (e.g., Elvis Presley's gyrations), appearance and dress (e.g., long hair in the 1960s and the bling and low pants of hip-hop in the 1980s), and the music itself (e.g., the volume of heavy metal).

Prolabor Songs

As the labor movement developed early in the 1900s, songs inspired workers around the country. "Bread and Roses" by James Oppenheim (1892–1932) and Caroline Kohlsaat became the anthem for striking textile workers in Lawrence, Massachusetts, in 1912; "Dump Your Bosses off Your Back" (1916) by John Brill was sung widely at rallies for several years, and "Which Side Are You On?" by Florence Reece (1900–1986) was first sung by the United Mine Workers in Harlan County, Kentucky, in 1931. However, the most influential pro-union activist and songwriter was Swedish American Joe Hill (1879–1915; born Joseph Emmanuel Hägglund). Among his most important songs are "Casey Jones: Union Scab," "There Is Power in a Union" (reworked by Billy Bragg in 1986), and "The Preacher and the Slave," which appropriates the melody of "In the Sweet Bye and Bye" and attacks organized religion for serving corporate interests and promising obedient workers, upon death, a "pie in the sky," a phrase coined by Hill. Executed after a suspicious murder conviction, Hill has lived on in the American consciousness through biographies (e.g., William M. Adler's *The Man Who Never Died,* 2011) and popular songs, especially Alfred Hayes's "I Dreamed I Saw Joe Hill Last Night" (1930), performed at Woodstock by Joan Baez (1941–) and recorded by Tom Morello (1964–) in 2011.

The most significant folksinging heirs to Hill have been Woody Guthrie (1912–1967) and Pete Seeger (1919–). Guthrie strummed his guitar, bearing the words "This Machine Kills Fascists," to compositions like "Union Burying Ground," "Union Maid," and "Plane Wreck at Los Gatos (Deportees)," which protests the dehumanization of illegal migrant workers. Consistently attacking corporate greed, Guthrie celebrated the outlaw hero in songs like "Pretty Boy Floyd," his sympathetic portrait of the notorious bank robber. In "This Land Is Your Land," his most famous song and written in response to the celebratory "God Bless America" by Irving Berlin (1888–1989), Guthrie calls on America to be faithful to its founding vision and to make its wealth and resources available to ordinary citizens—the controversial verses are generally omitted from the version sung by schoolchildren. Guthrie has been a hero to Bob Dylan (1941–), Billy Bragg (1957–), Wilco (1994–present), Anti-Flag (1988–1989, 1993–present), and the Dropkick Murphys (active 1996–present), among many others.

Pete Seeger emerged in 1940 as a core member of, first, the Almanac Singers (along with Guthrie, active 1940–1942/1943) and later, the Weavers (active 1948–1952, 1955–1964). In 1941 the Almanacs, founded to promote pro-union and other progressive causes, released *"Talking Union" & Other Songs,* which features powerful originals like "Talking Union" and "Get Thee Behind Me, Satan." Through the years Seeger, a central figure in antiestablishment music, has sounded a strong pro-worker, proenvironmental, and antiwar voice.

With the economy thriving immediately after World War II, other issues began to consume Americans. Yet

Underground Resistance in the 1980s and 1990s

American underground music scenes have always featured antiestablishment and protest messages. In the 1980s and 1990s American thrash metal and punk artists wrote thousands of songs critical of the establishment. Although thrash metal often criticizes those in power, the songs can seem ambiguous, because they can be written from the point of view of the aggressor or because the music itself is simultaneously elaborate, aggressive, and written from the point of view of a victim or someone seeking justice. Punk and hardcore, though no less aggressive, has taken a more direct stance, with easier-to-perform music reflecting its founders' embrace of their lower-class status. However, thrash metal and punk, much like early rap and acts like Public Enemy, had enormous underground influence during this time.

Thrash bands like Metallica (1982–present), Megadeth (1983–2002, 2004–present), Forbidden (1985–1997, 2001, 2007–present), Testament (1983–present), and Nuclear Assault (periodically 1984–present) have released songs dealing with social, economic, political, and environmental problems. These include war from the soldier's point of view, nuclear war, racism, rape, religious persecution, political and religious corruption, labor exploitation, economic inequality, species extinction, ozone depletion, and climate change. Metallica and Megadeth are the only two of these bands to achieve mass commercial success. Thrash metal's criticism of social ills has continued with contemporary bands like Heathen (1984–1993, 2002–present), Revocation (2006–present), and Lamb of God (1994–present).

Punk acts like Black Flag (1976–1986), Dead Kennedys (1978–1986, 2001–present), and Bad Religion (1979–present), and ska-punk crossover band Operation Ivy (1987–1989), have all dealt with similar topics but often at the street level, with songs about poverty, homelessness, racism, atheism and religious bigotry, street fights, and police brutality. Young punk fans have been among the most politically active youths over the last three decades, making up sizeable portions of the anarchist, antiglobalization, prolabor, vegan, and radical environmentalist movements.

Peter Buckland

prolabor and pro-working-class songs did not disappear: "Sixteen Tons" (written by Merle Travis [1917–1983] in 1946, a hit for Tennessee Ernie Ford [1919–1991] in 1955, and recorded by Tom Morello in 2011); Bob Dylan's "Maggie's Farm" (1965; covered by Silvertide [2001–2009] in 2006), "Union Sundown" (1983), and "Workingman's Blues #2" (2006); David Allan Coe's (1939–) "Take This Job and Shove It" (a hit for Johnny Paycheck [1938–2003] in 1977); Billy Joel's (1949–) "Allentown" (1982); Bruce Springsteen's (1949–) "Born in the U.S.A." (1984); Public Enemy's (active 1982–present) "Shut 'Em Down" (1991); and Steve Earle's (1955–) "Christmas Time in Washington" (1997), which evokes Joe Hill and Guthrie. In 2011, in response to the Wisconsin state government's efforts to weaken unions, Tom Morello, as the Nightwatchman and a founding member of Rage Against the Machine (active 1991–2000, 2007–present), released *Union Town,* featuring prolabor classics like "Solidarity Forever" (written by Ralph Chaplin (1897–1961) in 1915) and "Which Side Are You On?"

Individual Rights and the Civil Rights Movement

Since its founding the United States has given rise to impassioned songs whenever the empowered threaten or limit individual freedoms. At late nineteenth- and early twentieth-century suffragette rallies, women sang the ironic "Keep Woman in Her Sphere" (lyrics by D. Estabrook) to the tune of "Auld Lang Syne" and "Give the Ballot to the Mothers" (lyrics by Rebecca N. Hazard). In the 1960s the women's liberation movement inspired new anthems like Aretha Franklin's (1942–) 1967 version of Otis Redding's (1941–1967) "Respect" and "I Am Woman," a number one hit for Helen Reddy (1941–) in 1972. The 1990s saw a new wave of feminist singer-songwriters, groups, and movements, including Ani DiFranco (1970–), Sleater-Kinney (1994–), Riot Grrrl punk bands like Bikini Kill (active 1990–1998) and Bratmobile (active 1991–1994, 1999–2003), and the Lilith Fair festival series (1997–1999, revived in 2010), which brought together newer and older feminist voices like Jewel (1974–), Sarah McLachlan (1968–), and the Indigo Girls (active 1985–present). Hip-hop has produced several powerful feminist declarations, including "Ladies First" (1989) by Queen Latifah (1970–), "None of Your Business" (1993) by Salt-n-Pepa (active 1985–2002, 2007–present), and "Black Girl Pain" (2004) by Talib Kweli (1975–) featuring Jean Grae (1976–).

Music has been especially significant in the African American struggle for civil rights. "Lift Every Voice and Sing," a 1905 poem by James Weldon Johnson (1971–1938) set to music by his brother John Rosamond

Folk singer Pete Seeger strums a banjo on the bow of the 75-foot Hudson River sloop *Clearwater*, launched in South Bristol, Maine, on May 14, 1969. Seeger and a group of volunteers had the $150,000-vessel built to dramatize the fight against pollution of the Hudson River Valley. (AP Photo/Stephen Nichols)

Johnson (1873–1954), which presents images of hardship, implied racial abuse, and ultimate triumph, resonated throughout the century as the unofficial Negro national anthem. In 1990, after a recording led by Melba Moore and featuring, among others, Stevie Wonder (1950–), Anita Baker (1958–), and Bobby Brown (1969–), the song entered the congressional record as the official African American national hymn. Less triumphant but just as stirring was Billie Holiday's (1915–1959) recording of the intense lament "Strange Fruit" (1939), written by Abel Meeropol (a.k.a. Lewis Allan, 1903–1986), which contrasted images of southern beauty with the "strange fruit" of lynched African Americans.

Martin Luther King Jr. (1929–1968), at the height of the civil rights movement in the late 1950s and 1960s, often led followers in singing "We Shall Overcome," a prolabor anthem in the 1940s adopted by King after hearing a Pete Seeger performance of the song. Joan Baez delivered an especially moving version during the March on Washington in August 1963, an event at which Bob Dylan sang "Blowin' in the Wind." Other songs associated with the movement include "Keep Your Eyes on the Prize"; the gospel song "This Little Light of Mine," written around 1920 for children by Harry Dixon Loes; and the Staple Singers' (active 1948–1994) "When Will We Be Paid (For the Work We've Done)?" which calls for reparations. Nina Simone (1933–2003) wrote the jarring and ominous "Mississippi Goddam" (1964), made all the more chilling by its ironic show-tune melody and rhythm, and R&B great Sam Cooke (1931–1964) composed "A Change Is Gonna Come" (1964). In 1968, an especially contentious year in America with antiwar rallies and race riots, James Brown (1933–2006) led a chorus of children in his militant expression of empowerment, "Say It Loud—I'm Black and I'm Proud."

In spoken-word performances like "The Revolution Will Not Be Televised" (1970), Gil Scott-Heron (1949–2011) proved a forerunner of hip-hop's social consciousness. In 1982 Grandmaster Flash and the Furious Five (active 1978–1982, 1987–1988) updated Heron's depiction of inner-city angst with "The Message" song and video. Other hip-hop artists with similar rage followed:

among others, Public Enemy; N.W.A. (Niggaz With Attitude, active 1986–1991, 1999–2000); Ice-T (1958–), especially in the controversial "Cop Killer" with his heavy metal crossover band Body Count (active 1990–2006, 2009–present); Tupac Shakur (1972–1996), who celebrated thug life in his persona of the outlaw; and Notorious B.I.G. (a.k.a. Biggie Smalls, born Christopher Wallace, 1972–1997), whose gifted storytelling often captured the desperation of inner-city life. Often criticized for images of material and sexual excess, hip-hop maintains a strong social consciousness through artists like Eminem (1972–), The Roots (active 1987–present), Nas (1973–), Mos Def (1973–), Lupe Fiasco (1982–), J. Cole (1985–), and Common (active 1972–).

Antiwar Songs

Although antiwar songs appeared before America's entrance into World Wars I and II (e.g., the 1915 hit "I Didn't Raise My Boy to Be a Soldier" by Alfred Bryan [1871–1958] and Al Piantadosi, and the 1941 album *Songs for John Doe* by the Almanac Singers), the impulse to protest diminished greatly after America entered those wars. The Almanacs pulled *John Doe* after Germany invaded the Soviet Union. After World War II and the atomic bombings of Japan, antinuclear songs proliferated. Newspaper reporter and folksinger Vern Partlow (1910–1987), blacklisted during the McCarthy era, composed the satirical "Old Man Atom" in 1946, recorded in 1948 by Pete Seeger as "Talking Atom" and by others as "Atomic Talking Blues."

In 1961 Seeger wrote "Where Have All the Flowers Gone?" a lament in which young girls pick flowers for the grave sites of soldiers, and in 1963, two years before American combats troops fought in Vietnam, Bob Dylan wrote the diatribe "Masters of War," a condemnation of arms dealers and the growing military-industrial complex. But it was the Vietnam War in which songwriters of various genres galvanized the antiwar movement in song after song: the folk songs "I Ain't Marching Anymore" by Phil Ochs (1940–1976) and the popular singalong "I-Feel-Like-I'm-Fixin'-to-Die Rag" by Country Joe and the Fish (1965–1971); the soul of "I Should Be Proud" by Martha and the Vandellas (active 1962–1972); the rocking "Fortunate Son" by Creedence Clearwater Revival (active 1967–1972); the psychedelia of "Machine Gun" by Jimi Hendrix (1942–1970); the funk of "War" by Edwin Starr (1942–2003); and "Simple Song of Freedom" by Bobby Darin (1936–1973), largely regarded as a lounge act.

One of the bitterest songs of the era was Neil Young's (1945–) "Ohio," performed by Crosby, Stills, Nash & Young (active 1968–1970, 1974, 1977–present) and written in response to the fatal shooting of four college students during an antiwar protest at Kent State University on May 4, 1970. Featuring a piercing guitar riff above a marching beat, "Ohio," banned by many radio stations, attacks the National Guard, President Nixon, and the Vietnam War, and calls for increased protest. Similarly, other artists fused several antiestablishment themes in a single song, like Barry McGuire (1935–) in "Eve of Destruction" and The Temptations (active 1960–present) in "Ball of Confusion."

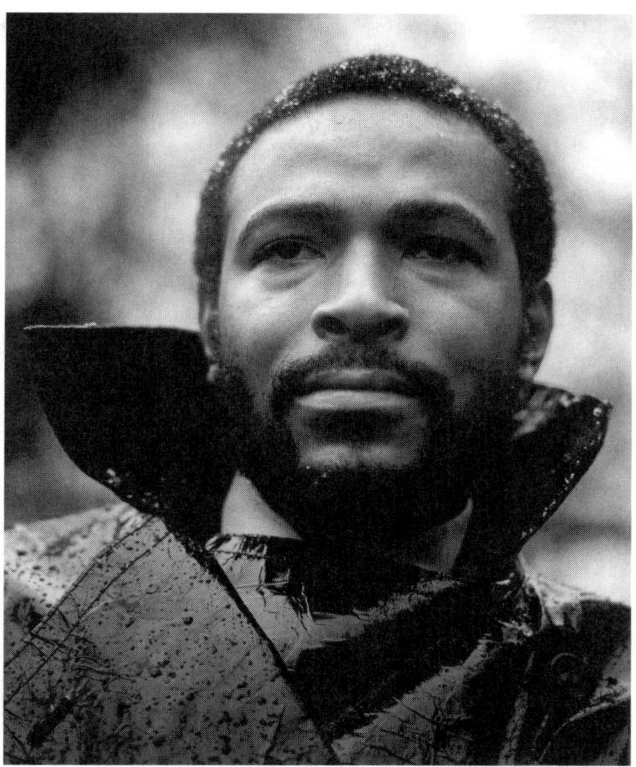

R&B singer Marvin Gaye poses for a portrait for his album *What's Going On* which was released on May 21, 1971. (Michael Ochs Archives/Getty Images)

Marvin Gaye (1939–1984) voiced one of the strongest antiestablishment statements in his epic concept album *What's Going On* (1971), and Johnny Cash (1932–2003) sang three protest songs in front of President Nixon in 1972: "What Is Truth?" "Man in Black," and "The Ballad of Ira Hayes."

Although antiwar songs were less prolific during the Iraq War (there was no draft), potent antiwar and anti–President George W. Bush songs were delivered by, among others, Eminem, "Mosh" and "White America"; Pink (1979–), "Dear Mr. President"; Bright Eyes (active 1995–present), "When the President Talks to God"; Pearl Jam (active 1990–present), "World Wide Suicide" and "Marker in the Sand"; Dar Williams (1967–) "Empire"; and John Mayer (1977–), "Waiting on the World to Change." Led by Fat Mike (Michael Burkett, 1967–), leader of NOFX and founder of Fat Wreck

Chords, new millennium punk bands joined with earlier punk bands to produce *Rock against Bush, Vol. 1* (April 2004) and *Vol. 2* (August 2004), featuring, among others, NOFX (active 1967–present), Green Day (active 1987–present), Anti-Flag (active 1988–1989, 1993–present), Rise Against (active 1999–present), Bad Religion (active 1979–present), Social Distortion (active 1978–1985, 1986–present), Henry Rollins (1961–), and Jello Biafra (1958–). In other acts, Lamb of God's (active 1994–present) album *Ashes of the Wake* (2004) contains only songs protesting the Iraq War. The industrial metal act Ministry, who had also written their 1993 song "New World Order" criticizing Bush's father, George H. W. Bush, released their album *Rio Grande Blood* (2007), which called Bush a "terrorist."

While mainstream country artists tended to support the Bush administration—for example, Toby Keith's (1961–) massive hit "Courtesy of the Red, White & Blue (The Angry American)" (2002)—some opposed the war. Most famously, the Dixie Chicks (active 1989–present), after making an anti-Bush statement on a London stage in 2003, were ostracized by many country music forums. Unapologetic, they released "Not Ready to Make Nice" in 2006. Other country music stars spoke out against the war, including Willie Nelson (1933–); Charlie Daniels (1936–); and, perhaps most surprisingly given his conservative anthems of the late 1960s, like "Okie from Muskogee," Merle Haggard (1937–), who released "That's the News" (2003) and "America First" (2005).

Perhaps the grandest counterculture statement came from punk band Green Day, with *American Idiot* in 2004 and its follow-up *21st Century Breakdown* in 2009, two powerful concept albums depicting a vacuous American landscape ruled by fear, the religious Right, and a short-sighted (to say the least) president manipulating a sycophantic media.

What George Washington wrote about Thomas Paine's radical pamphlet *Common Sense* could be said about antiestablishment songs then and now: "I find that [they are] working a powerful change . . . in the minds of many . . . [with] so dramatic an effect on political events." America would be a very different place without its antiestablishment music.

See also: Baez, Joan; Brown, James; Cash, Johnny; Counterculture in American Music; Country Music; Crosby, Stills & Nash; Dixie Chicks; Dylan, Bob; Folk Music; Franklin, Aretha; Gaye, Marvin; Green Day; Guthrie Family; Hendrix, Jimi; Hip-Hop; Holliday, Billie; Indigo Girls; Morello, Tom; Nelson, Willie; Ochs, Phil; Pearl Jam; Political Inscriptions on Musical Instruments; Presley, Elvis; Protest Music; Punk Rock; Queen Latifah; Rage Against the Machine; Seeger, Pete; Shakur, Tupac; Social Causes of Musicians; Springsteen, Bruce; War and Music; Young, Neil

Further Reading

Denisoff, R. Serge. 1998. *Sing a Song of Social Significance.* Bowling Green, OH: Bowling Green State University Popular Press.

Eyerman, Ron, and Andrew Jamison. 1998. *Music and Social Movements: Mobilizing Tradition in the Twentieth Century.* Cambridge, UK: Cambridge University Press.

Lynskey, Dorian. 2011. *33 Revolutions per Minute: A History of Protest Songs, from Billie Holiday to Green Day.* New York: HarperCollins.

Phull, Hardeep. 2008. *Story behind the Protest Song.* Westport, CT: Greenwood.

Pratt, Ray. 1990. *Rhythm and Resistance: Explorations in the Political Uses of Popular Music.* New York: Praeger.

Thomas M. Kitts

Antiwar Music

The Vietnam era remains one of the most culturally defining eras in American antiwar music, given the impact that this music and the artists who produced it had on American culture during that time and for decades to come. There are three major reasons for this large cultural footprint. First, many of the songs were top singles at that time and helped fuel antiwar sentiment. Many cultural historians have noted that Barry McGuire's 1965 folk-rock hit "Eve of Destruction," which rose to number one on the *Billboard* Hot 100 chart and stayed there for eleven weeks, helped to solidify the emerging youth movement by pointing out the hypocrisy of being asked to fight in a war when young people could not even vote and also portraying the ambivalence that many Americans felt toward the war: "You don't believe in war, but what's that gun you're totin'?"

Similarly, as the war raged on, other songs not only became huge hits but also reflected the growing antiwar movement, as troop levels surged to 451,000 in 1967 and then to 537,377 in 1968. Buffalo Springfield's 1967 rock classic, "For What It's Worth," charted at number seven on the top singles chart and encapsulated the era's uncertainty, particularly highlighting the clashes between antiwar demonstrators and the authorities: "I think it's time we stop, children, what's that sound, / Everybody look what's going down."

In 1969 John Lennon and Yoko Ono's Plastic Ono Band released "Give Peace a Chance," which rose to number fourteen on the *Billboard* charts and became the American antiwar movement's new sing-along. This was largely due to folksinger Pete Seeger's impromptu decision to lead a crowd of a half a million protestors in collectively singing the song at the antiwar protest, the "Moratorium to End the War in Vietnam," on October 15 in Washington, D.C.

Toward the war's end, many of the antiwar songs became more outwardly angry and reflective. The Guess Who's psychedelic-rock infused "American Woman" railed against American military imperialism, while Edwin Starr's funk diatribe, "War," asked rhetorically, "What is it good for? / Absolutely Nothing!" Both songs were number one hits in 1970 for fifteen weeks each and were followed by the soulful meditation of Marvin Gaye's 1971 hit, "What's Going On," which charted at number two for seventeen weeks. Gaye sang plaintively: "Father, father, we don't need to escalate."

The second reason that the Vietnam era was culturally significant was that a number of the artists' songs spoke truth to power, and as celebrity musicians they helped galvanize the emerging youth counterculture into the civil rights and antiwar movements. One of the most recognizable artist leaders of this period was Bob Dylan. *The Freewheelin' Bob Dylan,* his second album, released in 1963, prominently featured numerous protest songs such as "Blowin' in the Wind" and "Masters of War," and demonstrated that Dylan was following in the footsteps of political folk music hero Woody Guthrie. This association was further solidified by the release of Dylan's third album in 1965, *The Times They Are a-Changin',* as the title track became another protest anthem. This song in particular depicted the generational divide between the progressive, free-thinking 1960s flower children who were forming the new counterculture and their parents.

During this time Dylan, as well as Joan Baez, the folksinger known for her clear, high soprano voice, and the folk trio Peter, Paul and Mary, gained increasing fame and notoriety and displayed how the cult of celebrity could be used by social movements. In particular, all of these artists were strongly linked to the civil rights movement, performing in front of hundreds of thousands of protestors who participated in the August 28, 1963, March on Washington for Jobs and Freedom, where Martin Luther King Jr. gave his famous "I Have a Dream" speech, as well as performing at numerous other civil rights demonstrations and concerts.

By the mid-1960s Dylan had separated himself from the folk protest music tradition and severed his explicit ties to social movements. However, Joan Baez and Peter, Paul and Mary continued to use their platforms as famous singers to try to effect social change. These artists performed at numerous teach-ins against the war and prominent antiwar demonstrations, including the aforementioned "Moratorium to End the War in Vietnam" in October 1969, which Peter Yarrow (of Peter, Paul and Mary) co-organized. And Baez was particularly outspoken against the war, withholding her federal income taxes and becoming a strong proponent of draft resistance.

The third reason that much of the anti-Vietnam war music has maintained a place in our nation's collective cultural memory is its continued presence in the mainstream media. More than sixty commercially released antiwar songs from the Vietnam era have been subsequently covered by artists in more recent years, with John Lennon's "Imagine" (176 covers tracked) and Bob Dylan's "Blowin' in the Wind" (159 covers tracked) garnering the first and second places, respectively.

Furthermore, the placement of antiwar music from the Vietnam era on successful sound tracks has added to this music's lasting cultural resonance. The 1967 release of Country Joe McDonald's "Fish Chant/Fixin' to Die Rag" was not widely played on the radio at that time, given the lyrics' caustic satire (e.g., "Be the first one on your block to have your boy come home in a box"). However, Country Joe's performance of the song as a group sing-along with hundreds of thousands of hippies at the August 1969 Woodstock Festival was immortalized in the best-selling 1970 documentary *Woodstock.* Likewise, popular anti-Vietnam songs were featured in many successful Hollywood movies about the Vietnam War era, such as *Born on the Fourth of July* (1989) and *Forrest Gump* (1994), as well as in movies without any connection to that era. For example, Guess Who's "American Woman" was featured in the *Cable Guy* (1996) and *American Beauty* (1999), and Lenny Kravitz's cover version was in *Austin Powers 2: The Spy Who Shagged Me* (1999).

Likewise, many of these songs were highlighted in television advertising. "American Woman" was featured in commercials for Castor Motor Oil, Tommy Hilfiger, and Nike. The Beatles' antiwar classic "Revolution" (written originally by John Lennon) was used in a 1987 Nike commercial after rights to the song's use were bought for a year from Michael Jackson and Capitol Records, only to be discontinued after legal challenges from the three surviving Beatles and severe fan backlash.

After the Vietnam War ended, songwriters still expressed antiwar sentiment in their lyrics on various issues: (1) the threat of nuclear holocaust due to the Cold War (e.g., Frankie Goes to Hollywood's "Relax" [1984], Nena's "99 Luftaballoons" [1984], and Sting's "Russians" [1985]); (2) U.S. intervention in Central America (e.g., the Clash's "Washington Bullets" [1980], Don Henley's "All She Wants [to Do Is Dance]" [1984], and U2's "Bullet the Blue Sky" [1987]); and (3) the first Persian Gulf War (e.g., Bette Midler's "From a Distance" [1990], Oletta Adams's "Get Here" [1990], and

Offspring's "Baghdad" [1991]). Many of these songs were top 40 hits.

Afghanistan/Iraq: A Renaissance of American Antiwar Music

No period in U.S. history has witnessed such an outpouring of antiwar music as the post–September 11, 2001, Afghanistan/Iraq war era, even compared to the Vietnam era. Almost half of the 2,940 antiwar songs commercially released from 1963 to 2007 were released after 2001, compared to 484 songs released during the Vietnam era.

The difference in output between the two eras can mostly be explained by the increasing affordability and quality of new recording technology, which has greatly democratized musical production. Artists in the Afghanistan/Iraq war era can now produce their own music on independent labels and are often able to achieve sound quality that rivals that of the major labels. Yet given changes in the radio landscape since the Vietnam era, much of this independent music did not receive mainstream radio airplay.

Many critics trace the problems of radio back to the 1996 Telecommunications Act, which dramatically increased consolidation of the radio industry. With this act, national radio station ownership limits were abolished altogether, and limits in local markets went from four to as many as eight stations, allowing a handful of radio companies to accumulate hundreds of stations and to control many markets.

These large radio companies—such as Clear Channel, with 1,240 radio stations nationwide—have consistently sought to maximize profits by using computerized programming that plays a small sample of songs (i.e., the "hits"), thus eliminating the costs associated with having live disc jockeys who would have some say in their playlists. The diminishment of the field of disc jockeys overall has greatly decreased the creative flair that new FM radio programming had in the 1960s and 1970s and thus limited the possibility of new antiwar music breaking through to the mainstream. Music scholar Jim Pennea notes how different the radio landscape was in the Vietnam era: "In the sixties . . . the birth of FM changed the whole rules for everything, because then you could do album cuts and DJs were free to play pretty much what they wanted" (Brooks 2009).

In this increasingly consolidated environment, even mainstream artists who expressed concern about the use of violence as a foreign policy solution found that they did not receive mainstream radio play. It is interesting to note that not a single song from Bruce Springsteen's *The Rising,* one of the most critically acclaimed and popular albums recorded in response to 9/11, made it to the top 40. The album, which debuted at number one on the *Billboard* Top 200 (best-selling albums chart) when it was released in July 2002, ten months after the attacks and nine months after the United States began the war in Afghanistan (i.e., October 7, 2001), honored the victims of 9/11 and provided a pensive reflection on the repercussions of violence. Likewise, Neil Young's *Living with War,* released in 2006, which offered a strong rebuke to then-president George W. Bush for his handling of the Iraq War, did not receive radio play despite having charted at number fifteen on the best-selling albums chart.

The lack of radio play of major artists' antiwar songs in the Afghanistan/Iraq war era compared to the Vietnam era has been well-documented. Comparing top singles' charts (which measure not only sales strength but also the frequency of radio play), thirty antiwar songs in the Vietnam era reached the top 10, and ten songs were actually number one hits, whereas in the Afghanistan/Iraq era, only four songs reached the top 10, and there were no number one hits. The antiwar song that received the most radio play was "Where Is the Love" (2003) by hip-hop group Black Eyed Peas, which reached number eight on the *Billboard* 100 and spent 164 weeks on this chart.

When one examines the huge number of antiwar songs that were released on best-selling albums during the Afghanistan/Iraq war era, the fact that there were so few top singles in this period becomes even more evident. There were 41 antiwar songs released on *Billboard* 200 albums during the Vietnam era, compared with 183 antiwar songs released on *Billboard* 200 albums during the Afghanistan/Iraq war era. In fact, many antiwar songs were featured on number one albums (e.g., Green Day's *American Idiot* [2004], System of a Down's *Mesmerize* [2005], Dave Matthews's *Stand Up* [2005], and Nine Inch Nails' *With Teeth* [2005]) (Brooks 2009). It is clear that in this consolidated radio landscape environment, few radio chains have taken the risk of including anything as controversial as an antiwar song on their standardized radio playlists.

Radio chains have also removed artists' songs from radio play if artists expressed antiwar dissent in other contexts. The Dixie Chicks' number one antiwar hit on *Billboard* Country Singles, "Travelin' Soldier," dropped 15 percent in one week after lead singer Natalie Maines's infamous comment days before the second war in Iraq began: "We're ashamed that the president of the United States is from Texas" (Mansfield 2003). Upon further investigation, journalist Mansfield learned that "Cumulus Media has instructed all 42 of its country stations to stop playing the group's music until further notice." This type of censorship gave birth to the colloquialism "getting Dixie Chicked."

This lack of diversity of opinions in the mainstream media and the potentially harmful effects it has had on American civil discourse was highlighted in the neopunk band Green Day's song, "American Idiot" (2004), whose first line was, "Don't want to be an American idiot."

Yet despite the drawbacks of this increasingly consolidated media field, there is cause for hope that antiwar music will be disseminated in this continuing Afghanistan/Iraq war era, given the powers of our technological advances and the growth of the Internet. First, as mentioned previously, the affordability of new recording software has democratized music production. Second, Internet technologies allow artists to disseminate music for public consumption at minimal cost through iTunes and CD Baby, through social networking sites like Facebook and Twitter, and through artists' individual Web sites and MySpace pages. And third, the power of the Internet as a source of coordination and collaboration for social movement activists, in general, as witnessed by the 2011 and 2012 uprising in Egypt and other Middle Eastern countries, makes resurgence of a strong antiwar music movement in the future more likely. Current examples of this burgeoning movement are Neil Young's Living with War Today Web site (http://www.neilyoung.com/lwwtoday/index.html) and Peace Not War (http://www.peace.fm/), both of which provide listenable databases of current antiwar songs.

See also: Baez; Joan; Commercials and Advertisements; Dylan, Bob; Festivals; Film Music; Gaye, Marvin; Guthrie Family; Jackson, Michael; Midler, Bette; Peter, Paul and Mary; Psychedelic Music; Radio; Seeger, Pete; September 11th Commemorations; Springsteen, Bruce

Further Reading

Blecha, Peter. 2004. *Taboo Tunes: A History of Banned Bands & Censored Songs.* Berkeley, CA: Backbeat Books.

Brooks, Jeneve. R. 2009. "The Silent Soundtrack: Anti-war Music from Vietnam to Iraq." PhD diss., Fordham University, Bronx, New York.

D'Entremont, Jim. 2003. "Clear and Present Danger." *Index on Censorship* 3: 124–128.

Lynskey, Dorian. 2011. *33 Revolutions Per Minute.* New York: HarperCollins.

Mansfield, Brian. 2003. "Dixie Chicks' Chart Wings Get Clipped." *USA Today,* March 18. http://www.usatoday.com/life/music/news/2003-03-18-chicks-chart_x.htm.

Jeneve R. Brooks

Armstrong, Louis (1901–1971)

Jazz has produced countless geniuses, but only one Louis Armstrong. As a trumpeter, Armstrong taught the world how to swing, creating the foundations for just about every kind of American music that followed in his wake. As a singer, he had just as much of an impact, armed with only his, as he once put it, "sawmill voice." His daring rhythmic inventiveness and creative use of scat singing was a major influence on singers such as Bing Crosby and Billie Holiday.

But there was also Armstrong's persona; known as "Satchmo," he possessed a smile that might have been the most famous of the twentieth century. Armed with his horn, his voice, and that smile, Armstrong rose up from the deepest level of poverty while growing up in New Orleans to become an ambassador of goodwill.

Few could match Armstrong's impact on twentieth-century American culture. Perhaps because he was born at the right time, August 4, 1901, Armstrong was able to conquer each and every new medium that he encountered. He began making records in 1923, allowing his remarkable improvisations to spread around the country, influencing countless musicians, and proving definitively that jazz was a serious art form and not just a passing fancy. By 1929 Armstrong was appearing in the Broadway revue *Hot Chocolates,* where his performance of "Ain't Misbehavin'" won him rave reviews and a new audience. The following year he made his first of over thirty films. Though Hollywood didn't always know how to use him—often wasting his presence in demeaning, comic relief roles—he always managed to light up the silver screen. Armstrong was also a frequent presence on radio dating back to the late 1920s, and he became the first black entertainer to host a nationally sponsored show when he took over Rudy Vallee's *Flesichmann's Yeast Show* for a period in 1937. But Armstrong really flourished on television, where his genius as a musician *and* an entertainer came to the fore as he often displayed impeccable comic timing and a vivacious personality (Armstrong is credited with popularizing words such as "dig" and "cat," to name two of many).

By the 1950s Armstrong had started coming under attack by younger black musicians for being an "Uncle Tom," mainly because of his smiling persona, though

Artists Influenced by Louis Armstrong

Billie Holiday	Bunny Berigan	Duke Ellington	Harry James	Louis Prima
Bing Crosby	Cab Calloway	Ella Fitzgerald	Lester Young	Tony Bennett
Bobby Hackett	Dizzy Gillespie	Frank Sinatra	Louis Jordan	

Louis Armstrong was one of the 20th century's most important jazz innovators and performers. (Library of Congress)

such showmanship had always been part of his act. Offstage he always pioneered on issues of civil rights, and in 1957, when he became disgusted with President Dwight Eisenhower's slow reaction to the Little Rock school integration crisis, Armstrong went public with his feelings, saying the president had "no guts." This was a time when criticism of the president by a black entertainer was unthinkable, but Armstrong stood his ground, even though he received little public support from his fellow jazz musicians at the time.

During the 1950s and 1960s Armstrong's worldwide tours became something of a phenomenon. Thousands greeted him at airports when he landed in places such as Sweden, West Germany, and African countries. (CBS newsman Edward R. Murrow filmed two of Armstrong's tours.). In 1965 he cracked the Iron Curtain with a historic tour of Eastern Europe, including Prague and East Berlin. Each place he went, "Ambassador Satch" brought American culture—and specifically African American culture—with him, as fans could not get enough of his music and his personality.

Though Armstrong conquered every medium available during his lifetime, his greatest legacy will always be his records. At a time when jazz was growing less and less popular, Armstrong continued making hit records, including "Blueberry Hill" in 1949, "Mack the Knife" in 1955, and most surprisingly, "Hello, Dolly," a Broadway show tune that knocked The Beatles off the top of the charts at the height of Beatlemania in May 1964, when the trumpeter was already in his early sixties. Sixteen years after he passed away in 1971, Armstrong's recording of "What a Wonderful World" hit the popular music charts, quite a feat for someone who first made an impact in the 1920s and further proof that his influence on American culture will be felt for a long time.

See also: Crosby, Bing; Holiday, Billie; Jazz; Swing Music

Official Web Site: http://www.louisarmstronghouse.org/

Further Reading

Armstrong, Louis. 1986. *Satchmo: My Life in New Orleans.* New York: Da Capo Press.

Riccardi, Ricky. 2011. *What a Wonderful World: The Magic of Louis Armstrong's Later Years.* New York: Pantheon.

Teachout, Terry. 2009. *Pops: A Life of Louis Armstrong.* New York: Houghton Mifflin Harcourt.

Ricky Riccardi

Art Music (Experimental)

Experimentalism refers to the musical compositions of those twentieth-century American composers who rejected European-derived art music, even that which was considered avant-garde. They strove to create a new music that had a deep connection with some aspect of American cultural fabric, in the way folk music had already done. These Americanists, as they are called (Chase 1987; Zuck 1980), were also reacting to the musical class system that had emerged in the nineteenth century, which favored foreign-born musicians, composers, and conductors in the halls of high culture, the concert hall, and music conservatories. They rejected the convention of the time that required talented American musicians to go to France or Germany to study in order to be properly credentialed back home.

Henry Cowell may have been the first to use the term experimentalism, in his book, *American Composers on American Music.* John Cage used it frequently in *Silence* (1961) to refer to musical compositions whose outcomes were not known in advance. The critic Yates (1967) defined it as music that is a radical departure from traditional forms and draws on a wide range of cultural sources. Nicholls (1990) stressed that experimentalism applies to American music that is unlike any of its European antecedents.

Experimentalism was (and is) a musical movement with perhaps three core features (Cameron 1996). The first is an ideological framework in which experimental composers talked a lot about disavowing tradition and pursuing fundamental change. They were a vociferous lot, who wrote as much *about* music in journals and books as they actually wrote music. The second is the exploration of highly unorthodox sound sources and ideas. Examples of the former include natural sounds, non-Western musical cultures, altered or newly built instruments, and electronic sources; examples of the latter include chance and silence in compositions. Composers often regarded their explorations as *experiments* to find fresh ideas to see if the outcome was interesting in some musical or intellectual way. The third feature is the production of highly diverse music different from other new music. One sees a tangle of new directions rather than any stylistic consolidation in experimental composers' works.

In the 1920s experimentalists were not a group but a dispersed network of composers whose common goal was musical exploration and innovation. Arthur Farwell (1872–1952) from the Midwest believed that American composers were on the brink of creative foment. Not only did he write compositions that were inspired by vernacular styles (ragtime, cowboy songs, Native American music), but he established Wa-Wan Press, which was devoted to publishing scores of native composers. Henry Cowell (1897–1965), who studied briefly with the influential musicologist Charles Seeger at Berkeley, wrote music inspired by the unusual sounds he heard in the San Francisco neighborhood of his childhood. Seeger prompted him to write up his new music theory, which he did in the book *New Musical Resources.* Soon afterward he founded the journal *New Music,* which published scores and biographies of Americanist composers. After moving to New York City, Cowell founded the Pan-American Association of Composers (PAAC) with the French composer Edgard Varèse. He discovered the New Englander Charles Ives (1874–1954), who wrote music inspired by various sources: marching band music, popular songs, and hymns. Ives's music was first performed at the PAAC tours in the United States and Europe. He later provided generous support to *New Music* and concert tours in the early 1930s.

The grim times of the Great Depression inspired a serious approach to the arts among radical composers. They joined with left-wing artists in the "Popular Front," a movement that opposed fascism and promoted socially relevant art and music. Composers put out the *Workers' Song Book* to link expressive forms with political action. In the nadir of the Depression, the Roosevelt administration created the Arts Project, of which the Federal Music Project (FMP) was a unit. The FMP was charged with bringing music and music education to towns and cities across the country.

The West Coast has been a de facto breeding ground for innovative composers. Notable among them were Harry Partch (1901–1974), Lou Harrison (1917–2003), and John Cage (1912–1992). In the 1940s and 1950s Partch experimented with microtonal scales, eventually developing a forty-three-tone scale, for which he had to adapt existing instruments or build new ones. He is well known for his dramatic theater pieces inspired by Noh and Greek theater, in which actors, singers, and musicians shared the stage with their instruments.

Cage, the most visible of the experimentalists, made New York his creative home for most of his life. He collaborated with abstract expressionist painters and dancers such as Merce Cunningham. Such collaboration led to the first "happening" at Black Mountain College in North Carolina in 1952, in which dance, music, poetry, films, slides, and radio were played simultaneously.

Henry Cowell was a music trailblazer who plucked and played piano strings under the lid and also invented the Rhythmicon with Leon Theremin. (Bettmann/Corbis)

Cage is best known for the compositional method and philosophy he eventually called *indeterminacy,* in which the composer or performer uses chance, random, or stochastic processes to guide the piece. Cage meant indeterminacy as a celebration of process and becoming, the antithesis of deliberateness and craft in composition. No composition has inspired more controversy than his silent piece, *4'33"*, of 1952. In its debut, David Tudor, the pianist, walked onstage and sat at the keyboard. He gestured as if he would play three times, but did not, and left the stage at the end of the allotted time. Tudor remembers the event as one of the most intense listening experiences in performance. Critics of the time excoriated Cage.

During the interwar period, experimental composers struggled to support themselves. The lucky ones attracted patrician patrons such as Blanche Wetherill Walton and Gertrude Vanderbilt Whitney. In the post–World War II period, with the expansion of university campuses across the country, music and theater departments brought experimental composers to campus as composers-in-residence. Some taught classes or mentored students; many simply staged performances of their work. They inspired a new generation of young composers such as Steve Reich (1936–) and Philip Glass (1937–). The postwar campus climate, which fostered exploration in the sciences, was a congenial environment for new music, as well. The audience for new music grew significantly; people began to appreciate that there was a vibrant, homegrown avant-garde in music.

A measure of the success of the experimental movement is the antagonism and antipathy it has generated in many circles. Critics of new music worry that the value placed on craftsmanship has been lost, that stylistic consolidation will disappear, that newness and innovativeness are the main criteria by which to judge compositions. These fears are largely unfounded, for experimental music has not displaced the canon in the concert hall.

On the other hand, this new music is a vivid illustration of the power of the dialectic in the contemporary arts.

See also: Avant-garde in American Music, The; Cage, John; Federal Music Project; Glass, Philip; Ives, Charles; Music Patrons and Supporters; Partch, Harry; Reich, Steve; Seeger Family

Further Reading

Cameron, Catherine. 1996. *Dialectics in the Arts: The Rise of Experimentalism in American Music.* Westport, CT: Praeger.

Chase, Gilbert. 1987. *America's Music: From the Pilgrims to the Present.* 3rd ed. Urbana: University of Illinois Press

Nicholls, David. 1990. *American Experimental Music, 1890–1940.* New York: Cambridge University Press.

Yates, Peter. 1967. *Twentieth Century Music.* New York: Pantheon Books.

Zuck, Barbara. 1980. *A History of Musical Americanisms.* Ann Arbor, MI: UMI Research Press.

Catherine Mary Cameron

Art Music (Mainstream)

Art music can be defined in most Western cultures as music that takes a written musical score as its primary source; it may also be known as American classical music or music in the American cultivated tradition. In the United States, art music can be historically linked with that of European traditions until the twentieth century, when American composers began to deviate from the stylistic influence of their European counterparts in the name of innovation and the seeking of a true "American music." In most histories of American music, scholars contrast American art music with American vernacular music, encompassing styles ranging from folk to popular. Although vernacular music may seem more clearly associated with culture, American art music's links to cultural context are deep and defining, in contradistinction to the European concept of score-based music as divorced from the influence of any person or event.

Because of American history's direct connection with Europe, early American musical life revolved almost exclusively around music brought with settlers to the New World. On the East Coast music from English sources provided the primary written material prior to American independence; music in the western territories often reflected the musical influence of Spain. Religious services, whether Catholic in the West or Protestant in the East, often provided the initial context for the hearing of art music in America. This music exerted an early influence on those very first American composers, whom we may define as either born in the United States or having the majority of their careers within the United States after immigration. Because of the complex history of immigration to the United States, its composers have often created their works from multiple standpoints, for example, from that of a Russian Jew living in Brooklyn (George Gershwin) or a Latina woman raised in Texas on the Mexican border (Pauline Oliveros). Part of studying the relationship between art music and culture, then, is the negotiation of identity politics: What is the composer's background? What kind of music is he or she writing? and For what performance setting is it written? are three crucial queries for any investigator of American art music.

Before delving into a chronological exploration of American art music and culture, it should be noted that American art music itself cannot be materially separated from American popular and folk music, nor can one separate art music works from jazz and its antecedents. From the earliest examples, American composers have drawn upon culturally significant music—such as folk and popular musical sources—in their work. But as the American twentieth century approached, the use of local or indigenous musical material became almost a defining factor of American concert music. Ironically, this phenomenon can be traced to the influence of an Eastern European composer and teacher, Antonín Dvořák, who landed in New York at the end of his career, and to an

Art Music: Mrs. Beach and Her Birds

Amy Cheney Beach (1867–1944) began her career as a piano prodigy, but turned to composition after her marriage to Dr. Henry Beach. Among the composer's many gifts was the ability to hear very accurately the high pitches and complex rhythms of birdcalls and then to write them down in musical notation. Her 1921 piano work, *The Hermit Thrush*, op. 92, reflects her virtuosic piano skill as well as her love for bird song. There is a photograph of her at the MacDowell Colony, a haven in New Hampshire for composers and artists, where she composed many of her nature-centered works.

insurance salesman, Charles Ives, who composed in secret rather than succumbing to outside influences. These two examples demonstrate that, despite the stylistic breadth of American art music, it is first and foremost a concert music that has been written explicitly in the context of vernacular music, free from the aristocratic patronage system that funded the composition of many European classical works.

American Art Music: A Semichronological Survey

The first documented, score-based music composed in America was written in the early eighteenth century by New England singing masters known collectively as the First New England School. Chief among these composers was the idiosyncratic William Billings (1746–1800), whose first career as a hog reeve (gatherer of wayward swine) did not presage his innovations in the composition of choral music. Billings, a disabled Boston-based music master, composed four-part music meant to be sung in a colonial social setting called a singing school. Although music for these singing schools resembled four-part chorales by European masters such as J. S. Bach, Billings's works declaim a certain Yankee inscrutability, in that they do not adhere to the typical rules established for this genre of composition at the time. One example of Billings's composition is "Chester," from his 1770 publication *The New England Psalm Singer.* The influence of American revolutionary culture cannot be denied within this supposedly sacred text, which creates an allegory to England as a "tyrant" who rules her slaves with an "iron rod." Billings's close friendship with Paul Revere certainly colored his thoughts about politics, and "Chester" remains an example of the early influence of culture on American art music.

During the later eighteenth century and into the nineteenth, other New England patriots turned to music composition to forward both political and social agendas. Early American music iconography (images such as drawings and paintings that depict musical activities) indicates that not only sacred but secular music making was a major social activity during the post-revolutionary period. Music for small ensembles prevailed because of the general lack of large groups such as orchestras and bands. Primary genres at the time were vocal music—usually songs for voice and piano, as well as choruses—and instrumental music designed for dancing or as marches. Although this music certainly had social functions—in other words, it was not simply "music for music's sake"—it can still be considered art music because of its reliance on a score, and because it represents the beginnings of an American compositional tradition. Francis Hopkinson (1737–1791), a Philadelphia-based composer and patriot, composed vocal music during this period and also played organ and harpsichord. The famous "President's March," composed by immigrant theater worker Philip Phile (ca. 1734–1793) and also known as "Hail Columbia," provided esprit de corps for militias of the time. Phile's march, arranged skillfully by Hopkinson, was a contender for the national anthem. Meanwhile, in Virginia Benjamin Franklin was keeping up a correspondence with Wolfgang Amadeus Mozart regarding innovations in music and musical instruments.

As American culture began to re-form itself as that of an independent nation, the romantic era sensibilities that had taken hold after the tumult of European revolutions began to influence American artistic endeavors. Romanticism as a stylistic movement in music places emphasis on the composer as an individual and generally rejects classical era ideals of simplicity, symmetry, and balance. Alexander Reinagle (1756–1809), who wrote music in a late-classical style, helped bridge the gap in American concertgoers' ears between classical and romantic sounds. Romantic era composers took musical elements (e.g., dynamics, the length of pieces, the size of ensembles) to extremes and relished the growing virtuosity of musicians by writing increasingly difficult repertoires. American composers and musicians certainly took part in the production and performance of romantic era music concerts. Along with these concert performances came the construction of great concert halls in the larger cities to accommodate the increase in music making by larger ensembles, as well as the formation of symphony orchestras. Theodore Thomas (1835–1905) was one of the most powerful conductors and musicians in the United States in the nineteenth century, playing first violin for and eventually conducting the New York Philharmonic Society, formed originally by Louis Jullien (1812–1860). The formation of these ensembles influenced the composition by Americans of symphonic music. Concert programs from events in the early- to mid-nineteenth century indicate that works by American composers such as William Henry Fry (1813–1864) and Anthony Philip Heinrich (1781–1861) were performed alongside those of romantic era European composers Beethoven, Meyerbeer, and Brahms.

The American railway system that both marked and propelled the Industrial Revolution and fueled the California gold rush had the unexpected side effect of providing transportation for traveling musicians and musical productions such as operas. Louis Moreau Gottschalk (1829–1869), an American pianist and composer from New Orleans, toured extensively as a virtuoso pianist, performing as many as eight concerts in one week. Despite his grueling tour schedule, he composed several bravura piano works, the most famous of which is *The Banjo,* which imitates the sound of that instrument. Gottschalk's other works draw upon his memory of

Creole tunes, as filtered through the training he received as a teen while studying with a disciple of Chopin in Paris. Minstrel shows, another genre of touring music, generally featured only parodies of European opera arias, in addition to popular tunes. Yet Stephen Foster's songs, such as "Jeanie with the Light Brown Hair" (1851), presaged the deep connection between popular song and art music. While "Jeanie" was a popular hit, its sensitive compositional traits and performance by operatic singers places it within the realm of art music.

While Gottschalk's audiences were falling prey to his remarkable pianistic skills, the first academic music department had been formed at Harvard University, where many of America's great composers would be trained and would serve on faculty in future years. Composer John Knowles Paine (1839–1906) taught at Harvard for forty-three years, establishing himself as a major composer and the university as a center of art music composition in the United States. Paine was one of the composers making music within what is now known as the Second New England School. Other notable names from that list include George Chadwick (1854–1931), Horatio Parker (1863–1919), Arthur Foote (1853–1937), and Amy Cheney Beach (1867–1944). Amy Beach is particularly noteworthy because of her early career as a piano prodigy and her flourishing compositional career after her marriage, despite the social mores that would prevent many women from becoming composers during the Victorian era in the United States. Edward MacDowell (1860–1908) is another important name from New England at this time, because of his own innovative compositions incorporating naturalist themes, but also because of his legacy, the MacDowell Colony in New Hampshire, where many of the finest composers of the twentieth century spent summers creating new works.

The Boston "Six" were all white American composers working in a primarily European style. The advantages they had in terms of education and training were not shared by all American composers of the postbellum era. Specifically, African American composers were shunned, even after emancipation, by many of the colleges and conservatories where music composition was taught. Composers such as Scott Joplin (1867–1916) and James Reese Europe (1881–1919) added their individual styles to a growing American compositional voice. Joplin, who is best known for his popular ragtime hits, including "The Maple Leaf Rag," composed his opera *Treemonisha* based on concepts of African American spirituality and Caribbean identity. Europe conducted bands and composed music for his ensembles. Antonín Dvořák, a celebrated Czech composer who had landed a teaching position at the National Conservatory in New York City, composed his ninth symphony, "The New World," based on African American songs he had heard while traveling in the Midwest. These themes formed the basis for his work, but also encapsulated his teaching philosophy, for he was one of the only composition instructors at the turn of the twentieth century to accept black composition students, such as the successful Will Marion Cook (1869–1944), among others. Dvořák passionately called upon American composers to make an art music of their own, based on folk songs of their own people. At the same time, John Philip Sousa (1854–1932) was creating march music for and with the Marine Corps Band that would become inexplicably linked with American patriotic culture.

Charles Ives (1874–1954) also espoused the use of American vernacular tunes within his compositions, but he did so in a way that ushered in a new era in American composition, and indeed, the twentieth century. Ives's father was a band leader in Danbury, Connecticut, and was a musical experimenter. He asked his sons, particularly Charlie, to play music in different keys simultaneously; he created new musical instruments that sounded different from ordinary ones. These early aural experiences certainly affected Charles Ives's compositions, signaling the dawn of American experimentalism. He attended Yale, studying with Horatio Parker, but decided that he didn't want his family to "starve" on his "dissonances," and therefore composed in private while making a very good living in insurance sales; this "seclusion" also allowed him to remain relatively free of musical influences, an idea which would later be carried on by individualist composer George Crumb (1929–). When modern composers of the early twentieth century heard Ives's works, some written before 1900, they were astonished at his use of polytonality, extreme dissonance, and collage technique (a kind of pasting together of several different borrowed tunes within one piece, but happening simultaneously). One of the works from his suite *Three Places in New England* quotes "Hail Columbia" while also creating a musical Doppler effect, in which a parade seems to be going by and we hear several melodies simultaneously in the distance.

Ives took up the mantle of American experimentalism, which would be carried on by many other composers in the twentieth century. Henry Cowell (1897–1965) and Ruth Crawford Seeger (1901–1953) each created highly individual works that relied on extreme dissonance and railed against the lush harmonies of romantic music. These composers and their colleagues, most active in the 1920s and 1930s, subscribed to compositional tools that did not rely on any kind of tonal structure. In other words, many had no melody and no key, but created sound in new ways. Although influenced by European music of the twentieth century, modern American "ultramodernist" composers brought their individual identities and political affiliations to bear on their music. Henry Cowell, in addition to writing compositions such as *The Banshee,* which used the piano more like a harp or a percussion instrument, created the journal *New Music,* a publication of the Composer's Collective, which he founded to discuss and print the work of composers in the United States. Crawford Seeger, whose work could be found in *New Music,* composed overtly political pieces that reflected her leftist bent, as well as highly dissonant works such as her *String Quartet 1931,* in which the slow movement has no rhythmic pulse of any kind, but uses the dynamics of long held notes in each part to indicate motion and life. Crawford Seeger and her husband, Charles Seeger (1886–1979), also worked together tirelessly in gathering American folk songs from untrained musicians of all backgrounds and races, which would in turn be used by the next generation of American composers as the basis for their art music.

Contrary to the ultramodernists, George Gershwin (1898–1937), Aaron Copland (1901–1990), and later Leonard Bernstein (1918–1990) represented a new generation of composers who sought rich melodic content and lush orchestration in their works. These three composers were all children of Jewish immigrant families, and although each approached composition in a very different way, their works can be linked by their use in art music of materials from vernacular music. In addition, two of the three composers studied with the French composition teacher Nadia Boulanger, who was said to have influenced American twentieth-century composition more than any single composer through her American Institute at Fontainebleau. Gershwin, who began as a popular song composer, debuted his celebrated *Rhapsody in Blue* using Paul Whiteman's all-black jazz orchestra the Clef Club at Carnegie Hall in 1924. The piano rhapsody, though virtuosic and highly melodic, was initially dismissed as a jazz interloper to the hallowed classical halls of New York. (Boulanger had rejected him as a pupil based on the "corruptive" influence of jazz on his works.) Yet the *Rhapsody* has become one of the most performed works in classical music arenas. Aaron Copland—whom many have labeled the "first" American composer—garnered several of Seeger's American folk tunes for his ballets, created in collaboration with Martha Graham. His ballets *Appalachian Spring* and *Rodeo* feature some of the most recognizably "American" music because of their use of wide intervals in the orchestration, as well as their borrowing of folk tunes from the American South and West. Bernstein, who became the preeminent conductor of the New York Philharmonic later in his career, composed several operas and symphonic works, but is best known for his distinguished contributions to Broadway literature. His musicals *West Side Story* and *Candide,* with their complex compositional language and difficult vocal parts, call into question the need for a generic separation between opera and musical theater works.

In the 1940s and 1950s American art music composition became even more divided along academic lines. Two streams of composition emerged; one, eventually called American serialism, built upon the work of the ultramodernists, whereas the other built on the foundation of Copland and his colleagues. The American serialists found inspiration in the work of Arnold Schoenberg, Anton Webern, and the Second Viennese School. Finding a home in American universities provided the American serialists with the financial support they needed to create works within a largely mathematical framework, without having to rely as much on commissions, and hardly at all on ticket sales. Roger Sessions (1896–1985), Milton Babbitt (1916–), Elliot Carter (1908–2012), and Miriam Gideon (1906–1996) all wrote within this system outside of tonality, yet each composed in a unique way and with definite personal style. Babbitt sought to serialize (place in an ordered, mathematical set) each element of music, from rhythm to dynamics to pitch, creating what is known as "total serialism." His 1958 article "Who Cares If You Listen" exemplifies the increasing divide between composer and listener created by this movement. Carter's music was said to insist on both heart and mind and therefore required incredible rigor from performers, but provided a sense of constant movement and, indeed, satisfaction to listeners. Gideon used serialism in more subtle ways, preferring to let her pieces, which were often vocal chamber music or art song, be freely atonal. Her economy of ensemble is emblematic of composers' reserve in terms of the numbers of performers they required. Chamber music thrived in the twentieth century in America due to wartime economics: players were not always available in large numbers, and money was tight when it came to funding the arts.

Nonacademic composers who made a living through other musical means formed the second midcentury stream. Virgil Thomson (1896–1989), Marc Blizstein (1905–1964), Gian Carlo Menotti (1911–2007), and Samuel Barber (1910–1981) each provide a different example of art music composition that did not subscribe to "academic" discourses, and in some cases expressed direct disdain for them. Virgil Thomson, a longtime music critic for the New York *Herald Tribune,* composed with both whimsy and complexity, but in time found his real genius in overt simplicity. His opera *Four Saints in Three Acts* exemplifies his musical wit in the setting of Gertrude Stein's libretto; the opera is filled with final cadences from start to finish and therefore confounds the listener at once and throughout. He called for an all-black cast, not because the libretto indicated this in any way, but because he liked the idea. Marc Blizstein also composed operas and works that could be construed as operatic musical theater with a political agenda. In his opera *The Cradle Will Rock,* Blizstein writes an aria dedicated to the destruction of all "art for art's sake," a telling comment on the state of art music in the United States at that time. Another rebel of opera theater was Italian-born Gian Carlo Menotti, who experienced very early and intense success with his first handful of operas, including the operatic ghost story *The Medium,* which was mounted on Broadway. Menotti's accessible, tonal, Italianate style appealed to a broad audience, and his opera *Amahl and the Night Visitors* was thus the first to be commissioned for television with the NBC Opera Company. Menotti's longtime partner Samuel Barber had attended school with him at Curtis Institute in Philadelphia and took a more gradual approach to notoriety as a composer than did his friend. Barber achieved more lasting recognition, however, with his neoromantic style, which, combined with economy of melody, gave him the very sincere compositional voice that we hear in his art songs and in the *Adagio for Strings.*

In connection with the beginnings of counterculture in the United States in the 1960s, American art music began to reflect the works of Pollock and Rauschenberg in visual art. Indeterminacy, or aleatoric music, brought about a natural link between sound and vision; spattered paint on a canvas aligns aurally with random sounds, or as some may call it, noise. At the center of the postmodern deconstruction of music we find John Cage (1912–1992), who thought that the most beautiful music was the sound of Manhattan's Sixth Avenue through his window. Cage composed a silent piece, *4'33"*, which called for a pianist to open and close the lid of the piano after a certain amount of time had elapsed, finally totaling four minutes and thirty-three seconds. Cage also composed using the I-ching system to aid in deciding which notes to write on the page. His unaccompanied vocal work *Aria* calls on the singer to follow squiggly lines in different colors and formations from page to page, each color signifying a different language, and each line calling for a new, extended vocal technique, from growling to singing operatically. Composer Morton Feldman (1926–1987) was deeply influenced by these works, and took Cage's general brevity of timing to a different extreme, composing lengthy works such as his second String Quartet, which lasts six hours.

Minimalism and electronic music are linked to Cage through opposing impulses: from Cage's aleatoric pieces, where no element is certain, electronic music ensures that one part of the performance will always be the same because it is prerecorded, and minimalism uses only a very small number of materials, all written, but perhaps defying all musical structure through their use. Milton Babbitt's *Philomel* calls for soprano and tape, where the soprano has actually recorded some of the sounds on the tape, but others are synthesized; to modern listeners, the sounds on the tape recall sci-fi movies of the 1960s and 1970s. The increasing use of recorded sound in composition—a direct reflection of radio and record culture growing exponentially in the United States—led Steve Reich (1936–) to re-create, with acoustic instruments, a tape loop. The result was one example of what we now call minimalism, and it required incredible virtuosity on the part of the performers. His work *Piano Phase* for two keyboardists required just this technique. Philip Glass (1937–) is now most recognized for his many film scores, but his work with downtown Manhattan visual artists and poets initially led him to explore minimalist composition (around the same time as Reich) with his own ensemble. Glass's 1976 postmodern opera *Einstein on the Beach* has no plot, no melody, and no characters, and lasts five hours. Yet his piano works, operas, and film scores have slowly indoctrinated American listeners to the sounds of minimalism, until we no longer recognize it as revolutionary. But it was Terry Riley (1935–) who created the first true cornerstone work of minimalism and aleatory, his 1964 piece *In C,* a one-page work with fifty-three melodic motives to be performed for any length of time by any number of musicians.

The San Francisco Tape Music Center was a haven for modern composers in the 1970s and 1980s and has since created a movement of electronic composers and performance artists. Many of the major voices to emerge from the center have been women, perhaps because of San Francisco's ties to movements in feminism and gay rights, but certainly because of the new avenues that performance art through electronic media presented to a new generation of performer-composers. Pauline Oliveros (1932–), an accordionist and composer, actually collaborated with Donald Buchla (1937–), one of the first synthesizer makers from the same era as Moog (1934–). Oliveros used both acoustic and synthesized sound in her initial electronic works and later experimented with her own concept of deep listening. Though based on the East Coast, George Crumb found his compositional voice in *Black Angels,* scored for electric string quartet. Laurie Anderson (1947–), a self-proclaimed wizard of high tech, creates versatile works that span the artistic disciplines, encompassing poetry, sculpture, photography, music, and of course, politics. Her works have been received as popular music, art music, and electronica: "O Superman" was a pop hit in Britain in 1981, and her one-woman opera *United States* elaborated at length on the same populist themes. Pamela Z (1956–), a San Francisco–based performance artist and composer, creates works by singing and playing invented percussion instruments while using a specially designed body synthesizer that creates sounds according to her movements. Her performance *A Delay Is Better* plays on the ideas of time, electronic loops, and life's whimsy and melancholy.

In conclusion, it is clear that millennium-era composers continue to draw upon the many themes established by the composers discussed here in new and interesting ways. In Tania Leon's (1943–) extraordinary opera *Scourge of Hyacinths,* with its complex use of time and memory, and Robert Ashley's (1930–) overtly sexual operatic works, we find indirectly the freedom gained through the creation and staging of Glass's *Einstein.* In David Del Tredeci's (1937–) Pulitzer-winning *Final Alice,* the polytonality that expresses multiple imaginations operating simultaneously could be a relative of Ives and his collage technique. And in Tobias Picker's (1954–) *Keys to the City,* the open-handed lyricism of Copland combines with the mathematical underpinnings of Sessions. Joan Tower's (1938–) symphony *Made in America* calls to arms the supporters of art music in America. Although the scope of this entry prevents the mention of every American composer of consequence, those listed here represent larger movements within the realm of music that can be categorized as "art." With or without funding, American art music continues to flourish through innovation and experimentation.

See also: African American Influences on American Music; Broadway; Bernstein, Leonard; Cage, John; Copland, Aaron; Cajun and Creole Music; Electronic and Computer Music; Folk Music; Foster, Stephen; Gershwin, George; Glass, Philip; Ives, Charles; Jazz; Joplin, Scott; Minimalism; Opera in America; Pop Music; Reich, Steve; Sacred Music; Seeger Family; Sousa, John Philip

Further Reading

Cage, John. 1961. *Silence: Lectures and Writings.* Middletown, CT: Wesleyan University Press.

Copland, Aaron. 1968. *The New Music, 1900–1960.* New York: W.W. Norton.

Cowell, Henry, and Sidney Cowell. 1955. *Charles Ives and His Music.* New York: Oxford University Press.

Crawford, Richard. 2001. *An Introduction to America's Music.* New York: W.W. Norton.

Cripe, Helen. 1974. *Thomas Jefferson and Music.* Charlottesville: University Press of Virginia.

Duckworth, William. 1995. *Talking Music: Conversations with John Cage, Philip Glass, Laurie Anderson, and Five Generations of American Experimental Composers.* New York: Schirmer.

Floyd, Samuel, Jr. 1999. *International Dictionary of Black Composers.* Chicago: Fitzroy Deaborn.

Gann, Kyle. 1997. *American Music in the Twentieth Century.* New York: Schirmer.

Garrett, Charles Hiroshi. 2008. *Struggling to Define a Nation: America in the Twentieth Century.* Berkeley: University of California Press.

Glass, Philip. 1987. *Music by Philip Glass.* New York: Harper & Row.

Hamm, Charles. 1983. *Music in the New World.* New York: W.W. Norton.

Hisama, Ellie M. 2001. *Gendering Musical Modernism: The Music of Ruth Crawford, Marion Bauer, and Miriam Gideon.* New York: Cambridge University Press.

Hitchcock, H. Wiley, with Kyle Gann. 2000. *Music in the United States: A Historical Introduction.* Upper Saddle River, NJ: Prentice Hall.

Jablonski, Edward. 1987. *Gershwin.* New York: Doubleday.

Kirk, Elise K. 2001. *American Opera.* Chicago: University of Illinois Press.

Kostelanetz, Richard, and Robert Flemming, eds. 1997. *Writings on Glass: Essays, Interviews, Criticism.* Berkeley: University of California Press.

Nicholls, David, ed. 1998. *The Cambridge History of American Music.* Cambridge: Cambridge University Press.

Oja, Carol. 2000. *Making Music Modern: New York in the 1920s.* New York: Oxford University Press.

Reyes, Adelaida. 2005. *Music in America: Experiencing Music, Expressing Culture.* New York: Oxford University Press.

Straus, Joseph N. 1995. *The Music of Ruth Crawford Seeger.* New York: Cambridge University Press.

Straus, Joseph N. 2009. *Twelve-tone Music in America.* New York: Cambridge University Press.

Tick, Judith, and Paul Beaudoin, eds. 2008. *Music in the USA: A Documentary Companion.* New York: Oxford University Press.

Stephanie Jensen-Moulton

Artist Musicians

Art takes on many forms, from the musical to the written to the visual. Yet at its heart lies the insuppressible human need to express the feelings of joy, suffering, hope, bleakness, courage, and doubt. It is essential that the artist, the conveyor of emotion, choose the best artistic form to transmit these feelings to others so that little is lost in translation. Traditionally one artistic form is chosen; but at times combining multiple forms allows for a better expression of feeling. History shows the crossover of art and music, but it is not a thing of the past. Many current musicians also produce works of art, finding a shared need to express themselves outside their defined box.

While artists such as Andy Warhol (1928–1987) with The Velvet Underground (active 1964–1973, 1990, 1992–1994, 1996) and his numerous album cover designs, have influenced the American music scene, musicians who actively take part in and influence the art scene are numerous and stretch across music genres. Musicians like Tony Bennett (1926–), Grace Slick (1939–), Bob Dylan (1941–), Don Van Vliet (Captain Beefheart, 1941–2010), Jerry Garcia (1942–1995), Jimi Hendrix (1942–1970), Janis Joplin (1943–1970), Tico Torres (1953–), Marilyn Manson (1969–), Beck (1970–), and Brandon Boyd (1976–) are some of the artist musicians who have been featured in gallery and museum exhibitions.

Following up his childhood interest in art with serious training at the School of Industrial Arts (now known as the School of Art and Design) in Manhattan and multiple museum visits throughout his life, Tony Bennett has flourished as a painter. Working under his given name of Benedetto, Bennett draws or paints every day, often while looking out of hotel windows while he is on tour. His paintings have been exhibited in many museums and galleries, including the Butler Institute of American Art in Youngstown, Ohio; the National Arts Club in Gramercy Park in New York City, New York; and the Smithsonian American Art Museum in Washington, D.C. The Kentucky Derby selected Bennett as its official artist for 2001, and the United Nations has commissioned numerous paintings, including one for its fiftieth anniversary. Bennett balances his love of painting with his love for performing. His work touches on familiar subjects and uses various styles, reflecting his awareness of art history. With the desire to communicate, Bennett found painting and sketching another avenue besides music to connect with his audience.

After retiring from music, Grace Slick turned to drawing and painting animals to get through a difficult period in her life. Approached to write her autobiography not long after, Slick agreed to paint portraits of her various contemporaries, finding that she enjoyed it. Color renditions of Janis Joplin, Jimi Hendrix, and Jerry Garcia appeared in her completed book. In addition, an *Alice in Wonderland* painting and various other sketches were first seen in her autobiography. Though Slick began painting and drawing as a child, she admits not being able to multitask and therefore did not turn to paper or canvas often while active in her musical career. Not faithful to any particular style or medium, she uses acrylic, canvas, ink, pen, scratchboard, pencil, and watercolors and often mixes media. Her subjects tend to be animals, colleagues from the music industry, and various themes on *Alice in Wonderland,* the latter so popular it led to the development of stationery and journals based on her work. She views her paintings and drawings as another extension of her artistic temperament that led her to the music industry initially. Slick's work has been featured at galleries such as Peabody Gallery in Menlo Park, California, and Alexander Salazar Gallery in San Diego, California.

Known predominantly as one of the most influential and at times controversial figures on the American music scene, Bob Dylan has long been drawing and painting as well. The first exhibit of his drawings opened in October 2007 at the Kunstsammlungen in Chemnitz, Germany, thirteen years after the publication of *Drawn Blank,* which featured many of Dylan's drawings. Dylan's first public exhibition, which was timed with the release of his second book, included more than two hundred paintings. He uses watercolor, gouache, and acrylic in his work. The National Gallery of Denmark exhibited acrylic paintings by Dylan in 2010. The Gagosian Gallery hosted an exhibition of his art, *The Asia Series,* at its Madison Avenue Gallery in the fall of 2011. Without any formal training, Dylan's subjects tend to be drawn from sketches he made on previous worldwide tours.

Throughout his musical career Don Van Vliet, better known as Captain Beefheart, remained interested in art, and many of his own paintings appear on several of his albums. Van Vliet abandoned music in the mid-1980s to focus on painting, inspired to focus on his art career by a fan who admired the album artwork. Van Vliet has been described as a modernist, a primitivist, an abstract expressionist, and an outsider artist. As a self-taught artist, his style is influenced by his rural desert environment, giving his art a distinctly naturalistic tone. He claims he has no outside influences, but is trying to figure himself out on canvas. Some believe Van Vliet stopped painting in the late 1990s, but as late as 2007 he was still artistically active. However, few paintings were seen, as he immediately destroyed any that did not satisfy him. Waddington Galleries in London, England; the San Francisco Museum of Modern Art in San Francisco, California; and the Michael Werner Gallery in New York City, New York, are just a few who have hosted Van Vliet's exhibitions through the years.

Jerry Garcia of the Grateful Dead (active 1965–1995) was a unique artist who both symbolized and transcended his era. Garcia also was known to draw prolifically as he hung out backstage at concerts or during breaks in rehearsal sessions. He studied art for a short time at the San Francisco Art Institute, yet mostly he was self-taught. Garcia experimented with water colors, inks, and markers, and he also used computer technology to create

Don Van Vliet (Captain Beefheart) paints a canvas in the California desert, November 3, 1982. (Neal Preston/Corbis)

surrealistic designs and drawings. His art is now found on a tie collection named in his honor, and exhibits of his work have been displayed in cities around the world.

As a young child Jimi Hendrix displayed interest and talent in art, but very little early interest in music. By the time he was twelve his interest in drawing automobiles was so great that he sent some of his designs to the Ford Motor Company. Many of his paintings and drawings began as small doodles, then evolved into highly intricate and fanciful figures and inventive forms in various shapes and sizes. His work is psychedelic, immediate, and precise. Hendrix often spoke of how he related colors to emotions and that his music was an effort to play in colors, linking back to his love of the visual arts. The Experience Music Project exhibited many of his artworks in a 2007 exhibition.

Although the body of remaining work by Janis Joplin is limited, she once told her brother she only took singing gigs to help pay for art supplies. Painting was a part of Joplin's life from grade school and continued until she joined the music scene. Singing and performing took precedence over painting and fashion design, although her love of visual art remained visible in her performances. The majority of Joplin's body of work was completed between the ages of twelve and twenty and ranges from large-scale oil paintings to fashion design sketches for a clothing line Joplin was working on. Her style tends towards realism, with greater maturity of visualizing images and connecting emotions through a different avenue.

Exhibiting his paintings since 1994, Bon Jovi (active 1983–present) drummer Tico Torres has created many expressive scenes of his vast travels and life experiences. Not sticking to a particular style or medium, Torres has also created works in bronze, ceramics, glass, and mixed media. His style ranges from classical to abstract to expressionistic, predominantly confronting his subjects in a figurative way. Believing there are fewer limitations in the visual arts world, Torres thinks there is more freedom to explore feelings on canvas than as a drummer. His work has been featured in galleries such as Ambassador Galleries in New York City, Art Avenue Galleries, Robbins Gallery, Park West Gallery, and more.

Allegedly beginning his artistic career as a watercolor painter in 1999, Marilyn Manson paints dark and disturbing images. His subjects range from portraits of people he knows to comments on religion. His watercolors reveal the same aesthetic sense as his music presence, where his personality covers topics such as death, violence, addictions, and other modern media obsessions. Manson uses watercolors in his artwork and has started a movement called Celebritarian Corporation, which is based on the belief that art is the only true form of spirituality in the world. Manson has been developing Celebritarian Corporation since 1998, weaving its predominant belief that religion is based on death throughout his musical and visual work. A gallery named Celebritarian Corporation Gallery of Fine Art opened in Los Angeles in 2007 and features Manson's watercolors predominantly.

Born into an artistic family, Beck Hansen was always surrounded by music and art. His mother and maternal grandfather in particular influenced his artistic leanings. As in his music, Hansen's visual art tends to be pop art collages, crossing over the traditional bounds of media. For his first exhibit in 1998, Hansen collaborated with his grandfather, Al Hansen, on numerous collages, transforming commercial items and perceptions back on themselves to better evaluate consumer society. The exhibit *Playing with Matches* toured from the Santa Monica Museum of Art to galleries in New York City and Winnipeg, Manitoba, in Canada.

With a first memory of art drawn from a painting his mother did while she was at art school, Brandon Boyd of Incubus (active 1991–present) has been surrounded by creativity and art all of his life. Beginning his artistic explorations as doodles in small notebooks, Boyd now draws and paints on a much grander scale, utilizing canvas and acrylic paints. Without any formal training, Boyd focuses on bringing his thoughts to life. His work tends to be observational and expressive, gravitating toward the unusual, dark, and absurd. His first exhibition debuted at Mr. Musichead Gallery in Los Angeles, California, in 2008.

In addition to these artists who have been featured in gallery or museum exhibitions, many other musicians also seek other avenues of artistic expression, but have not focused time and energy on gallery or museum exhibitions. Many attended art schools or enrolled in art programs in larger colleges and universities. Fleetwood Mac (active 1967–present) guitarist Lindsey Buckingham (1949–) attended San Jose State to major in art before pursuing music. Maynard James Keenan (1964–) of Tool (active 1990–present) studied art at Kendall College of Art and Design in Grand Rapids, Michigan. Fiona Apple (1977–) and many others spend large spans of time away from making music to paint or draw, without actively exhibiting their creations. Some artists, such as vocalist Wayne Coyne (1961–) of The Flaming Lips (active 1983–present), only share glimpses of their work on their album covers and liner notes.

Combining multiple avenues of artistic expression enables artists and musicians to more fully express their thoughts and feelings. Many musicians travel with sketchpads on tour, taking visual notes that might be further elaborated on canvas at the conclusion of the tour. Some are classically trained in art and design schools, some are not, but all seek another avenue of creativity.

See also: Album Art; Dylan, Bob; Garcia, Jerry; Grateful Dead; Hendrix, Jimi; Joplin, Janis; Manson, Marilyn; Velvet Underground, The

Official Web Sites:

Tony Bennett: http://www.benedettoarts.com

Bob Dylan: http://www.bobdylanart.com

Tico Torres: http://www.ticoshow.com/

Marilyn Manson: http://marilynmanson.com/art/paintings/

Area Arts (representing Grace Slick, Jimi Hendrix, and Janis Joplin): http://www.areaarts.com/

Further Reading

Bennett, Tony, Robert Sullivan, Mitch Albom, and Mario Cuomo. 2007. *Tony Bennett in the Studio: A Life of Art & Music.* New York: Sterling Publishing Company.

Dylan, Bob. 1994. *Drawn Blank.* New York: Random House

Dylan, Bob, Ingrid Mossinger, and Kerstin Dreschel. 2007. *Bob Dylan: The Drawn Blank series.* New York: Prestel Publishing.

Slick, Grace, and Andrea Cagan. 1999. *Somebody to Love? A Rock-and-Roll Memoir.* New York: Grand Central Publishing.

Van Vliet, Don. 1994. *Stand Up to Be Discontinued.* New York: Distributed Art Publishers, Inc.

Van Vliet, Don. 2003. *Riding Some Kind of Unusual Skull Sleigh.* New York: Artist Ink Editions.

Danielle Lewis

Asian American Music

Given that Asian Americans come from different social classes and ethnic heritages and have very dissimilar relationships with Asia and knowledge of Asian cultures, it is no surprise that they participate in a wide variety of musical activities. This entry surveys several musical traditions with significant Asian American participation, but it is important to note that many would not apply the label "Asian American music" to any or all of them. "Asian American music" is a highly contested term that is used to denote anything from "any music made by Asian Americans" to "music made by Asian Americans about the Asian American experience" (Wong 2004).

People of Asian descent have settled in North America since the mid-eighteenth century. The first known permanent residents were Filipino sailors; when the Spanish ships they were forced to work on docked in New Orleans, the "Manilamen" fled and established fishing villages in the Louisiana bayous. In the nineteenth and early twentieth centuries, hundreds of thousands of Chinese, Japanese, and Filipinos, as well as smaller numbers of Koreans and Indians, came to the United States, primarily to work on plantations, in factories, and on railroads.

During the first waves of Asian immigration racial tension was high, as white laborers feared that they would lose their jobs to or have their salaries undercut by new immigrants. As the notion of a "Yellow Peril" gained prominence, Chinese and Filipino laborers in particular became frequent targets of mob violence and lynchings in the American West. Fear also led to the passage of the Chinese Exclusion Act of 1882 (expanded into the Asian Exclusion Act of 1924), which barred further immigration from Asia, and Executive Order 9066, which gave the U.S. government the authority to relocate Japanese Americans to internment camps during World War II. One effect of all this discrimination was the growth of ethnic enclaves, where musical cultures that influenced both America and Asia thrived.

The Magnuson Act of 1943 repealed the Asian Exclusion Act, but the law that ultimately reopened Asian immigration to the United States was the 1965 Immigration and Nationality Act. Asian immigrants of the past half century have diverse backgrounds and moved to the United States for a wide variety of reasons: to take advantage of educational and economic opportunities, to escape political persecution, to reunite with family members, and so forth. According to the U.S. Census Bureau, in 2010 there were approximately seventeen million people of Asian descent in the United States (including almost two million who identify as multiracial); this was approximately 5 percent of the country's population. The 2008 Census Bureau Population Projection foresaw the Asian American population exceeding 40 million (9.2 percent of the population) by 2050.

Asian American Music Before 1965

Most Chinese immigrants in the nineteenth and early twentieth centuries came from the coastal regions (particularly Taishan, located just west of Macau) of Guangdong province in southern China, and they brought with them their love of Cantonese opera (*Yueju*) and a narrative song tradition from Taishan called *muyu* (literally "wooden fish"). Often sung without instrumental accompaniment by one singer or a group of alternating singers, many *muyu* texts are based either on historical, mythical, and folk romances, or on the immigrant experience. A particularly popular *muyu* among Chinese Americans, "Xiu Hua Ge" ("The Embroidery Song"), depicts the sorrows of a wife who was left behind in China after her husband came to America (Zheng 2010).

To fulfill their desire to enjoy Cantonese opera, Chinese Americans not only formed musical clubs that put on operas, but also sponsored tours by well-known troupes from China and Hong Kong during the late nineteenth and early twentieth centuries, with the 1920s being a particular "golden age." It is worth noting that these tours took place during the exclusion era; the United States banned permanent immigration from China, but well-known performers were granted short-term work visas. (Bruce Lee's father, Lee Hoi-Chuen, was a member of one of these touring troupes.)

Many non-Chinese attended performances of Cantonese operas in various Chinatowns. As a child, maverick composer Henry Cowell (1897–1965) lived in close proximity to San Francisco's Chinatown and became fascinated with the sliding tones he heard in these theaters (Rao 2005). Later he incorporated these techniques into his music and discussed them in his writings, which are still considered seminal in the American experimental music tradition. Cantonese opera performances in Chinatown also affected the course of Cantonese opera performances in Asia. Although the top performers of a Cantonese opera troupe are traditionally all male or all female, male and female stars began performing together in the United States. When they returned to China and Hong Kong, some of them began forming mixed troupes.

Because of the passing of the Asian Exclusion Act in 1924, the history of Japanese America before 1965 can be divided generationally (Asai 1995). The first generation, the *Issei,* moved to the United States between the onset of significant Japanese immigration in 1890 and 1924. For the most part these immigrants continued to play, teach, and listen to folk, classical. and popular Japanese music in America. The second generation, the *Nisei,* were born in America between 1910 and 1940. Although they often learned some type of Japanese music as children, the *Nisei* increasingly turned toward American and European idioms, such as jazz (forming such groups as the Cathayans in San Francisco and the Japanese Sandmen and the Sho Tokyans in Los Angeles in the 1930s), glee club singing, Western classical music, and Hawaiian music.

This trend toward Americanization peaked after anti-Japanese hysteria during World War II led to the forced internment of 110,000 Americans of Japanese descent in ten camps located in desert/semiarid areas in the western states or a swampy area in Arkansas. Although some Japanese music, played primarily by the *Issei,* could be heard at the internment camps, most *Nisei* wanted to demonstrate their American-ness. As a result, the sounds of big bands, the most famous of which was called the Manzanar Jive Bombers, permeated the camps. They performed at Christmas concerts, variety shows, camp dances, and other events. After Word War II, several of these jazz musicians moved to Japan and helped launch the jazz scene there (Yang 2001).

Asian American Music After 1965

After 1965 Asian American music was transformed by two developments. One is the large and continuing influx of immigrants. Some are laborers from China, Japan, and the Philippines, but others do not resemble the early Asian immigrants. There are refugees from mainland Southeast Asia (Vietnamese, Hmong, Cambodian, Laotian) as well as well-educated professionals and wealthy entrepreneurs from many countries. The other is the emergence of an Asian American movement. Led initially by descendants of the early immigrants, the movement formed a multiethnic coalition to fight discrimination against and bring greater political recognition to Asian Americans. Together, these developments created active scenes for Asian traditional and classical music in almost all major American cities and the proliferation of new Asian American styles that combined elements of various musical traditions.

Over the past four decades, numerous masters of Asian traditional and classical music have moved to the United States. The most successful tend to perform not only canonical repertories from their homeland, but also new music and fusion works. While Ravi Shankar (North Indian sitar) has written three concertos for sitar and orchestra, Wu Man (Chinese pipa) has a longstanding collaboration with the Kronos Quartet, and Kyaw Kyaw Naing (Burmese drum circle) has performed with the Bang on Can All-Stars. Some, such as Sumarsam (Javanese gamelan) and Swapan Chaudhuri (North Indian tabla), have also spent many years teaching at the college level, but others, such as Wang Guowei (Chinese erhu) and Masayo Ishigure (Japanese koto), teach primarily within their own ethnic communities.

Today, thousands of Americans regularly perform on Asian instruments and in Asian music ensembles. While some groups, such as Chinese youth orchestras, attract primarily participants from within their own ethnic communities, some others, such as Japanese taiko, are more pan-Asian in membership (Yoon 2001). Most of the over one hundred gamelans in the United States consist mainly of non-Asian Americans.

Asian Americans have been very active in Western classical music. Since East Asian countries adopted Western music education in the late nineteenth and early twentieth centuries, most post-1965 immigrants from China, Taiwan, Hong Kong, South Korea, and Japan

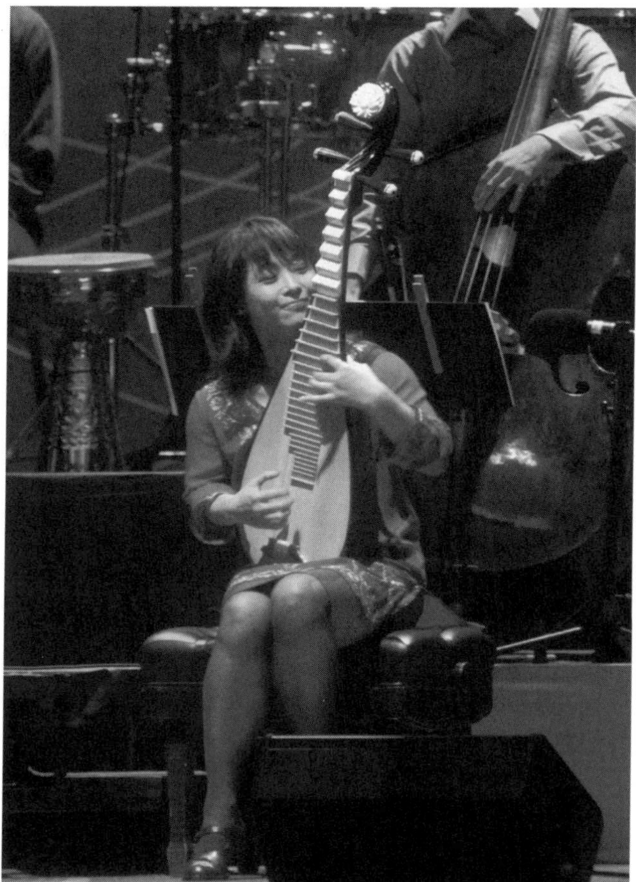

Wu Man plays the pipa during a performance by the Silk Road Ensemble in New York City on June 9, 2009. (Hiroyuki Ito/Getty Images)

have had at least some familiarity with Western classical music. Many also saw knowledge of this tradition as a kind of cultural capital that can lead to upward mobility, and they booked piano and violin lessons for their children. By the late 1970s Asian Americans began flooding major music conservatories in the United States. Today major Asian American performers of Western classical music include cellist Yo-Yo Ma; violinist Sarah Chang; conductor Kent Nagano; the concertmasters of the Chicago Symphony and the Philadelphia Orchestra; and members of the Tokyo, Ying, and Parker Quartets.

Ever since Henry Cowell, American experimental composers, such as Lou Harrison, John Cage, and George Crumb, have incorporated Asian philosophies and sounds in their works. The past three decades have also witnessed the rise of numerous Asian American composers, such as Tan Dun, Chen Yi, Chinary Ung, Bright Sheng, Zhou Long, and Bun-Ching Lam. They write mostly for Western classical instruments and ensembles, but many use aspects of Asian traditional music in their works. This use of traditional elements and the ways audiences hear them have been a great source of debate among scholars of Asian American music (Lam 2000; Sheppard 2009).

Since the 1930s jazz has played an important role in Asian American history. In the 1960s jazz pianist-composer Toshiko Akiyoshi was among the first Asian American musical acts to achieve mainstream success. A decade later a younger generation of Asian Americans, including Jon Jang, Mark Izu, Francis Wong, Glenn Horiuchi, Fred Ho, Anthony Brown, and Jason Kao Hwang, began developing an experimental and hybrid genre that is rooted in jazz, but is also reflective of their ancestry and experiences as Asian Americans. They valued the balance between individuality and group cohesion in jazz and the music's American-ness. Most of those involved in this movement are committed to building multicultural coalitions (reflected in the multiethnic lineup of many of their ensembles) and progressive politics. Many of their works attack common American stereotypes of Asians and, especially in the early years of the movement, reflected on the Japanese internment experience.

Numerous Asian Americans, especially recent immigrants, keep a connection to their heritage by listening to popular music from their ethnic homelands. Many sing these songs in karaoke, and some even compete in singing competitions (Lum 1996). A few of the top pop stars in Asia today, such as Wang Leehom, were in fact born and raised in America.

At the same time, many form or join bands that play a wide variety of music that has nothing to do with recent top 40 hits in Asia. While some, such as happyfunsmile and Dzian!, are inspired by Asian popular music of earlier decades and incorporate Asian instruments in their bands, others have become successful singer-songwriters (Magdalen Hsu-Li, Rachel Yamagata), rappers (Jin, Mountain Brothers, Blue Scholars), and bhangra musicians (DJ Rekha) (Maira 2002). A number of extremely successful mainstream bands also have Asian American members (Metallica, Deftones, Smashing Pumpkins, Linkin Park, The Black Eyed Peas, The Yeah Yeah Yeahs).

In the early twenty-first century Asian Americans make and listen to all kinds of music. Some are involved in traditional music from their ancestral homelands or some other part of the world; others connect most with Western classical music, jazz, or some form of popular music. As the experiences of Asian Americans are becoming increasingly diverse and entangled in the American fabric, the musical activities that they participate in are bound to become even more varied in the future.

See also: Art Music (Experimental); Big Band Music; Cage, John; Hawaiian Music; Jazz; Karaoke; Ma, Yo-Yo; Metallica; Orchestras; Rap and Rappers; Singer-Songwriters

Further Reading

Asai, Susan Miyo. 1995. "Transformations of Tradition: Three Generations of Japanese American Music Making." *The Musical Quarterly* 79, no. 3: 429–453.

Garland Encyclopedia of World Music, Volume 3: The United States and Canada. 2001. Edited by Ellen Koskoff. New York: Routledge.

Lam, Joseph. 2000. "Exotica for Sale or the New American Music? How Should We Listen to Music by Asian-American Composers?" http://www.americancomposers.org/pacifica_lam_article.htm (accessed January 17, 2011).

Lum, Casey Man Kong. 1996. *In Search of a Voice: Karaoke and the Construction of Identity in Chinese America.* Mahwah, NJ: Lawrence Erlbaum Associates.

Maira, Sunaina Marr. 2002. *Desis in the House: Indian American Youth Culture in New York City.* Philadelphia: Temple University Press.

Rao, Nancy Yunhwa. 2005. "Cowell's Sliding Tone and the American Ultramodernist Tradition." *American Music* 23, no. 3 (Fall): 281–323.

Sheppard, W. Anthony. 2009. "Blurring the Boundaries: Tan Dun's *Tinte* and *The First Emperor.*" *The Journal of Musicology* 26, no. 3 (Summer): 285–326.

Wong, Deborah. 2004. *Speak It Louder: Asian Americans Making Music.* New York: Routledge.

Yang, Mina. 2001. "Orientalism and the Music of Asian Immigrant Communities in California, 1924–1945." *American Music* 19, no. 4 (Winter): 385–416.

Yoon, Paul Jong-Chul. 2001. "'She's Really Become Japanese Now!' Taiko Drumming and Asian American Identifications." *American Music* 19, no. 4 (Winter): 417–438.

Zheng, Su. 2010. *Claiming Diaspora: Music, Transnationalism, and Cultural Politics in Asian/Chinese America.* Oxford: Oxford University Press.

Eric Hung

Astaire, Fred (1899–1987)

From vaudeville and nightclubs, to Broadway and the silver screen, Fred Astaire danced, acted, and sang his way into the hearts and admiration of generations of Americans. Dubbed the greatest dancer in the world by critics and fans alike, Astaire rose from humble beginnings to heights of fame and wealth over his seventy-four-year career. His sense of elegance, charm, and grace influenced fashion, fellow performers, and the American public's entertainment tastes.

Born Fredrick Austerlitz II on May 10, 1899, in Omaha, Nebraska, Fred, his mother Johanna, and his sister Adele moved to New York City in 1905 in pursuit of stardom. Upon their dance teacher's advice, they changed their name to the less-ethnic Astaire. Though they were a working-class family, Astaire's socially astute mother continually placed her children in luxurious and affluent milieus, which greatly influenced Astaire's personal bearing. Most nights the children performed in small theaters and vaudeville shows, but by 1920, they were dancing in the finest nightclubs and on Broadway, and they toured Europe. Adele retired from dancing upon her marriage in 1932.

Astaire's big break in films came during the Great Depression, when cinemagoers desired escapist entertainment; elegant frivolity, quick-witted banter, and extravagant dance numbers helped Americans forget their financial woes. His dancing grace, personal charm, and sense of timing translated well to romantic musical comedies. Studios paired him with many talented and beautiful leading ladies, but most often with Ginger Rogers. Their onscreen chemistry and fluid synchronized dancing made instant hits of musicals such as *Top Hat* (1935), *Shall We Dance* (1937), and *Swing Time* (1937). As Astaire aged he appeared in televised musical variety shows such as *An Evening with Fred Astaire* (1958), performed voice-over work on the animated classics *Santa Claus Is Coming to Town* (1970) and *Here Comes the Easter Bunny* (1977), and acted in character roles in made-for-television movies such as *Better Late Than Never* (1979) and *The Man in the Santa Claus Suit* (1979). He also appeared in guest spots on a number of television series and commercials throughout the 1970s and 1980s.

Fred Astaire was the embodiment of elegance both on and off the dance floor. Always dressed impeccably, biographers note his casually elegant style continues to be popular with designers such as Ralph Lauren. They attribute his onscreen performances with popularizing romantic musical comedies and setting high standards for other performers. A number of dancer-actors point to his influence on their own careers. John Travolta, who danced his way though *Grease* (1978), *Saturday Night Fever* (1977), and *Staying Alive* (1983), claimed Astaire was the first cinema icon to invite the American public "to watch a man dance. And he inspired a man to want to dance . . . in elegant ways" (Levinson 2009, 386). With his clear voice and meticulous diction, he had the ability to convey a story in song. Astaire's onscreen performances popularized a number of songs by Tin Pan Alley songwriters Irving Berlin, Cole Porter, George Gershwin and Ira Gershwin, and Jerome Kern. Fred Astaire died of pneumonia on June 22, 1987, in Los Angeles, California.

One of America's favorite entertainers, Fred Astaire danced with a winning, effortless style that drew life from ingenious combinations of tap, ballroom, and ballet dancing. (AP Photo)

See also: Berlin, Irving; Gershwin, George; Gershwin, Ira; Kern, Jerome; Porter, Cole; Television Variety Shows; Tin Pan Alley; Vaudeville and Burlesque

Further Reading

Epstein, Joseph. 2008. *Fred Astaire.* New Haven, CT: Yale University Press.

Gallafent, Edward. 2002. *Astaire and Rogers.* New York: Columbia University Press.

Levinson, Peter J. 2009. *Puttin' on the Ritz: Fred Astaire and the Fine Art of Panache.* New York: St. Martin's Press.

Jennifer Robin Terry

Astronaut Music

The first four years of NASA's human spaceflight program (1961–1965) involved missions of a day or less, designed to test astronauts' ability to do useful work in space. Beginning with the Gemini V mission of August 1965, however, NASA turned its attention to the problems associated with living in space, laying the groundwork for the seven- to ten-day lunar missions of Project Apollo planned for the end of the decade. Gemini V was scheduled to spend eight days in orbit, and NASA anticipated that the crew—Project Mercury veteran Gordon Cooper and newcomer Charles "Pete" Conrad—would be susceptible to boredom and loneliness. To combat both, NASA flight controllers played music for the astronauts over the radio, making Gemini V the first American space flight with a sound track. Music, some beamed from the ground and some carried into space by the astronauts themselves, was a part of every subsequent American spaceflight through the end of the space shuttle era in 2011. It has served—as NASA envisioned it originally—as an antidote to boredom and loneliness, but also as a way to help astronauts feel connected to flight controllers and to loved ones left behind on Earth.

The ways in which NASA astronauts experienced music in space changed as recording technology changed. The music played for Cooper and Conrad came from playback equipment at Mission Control in Houston, but by the late 1960s, cassette tapes and compact battery-powered tape players allowed the astronauts of Project Apollo to bring music with them. The Sony Walkman personal stereo came on the market in 1979, as the first space shuttle missions were being planned, and over the three decades and 135 missions of the shuttle program portable cassette players, CD players, and finally MP3 players made astronauts' experience of music steadily more personal and less communal. Despite this move toward individualized playlists, however, one form of shared listening remained: the wake-up call. These pieces of music, played over the spacecraft's communication link to mark the end of the astronauts' sleep period and the beginning of a new workday, began on the Gemini VI mission and remained a NASA tradition for nearly fifty years.

The NASA astronauts and flight controllers of the 1960s and 1970s were predominantly middle-aged white men from military and engineering backgrounds, with culturally conservative tastes. The music played aboard the Gemini and Apollo spacecraft reflected those tastes, leaning heavily to country, easy listening, and traditional jazz. Recordings of Al Hirt (1922–1999) playing "Muskrat Ramble" and "Birth of the Blues" serenaded astronauts Cooper and Conrad on Gemini V, and later in 1965 the crew of Gemini VII woke to Louis Armstrong (1901–1971) singing "Hey Look Me Over" and Bing Crosby (1903–1977) crooning "High Hopes." Apollo 8, the first mission to carry its own music on cassette, did so in the form of a tape of Buck Owens (1929–2006) songs. The crew of Apollo 10—the "dress rehearsal" mission that paved the way for the first moon landing—were wakened on the first three mornings of their flight by Mission Control wake-up calls featuring the songs of Robert Goulet (1933–2007), Frank Sinatra (1915–1998), and Tony Bennett (1926–). Sinatra also appeared (singing, fittingly, "Fly Me to the Moon") on a cassette tape that Apollo 10 astronaut Gene Cernan and Boeing engineer Al Bishop made for the flight, along with songs by Dean Martin (1917–1995) and the Kingston Trio (active 1957–present), and several jazz instrumentals. The crews of the first two lunar-landing missions favored easy listening and country, although Apollo 12 command module pilot Dick Gordon drove his crewmates to distraction by bringing (and enthusiastically singing along to) the Archies' hit "Sugar, Sugar" (1968–1972).

The classical selections that occasionally played over the speakers of Gemini and Apollo spacecraft had a similar middle-of-the-road quality. Selections played for the crew of Gemini VII by Mission Control included Beethoven's Symphony no. 6 and Rachmaninoff's Symphony no. 2, Bach's "Air on the G String" Liszt's Hungarian Dance no. 2, and excerpts from Puccini's *La Boheme* and *Madame Butterfly.* The quietly thoughtful Neil Armstrong—thinking, perhaps, of his place in history as commander of the first lunar landing mission—put Dvořák's "New World" symphony on his personal audiotape, along with excerpts from Harry Revel's 1947 easy listening album *Music Out of the Moon.* The latter featured a theremin, an early electronic instrument played by moving the user's hands near its twin antennas, whose eerie *glissando* sounds added an unearthly quality to the sound tracks of films like *The Day the Earth Stood Still* and *The Thing (from Another World)*. Thomas Mattingly, command module pilot on the Apollo 16 mission, played Berlioz's *Symphony Fantastique* as he circled the moon alone, waiting for his crewmates to return from the surface.

More exotic musical choices began to filter into NASA spacecraft as the 1960s gave way to the 1970s. Apollo 13 commander Jim Lovell brought Strauss's "Also Sprach Zarathustra," newly famous because of its prominence on the sound track of the film *2001: A Space Odyssey* (1968). Music from the hit musical *Hair* also made the trip to the moon. Lunar module pilot Fred Haise included "Age of Aquarius" among his musical selections, and Mission Control played "Good Morning, Starshine" one morning as a wake-up call. The names of the Apollo 13 spacecraft echoed the crew's choices in music: the command module was *Odyssey* and the lunar module *Aquarius.* Al Worden's tapes for the 1971 Apollo 15 mission included Sinatra and Sousa (1854–1932), but also music by Judy Collins (1939–), Simon and Garfunkel (active 1970–1981), and The Moody Blues (active 1964–1988). George Harrison ("My Sweet Lord"; 1943–2001), The Beatles ("Yellow Submarine" and "Yesterday"; active 1960–1970), Bill Haley ("Rock Around the Clock"; 1925–1981), and the Animals ("House of the Rising Sun"; active 1960–1966) all found a place on Worden's dozen hour-long cassettes.

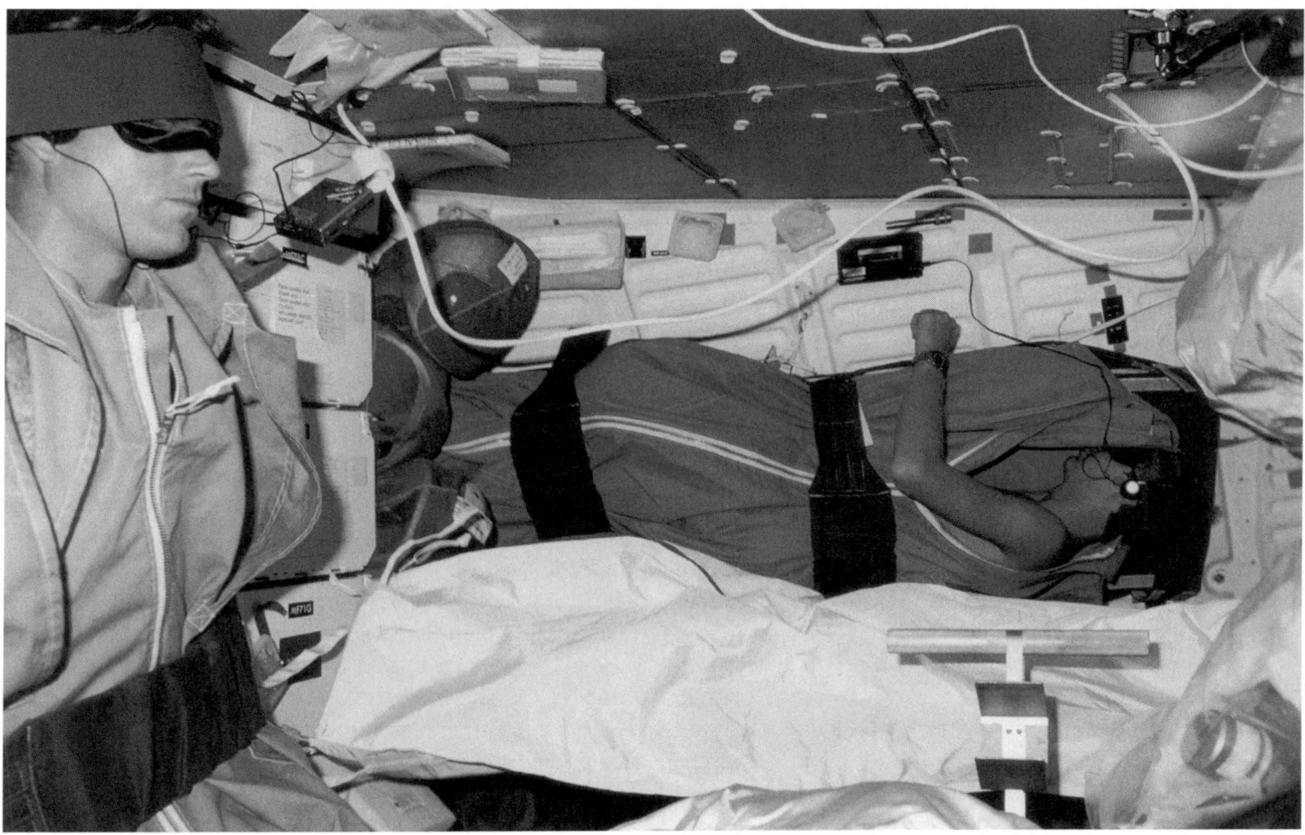

STS-41-D crew members Michael L. Coats (pilot, left) and Steven A. Hawley (mission specialist, right) fall asleep listening to music on the lower deck of the shuttle *Discovery*, 1984. (Space Frontiers/Getty Images)

Humor, usually tightly controlled by the image-conscious space agency, periodically crept into musical broadcasts to and from orbit. While the crew of Gemini V waited, on a Saturday afternoon, for the go-ahead to remain in orbit one more day, flight controllers in Houston teased them by playing "Never on Sunday." Just before Christmas in 1965, Gemini VI mission commander Wally Schirra played "Jingle Bells" from orbit on a contraband harmonica, accompanied by pilot Tom Stafford on a smuggled set of bells. The all-navy crew of Apollo 12 was woken, on their first morning in space, first by a bugle and then by its naval equivalent: a boatswain's whistle. Astronauts on *Skylab*—a three-person space station that hosted three NASA crews in 1973–1974—were woken up at least twice by Legendary Stardust Cowboy's (1947–) famously dissonant novelty song "Paralyzed," and twice by Jerry Jeff Walker's (1942–) "Up Against the Wall, Redneck Mother."

The tradition of NASA controllers choosing wake-up songs with significant titles began early in the space program. Mission control was headquartered, and most astronauts lived, in Houston, so Dean Martin's (1917–1995) "[Goin' Back to] Houston" became a traditional last-morning-in-orbit wake-up call. Flight controllers for Apollo 17—the final lunar landing—played The Doors' (active 1965–1973) classic "Light My Fire" the morning that the crew prepared to lift off from the moon and (striking a hopeful note at a bittersweet moment) "We've Only Just Begun" as they flew home toward Earth. The third *Skylab* crew, spending the holidays in orbit in 1973, woke to "Ring Christmas Bells" on December 25 and Guy Lombardo's (1902–1977) rendition of "Auld Lang Syne" on New Year's Day. It was during the shuttle era, however, that carefully chosen wake-up calls from Mission Control came into their own. The advent of personal stereo systems meant that the wake-up music from Houston was frequently the only music that shuttle crews listened to *as* a crew: a moment for bonding between crew members and between the crew as a whole and flight controllers in Houston.

The wake-up songs played for shuttle crews continued the NASA tradition, now decades old, of commenting musically on mission milestones. Dean Martin's "Houston" remained a last-day fixture, as did "I'll Be Home for Christmas" and "Home for the Holidays" on missions flown in December. A crew assigned to recover two malfunctioning communication satellites—whose insurers had agreed to pay NASA $5.5 million—woke on the morning of the recovery to the theme from the Clint Eastwood film *For A Few Dollars More.* "Believe It or Not [I'm Walking on Air]," the theme to the then-popular television series *The Greatest American Hero,* heralded several spacewalks in the mid-1980s; "Shake, Rattle, and Roll" alluded to the release of a satellite designed to study the movement of Earth's crustal plates; and a crew preparing to link up with the Russian space station *Mir* woke to "Dance of the Flowers" from Tchaikovsky's *Nutcracker*—a symbolic reference to the delicate "orbital ballet" that would precede the docking. Songs that alluded to spaceflight in general—symbolically, like Carole King's (1942–) "I Feel the Earth Move [Under My Feet]" and Tom Petty's (1950–) "Freefalling," or literally, like Elton John's (1947–) "Rocket Man" or David Bowie's (1947–) "Space Oddity"—also figured prominently. The last two were ironic choices, given that they tell the stories of a lonely, disillusioned astronaut and an astronaut who loses his mind during a spacewalk.

Flight controllers also used wake-up songs to single out specific shuttle astronauts, musically acknowledging their national, educational, or professional backgrounds. "The Air Force Song" and "The Marine Hymn" were, like the U. S. Naval Academy fight song "Anchors Aweigh," played dozens of times in honor of veterans and active-duty members of those services among the shuttle crews, and the presence of U.S. Coast Guard officer Bruce Melnick on two flights in the 1990s was acknowledged with "Semper Paratus," the official Coast Guard march. Musical nods to crew members' alma maters became a tradition early in the shuttle program, giving momentary exposure to college fight songs both famous ("Ramblin' Wreck from Georgia Tech" and the "Notre Dame Victory March") and obscure (the University of Wisconsin–River Falls' "Falcon Fight Song"). Astronauts from other countries were acknowledged with wake-up music from their native cultures. The crew of the STS-84 mission, whose seven members had been born in five different countries, were wakened on five successive mornings by the national anthems of Russia, France, Peru, the United Kingdom, and the United States.

Flight controllers also used songs to acknowledge special events and send "thinking of you" messages to individual astronauts from loved ones on Earth. The crew of STS-43 woke one morning to a medley of songs sung by friends in the aerospace industry, and on another morning to selections from *Phantom of the Opera* played by a high school orchestra that included mission commander John Blaha's daughter. Astronauts who played and sang in their spare time—particularly members of the all-astronaut rock band Max Q—were sometimes serenaded by music they had helped to record, and at least one astronaut-alumnus of Notre Dame woke to a rendition of the Notre Dame fight song performed, in four-part harmony, by a quartet of fellow alumni who worked in Mission Control. Flight controllers played "The Bare Necessities," from Walt Disney Studios' animated film *The Jungle Book,* for the crew of STS-48 as a nod to astronaut Ken Reightler's daughters, who were visiting Mission Control. One morning during the STS-79 mission, "Duke of Earl" acknowledged the twentieth wedding anniversary of astronaut Carl Walz, who (as a member of a band called The Blue Moons) had sung it to his wife during their courtship.

Over the thirty years of the space shuttle program, such musical gestures served not only to create relaxed moments and the beginnings of long, tightly scheduled workdays but also—when reported in press coverage of shuttle missions, as they often were—to humanize and individualize the increasingly anonymous members of astronaut corps. They allowed the public glimpses behind the relentlessly serious, work-focused image that the astronauts maintained while at work. Through their music, the public could see the astronauts as people who—even if they commuted to work at Mach 24 and could see the curvature of Earth from their office window—still attended their children's band concerts, played rock 'n' roll with their buddies on the weekends, and (even in orbit) sang along when their favorite songs came on the radio.

See also: Armstrong, Louis; Comedy and Satire in American Music; Country Music; Crosby, Bing; Disney Music; Doors, The; Fight Songs; Haley, Bill; Jazz; King, Carole; Military Bands and Songs; Petty, Tom; Personal Music Devices; Rock Musicals; Sinatra, Frank; Sousa, John Philip

Further Reading

Fries, Colin. 2011. "Chronology of Wakeup Calls." Compiled for the NASA History Division. http://history.nasa.gov/wakeup%20calls.pdf.

Knopper, Steve. 2000. "Rocket & Roll: What Do Astronauts Listen to in Outer Space?" *Details* (January). http://www.knopps.com/DetailsRockSpacemen.html

Smith, Andrew. 2005. *Moondust: In Search of the Men Who Fell to Earth.* New York: Harper.

A. Bowdoin Van Riper

Audiences

The conventions of audience listening vary markedly between genres, and although often unstated are quickly learned by new audience members in order to feel part of the social group. Pop and rock audiences are the most demonstrative, screaming as the introduction to a well-loved song is recognized and sometimes being encouraged by the band on stage to sing along, creating a communal experience of a familiar song. Classical music listeners are more restrained, applauding only at the end of a three- or four-movement work rather than in the gaps between, and listening quietly, with the aim of not distracting other audience members. Jazz, folk, and world music audiences fall somewhere in between, and audience members learn through experience of live listening when to applaud an impressive improvised solo and how much talking during the performance is acceptable in different venues. These conventions have developed over time and are not intrinsic to the music: contemporary audiences for Haydn and Mozart's symphonies, for instance, talked, ate, and drank through performances, and some of the sudden changes in dynamics in those works are thought to be the composers' attempts to grab the attention of their listeners.

Within any audience, there will be different levels of past listening experience, musical knowledge, and devotion to the music being performed. In pop music this is clearly manifested as fan behavior, wherein some listeners pride themselves on being the first to get tickets for a gig and are willing to travel long distances to hear their musical idols, while others in the same audience will have a casual interest, perhaps attending as a social or celebratory occasion with friends. Classical and jazz audiences are less likely to describe themselves as fans, but the same hierarchies of listening enthusiasm are evident: some listeners will have researched the performers or repertoire through recordings in advance of the concert, whereas others will feel that supporting a particular venue or festival is a culturally valuable activity, perhaps preferring to hear familiar music or performers to be sure of gaining value for the cost of their tickets. Whatever the genre and setting, audience members typically gain pleasure from being among like-minded people, knowing that their musical interests are shared by others, and feeling a sense of connection and group experience.

Many factors other than the music itself have an effect on audience enjoyment, including the appropriateness of the venue, which needs to be comfortable and accessible for both new and established audience members if a musical organization is to thrive and attract new listeners. The ethnomusicologist Christopher Small has written about the social values that are communicated by symphony halls, the grand buildings purpose-built for the performance of orchestral music that are a feature of major cities throughout Europe, America, and other industrialized countries. He suggests that the architecture and ethos of such buildings reinforce the social perception of classical music as elitist, providing a welcome for people who are affluent and well-educated, but putting up barriers to less-privileged groups who might feel uncomfortable in grand, institutional buildings. Once inside the concert hall, the rituals of buying a ticket, having an allocated seat, and knowing how to behave in the interval might all alienate people who are not familiar with the setting. Frequent attendees at classical concerts experience the buildings differently, of course: the grandeur of the setting quickly becomes familiar, and so less impressive or intimidating. Over time and with repeat attendance, memories build up of having previously enjoyed occasions there, giving people a sense of attachment and loyalty to the venue. A regular orchestral concert-goer might feel equally out of place at a pop gig or a folk club, though this has been less commented on by researchers, perhaps because those activities are not often supported by public funding, so attendance is viewed as a personal choice rather than a cultural obligation.

Internationally, audiences for classical music are perceived to be aging, with a predominance of middle-aged or retired listeners choosing to hear this kind of music live. Some orchestras have made deliberate attempts to appeal to younger listeners: the Boston Pops (www.bso.org) in Boston, Massachusetts, and the Night Shift concerts run by the Orchestra of the Age of Enlightenment in London (www.oae.co.uk/thenightshift/) both aim to relax the rules of classical music and break down something of its stuffy image. First-time attendees in their twenties and thirties at the Night Shift have welcomed the spoken introductions that guide them in their listening, but nonetheless retain a preference for some of the formality and ritual of classical music concerts (see Dobson and Pitts 2011). Audiences might be getting older because of changes in music education in schools, which is less focused on classical music now than it was three or four decades ago, or because the genre is perceived to require the concentration and experience associated with older listeners (Kolb 2001). Music of all kinds is also more widely available through portable media devices, which might over time reduce the demand for live performance, though so far this decline is not in evidence in other genres. Whatever the reasons, recruiting and retaining audiences is a major concern for classical music promoters, as well as dictating the short career span of many popular artists and groups.

Audiences and Performers

Research in the psychology of music (e.g., Juslin and Sloboda 2001) has investigated the communication between performers and listeners, considering the ways in which music can provoke an emotional response, and the factors involved in making a successful performance. There is some debate about whether music "represents" or "generates" emotion: listeners vary in the extent to which they have strong emotional responses to music, but there is agreement about some of the factors that elicit such experiences. John Sloboda has called these "chills and thrills," features of music such as an orchestral crescendo or a sequence of falling intervals that cause sensations including shivers down the spine or hairs standing up on the back of the neck. These effects come partly through the structure of the music and its sense of tension and release, or predictability and surprise: getting the balance right between familiarity and novelty is the secret of all good music, from an hour-long symphony to a three-minute pop song.

For notated music (though not for improvised jazz or many world music traditions), the mood or emotion of a piece of music is the joint responsibility of the composer, the performer(s), and the listeners who hear the performance. The parameters set by the composer determine the speed, tonality, and sounds of the music, and these will dictate whether the piece is slow, minor and melancholy, or upbeat and joyful. Within these broad terms, the performers and/or conductor play a vital role in deciding the intensity, pace, and tone color that contribute to a more nuanced interpretation of the music. And at an even finer level of detail, each listener in an auditorium will hear the piece with slightly different emotional effects, depending on his or her own temperament, mood in the moment of listening, and the associations that the piece has for each individual.

Consider, for example, the "Ride of the Valkyries," the dramatic orchestral prelude that begins Act III of Wagner's opera *Die Walküre*. Heard for the first time, this is an exciting piece, with the orchestra at its full force, a strong brass fanfare theme emerging through swirls of rapid violin passages and high flute flourishes. Clearly Wagner wished the audience for his opera to be on the edge of their seats: the music tells them that something exciting is about to happen and demands their attention and full emotional engagement. Sixty years after the piece was composed, however, the music might have lost its emotional impact for some listeners: the musical material is quite repetitive and might become dull and familiar after a few listenings, perhaps losing its sense of drama and seeming rather overblown and unsubtle. For other listeners, the music will have acquired nonmusical associations: it might be recognized from the film *Apocalypse Now* or, for German listeners of the 1940s, have been a disturbing reminder of the recent horrors of the Second World War, since it was used to accompany news footage of German bombing raids. From this example, it can be seen that the emotional impact of any piece of music lies partly in its sounds and the way that these are performed, but also in the cultural context and associations of the music, and the interpretations and responses that each listener brings to the work.

Audience members are also affected by the visual components of a musical performance in making their judgments of and responses to a performance. The appearance of the performers sends implicit messages about the level of formality of a concert, with performers' dress often reflecting a more conservative style than that of everyday life, even though the traditional evening dress of chamber music concerts has now largely been replaced by colorful shirts for men and more individual styles of dresses or trousers for women. Orchestras still tend to wear a uniform of sorts, emphasizing their unity as an ensemble and distinguishing themselves from any soloists who join them for a concerto or oratorio performance. Classical performers who deviate too much from these norms might be judged to be less serious, or even less competent: in one experiment, the same performance apparently played by a violinist in formal, casual, and clubbing wear was rated differently by listeners, who preferred the performer to be dressed according to their expectations of formal concert dress (Griffiths 2010). Regrettably, studies have also shown that performers are sometimes judged differently according to race and gender (Davidson and Edgar 2003), a situation made worse by the many decades of deliberate male-only recruitment to major international orchestras. "Blind" auditioning, in which performers audition for orchestras behind a screen, has increased the number of women in orchestral positions, though the Vienna Philharmonic was the last to change its policy, admitting its first female player as recently as 2003 and still employing relatively few female musicians.

Although the majority of the intended communication in a live concert is from the performers to the audience, feedback in the other direction can have a strong effect on the performers' experience and therefore on the success of an event. Jazz listeners are perhaps most aware of this (see Monson 1997), recognizing that their convention of applauding after an improvised solo can encourage (or discourage) players, as well as contributing to the atmosphere of a gig. Classical listeners conventionally respond at the end of a performance, and this lack of ongoing feedback can be a source of performance anxiety for inexperienced players, who might wrongly assume that their silent audience is being judgmental, rather than attentive.

Recorded Music and its Effects on Audience Listening

By far the most music listening in the twenty-first century takes place not in concert halls or other live music venues, but privately in the home, car, or through portable listening devices. Recorded music forms a sound track to everyday life, whether selected by individual listeners or imposed upon them in public spaces. Commercial organizations, including shops and restaurants, have become very sophisticated in their uses of music to attract some customers and put off others: the choice, volume, and tempo of music will draw in people of particular age groups, spending power, and style preferences, allowing commercial businesses to shape their clientele in unspoken ways. In a restaurant where the aim is to achieve high customer turnover, for example, the music is likely to be fast-paced, mainstream pop, and there is evidence that customers will chew more quickly as the music drives their sense of arousal, leaving the table free for the next paying customers more quickly than would otherwise have been the case. In a more expensive establishment, where the aim is to encourage people to linger over their meals, spending more money by ordering an extra coffee or staying for dessert, the music will usually be quieter, less frenetic, and probably jazz or classical, and the older, more affluent customers will enjoy a leisurely meal and be more likely to return to the restaurant in future.

Music therefore establishes the ambience of a restaurant or shop; it also reduces anxiety in a dentist's waiting room and causes listeners to stay on hold longer as they wait to get through a call center switchboard (see North and Hargreaves 2008). In all these ways, recorded music shapes people's emotional experience of everyday life. Some concern has been expressed that the pervasive presence of background music reduces the ability to listen "in audience," encouraging listeners to process music as background sound and making them less able to listen attentively. Campaigns against the use of music in public spaces (e.g., www.pipedown.info) argue particularly for the abolition of "piped music" or "muzak" in airports, hospitals, and other public spaces. However, the extent to which individuals construct their own sound tracks to daily life, through MP3 players and other portable music devices, suggests that there is little opposition to the quantity of music experienced, and more to the lack of choice that comes with externally imposed music.

When people select their own recorded music to listen to, they do so for a variety of reasons: to fill time during a commute to work, to set the mood for a night in, to share their music preferences with friends, or to change or deepen their emotional state (DeNora 2000). As with the response to music in the concert hall, individual listeners will bring their own past experiences of music and life to their choices of repertoire. Musical tastes and preferences change over time, through the influences of friends as well as the media; there is some evidence, however, that music experienced during adolescent years has a lasting impact, remaining significant into later life, even while additional preferences may be acquired. For adolescents, music is also a valuable means of exploring and expressing identities, giving them solidarity with a particular group of friends, sometimes displayed visibly through clothing, appearance, and other lifestyle choices. While adults, constrained more by work and other responsibilities, are typically less demonstrative in their musical preferences, music plays a powerful role in emotional well-being for many people.

For the smaller proportion of the population who attend live concerts as well as listening to recorded music, the relationship between the two kinds of musical experience has several possible effects. For fans of specific performers or repertoire—whether classical music devotees or pop groupies—live listening is likely to be the culmination of acquiring familiarity with a performer or his or her music through repeated listening and informal self-education. This is demonstrated through the expectation of many pop performers that audiences will sing along with well-known lyrics: in YouTube recordings of Robbie Williams's singing "Angels," for example, the audience typically sings along from the start of the song, with Williams holding out the microphone to them in the chorus as they take over the performance (see http://www.youtube.com/watch?v=lUCdDzfEsF4). This kind of response would be frowned upon in a classical concert, of course, but nonetheless experienced listeners there might compare interpretations and performances, seeking out a particular exponent of Beethoven piano sonatas or the Elgar cello concerto, and relishing the opportunity to hear live a performance that they already know well. The relationship between live and recorded listening might continue after the event: performers selling CDs at their live gigs is commonplace across all genres and can provide a lasting reminder of an enjoyable experience, as well as encouraging audience members to broaden their listening to other repertoire by the same performers.

Despite its relationship to more widely accessible recorded music, live music is a distinctive experience, and for jazz audiences particularly the sense of spontaneity in improvised solos provides a feeling of "having to be there" that motivates continued attendance at live performances. For classical music audiences also, the sense of hearing a performance unfold live gives it an immediacy lost in repeated listening to a recording, even though there may be imperfections in a live performance that would usually have been edited out in a recording. Listening to a performance alongside other like-minded music lovers can also provide a sense of collective enjoyment that surpasses individual listening to recorded music. Nonetheless, there are barriers to live attendance, not least the fact that a ticket to a concert or gig will usually cost significantly more than a CD or download. The sense of financial risk can inhibit concertgoers' attendance habits, often making classical music listeners more conservative in their choice of program. Many concert promoters know all too well that a new or unfamiliar work needs to be sandwiched between more popular repertoire to ensure ticket sales.

Although there are obviously differences in cost, convenience, and experience between live and recorded music listening, there has so far been relatively little exploration of how listeners respond differently to music in the two contexts. New audiences at a classical music event have been shown to believe that more experienced listeners are more knowledgeable and focused than they are (Dobson and Pitts 2011), but it may be that many listeners "zone out" and relax to music in the ways described by first-time attenders, but are less prepared to admit to this. The use of recorded music to shape and enhance moods in everyday life is unlikely to be completely forgotten in the concert hall, even if being in a venue specifically designed for music invites the greater concentration and intellectual engagement that it is often assumed are characteristic of classical audiences.

Understanding and Developing Audiences

Understanding audience experience is a growing area of interest for researchers, who seek insight on how live music is experienced and what this reveals about musical communication and the role of music in personal and social identity. More pragmatically, the experiences of audiences are also of value to arts promoters, who need to understand who goes to their events and why, and how more people could be encouraged to come more often.

Many arts organizations now devote considerable energy to their outreach activities: programs designed to appeal to young people and others typically beyond the reach of the organization's main work. Such programs contribute to music education in many schools, supplementing the school curriculum with a valuable opportunity for children to see professional musicians playing live and to interact with them, often on imaginative composition or improvisation projects. Among many such examples are Classical Music for Kids, run by the American Classical Orchestra (see http://www.amerclassorch.org/education.shtml), and LSO Discovery, the community and education program of the London Symphony Orchestra (http://lso.co.uk/page/3/LSO+Discovery). The prevalence of these projects has changed the nature of orchestral musicians' careers, requiring them to become expert in communicating with young children, a task for which their conservatoire education will not always have prepared them thoroughly. There are challenges for schools, too, in accommodating professional input without undermining the regular music provision in the school, and the most successful programs work carefully to mentor teachers and ensure that the short-term intervention from an orchestra or other organization is followed up on and supported. At their most effective, these programs are inspiring and innovative, bringing classical music to children who might not otherwise have had that experience. There are some doubts, however, about whether these programs achieve their other stated purpose, of drawing in audiences for the future (see Kolb 2001). Progress in this area seems to depend more heavily on parents' concertgoing habits and on the provision of accessible, affordable events at which new audience members are made to feel welcome.

The marketing and advertising of arts events is another area in which understanding of audience experience is beneficial. Historically, much arts marketing research has focused on demographics: where typical audience members live, how old they are, how much they earn, and how frequently they tend to go to concerts. Once an audience's attendance habits have been identified, arts promoters can focus on extending these listeners' commitment to an organization, through the Friends schemes that reward loyalty and the discount ticket offers that aim to increase attendance and so establish new habits of concertgoing. In England the Arts Council engaged in a detailed audience segmentation study, identifying types of listeners and their likely behaviors, ranging from "traditional culture vultures" (estimated at 4 percent of English adults), who are typically middle-aged and well educated and have an active leisure life, to "time-poor dreamers" (7 percent of English adults), who are more likely to be parents of young children, live in urban areas, and use their leisure time to meet friends or watch television (Arts Council England 2008). This research can be seen as a first step toward greater collaboration between the consumer satisfaction style of much arts marketing research and the deeper understanding of audience experience afforded by considering the role of music in people's lives and well-being.

Attempts to appeal to new audiences can also be seen in the marketing of individual artists, most notably classical musicians who engage in crossover playing: performing popular repertoire and taking on a celebrity persona to go with it. There has been some criticism of the tendency to market female classical artists in provocative clothing, the implication being that this debases the music as well as the performers. While established audiences may be concerned about these forays into pop culture, the greater success of commercial classical radio stations over traditional broadcasting styles shows that there is an appetite for classical music among a wider audience than those who typically attend live events. Marketing the music and its performers to new listeners seems to be essential to securing the future of arts organizations; time will tell whether classical music is something to grow into, as some current older listeners suggest, or the nature of live performance will have to change substantially to accommodate the changing pace and preferences of contemporary listeners.

See also: Deadheads; Film Music; Folk; Improvisation; Jazz; Orchestras; Pop Music; Personal Music Devices; Psychology of Music; Rock 'n' Roll (Rock); Theaters and Other Venues; World Music

Further Reading

Davidson, Jane W., and Richard Edgar. 2003. "Gender and Race Bias in the Judgment of Western Art Music Performance." *Music Education Research* 5: 169–182.

DeNora, Tia. 2000. *Music in Everyday Life.* Cambridge, UK: Cambridge University Press.

Dobson, Melissa C., and Stephanie E. Pitts. 2011. "Classical Cult or Learning Community? Exploring New Audience Members' Social and Musical Responses to First-time Concert Attendance." *Ethnomusicology Forum* 20, no. 3: 353–383.

Griffiths, Noola K. 2010. "Posh Music Should Equal Posh Dress: An Investigation into the Concert Dress and Physical Appearance of Female Soloists." *Psychology of Music* 38: 159–177.

Juslin, Patrik, and John A. Sloboda. 2001. *Music and Emotion: Theory and Research.* Oxford: Oxford University Press.

Kolb, Bonita M. 2001. "The Effect of Generational Change on Classical Music Concert Attendance and Orchestras' Responses in the UK and US." *Cultural Trends* 11: 1–35.

Monson, Ingrid. 1997. *Saying Something: Jazz Improvisation and Interaction.* Chicago: University of Chicago Press.

North, Adrian C., and David J. Hargreaves. 2008. *The Social and Applied Psychology of Music.* Oxford: Oxford University Press.

Small, Christopher. 1998. *Musicking: The Meanings of Performing and Listening.* Middletown, CT: Wesleyan University Press.

Stephanie E. Pitts

Autry, Gene (1907–1998)

Best known for his roles as a singing cowboy in Western films, Gene Autry was a singer, songwriter, and actor who performed on radio, film, and television for over three decades. Throughout his career Autry and his music were closely associated with heartland values and American national identity.

Born Orvon Gene Autry in Tioga, Texas, on September 29, 1907, he was the son of a poor tenant farmer. He learned to ride, sing, and play guitar in his youth, skills that would form the foundation for his later career. One day, when patronizing the telegraph office where the young Autry worked, well-known actor and humorist Will Rogers (1897–1935) heard his voice and suggested that he should sing professionally. This encouraged Autry to audition for his first radio performance in 1928, on station KVOO in Tulsa. One year later he signed a contract with the American Record Corporation (ARC); he made his first six recordings in 1931, including his signature ballad, "That Silver-Haired Daddy of Mine," which was written during his long hours at the Chelsea telegraph depot. When the record sold its one-millionth copy, ARC presented Autry with a gold record, beginning an award tradition that continues to the present day.

By 1930 Autry was featured on NBC's popular "National Barn Dance" program on radio station WLS, where he was billed as "Oklahoma's Yodeling Cowboy." Autry's radio fame led to a bit part in Mascot Pictures' B Western *In Old Santa Fe* (1934), followed by his first leading role, in the twelve-part serial *Phantom Empire* (1935). Autry was so successful in his role as a singing cowboy that he was signed to a long-term contract with the newly formed Republic Pictures; for six years he was the studio's top-grossing performer. With each successive film, Autry's music was featured more prominently, propelling Western songs such as "Tumbling Tumbleweeds" (1935) into mainstream popularity, along with hits such as "Have I Told You Lately That I Love You" (1948) and the second all-time best-selling Christmas single, "Rudolph the Red Nosed Reindeer" (1949). Autry produced 640 recordings, nearly half of which were written by him. In 1950 he turned his production efforts toward the medium of television. He starred in ninety-one episodes of *The Gene Autry Show* for CBS-TV. The series ran until 1956.

Autry's career slowed as a rougher, troubled, and more complex sound grew in popularity in country and western music, promoted by singers like Johnny Cash (1932–2003) and Waylon Jennings (1937–2002). In the early 1960s Autry retired to California, where he embarked on a second career as owner of the Los Angeles Angels baseball team, along with a television station, Flying A Productions, and several radio stations. Autry died in his home in Studio City, California, on October 2, 1998, at the age of ninety-one. He was inducted into the Western Performers Hall of Fame in 1972 and was also posthumously inducted into the Radio Hall of Fame (2003). He is the only entertainer to have been awarded stars in every category on the Hollywood Walk of Fame: Radio, Recording, Motion Pictures, Television, and Film.

Gene Autry, seen here in the 1950s, was a Hollywood legend who started his career as a popular western singer in the 1930s and 1940s. (Library of Congress)

See also: Cash, Johnny; Country Music; Halls of Fame; Radio; Television Variety Shows

Further Reading

George-Warren, Holly. 2009. *Public Cowboy No. 1: The Life and Times of Gene Autry.* New York: Oxford University Press.

Cynthia J. Miller

The Avant-garde in American Music

The avant-garde of one age is the commonplace of another. Its definition will vary with every commentator, but one way to consider the avant-garde in music is to explore composers and movements that have jolted what may be perceived as the mainstream and, through a high level of originality of thought, have diverted this mainstream of musical thought. Avant-garde music generally refers to music after 1945 that is more radical or subversive in nature and is not easily defined within the modernist genre of art music.

At the opening of the twentieth century music in the United States was essentially conservative, and part of the opening salvos fired at the establishment coincided with the arrival of some key European musical figures as well as homegrown composers who challenged the status quo. These individuals very quickly sought each other out and formed at least some sort of front in the battle for new music. European unrest and the First World War as well as its aftermath benefited the United States by bringing musical presences and innovative composers to the country. Composer Charles Griffes, for example, studied in Berlin and then returned to the United States to teach in a private boys' school for many years. His contribution to American music included an interest in exotic scales, Asian and Native American melodies, and strong influences from composers such as Scriabin, Busoni, Debussy, Stravinsky, and Mussorgsky. His early death prevented the full development of his experimental compositional technique.

Other notable composers in the early twentieth century were Edgard Varèse, Ernest Bloch, Dane Rudhyar, Leo Ornstein, and Charles Martin Loeffler. These "imports" from France arrived at a time when anti-German feeling influenced program building, so Loeffler, Griffes, Varèse, and Rudhyar came to America as representatives of a friendly nation, and they brought with them an introduction to early-twentieth-century French music. Varèse, a composer, conductor, and organizer, became a vital element in the move toward modernism, and his works are foundations of the orchestral repertoire from this era. Ferruccio Busoni, who taught some of these composers, also toured America at that time and composed his *Indian Diary* and *Indian Fantasy,* demonstrating how Native American melodies could be used even by a European composer.

With the rise of a national musical confidence in America, a number of small journals emerged (a fine example is *Modern Music*), catering to a voluble elite group and to composers with strongly held opinions who were not averse to airing them in public. A feature of the avant-garde then, as now, is that initially such movements were a vocal minority, loud well out of proportion to their numbers. Eventually the world sits up and takes notice of the loud propaganda, so certain aspects survive and later become conservative. This has occurred many times and is descriptive of what happened with avant-garde music in America.

Travel to Europe and especially Paris was ongoing in the early twentieth century and became almost a professional necessity after the First World War ended. A second wave of Americans seeking to study in Europe also occurred after World War II, but by then it was less essential, and many Europeans were traveling to America to study. A well-known example was composer

American composer Conlon Nancarrow, 1985. (Neil Libbert/Lebrecht Music & Arts/Corbis)

George Antheil and his *Ballet Mecanique,* which caused a sensation on at least two continents and has in more recent years had successful revivals and recordings. This work brought the idea of "machine music" to America and was an offshoot of the Dadaist and futurist European movements. The score incorporated airplane propellers as well as multiple pianos and percussion, both characteristics of the new music.

It is no accident that instruments such as the theremin, an early electronic musical instrument, and the rhythmicon, an electronic drum machine, made an appearance at this time. There were serious attempts to study music scientifically and mathematically, and immigrants such as Joseph Schillinger (who later taught George Gershwin) and Lazare Saminsky wrote voluminously on such topics. The pianola, or player piano, became a minor obsession for some composers (including Igor Stravinsky, yet another Russian who eventually moved to the United States), who used what they saw as a mechanical instrument in their compositions, although this was not exactly an accurate description of the pianola. The pianola was also important to composer Conlon Nancarrow, who wrote most of his music for it, developing musically complex rhythms too difficult for human hands but possible on a hand-cut piano roll. Eventually the pianola gave way to the tape recorder and the computer as a compositional tool; these latter are further manifestations of a fascination with the machine in composition.

This new relationship with the piano as a concert instrument also produced a percussive and coloristic approach to the instrument, moving away from its traditional role as a product of grand romanticism. It was probably first heard in this new guise in the music of Leo Ornstein (another Russian refugee from anti-Semitism), especially in pieces such as *The Wild Mens' Dance.* At roughly the same time, Henry Cowell began to play the piano using his fists and elbows and reaching under the lid to pluck and strum the strings. It was only a matter of time before others, such as John Cage and Lou Harrison, found new sounds by attaching different materials such as paper, screws, and various other materials to the strings to radically alter the sound. Some composers became dissatisfied with the Western tuning system and the division of the octave into twelve steps. Using Eastern music as a launching pad, they began to search for new instruments to produce microtonal divisions of the octave. Harry Partch (*Delusion of the Fury*) was the archetypal American loner, who devoted his entire life to building new instruments and then composing music for them. Another rugged individualist was Charles Ives (*Three Places in New England*), who wrote in a vacuum early in the century and, after producing a mass of works, burnt himself out, but did live to see the beginnings of recognition of his undoubted status as a pioneer American composer.

The period between the two world wars was a high point for the avant-garde movement in the United States. The early twelve-tone music of the Second Viennese School began to filter into the American compositional psyche, and with it occurred the birth of what can be loosely called "systems music," with various mathematical applications applied at first to the pitch successions and in due course to parameters such as dynamics, durations, and attack, transforming from twelve-tone music to total serialism. Milton Babbitt was an early proponent of such music, which in the post–World War II era became a compulsory language of the progressive composer.

Other forces also shaped the avant-garde in American music. The machines were countered by a fresh interest in spirituality, partly as a reaction to war, partly as an extension of the theosophical movement, which had originated in Russia and quickly spread to many other countries. Theosophy, a doctrine of religious philosophy and mysticism, brought with it a growing interest in Eastern thought, including music. This meant opening up the whole world of different scale construction, new, exotic instruments, and eventually multiculturalism. Many composers claimed to tap into the spiritual, including important Americans like Dane Rudhyar, Ruth Crawford-Seeger, John Cage, James Tenney, Lou

American composer Lou Harrison, undated photo. (Oscar White/Corbis)

Harrison, and Harold Budd. Theosophy sowed the seed of the growth of Buddhism in the United States and eventually the new age movement.

The aesthetic philosophy of what was "dissonant" in music occupied many minds, and at least one result was a movement that utilized neoclassicism, whose composers sought to return to the order, balance, and clarity of classicism as its structural base, but within the structure turned to polyphonic technique, which consisted of two or more independent melodic voices in the same piece. Composers such as Roger Sessions, Walter Piston, and Aaron Copland figured largely in this approach. Since the Second Viennese School was also essentially neoclassical in its structural orientation, composers who employed the serial method (and there were many) rubbed shoulders with the composers who were experimenting with dissonant counterpoint. Igor Stravinsky encompassed both the neoclassical as well as the serial movements during his long life, leaving his personal stamp on everything that he composed.

The exodus to Europe and especially Paris throughout the twentieth century involved the major influence of composer and teacher Nadia Boulanger on the course of American music, especially in the period between the two world wars. In contrast to some of the highly constructed/invented music of some American composers, a fresh simplicity also emerged, perhaps attributable to Boulanger's teaching. This simpler, almost folk-like music, in scores such as Virgil Thomson's *Four Saints in Three Acts,* has links with the French group *Les Six* (one of whom, Darius Milhaud, taught in the United States) and the music of Erik Satie. It in turn led composers to consider their own indigenous sources as raw material (the symphonies of Roy Harris are a fine example).

Although this type of nationalism also opened the doors to a cosmopolitan internationalism in music, Americans increasingly recognized jazz music as their own, and serious attempts were made to blend the jazz style with the so-called serious concert style then in vogue. It was because of this development that George Gershwin rocketed to fame with his *Rhapsody in Blue.* Other composers worked from a European background and made the new combination work for them: Kurt Weill (in the musical *Johnny Johnson*), Louis Gruenberg (in the orchestral *The Daniel Jazz*), John Alden Carpenter (in the ballet *Skyscrapers*), and Marc Blitzstein (in the musical *The Cradle Will Rock*) in the interwar years, and after World War II, Leonard Bernstein (in Symphony No. 2, *The Age of Anxiety*) and Duke Ellington (in the jazz composition *In the Beginning*).

The twelve-tone procedure, a technique pioneered by composer Arnold Schoenberg, is a means of ensuring that all twelve notes of the chromatic scale are sounded in a composition. It had its heyday in the immediate postwar period of the 1950s. Early users of the technique included Wallingford Riegger (String Quartet no. 1), George Perle (String Quartets nos. 3 and 4), Roger Sessions (Violin Sonata), Ernst Krenek, and Stefan Wolpe (String Quartet in Two Parts). The last two were imports from Europe. Babbitt began using the twelve-tone technique quite early and moved to total serialism before the Europeans (3 Compositions for Piano). Soon after, he began work with electronic music synthesis as a wave of composers embraced the latest manifestations of the machine: the tape recorder, the music synthesizer, and eventually the computer. This last was of course the ideal instrument for the realization of mathematically complex relationships. Total serialism became the favorite vehicle for the academic arm of the avant-garde and was widely taught in tertiary institutions. One unique practitioner was Elliott Carter, a composer who developed a style all his own, using "metrical modulation" (frequent precise tempo changes) as a form of control, resulting in a highly complex, individual style that nevertheless left room for intuitive action. The rapid development of electronic music in the late 1950s, using the computer as a compositional device, pioneered by Lejaren Hiller (*Illiac Suite*), allowed for interaction between people and machines, and composers began to invent ways to achieve such collaboration, with varying levels of success and complexity.

Parallel to the strong wave of serial thinking, during the 1960s negative reactions to it, especially as scores became less and less user-friendly and performers, began to voice opposition to the exact notations that were a hallmark of the serial schools. Lukas Foss, in many works such as *Echoi,* exercised much looser control over his materials and introduced improvisation as a key element of his scores. Alan Hovhaness, with his huge output, managed to create complex-sounding passages using the simplest of means. Gradually new scores were decorated with "boxes" containing instructions like "play these pitches in any order," or "improvise on these pitches until cued to stop," and many ingenious variations on this idea. The logical outcome of such an approach was a move toward what became known as "indeterminacy," probably first used by John Cage and then further elaborated by Earle Brown (*Folio*), Morton Feldman (*Projections*), Christian Wolff (*For 5 or 10 Players*), and others in New York. These developments drove the first nail into the coffin of serialism, and in the end the reaction was extreme. Minimalism was born, with composers such as La Monte Young (*The Four Dreams of China*), Steve Reich (*Come Out*), Terry Riley (*in C*), Morton Feldman (String Quartet 2), and Philip Glass (*Akhenaton*) leading the movement to limit music to its most basic elements and fundamental features. Arnold Schoenberg's "endless variations" had become minimalism's "endless repetitions."

With the end of the twentieth and the beginning of the twenty-first centuries, music entered a period of extreme freedom and interaction between art forms and instruments. Polystylism, the use of multiple styles or techniques, was heard in John C. Adams's *Nixon in China* and has by now become a universal truth. Further, there has been an explosion of new tendencies in music, labeled with terms that still await clear definition: postminimalism, postmodernism, laptop music, computer games music, spectralism, and so forth. The new complexity (which I cannot resist calling maximalism) is still around, carrying the wilting banner of serial complexity to new heights. Brian Ferneyhough (String Quartet no. 3) represents the movement in the United States as well as anyone else. There are many other movements, each with its small coterie of adherents. Is multimedia the contemporary version of Scriabin's *Prometheus*? Has this type of new romanticism finally won out over mechanical music and mathematical music? Nobody knows, but we can be certain that composers will evolve, and the art of music will morph yet again.

See also: Adams, John C.; Bernstein, Leonard; Cage, John; Copland, Aaron; Ellington, Duke; Gershwin, George; Glass, Philip; Ives, Charles; Partch, Harry; Reich, Steve

Further Reading

Adlington, Robert. 2009. *Sound Commitments: Avant-Garde Music and the Sixties.* New York: Oxford University Press.

Piekut, Benjamin. 2011. *Experimentalism Otherwise: The New York Avant-Garde and Its Limits.* Berkeley: University of California Press.

Sitsky, Larry. 2002 *Music of the Twentieth-Century Avant-Garde: A Biocritical Sourcebook.* Westport, CT: Greenwood Press.

Larry Sitsky

Awards and Prizes for Music

Awards in Performance Competitions

Musical competitions have long been utilized to identify and celebrate the outstanding talent of an ensemble or soloist. Awards for such competitions have expanded, from the respect and adulation of the community, to money, to recording contracts and other monetary devices. Awards in music have signified the talent in our society and the resulting adoration that such awards warrant.

The foundation of musical performance competitions can be traced back to ancient Greece, where the arts played an important function in the Pythian games of Delphi. The Pythian games can be viewed as a forerunner to the contemporary Olympic Games and involved competition organized at the residence of Apollo, the Greek god of the arts. The competition commemorated the tale of Apollo slaying a python that was terrorizing the local people.

As part of the competition, participants had to display their artistic skills in several ways. Examples included singing a song to Apollo, playing the flute, and other musical tasks. Although the winner of the games did not receive any fiscal advantages, he was given a twig from a laurel plant, which Apollo admired, as well as the respect of the city.

Beginning around the twelfth century AD, the Welsh festival known as Eisteddfod was launched as a means to display the artistic talents of the Welsh people. From its humble beginnings, the competition was restricted to professionally certified individuals as a means of achieving the best criteria possible.

Although the precise date is subject to dispute, the Eisteddfod began in 1176 when Lord Rhys of Deheubarth held an assembly at his castle, to which he invited performers of both musical and literary disciplines to compete. The winner received the prestigious honor of a chair at his table. Since then several different Eisteddfodau have taken place, but one of the largest gatherings was in Caerys in 1568. Awards for the various areas included trophies or other paraphernalia associated with the discipline.

As awareness of Welsh arts declined, the quality of the Eisteddfod depreciated. In 1789 government worker Thomas Jones arranged an Eisteddfod in Corwen, where public artists were allowed to enter the competition. This event increased the awareness of the Eisteddfod to the level that it is today. The competition has even made its way to the United States (Koch 2005, 665).

Another example of artistic competition, the Puy or Pui, was widespread in England and France. Consisting of a religious organization for the expansion of music and poetry, the term draws from the Latin phrase meaning "a place to stand." Puys were mainstays in several English and French cities during the Middle Ages and the Renaissance.

The archetypal Puy was steeped in religious thought and was often dedicated to the Virgin Mary. The participants were held to certain provisions and policies and could be anyone from any social or economic background. The most basic of these events were arranged in close proximity to religious festivities of the Marian feast days, although these developed into poetry competitions and eventually became the focal point of the festivities.

The pinnacle of the French Puy was in the late Middle Ages, when there was an open invitation for contestants in numerous categories, with each following a certain theme and form. The musical category of the Puy contained works arranged for a single melody or for several melodic lines. The winner was often given flowers as a prize, which could be redeemed for money. Other awards included engraved rings and other articles of decoration.

Often a musical award or competition can advance the artistic integrity of a nation or group of people. One example is the Feis Ceoil, which significantly increased the growth of musical talent among the Irish people. The competition dates back to one Mr. T. O'Neill, who wrote to the Dublin-based newspaper the *Evening Telegraph* in the early 1900s, complaining about the lack of attention to Irish music. In response, educator Dr. Annie Patterson and journalist Edward Martyn, to counteract the neglect of musical development in Ireland, first organized the competition in 1897.

The competition included both performance and composition events and was supported by musicians of the day. In the beginning the festival had thirty-two competitions: twelve for composition, six for vocal ensembles, and fourteen for solo performance (the Feis). Many famous Irish men and women have competed in the festival, including singers John McCormack and Anne Murray and even writer James Joyce. The winners are given money or a trophy to celebrate their victory.

In the twentieth and twenty-first centuries, several awards have been given by the recording industry. The archetypal American recording industry award is the Grammy. The Grammy is given to an individual artist, performing ensemble, or producer for accomplishments in the recording industry for a given year.

The Grammy is bestowed by the National Academy of Recording Arts and Sciences, a governing body made up of artists, musicians, producers, recording engineers, and other recording industry figures who have a passion to enhance the professional and personal satisfaction of those involved in the recording industry.

On May 28, 1957, several recording industry professionals met at the Brown Derby Restaurant in Hollywood to discuss plans to form an organization dedicated to the recording arts. Included at this meeting were Sonny Burke of Decca Records, James B. Conklin of Columbia Records, Denis Famon of RCA Victor Records, and others. After several days the committee finalized the name the National Academy of Recording Arts and Sciences, better known as NARAS. In August 1957 the original chapter of NARAS was born in Los Angeles, with Columbia Records executive Paul Weston acting as its first president. Some early members were singer Nat King Cole (1919–1965), composer Henry Mancini (1924–1994), and bandleader Stan Kenton (1912–1979).

The name of the award went through several drafts. One suggestion was "Eddie," after Thomas Edison (1847–1921), the inventor of the gramophone. Taking a cue from Edison's famed invention, the award was eventually named the "Grammy" in 1959.

In its infancy the purpose of the Grammy was to gain recognition for accomplishments in music within the entertainment industry, as the Academy Award had done for the movie industry and as the Emmy did for the television industry. Paul Weston explained: "We feel it's about time the record industry grows up and gets a little recognition for its part in the entertainment industry. The record companies never promote records as a form of entertainment the way movie and TV companies promote themselves" (Mosby 1957, 8).

On May 1, 1959, the first annual Grammy Awards ceremony was held, honoring the recording achievements for music released in 1958. It was held at two locations, the Beverly Hilton in Beverly Hills and the Park Sheraton Hotel in New York City. Since then the Grammy categories have been increased to more than sixty-five, honoring all genres, such as classical, country, jazz, and rock.

Although a trophy is the physical award for being a Grammy winner, past winners have experienced a surge in their music's sales as a result of winning. For example, singer Norah Jones (1979–) saw the sales of her debut album *Come Away from Me* increase by nearly 237 percent after winning "Album of the Year" in 2003.

The Grammy Awards have been met with a fair amount of criticism throughout the years. Record executive Steve Stoute has criticized the importance attached to the Grammy: "Over the course of my 20-year history as an executive in the music business and as the owner of a firm that specializes in in-culture advertising, I have come to the conclusion that the Grammy Awards have clearly lost touch with contemporary popular culture" (Stoute 2011). Stoute's attitude reflects a greater belief that the Grammy Awards no longer celebrate the talent that the recording industry has to offer.

Even musicians have criticized what the Grammy means in contemporary society. Singer Maynard James Keenan (1964–) of the band Tool (1990–present) stated; "I think the Grammys are nothing more than some gigantic promotional machine for the music industry. They cater to a low intellect and they feed the masses. They don't honor the arts or the artist for what he created. It's the music business celebrating itself. That's basically what it's all about" (Gabriella 2002).

Wanting to compete with the Grammy Awards, radio legend Dick Clark (1929–) created the American Music Award in 1973. One of the main differences between the AMA and the Grammy is that whereas the Grammy Awards are awarded based on votes by members of the entertainment industry, the AMA is determined by a poll of music buyers, resulting in a better representation of the viewpoints of the listening public. The AMA nominations are based on physical sales, radio airplay, and social/new media exposure.

Music critics throughout the years have created their own polls and awards for music as a means of getting their voices heard. One such poll is the Pazz & Jop critics poll taken by the New York–based newspaper *The Village Voice*. The poll's name is a play on the words "Jazz & Pop," intended to discourage claims that a certain work is unworthy because it does not fit into a specific category. Because the words "pazz" and "jop" do not exist, voters will concentrate on the actual merits of a work rather than arguing over whether it fits into a particular genre (Doughty 2001).

The poll is compiled every year from the top 10 lists of hundreds of music critics. Beginning in 1971, the poll voted The Who's *Who's Next* album of the year. The poll expanded to include critics in 1979, with singer Ian Dury's (1942–2000) "Hit Me with Your Rhythm Stick" being named the winner. For the poll's first thirty-three years, music critic Robert Christgau was its figurehead; he wrote an essay every year that correlated with that year's list (Christgau 1975).

Although the Pazz & Jop poll has striven to be a different kind of award, it has had its fair share of detractors. Mike Doughty of the *New York Press* has criticized those critics who have participated in the poll: "In the guise of a love of music, you've taken the most beautifully nebulous form of human expression, squeezed it through an asinine points-scoring system specially cooked up for this pointless perennial, and forced it into this baffling, heinous chart system" (Doughty 2001).

Awards in Composition Competitions

Awards and competitions in musical composition date back to European art movements. One of the first was the Prix de Rome. The competition was initially started as a monetary award for students of the arts. Established in 1663 in France, the competition featured young artists competing against each other by showcasing their artistic talents in either painting or sculpting. Beginning in 1803, the competition added music as part of the curriculum.

Within the music portion of the program, students had to display their musical talents by composing both a choral piece and a work developed in the fugue form. If their results were accepted into the competition, they were then commissioned to compose a cantata for solo voices and orchestra, which was to be completed in four weeks.

If chosen as a winner, a student was given the title "Premier Grand Prix de Rome" and was given a stipend by the state to spend a minimum of two years in Rome and another two years in another cultural area. Past winners include Hector Berlioz (1803–1869), Charles Gounod (1818–1893), Georges Bizet (1838–1875), Claude Debussy (1862–1918), and Henri Dutilleux (1916–). Famous participants include Olivier Messiaen (1908–1992), Camille Saint-Saens (1835–1921), and Maurice Ravel (1875–1937), who competed five times. The Prix de Rome was abolished in 1968 by France's then minister of culture, Andre Malraux.

In 1984 industrialist and entrepreneur H. Charles Grawemeyer (1912–1993) established the Grawemeyer Award for Music Composition. The annual prize is given by the University of Louisville as a means of recognizing the "outstanding achievement by a living composer in a large musical genre: choral, orchestral, chamber, electronic, song-cycle, dance, opera, musical theater, extended solo work and more" (Grawemeyer Award n.d.) The initial award was for music, but it has since expanded into other categories such as "Ideas Improving World Order," "Education," "Religion," and "Psychology."

The selection process includes three panels of judges. The initial panel consists of faculty from the University of Louisville, followed by a panel of music professionals, often conductors, performers, and composers, usually including the previous year's winner. The final decision is made by a committee of general music enthusiasts who are interested in new music. The award has most often been awarded to large-scale works, such as symphonies, concerti, and operas. The winner originally was given $150,000, which was increased to $200,000 in 2000. Winners include Harrison Birtwistle (1934–), Witold Lutoslawski (1913–1994), John Corigliano (1938–), John Adams (1947–), and Louis Andriessen (1939–).

The Grawemeyer Award is one of many supporters of music that have used their influence and fiscal power to increase the presence of music throughout society. Another such figure is Joseph Pulitzer, who instituted the "Pulitzer Prize" as a means of celebrating achievements in several media forms, including literature, journalism, and musical composition.

The mission statement of the Pulitzer Prize for music states: "For distinguished musical composition in the larger forms of chamber, orchestral, or choral work, or for an operatic work (including ballet), first performed or published by a composer of established residence in the United States" (Benner 2004). Although Pulitzer had a strong enthusiasm for music, his initial awards did not include one for music. Instead, he established an annual scholarship in music for a student before inaugurating the first Pulitzer Prize in 1943, with the first recipient being composer William Schuman's Secular Cantata no. 2: "A Free Song" for full chorus of mixed voices, with accompaniment of orchestra. Currently, recipients receive a certificate and $10,000.

The Pulitzer Prize's standards have met with a certain amount of criticism. For many years the award was given to classical works and excluded other genres such as jazz and movie scoring. In 1965 composer Duke Ellington (1899–1974) was voted the winner of the Pulitzer Prize, but the Pulitzer Board refused to accept the ruling and decided not to give an award that year. Upon hearing this, Ellington stated, "I'm hardly surprised that my kind of music is still without, let us say, official honor at home. Most Americans still take it for granted that European-based music—classical music, if you will—is the only really respectable kind" (Hentoff 1984, 29).

Even some past recipients have expressed disdain for certain elements of the selection process. Composer Donald Martino (1931–2005) has stated: "If you write music long enough, sooner or later, someone is going to take pity on you and give you the damn thing. It is not always the award for the best piece of the year; it has gone to whoever hasn't gotten it before" (Dyer 2004). Composer Lewis Spratlan (1940–; awarded in 2000) voiced his concern: "The Pulitzer is one of the very few prizes that award artistic distinction in front-edge, risk-taking music. To dilute this objective by inviting . . . musicals and movie scores, no matter how excellent, is to undermine the distinctiveness and capability for artistic advancement" (Dyer 2004).

Beginning in 1996, the Pulitzer Board decided to broaden the definition of its processes "so as to attract the best of a wider range of American music" (Kaplan 2006). Since then several jazz composers have been awarded the prize, including Wynton Marsalis (1961–) for his oratorio *Blood on the Fields* (1997) and Ornette Coleman (1930–) for *Sound Grammar* (2007). The board has also retroactively awarded Pulitzers to composers whom it failed to name in the past, including composer George Gershwin (1898–1937) in 1998 and Ellington in 1999.

Present-day Competitions and Awards

Music competition was forever changed upon the debut of the TV show *American Idol.* The show grew out of the British television program *Pop Idol,* itself based on the Australian program *Popstars,* which was brought over to England by TV producer Nigel Lythgoe (Armstrong 2010). A panel of judges selects singers to audition to compete on live showings of the program. Their performances that will go on, and ultimately the winner, are then selected by the viewing public via telephone or e-mail, giving the voting power completely to the public. The show is augmented by discussing the history of the contestants as well as documenting their lives as the show progresses.

Judge Simon Cowell (1959–) and producer Simon Fuller (1960–) sold the format to the U.S. television network Fox. The show debuted in the summer of 2002 and was an immediate success. With the original panel consisting of the often brazen Cowell, choreographer/dancer Paula Abdul (1962–), and music producer Randy Jackson (1956–), the viewing public was and is easily drawn to the contestants as much as to what the judges have to say about the performances.

The winner of each season receives a major record label deal as well as a management contract. All of the winners prior to season 9 earned a minimum of $1 million in their first year. All the runners-up, as well as some of the other finalists, have received record contracts and high-paying performance opportunities. All of the top 10 finalists earn the opportunity of going on a tour for which the participants may each earn a six-figure sum. *American Idol* is a perfect example of not having to win the top spot to be awarded a career in music and how important exposure is in our current cultural climate (Wyatt 2010).

With the advent of the Internet and other new media enterprises, awards for music have branched out into online environments. An example is The Webby Awards, established in 1997 as a way of celebrating the very best in online content. The Webby Awards include an award for music that is given to music blogs and a special achievement award that has been given to musicians, including LCD Soundsystem, Trent Reznor of Nine Inch Nails, and others.

Awards for music continue to celebrate the output of composers, performers, and music-minded individuals as a means to enhance the art form and the global music community.

See also: Cage, John; Cole, Nat "King"; Ellington, Duke; Gershwin, George; Jones, Norah; Marsalis, Wynton

Official Web Sites:

Grammy Awards: http://www.grammy.com/

Pulitzer Prize for Music: http://www.pulitzer.org/bycat/Music

Webby Award: http://www.webbyawards.com/

Further Reading

Armstrong, Stephen. 2010. "Nice Work for Nasty Nigel Lythgoe." *Guardian,* January 10, 2010. http://www.guardian.co.uk/media/2010/jan/11/nigel-lythgoe-television-dance (accessed October 20, 2011).

Benner, Al. 2004. "Pulitzer Changes." *Composer/USA* (Spring). http://faculty.lsmsa.edu/ABenner/NACUSA/CUSA-Sp04.htm (accessed October 1, 2011).

Christgau, Robert. 1975. "Our Own Critics' Poll." *Village Voice,* January 20.

Dornbrook, Don. 1959. "And Now the Grammy Award." *Milwaukee Journal,* 24 (May): 58.

Doughty, Mike. 2001. "*The Voice*'s Jerky 'Pazz and Jop' Proves That Rock Critics Are Just Failed Writers." *New York Press,* March.

Dyer, Richard. 2004. "Changes to Definition of Pulitzer for Music Spark Dissonance." *Boston Globe,* June 1.

Fuller, Simon. 2011. "Simon Fuller on How 'Idol' Began." *Variety,* May 20. http://www.variety.com/article/VR1118037190?refcatid=14&printerfriendly=true (accessed October 19, 2011).

Gabriella. 2002. "Interview with Maynard James Keenan of Tool." *NY Rock.com.* http://www.nyrock.com/interviews/2002/tool_int.asp (accessed October 8, 2011).

"The Grammy Bump." [2011]. *Washington Post,* [February 11]. http://www.washingtonpost.com/wp-srv/special/artsandliving/the-grammy-bump/ (accessed October 8, 2011).

Grawemeyer Awards Official Website. n.d. "About." http://grawemeyer.org/about/history.html (accessed October 8, 2011).

Hentoff, Nat. 1984. *Jazz Is.* New York: Limelight Editions.

Jackson, John. 1991. *"American Bandstand": Dick Clark and the Making of a Rock 'n' Roll Empire.* New York: Oxford University Press.

Kaplan, Fred. 2006. "Sour Note: When Will the Pulitzer Prize in Music Get It Right?" *Slate Magazine,* April 19. http://www.slate.com/articles/arts/music_box/2006/04/sour_note.html (accessed October 20, 2011).

Koch, John Thomas, ed. 2005. "Eisteddfod." In *Celtic Culture: A Historical Encyclopedia,* 65. Santa Barbara, CA: ABC-CLIO.

Stoute, Steve. 2011. "An Open Letter to Neil Portnow, NARAS and the Grammy Awards." http://www.huffingtonpost.com/steve-stoute/steve-stoute-grammys_b_825377.html (accessed October 14, 2011).

Teviotdale, Elizabeth C. n.d. "Puy [pui]." *Oxford Music Online.* http://www.oxfordmusiconline.com.queens.ezproxy.cuny.edu:2048/subscriber/article/grove/music/22580 (accessed September 31, 2011).

Topping, Seymour. n.d. "History of the Pulitzer Prize." http://www.pulitzer.org/historyofprizes. Retrieved September 31, 2011.

Wyatt, Edward. 2010. " 'Idol' Winners: Not Just Fame but Big Bucks." *New York Times,* February 23.

Eric Wendell

B

The B-52s (Active 1976–Present)

Dubbed the "World's Greatest Party Band," the B-52s (originally B-52's) has provided entertainment and energizing dance music to audiences since 1976. The band's distinctive mixture of post-punk, new wave, rock 'n' roll, pop rock, and electronica, combined with clear vocals, compelling rhythms, creative songwriting, and memorable music videos like "Love Shack" have solidified the group as a uniquely American institution. The thrift-shop clothing style and trailer park chic that characterize the band's kitschy appearance only add to its allure.

The B-52s originated in Athens, Georgia, when five friends—Fred Schneider, Kate Pierson, Keith Strickland, Cindy Wilson, and her brother Ricky Wilson—decided to form a group after an impromptu jam session that followed dinner and drinks at a Chinese restaurant. The group had little formal musical training. Ricky suggested the band's unusual name, which was southern slang for a large beehive hairstyle that resembled the nose cone of the B-52 aircraft.

The band's first performance, on Valentine's Day in 1977, was soon followed by success with its first singles, "Rock Lobster" and "52 Girls." The debut album *The B-52's* (1979) peaked at number fifty-two on the *Billboard* 200 chart. *Wild Planet* (1980) followed, with the band's first electronic drum machine experiments and the popular single "Private Idaho." *Mesopotamia* (1982), produced by David Byrne of the Talking Heads, and *Whammy!* (1983) continued the band's successes.

While the band was recording *Bouncing off the Satellites* (1986), tragedy struck. Ricky Wilson died from HIV/AIDs-related illness. The remaining band members, who were too distraught to tour and promote the album, decided to take a hiatus from their musical careers. When they reunited, they recorded *Cosmic Thing* (1989). Singles released from this album became immediate hits on college campuses and in music venues across the country: "Channel Z," "Love Shack," and "Roam." "Love Shack" became the band's first top 40 hit, and the music video received significant airplay on MTV and other television music channels. The album *Good Stuff* followed in 1992, the only album that did not include Cindy Wilson, who was taking a break from the band at the time.

Over the years band members have performed with other notable musicians and groups. Kate Pierson sang with R.E.M. on the single "Shiny, Happy People"; Cindy Wilson and Kate Pierson sang with the Ramones on the song "Chop Suey"; and Fred Schneider provided vocals for the Foo Fighters' cover of "Planet Claire." Keith, Fred, and Kate appeared as the BC-52s in *The Flintstones* movie (1994), and the band's music has been used in Buick car advertisements and other commercial venues, solidifying its position in mainstream American culture.

In 2008 the band dropped the apostrophe from its name and released its first original album in sixteen years, *Funplex.* The dance-oriented album debuted at number eleven on the U.S. *Billboard* charts.

See also: R.E.M.

Further Reading

Martini, Della. 1990. *The B-52s.* New York: Wise Publications.

Sexton, Mats. 2002. *The B-52's Universe: The Essential Guide to the World's Greatest Party Band.* Glasgow, UK: Plan B Books.

Jacqueline Edmondson

Members of the B-52s, from left, Cindy Wilson, Fred Schneider, and Kate Pierson, perform during the TV Land Awards in New York City, April 14, 2012. (AP Photo/Jason DeCrow)

The B-Side

According to popular adages, there are "two sides to every story" and "two sides to every coin." There are also two sides to every record, the "A-side" and the "B-side." These designations originated in popular music with 78 rpm shellac records and became more significant as formats evolved to 45-rpm seven-inch vinyl. The "B-side" was also known as "the flip" or "b/w," an abbreviation for "backed with." Initially, "taking sides" was not an issue. Radio station programmers had little preference, as disc jockeys played songs on either face of the record. In the view of Jim Dawson and Steve Propes, coauthors of *45 RPM: The History, Heroes, and Villains of a Pop Music Revolution,* "The B-side's job is to complement the A-side" (2003, 72).

In the early 1950s, with the advent of the 45-rpm record, "singles" became the standard. Unlike in the previous era, when there was often more than one song to a side, the conventional record release now contained two songs, one on each side of a record. Initially most record labels randomly assigned which song was the A-side and which was the B-side. As a result, several artists had "double-sided hits" when both songs made the national sales charts. Among the more notable were Elvis Presley's "Don't Be Cruel"/"Hound Dog" and Ritchie Valens's "Donna"/"LaBamba."

By the 1960s, perhaps one of the most prolific periods for hit singles in popular music, the terms "A-side" and "B-side" had become more common vinyl vernacular, and they were more differentiated. The A-side was synonymous with "airplay." It was the song the record company wanted radio stations to play; the hopeful hit, the catchy tune that would also help promote the artist's 33⅓ long-playing album. The record's reverse side, the B-side, for the most part became the disc deposit for a comparably "inferior" recording. Materials commonly found on the B-side included nonalbum tracks, "throwaway" songs that may have been considered stylistically unsuitable for an album, experimental or instrumental songs, acoustic or a cappella versions, and alternate renditions of the A-side. The B-side also provided a three-minute platform of exposure and potential income for songwriters looking for a breakthrough. For example, in 1967, Howard Kaylan and Mark Volman of The Turtles selflessly selected then unknown songwriter Warren Zevon's song, "Like the Seasons," as the B-side of the band's number one hit "Happy Together."

Symbolically, and perhaps idealistically, the B-side offered a metaphor for musicians, a place of possibility. The "flip side" was an outlet for conceiving and dividing their work, a line of demarcation, a detachment or diversion from the commercially viable art, airplay, and industry expectations that accompanied the A-side. There was little to lose and much to gain from the grooves of least resistance that were the B-side.

Not all B-sides were rejects or remixes. Some would occasionally catch the attention of a radio station music or program director or a maverick disc jockey and receive airplay, though not as routinely in the rotation as the designated single side. At Chicago's legendary station WLS-890 AM, such record releases were billed as "TSWs"—two-sided winners. For a generation of listeners, record consumers, and collectors, these 45s represented a "two for one" bargain. Discovering a three-minute gem or curiosity on a B-side was an iconic era experience analogous with artifact expeditions: digging for the cool prize in a box of Cracker Jack or opening a nickel pack of baseball cards to find a favorite player and get a powdery stick of pink bubblegum.

Popular B-sides frequently originated from bands that produced strings of chartable songs in assembly line fashion in the 1960s hit factory, among them The Byrds' ("All I Really Want to Do"/"I'll Feel a Whole Lot Better" and "Turn, Turn Turn"/"She Don't Care About Time") and Creedence Clearwater Revival's ("Down on the Corner"/"Fortunate Son"). And there was The Beatles' remarkable record run, twenty-seven number one songs during an eight-year period, from their first single in 1962, "Love Me Do," to "The Long and Winding Road" in 1970. At one point in the mid-1960s the Fab Four held the first five spots on the U.S. Hot 100 singles charts. Just as their melodic A-sides were abundant and automatic hits, their B-sides were bountiful bonuses that underscore the breadth and enduring magnificence of the Lennon/McCartney songbook.

The accumulation of B-sides that appeared on the U.S. and UK versions of The Beatles' singles remains a pop treasure trove: "P.S. I Love You," "Thank You Girl," "She's a Woman," "This Boy," "I Saw Her Standing There," "Things We Said Today," "I Should Have Known Better," "I'm a Loser," "Baby's in Black," "I Don't Want to Spoil the Party," "Rock and Roll Music," "Act Naturally," "I'm Down," "Yes It Is," "You Can't Do That," "Rain," and "Day Tripper." During the second half of the decade, song symmetry between the sides of Beatles singles was standard: "Yellow Submarine"/"Eleanor Rigby," "Penny Lane"/"Strawberry Fields Forever," "Hey Jude"/"Revolution," "Get Back"/"Don't Let Me Down," and "Come Together"/"Something." Even songs that The Beatles wrote but did not record had a B-side knack. "Bad to Me," recorded by Billy J. Kramer, reached number nine as the flip side of his hit "Little Children," which charted at number seven in 1964. Whether amused or insulted by the B-side designation, The Beatles preferred the label "double A-side" for their two-sided singles.

Beyond The Beatles, the list of B-sides that eclipsed their A-sides during the 45 era is significant. "Earth Angel" (The Penguins), "The Twist" (Hank Ballard and the Midnighters), "Louie Louie" (Richard Berry), "You Send Me" (Sam Cooke), "Rockin' Robin" (Bobby Day), "Hushabye" (The Mystics), "The Wanderer" (Dion), "The Lion Sleeps Tonight" (The Tokens), "Save the Last Dance for Me" (The Drifters), "Surfin' Safari" (The Beach Boys), "To Sir with Love" (Lulu), "Incense and Peppermints" (Strawberry Alarm Clock), "Signs" (Five Man Electrical Band), and "Na Na Hey Hey Kiss Him Good Bye" (Steam) are among hit songs that were originally slated to be B-sides. Likewise, in 1971 Rod Stewart's signature song, "Maggie May," began as the flip side to "Reason to Believe," the first single from his album *Every Picture Tells a Story.* "Maggie May" transformed the single from minor hit to sustaining chart topper, as it reached and remained at number one in the United States and UK for five weeks. Whether because of record executives' inability to recognize hits or savvy, bored, curious, or influential disc jockeys turning an A-side over determined to design their own playlists, these B-sides were converted from backside tagalong tunes to chart climbers. To counter the side swiping, producer Phil Spector routinely put instrumental jams with obscure titles on the B-sides of singles to assure that disc jockeys would play only the intended hit sides.

The rock 'n' roll B-side began to recede as early as the late 1970s, with KISS's "Beth" among the last "surprise" flip-side hits in 1976. The B-side, or "flip," became widely viewed as an inconvenience to record companies because of additional royalty fees and as potential competition to the hit side. As music formats continued to downsize and digitalize, the A-side/B-side dichotomy gradually diminished. The advent of the cassette and compact disc singles in the 1980s foreshadowed the imminent obsolescence of the B-side. Cassettes briefly matched the vinyl arrangement of a song per side, but maxi singles with more than two songs became the music marketplace preference.

By the early 1980s the B-side was used primarily as a marketing ploy geared to the predominantly album-oriented audience. Record companies employed the same strategy they had used in the 1960s with The Beatles, The Who, and Bob Dylan, placing songs on B-sides that were unavailable anywhere else. A few major artists such as John Mellencamp and Bruce Springsteen remained faithful to the B-side tradition by routinely including "previously unavailable" songs on the flip sides of their numerous hit singles during the decade. The Springsteen B-sides were original compositions. For example, "Shut Out the Light" on the flip side of "Born in the U.S.A." and "Pink Cadillac" from "Dancing in the Dark" were nonalbum tracks. Mellencamp's B-sides were predominantly cover versions ("Pretty Ballerina," "Shama Lama Ding Dong," "Under the Boardwalk") and acoustic renditions of his own songs ("Small Town," "Little Pink Houses," "Jackie Brown"). Attractive picture sleeve packaging further enhanced the appeal of these vinyl 45s. The songs eventually resurfaced in other convenient collector configurations such as the box set (Springsteen's *Tracks* [1998]) and the compilation (Mellencamp's *Rough Harvest* (1999). In 1984 seventeen of *Billboard*'s top 40 singles, including songs by Madonna, R.E.M., and the Bangles, had nonalbum B-sides, ranging from remixes to instrumentals, often of the A-side. Warner Brothers employed the strategy so extensively with its releases that it was able to compile non-LP sides by artists such as Prince, the Pretenders, and the Talking Heads into two albums, *Attack of the Killer B's* and *Revenge of the Killer B's.*

In the 1990s, with the vinylogical time clock ticking as the compact disc replaced vinyl and cassette as the dominant music medium and digital downloading was rapidly developing, the physical flip-side distinction of the B-side teetered on the brink of extinction, a casualty of progress, both technological and economic. However, the term "B-side" persists, its meaning and application slightly modified in the music marketplace. Not only has "B-side" been adapted into a common referent to "bonus" tracks on CD singles and EPs, it continues to be a familiar catchphrase loosely linked with "previously unreleased materials" such as demos, rarities, outtakes, alternate versions, and other nonalbum tracks. The rare recordings are commonly compiled for collections and multidisc anthologies that attract curious consumers and have profit potential that appeals to record labels. For artists, the projects provide an opportunity to revisit their vaults and versions of their songs. "B-sides and rarities" has become a music market standard and distinct record subgenre. Nick Cave, Moby, Cake, Smashing Pumpkins, Pixies, Cure, Cowboy Junkies, Sonic Youth, Deftones, Steve Earle, Tori Amos, Prince, and Sarah McLachlan are among the countless artists who have released the requisite record of B-side material. Though not marketed purely as B-sides, other career-spanning box set collections such as the Bob Dylan Bootleg Series and Neil Young *Archives* volumes and special editions such as Bruce Springsteen's *The Promise: The Darkness on the Edge of Town Story* are brimming with characteristic B-side recordings.

As the digital mode continues to develop, deepen, and dominate, the B-side's parallel progression accumulates a hint of irony. The noncommercial nature of the material that was a defining characteristic of the B-side became a primary marketing tool and a commercially viable selling point. The music industry engaged in a constant cycle of customizing, expanding, and upgrading records. Following the involuntary vinyl replacement revolution, fans were more easily swayed to buy recordings for a second, if not third time, if their reward was a visit to an artist's music vault. The early Elvis Costello albums—*My Aim Is True, This Year's Model, Blood and Chocolate*—are representative of an artist's catalog being remastered and reissued, often by archival label Rhino Records, with standard repackaging that includes a (B)onus disc of demos, rarities, and live and alternative takes transformed from their original neglected status on the B-side. The B-side staple, cover versions, were also common content of the enhanced packaging.

The B-side concept has been adapted into anniversary editions commemorating debuts such as Counting Crows' *August and Everything After,* classics like *Born to Run* and *Thriller,* Lucinda Williams's masterpiece *Car Wheels on a Gravel Road,* and the long-awaited completion of Brian Wilson's *Smile.* Artists' discographies expanded with multiple greatest hits and essential collections. Like sound track snowflakes, no two were exactly alike, as each contained "previously unavailable" songs.

Even box sets suggested that "definitive" is fleeting. In 2001 Columbia released *18 Tracks,* "highlights" from Springsteen's B-side box *Tracks.* The condensed album contained three songs bearing the B-side badge and bait: "previously unavailable." The trio of tunes were conspicuously absent from *Tracks*' comprehensive four discs. *18 Tracks* suggested a new niche, "the B-side of B-sides," and foreshadowed a maximum marketing strategy and B-side branding. The Byrds' *There Is a Season* (2006) reprised its box set from 1990 and a number of the band's greatest hits compilations in between, including *20 Essential Tracks from the Boxed Set.* The only distinguishable difference between The Byrds' boxes was an impressive deal breaker, a hard-core collector appealing DVD of the group's early television performances. The Band's epic *A Musical History* (2005) provides a five-disc encore to its previous three-disc box *Across the Great Divide* (1994), suggesting that Robbie Robertson and Levon Helm located more tapes in the basement. Artists themselves fostered the B-side revival and brand via music and video downloads available exclusively at their Web sites.

"Deluxe," "limited," "exclusive," "special," "expanded," and "legacy" were among the labels affixed to editions of records. The B-side brand and packaging became a confounding constant and seductive siren song for music consumers, particularly when bonus materials commonly showed up in special editions months after the initial release, or when retailers such as Target, Walmart, and Best Buy each had exclusive editions of a record. Music consumers were confronted with a deluxe dilemma.

By 2004, in the midst of the one-sided compact disc and digital downloads of the iPod age, the technological advances that contributed to the gradual fading of the B-side in its purest form further reconfigured the flip-side concept into a visual variation—the dual disc. Designed to provide multimedia music consumers with an alternative to the conventional CD, the dual disc was a slightly higher priced ($1.50–$2.50), enhanced package that basically converted the B-Side into a DVD. This technological twin contained the familiar B-side "bonus" trait incentives for music consumers. Common content on the DVD included the entire album in higher quality stereophonic and/or surround sound, documentaries, interviews, music videos, footage from live performances, studio recording sessions, artist discography, and Web site links. Record companies hoped that the dual disc format would eventually replace the CD as the preferred medium in the music marketplace. By the end of 2005 there were approximately 200 dual disc titles, with sales reaching over two million units. Some major titles, such as Bruce Springsteen's *Devils and Dust* (2005), were released exclusively in the dual disc format.

Although the dual disc did not sustain the B-side in its purest form, the pervasiveness of remastered reissues; special, deluxe, and limited editions; multiple versions of greatest hits; "essential" collections; and box sets was innately, conceptually "dual discs." The B-side—whether viewed as an authentic aural artifact, a brand, bonus, betrayal, or downloading backlash—endures in the music marketplace as a flip-side phenomenon, cultural catchphrase, and icon of an era, reinvented, reconfigured and repackaged from its spinning 45-rpm roots.

See also: Dylan, Bob; KISS; Madonna; Mellencamp, John; Presley, Elvis; Prince; Producers; R.E.M.; Springsteen, Bruce; Talking Heads; Vinyl Records; Young, Neil

Further Reading

Dawson, Jim, and Steve Propes. 2003. *45 RPM: The History, Heroes, and Villains of a Pop Music Revolution.* San Francisco: Backbeat Books.

Plasketes, George. 2009. *B-Sides, Undercurrents and Overtones: Peripheries to Popular in Music, 1960 to the Present.* Surry, UK: Ashgate Publishing.

George Plasketes

Badu, Erykah (1971–)

Grammy Award–winning Erykah Badu is known as the First Lady or Queen of neo-soul, a genre that emerged in the late 1990s and combines soul and R&B, but also infuses different rhythms and sounds from hip-hop, funk, fusion, and other music to create a more unconventional sound. Badu has rejected being identified with a single genre, and her body of work as a singer-songwriter and producer reflects numerous influences and innovations.

Born Erica Abi Wright in Dallas, Texas, Badu attended the Booker T. Washington High School for the Performing Arts in Dallas before studying theater at Grambling State University in Louisiana. Her actress mother, Kolleen Wright, is credited with introducing Badu to a range of music when she was a child and encouraging her interest in the performing arts. Badu began to perform for audiences, singing and dancing as a young child, and she turned her full attention to music in 1993 when she joined a group called Apple Tree with her cousin. The group did not work out, and Badu moved to New York, where Kedar Massenberg, who was managing R&B/soul artist D'Angelo (1974–), noticed her and asked her to open for D'Angelo's show in Texas. Massenberg liked what he heard and helped Badu secure a record deal with Universal.

The year 1997 was an eventful one for Badu. Her first album, *Baduizm* (1997), shared her personal philosophies on life, which are influenced by African ideas, the Nation of Islam, and African American folklore. The album won two Grammy Awards: Best R&B Vocal Performance and Best R&B Album. Wearing her signature head wraps early in her career, Badu's performances were memorable for her cerebral, creative, and often eccentric approaches to music. *Entertainment Weekly* named her the best new artist of the year. Her first child was born on the same day her second album, *Live* (1997), was released, and it went double-platinum. Badu then took some time away from her career to be with her son.

Badu acted in the *Blues Brothers 2000* film and in *The Cider House Rules* (1999), in which she played the character Rose Rose. She also had a role in *House of D* (2005) and appeared in the documentaries *Before the Music Dies* (2006), which critiqued the American music industry and its commercialization, and *Dave Chappelle's Block Party* (2006).

In 2000 Badu won a second Grammy for her rap with The Roots in "You Got Me." That same year, she released her second studio album, *Mama's Gun* (2000), followed by *Worldwide Underground* (2003) and *New Amerykah Part I: 4th World War* (2008), which was a political statement about social problems in the

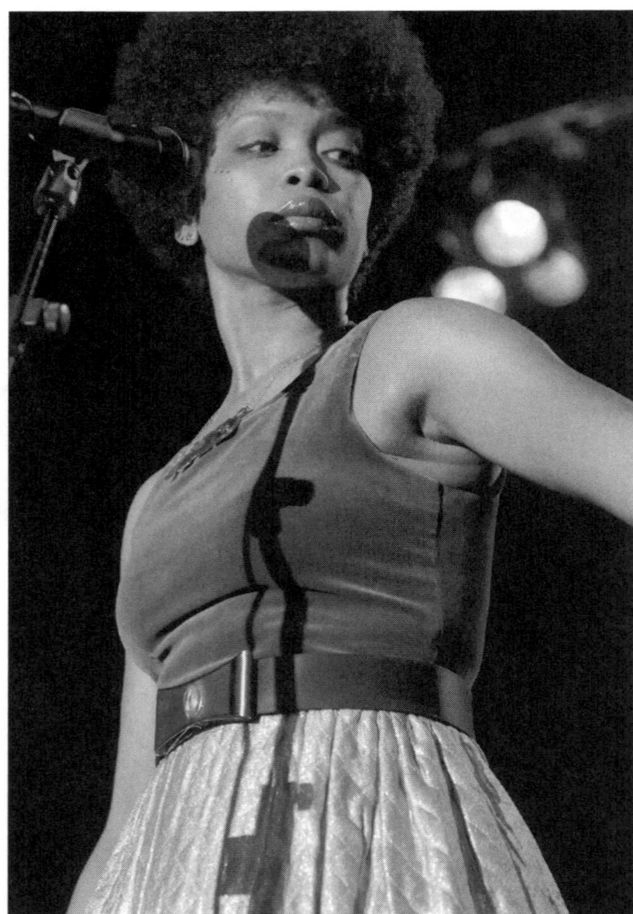

Erykah Badu performs at the Hollywood Palladium in September, 2009. (Aaron Settipane/Dreamstime.com)

United States, including poverty, urban violence, and U.S. involvement in war. *New Amerykah Part Two: Return of the Ankh* (2010) contained songs with more personal themes. The album had three hit singles, including "Window Seat," which raised some controversy for Badu when she filmed the video in Dallas, Texas. Badu walked down a street in Dallas, shedding her clothes, until she was completely naked at the site where John F. Kennedy was assassinated. When a bullet shot sounds in the video, Badu crumbles to the ground and appears to be shot. Badu explained that her video was a statement against groupthink and not a criticism of Kennedy, whom she claimed to admire. Badu was fined $500 for public nudity.

Badu launched her own label, Control FreaQ Records, in 2005. She has three children: her oldest son, Seven Sirius Benjamin, born in 1997 to Badu and rapper André 3000 (formerly known as Dré); daughter Puma Sabti Curry, born in 2004 to Badu and rapper the D.O.C.; and her youngest child, daughter Mars Merkaba Thedford, born in 2009 to Badu and rapper Jay Electronica. Badu has been an activist through her nonprofit organization B.L.I.N.D. (Beautiful Love Incorporated Non-Profit Development), which is intended to bring social change through artistic and cultural efforts. She is a vegan and speaks openly about her dietary choices.

See also: African American Women's Influences on American Music; Funk and Postpsychedelic Funk; Fusion; Hip-Hop; R&B; Social Causes of Musicians; Soul

Official Web Site: http://www.erykah-badu.com/

Further Reading

McIver, Joel. 2003. *Erykah Badu: The First Lady of Neo-Soul.* London: Sanctuary.

O'Brien, Lucy. 2002. *She Bop II: The Definitive History of Women in Rock, Pop, and Soul.* New York: Continuum.

Jacqueline Edmondson

Baez, Joan (1941–)

Joan Chandos Baez once described herself as a humanist, pacifist, and folksinger, in that order. She has a deep passion for human rights and social justice and a longstanding commitment to nonviolence. Baez became a public figure in the late 1950s when she took the stage to sing folk music. She is known for her distinct soprano voice and unique finger-picking style on the guitar. Influenced early in her career by Pete Seeger (1919–) and Bob Dylan (1941–), she learned to combine music with her political agenda. Baez used her public image to bring attention to civil rights issues, human rights violations, and environmental causes, even when it meant risking her own personal safety and her musical career.

Baez was born in New York City to Albert Baez, a Mexican American, and Joan Bridge Baez, a Scottish American. Raised in the Quaker religion, Baez and her sisters Pauline and Mimi (1945–2001), who was also a folksinger and activist, learned from an early age to advocate for peace. The Baez family moved frequently, living in many U.S. cities and abroad, because Albert worked in health care and was involved with UNESCO.

After the Baez family moved from California to Boston in 1958, Joan began to play her guitar and sing folk music in coffeehouses. She was a regular at Club 47, and after her 1959 performance at the Newport Folk Festival in front of thirteen thousand people, her popularity soared. Baez began her recording career in 1960. Her first three albums went gold: *Joan Baez* (1960), *Joan Baez 2* (1961), and *Joan Baez in Concert Part 1* (1962).

Bob Dylan listened to Baez's music and was among her fans. The two met in 1961 in Greenwich Village, and a relationship developed between them. Baez invited

Joan Baez

Artists Who Influenced Joan Baez	Artists Influenced by Joan Baez
Bob Dylan	Bob Dylan
Marian Anderson	Bonnie Raitt
Odetta	Emily Lou Harris
Pete Seeger	Joni Mitchell
	Judy Collins

Singer, songwriter, and political activist Joan Baez performs during a protest against the Vietnam War, London, May 29, 1965. Baez has been called the queen of folk music and epitomized the flower child image of the 1960s through her music, dress, and outspoken involvement in pacifist causes. (Bettmann/Corbis)

Dylan, who was not as well known as she was at the time, to join her onstage at the 1963 Newport Folk Festival. Baez, who advocated for civil rights and school integration in the south alongside Martin Luther King Jr., also performed with Dylan during the March on Washington in 1963. Although their personal relationship was relatively short-lived, their influence on each other's music was long-standing. Baez later wrote two songs for Dylan, "To Bobby" (1972) and "Diamonds and Rust" (1975).

As the Vietnam War raged, Baez worked tirelessly to help young men avoid the draft. She was jailed several times for her activism, and during one of her arrests she met David Harris, a draft-resister and activist. The two married in March 1968, and just over a year later Harris was imprisoned for fifteen months for refusing to be drafted into the military. Their son Gabriel was born while Harris was in jail. Their marriage ended soon after his release.

Baez performed in George Harrison (1943–2001) and Ravi Shankar's (1920–) Concert for Bangladesh in 1971, and she traveled the world to share her music and advocate for human rights. In 1972 she spent eleven days in Hanoi, North Vietnam, surviving the Christmas Bombings, in which over sixteen hundred people were killed.

In the 1980s and 1990s Baez performed at Live Aid and on behalf of Amnesty International. She traveled to Czechoslovakia, where she met with Vaclav Havel and performed for thousands of people. Havel later claimed that Baez influenced the Velvet Revolution, a nonviolent revolution that resulted in the overthrow of the communist government in that country. She also performed in Sarajevo during the Yugoslav civil war.

Baez continues to record and tour more than fifty years after she first took the stage in the coffeehouses of Boston, and she continues to take on human rights projects, including advocating for gay and lesbian rights, protesting the U.S. invasion of Iraq in 2003, and joining those trying to fight poverty and environmental problems. She has recorded thirty-four studio and live albums, eight of which are gold, and nineteen compilations. Baez received seven Grammy nominations, and in 2007 she was honored with the Grammy Lifetime Achievement Award.

See also: Awards and Prizes for Music; Coffee Shops and American Music; Dylan, Bob; Folk Music; Odetta; Seeger, Pete; Social Causes of Musicians

Official Web Site: http://joanbaez.com/contents.html

Further Reading

Baez, J. 2009. *And a Voice to Sing With.* New York: Simon & Schuster.

Baez, J. 1968. *Daybreak.* New York: The Dial Press.

Hajdu, David. 2011. *Positively 4th Street: The Lives and Times of Joan Baez, Bob Dylan, Mimi Baez Fariña and Richard Fariña.* New York: Picador.

Jacqueline Edmondson

Banjo

The banjo is a plucked string instrument used in both popular and vernacular (or "folk") music traditions around the world. It was developed by enslaved Africans in the Caribbean during the seventeenth and eighteenth centuries and arrived in North America by the 1730s. The banjo was exclusively identified as an African and African American instrument through the turn of the nineteenth century. In the 1830s European Americans took the banjo and made it one of the central instruments in blackface minstrelsy, America's first major popular music form. Since that time the banjo has been widely used in a variety of music both in the United States and internationally, although it is frequently associated with American old-time, bluegrass, and country music genres.

African and African American Origins

Period writers consistently cite the banjo as having African and African American origins. These claims cover references to gourd-bodied, plucked string instruments in the Caribbean and later in North America with the expansion of the slave trade. Throughout the Caribbean and the northern port regions of South America, European colonists, settlers, and travelers reported many names for the instrument, including *bangil, banshaw, banjar,* and *banza* (Epstein 2003, 359–362). In 1687 Sir Hans Sloane observed enslaved Africans in Jamaica playing "strum-strumps," describing them as an "imitation of Lutes, made of small Gourds fitted with Necks, strung with Horse hairs, or the peeled stalks of climbing Plants or Withs" (Sloane 1707, 68–69).

The earliest-known reference to the banjo in North America comes from John Peter Zenger's March 7, 1736, edition of the *New-York Weekly Journal,* in which a writer described an African American musician tuning and playing his "banger" in preparation for a holiday event ("The Spy" 1736, 1). Subsequent observations of the banjo accompany descriptions in runaway slave ads, newspapers, books and diaries, and by the 1790s, artistic renderings. Other North American references to the banjo before 1840 appear as far north as Pennsylvania and throughout the South (Gura and Bollman 1999, 13–14; Conway 1995, 61). In the Caribbean and North America, period documentation generally describes or depicts the banjo in use with various percussion instruments to support dancing and singing.

Collectively, these numerous descriptions, depictions, and at least two surviving instruments provide insight into how some early banjos were built. In general, they had drum-like bodies made from a hollowed-out gourd or sometimes a calabash. An animal hide sound table (also known as a *head*) was tacked into place over the opened part of the gourd. A neck was inserted through additional openings at either end of the gourd body. The exposed upper end of the neck (the part the player can see) extended out from the body in the form of a flat fingerboard like a guitar neck. The lower end of the neck (the part not visible to the player) was narrower and protruded through the opposite end of the body. On the upper part of the neck, tuning pegs held the strings in place on a *peg head.* The strings then ran down the playing surface of the neck and were suspended above the head with a carved bridge held in place by the strings. In some cases a tailpiece was attached to the small part of the neck protruding from the lower end of the body and used to anchor the strings. These early instruments most commonly (but not exclusively) included four strings—three long strings running the full length of the instrument and one short thumb string that stopped at a midpoint on the neck between the gourd body and top of the neck on the side closest to the player's chest. Examples of this type of construction include Captain John Gabriel Stedman's 1770s depiction and description of a "creole-bania" in Suriname, South America, and South Carolina slaveholder and amateur artist John Rose's painting *The Old Plantation* (ca. 1785–1795) (Price and Price 1992, 278–279; Shames 2010, 50).

The Banjo in the Nineteenth Century

By the 1820s and 1830s European American observation of the banjo had moved beyond mere associations with African American music and culture; the banjo was appropriated as part of the rise of American blackface minstrelsy. Minstrelsy was a popular form of entertainment largely centered on European American performers using caricatures of African American racial identity as a masking device. Performers created dark complexions by applying burnt cork to their faces, wearing wigs and exaggerated clothing, and attempting to speak in dialects based on their misperceptions of African American language patterns. Minstrelsy combined these misrepresentations with traditions of European and European American music and culture to express contradictory beliefs regarding race, gender, class, politics, competition, and masculinity, and to portray sexual and domestic marginalization of women (Mahar 1999, 1–8). Here the banjo was used with the violin, rhythm bones (percussion castanets typically made from animal ribs),

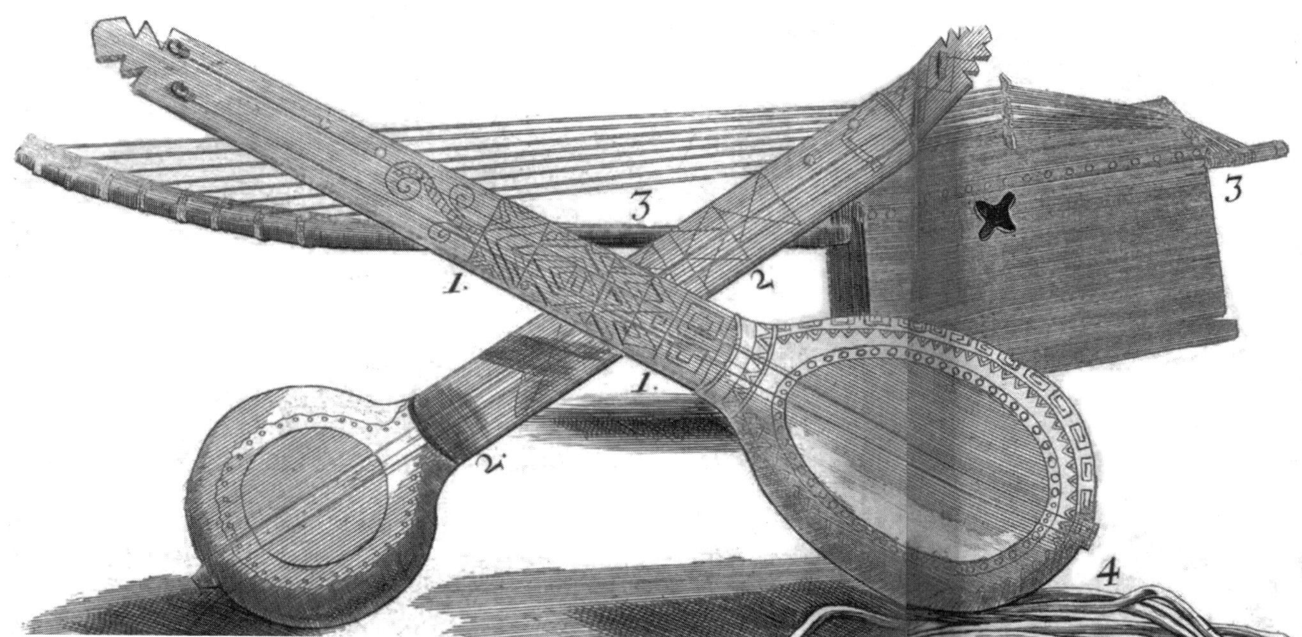

Strum-strumps, illustration by Sir Hans Sloane. (Sloane, Hans. *A Voyage to the Islands Madera, Barbados, Nieves, S. Christophers and Jamaica . . .* 1707)

tambourine, and other instruments such as flutes, fifes, accordions, and guitars.

Joel Walker Sweeney (1810–1860) was the first person to popularize the banjo's use in early minstrelsy. He learned how to play and build banjos from African Americans in and around his home in Appomattox, Virginia. From 1836 through the 1850s Sweeney performed and toured with the banjo throughout the urban Northeast; in the South; and in England, Scotland, and Ireland (Carlin 2007, 163–166). By 1843 minstrelsy became a full evening's entertainment, and the banjo was a common musical fixture in performances by groups like the Virginia Minstrels, Christy's Minstrels, and in the hands of many other professional and nonprofessional musicians (see Schreyer 2007).

Broadened awareness of the banjo in minstrelsy led to the publication of banjo instruction books, advertisements for teachers offering services to students, and continuous innovations in banjo construction. For example, the gourd banjo became a blueprint for commercially manufactured banjos, especially in the Northeast and Upper South (Gura and Bollman 1999, 43–48). In the 1840s and 1850s builders like James Ashborn of Wolcottville, Connecticut, and William E. Boucher Jr. of Baltimore, Maryland, were making five-string banjos (four long strings and one short thumb string) with wooden hoops instead of gourds (Gura and Bollman 1999, 5). The necks were carved and shaped to help improve intonation as musicians played in higher positions on the fingerboard of the neck. In addition to using tacks, an increasing number of builders used alternate methods for attaching the head to the body. One such method consisted of two metal hoops (a *flesh hoop* and a *tension hoop*) and hardware (a series of *hooks, shoes,* and *nuts*). The flesh hoop was used to fit the head over the wooden body. The tension hoop, used in conjunction with the hardware, was placed above the flesh hoop to tighten the head against the body. The hooks were hung over the tension hoop, inserted through the shoes fixed on the side of the body, and tightened with the nuts.

This commercialized form of the banjo also became known internationally in places such as England, Japan, Australia, and South Africa. In England players and builders distinguished the banjo from its American counterparts by uniquely innovating the instrument with additional bass strings, short thumb strings, and building materials (Winans and Kaufman 1994, 10). In the mid-1850s, Commodore Matthew Perry introduced the banjo to Japanese audiences with blackface minstrel performances given by American crewmembers on the deck of the USS *Powhatan* (Roxworthy 2008, 27–28). Because of well-established trade routes, Australians became involved with both American and English banjo traditions through blackface performances in the 1850s (Carlin 2007, 84–85). Blackface performance and the banjo were also featured in South Africa as early as 1865 and persisted throughout the nineteenth and twentieth centuries (Cockrell 1987, 419).

After the American Civil War (1861–1865) commercial manufacturers, musicians, and innovators in the

Detail of folk artist John Rose's *The Old Plantation*, ca. 1785–1795. (MPI/Getty Images)

United States worked to distinguish the banjo from its association with African Americans and blackface minstrelsy. By the 1870s and 1880s they were increasingly marketing the banjo as a woman's parlor instrument, an instrument appropriate for formal concert settings, and to the growing number of urban music clubs (Linn 1991, 5–36). For example, in the 1880s Philadelphia businessman Samuel Swain Stewart (1855–1898) sought to "elevate" the banjo through strong public outreach; innovating the construction of the instrument; and promoting specific artists, instrument types, and music instruction (Gura and Bollman 1999, 124–140). Other like-minded competitors of this time period included J. H. Buckbee and the Dobson brothers of New York, A. C. Fairbanks and William A. and Frank Cole of Boston, and Lyon and Healy and J. B. Schall of Chicago (Linn 1991, 9).

Late nineteenth-century banjos generally continued to exhibit the five-string configuration, but were more streamlined and mechanized in their production. A combination of both wood and metal parts—for example, wooden hoops with spun-over metal rims—enhanced the sound. Manufacturers added *frets* (metal wire, as on guitars) and other types of flush inlays to the fingerboard of the neck to improve a player's intonation and precision of pitch. Another innovation during this period was the addition of a *tone ring,* a metal ring that rested between the body of the banjo and the head, altering the sound of the banjo (Gura and Bollman 1999, 8). More expensive banjos were also endowed with ornamentation (inlay, marquetry, and carving) that further transformed the instrument into a visual work of art.

To maintain the banjo's popularity with changing public tastes in music, manufacturers adapted the ways they built their instruments. For example, with the popularity of the mandolin in the United States by the 1890s, banjos were built with necks that incorporated the eight-string arrangement of the mandolin (Linn 1991, 83–84). Builders also made banjos with six-string, guitar-style necks. Still other banjos were built to reflect the sound qualities associated with instruments like the string bass, cello, and piccolo, as well as small-scale instruments such as the ukulele (Linn 1991, 12, 84).

The Banjo in the Twentieth and Twenty-First Centuries

By the turn of the twentieth century, evolving playing techniques affected banjo construction as musicians moved from sounding the strings with their fingers to holding, plucking, and strumming banjos with a flat pick or *plectrum.* These plectrum banjos—with the short fifth string removed—provided players with a different kind of musical flexibility for the theater, vaudeville, ragtime, and jazz (Linn 1991, 83). From the mid-1910s through the end of the 1920s another four-string version of the banjo—the *tango* or *tenor* banjo—was popular in dance music. This banjo was of particular interest to multi-instrumentalists who were accustomed to the mandolin (Linn 1991, 84–88). To help project the sound of plectrum and tenor banjos, builders applied a slightly concave wooden bowl—a *resonator*—to the back of the banjo, making it a *closed-back* banjo (Linn 1991, 82). The tenor banjo was further distinguished from the plectrum and other five-string banjos in that it had a shorter scale and was tuned differently (see section on banjo tuning below). Although many fretted banjos in the nineteenth and twentieth centuries had eighteen to twenty-two frets, tenor banjos generally included seventeen to nineteen frets. Some of the more notable musicians who used plectrum and tenor banjos during this era were Harry Reser (1896–1965), Elmer Snowden (1900–1973), Roy Smeck (1900–1994), and Eddie Peabody (1902–1970). Plectrum and tenor banjos generally found a home in a variety of jazz and dance bands alongside horns, strings, and other percussion instruments.

With the increasing impact of commercial recorded sound and broadcast radio by the 1920s and '30s, musicians used the banjo in the budding genre of country music, which incorporated the banjo's cultural associations with the American South (Malone 2002, 31–76). Banjoists such as Charlie Poole (1892–1931), along with his North Carolina Ramblers, helped to bridge multiple influences between popular music and localized, regional styles. Entertainers such as Uncle Dave Macon (1870–1952) also contributed to this phenomenon, in part by maintaining cultural links to minstrelsy, medicine shows, and vaudeville.

In addition to the growing country music industry, Bill Monroe (1911–1996) and his Blue Grass Boys incorporated the banjo into the fast-paced, syncopated music now characterized as *bluegrass*. Of those banjoists with whom Monroe worked in the 1940s, Earl Scruggs (1924–2012) innovated and popularized a three-finger plucking technique that brought new generations of musicians to the five-string banjo. In particular, resonator banjos with heavy tone rings helped give bluegrass banjo music its distinctive sound. Other notable contemporaries of Scruggs and more recent influential bluegrass banjoists include Snuffy Jenkins (1908–1990), Don Reno (1924–1984), Ralph Stanley (1927–), Sonny Osborne (1937–), Eddie Adcock (1938–), Bill Keith (1939–), Eric Weissberg (1939–), Tony Trischka (1949–), Bill Evans (ca. 1956–), and Béla Fleck (1958–). In many bluegrass bands the banjo is regularly used with the guitar, violin, mandolin, dobro, and bass.

Alternately, vernacular musicians from rural regions in the South and along the Appalachian Mountains used factory-made and homemade five-string banjos to maintain local music traditions. Musicologists, folklorists, and song and music collectors documented aspects of these traditions, placing value on early sound recordings, tune collections, oral histories, and performances in what is now commonly identified as *old-time* music. Some of the most-emulated banjoists of this tradition are Gus Cannon (1883–1979), Tommy Jarrell (1886–1975), Wade Ward (1892–1971), Dink Roberts (1894–1989), Elizabeth Cotton (1895–1987), Clarence Ashley (1895–1967), Dock Boggs (1898–1971), Fred Cockerham (1905–1980), John Snipes (ca. 1906–1981), Odell Thompson (1911–1994), Roscoe Holcomb (1911–1981), Kyle Creed (1912–1982), and members of the Hammons family. Many of these musicians used the banjo to support ballad singing and other vocal music as well as dance music. In old-time music, the banjo generally accompanies the violin, along with the guitar and other ensemble instruments such as the accordion, banjo-ukulele, dulcimer, and autoharp.

By the 1940s and '50s and into the '60s and '70s a American *folk revival* took shape, with growing public interest in songs with mixed associations in old-time, Appalachian, and other regional music (Cohen 2005, xv–xx). Popular success by groups like the Weavers, and later, the Kingston Trio, reinforced the commercial use of the five-string banjo. In other contexts, transformative figures such as Pete Seeger (1919–) and his half-brother Mike Seeger (1933–2009) further popularized the banjo in both popular and vernacular circles as educators, entertainers, and advocates.

Today, the banjo continues to be used in a variety of ways. For example, people develop musical and social networks centered on other aspects of banjo history. These communities of musicians meet online (e.g., through social sites and listservs while sharing video and audio content) and in-person at gatherings, festivals, and conferences. Since the 1970s a growing number of musicians studying early banjo instruction books of the 1850s and 1860s are regularly found at Civil War reenactments, living history events, and old-time music festivals. Since the 1940s the members of the *American Banjo Fraternity* have maintained an ongoing link to classic and ragtime banjo players from the late nineteenth and early twentieth centuries, emulating players and composers like Horace Weston (1825–1890), Alfred D. Cammeyer (1862–1949), Alfred A. Farland (1864–1954), Joe Morley (1867–1937), Vess Ossman (1868–1923), Parke Hunter (1876–1912), Fred Van Eps (1878–1960), and Emile Grimshaw (1880–1943). Organizations such as the Pittsburgh Banjo Club maintain musical connections to four-string tenor and plectrum banjo music from the 1920s and 1930s while traditional Irish musicians now incorporate the four-string tenor banjo as part of a standard musical lineup. Multiple generations of scholars and musicians are now also actively emphasizing greater public awareness of the banjo's African American past and present. Some of the notable artists involved with this work are Taj Mahal, Otis Taylor, Don Vappie, Sule Greg Wilson, Tony Thomas, and groups such as the Ebony Hillbillies, the Carolina Chocolate Drops (formed in 2005), and the Turbo Project (formed in 2007).

Recent Investigations into the Banjo's West African Heritage

West Africa is home to dozens of culturally distinct *plucked spike lute* traditions. Limited in-depth knowledge of these traditions is available outside the communities that maintain them (for a partial list of these traditions, see Charry 2000, 123–126). Since the 1950s American and European scholars, musicians, and collectors have been exploring different aspects of the banjo's West African heritage. Early scholarship in this area considered the history of lutes associated with Mande and neighboring music cultures as potential antecedents to the banjo (e.g., the Wolof *xalam* and the Bamana *ngoni*) (Coolen 1991, Conway 1995). More recent scholarship advocates that greater consideration be given to additional traditions such as the Jola *ekonting* and the Manjak *bunchundo* (Jägfors 2003). New, forthcoming research is currently needed to more effectively determine how these traditions, or others, may be related to the development of the banjo before, during, and after the period of the transatlantic slave trade.

Playing Techniques

Documented banjo playing techniques since the mid-nineteenth century consist of at least three primary ways of sounding the strings: 1) striking the strings in a downward motion (a downstroke technique) with at least one finger and the thumb, 2) plucking the strings in an upward motion (similar to a guitar), or 3) using a flat pick held by the playing hand to pluck and strum the strings. The first fully described way of playing is a down-stroke technique for five-string banjo found in *Briggs' Banjo Instructor* (1855). The author describes how to play "banjo" style by using "the ball of the thumb and the nail of the 1st finger [where the] first finger should strike the strings with the *back* of the *nail* and then slide to" (Briggs 1855, 8). This style of playing was also known as *thimble* style or *stroke* style. Versions of this down-stroke technique remain common in Appalachian and old-time music traditions today and are recognized by such names as *clawhammer, frailing, thumping,* and *rapping.*

Later nineteenth-century playing techniques increasingly focused on plucking the strings like a guitar. This style of playing was foundational to parlor music, ragtime, and European social music forms. Twentieth-century old-time and bluegrass banjo playing also relies on finger style techniques. Some old-time musicians use two- and three-finger plucking techniques, whereas bluegrass musicians use a three-finger technique in which each finger—index, middle, and thumb—is covered with an individual pick to support rapidly plucking the strings with greater brightness and volume. Musicians who use these fingerpicking styles often plant their little finger and sometimes the ring finger to stabilize the picking hand next to the strings.

Banjo players who use a flat pick are most closely associated with plectrum and tenor banjo music. This includes ragtime, jazz, Dixieland, Irish, and other international traditions that use the banjo. The single flat pick can be used to pluck individual notes, strum chords, or do a combination of the two.

Banjo Tuning

Dozens of tunings mark the history of the banjo. Beginning with the modern five-string banjo, one of the more commonly emphasized tunings is an *open-G* tuning, represented with the following upper- and lower-case pitch names: *g-D-G-B-D.* It is called open-G because all of the pitches of the strings are tuned to the three pitches that constitute a *G chord*—G, B, and D. What makes this and other five-string banjo tunings unique is that the pitch order of the strings is not from lowest to highest (or highest to lowest). Rather, the fifth string (represented with the lowercase "*g*") is the highest pitched open string of the banjo, located closest to the player's chest. Following the fifth string is the lowest-pitched fourth string, "*D*" (also considered the *bass* string), which is tuned an octave and a fourth below the fifth string. From the fourth string, the third, second, and first strings (closest to the player's lap) are tuned to increasingly higher pitches.

The open-G tuning is the most popular tuning in bluegrass music and is used with great frequency in old-time banjo music. A common alternative to the open-G tuning is *C-tuning* (or *low-bass* tuning). Low-bass tuning is identical to open-G tuning except that the fourth string, the lowest-pitched "bass" string, is tuned down a whole step to "*C*" with the following order: *g-C-G-B-D.* In nineteenth-century popular music (early blackface minstrelsy through the turn of the twentieth century), both open and low-bass tunings were used, but in contrast to today, the low-bass tuning was the most common. The nineteenth-century banjo was also generally pitched a third, fourth, or fifth below a modern instrument. This means that the interval relationship between the pitches of the strings is equivalent to a modern low-bass tuning, but the entire instrument is pitched in a lower register. As early as 1851 one author described *F-tuning* (*c-F-C-E-G*), a fifth below modern low-bass C-tuning (Gumbo Chaff 1851). Between 1855 and 1865, the pitches would have been a low G-tuning (*d-G-D-F#-A*) and a low A-tuning (*e-A-E-G#-B*), a fourth and a minor third below modern C-tuning.

By the late 1880s and 1890s, although the actual pitch of commercially produced banjos was raised from lower registers (like F-, G-, and A-tuning) to the modern C-tuning (*g-C-G-B-D*), the music continued to be written in the keys of *A* (a key signature with three sharps) and *E* (a key signature with four sharps). This distinguishing feature meant that the banjo was a transposing instrument, because the pitches produced by the instrument were not those written in the musical notation. In banjo orchestras of the late nineteenth century, even though banjos were constructed and tuned in the range of basses, cellos, and piccolos, they all generally relied on playing formations largely represented by C-tuning and open-G tuning.

In old-time music, clawhammer banjo players use a much wider diversity of banjo tunings that are representative of specific geographic regions, tune types, and ensemble experiences. The more prevalent tunings beyond low-bass C-tuning and open G-tuning include a double-C tuning (*g-C-G-C-D*), which is often raised to play in the key of *D* (*a-D-A-D-E*), and *sawmill tuning* (*g-D-G-C-D*) (see Conway 1995, 224–225).

The four-string plectrum banjo generally used the late nineteenth-century C-tuning, minus the fifth string (*C-G-B-D*), whereas the four-string tenor banjo used an open-fifths tuning (*C-G-D-A*). Variant tunings for tenor banjo also exist in Irish music and other regional styles. Tenor banjo tuning is based on the open-fifths tunings found on the mandolin as well as the violin.

See also: African American Influences on American Music; Bluegrass; Dixieland Jazz; Fleck, Bela; Folk Music; Immigrant Music; Jazz; Monroe, Bill; Ragtime; Seeger, Mike; Seeger, Pete

Further Reading

Briggs, Thomas F. 1855. *Briggs' Banjo Instructor.* New York: Oliver Ditson.

Carlin, Bob. 2007. *The Birth of the Banjo: Joel Walker Sweeney and Early Minstrelsy.* Jefferson, NC: McFarland and Company.

Charry, Eric. 2000. *Mande Music: Traditional and Modern Music of the Maninka and Mandinka of Western Africa.* Chicago: University of Chicago Press.

Cockrell, Dale. 1987. "Of Gospel Hymns, Minstrel Shows, and Jubilee Singers: Toward Some Black South African Musics." *American Music* 5, no. 4 (Winter): 417–432.

Cohen, Norm. 2005. *Folk Music: A Regional Exploration.* Westport, CT: Greenwood Press.

Conway, Cecelia. 1995. *African Banjo Echoes in Appalachia: A Study of Folk Traditions.* Knoxville: University of Tennessee Press.

Coolen, Michael T. 1991. *Black Music Research Journal* 11, no. 1 (Spring): 1–18.

Epstein, Dena. 2003. *Sinful Tunes and Spirituals.* Chicago: University of Illinois Press.

Gumbo Chaff [Elias Howe]. 1851. *The Complete Preceptor for the Banjo.* Boston: Oliver Ditson and Company.

Gura, Philip F., and James F. Bollman. 1999. *America's Instrument: The Banjo in the Nineteenth Century.* Chapel Hill: University of North Carolina Press.

Jägfors, Ulf. 2003–2004. "The African Akonting and the Origin of the Banjo." *Old Time Herald* 9, no. 2 (Winter): 26–33.

Linn, Karen. 1991. *That Half-Barbaric Twang: The Banjo in American Popular Culture.* Chicago: University of Illinois Press.

Mahar, William J. 1999. *Behind the Burnt Cork Mask: Early Blackface Minstrelsy and Antebellum American Popular Culture.* Chicago: University of Illinois Press.

Malone, Bill C. 2002. *Country Music U.S.A.* 2nd rev. ed. Austin: University of Texas Press.

Price, Sally, and Richard Price. 2002. *Stedman's Surinam: Life in Eighteenth-Century Slave Society.* Baltimore, MD: Johns Hopkins University Press.

Roxworthy, Emily. 2008. *The Spectacle of Japanese American Trauma.* Honolulu: University of Hawai'i Press.

Schreyer, Lowell. 2007. *The Banjo Entertainers: Roots to Ragtime, a Banjo History.* Mankato: Minnesota Heritage Publishing.

Shames, Susan P. 2010. *The Old Plantation: The Artist Revealed.* Williamsburg, VA: Colonial Williamsburg Foundation.

Sloane, Hans. 1707. *A Voyage to the Islands of Madera, Barbados, Nieves, S. Christophers and Jamaica.* London: Printed by B.M. for the Author.

"The Spy." 1736. *New-York Weekly Journal,* March 7, 1–2.

Winans, Robert B., and Elias J. Kaufman. 1994. "Minstrel and Classic Banjo: American and English Connections." *American Music* 12, no. 1 (Spring): 1–30.

Greg Adams

Barrio Rhythm

"Barrio" and "Rhythm"

The words *barrio* and *rhythm* are both metaphors, and also synecdoches, in the sense that *barrio* represents "urban life," as especially applied to Latinos, and *rhythm* sometimes represents nonmusical "life processes and interactions." In a more restricted sense, *rhythm* can also serve as a synecdoche for *music,* inasmuch as Latinos are often essentialized as being full of "hot passionate energy," and the rhythmic aspect of music probably most overtly represents that characteristic. This entry discusses rhythm only as a component of the larger subject of music.

Barrio Latin Ethnicities

In modern America, the term *barrio,* originally referring to "neighborhood," now more specifically refers to groups of neighborhoods, comprising entire sections of towns or cities with large percentages of Latin population and the critical masses to maintain a rich and coherent culture. Three principal groups of Latinos comprise the bulk of the urban barrio population in America, each with its own set of music and dance preferences (with considerable overlap among the three in some cases). These groups are (1) Puerto Rican and Dominican Americans of Northeast urban centers; (2) Cuban Americans of metropolitan Miami (and in much smaller concentrations in other urban areas); and (3) Mexican Americans of urban California, other southwestern states, and an increasing number of midwestern urban areas, notably including Chicago. Spanish-speaking Latinos from other countries, for example in Central and South America, have their own self-identified national folk music and dance repertoires, but in mass media (television, radio, recordings) primarily tend to relate to the preferences of one or more of the three groups, as these are the most available in mass media.

Traditional Music/Dance Styles Perpetuated in Barrios

Virtually all of the most popular traditional genres in the repertoires of both Mexican and Caribbean American Hispanics emphasize lyrics and the voice, and most are associated with dance as well. Puerto Ricans often enjoy group participatory performances of *plena* and *bomba* (Afro-Puerto Rican vocal/percussion genres) playing, singing, and dancing, especially at folkloric occasions. Latinos of Caribbean descent (and many others) enjoy participating in informal Cuban-style *rumba* drumming, singing, and dancing.

First-generation Mexican Americans from many regions enjoy a wide variety of regional music. Some of these regional Mexican ensembles and genres have become nationally popular in Mexico, as well as among a large cross-section of the Mexican American immigrant population. These styles include *mariachi, banda,* and *Norteño* music. The *mariachi* (string and brass ensemble originally from the state of Jalisco) repertoire prominently includes *son, huapango, bolero,* and *rancheras* (love or nationalistic songs that often extol the virtues of rural life) most typically using polka, waltz, or slow *bolero* rhythms. *Banda* (wind and percussion band ensemble from the state of Sinaloa) also emphasizes *rancheras*; and *Norteño* (closely related to "Tex-Mex" music) built around the accordion plus bass, guitars, saxophones, and so forth as desired, emphasizes *corrido* (a kind of narrative and topical ballad, with either polka or waltz rhythms). Radio stations in areas with large Mexican populations prominently feature all three of these traditional folk ensembles.

"Pan-Tropical" Music Popular in Barrios

Mexicans apply the term "*música tropical*" to Afro-tinged upbeat dance music (mostly vocal), of the circum-Caribbean area. Currently the most popular such genres are Nuyorican/Cuban *salsa,* Dominican *merengue,* and Colombian *cumbia,* all of which have also become popular throughout Latin America. Some Mexican and U.S. barrio radio stations specialize in this kind of music; others emphasize traditional genres such as *mariachi, banda,* and *Norteño,* as well as in *Rock en Español* (Spanish-language rock) and hip-hop.

Influences of Mexican, Puerto Rican, and Cuban music on each other are not symmetrical; Cuban music has in general had a far more extensive influence on preferences and styles of other groups than they in turn have had upon it. Cuban music and dance genres had pervaded most of Hispanic Latin America even before the extensive migrations to the United States around the mid-twentieth century and are now considered part of the core repertoires in many countries. Puerto Ricans, for example, have adapted Cuban genres such as the *bolero* and *guaracha* to such extent that these are now considered Puerto Rican. The *bolero,* a lyrical romantic song/dance of Cuban origin often performed by popular trios, is hugely popular in Mexico, in Mexican American areas of the United States, throughout Hispanic Latin America, and among immigrants from those countries. The *cumbia,* originally from Colombia, is popular throughout Mexico, Central America, and many parts of South America, but somewhat less popular among *Caribeños* (Caribbean Hispanics). Dominican *merengue* is now almost as popular among Puerto Ricans as among Dominicans. *Salsa* is an urban Hispanic music most identified with *Nuyoricans* (Puerto Ricans of New York City), whose texts often reflect New York urban angst. *Salsa* instrumentation, harmonies, and arrangements reflect a long engagement of Latin music with American jazz; the formal and rhythmic structures and improvisational procedures of *salsa,* however, largely derive from those of the Cuban *guaracha* and *son.* The A + B structure is typical for *salsa* compositions and performances; the "A" part consists of poetic verses, and the "B" part, of a call and response between the vocal soloist (who improvises music and text based on part A) and a chorus drawn from within the band, which provides a fixed response. *Salsa* is popular nearly everywhere in Hispanic Latin America and among all U.S. Hispanic groups.

Modern Styles Based on U.S. Mainstream Popular Music

Young Hispanics in all urban areas enjoy varieties of the same music as other American youth: rock, hip-hop, rap, and reggae, whether in mainstream African American–tinged English, Spanish, or "Spanglish" (mixed English and Spanish, often with very local in-group slang drawing upon both languages). Immigrants themselves may have already enjoyed these now universally popular styles before moving to the United States; the second-generation children of immigrants very quickly change their preferences from those traditional styles discussed above to these more modern styles. *Rock en Español* ("rock in Spanish") has a history going back to the 1950s in Latin America and (by contrast with local folk and popular styles) was often associated throughout the region with the more cosmopolitan, "modern" classes in various countries. Forms of rock found in U.S. barrios are more syncretic; Chicano rock, in Los Angeles and the Southwest, typically draws on the R&B roots of rock, as well as many influences from other parts of Latin America. Chicano rockers commonly incorporate instruments and rhythms of Afro-Cubans and Andean Indians and use nationalistic or pan-Indigenous textual themes.

Rap and hip-hop have developed Chicano and Puerto Rican varieties. They typically draw upon both local musical and textual reference influences (i.e., New York, Los Angeles) and the rhythms and styles of the "mother cultures" involved. *Reggaeton,* developed in Puerto Rico, blends influences from reggae, Latin dance rhythms, and rapping, and is especially popular on the East Coast. It is a prime example of the blending and adaptation so characteristic of U.S. Latin populations in every domain of culture.

See also: African American Influences on American Music; Hip-Hop; Immigrant Music; Jazz; Latin Music in the United States; Rap and Rappers; Rock 'n' Roll (Rock)

Further Reading

Allen, Ray, and Lois Wilcken, eds. 1998. *Island Sounds in the Global City: Caribbean Popular Music and Identity in New York.* New York: New York Folklore Society.

Flores, Juan. 2000. "Puerto Rocks: Rap, Roots, and Amnesia." in *From Bomba to Hip-Hop: Puerto Rican Culture and Latin Identity.* New York: Columbia University Press.

Kelly, Raegan. 2004. "Hip Hop Chicano: A Separate But Parallel Story." In *That's The Joint: The Hip Hop Studies Reader,* edited by Murray Foreman and Mark Anthony Neal. New York and London: Routledge.

Loza, Steven. 1993. *Barrio Rhythm: Mexican American Music in Los Angeles.* Urbana: University of Illinois Press.

Sheehy, Daniel. 2005. *Mariachi in America: Experiencing Music, Expressing Culture.* New York: Oxford University Press.

Simonett, Helena. 2001. *Banda: Mexican Musical Life Across Borders.* Middletown, CT: Wesleyan University Press.

Theodore Solís

Basie, William "Count" (1904–1984)

A member of America's jazz aristocracy, William James "Count" Basie played a major role in the development of the swing era of jazz music. Basie's introduction to music occurred early in his life. He learned piano from his mother in Red Bank, New Jersey, then moved across the Hudson River to New York City, where he learned to play Harlem stride piano from James P. Johnson and Fats Waller. While still in his teens Basie entered the vaudeville circuit as a pianist and musical director.

The turning point in Basie's musical development occurred in 1927. After being stranded in Kansas City, Missouri, when his touring vaudeville show disbanded, Basie stumbled upon Walter Page's Blue Devils (active 1920s–1930s), a band that he went on to join and that changed his perspective on music.

Basie played with several other Kansas City bands in the coming years, eventually forming an eight-piece ensemble that came to be known as the Barons of Rhythm. Basie's band established a long-standing relationship with the Reno Club in Kansas City, and it was during this period that Basie achieved national success. Radio broadcasts in 1936 attracted attention from the Decca Record Company, and the newly renamed Count Basie Orchestra expanded to thirteen members and soon became one of the leading swing era big bands, with recordings such as "One O'clock Jump" (1937), "Jumpin' at the Woodside" (1938), and "Taxi War Dance" (1939). The Count Basie Orchestra began touring the country, with notable performances in Chicago and New York.

In contrast to the more orchestrated sounds exemplified by most big bands of the 1930s, Basie's big band was known for a loose style of swing more typical of a smaller ensemble and provided a stage for soloists such as Lester Young (1909–1959), Herschel Evans (1909–1939), and Harry "Sweets" Edison (1915–1999). Further, as a pioneering musician who pushed the Kansas City sound forward, Basie's All American Rhythm Section, with Jo Jones (1911–1985) on drums, Walter Page (1900–1957) on bass, and Freddie Green (1911–1987) on guitar, was especially influential in helping jazz continue its shift away from the rigidity of two-beats to a measure toward the more flowing four-four time.

The Count Basie Orchestra's swing-era heyday ended with the declining popularity of the big bands after World War II, and it was forced to disband for a short period starting in 1950. Basie, however, remained active on the music scene and performed with a smaller, six- to nine-piece group, which included notable musicians such as Clark Terry (1920–), Buddy DeFranco (1923–), and Buddy Rich (1917–1987). In 1952 Basie reorganized a new big band, launched a national tour, and embarked on new recording sessions. Continuing to partner with new talent and soloists, including Frank Sinatra (1915–1998), Ella Fitzgerald (1917–1996), Sammy Davis Jr. (1925–1990), Nat King Cole (1919–1965), and Tony Bennett (1926–), Basie continued building a jazz institution that established his international legacy.

Count Basie, American bandleader, jazz pianist, and composer. (Library of Congress)

Basie had a prolific career, releasing more than one hundred albums with his band and other ensembles, winning nine Grammy Awards during his lifetime, and having four recordings inducted into the Grammy Hall of Fame. Basie died on April 26, 1984, at the age of seventy-nine.

See also: Big Band Music; Cole, Nat King; Fitzgerald, Ella; Jazz; Halls of Fame; Radio; Sinatra, Frank; Vaudeville and Burlesque

Further Reading

Murray, Albert. 1995. *Good Morning Blues: The Autobiography of Count Basie.* New York: Da Capo Press.

Sheridan, Chris. 1986. *Count Basie—A Bio-Discography.* New York: Greenwood Press.

Stanley, Dance. 1980. *The World of Count Basie.* New York: Charles Scribner's Sons.

Vail, Ken. 2003. *Count Basie: Swingin' the Blues, 1936–1950.* Lanham, MD: Scarecrow Press.

Hans C. Schmidt

The Beach Boys (Active 1961–Present)

The Beach Boys emerged as America's preeminent pop group, with their close vocal harmonies and lyrics reflecting a Southern California youth culture of surfing, hot rods, and romance. From 1962 through 1988 the group topped the charts four times and scored seventeen top 10 hits on *Billboard*'s Hot 100 chart. During the mid-1960s The Beach Boys, who were 1988 Rock and Roll Hall of Fame inductees, were the only act that challenged the phenomenal success of The Beatles with both mainstream record buyers and music critics. In addition to their unmistakable vocal harmonies and enduring chart appeal, The Beach Boys' 1966 critically acclaimed album *Pet Sounds,* with its evolving psychedelic rock style, and the single "Good Vibrations" frequently rank among critics' lists of the greatest albums and singles of all time.

Founded in Hawthorne, California, in 1961, the band comprised three brothers, Brian (1942–), Carl (1946–1998), and Dennis (1944–1983) Wilson, along with their cousin Mike Love (1941–) and Brian's football teammate Alan Jardine (1942–), who was replaced by David Marks between 1962 and 1963; he later rejoined the band. With their father Murry also being an aspiring musician and songwriter, the Wilson brothers were exposed to music from an early age. Due to Brian's intense passion for harmony groups such as The Four Freshmen (active 1948–present), the quintet frequently harmonized together, under the names Carl and the Passions and the Pendletones.

In the fall of 1961 the group visited Hite Morgan and Doreen Morgan, their father's music publishers, to discuss recording a song. The Morgans were interested only in original material, so Dennis, the only group member who surfed, suggested they write a song about surfing. Days later they recorded "Surfin'," cowritten by Brian and Mike. Released on the Candix label, it became a local smash hit and peaked at number seventy-five on the *Billboard* Hot 100 chart, and the label's promotion man renamed the group The Beach Boys.

Initially managed by the Wilsons' father, The Beach Boys were signed to Capitol Records in 1962 and scored a top 15 hit with "Surfin' Safari." Beginning in 1963 the group had a consistent run of top 10 smash hits and the chart-toppers "I Get Around" and "Help Me Rhonda" in 1964 and 1965, respectively. Although the band was charting hit after hit and touring the world, Brian Wilson suffered a "nervous breakdown" on a flight to Houston in late 1964 and was replaced on tour by Bruce Johnston (1944–).

While the band was touring, Brian began work in January 1966 on the *Pet Sounds* album, which was

The Beach Boys pose for a photo at the Finsbury Astoria, November 6, 1966. Pictured from the left are Bruce Johnston, Al Jardine (front), Carl Wilson, Dennis Wilson, and Mike Love. (Clive Limpkin/Express/Getty Images)

inspired by The Beatles' (active 1960–1970) *Rubber Soul* album. For nearly four months he worked continuously on the production, enlisting a genuine orchestra of session musicians to help him chase the "pet sounds" he heard in his head. Brian used a number of creative, extended techniques to achieve the various sound effects he sought, including bicycle bells, barking dogs, and various flutes. In spite of its innovation, *Pet Sounds* sold disappointingly as an album, although it produced the singles "Wouldn't It Be Nice," "God Only Knows," and "Sloop John B." That same year the group returned to the top spot on the singles chart with "Good Vibrations," which Brian described as a "pocket symphony."

In 1970 The Beach Boys established their own label, Brother Records, when they changed labels, leaving Capitol to go to Reprise. As they were recording on their own label, in 1974 Capitol released *Endless Summer,* a double album compilation of the group's pre–*Pet Sounds* hits, which surged to the top of the *Billboard* album charts. The Beach Boys remained consistently on the singles and album charts throughout the 1970s and 1980s, including the number five remake of Chuck Berry's (1926–) "Rock and Roll Music" in 1976. In 1988 they scored their first number one hit single in twenty-two years with "Kokomo," which was written for the movie *Cocktail.*

Over the last few decades there have been several ongoing legal battles among band members. Despite these issues, The Beach Boys have received countless acknowledgments for their musical contributions, including the Grammy Lifetime Achievement Award in 2001.

See also: Awards and Prizes for Music; Berry, Chuck; Halls of Fame

Further Reading

Doe, Andrew G., and John Tobler. 2004. *Brian Wilson & The Beach Boys: The Complete Guide to Their Music.* London: Omnibus Press.

Gaines, Steven S. 1995. *Heroes and Villains: The True Story of the Beach Boys.* New York: Da Capo Press.

Golden, Bruce. 1991. *The Beach Boys: Southern California Pastoral.* San Bernardino, CA: Borgo Press.

White, Timothy. 1994. *The Nearest Faraway Place: Brian Wilson, the Beach Boys, and the Southern California Experience.* New York: Henry Holt and Company.

Susie Skarl

Benatar, Pat (1953–)

Pat Benatar seemingly exploded onto the American scene with her 1979 album *In the Heat of the Night,* a rare rock album with a band fronted by a female vocalist. Benatar's sudden fame belied years of singing in small clubs and the prevalent belief that a woman could not lead a male rock band.

Born Patricia Andrzejewski on January 10, 1953, in Brooklyn, and raised in Long Island's Lindenhurst, she married—and later divorced—Dennis Benatar (Benatar/Cox 2010, 30). She later married her guitarist, Neil Giraldo, who was significantly involved in crafting her music.

In the Heat of the Night brought Benatar quick fame and criticism. She caught the attention of crowds and the recording industry at the Catch a Rising Star club after wearing a catwoman outfit during a Halloween show (Benatar/Cox 2010, 47–48). Chrysalis Records played up her sex appeal, including doctoring photographs of her for a publicity campaign. Benatar's sex appeal brought her additional media attention, but some critics assumed she was more interested in appearances than her music, although she was called a "pioneer" of "teen-oriented hard rock" (Holden 1982).

Benatar's success continued with 1980's *Crimes of Passion* and *Precious Time* (1981). "You Better Run," a remake of the Rascals' song appearing on *Crimes of Passion,* was the second video to appear on MTV (Benatar/Cox 2010, 107). It was the first of several videos she made that were significant in music video history. "Shadows of the Night" from *Get Nervous* (1982) was a fictional, World War II–based story, and is an early example of narrative music video. "Love Is a Battlefield" from *Live from Earth* (1983) portrayed Benatar as a runaway working as a dancer in a sleazy club. At the time the rock video was notable for its moral storytelling and extensive use of dancing.

She was increasingly in conflict with Chrysalis, and the album art for *Get Nervous* was a product of their arguments over her public image. Benatar wanted to break away from the overt sexuality desired by Chrysalis. It is no surprise that Benatar's signature look was one Chrysalis wanted to maintain. Her look was specifically copied in the movie *Fast Times at Ridgemont High* (1982), and Benatar was one of music's major style influences for girls and young women before Madonna (1958–). Benatar described this era as one when women in rock were expected to be "girlfriends or groupies" (Benatar/Cox 2010, 135).

She took a break from rock and pursued blues music in 1991 with *True Love,* before returning to a more subdued rock style with three later albums. Benatar's music remains in the public's ears, being replayed in movies and television shows. The Internet Movie Database (2011) lists more than forty movie and television uses of her songs.

See also: Blues; Groupies; Madonna; Music Television; Rock 'n' Roll (Rock); Rock 'n' Roll (Rock), Women In

Official Web Site: http://www.benatar.com

Further Reading

Benatar, Pat, with Patsi Bale Cox. 2010. *Between a Heart and a Rock Place.* New York: HarperCollins.

Holden, Stephen. 1982. "Rock: Pat Benatar at Garden." December 17. http://www.nytimes.com/1982/12/17/arts/rock-pat-benatar-at-garden.html.

Timothy R. Gleason

Benson, George (1943–)

George Benson's refined approach to the guitar grew out of the synthesis of the advancements made by his idols and his genre-blending observations on music. His achievements as both a guitarist and vocalist displayed a polished technique that has transcended the genre and satisfied numerous harmonic territories. Benson's characteristic incorporation of scat singing with his guitar playing has added subtle melodicism to his repertoire.

Benson was born on March 22, 1943, in Pittsburgh, Pennsylvania. At the age of four Benson sang for the first time at a local contest; he won $7. By the age of eight he was performing on street corners, where he earned close to $40 a night. A year later, at the age of nine, Benson received his first guitar, which was handmade for him by his stepfather from his mother's oak chest.

In 1954 Benson recorded his first single, "It Should Have Been Me," written by Ray Charles (1930–2004). Beginning in 1962, he began to perform with the quartet of organist Brother Jack MacDuff (1926–2001). At the age of twenty-one Benson started his solo career with his first album, *The New Boss Guitar,* the title serving as an homage to his idol Wes Montgomery's album *Boss Guitar.*

Shortly afterward Benson signed with Columbia Records under the tutelage of producer John Hammond (1910–1987). After releasing several albums throughout the 1960s, Benson began to receive attention from major performers, including trumpeter Miles Davis (1926–1991), who recruited him to perform on the song "Paraphernalia" on Davis's 1968 release *Miles in the Sky.* The following year Benson released the highly ambitious album *The Other Side of Abbey Road,* which

Jazz guitarist George Benson performs at the Universal Amphitheatre in Universal City, California, July 6, 1978. (AP Photo/G. Paul Burnett)

included several reworked songs from The Beatles' album *Abbey Road.* Benson's album also featured contributions from pianist Herbie Hancock (1940–) and bassist Ron Carter (1937–).

In the early 1970s Benson signed with CTI Records and released several albums, including *Beyond the Blue Horizon* (1971) and *Bad Benson* (1974). He achieved true mainstream success with his 1976 release *Breezin'*. Produced by Tommy LiPuma (1936–), the album was met with critical acclaim and commercial success and won several Grammy Awards, including for Best Pop Instrumental Performance and Record of the Year for the single "This Masquerade."

Benson began the 1980s with the album *Give Me the Night,* which was produced by Quincy Jones (1933–). The album introduced Benson to a younger demographic due to its inclusion of funk and disco sounds. During the 1980s Benson continued to incorporate other sounds in his work, including R&B and soul, which served to broaden his audience throughout several genres.

In the mid-1990s Benson signed with GRP Records, where his former producer Tommy LiPuma was president at the time. Benson's first album for the label, *That's Right* (1996), was a success, reaching number one on *Billboard*'s Top Jazz Album Chart. Their working relationship continued to flourish with the release of *Standing Together* (1998), an album that charted on both the R&B and jazz charts.

Since the millennium Benson has continued to record and perform at a prolific pace. Recent offerings include *Irreplaceable* (2004), *Givin' It Up* (2006), and *Guitar Man* (2011).

See also: Awards and Prizes for Music; Charles, Ray; Davis, Miles; Disco; Funk and Postpsychedelic Funk; Hancock, Herbie; Jazz; Jones, Quincy; R&B

Official Web Site: http://georgebenson.com/biography/

Further Reading

Orth, Maureen. 1977. "Four Faces of Benson." *Newsweek,* May 23.

Pauley, Jared. 2011. "George Benson." http://www.jazz.com/encyclopedia/benson-george (accessed September 2, 2011).

Eric Wendell

Berlin, Irving (1888–1989)

Composer of almost fifteen hundred songs, nineteen Broadway musical scores, and eighteen Hollywood movies, and twenty-five times conqueror of the charts, Irving Berlin was one of the most productive, successful, and famous American composers. His obituary in the *New York Times* expressed his life's work, quoting him: "My ambition is to reach the heart of the average American, not the highbrow or lowbrow but that vast intermediate crew which is the real soul of the country. . . . My public is the real people." He certainly reached his target; among his compositions were songs that have become holiday anthems (e.g., "White Christmas," "Easter Parade," "Happy Holiday") and the unofficial anthem of the United States, "God Bless America," which hit number one after 9/11 and is constantly played at sports events.

Berlin's biography is a rags-to-riches story. Born on May 11, 1888, his family emigrated in 1893 from rural Russia (near Mogilyov, Belarus) to New York. After his father died when Berlin was eight, he left school and supported the family as a newspaper boy. Music started to play an important role in his life only in his teenage years. He earned a living singing in saloons on the Bowery and as a singing waiter. In 1909 he turned his back on waiting tables when the Ted Snyder Company hired him as a staff lyricist.

Irving Berlin, perhaps the most prolific songwriter of the 20th century, responded to changing times and tastes with main-street language and down-home images in such irresistible melodies as "Alexander's Ragtime Band" and "White Christmas." (Library of Congress)

Berlin's compositions have a wide scope, but they share one characteristic: connection to the pulse of the time. In 1911 Berlin wrote his first world-famous song: "Alexander's Ragtime Band." As an instrumental version, the song was overlooked. Once Berlin added lyrics, however, the song became so successful that it was interpreted by various artists. It was on the charts on a regular basis for five decades.

Many of Berlin's compositions were connected to dancing. The revue "Watch Your Step" (1914) featured the famous dancing couple Irene and Vernon Castle. Apart from the stage, a lot of songs were tailored to specific dances, like "The International Rag" (1913), which praised the "grizzly bear." Apart from writing songs for the dance craze, Berlin composed patriotic pieces during the two world wars. Most successful were his stage shows *Yip Yip Yaphank* (1918) and *This Is the Army* (1942), of which the latter one was shown at military bases throughout the world and transformed into a movie in 1943. His most famous patriotic song is "God Bless America." Composed in 1918, Berlin released it only in 1938 when Kate Smith (1907–1986) sang it on the twentieth anniversary of Armistice Day.

What sets Berlin apart from most composers is that he wrote lyrics as well as music and that he was an autodidact without a professional musical education. During his Bowery youth he taught himself to play the piano, but throughout his career he hired a musician to write the music under his supervision. Berlin's goal was not to combine different genres, but to write American vernacular music. For colleagues like George Gershwin (1898–1937), he highlighted the meaning of ragtime as American music. For others, Berlin was the personification of American music. After his death on September 22, 1989, the *New York Times* noted; "Irving Berlin set the tone and the tempo for the tunes America played and sang and danced to for much of the 20th century."

See also: Gershwin, George; Patriotic Music

Further Reading

Barrett, Mary Ellin. 1994. *Irving Berlin: A Daughter's Memoir.* New York: Alfred A. Knopf.

Furia, Philip. 1998. *Irving Berlin: A Life in Song.* New York: Shirmer Books.

Jablonski, Edward. 1999. *Irving Berlin: American Troubador.* New York: Alfred A. Knopf.

Linda Braun

Bernstein, Leonard (1918–1990)

Leonard Bernstein was one of the most influential composers and conductors of the twentieth century. Educated at Harvard University (BA, 1939) and the Curtis Institute of Music in Philadelphia, Bernstein concentrated on conducting while studying at the Boston Symphony Orchestra's summer institute with Serge Koussevitzky, one of his major influences. Bernstein gained instant fame when, standing in for Bruno Walter, he conducted the New York Philharmonic Orchestra on November 14, 1943. He served as music director for the New York Symphony Orchestra from 1945 to 1947, and he conducted a number of European orchestras during this same period. In 1956 Bernstein became music director for the New York Philharmonic, a position he held until 1969. Even after stepping down from the New York Philharmonic, Bernstein continued to appear with that group and the Vienna Philharmonic Orchestra on a regular basis, as well as conducting other orchestras.

In contrast to conductors like Herbert von Karajan (1908–1989), Bernstein did not focus on operas, but rather on symphonies and his own compositions. From

1967 to 1976 he conducted Gustav Mahler's symphonies with the Vienna Philharmonic. Cycles of Johannes Brahms's and Robert Schumann's symphonies followed in the 1980s. Bernstein performed a chronologically broad repertoire, from the baroque era to the twentieth century. With such conducting experience, it remains surprising that Bernstein led the Berlin Philharmonic Orchestra only in 1979 at two concerts.

In 1944 Bernstein started to gain influence as a composer by presenting his "Jeremiah Symphony," which was quickly developed into the musical *On the Town.* Bernstein's composition style can best be described as eclecticism for his fusion of the elements of different genres (e.g., jazz and Jewish music). In some of his pieces, like the "Kaddish Symphony" (1963), Bernstein included elements of the twelve-tone technique. Apart from these characteristics, his compositions are best known for bridging the gap between classical and popular music, as he did in *West Side Story* (1957).

One reason for Bernstein's popularity is his extensive recordings. He recorded from the 1950s until a few months before his death. His interpretations were highly appreciated and so successful that he acquired over the years sixteen Grammys, and one Lifetime Achievement Grammy in 1985.

Throughout his career Bernstein emphasized the importance of education, giving televised music lectures on topics ranging from Bach to jazz, presenting a series of fifty-three Young People's Concerts on CBS, and teaching at Brandeis and Harvard Universities. In addition, he was an influential teacher of conducting, mentoring Marin Alsop (1956–), for one.

Although his music was often praised, Bernstein's political activism was criticized. Involved in various left-wing organizations since the 1940s, he spread awareness of the governmental prosecution of members of the Black Panther Party. Critics highlighted how Bernstein's comfortable lifestyle stood in stark contrast to that of the Black Panthers.

For many people, Bernstein attained superstar status not only as a conductor, composer, lecturer, and author, but also as the first American-born director of the New York Philharmonic.

See also: Awards and Prizes for Music; Classical Music in America; Musical Theater

Official Web Site: http://www.leonardbernstein.com/

Further Reading

Bernstein, Burton, and Barbara Haws, eds. 2008. *Leonard Bernstein: American Original.* New York: HarperCollins.

Gottlieb, Jack. 2010. *Working with Bernstein.* New York: Amadeus Press.

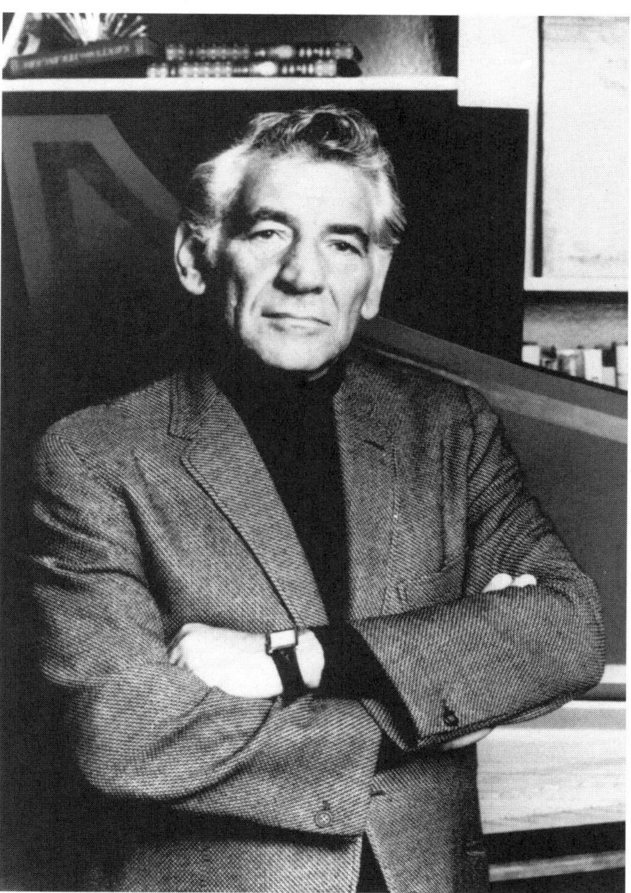

American composer, conductor, and pianist, Leonard Bernstein in 1978. (AP Photo)

Laird, Paul R. 2002. *Leonard Bernstein: A Guide to Research.* New York: Routledge.

Myers, Paul. 1998. *Leonard Bernstein.* London: Phaidon Press.

Peyser, Joan. 1998. *Leonard Bernstein: A Biography.* New York: Billboard Books.

Seldes, Barry. 2009. *The Political Life of an American Musician.* Berkeley: University of California Press.

Linda Braun

Berry, Chuck (1926–)

Chuck Berry, whose music mixed elements of country and R&B, is considered one of the fathers of rock 'n' roll. His signature guitar sound, coupled with lyrics that appealed to the hearts of 1950s teenagers, burst onto the music scene with success that crossed from the R&B to the pop charts. His influence had a lasting impact on a generation of fans and musicians who came of age in the

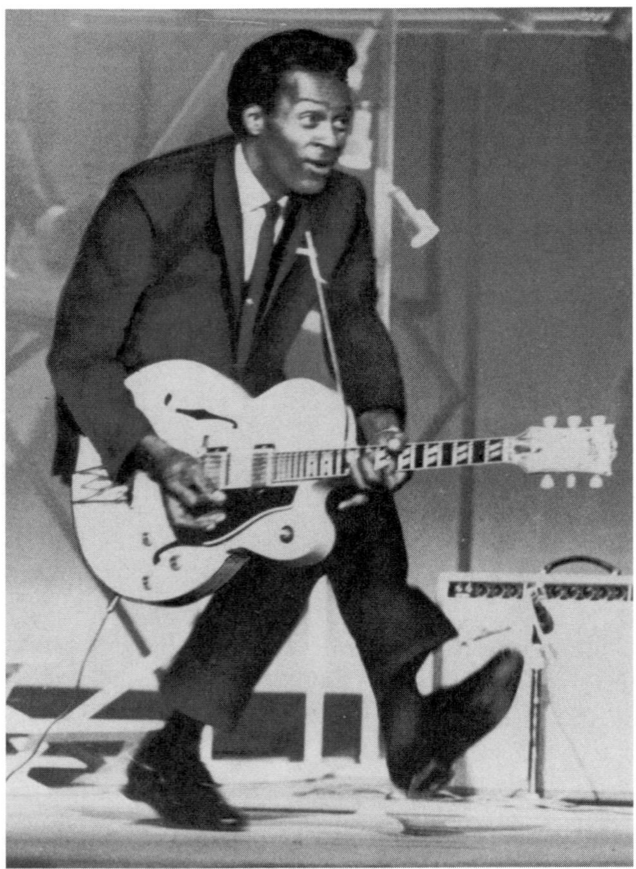
Chuck Berry performing in 1965. (Library of Congress)

post–World War II period, dancing to the electrified sounds of a new American musical genre.

Born October 18, 1926, and raised in the 'Ville, a suburb of St. Louis, Chuck Berry grew up singing in the Baptist church with his family. While training to be a beautician, he began his professional musical career in the clubs of East St. Louis, teaming up with Johnnie Johnson (1924–2005) on piano and Ebby Hardy on bass. Through the recommendation of Muddy Waters (1915–1983), Berry sought out producer Leonard Chess in Chicago. Chess, who had mostly produced blues artists, including Bo Diddley (1928–2008), saw the crossover potential in Berry's "jump blues" style of music. With the promotional help of disc jockey Alan Freed (1922–1965), Berry's first single on Chess Records, entitled "Maybellene" (1955), made him a national star. Combining aspects of country and R&B with lyrics about fast cars, chasing girls, and the doldrums of school days, Berry's music spoke to teenagers across racial boundaries in a way that no artist had before. His trademark two-string guitar solo in "Johnny B. Goode" (1958) is perhaps one of the most recognizable guitar licks in rock 'n' roll music, even finding fans a generation after it was released when it was prominently featured in the 1985 film *Back to the Future.*

Chuck Berry was a natural entertainer whose stage presence often stole the show. His signature "duck walk," snazzy wardrobe, and Cadillac cars were the marks of a showman. Offstage, however, Berry was a private person who shied away from the limelight when not performing. His scrapes with the law, both in his youth and at the height of his career in 1962, changed him. He developed a reputation for being difficult to work with, yet his music became larger than the man himself. He toured the country, starred in films, and proved to be more than a one-hit wonder with records such as "You Never Can Tell" (1964) and "My Ding-a-Ling" (1972). Though Berry never regained his 1950s popularity after his release from jail in 1964, his music inspired countless artists, including The Beatles (active 1960–1970) and The Rolling Stones (active 1960–present).

Along with Bill Haley (1925–1981), Jerry Lee Lewis (1935–), Buddy Holly (1936–1959), Carl Perkins (1932–1998), and Elvis Presley (1935–1977), Berry helped usher in the rock 'n' roll era. Berry's lyrics in several of his singles, including "Roll Over Beethoven" (1956), hailed the new genre as a turning point away from the established music of the day. His songs declared to 1950s youth that this new rebellious style of rock 'n' roll music was profoundly different from their parents' musical taste.

See also: Country Music; Diddley, Bo; Film Music; Guitar; Holly, Buddy; Lewis, Jerry Lee; Notorious Musicians; One-Hit Wonders; Perkins, Carl; Presley, Elvis; R&B; Rock 'n' Roll (Rock); Waters, Muddy

Official Web Site: http://www.chuckberry.com/

Further Reading

Berry, Chuck. 1987. *Chuck Berry, The Autobiography.* New York: Harmony Books.

Pegg, Bruce. 2002. *Brown Eyed Handsome Man: The Life and Hard Times of Chuck Berry, An Unauthorized Biography.* London: Routledge.

Lydon, Michael. 1971. "Chuck Berry." In *Rock Folk: Portraits from the Rock 'n' Roll Pantheon,* 1–23. New York: The Dial Press.

Hicks, Michael. 1997. "The Court of Star Chamber under Henry VII." In *The Reign of Henry VII,* edited by Michael Bennet, 23–39. Cambridge, MA: Harvard University Press.

Andrew D. A. Bozanic

Beyoncé (1981–)

Born on September 4, 1981, in Houston, Texas, Beyoncé Giselle Knowles is arguably one of the greatest entertainers of her generation, and perhaps of all time. Her image is one of perfection, regality, and decisive control. Through her girl power anthems and fierce dance moves aided with high fashion, Beyoncé, often compared to the legendary Diana Ross (1944–), has positioned herself as the quintessential pop star. She is known for her amazing vocal technique. Beyoncé's breath control has precision and a soulful, sultry sound like no other. She is a true entertainer and glam queen in her own right.

The third most honored woman in Grammy history, Beyoncé began performing as a young age in a vocal girl group, which eventually became known as Destiny's Child (active 1997–2006). Managed by her father, Mathew Knowles (1951–), Destiny's Child released five studio albums: *Destiny's Child* (1998), *The Writing's on the Wall* (1999), *Survivor* (2001), *8 Days of Christmas* (2001), and *Destiny Fulfilled* (2004). After breaking up in 2005, Destiny's Child was inducted into the Hollywood Walk of Fame, solidifying its spot as one of the most popular female groups of all time. As the lead singer of the group, it was clear that Beyoncé was destined for super stardom.

Using her powerful, sultry vocals as a catalyst for a strong career, Beyoncé has influenced American culture through her music, dance, fashion, and endorsement deals. In 2003 she released her first studio album, *Dangerously in Love.* It sold over four million copies in the United States alone. Her follow-up albums, *B'Day* (2006), *I Am . . . Sasha Fierce* (2008), and *4* (2011), also went multiplatinum, garnering awards and rave reviews. Some of her most popular singles are "Crazy in Love," "Baby Boy," "Single Ladies (Put a Ring on It)," "Irreplaceable," and "Run the World Girls." In particular, "Single Ladies (Put a Ring on It)" created a dance craze worldwide and on the Internet. Dance halls and raves everywhere were mimicking the choreography while paying homage to the legendary choreographer Bob Fosse (1927–1987), who inspired the moves.

Her mother, Tina Knowles (1954–), envisions Beyoncé's glitzy gowns and crystal-studded suits. From lavish gowns to eccentric brassieres, Beyoncé is always a sight to behold. Capitalizing on the popularity of her fashion, she and her mother launched a successful fashion line called House of Dereon. Beyoncé also has a perfume line with three fragrances, Heat, Pulse, and Heat Rush, and she has inked endorsement deals with L'Oreal, Pepsi, Tommy Hilfiger, and Giorgio Armani.

While her solo career was on the rise, Beyoncé also launched an acting career. She has appeared in seven feature films; *Carmen: A Hip Hopera* (2001), *Austin Powers in Gold Member* (2002), *Fighting Temptations* (2003), *The Pink Panther* (2006), *Dreamgirls* (2006), *Cadillac Records* (2008), and *Obsessed* (2009).

On April 4, 2008, Beyoncé Knowles wed hip-hop mogul and co-owner of the New Jersey Nets Shawn "Jay-Z" Carter (1969–). Their first child, a girl they named Blue Ivy Carter, was born in January 2012. She gave a stunning performance during the Superbowl XLVII Half-Time Show one year later.

Beyoncé performs at Revel in Atlantic City, New Jersey, May 26, 2012. (Kevin Mazur/WireImage)

See also: African American Women's Influence on American Music; Hip-Hop; Musicians as Actors; Pop Music; R&B

Official Web Site: http://www.beyonceonline.com

Further Reading

Arenofsky, Janice. 2009. Beyoncé *Knowles: A Biography.* Westport: Greenwood Press.

Easlea, Daryl. 2011. *Crazy in Love: The Beyoncé Knowles Biography.* Omnibus Press.

Sharrell Luckett

Big Band Music

In its heyday during the swing era (1935–1946), big band music was a popular form of jazz that dominated the radio airwaves and drew masses of teenagers and young adults to dance halls and clubs. Like sports fans today, big band lovers knew the names of everyone on

Members of the Bennie Moten Orchestra pose for a studio portrait at the Pearl Theatre in Philadelphia, 1931. Pictured from the left are Count Basie, Jimmie Rushing, Hot Lips Page, Willie McWashington, Booker Washington, Ed Lewis, Buster Berry, Thamon Hayes, Harland Leonard, Eddie Durham, Jack Washington, Vernon Page, Woodie Walder, Bennie Moten, and Buster Moten. (Gilles Petard/Redferns)

their favorite "team," even behind-the-scenes people like composers and arrangers; went to see them regularly; and collected recordings. Before and since that period, jazz in general and big band music in particular have not been so fashionable, attracting only a small fraction of music fans. In spite of its minority status, however, big band music, like the blues, has never completely disappeared, reviving and reinventing itself in various forms for new generations of musicians and fans.

Big bands evolved from several sources, including marching bands, dance orchestras, and traditional New Orleans–style jazz combos. Early jazz groups had a "rhythm section" and a "front line." In the former, drums kept the beat, tuba played bass lines, and banjo and/or piano filled in the harmonies of the particular song being performed. The front line, typically a trumpet (or cornet), clarinet, and trombone, occasionally other brass or woodwind instruments, was responsible for playing the melody and then inventing solos based on the song's form; sometimes everyone improvised together. From the 1910s, bandleaders like Ferdinand "Jellyroll" Morton began to write songs and organize them into specific arrangements that exploited these different musical roles for dramatic effect. Early big bands led by James Reese Europe, Art Hickman, George Morrison, Dave Peyton, and Paul Whiteman played arrangements of popular songs using ever larger ensembles, adding trumpets, trombones, and woodwinds to create sections of similar instruments, also employing vocalists, classical string instruments, and extra percussion. As band size increased, a front-line part once performed by a single musician might now be played by two to five instruments, but the basic division of roles—drums, bass, chording instruments, trumpet(s), trombone(s), woodwind(s)—remained the same. More people meant less freedom for each musician, less space to solo, but allowed for complex arrangements and big, impressive sounds.

In the late 1920s and early 1930s Paul Whiteman, Guy Lombardo, and others were developing the "sweet" sound, a polite, polished style that used jazzy syncopation (accenting "weak" instead of "strong" beats). Meanwhile, McKinney's Cotton Pickers; Glen Gray's Casa Loma Orchestra; and groups led by Bennie Moten, Jean Goldkette, and especially Fletcher Henderson were cultivating a new approach to rhythm that would come to be known as "swing." In the rhythm section, the low march-like "oompahs" of the tuba were replaced by an even four-beat ("walking") pulse on acoustic bass; drummers began to use cymbals instead of snare drums for steady timekeeping; banjoists switched to guitar; and pianists played with a lighter, less repetitious touch. Cumulatively, these changes produced a subtler, suppler rhythmic feel that was paradoxically loose yet precise, relaxed yet urgent.

Swing-style big bands developed in several areas simultaneously. Around Kansas City, Bennie Moten's and other "territory bands" created spontaneous "head arrangements" by playing horn "riffs" (short, repeated figures) over the twelve-bar blues and other well-known chord progressions. In New York City, borrowing techniques from Don Redman, Fletcher Henderson wrote "charts" (written arrangements) in which trumpet, trombone, and reed sections "called" and "responded" to each other, much like a preacher soliciting "Amens'" from the congregation; his influential style also featured playful reinterpretations of song melodies (a practice popularized by Louis Armstrong), danceable grooves, and exciting improvised ("hot") solos. Regional bands from around Chicago, Cleveland, Dallas, Detroit, Omaha, and other parts of the South and Southwest heard and assimilated these elements into a swinging jazz style that, in contrast to the sweet bands, had a stronger beat and more improvisation.

The stock market crash of September 1929 initiated the Great Depression. Wealthy Americans lost their fortunes and workers lost their jobs, eating in soup kitchens and standing in bread lines to survive; many sought lighthearted music to ease economic hardships, reflecting a popular mood that was perhaps more romantic and sentimental, less cynical, than today. Before television, home video, digital recording, and the Internet, people relied on vinyl records, jukeboxes, radio broadcasts, and live performances to hear music. Across the country, "jitterbugs" (swing dancers) flocked to hotel lounges, ballrooms, nightclubs, movie theaters, supper clubs, and colleges to do the Lindy hop (a Harlem style imitating the takeoff and landing of Charles Lindbergh's epic transatlantic flight), the black bottom, the Charleston, the shag, and other popular steps; some preferred to listen, gathering around the stages to admire the impressive sounds and deft musicianship up close. Some of the most famous ballrooms and theaters were Atlantic City's Steel Pier; Boston's Raymor; Chicago's Aragon, Grand Terrace, and Trianon; Hollywood's Palomar; Cedar Grove's Meadowbrook; New Orleans' Blue Room at the Hotel Roosevelt; New Rochelle's Glen Island Casino; New York City's Palladium, Paramount, Roseland, and Savoy; and San Francisco's Mark Hopkins Hotel.

Over the airwaves the four major radio networks featured big bands every night on primetime radio shows and after 11 PM on direct broadcasts from various venues via remote "wires." Duke Ellington's early career was boosted by radio coverage of his regular gig at the Cotton Club in Times Square, while Count Basie was "discovered" by John Hammond, a wealthy New York producer who picked up his Kansas City shows over shortwave receiver. Collectors could buy their favorite vinyl recordings on the Columbia, Decca, and RCA Victor/Bluebird labels or hear them on local jukeboxes.

The innovations of African American bands led by Edward Kennedy "Duke" Ellington, Fletcher Henderson, Jimmie Lunceford, Bennie Moten (later led by William "Count" Basie), and Chick Webb were widely admired and imitated by musicians, but it was not until Glen Gray's Casa Loma Orchestra, a white band incorporating these innovations, caught the attention of college students that mainstream culture began to notice the latest jazz style. The big breakout came when another white musician, Benny Goodman, using arrangements Henderson had written for him, was featured on a coast-to-coast broadcast, followed by a rave performance at the Palomar on August 21, 1935, the latter effectively launching the swing era. In the decade that followed Basie, Tommy Dorsey, Ellington, Goodman, and Glenn Miller became household names, while hundreds of other bandleaders enjoyed lucrative and artistically successful careers.

At the peak of the swing era, annual *Metronome* (a top trade magazine) polls listed nearly three hundred groups in each of three categories. The proliferation of big band styles included swing, sweet, novelty/gimmick ("Mickey Mouse music"), and Dixieland (traditional New Orleans jazz), while Ellington's approach was so unique that he could almost be considered in a class by himself. Some of the best-known sweet bands were led by Glen Gray, Hal Kemp, Guy Lombardo, Glenn Miller, and Ray Noble (an Englishman), while popular swing band leaders included Les Brown, Cab Calloway, Jimmy Dorsey, Lionel Hampton, Woody Herman, Earl Hines, Harry James, Stan Kenton, Andy Kirk, Gene Krupa, Artie Shaw, Claude Thornhill, and Chick Webb. Within the swing category, leaders like Ellington, Herman, Kenton, Red Norvo, Boyd Raeburn, and Thornhill favored complicated arrangements aimed at serious listeners, whereas Basie, Goodman, Lunceford, and others kept the focus on danceable tempos and catchy melodies. Other big band styles were represented by Bob Crosby

Glenn Miller and his orchestra, ca. 1930–1944. (Underwood & Underwood/Corbis)

(Dixieland), Xavier Cugat (Latin dance), Billy Eckstein (bebop-influenced), Horace Heidt (gimmicks), Sammy Kaye (Mickey Mouse), Kay Kyser (sweet and gimmicks), Lawrence Welk (Mickey Mouse and polka), and Bob Wills (Western swing). A few bands altered styles within a performance or changed direction in the course of their careers.

A majority of big band fans were white, and nearly all of the groups were racially segregated. Blacks were not allowed to attend or perform in certain venues, especially in the South, where Jim Crow laws enforced racial segregation in public places. Musicians of all races, attracted by mutual talent, associated at informal, after-hours jam sessions; in public performances, however, black and white bands appeared on separate stages at separate times, even when they shared a billing. In *Check and Double Check,* a 1930 film featuring a short clip of Duke Ellington's band, producers worried that the light skin-tones of Puerto Rican trombonist Juan Tizol and Creole (mixed-race) clarinetist Barney Bigard would provoke a reaction when the movie was shown in the South, so they made the musicians wear blackface (skin-darkening) makeup. Benny Goodman, hailed as the "The King of Swing," yet resented by some because his success was built on musical innovations appropriated from African Americans, was also the first to tour with an integrated band, hiring black pianist Teddy Wilson in 1936 and black vibraphonist Lionel Hampton shortly afterward. Artie Shaw and Charlie Barnet had previously recorded with Wilson in 1934, as had Louis Armstrong and Jimmy Dorsey in 1936, but these musicians did not appear onstage together. More challenges to the color barrier followed when black singers and instrumentalists were featured with white bands: Billie Holiday in Artie Shaw's; June Richmond in Jimmy Dorsey's; Roy Eldridge in Gene Krupa's; Charlie Shavers in Tommy Dorsey's; and Roy Eldridge, Oscar Pettiford, Peanuts Holland, and Lena Horne in Charlie Barnet's. Results were mixed: although Goodman's half-white/half-black quartet was well received, Holiday was so disillusioned by hostile audiences in the South that she quit Shaw's band soon afterward.

Much of big band music was instrumental, but vocalists, whether soloists or harmonizing groups, were an important part of the scene, delivering the popular songs of the day and connecting to audiences. Early innovators included Bing Crosby, who took advantage of the newly invented microphone to sing in a soft, more intimate, "crooning" manner; Mildred Bailey, who incorporated jazz influences into her style; and Connee Boswell, who popularized "scat" singing (using nonsense syllables to imitate jazz instruments), invented by Louis Armstrong and developed into a high art by Ella Fitzgerald. The three most influential female jazz singers, Fitzgerald, Holiday, and Sarah Vaughn, all sang with big bands, while more commercially oriented vocalists like Doris Day, Perry Como, Dick Haymes, Lena Horne, Peggy Lee, Dinah Shore, Frank Sinatra, and Dinah Washington went on to successful solo careers. Other notable big band singers included June Christy, Bob Eberly, Billy Eckstein, Helen Forrest, Dick Haymes, Helen O'Connell, Anita O'Day, Jimmy Rushing, Jo Stafford, and Kay Starr; important vocal groups were The Andrews Sisters, The Boswell Sisters, and the Pied Pipers.

The male-dominated big band scene was highly competitive, with groups vying to outdo each other with complicated arrangements, athletic playing, and aggressive showmanship. Harlem's block-long Savoy Ballroom, one of the nation's first to allow blacks and whites on the same dance floor, staged several famous battles of the bands; Chick Webb's "house band" was bested by Duke Ellington's in March 1937, trounced Benny Goodman's the following June, and narrowly defeated Count Basie's in January of the next year. Women had a large role as singers, but very few played instruments or wrote songs and arrangements. All-girl groups included Rita Rio's, The Darlings of Rhythm, The Prairie View Co-eds, Phil Spitalny's Hour of Charm, Ina Ray Hutton and Her Melodears Orchestra, and The International Sweethearts of Rhythm. The Sweethearts, easily the best known and artistically acclaimed of the female bands, featured tenor saxist Viola Burnside, trumpeter Ernestine "Tiny" Davis, and drummer Johnnie Mae Rice. Standout female instrumentalists in male bands were trumpeters Billie Rogers and Valaida Snow, trombonist/arranger Melba Liston, and pianist/composer/arranger Mary Lou Williams, a featured star with Andy Kirk's band.

Several important economic and political events diminished the dominance of big band music. The American Society for Composers, Authors, and Publishers' 1941 dispute with major networks over songwriting royalties eliminated most popular songs from the radio for ten months; the establishment of Broadcast Music Incorporated provided licensing for roots and regional music; and the American Federation of Musicians' two-year ban on instrumental recordings led to a proliferation of vocal records and small-group sessions on smaller labels. When the United States entered World War II, many musicians were drafted. Gas rationing, a midnight curfew for nightclubs, plus a 20 percent "entertainment" tax levied on bands using a singer or playing dance music all made touring and performing expensive. The postwar recession, the rise of television, public taste for solo singers, and musicians' taste for modern jazz also contributed to the end of the swing era, officially decreed in December 1945 when eight of the most prominent leaders disbanded their groups.

Although big band music has never been as widely popular as it was in those years, it has continued to develop and diversify. A handful of bands continued to tour, while new ones led by Toshiko Akiyoshi, David Baker, Carla Bley, Bob Brookmeyer, Ray Charles, Don Ellis, Gil Evans, John Faddis, Maynard Ferguson, Frank Foster, Russ Gershon, Dizzy Gillespie, Charlie Haden, Andrew Hill, Quincy Jones, Thad Jones and Mel Lewis, Sherrie Maricle, Wynton Marsalis, Tina Marsh, Charles Mingus, Bob Mintzer, John Mosca, Gerry Mulligan, Arturo O'Farrill, Chico O'Farrill, William Parker, Tito Puente, Buddy Rich, Ray Santos, Alexander von Schlippenbach, Maria Schneider, and Sun Ra have experimented with instrumentation, musical form, harmonic language, rhythmic structures, and improvisational approaches, adapting elements of bebop (modern jazz), avant-garde, Latin, R&B, and rock music. Today, big bands thrive in recording studios, college music departments, and the armed forces, and on television programs and concert stages. Many are part-time outfits, assembled for rehearsals or special projects and events. Repertory bands, often institutionally sponsored, perform the works of great composer/arrangers, while "ghost bands" keep a former leader's music alive. In spite of difficult economic conditions, innovative artists have found alternative ways to do business: multiple Grammy-winner Maria Schneider raises funds for future recording projects entirely through fan contributions to her Web site. Latin, R&B, and funk-influenced groups still play for dancing, but most big bands perform concert music for serious listeners. The latest generation of young composer/bandleaders, including Darcy James Argue, John Hollenbeck, Guillermo Klein, Jason Lindler, Paul Neufeld, and Michael Occhipinti, continues to push artistic boundaries, bringing new cultural and musical influences to the mix.

See also: African American Influences on American Music; American Federation of Musicians; Armstrong, Louis; Basie, Count; Bop and Hard Bop; Blues; Charles, Ray; Club Venues; Dixieland Jazz; Ellington, Duke; Fitzgerald, Ella; Goodman, Benny; Holliday, Billie; Jazz; Jazz, Women In; Jones, Quincy; Latin Music in the United States; Marching Bands; Marsalis, Wynton; Polka; Radio; Sinatra, Frank; Swing Music; Vinyl Records

Further Reading

Basie, William "Count," with Albert Murray. 1995. *Good Morning Blues: The Autobiography of Count Basie.* New York: Da Capo Press.

Dahl, Linda. 1999. *Morning Glory: A Biography of Mary Lou Williams.* Berkeley: University of California Press.

Hasse, John Edward. 1927–1967. *Beyond Category: The Life & Genius of Duke Ellington.* New York: Da Capo Press, 1995. RCA: RD 104 DMC2-1141 (Victor/Bluebird/RCA) (2 CD set, rec. 1927–1967).

Kirchner, Bill. 1941–1989. *Big Band Renaissance: The Evolution of the Jazz Orchestra, the 1940s and Beyond.* Washington, DC: Smithsonian Institution Press, 1995. Smithsonian: RD 108 S25-17618 (5 CD set, rec. 1941–1989).

Schuller, Gunther, and Martin Williams. 1983. *Big Band Jazz: From the Beginnings to the Fifties.* Washington, DC: Smithsonian Institution Press. Smithsonian: RD 030-1R, 2R, 3R, 4R (4 CD set, rec. 1924–1956).

Simon, George T. 1982. *The Big Bands.* 4th ed. New York: Schirmer Books.

Stewart, Alex. 2007. *Making the Scene: Contemporary New York City Big Band Jazz.* Berkeley: University of California Press.

Tirro, Frank. 1993. *Jazz: A History.* 2nd ed. New York: W. W. Norton & Co.

Tom Greenland

Bluegrass

Bluegrass is a distinct form of popular music that developed during the 1940s out of America's pre–World War II commercial country music industry. The genre derived its name from the band of mandolinist Bill Monroe (1911–1996), an innovative musician who formed his first group in 1938. He settled on the Blue Grass Boys as a name in honor of his roots in Kentucky, the Blue Grass State. Monroe's unique style of country music inspired other musicians to adopt his band's sound as a model, which eventually led to the establishment of the genre.

While debate persists concerning definitions of bluegrass, certain characteristics remain central to the music's identity. One of these is acoustic string instrumentation. It generally consists of a mandolin, steel-stringed guitar, five-string banjo, fiddle, double bass, and occasionally a resonator slide guitar (dobro), or some combination thereof. Although the electric bass guitar has been the most common exception in this regard, even its use has become more infrequent since the 1990s. Other signature features are high-pitched singing and thematically traditional songs focusing on love, loss, death, homesickness, family, and Christian religion. These traits in particular led to the nickname "the high lonesome sound" in the 1960s, a phrase that remains popular in reference to the genre.

In addition to vocal solos, close harmony singing is a key aspect of bluegrass. Duets, trios, and quartets are all equally important components of its song canon. In bluegrass parlance, these textures typically position the melody or "lead" vocal part in the middle with a "tenor" part above for a duet and an additional "baritone" part below for a trio. Performers reserve quartets mainly for sacred material, adding a bass part below the baritone. The added parts primarily serve a homophonic, harmonic function, but they occasionally assume a melodic independence of their own amid textures of a more antiphonal or contrapuntal nature. The most common bluegrass song structure employs a strophic verse-refrain form that contrasts solo verses with a harmonized refrain.

Various preexisting forms of American popular music influenced the creation of bluegrass and provide insight into its current varieties. These include early country and old-time music, ballad singing, dance fiddle styles (especially those of the southern Appalachian region), early blues and jazz, Tin Pan Alley and parlor song repertories, and white and black gospel music traditions. Harmonic accompaniment remains largely confined to basic progressions of tonic, subdominant, and dominant chords, although certain contemporary styles of bluegrass have ventured considerably beyond such confines since at least the 1970s.

Similar to jazz, virtuosic instrumental solos form an important facet of bluegrass performance. Often based on the melody, such solos occur between verses of a song or in alternating succession during instrumental pieces, with the guitar and bass functioning as the rhythm section. During songs, these soloists also back the vocal parts with harmonic, rhythmic, and melodic embellishments, often in a responsorial fashion. The underlying rhythmic structure of bluegrass is quite uniform. Bass notes in the guitar and bass alternate with punctuated chords and accents from the other instruments to create an oompah-like accompaniment. A penchant for fast tempos, especially among instrumental works, prompted early descriptions of bluegrass to emphasize the music's "overdrive" quality and "breakneck" speeds.

Before Bill Monroe formed his first band, he and his older brother Charlie performed extensively in the Carolinas and Georgia as the Monroe Brothers, a successful mid-1930s musical duo. Along with old-time string bands, musical families, and yodeling singers, "brother duets" were a common fixture of early "hillbilly" music, the preferred term at the time. The music was especially

Lester Flatt (right) and Earl Scruggs (left) perform with the Foggy Mountain Boys at the Grand Ole Opry in Nashville, ca. 1960. (Michael Ochs Archives/Getty Images)

prevalent in southern Appalachia, an area that contributed significantly to the formation of bluegrass and that remains the strongest among the genre's regional identities. However, hillbilly music was popular throughout the American South and Southeast, and Bill Monroe, the "father of bluegrass," actually hailed from western Kentucky, far from the Appalachian Mountains.

Under the strain of their working relationship, the Monroe Brothers parted ways in 1938. Each organized his own group, and Bill Monroe soon hired a guitarist, fiddler, and bass player as the first lineup of Blue Grass Boys. By 1939 the group had earned a spot on WSM's *Grand Ole Opry* in Nashville, Tennessee, the most prominent "barn dance" radio program in the nation. This gave Monroe and his special brand of country music a national radio audience. However, he continued to refine his band's repertoire and sound over the next several years, and most scholars believe that Monroe's first true bluegrass band (and to some, his finest) did not coalesce until 1946, when his lineup included singer/guitarist Lester Flatt, Robert "Chubby" Wise on fiddle, Howard Watts on bass, and a young banjo player named Earl Scruggs.

Scruggs was a native of western North Carolina, a region with a deep heritage of banjo playing and the birthplace of a unique, three-finger style. Scruggs had mastered this technique, allowing him to execute clear, rapid sequences of notes and ably match the virtuosity of Monroe's mandolin and his skilled fiddlers. His brilliant playing was a distinct departure from the old-timey brushing, clawhammer style of Monroe's previous banjoist. Furthermore, he was uninterested in the comedic role that most banjo players assumed within the country music entertainment of the era. Instead, he elevated the instrument to a new level of musicianship and respect and established his three-finger style as an essential element of Monroe's music. Scruggs also added apt singing talents to Monroe's existing stable of strong vocalists, which included himself, Flatt, and Watts, enabling the bandleader to produce some of the finest quartet recordings of his career.

Unfortunately for Monroe, this "classic" band was short-lived, and all the members were gone by early 1948. Most notably, Flatt and Scruggs left to form their own band, the Foggy Mountain Boys, and Watts went with them. To distinguish their music from Monroe's, they minimized the mandolin's exposure and made Scruggs the main attraction. Nevertheless, Flatt and Scruggs featured a sound that clearly reproduced their recent work with the Blue Grass Boys and even carried over material from their time with Monroe. In 1955 the addition of dobro player Burkett "Buck" Graves was much more effective in giving Flatt and Scruggs a distinctiveness of their own. By this time their group had reached a level of polish and execution that was nearly flawless. As a result, Flatt and Scruggs became far and away America's most popular bluegrass performers, until their breakup in 1969.

Another group, the Stanley Brothers and the Clinch Mountain Boys, also began imitating the sound of Monroe's band during the late 1940s. Brothers Carter and Ralph were from the mountains of western Virginia. The former was a guitarist and lead singer, while the latter played banjo and sang harmony. In 1947 they achieved regional popularity after their band landed a daily radio slot on WCYB in Bristol, on the Tennessee–Virginia border. The Stanleys deeply admired Monroe's music as well as that of Flatt and Scruggs once the latter had formed the Foggy Mountain Boys. They reportedly developed a habit of appropriating material from Monroe's *Opry* broadcasts and performing it the following week on WCYB. In one case the Stanleys' commercial recording of a Monroe-derived song actually appeared on the market before Monroe's did. Nevertheless, the Stanley Brothers were bluegrass pioneers who cultivated a distinct vocal blend that captivated listeners until the untimely death of Carter Stanley in 1966. Ralph continued with the Clinch Mountain Boys on his own and as of 2011 was still one of the music's living legends.

While Monroe was apparently upset about his new competition in the late 1940s, the emergence of the Stanley Brothers and the Foggy Mountain Boys marked a significant milestone in bluegrass music's evolution. It was clear evidence that multiple groups were directly patterning their sound after Monroe's and represented the beginning of the music's transformation into becoming its own genre. This process continued as more bandleaders appeared during the late 1940s and early 1950s who, in addition to the Stanley Brothers and Flatt and Scruggs, exhibited the clear influence of Monroe's classic lineup from 1946 to 1948. However, most of these artists also advanced the music by making creative contributions of their own. Tennessean Jimmy Martin possessed singular talents as a guitarist and singer. Jim and Jesse McReynolds of western Virginia successfully adapted their sweet brother duet to the context of a bluegrass band. Bobby and Sonny Osborne, from southeastern Kentucky via Dayton, Ohio, contributed respective innovations to tenor singing and banjo playing as the Osborne Brothers. Don Reno, another extraordinary banjoist, joined with vocalist and fellow Carolinian Red Smiley to mix sparkling banjo work with a smoother, more crooning vocal approach. Mac Wiseman, also a Virginian, became one of bluegrass music's most respected solo singers. Perhaps unsurprisingly, several of these individuals (Martin, Sonny Osborne, Reno, and Wiseman) were direct alumni of Monroe's band.

By 1950 these performers, including Monroe, were not yet calling their music "bluegrass." To them it remained under the umbrella of "country" or "hillbilly" music. However, as consumer interest in the music of Monroe, Flatt and Scruggs, the Stanley Brothers, and similar groups began to grow during the 1950s, such consumers reportedly began to distinguish this more traditional music from the increasingly modern sounds of mainstream country by using the word "bluegrass" in their requests to performers, disc jockeys, promoters, and record store owners.

In the mid-1950s musicians from America's folk music revival began discovering bluegrass. Mike Seeger, Ralph Rinzler, and other major revival figures embraced the genre as a distinct, exciting, and authentic form of American folk music. Significantly, they represented a new segment of consumers and enthusiasts from outside the realm of country music who prized the acoustic instrumentation (especially the banjo), traditional songs, and old-fashioned ethos of bluegrass. To promote their discovery, Seeger produced the first bluegrass LP, *American Banjo Scruggs Style* (Folkways, 1957). This album's accompanying notes contain, according to Neil Rosenberg, the first print appearance of the word "bluegrass" in reference to the music and marks the completion of its evolution into a special, separate genre.

The folk revival provided bluegrass with a crucial new audience that helped its artists weather the storm of rock 'n' roll's new market dominance. Folk festivals and college campuses became new venue opportunities, and scholars began legitimizing bluegrass as a unique American art form via articles, concert promotion, and anthologies of recordings. The music also changed as a result. Certain performers began altering their repertoire to include more old-time traditional songs and material popularized by revivalists themselves. In particular, Flatt and Scruggs and the Stanley Brothers became darlings of the folk revival's college circuit. Monroe himself hired young urban bluegrass musicians reared in the metropolitan folk scenes of the North and the West Coast, and he even allowed Ralph Rinzler to manage his band for several months in 1964.

Folk revivalists' interest in bluegrass was evidence of a larger trend in the music: its continuing spread beyond the confines of the South. The most important regional scenes developed in urban centers that had experienced an influx of working-class migrants from the South during the early and mid-twentieth century. One of the earliest examples was Boston, where the Lilly Brothers (Everett and Mitchell "Bea") served as a catalyst for the expansion of bluegrass when they moved there from West Virginia in the early 1950s. Some of these scenes produced characteristic flavors of bluegrass style. Such artists as Jimmy Martin, Red Allen, and Mac Martin added honky-tonk shadings to their bluegrass while playing the bars and nightclubs of Cincinnati, Detroit, Dayton, Pittsburgh, and other Rust Belt cities that had large communities of relocated industrial workers from the South.

The Washington, D.C., and Baltimore region provided perhaps the greatest urban reception of the music. Early exponents included the Stoneman Family, Buzz Busby, and Earl Taylor. However, the emergence of the Washington-based Country Gentlemen in 1957 permanently established the area as an important center for bluegrass music. The folk revival heavily influenced the group, and as a result, its repertoire contained a diverse mix of old traditional material, bluegrass mainstays, contemporary folk, classic country, and pop-oriented fare. The Country Gentlemen remains the first bluegrass band to effectively fuse the musical sensibilities of bluegrass and the folk revival, and the group's national success helped affix this amalgam as a signature trait of the Washington-Baltimore bluegrass scene.

By the early 1960s similar bluegrass blends began surfacing on the West Coast, particularly in Los Angeles. The Dillards were one such group, whose material and marketing targeted folk revival audiences. With an appealing mix of musical talent, eclecticism, and droll humor, the group gained national exposure when it began appearing regularly as the Darling family on *The Andy Griffith Show.* Other Southern California bluegrass bands with important ties to folk and folk-rock included the Kentucky Colonels (featuring bluegrass guitar pioneer Clarence White) and the Hillmen. While neither matched the success of the Dillards, personnel from both groups later left bluegrass to become members of the folk-rock group The Byrds.

Not all bluegrass bands took advantage of the music's new fan base among folk revivalists. Such Nashville-based artists as Jim McReynolds and Jesse McReynolds and the Osborne Brothers were content to keep their careers within the realm of mainstream country music. The Grand Ole Opry inducted both groups as members in 1964, evincing their success at the time of performing bluegrass that incorporated heavy doses of contemporary country.

As America's folk music revival began to lose steam in the late 1960s, bluegrass artists began losing revenue. They needed another performance outlet; fortunately, bluegrass festivals emerged to fulfill that need at precisely the right time. Although Bill Clifton organized a multi-artist, all-day bluegrass concert on July 4, 1961, in Luray, Virginia, historians consider Carlton Haney's three-day festival in Fincastle, Virginia, on September 3–5, 1965, as the first genuine bluegrass festival. Haney was a passionate bluegrass promoter and impresario who, with the help of Ralph Rinzler, modeled aspects of his Roanoke Bluegrass Festival on the successful Newport Folk Festival. He also incorporated programming that celebrated the history of bluegrass, inviting former Blue Grass Boys to join Monroe on stage for special reunion performances.

Haney's Roanoke event set the pattern for subsequent festivals, and by 1971 they had spread all over the United States and even internationally, to New Zealand, Japan, and Canada. Their success ignited fresh interest in bluegrass, and the genre entered a new period of economic viability. The music's first regular periodical, *Bluegrass Unlimited,* was founded in 1966, with two additional monthly bluegrass magazines, *Muleskinner News* and *Pickin',* in circulation by 1975. These publications were essential in disseminating information and advertising for festivals. By the early 1980s their event listings reported around three hundred such gatherings, a number that doubled by the late 1990s.

As of 2011 several hundred bluegrass festivals—both large and small—continue to take place across the globe and remain crucial to the music's survival. They supply vital income for performers and comprise the "bread and butter" of most artists' bookings. These events are just as important for bluegrass consumers as well, for whom the festival experience has become a sacrosanct element of fan identity in addition to simply offering live entertainment, merchandise, and interaction with artists. The customer base of bluegrass has long included a disproportionately high number of aspiring or hobby musicians in its ranks, and festivals remain the ideal place for not only consuming bluegrass, but also playing it with friends and strangers alike.

As the festival boom sparked major changes in the bluegrass industry's venue and revenue bases during the early 1970s, the music itself was dramatically changing as well. While Bill Monroe, Lester Flatt, Ralph Stanley, and other "first-generation" performers still adhered to the core traits of classic bluegrass, the innovations of such groups as the Country Gentlemen, particularly in terms of exploring repertoire from other genres and more adventurous soloing, had inspired a new vanguard of bands to do the same. The Seldom Scene and II Generation (both founded by former members of the Country Gentlemen), along with J. D. Crowe and the New South and the Earl Scruggs Revue, are prominent examples that included experienced performers still pushing the envelope. Younger bands and musicians, hailing anywhere from New York to California, were no less critical in their contributions to this new phase of the music. These included such artists as the Bluegrass Alliance, Breakfast Special, Country Gazette, David Grisman, John Hartford, and the New Deal String Band.

"Newgrass" eventually took hold as the most widespread and preferred term to delineate this brand of bluegrass from more traditional or classic styles. The name came from the New Grass Revival, the foremost band to emerge from the movement. Formed in early 1972, this group developed a matchless flair for delivering uncompromising performances of rock, jazz, and blues material within a bluegrass framework. Driven by the wild virtuosity of mandolinist/fiddler Sam Bush and the vocal acrobatics of bassist John Cowan, the New Grass Revival soon became the quintessential progressive bluegrass band. Its success reached further heights after the addition of banjo phenom Béla Fleck in 1981 and continued until the group disbanded in 1989.

Following the explosion of newgrass, new bluegrass performers were bound to surface with intentions of countering the music's shift toward eclecticism. In the early 1980s the Johnson Mountain Boys, Del McCoury, and the Bluegrass Album Band (a super group of top players) became three of the leading acts in this regard, taking great pains to preserve the sound and style of early bluegrass. The inevitable dichotomies of new versus old, progressive versus conservative, contemporary versus classic, and innovation versus tradition became established in earnest, and they continue today as a major component of authenticity discourses within bluegrass music.

Perhaps most significantly, the early 1980s also marked the emergence of bluegrass artists unafraid to fold both progressive and traditional ingredients into their music. Such fusion typically involved contemporary songwriting laced and contrasted with elements of classic bluegrass. Pioneering groups in this regard included the Denver-based band Hot Rize, Doyle Lawson's group Quicksilver, and the Nashville Bluegrass Band. As bluegrass songwriting trends drifted closer in manner and spirit to those of contemporary country music, such "middle-of-the-road" bands became the new bluegrass mainstream during the late 1980s. They distinguished themselves by the ways in which they incorporated and modified earmarks of traditional bluegrass in their repertoire. Two of the most successful artists of the early 1990s that epitomized the mainstream bluegrass of the period were the Lonesome River Band and IIIrd Tyme Out.

This era in bluegrass history also witnessed great progress with respect to a major social critique that had long plagued the music. Female artists began making astonishing breakthroughs in the industry, which had been almost exclusively the domain of male performers since its beginnings. Alison Krauss, who rose to fame during the late 1980s and early 1990s, surpassed all others in this regard and became the first genuine bluegrass megastar. While Krauss was a consummate fiddler, her delicate singing mesmerized audiences and ultimately spelled her success. As a result, she and other such female performers as Dale Ann Bradley, Laurie Lewis, Claire Lynch, Lynn Morris, and Rhonda Vincent soon became main acts at festivals, on charts, and within the industry. While the achievements of this first generation of female stars rested chiefly on their vocal talents, women also became more common as instrumentalists. Today each instrument boasts several female players who compete professionally as top-caliber musicians, including Kristen Scott Benson, Alison Brown, Sierra Hull, and Missy Raines.

Despite these advances in counteracting the gender imbalance in bluegrass, the music's other glaring social issue, its whiteness, continued to persist. As in country music in general, whites had dominated the production and consumption of bluegrass since its beginnings. Although discourse about this fact has been steadily increasing since the 1980s, especially within bluegrass scholarship, it nevertheless remains a blemish on the industry that shows little sign of changing at present.

At the time of Bill Monroe's death in 1996, bluegrass had fully blossomed into a unique genre of American popular music with an international audience. Since the 1970s the aging Monroe had become increasingly comfortable and cordial in his role as the music's patriarch. Indeed, the legacy of bluegrass was in no danger of disappearing as it approached the new millennium. Two trade organizations, the Society for the Preservation of Bluegrass Music in America (SPBGMA) and the International Bluegrass Music Association (IBMA), had been in place for over a decade. The IBMA in particular, formed in 1985, elevated the industry to a new level of professionalism, providing members with a centralized resource for career training, business development, networking, and artistic recognition as well as exposure through an annual trade show and showcase. The International Bluegrass Music Museum, a sister organization of IBMA, became the hub for the music's history and preservation in 1995 when it opened its doors in Owensboro, Kentucky.

Since Monroe's passing, bluegrass has continued to advance and expand on a variety of levels. Television and film sound tracks have provided consistent spikes in the music's popularity since the debut of Flatt and Scruggs's theme song for *The Beverly Hillbillies,* a hit television series during the 1960s. Prominent film sound tracks include *Bonnie and Clyde* (1967), *Deliverance* (1972), and most recently, *O Brother, Where Art Thou?* (2000). The latter took the American popular music industry by complete surprise as it reached multiplatinum status shortly following its release and garnered five Grammy awards in 2002, including the coveted Album of the Year award. The success of this sound track was a huge boost to the bluegrass industry, thrusting it and other American roots music into the national spotlight.

Bluegrass has also benefited in recent years from a surge in mainstream country stars commercially experimenting with the music. Since 1999 Dierks Bently, Vince Gill, Merle Haggard, Patty Loveless, and Dolly Parton have all released bluegrass-inspired albums. Ricky Skaggs returned to bluegrass from country music in 1997 and has not looked back since, becoming one of the genre's most sought-after performers. Artists aligned with the alternative country and Americana wings of popular music have also helped advance bluegrass, including Steve Earle, Emmylou Harris, Jim Lauderdale, and Gillian Welch.

This attention from individuals connected to more mainstream realms of popular music has aided in the current vitality and prosperity of bluegrass. The international markets for the music that have existed for decades are more robust than ever, especially in Europe and Japan. The European World of Bluegrass event, inaugurated in the Netherlands in 1998, offers a European equivalent to IBMA's annual trade show and awards ceremony. Japan boasts numerous festivals and even its own bluegrass periodical, *Moonshiner Bluegrass Journal.* Bluegrass scholarship has also been steadily rising since the publication of Neil V. Rosenberg's landmark book, *Bluegrass: A History.* Under the editorship of Judith McCulloh, the University of Illinois Press began publishing a number of important titles in this regard. Recent academic symposia devoted to bluegrass at Western Kentucky University (2005) and Harvard (2010) provide further evidence of growing interest in the music among researchers and scholars.

Nevertheless, at its core bluegrass remains a niche music that is largely self-sufficient and grassroots, using a spectrum of traditionalism and innovation to fuel its creative growth. Today important artists remain across that spectrum. J. D. Crowe, Del McCoury, Danny Paisley, and Skaggs are examples of those who maintain identities as traditionalists. Prominent mainstream performers continue to draw inspiration from modern country music, including such acts as Blue Highway, Daily and Vincent, the Grascals, Mountain Heart, and Rhonda Vincent, among many others. Newgrass, with its emphasis on mixing bluegrass with other popular styles of music, has had perhaps the greatest impact and success. While many terms now appear in reference to more progressive, hybrid styles of bluegrass, the heritage of newgrass lives on among a wide variety of artists, including Jerry Douglas, Béla Fleck, Nickel Creek, the Punch Brothers, and the Yonder Mountain String Band. If the first decade of the new millennium is any indication, the future of bluegrass is in capable hands. Contrasting forces of tradition and innovation still complement each other and have yet to cease producing music that is compelling, appealing, and, in the words of an Osborne Brothers album title, uniquely up to date and down to earth.

See also: Banjo; Blues; Country Music; Fleck, Béla; Folk Music; Grand Ole Opry; Jazz; Krauss, Alison; Monroe, Bill; Parton, Dolly; Rock 'n' Roll (Rock); Seeger, Mike; Skaggs, Ricky; Tin Pan Alley

Further Reading

Artis, Bob. 1975. *Bluegrass.* New York: Hawthorn Books.

Cantwell, Robert. 1984. *Bluegrass Breakdown: The Making of the Old Southern Sound.* Urbana: University of Illinois Press.

Ewing, Tom, ed. 2000. *The Bill Monroe Reader.* Urbana: University of Illinois Press.

Goldsmith, Thomas, ed. 2004. *The Bluegrass Reader.* Urbana: University of Illinois Press.

Malone, Bill C. 2002. *Country Music, U.S.A.* 2nd rev. ed. Austin: University of Texas Press.

Rosenberg, Neil V. 1985. *Bluegrass: A History.* Urbana: University of Illinois Press.

Rosenberg, Neil V., and Charles K. Wolfe. 2007. *The Music of Bill Monroe.* Urbana: University of Illinois Press.

Smith, Richard D. 2000. *Can't You Hear Me Callin': The Life of Bill Monroe, Father of Bluegrass.* New York: Little, Brown.

Stanley, Ralph, with Eddie Dean. 2009. *Man of Constant Sorrow: My Life and Times.* New York: Gotham Books.

Wolfe, Charles K. 1996. *Kentucky Country: Folk and Country Music of Kentucky.* Rev. ed. Lexington: University of Kentucky Press.

Wright, John. 1993. *Traveling the Highway Home: Ralph Stanley and the World of Traditional Bluegrass Music.* Urbana: University of Illinois Press.

Kevin Kehrberg

Blues

The blues pervades American culture. But much like the light refracted through a glass prism, the kinds of blues heard as well as seen vary according to how and where they are enjoyed. The blues is a culture of *today.* Since the blues has had 120 years of "todays," its rich history may be explored through performances, recordings, books, and other media.

Blues Present

The blues is music for people who work hard, who expect it to be sung and played by musicians who also work hard. For many years the blues was played in bars and other places for adults only. Recently, however, it has been presented for free at outdoor concerts and festivals. A festival is a great way to hear the blues for the first time. During an afternoon or evening, you can listen to several different kinds of musicians: some sing the blues, others play them as wordless solos on their instruments. People can be seen dancing as the spirit moves them.

How to Sing the Blues

One way of defining the blues is by singing the blues. Blues songs are easy to create, but they do have some characteristics that make them the blues. The unit of a blues line is the beat, and usually a blues line may have sixteen beats:

1 2 3 4 5 6 7 8 9 10 11 12 13 14 15 16

Example 1

Most people gather them in groups of four units:

1 2 3 4 | 5 6 7 8 | 9 10 11 12 | 13 14 15 16 |

Example 2

Musicians often refer to such gathering as "meter":

4/4 1 2 3 4 | 1 2 3 4 | 1 2 3 4 | 1 2 3 4 |

Example 3

But let us return to our group of sixteen:

4/4 1 2 3 4 | 5 6 7 8 | 9 10 11 12 | 13 14 15 16 |

Example 4

The classic blues singer will sing the last syllable on beat 9:

4/4 1 2 3 4 | 5 6 7 8 | (9) 10 11 12 | 13 14 15 16 |

Example 5

Now for some words, such as, "If I had a million dollars, I wouldn't know what to do," we'll need to sing the word "do" on beat 9:

4/4 1 2 3 4 | 5 6 7 8 | (9) 10 11 12 | 13 14 15 16 |
(do)

Example 6

We have fifteen syllables to fit within nine beats. We can help ourselves by dividing each beat in two:

from 4/4 1 2 3 4

to 4/4 1 and 2 and 3 and 4 and

Example 7

So we can recite our words within nine beats:

4/4 1 and 2 and 3 and 4 and |
if I had a million dollars |

5 and 6 and 7 and 8 and
I __ wouldn't know __ what to

(9) and 10 and 11 and 12
(do) ____________

Example 8

Think about how long you may say some words for a longer time than other words. In our lines, I say "I" and "know" longer, so I give them an extra half-beat than the rest of my words.

So we have used nine of our sixteen beats. What do we do with the remaining seven beats in the line? If we think of our lyric as a "call," we can have a friend speak freely a "response" during the remaining beats:

4/4 1 and 2 and 3 and 4 and |
if I had a million dollars |

4/4 5 and 6 and 7 and 8 and |
I __ wouldn't know __ what to |

4/4 (9) and 10 and 11 and 12 and |
(do) ____________ |

13 and 14 and 15 and 16 and |
freely: (Do you know how many are in a million?) |

Example 9

Musicians often refer to a wordless response as a "fill," which they play on an instrument.

Many blues consist of three lines of the kind we constructed. The two lines (AA) are the same:

If I had a million dollars, I wouldn't know what to do.
If I had a million dollars, I wouldn't know what to do.
But if I had a hundred dollars, I wouldn't give it to you.

The third line (B) is different, but it has to rhyme with the repeated A line and also fit within nine beats:

4/4 1 and 2 and 3 and 4 and |
But if I had a hundred dollars, |

4/4 5 and 6 and 7 and 8 and |
I ___ wouldn't give __ it to |

4/4 (9) and 10 and 11 and 12 and |
(you) ____________ |

Example 10

We are writing lyrics to be sung and heard, so sometimes sound and rhyme take priority over meaning. Even so, the more that the words in the third line refer to those in the first line, the better. Some blues singers may set up their lines in the form of a joke, or as a story. But like rappers, blues singers are expected to create a flow of lines. Each set of lines—such as the A line and its repeat, and the B line—is called a blues chorus. The more choruses a blues singer can think up and sing, the more respect is given to the singer.

The blues is sung not just to meter—those groups of four beats—but also to musical melodies and chords. Broadly speaking, blues singers and musicians use a somewhat altered form of the diatonic major scale (the do-re-mi scale):

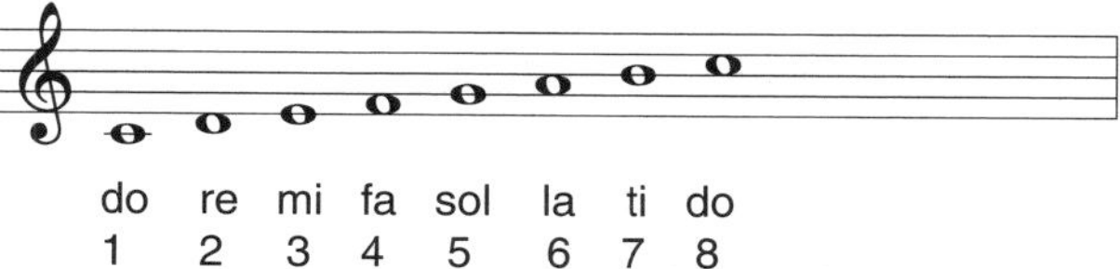

Example 11

The alterations to this scale are slight lowering ("flattenings") at the "mi" and "ti" tones (the third and seventh scale steps):

Example 12

These flatted tones are often known as "blue notes."

Using this group of scale tones, we can sing our blues line:

Example 13

The instrumentalists in a blues band play according to chords built with the same tones of the diatonic scale:

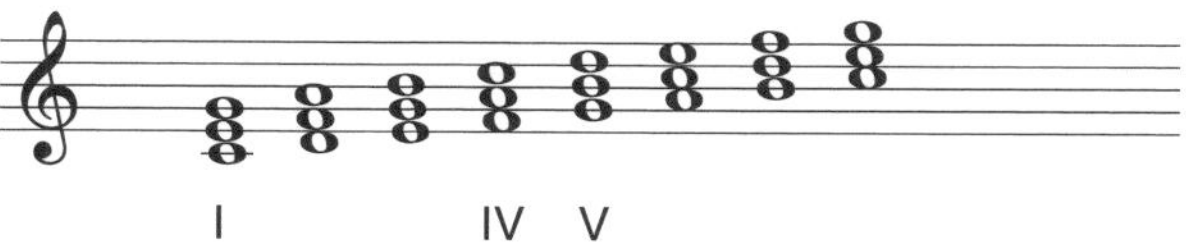

Example 14

They won't play all of these chords. They will use the one on "do" (I) for the first lyric line, the one on "fa" (IV) for the repeated line, and the one on "sol" (V) for the third line. These three chords are the basis of the harmonic blues chorus. Seldom will the altered tones of the classic blues scales be used in chords, except occasionally during the wordless "fill" between lyrics:

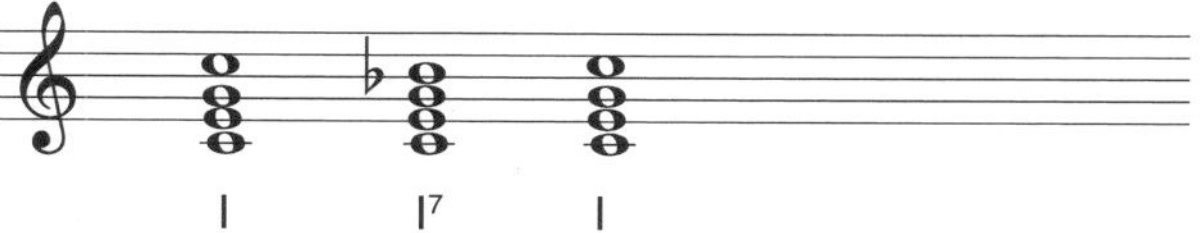

Example 15

These characteristics may be heard in the majority of songs by blues singers and their bands. But every so often they may sing or play differently from these basics. At such times, listeners should pay attention. And learn.

Knowing what to sing in a blues song is one thing, but knowing how to sing the blues is quite another. The greatest blues singers stay rooted in their life experiences, using their habits and ways of speaking to shape their singing. Here are some common backgrounds for the blues:

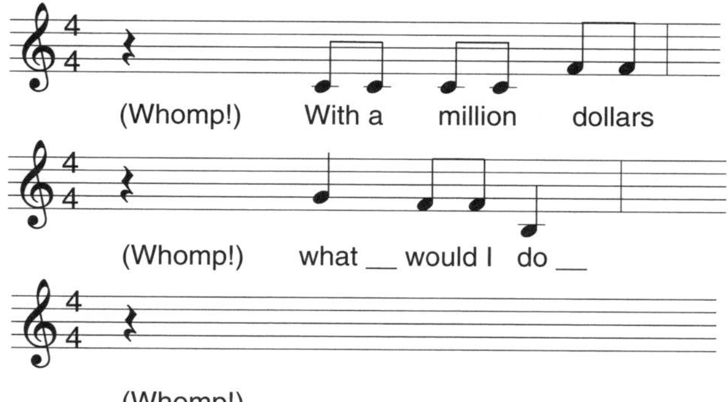

Example 16

- *Work:* Many of the earliest blues singers in the southern United States were farmworkers. Even before the first blues were created, these field laborers sang a kind of work song often now called a "field holler." These hollers were simple melodies of eight beats or sixteen beats, with words about bosses, mules, women, or some combination of all three. Workers sang hollers for two reasons: to pace themselves during the long summer days in the broiling sun and to ensure a safe execution of the task at hand—this is especially true for singing while swinging an ax or a hammer. Work song phrasing requires that there be a silent beat for the ax or hammer to fall before each song phrase is sung. So we can change our blues line about a million dollars into the style of a field holler by applying an ax-fall (or hammer blow) to the beginning of each subphrase, changing some words where need be:
- *Dance:* Audience dancing and the blues have been inseparable. The three-line, twelve-measure form may be found in nineteenth-century American dances, but not in spirituals and ballads. This suggests that the twelve-measure blues was always meant to be danced to, even if the blues was not born from dances. Many of the early African American dances to the blues had formal steps and names like shimmy, stomp, and slow drag. Today's dances may be informal and may no longer have names, but people still shake and bounce and sway wherever blues are played.

- *Social:* Sung slowly, the blues can be an expression of relief from personal hurts and worries, especially those concerning love, sex, or hunger. Some people have thought that singing the blues to oneself can be good individual therapy. Many of the classic blues songs are laments. But also, when sung by or for a group of people, a blues song can deal with loneliness, social wrongs, and concerns, whether they are about government programs, murders, jail, court trials for murder, or responses (or lack of them) to natural disasters. These songs are often like ballads, and they are of great appeal to people who prefer hearing their news from a witness instead of a reporter.

Venues

- *Markets:* Blues makes a loud noise—only a brass band may be louder—and it attracts people wherever it is played. Since the 1920s, business owners and entrepreneurs often hire bluesmen to play. In the 1920s an Atlanta musician named Robert Hicks became famous as "Barbecue Bob" for working and performing at a local barbecue business. For many years the Maxwell Street Market and the Delta Fish Market featured live blues performances in Chicago. To this day, blues may be heard in radio and television ads for supermarkets and restaurants, especially those offering barbecue and other southern foods.
- *Clubs:* The blues may be experienced at its cultural roots in clubs. In the cities they are bars and nightclubs, and in the rural counties they are juke joints and road houses. In the blues culture, such places are known by name: for example, Junior's, Sacone's, Joe's, Proud Larry's, Sarah's, Smitty's. Each of these spaces is small, containing a few hundred people at most, and they are frequented by local regular customers who often notice who is visiting from outside the neighborhood. Admission is paid at the door as a "cover charge" on the night of the show; rarely are tickets sold in advance, and then only for better-known performers. Since the clubs are the training grounds for young musicians, the music is often raw, its words and melodies being combined awkwardly. Still, a future star may be heard in such a small space, or a blues legend.
- *Concerts:* Many people listen to blues in formal, nondancing performances in concert halls and other kinds of seated venues. Over the years as blues became well-known and influential, people outside the culture of "working hard, playing hard" became interested in hearing the music. The kinds of blues performed in concerts are generally social blues for groups, yet on occasion a great blues singer may perform some of the older personal lament type. Blues musicians may be invited to perform at rock venues, including ballrooms, auditoriums, and rock festivals. These settings are less formal than concerts, and the style of blues may emphasize more the guitar solos and other instrumental features of the music than the words.

Blues Past

Even though the blues is powerful and immediate, it has been heard through many musical styles, each associated with a city or region. The following survey of blues history proceeds through the creative homes of the blues in the approximate order that they sprang up.

Many of the earliest blues may be dated to the late 1890s, as they are based on actual people living in St. Louis, Missouri, including Frankie Baker ("Frankie and Albert"), Stagger Lee, and Bob McKinney. In the 1930s many St. Louis musicians became known enough to make some records—a rare opportunity in those days—among them the superb guitarist and singer Lonnie Johnson, and the popular pianists-singers Peetie Wheatstraw, Roosevelt Sykes, and Walter Davis.

Blues History by Location For the last hundred years, Beale Street in Memphis, Tennessee, has been a center for the blues. "Father of the Blues" W. C. Handy wrote his first blues songs there in the early 1910s. Many Memphis musicians in the late 1920s made great blues records, including Gus Cannon, Will Shade and the Memphis Jug Band, Robert Wilkins, and Furry Lewis. Since 1948 the radio station WDIA has programmed blues and community news for black Memphians; Rufus Thomas was a radio host on that station for over fifty years. Through recording artists like Carla Thomas, Otis Redding, Ann Peebles, and Al Green, contemporary soul blues evolved at local record labels Stax and Hi Records in the 1960s and 1970s. Since the 1990s Beale Street has continued to be a popular blues destination for interested visitors, with the great blues performer B. B. King's club a key location.

Just south of Memphis is the state of Mississippi and its "Mississippi Delta," a vast region of cotton farmland stretching from the north and west state borders to the city of Vicksburg. The influence of early Delta blues on later city blues has led Mississippi to be called "the home of the blues." Through the 1940s many Mississippi Delta blues singers sang in the style of field hollers, especially Charlie Patton, Son House, and the legendary Robert Johnson. After World War II young musicians like Ike Turner and Little Milton helped to bring an urban R&B style to the Delta. Meanwhile, in the central state capital Jackson, many artists worked with local business people toward making records. Since the 1970s Malaco has been the leading record label for southern blues and soul. An abiding African American music tradition is the fife-and-drum music of the north-central "hill country" in the state, which may be heard in the recordings made of fife player Othar Turner, and its influence may be heard in the music of Junior Kimbrough , R. L. Burnside, and their sons.

New Orleans has long been famous for jazz, but its importance in blues has been around just as long. Many of the earliest blues masters in that city were the piano "professors" such as Jelly Roll Morton and Professor Longhair. After World War II a distinct piano-based R&B style became well-known through the performances of Fats Domino and Smiley Lewis. North Louisiana cities like Shreveport and the state capital Baton Rouge had pockets of local blues, with musicians like Slim Harpo, Lightnin' Slim, Tabby Thomas, and Lazy Lester; much of their music used to be known as "swamp blues." The bayou region with the Cajuns and Creoles engendered zydeco music—the blues of the bayou—featuring fiddles and accordions, and enjoyable and danceable records have been made by the late Clifton Chenier and others who followed, such as Boozoo Chavis, Beau Jocque, and Rosie Ledet.

North and South Carolina and Georgia contain what is popularly known as the Piedmont region, where many African Americans worked in the tobacco fields and textile mills. Leading pre-1940s musicians were guitarists Blind Blake, Reverend Gary Davis, Willie McTell, and Blind Boy Fuller. Their music retained more of the preceding ragtime style than had Memphis music, but it was played on guitars instead of pianos. For many years afterwards, the Piedmont style was kept alive by the next generations, including John Cephas with Phil Wiggins, Etta Baker, and Drink Small, along with white students of Piedmont music Roy Book Binder and Paul Geremia.

Texas blues has been around for as long as the blues in St. Louis, Memphis, and Mississippi; much of the earliest east Texas blues music was recorded by Henry Thomas, Leadbelly, and Blind Lemon Jefferson. In the 1940s T-Bone Walker formulated the modern blues electric guitar style that would influence early rock 'n' roll guitarists like Chuck Berry. Dallas was an early center of Texas styles, initially in the local "Deep Ellum" district, and later broadly in the Dallas-Fort Worth "Metroplex" region. In the 1970s and early 1980s Z. Z. Hill was a popular singer in the soul/blues vein.

The great migration of African Americans from the southern United States to the North and West during and after World War II led to the creation of new blues centers. Detroit was one destination, whose Hastings Street rivaled Memphis's Beale Street for blues music and black entertainment. John Lee Hooker is the most famous bluesman to have emerged from the postwar Detroit scene, yet pianist "Big Maceo" Merriweather and guitarist Eddie Burns were popular in their times, too. Hastings Street was converted to Interstate 75 during the 1950s, removing the venues where blues musicians played, but the local blues persist due to older local musicians like Johnnie Bassett.

Chicago attracted many musicians from the South, especially from Mississippi. For many years into the 1990s Maxwell Street was the site of a weekly bazaar where goods could be purchased, gossip could be shared, and live music could be heard, especially the blues. Before 1940 Chicago was already a notable blues town, the home of Tampa Red (Hudson Whittaker) and "Georgia Tom" (Thomas A.) Dorsey, the duo who had written and performed the monster 1928 hit "Tight Like That"; Memphis Minnie, one of the great women singer-guitarists; the pianist and arranger Lovie Austin; John Lee "Sonny Boy" Williamson; and Big Bill Broonzy. The later wave during and shortly after World War II brought the bluesmen who were most influential on what would be rock 'n' roll, especially Muddy Waters, Howlin' Wolf, Sonny Boy Williamson (born Aleck Miller, often numbered "II" to distinguish him from John Lee Williamson), Jimmy Reed, and Elmore James. Later greats based in Chicago were Koko Taylor, Junior Wells, Buddy Guy, and J. B. Lenoir, among many others. Several record labels have documented the changing sound of Chicago blues, chiefly RCA Victor Bluebird (1930s–1940s), Chess (1940s–1970s), Delmark (1950s–present), and Alligator (1970s–present). The annual Chicago Blues Festival is one of the leading showcases for the blues in the country.

The heyday of Kansas City nightlife was during the 1930s, when its clubs provided alcohol, gambling, and live music under the encouraging eye of local political boss Thomas Pendergast. Blues about the city were recorded by Jim Jackson and, a little later, by Wilbert Harrison. The great "blues shouters" Jimmy Rushing, Helen Humes, and Big Joe Turner developed their styles here. Today's Kansas City blues performers may not be as famous as their predecessors, but they are featured in local clubs and at the annual city blues festival.

California has had blues scenes in Los Angeles and the Oakland/Bay Area. Many of its performers were those who had moved there as part of the great migration, quite a few of them continuing the shout blues and jump blues of Kansas City. Louis Jordan, Wynonie Harris, and Roy Brown made records in the 1940s and 1950s that still swing hard today. Many older southern musicians who revived their performing careers in the 1960s often performed at the Ash Grove in Los Angeles and other folk-music venues for white audiences. Occasionally Hollywood directors notice the blues, whether in feature films like *The Blues Brothers* (1980) and *Crossroads* (1986), or in a series of short films such as *Martin Scorsese Presents The Blues,* aired on PBS in 2003.

New York tends to be a city where blues musicians visit instead of stay. Nonetheless, many of the classic blues women singers of the 1920s and their pianists made many fine records in New York recording studios, including Mamie Smith, who with a band led by the great pianist Willie "The Lion" Smith made the first blues record ("Crazy Blues," for Okeh Records) in 1920, and Bessie Smith, "the Empress of the Blues" as she was known. Those who moved to New York in the 1940s tended to have come from the eastern South, including the Carolinas, among them Reverend Gary Davis, Sonny Terry, and Brownie McGhee. The finest concert presentations of blues have been in New York, whether at Carnegie Hall or at Town Hall, and the city is often a lucrative stop for touring musicians.

During the first twenty years after World War II, Houston, Texas, had a wide blues scene, from the guitar-based blues of Lightnin' Hopkins, to the electric guitar flash of Clarence "Gatemouth" Brown, Albert Collins, and Johnny Clyde Copeland, to the singing of Big Mama Thornton and Esther Phillips. In recent decades the state capital, Austin, has had a blues style set by the late electric guitarist Stevie Ray Vaughan, pianist Marcia Ball, and singers Angela Strehli and W. C. Clark. Many resident and visiting blues acts may be seen on the long-running PBS series *Austin City Limits.*

Festivals Since the 1960s blues acts have been featured in music festivals, many devoted exclusively to the blues. Often they may be sponsored by a local blues society with the cooperation and assistance of the host city. Since all or nearly all of these events are outdoors, with programs that run through the afternoon into the evening, several blues musicians may be heard in one day. Also, festivals allow younger listeners to attend, unlike the clubs and bars, where attendees have to be as old as or older than the legal drinking age of twenty-one. Nearly all of the states now have festivals featuring blues. The spring issues of the magazines *Living Blues* and *Blues Revue* have lists of festivals for the coming summer and fall, as does the Web site Blues Festival Guide (http://www.bluesfestivalguide.com/).

Finding Out More About the Blues

Reference Books for Blues Names, Dates, and Records *The Encyclopedia of the Blues,* edited by Edward Komara (New York: Routledge, 2006) is a standard reference work for the blues, with subject entries, biographies, and suggestions for more reading. The *New Grove Dictionary of Music and Musicians* (New York: Oxford University Press, 2001) and the *New Grove Dictionary of American Music* (New York: Macmillan, 1986) have basic entries on blues with additional entries for the leading blues musicians.

Discographies are to records as bibliographies are to books. The standard discographies for blues are Robert M. W. Dixon, John Godrich, and Howard Rye, *Blues and Gospel Records 1890–1943* (Oxford University Press, 1997); *Blues Discography 1943–1970* (Eyeball Productions, 2006); and *Blues Discography 1971–2000* (Eyeball Production, 2010). However, these are straightforward lists of performers and recording session data, which are of use to knowledgeable blues listeners wanting to know the musicians on a recording and what the date of recording was. For the newcomer to the blues, a record guide like the *Penguin Guide to the Blues* or the *All Music Guide to the Blues* will be of enormous help for identifying the most important recording acts, suggesting the next performers to explore, and pointing out their best records.

Blues Magazines Magazines have lots of profiles of bluesmen and blueswomen. It is sometimes surprising how even the most famous of the living ones have not been written about in books. *Living Blues* concentrates on current African American blues, with many articles being interviews; even the obscure people have great stories to tell. *Blues Revue* includes white musicians in blues and blues/rock, and its articles tend to be reports rather than interviews. Both magazines have reviews of new CDs, DVDs, and books, as well as obituaries of recently deceased musicians. Also notable are two British magazines, *Blues and Rhythm: The Gospel Truth* and *Juke Blues.* They may be more expensive than the American blues magazines, but their articles are often worth re-reading.

Hearing the Blues: Some First Choices There are more blues recordings in print today than at any previous time through the 1980s. Virtually all of the music recorded before 1943 is now on CD, and for blues since 1943, at least excellent anthologies are available, if not a musician's complete recordings. Many performances may be accessible through online music resources like Pandora, Rhapsody, and Emusic. A few blues records are essential to novices and collectors alike:

- **Bessie Smith** (1894–1937): Her complete recordings of classic blues have been reissued on the labels Sony/Columbia and Frog. An exemplary singer of the 1920s who really leaned on the blue notes.
- **Robert Johnson** (1911–1938): His complete recordings were reissued on Sony/Columbia in 1990, 1996, and 2011. In his lifetime, he had only one hit ("Terraplane Blues," released 1937), but his recorded performances show him in the center of southern blues styles, including those of the Mississippi Delta. His songs were copied in the 1960s by white rock bands and performers, including Eric Clapton.
- **B. B. King** (1925–): *Live at the Regal* (MCA, released 1965). The Regal Theater was the leading venue for African Americans in Chicago through the early 1970s. B. B. King has been the elder statesman of the blues for the last twenty years, but this recording, taped live in 1964, preserves his younger self with a band that

doesn't let up on him by playing softly. And the Regal audience is an extra performer, too, with its vocal encouragement and screams.

- **Magic Sam** (1937–1969): *West Side Soul* (Delmark, released 1967). "Magic Sam" Maghett was a promising musician who mastered the tough transplanted electric Chicago guitar blues of the 1960s. *West Side Soul* is a cross-section of then-current blues done the Magic Sam way. And it rocks hard, too.
- **Current artists:** If you like an artist whom you have heard in person, find and buy any CDs you can find. With the number of CD stores and the availability of new blues CD decreasing, you may have to buy what you can whenever you can. Sometimes you may have to buy a CD at the artist's show (in which case, get it autographed). And some recordings are available as MP3 and MP4 files, such as through iTunes.

Books about the Blues Find and read what you can. Most libraries will have books by Paul Oliver, Peter Guralnick, and Samuel Charters, some of them tattered copies. If you can choose, start with *Nothing But Blues,* edited by Lawrence Cohn (New York: Abbeville Press, 1991), which offers an overview of blues history, each chapter written by an expert who has written a book worth seeking. Another good first book to read is Paul Oliver's *Blues Fell This Morning: Meaning in the Blues* (Cambridge, UK: Cambridge University Press, 1960; reprinted 1990), a foundational study of African American culture through blues lyrics.

Watching Classic Blues Bear in mind that for the most part blues musicians were not filmed until the 1960s. This was because of the expensive and cumbersome filming equipment, and also because blues was a lowbrow music compared to mainstream American popular music, even other African American kinds of music like popular theater, jazz, theatrical dance, and art composition. Also, for the 1960s, 1970s, and 1980s, not all blues musicians were captured on film or video. However, the *American Folk Blues Festival* DVDs (Hip-O Records) from 1960s European television broadcasts captured many precious performances from the mid-century legends. Since the 1990s many blues performers may be seen on DVD, some of their own production. My personal favorite of those by living artists is Bobby Rush, *Live at Ground Zero* (MVD Visual, 2007), shot at a Mississippi Delta blues club owned by actor Morgan Freeman. Rush has been one of the top showmen in blues and soul for the last twenty years: great music, funny (and true) lyrics, and earthy dancing.

See also: African American Influences on American Music; African American Women's Influences on American Music; Berry, Chuck; Blues, Women In; Cajun and Creole Music; Davis, Gary (Reverend); Domino, Fats; Dorsey, Jimmy, and Dorsey, Tommy; Guy, Buddy; Hooker, John Lee; Jazz; Jefferson, Blind Lemon; Johnson, Robert; King, B. B.; Lead Belly; Morton, Jelly Roll; Ragtime; Redding, Otis; Rock 'n' Roll (Rock); Smith, Bessie; Smith, Mamie; Taylor, Koko; Thornton, Willie Mae; Walker, T-Bone; Waters, Muddy; Zydeco

Further Reading

Komara, Edward, ed. 2006. *The Encyclopedia of the Blues.* New York: Routledge.

Hitchcock, H. Wiley, and Stanley Sadie. 2002. *New Grove Dictionary of American Music.* New York: Oxford University Press.

Edward Komara

The Blues Brothers (Active 1978–1982, 1988–Present)

The Blues Brothers was a band formed by *Saturday Night Live* (*SNL*) cast members John Belushi (1949–1982) and Dan Aykroyd (1952–). They went on to have several successful tours and a critically panned but successful film before Belushi's death from a drug overdose in 1982.

John Belushi had long been a fan of old blues recordings, and along with Aykroyd had chafed at not being allowed to perform musical comedy on *Saturday Night Live.* As their popularity grew, Belushi and Aykroyd were allowed more leeway, and Belushi appeared with the *SNL* band in a bee costume (the killer bees were an early recurring skit) singing the song "King Bee," to much applause. Encouraged by audience response, the duo developed the characters of Jake and Elwood Blues. Director Howard Shore (1946–) dubbed them The Blues Brothers, and they premiered the characters on *Saturday Night Live* on April 22, 1978.

The group was introduced by SNL music director Paul Schaffer who was imitating the ubiquitous rock promoter Don Kirshner (1934–2011). Schaffer (1949–) snidely told the audience that The Blues Brothers was "no longer an authentic blues act but [has] managed to become a viable commercial product." With that, the act took the stage backed by the *Saturday Night Live* band and ripped through the old blues classic "Hey Bartender." Later in the show they played "I Don't Know" to much applause. After this appearance, Belushi had his and Aykoryd's manager, Bernie Brillstein (1931–2008), negotiate a record deal. He also worked the band into an opening slot for a nine-date set with fellow *SNL* comedian Steve Martin (1945–) at the Universal Amphitheater in Los Angeles in fall 1978.

With the act's popularity increasing, Belushi hired the official Blues Brothers band members, most of whom appeared in the 1980 movie, *The Blues Brothers.* The band included Paul Schaffer as the bandleader on keyboards, Steve Jordan (1957–) on drums, Tom Malone (1947–) and Lou Marini (1945–) on saxophones, and Alan Rubin (1943–2011) on trumpet, all from the *SNL* band. Belushi also hired Matt "Guitar" Murphy (1929–), who had played with Muddy Waters (1913–1983) and Chuck Berry (1926–) and was a highly acclaimed session musician in blues and R&B. Two of Belushi's favorite musicians from Booker T and the MG's (active 1962–1971, 1973–1977, 1994–present), Steve "The Colonel" Cropper (1941–) on guitar and Donald "Duck" Dunn (1941–) on bass, completed the band.

Belushi invested $100,000 of his own money, and Atlantic Records recorded the sets of the band opening for Steve Martin. In December 1978 the live Blues Brothers record, *Briefcase Full of Blues,* was released. The record sold over a million copies and was certified platinum within a few months.

The Blues Brothers' success as a viable live band led to *The Blues Brothers* movie (1980), directed by John Landis (1950–). Landis had previously directed Belushi in *Animal House.* The filming was rife with problems, and Belushi and Aykroyd ended up leaving *SNL* before the start of the sixth season in order to complete the film. Despite their talent and top-notch cameo performances by Aretha Franklin (1942–), Ray Charles (1930–2004), and Cab Calloway (1907–1994), the film received mostly negative reviews. The movie, though, earned $57 million at the box office and has had a solid place on cable television for at least twenty-five years.

The Blues Brothers ended with Belushi's death in 1982. The band was dormant for almost two decades, until Aykroyd resurrected the group with Belushi's younger brother Jim Belushi (1954–) for new recordings and John Goodman (1952–) for the film *Blues Brothers 2000.* Aykroyd continues to tour with the younger Belushi as The Blues Brothers. There are licensed Blues Brothers tribute acts across the country.

See also: Berry, Chuck; Blues; Franklin, Aretha; R&B; *Saturday Night Live*; Tribute Bands; Waters, Muddy

Further Reading

Hill, Doug, and Weingrad, Jeff. 1986. *Saturday Night: A Backstage History of "Saturday Night Live".* New York: Vintage Books.

Woodward, Bob. 1984. *Wired: The Short Life and Fast Times of John Belushi.* New York: Pocket Books.

Brian Cogan

Blues, Women In

Blues are songs about life in its boldest and bluntest form. They exist as a way for people to tell their own stories and express individual emotions through their own words and melodies. Women have sung the blues from the very beginning on and off stage, through many different styles and eras, and these songs have given women a place to express not only the universal experiences relevant to all people, but concerns specific to women, according to women's points of view. From the nineteenth to the twenty-first centuries, the blues have permeated American music and have continually changed and been changed by it. They have formed the foundations of jazz, R&B, rock 'n' roll, funk, and hip-hop. What has remained consistent through the changes is the durability of its connection to raw and real life and the strength and suppleness of its structure, which bends and sways, but never breaks. As the blues themselves have changed from the jazz-inspired classic blues of the 1920s, through the electric-guitar-based sounds of the 1940s urban blues, to the hip-hop inflections of the twenty-first century, as long as the words speak about the realities of life, the happy and sad times, rich and poor, good sex and painful betrayal, the songs are the blues, and they help all of us speak, sing, and hear truths about real life.

Blues started in the nineteenth-century American South as the communal concerns of an enslaved people gave way to the individual concerns of the free but oppressed, and the work songs of slaves became the blues of sharecroppers. The term *blues* can refer to a general feeling, but it can also mean a very specific set of formal and harmonic traits. The eight-bar, twelve-bar, and sixteen-bar blues formats are the most common and share an AAB melodic pattern and rhyme scheme. A common chord progression overlays this formal structure, rendering the blues the only genre in American music whose core songs all share exactly the same harmonic structure. The strength of this structure is in the flexibility that this universal harmony provides, for the focus then becomes the improvisatory melody and lyric that is sung above it. Improvisation and individual creativity and expression, then, are the keys to these songs, which then can furnish a platform for the voices and concerns of women in a world where most of the accepted published and popular songs are written by white men. Women's blues has provided a unique and powerful vehicle for the concerns of people who have no other outlet for the expression of what they suffer; the first professional purveyors of the blues were black women.

After untold decades as an oral, folk tradition of the rural South, the blues got its professional start on the black vaudeville stage at the end of the nineteenth century. Women who could sing as well as dance found that traveling tent shows would hire them to sing the songs that black audiences loved to hear. These vaudeville shows gave black women not only a way of earning money outside of sharecropping and domestic service, but also a place to tell their own stories and the stories common to thousands of women like them. The most successful performers toured the North and South, finding success also with white audiences. As its popularity on stage grew, the young recording industry began to take notice, and the classic blues was born.

Gertrude "Ma" Rainey (1886–1939) started performing in tent shows in her home state of Georgia at the turn of the century and by the middle of the second decade was the most popular blues singer on the vaudeville stage. In 1920 another popular singer, Mamie Smith (1884–1946), recorded "Crazy Blues," which went on to become so successful that other companies flocked to record more blues singers. Stars of the vaudeville stage like Ma Rainey, Mamie Smith, Bessie Smith (1894–1937), Sippie Wallace (1898–1986), Ida Cox (1896–1967), Alberta Hunter (1895–1984), Ethel Waters (1896–1977), and Victoria Spivey (1906–1976) soon became recording artists as well.

Many of these classic blues singers wrote their own material as well as singing songs by others. Because the success of the blues depends so heavily on improvisation, blues singers imbue each performance of every song with originality, whether the song is their own or written by someone else; each performance is unique. Classic blues texts might portray a flamboyant picture of life for African American women in the 1920s, but the subjects are more down to earth than the idealized love songs also popular during these years. More often than romantic love, the songs tell stories of relationships from the point of view of women, often presenting the narrator as an active agent rather than a passive victim. Ma Rainey's "See See Rider" tells the tale of a woman in love with a two-timing man, but rather than putting up with it, she says she'll buy a pistol and kill her man, and "If he don't have me, he won't have no gal at all" (Davis 1998, 241).

Some songs talk about daily struggles of living in poverty, like Bessie Smith's "Poor Man's Blues," while others talk about the upside of life. There are party songs, like Smith's "Gimme a Pigsfoot," and songs about sex, like Alberta Hunter's "My Handy Man."

Toward the end of the 1920s two events catalyzed the end of vaudeville and the classic blues. The first sound movie eventually put much stage-based entertainment out of business, and the stock market crash led to a rejection of sad songs. By the middle of the 1930s companies stopped recording blues, and theaters stopped booking singers who only sang the blues. Some women, like Ma Rainey and Bessie Smith, faded into obscurity for decades, whereas others, such as Alberta Hunter and Ethel Waters, moved into musical theater and pop music, and their careers survived.

From the 1930s blues ceased to be a relatively unified style, but has since manifested in great variety of sounds and subgenres. Billie Holiday (1915–1939) began her career in the early 1930s as classic blues was fading. She sang primarily with jazz bands, merging blues inflections with jazz and pop; as one of the singularly most influential of all American singers, her work and contributions range far beyond the limits of any one style. Although the songs she sang tended to come from white popular repertoires rather than black, she sang them as if they were blues, applying the same improvisational process that the blues singers did, making them, in essence, blues songs (Davis 1998, 161–165).

American blues singer Ma Rainey, ca. 1923. (Frank Driggs Collection/Getty Images)

As many African Americans moved from the rural South to the urban North in response to the industrial needs of World War II, the blues regained its earlier popularity, but men with guitars dominated this incarnation. The urban blues of this era featured rough sounds from amplified guitars and guttural voices and texts about city woes on the one hand, and parties on the other, without losing focus on sex and relationships. Memphis Minnie (1897–1973) was one of the few blueswomen to play guitar and was at the vanguard of shifting to electric instruments in the early 1940s. Koko Taylor (1928–2009) reigned for decades as the Queen of the Blues. The songs she sang were built on the classic blues format accompanied by an up-tempo, hard-driving, electric guitar, bass, and drum set; she sang of good times and bad times,

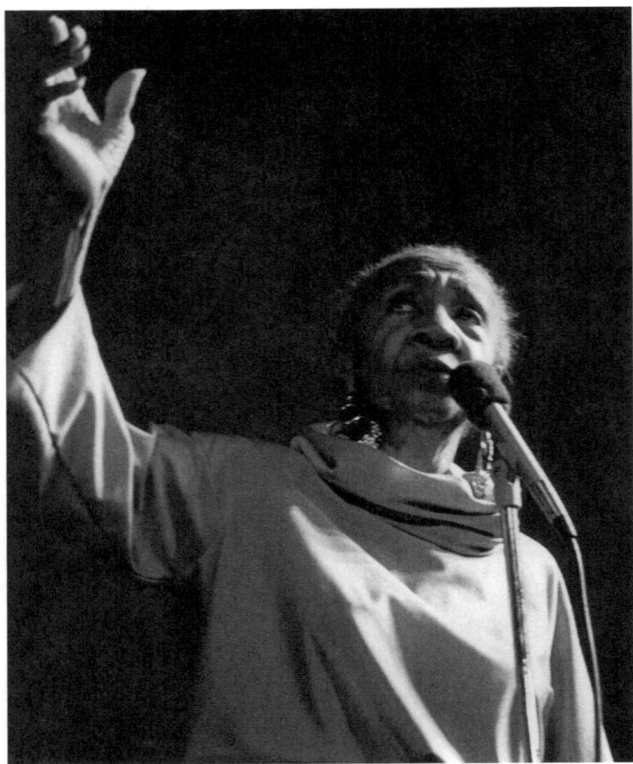

Blues singer Alberta Hunter, ca. 1970. (David Redfern/Redferns)

often mixing humor with tears. Her song "I Cried Like a Baby" tells the story of a woman who, after losing her man, finds comfort with a long list of other men.

When, at the end of the 1940s, "rhythm and blues" replaced "race records" as the commercial term for music created primarily for and by African Americans, musical styles proliferated. While some singers, like Koko Taylor and Willie Mae "Big Mama" Thornton (1926–1984), preferred the more traditional sounds of urban blues, other women took different routes. Dinah Washington (1924–1963) leaned toward jazz, Marie Adams (1925–) and Esther Phillips (1935–1984) sang a mixture of blues and big band called jump blues, and Etta James (1938–) and Ruth Brown (1928–2006) took blues to its rockiest edge. No matter the changes and diversity in styles, however, the fundamental principles of improvisation and real-life stories remained consistent.

By the 1960s, when blues singers were singing in all types of musical styles, the folk revival brought back an appreciation for traditional classic blues. As new singers like Janis Joplin (1943–1970) and Bonnie Raitt (1949–2012) took up the blues mantle with a modern sound, older singers who had lost their original popularity, such as Alberta Hunter and Sippie Wallace, got new opportunities to perform and record.

Alberta Hunter sang jazz and blues in the early years of the twentieth century, beginning a long and successful career that shifted from classic blues into musical theater and pop in the 1930s and 1940s. To help keep her career going, she joined the USO and sang for the troops during World War II and the Korean War, after which she retired from music the first time. In the mid-1970s, encouraged by the success of other blues singers in the folk revival, Hunter again began performing and recording, appealing to brand new audiences. One of her most popular songs, "My Handy Man," presents a long list of double entendres describing exactly what her man does for her, from shaking her ashes to churning her butter. Her entertaining approach to some of the grittier aspects of real life, even at age eighty, ensured the continuity not only of her career, but of the blues itself.

Since the number of styles exploded in American music in the 1950s and 1960s, women have sung the blues under many different labels. In addition to the singers mentioned above, blueswomen at the turn of this century include La Vern Baker (1929–1997), Odetta (1930–2008), Bonnie Lee (1931–2006), Katie Webster (1936–1999), Denise Lasalle (1939–), Irma Thomas (1941–), Millie Jackson (1944–), Bettye LaVette (1946–), Zora Young (1948–), Marcia Ball (1949–), Rory Block (1949–), Shirley King (1949–), Sarah Streeter (1953–), Valerie Wellington (1959–1993), and Shemekia Copeland (1979–). All have kept the music gritty, the stories real, and the blues feeling alive and well.

Although the blues revival rekindled the careers of several of the classic blues singers, blues has remained on the periphery of the music industry, and women have remained on the periphery of the blues world. In 1980 the Blues Foundation was established, with both a Hall of Fame and its own music awards. The list of twenty inductees in 1980 included only two women, Memphis Minnie and Bessie Smith; Ma Rainey, the next woman, was not inducted until 1983. The only other classic blues singer to be inducted was Alberta Hunter, in 2011. The other women included have been Big Mama Thornton in 1984, Billie Holiday in 1991, Koko Taylor in 1997, Etta James in 2001, Ruth Brown in 2002, Dinah Washington in 2003, Sister Rosetta Tharpe (primarily known as a gospel singer) in 2007, Irma Thomas in 2009, Bonnie Raitt in 2010, and Big Maybelle and Denise LaSalle in 2011 (http://www.blues.org/#ref=halloffame_inductees).

Recognition might be lacking, but women's contributions have been essential to a genre that has shaped American music. Women established the public form of classic blues in the 1920s and have helped to keep the fundamental principles of what makes it the blues alive through all of the shifts and eddies of American popular culture since then. They have told stories that no one else would tell, with improvised tunes no one else could sing. Not only would we have no jazz and rock without blues, but without the women's voices and stories, we would only have half of the truth. The blues gave women a platform, and women gave the blues its meaning.

See also: African American Influences on American Music; Blues; Funk and Postpsychedelic Funk; Halls of Fame; Hip-Hop; Holiday, Billie; Improvisation; James, Etta; Jazz; Joplin, Janice; Music Theater; Odetta; Pop Music; R&B; Rainey, Gertrude "Ma"; Raitt, Bonnie; Rock 'n' Roll (Rock); Smith, Bessie; Smith, Mamie; Thornton, Willie Mae; Vaudeville and Burlesque

Further Reading

Blues Foundation. 2011. "Inductees." http://www.blues.org/#ref=halloffame_inductees.

Dahl, Linda. 1984. *Stormy Weather: The Music and Lives of a Century of Jazzwomen.* New York: Pantheon Press.

Davis, Angela Y. 1998. *Blues Legacies and Black Feminism.* New York: Vintage Books.

Falkenburg, Carole van, and Christine Dall. 1989. *Wild Women Don't Have the Blues.* San Francisco: Calliope Film Resources, Inc./California Newsreel. Videocassette (VHS). 58 min.

Flandreau, Suzanne. 2002. "Blues." In *Women and Music in America Since 1900: An Encyclopedia,* edited by Kristine H. Burns, I: 58–62. Westport, CT: Greenwood Press.

Goldman, Stuart. 2001. *Alberta Hunter: My Castle's Rockin'.* View Video Jazz Series, deluxe ed. New York: View Video. 1 videodisc. 58 min.

Harrison, Daphne Duval. 1988. *Black Pearls: Blues Queens of the 1920s.* New Brunswick: Rutgers University Press.

Taylor, Koko. 1990. *Live from Chicago: An Audience with the Queen.* Chicago: Alligator Records.

Robin Armstrong

Bop and Hard Bop

One of the most remarkable features of bop in American jazz is its longevity. It began in the late 1930s or the 1940s and continues today. Even a brief excursion into the music department on any college campus with a jazz program in the United States will provide ample opportunity to hear a multiplicity of bop and hard-bop sounds. This is true despite the fact that early bop experiments began before the twentieth century was even half completed, in contrast to blues, ragtime, New Orleans combos, dance bands, and swing bands, which in the early years of the twentieth century all made their mark within a relatively brief period of about four decades.

Of course, bop and its hard-bop successor enjoyed a comparatively brief heyday, just as their predecessors had. But unlike the styles that dominated in the early twentieth century, bop's influence and appeal in the jazz community never fully dissipated. Certainly other styles (such as third-stream music, free jazz, fusion, and jazz rock) enjoyed a run of limited popularity, but a trip to the jazz training grounds of the first decades of the twenty-first century will yield a valuable lesson. Jazz auditions on college campuses and elsewhere throughout the United States consist not of Dixieland solos or ragtime riffs or swing-era styling, but rather bop. It is the common currency of jazz; any artist who expects to be taken seriously needs to have thoroughly immersed himself or herself in the bop repertoire and culture.

In the 1960s it was difficult to imagine that bop would have such staying power. But its allure might have been more predictable if the roots of bop had been more clearly understood.

The precursors of the bop movement occurred in the melodic shapes, harmonic complexities, and rhythmic subtleties of forward-thinking soloists of the swing period, such as Art Tatum, Coleman Hawkins, and Bix Beiderbecke. Even earlier examples like James Europe's 1913 *Down Home Rag* and Jabbo Smith's *Till Times Get Better* from 1929 demonstrate that the music many musicians and listeners viewed as "experimental" in the early 1940s came to embody the mainstream of jazz expression.

As World War II came to a close in the mid-1940s, many musicians who paid their dues in the big bands of the 1930s and 1940s longed for the opportunity to more freely express their soloistic ambitions. As a rule the swing era was one of expansion when gauged by numbers of musicians within the bands, so not surprisingly, emphasis was on the sound of the ensemble rather than the skills of the aspiring soloists. Bop sought to redress this inequity. Ensembles (as in the early days of the twentieth century) became smaller—usually piano, bass, and drums in the rhythm section with one or two horns—and the ensemble served the desires of the individual soloist rather than the musicians serving the needs of the ensemble, which had been the case during the period of the big bands. In a dramatic departure from swing-era aesthetics, bop's simple statement of the melodic idea and its underlying chord changes (that is, once through the tune's "head" or form) only served to set the stage for a succession of solos. Most of these improvisations were played with blistering intensity; the emphasis on complexity of expression and intricacy of presentation made even some seasoned musical veterans envious.

The genesis of this movement is generally traced to a series of sessions at Minton's Playhouse or Monroe's Uptown House, nightclubs in the Harlem section of New York, beginning in 1940. In attendance at these early sessions (usually convened after the players had finished their requisite big-band gigs) were now-legendary

Bop/Hard-bop Timeline

1940 Minton's Playhouse (West 118th Street, New York) hires Kenny Clarke as leader of its house band. Clarke in turn hires Thelonius Monk on piano. Many musicians stop by Minton's (and similar clubs) after their regular gigs. The resulting "jam sessions" include guitarist Charlie Christian and form the foundation for an emerging bop genre.

1941 The United States formally enters World War II, effectively beginning the decline of big band swing as America's dominant popular music.

1942 The American Federation of Musicians calls a strike, which includes a recording ban. It protests lack of compensation to musicians whose recordings are played on radio. The strike ends in 1944.

1942 Pianist Earl Hines recruits Dizzy Gillespie on trumpet and Charlie Parker on tenor saxophone (no alto slots are available) for his bop big band. This is the first time Gillespie and Parker appear together.

1944 Over the next two years, West Fifty-Second Street (between Fifth Avenue and Broadway) becomes the center of jazz in New York, and bop bands mature in these clubs.

1944 Gillespie leaves the Billy Eckstine band. He forms the first bop group at the Onyx Club with bassist Oscar Pettiford and drummer Max Roach.

1944 The Onyx Club band plus Coleman Hawkins on tenor saxophone assemble in a studio to lay down tracks of what are considered the earliest bop recordings.

1945 Gillespie and Parker form a bop ensemble at Three Deuces on Fifty-Second Street. They record many of the tunes that become anthems of the bop movement. The two continue to tour and record, but the group disbands at the end of the year.

1947 Parker forms a group with Miles Davis on trumpet, bassist Tommy Potter, Duke Jordan on piano, and Max Roach on drums. The next four years are arguably the most productive of Parker's career.

1947 Drummer Art Blakey forms his first group. It is originally dubbed the Seventeen Messengers, but is later reduced to an octet and renamed The Messengers.

1954 Trumpeter Clifford Brown forms a quintet coled by Max Roach. The group records a number of Brown's compositions, which become jazz standards.

1955 Charlie Parker dies in New York at age thirty-four. The coroner estimates his age as fifty-three.

1955 Blakey forms a second group, this time with pianist Horace Silver. It is named The Jazz Messengers and becomes the seminal band of the hard-bop movement.

1956 Clifford Brown and pianist Richie Powell die in a car accident. Brown is twenty-five and Powell, twenty-three.

performers such as trumpeter Dizzy Gillespie, Thelonious Monk on piano, Charlie Parker on alto saxophone, guitarist Charlie Christian, and drummer Kenny Clarke. By the end of the war the sessions moved to downtown New York in an area centered on West 52nd Street (dubbed "Swing Street" by the musicians). The clubs included the Hickory House, the Onyx, and the Famous Door, among dozens of others.

The musical experiments that began in Harlem centered on what are now termed "contrafacts," which use the underlying chords of an earlier song standard with the original tune replaced by a new melodic concept. Tempos were generally fast, and the chord structure, while retaining the essentials of the original tune, became more complex through the addition of added-note chords and alterations to the original structure (commonly referred to as "chord substitutions"). The best known of these contrafacts include Charlie Parker's modifications on the Ray Noble classic "Cherokee," which Parker retitled "Ko-Ko"; Dizzy Gillespie's reworking of the John Schonberger tune "Whispering," renamed "Groovin' High"; and Parker's "Ornithology," modeled on the composition "How High the Moon" by Morgan Lewis. Of course the move to this hybrid repertoire did not happen overnight. Like many innovations, the bop contrafacts went through a gradual process of first erasing the surface elements of the existing tune while maintaining its underlying changes and form. Two such transitional pieces are "I Got Rhythm" and "All the Things You Are," by George Gershwin and Jerome Kern, respectively. These two tunes achieved near-mythic status among jazz musicians, partly because of the nature of the chord changes. In the case of the Gershwin anthem, the chord progression even today is referred to simply as "rhythm changes" by musicians; this chordal underpinning serves as the jumping-off point for a freewheeling improvisational session. In Kern's standard, the chords and the tune's original and rare phrase configuration are sufficiently difficult and fast moving (one chord per measure) to merit the attention of the bop community and be included in the canon of melodies that virtually every accomplished bop musician knows in various keys.

The rhythm section players began to change the way in which their instruments were used within the context of the group. No longer was the drummer only a timekeeper; the juxtaposition between a steady beat on one section of the drum set and syncopated accents on other parts of the set became common to the bop drummer's collection of techniques. The bassist (following the advanced notions of Jimmy Blanton) now used the instrument as an integral part of the melodic component of the ensemble and explored the nether reaches of the instrument's range more frequently than had bassists of the swing period. Pianists comped much more irregularly and unpredictably, so the instrument was rarely used in a timekeeping role. Their task became one of primarily complementing (as the term "comping" would indicate) the efforts of the soloist.

As important as the superficial aspects of this new music were, they paled by comparison to the less-apparent aesthetics of the movement itself. Bop represented a dramatic departure from the conventions of the swing period in many ways. The latter aspired to be—and indeed, was—the popular music of the 1930s and early 1940s. Musical polish, showmanship, and visual interest all played a part in the enormous success of the big bands. Bop, by stark contrast, was from its very inception music for listening and music for musicians (and a musically educated public), with little pretension to commercial success or public acclaim. Not everyone (including many musicians) eagerly welcomed the new music. Reactions to bop ranged from the puzzled to the downright hostile. As a result, with some notable exceptions, bop marked the end of jazz as commercially viable music in the United States.

Bop also signified both political and racial reactions to conditions in the United States for African Americans. Younger black musicians tended to regard older ones as conformists ("moldy figs") who accepted the racial stereotypes of black entertainers. The older musicians viewed the bop stylists as annoying, unappealing, and musically disorganized. As bop continued to evolve throughout the 1950s and 1960s, nationwide racial segregation came under increasing attack, and the bop movement was perceived as another vehicle for protesting the political status quo. In this context it is certainly possible to consider the longevity of bop as the foundation of "modern" jazz, because it simultaneously brought together the conventions of the music and the political beliefs of its performers.

Despite the notion that this new music was a radical experiment, bop, like many movements before it, did not completely discard the conventions bequeathed to it by previous generations. Swing and bop, in fact, had many musical elements in common. Among them were the use of the standard formal designs (AABA, AA', blues), instruments (though the ensembles differed in size), uneven eighth-note division (though this "swing" style was not used as extensively by the boppers on tunes where a very fast tempo prohibited it), improvisation based on underlying chord changes, and other such similarities. Though a complete recitation of the differences between swing and bop is beyond the scope of this discussion, Richard J. Lawn has provided an excellent side-by-side comparison table in *Experiencing Jazz* (Lawn 2007, 210).

By 1950 many of the country's major recording labels had declared that bop, as commercially feasible music, was dead. That assessment was premature. Bop survived by embracing its own evolution. Successive styles such as "cool" and "West Coast" followed bop in the 1950s and 1960s, but eventually bop reacted to a desire by musicians to return to simpler roots. The result came to be known as "hard bop." Though there are definable differences between "classic" bop and hard bop, it would be a mistake to try to relegate most jazz artists to one style or the other. Bop significantly influenced the tone and direction of both the cool school and the West Coast style, but hard bop was the most recognizable successor to the bop sound that originated in New York in the late 1940s. These styles overlapped each other and grew more or less contemporaneously at the beginning of the second half of the twentieth century.

One of the most significant of the influences that helped give birth to hard bop was a competing trend of the 1940s labeled rhythm and blues (R&B). It existed alongside bop but took a more "grassroots" approach to music, with its exuberant showmanship and small-group extension of the hard-driving big bands of Cab Calloway, Lionel Hampton, and Jay McShann. This "jump band" style enjoyed a brief revival in the 1990s. Although critics tend to classify bop and R&B as distinct musical entities in this country, the fact is that, like the populace of the United States itself, jazz was—and is—a mixed salad, with each ingredient influencing the flavor of everything it touches. Bop touched off the move to the cool school, which led to a reaction of the hard-bop advocates, which had in turn been sparked by blues-based R&B bands.

One reason for the emergence of hard bop on the heels of the West Coast and cool movements was that many musicians never accepted the more laid-back aesthetics inherent in the cool school; they favored a return to the energy and emotional expression that first characterized bop innovations. A second reason, closely allied

Art Blakey performs with his Jazz Messengers at the New Morning Club in Geneva, Switzerland, March, 1981. Pictured from the left are Bobby Watson, Charles Fambrough (hidden), Art Blakey, and Billy Pierce. (Howard Denner/Photoshot/Getty Images)

with the first, was the desire on the part of the East Coast musicians to break with the performance techniques and values of the West Coast. In the view of hard-bop advocates, jazz was a music that should, above all else, express the vitality and exuberance that first brought jazz into existence. In their opinion, the idea of distancing oneself from the music, decreasing the dynamic levels, and playing with less fervor was the antithesis of how the music should be played. In the merging of bop and hard bop (though this would take some time to accomplish), jazz established the two closely allied styles as the synthesis of "mainstream" jazz.

If one views hard bop as merely a chronological extension of the original bop movement, a lot of the subtle—but very real—differences between the two categories are missed. For one thing, hard boppers were to some extent a retrospective group. They sought inspiration in the very roots of American music itself; blues, gospel, African call and response techniques, and similarly inflected idioms found their way into the hard-bop vocabulary. Another characteristic of hard bop was its increasing reliance on original music (as opposed to the contrafact-based tunes of bop). Much of hard bop was written in minor tonalities and relied on a more extensive use of arrangements that sought to split the difference between the freewheeling approach of the boppers and the write-it-all-down method of the big bands. Backgrounds for soloists were preconceived, as were introductions, out-choruses, and episodic interludes between solos. Finally, hard bop slowed the tempos that prevailed in the original bop style and, led by the drummer, provided a relentlessly driving rhythm that projected energy and momentum onto the music. This latter characteristic reclaimed some of the audience that had deserted jazz over its disillusionment with early bop.

Whereas bop was primarily centered in the clubs of New York, hard-bop venues were more widely disbursed, with centers of activity in Los Angeles, Philadelphia, Detroit, San Francisco, Boston, and Chicago. Because of a resurgence of audience interest in the music, many bop and hard-bop performers enjoyed long and stable careers. Among them were Horace Silver, Max Roach, Cannonball Adderley, Lee Morgan, and perhaps most important, drummer Art Blakey and The Jazz Messengers.

One reason for Blakey's success can be found in even the most superficial analysis of the group's recordings.

They emphasized a simple but incessant and driving rhythm and melodically meaningful tunes underpinned by innovative and inspired chord changes. Similar characteristics were featured by many of hard bop's practitioners, and some went on to incorporate even more of the R&B and religious characteristics of the American musical scene. These spin-off styles were known by various monikers such as "funk" and "soul jazz."

Although the majority of the hard-bop artists were more cognizant of audience response to their efforts than was true of the original bop players, there were exceptions. The most notable example was perhaps trumpeter Clifford Brown, a highly talented musician whose allegiance was primarily to the music. His brief but spectacular career made a major impact and lasting impression on jazz musicians who followed in his wake. Brown formed one of the great ensembles in jazz history when he coled a quintet with Max Roach in the 1950s.

The 1960s were a particularly difficult time for jazz, no matter what style one preferred. The primary reasons were twofold. First, bop was seen to have run its course (and in any event, the music was never especially popular during the period of its birth), and the free jazz and fusion species were not sufficiently attractive or powerful to engage a new audience. Second, jazz was competing with the still-emerging genre of rock 'n' roll and the attendant national obsession with Elvis and The Beatles. But by the 1970s things had begun to tilt back (at least in the field of jazz) toward the more approachable bop and hard-bop styles. While this assertion may seem odd given the lack of popularity of bop at its inception, one must remember that more than a quarter century had passed by the mid- to late 1960s. Many musicians now considered bop "classic" or "straight-ahead" music when viewed against the alternatives. In addition, bop and hard bop have both continued to evolve and attract new, younger players. The music today is seen as not just simple reverence for early artists, but rather a constantly developing creative art form that does not need commercial acceptance to be either significant or artistically valid.

What began as a fundamental and uncompromising turn from swing aesthetics became, ironically, an embodiment of the jazz status quo. What started as a sweeping (and some would say, extreme) departure from the conventions of the 1930s has come to symbolize everything that jazz stands for and is now viewed as the "conservative" alternative to current American musical trends.

See also: African American Influences on American Music; Club Venues; Funk and Postpsychedelic Funk; Gershwin, George; Gillespie, Dizzy; Jazz; Kern, Jerome; Monk, Thelonius; Parker, Charlie; Presley, Elvis; R&B; Rock 'n' Roll (Rock); Route 66 Neighborhoods and Music Culture; Swing Music

Further Reading

Gridley, Mark C. 2009. *Jazz Styles.* 10th ed. Upper Saddle River, NJ: Pearson/Prentice-Hall.

Kernfeld, Barry, ed. 1996. *The New Grove Dictionary of Jazz.* New York: St. Martin's Press.

Kirchner, Bill, ed. 2000. *The Oxford Companion to Jazz.* Oxford: Oxford University Press.

Lawn, Richard J. 2007. *Experiencing Jazz.* New York: McGraw-Hill.

Martin, Henry, and Keith Waters. 2002. *Jazz: The First 100 Years.* Belmont, CA: Schirmer/Wadsworth.

Meadows, Eddie. S. 2003. *Bebop to Cool: Context, Ideology, and Musical Identity.* Westport, CT: Praeger Publishers.

Tirro, Frank. 1993. *Jazz: A History.* 2nd ed. New York: W. W. Norton & Co.

Yanow, Scott. 2000. *Bebop.* San Francisco: Miller Freeman Books.

Ralph D. Converse

Border Music

The production of border music is not limited to the U.S.–Mexican border. From the Scottish to the North African borderlands, musical creation—involving rich balladry traditions, language switch, and innovation—is a hallmark of these regions across time and place. In addition, borderlanders and their music circulate; thus we hear border music in and outside of border regions. One can hear Khaled (1960–) singing rai (a form of colloquial Arabic that also uses Spanish, French, and Berber) in Paris, and Selena (1971–1995) in Mexico City and Washington (Swedenburg 2010).

For many scholars of U.S.–Mexican border music, the *corrido* is a text that defines the genre. It is a song that tells a story: in other words, a ballad. In the early twentieth century a corrido functioned like Yahoo news does today—with a catchy melody; it often told captivating stories, more specifically stories of the heroic exploits of a good person in a tragic situation. In the case of Jim Crow Texas in the early 1900s, this encompassed the experience of most working-class and upper-middle-class Mexican Americans. The border song that Américo Paredes (1915–1999) immortalized in his work is the story of Gregorio Cortez, an upright man fighting with a pistol in his hand (Paredes 1958). Iterations of the song inform us that Cortez was an honest, hard-working, and peaceful man until an Anglo Texan shot his brother. This set off a series of events, including Gregorio Cortez's turn to violence and incredible horseback rides across

Border Music Further Listening

Ayala, Pedro. *Pedro Ayala: El Monarca del Acordeon.* Arhoolie Productions (reissue) 9022, 2001.

Best of the 16th Annual Tejano Conjunto Festival. Various Artists. Guadalupe Cultural Arts Center 090927-23092-5, 1998.

Borderlands: From Conjunto to Chicken Scratch, Music of the Rio Grande Valley of South Texas and Southern Arizona. Various Artists. Smithsonian/Folkways SF CD40418, 1993.

The Chieftains, with Ry Cooder and Other Artists. *San Patricio.* Hear Music, 2010.

Los Donneños. *Mario y Ramiro: 16 Exitos de Oro Vol. 1.* Ramiro Cavazos Gutiérrez 1410, 2000.

Escobar, Linda. *Linda Escobar y Su Conjunto: Mi Cantina.* Escobar 1004, 2006.

Hinojosa, Tish. *The Best of the Sandia: Watermelon 1991–1992.* Watermelon CD1062, 1997.

Jiménez, Santiago. *Santiago Jiménez Jr. y Su Conjunto: El Corrido de Esequiel Hernández (La Tragedia de Redford, Texas).* Arhoolie Productions 9016, 1999.

Jordan, Steve, with Virginia Martinez. *The Many Sounds of Esteban "Steve" Jordan.* Arhoolie Productions 319, 1990.

Khaled. *Khaled.* Cohiba, 1992.

"Kenji y Los Gatos de Japon—La Unica Estrella." Posted on YouTube by Texmexdj on February 25, 2008. http://www.youtube.com/watch?v=wmYPVUerhDc.

La Rosa, Tony de. *Atotonilco.* Arhoolie Productions (reissue) 362, 1993.

Moreno, José. *José Moreno "El Patrullero": El Fidelero del Valle.* Arhoolie Productions 9014, n.d.

Rage Against the Machine. *Renegades.* Epic Associated Records, 2000.

Rolas de Aztlán: Songs of the Chicano Movement. Various Artists. Smithsonian/Folkways SFW CD40516, 2005.

Taquachito Nights: Conjunto Music from South Texas. Various Artists. Smithsonian/Folkways SFW CD40477, 1999.

Los Tigres del Norte. *Raíces.* Fonovisa, 2008.

Texas. The corrido of Gregorio Cortez provides singers with an opportunity to tell about the experience of Texans of Mexican descent, providing a counternarrative to that taught in required Texas history courses.

The formulaic nature of its sound, melody, and rhyme scheme make the corrido accessible to music makers and participants in the performance event. This song form follows a basic four-line quatrain structure with clear stops, and "the melody has four members only" (Paredes 1958, 206). The song form borrows from the Spanish romance and décima tradition and creates its own tradition for verse in the context of the Texas Mexican borderlands.

In his landmark work on border music, Américo Paredes argues that one cannot understand border music outside of the history of contact between Mexicanos and Americanos in South Texas. This story of conflict begins with the Spanish soldiers entering the northern territories of Mexico in the mid-1700s, which often involved violent and inhumane treatment of indigenous inhabitants. The next major event was the signing of the Treaty of Guadalupe Hidalgo in 1848, which led to the annexation of Texas—among other states—into the United States. Mexican representatives agreed to this "treaty" at the same time that U.S. armed forces successfully occupied Mexico City.

This history of conquest is central to understanding border music. In that context, border music provides an alternative voice or counterstatement to that of the conquering culture of the United States. How does this function? Musicians typically articulate border music in Spanish, English, Tex Mex, or a regional vernacular that incorporates code switch and words unique to the Northern Mexican–Southwestern U.S. border area.

Just as most scholars consider the corrido the urtext for border music, they also look to the South Texas conjunto ensemble as the evolution of that form (Peña 1985). Conjunto groups are not limited to playing corridos; in fact, they sing a variety of song types from corridos to rancheras, vals, huapangos, and English-language country and western music.

A basic conjunto ensemble includes an accordionist and a bajo sexto guitar player. Typically, the accordion player leads the band, and the group is often named after the accordionist. For example, on conjunto accordionist

Selected Border Music by Genre

Reggaetón

Calle 13. "Electro Movimiento." *Los de Atras Vienen Conmigo.* Sony Music Entertainment, 2009.

Wayne &Wax. "From Música Negra to Reggaetón Latino': Musical Examples." Last modified in July 2011. http://wayneandwax.com/?page_id=139.

Quebradita

"Banda Quebradita 2011." Posted on YouTube by Djcarlosb4 on December 21, 2010. http://www.youtube.com/watch?v=FmnFsqEwYDo.

Duranguense

El Trono de Mexico. *Almas Gemelas.* Universal Music, 2008.

"El Trono de Mexico: Almas Gemelas." Posted on YouTube by Latamboravaasonar on October 1, 2008. http://www.youtube.com/watch?v=BD1uSGxdjjQ.

Reggae

"Living Darfur (Official Music Video)." Posted on YouTube by Mattafixdarfur on September 19, 2007. http://www.youtube.com/watch?v=qQwCCm-H-sU&feature=related.

Mattafix. *Rhythm and Hymns.* Virgin, 2007.

Tohono O'odham

"Tohono O'odham Black Mountain Song." Posted on YouTube by TheLonelyBearCub on May 9, 2011. http://www.youtube.com/watch?v=7nphpJ8xOes.

Traditional Tohono O'Odham Songs. Various Artists. Canyon, 1998.

Yoreme

Indian Power. *Pazcola's Show.* Garmex Records, 2010.

Seminole

Songs of the Seminole Indians of Florida. Various Artists. Folkways FW04383, 1972.

Cumbia in Monterrey

Binomio de Oro de America. *En Vivo, Vol.1.* Disa, 2004.

Electronic and Mariachi

"Demetrio Gonzalez, Cocula." Posted on YouTube by Solitariodark on May 16, 2008. http://www.youtube.com/watch?v=_FG_1G0Vefw.

Esperon, Manuel. *El Mariachi Arriba Juarez—2.* 1996.

Narcocorridos

"Chalino-Corrido de Rosalino." Posted on YouTube by Chalinosanchez123 on August 2, 2007. http://www.youtube.com/watch?v=SicgxsYXkDA.

Sanchez, Chalino. *Alma Enamorada.* Balboa Recording Corporation (reissue) 1205523, 2003.

Santiago Jiménez Jr.'s (1944) album *El Corrido de Esequiel Hernández* (*La Tragedia de Redford, Texas*), the band is called Santiago Jiménez Jr. y su Conjunto (Jiménez 1999). Following the themes of contact and U.S. militarization, the lead song on this album is a corrido performed by a conjunto ensemble recounting the tragic encounter of a goatherder named Esequiel Hernández with the U.S. military (marines) on the border. Whereas the accordion and bajo sexto mark the conjunto ensemble, contemporary bands often include more instruments, such as the drums and electric bass.

Scholars have only recently turned their attention to the role of women in the production of border music (Broyles-González 2001; Dorsey 2006, 2011; Nájera-Ramírez 2003; Paredez 2009; Valdez and Halley 1996; Vargas 2006). This analysis—often from a Chicana feminist perspective—focuses on the ways in which female performers invert and call into question sexuality and traditional gender roles. The conjunto music performed by Linda Escobar (1957–), for example, questions standard gender roles and provides an alternative imaginary of female and male space (Dorsey 2011). Her song, "Mi Cantina," narrates a story in which the protagonist's spouse likes to frequent bars after work, spending his paycheck on beer. The song's female protagonist suggests that they rearrange the living room of their home and create a little cantina there that they can share, hence the title "Mi Cantina." In this song Escobar rearranges the furniture of everyday life bifurcated along the lines of gender roles.

Escobar's music also pushes the boundaries of how Mexican Americans view ethnicity and nation through conjunto music, and in the process of doing so, create new myths. For the past ten years on Veterans Day, Escobar has organized the El Veterano (The Veteran) music festival. The festival honors U.S. war veterans and features tejano conjunto music, culminating with a music scholarship (Dorsey and Díaz-Barriga 2011). Many of the veterans present at the event fought in World War II in Japan and are not particularly fond of Japanese

Conjunto group Roberto Palido y Los Classicos perform in Texas, 1989. (Philip Gould/Corbis)

people. One year the festival featured the Japanese conjunto ensemble Kenji Katsube y Los Gatos de Japon (2000). Despite complaints from some attendees—including relatives—Kenji y Los Gatos performed, and people still talk about their performance.

Scholars of borderlands music have widened their domain of study, no longer limiting their research to the corrido and conjunto or music related to them and their derivation. Contemporary scholarship on border music recognizes and explores the significance of and the ongoing musical conversation between music affiliated with and produced by indigenous people, African and African American people, and Mexican-origin populations. Indicative of this transformation in what constitutes border music are the prefix "trans" and the neologism "transnational." In other words, many scholars of border music today also consider themselves scholars of transborder or transnational music.

Alejandro Madrid's anthology *Transnational Encounters* exemplifies this range and significant opening of the field, discussing reggae, rock, *'Manitos,* reggaetón, and conjunto music within the context of border music (Madrid 2011). Emerging scholarship on border music also moves far beyond the place and issues of South Texas borderlanders, while at the same time—like border music itself—starting with contact, synthesis, and creation. One can learn about indigenous rap created by Yoreme musicians using digital technologies (Simonett 2001), black Seminole musicians in Coahuila singing spirituals through Capeyuye's work, or Tohono O'odham musicians mixing German and Mexican traditions to make their own sound in the U.S. border region in Arizona. Just as it has moved beyond the boundaries of place, people, and form, scholarship on border music has brought renewed attention to the performance event, heightening awareness of the interaction between the music and the dancers. Ramos-Kittrel (2011) takes us to a working-class club in northern Mexican industrial metropolis, Monterrey, to learn about Mexicanos dancing to cumbia, an African-based music traditionally affiliated with Colombia. Another scholar, Hutchinson (2011), draws attention to the ways in which body movement defines space in the brassy Duranguense tradition.

The themes and interests reflected in this new scholarship continue to encompass the core elements of border music. It is a repertoire based in contact and counterstatement. With these themes in mind, I conclude by sharing a new border music that provided a fuller history of the U.S. invasion of Mexico in the mid-nineteenth century.

"We are the San Patricios, a brave and gallant band. . . . We have but one demand: to see the Yankees safely across the Rio Grande." Irish actor Liam Neeson (1952–) voices this sentiment of a former conscript in the U.S. Army on the 2010 album *San Patricio* (*Saint Patrick*). An Irish band named the Chieftains (active 1962—present) joined with famous Mexicano musicians and Ry Cooder to record a series of songs that embody the spirit of borderlands music. The songs employ the talents of artists from a variety of backgrounds, coming together to tell stories not usually heard, often involving issues of justice. More specifically, accomplished Irish (the Chieftains), Mexicano (Los Tigres del Norte, active 1968–present; Chavela Vargas, 1919–), U.S. (Ry Cooder, 1947–), and borderland (Linda Rondstadt, 1946–) musical voices join on this album to tell an alternative history of the Mexican–American War of 1846, the story of Irish soldiers conscripted into the U.S. military. (The distinctions between Irish, Mexicano, U.S., and borderland are slippery. Some of these musicians could fit in different categories. A compelling argument can be made, for example, for categorizing Los Tigres del Norte as borderland artists. The point of the categories, however, is to show that individuals from various national and musical backgrounds were in dialogue when creating this album.)

A battalion that called itself the "San Patricios" deserted from the U.S. army and fought with the Mexican Army in five battles. These fights included the battles that helped defend Mexico City. The leader of the San Patricios was John Reilly. Most likely, John Reilly and the San Patricios connected with the plight of the Mexican people. As the musician Paddy Moloney of the Chieftains said, he envisioned that Reilly and the San Patricios related to "the injustice" the Mexican people were experiencing at the hands of the U.S. military. Moreover, Moloney explained that the San Patricios were also Catholic, and Ireland had been experiencing a similar sort of military presence for hundreds of years (NPR 2010). Ry Cooder's discussion of the impetus behind this album returns to the theme of providing a counterstatement: "I was never taught this story in LA public schools." He later revealed: "My own great-grandfather, whom I never knew, Jack O'Leary, was one of these conscripted Irish guys. He was a farmer. Stepped off the boat in the Ellis Island there. This is the family story. And as soon as he got down the gangplank, there were two officers, Army officers, waiting for him: Here's your uniform, and here's your gun" (NPR 2010).

Border music is integral to the music of the United States because border musics are what make "American" music the unique and constantly shifting hybrid that it is.

See also: Accordion; Guitar; Protest Music; Rap and Rappers; War and Music; Women in American Music

Further Reading

Broyles-González, Yolanda. 2001. *Lydia Mendoza's Life in Music/La Historia de Lydia Mendoza: Norteño Tejano Legacies.* New York: Oxford University Press.

Dorsey, Margaret. 2005. "Borderland Music as Symbolic Forms of Nationalism: The Best of Texas Tornados, Partners, and ¡Viva Luckenbach!" *Latin American Music Review/ Revista de Música Latinomericana* 26: 23–56.

Dorsey, Margaret. 2006. *Pachangas: Borderlands Music, U.S. Politics, and Transnational Marketing.* Austin: University of Texas Press.

Dorsey, Margaret. 2011. "Linda Escobar and Tejano Conjunto Music in South Texas." EVIA (Ethnographic/ Ethnomusicological Video for Instruction and Analysis). http://www.eviada.org/collection.cfm?mc=7&ctID=45.

Dorsey, Margaret, and Miguel Díaz-Barriga. 2011. "Patriotic Citizenship, the Border Wall and the 'El Veterano' Conjunto Festival." In *Transnational Encounters: Music and Performance at the U.S.-Mexico Border,* edited by Alejandro L. Madrid, 207–228. New York: Oxford University Press.

Gross, Joan, David McMurray, and Ted Swedenburg. 1994. "Arab Noise and Ramadan Nights: Rai, Rap, and Franco-Maghrebi Identity." *Diaspora* 3: 3–39.

Guadalupe, San Miguel, Jr. 1999. "The Rise of Recorded Tejano Music in the Post-World War II Years 1946–1964." *Journal of American Ethnic History* 19: 26–49.

Hutchinson, Sydney. 2011. "Breaking Borders/Quebrando fronteras: Dancing in the Borderscape" In *Transnational Encounters: Music and Performance at the U.S.-Mexico Border,* edited by Alejandro L. Madrid, 41–66. New York: Oxford University Press.

Jiménez, Santiago, Jr. 1999. *El Corrido de Esequiel Hernández* (*La Tragedia de Redford, Texas*). Performed by Santiago Jiménez Jr., Rufus Martínez, Victor Mermea, and Ruben Valle. Arhoolie Records. CD.

Kapchan, Deborah. 2006. "Performing Home and Anti-Home in Austin's Salsa Cultures." *American Ethnologist* 33: 361–377.

Kartomi, Maragaret, and Andrew D. McCredie. 2004. "Introduction: Musical Outcomes of Jewish Migration into Asia via the Northern and Southern Routes c. 1780–c.1950." *Ethnomusicology Forum* 13: 3–20.

Kenji Katsube y Los Gatos de Japon. 2000. "La Unica Estrella." http://www.youtube.com/watch?v=wmYPVUerhDc (accessed February 11, 2013).

Kloet, Jeroen de. 2005. "Popular Music and Youth in Urban China: The Dakou Generation." *The China Quarterly* 183: 609–626.

Kun, Josh D. 2000. "The Aural Border." *Theatre Journal* 52: 1–21.

Madrid, Alejandro L., ed. 2011. *Transnational Encounters: Music and Performance at the U.S.-Mexico Border.* New York: Oxford University Press.

Nájera-Ramírez, Olga. 2003. "Unruly Passions: Poetics, Performance, and Gender in the Ranchera Song." In *Chicana Feminisms: A Critical Reader,* edited by Gabriela F. Arredondo, Aida Hurtado, Norma Klahn, Olga Nájera-Ramírez, and Patricia Zavella, 184–210. Durham, NC: Duke University Press.

NPR. 2010. "The Chieftains and Ry Cooder Tell 'San Patricio' History." http://www.npr.org/templates/story/story.php?storyId=124333729 (modified March 7, 2010).

Paredes, Américo. 1958. *With His Pistol in His Hand: A Border Ballad and Its Hero.* Austin: University of Texas Press.

Paredez, Deborah. 2009. *Selenidad: Selena, Latinos, and the Performance of Memory.* Durham, NC: Duke University Press.

Peña, Manuel. 1985. *The Texas Mexican Conjunto.* Austin: University of Texas Press.

Ragland, Cathy. 1994. "La Voz del Pueblo Tejano: The Construction of Tejano Identity and Conjunto Music in South Texas." Master's thesis, University of Washington.

Ramos-Kittrell, Jesús A. 2011. "Transnational Cultural Constructions: Cumbia Music and the Making of Locality in Monterrey." In *Transnational Encounters: Music and Performance at the U.S.-Mexico Border,* edited by Alejandro L. Madrid, 191–206. New York: Oxford University Press.

Shannon, Johnathan H. 2003. "Sultans of Spin: Syrian Sacred Music on the World Stage." *American Anthropologist, New Series* 105: 266–277.

Simonett, Helena. 2001. "Narcocorridos: An Emerging Micromusic of Nuevo L.A." *Ethnomusicology* 45: 315–337.

Solomon, Thomas. 2006. "Hardcore Muslims: Islamic Themes in Turkish Rap in Diaspora and in the Homeland." *Yearbook for Traditional Music* 38: 59–78.

Soto, Amanda. 2008. "Conjunto in the Classroom." *Music Educators Journal* 95: 54–59.

Spinetti, Federico. 2005. "Open Borders. Tradition and Tajik Popular Music: Questions of Aesthetics, Identity and Political Economy." *Ethnomusicology Forum* 14: 185–211.

Swedenburg, Ted. 2010. "Rai Myths: Khaled (Repeat) and Cheikha Rimitti." *Hawgblawg: Broadcasts from NW Arkansas, Razorback Country,* September 12. http://swedenburg.blogspot.com/search?q=rai.

Valdez, Avelardo, and Jeffrey A. Halley. 1996. "Gender in the Culture of Mexican American Conjunto Music." *Gender and Society* 10: 148–167.

Vargas, Deborah. 2006. "Cruzando Frontejas: Remapping Selena's Tejano Music Crossover." In *The Chicana/o Cultural Studies Reader,* edited by Angie Chabram-Dernersesian, 314–323. New York: Routledge.

Wai-ming, Benjamin. 2003. "Japanese Popular Music in Singapore and the Hybridization of Asian Music." *Asian Music* 34: 1–18.

Margaret E. Dorsey

Boy Bands

A boy band is a pop music group, often assembled by a manager or producer, that features young males as vocalists and entertainers, performing songs written by outside songwriters. This contrasts with self-formed bands in rock music. Throughout popular music history, boy bands have been held in low regard by musicians and fans, who put a heavy emphasis on authenticity and artistry, although there are many critics and scholars who defend these groups on the grounds that they possess talent as singers.

The first boy band in American popular music was The Monkees (active 1966–1970). This quartet was formed through a casting call in Los Angeles, advertising for young actors and musicians to play a band on a television program. The concept of the show was inspired by The Beatles' first two feature films, *A Hard Day's Night* (1964) and *Help!* (1965). Both movies featured the members of the band living together and their encounters with the outside world. Of the four members of The Monkees, two—Englishman Davy Jones (1945–2012) and California native Micky Dolenz (1945–)—started as actors, while East Coaster Peter Tork (1942–) and Texan Michael Nesmith (1942–) had spent several years as semiprofessional musicians.

Although The Monkees earned admiration from The Beatles (active 1960–1970), Frank Zappa (1940–1993), and other rock luminaries, many journalists lambasted the group for the manufactured nature of its music and television program. In 1967 the group recorded *Headquarters* and *Pisces, Aquarius, Capricorn & Jones Ltd.,* two albums with the members of the band playing nearly every instrument. Although their show was a fast-paced comedy, they also made a film called *Head* in 1968. It was a commercial flop in its time, but has since gained appreciation as a work of experimental psychedelic cinema. The group disbanded in 1970, reuniting in 1976, 1986, 1996, 2006, and briefly in 2011. Jones and Tork have experienced middling continued success in music, while Dolenz found a new career directing television. Of the four, Nesmith is largely regarded as the most successful, both as a solo artist and as a businessman. His Grammy-winning 1981 film *Elephant Parts* led to the establishment of Music Television (MTV) later that same year. He also produced the 1984 cult film *Repo Man.*

The Monkees in 1966. Pictured from the left are Davy Jones, Peter Tork, Micky Dolenz and Mike Nesmith. (AP Photo)

Davy Jones, a successful entertainer and owner of racing horses, died of a heart attack in March 2012 in Florida.

In contrast to The Monkees, who were adults when their band formed, the two dominant boy bands in the 1970s consisted of adolescent boys: The Osmonds and Jackson 5. Formed in Gary, Indiana, Jackson 5 began when Joseph Jackson (1928–) saw potential talent in his sons, who enjoyed singing and dancing. He formed them into a quintet: Jackie (1951–), guitarist Tito (1953–), bassist Jermaine (1954–), Marlon (1957–), and Michael (1958–2009). After gaining a reputation on the local circuits, Motown Records founder Berry Gordy (1929–) signed the group to his label in 1968. As part of his marketing push for the band, Gordy fabricated the story that Motown starlet Diana Ross (1944–) had "discovered" the group; this myth even extended to its first album, entitled *Diana Ross Presents The Jackson 5* (1969).

The group was an instant success, with its debut record hitting number one on the *Billboard* charts for both pop and R&B. Two of the band's best-known songs, "I Want You Back" and "ABC," are sprightly, catchy pop songs, whereas "I'll Be There," another hit, is a heartfelt soul ballad. Joseph and Gordy were quick to capitalize on Michael's youthful good looks and skills as a dancer, and they promoted him as the lead singer of the quintet. The group became a trademarked commodity for the Motown label, including Jackson 5 merchandise and even a Saturday morning cartoon. Jermaine and Jackie released a few solo singles in 1973 and 1974, but Michael's solo releases earned the most acclaim and success. As the boys grew older, sales began to decline; Joseph blamed this in part on Motown for refusing to update the group's image into the independent songwriting musicians they had become.

In 1975 Joseph negotiated a generous contract with CBS Records. Motown held the rights to the Jackson 5 name, as they had trademarked it. As a result, the group released music simply as The Jacksons. Jermaine stayed at Motown out of loyalty to his now father-in-law, Berry Gordy. Jermaine was replaced in the lineup by younger brother Randy (1961–). Turning to a more dance-heavy, disco-inspired sound, The Jacksons were also given their own variety show on the CBS network.

Michael's work under composer Quincy Jones (1933–) on the film musical *The Wiz* (1978) led to the pair collaborating on more solo efforts, first *Off the Wall* (1979) and then *Thriller* (1982). *Thriller* propelled Michael to worldwide fame, earning him the title King of Pop from the music press. The album itself was a flashy dance-pop album in the R&B vein, although Michael and Jones made his music accessible to white audiences by having guitarist Eddie Van Halen (1955–) play on "Beat It" and having Michael perform a duet with former Beatle Paul McCartney (1942–), "The Girl Is Mine." Eager to publicize the rising star, MTV desperately wanted to show Michael's music videos. However, CBS Records demanded that MTV either feature more African American musicians in its programming or it would not be allowed to show any videos by any CBS artist. MTV agreed to the terms, and Michael Jackson became the most famous performer of his time. After winning an unprecedented eight Grammys in 1984, *Thriller* to this day is the best-selling album of all time.

Jackson 5 reunited in 1984 for the album *Victory,* which had Michael at the forefront of the band, including a duet with Rolling Stones front man Mick Jagger (1943–) on one song. The recording sessions were fraught with tension, and the band parted acrimoniously after *Victory*'s follow-up tour. The group had some sporadic reunions, but never again with the success that came with *Victory.* Michael's erratic lifestyle throughout the late 1990s and into the 2000s kept any hopes of another reunion out of reach.

The Osmond Brothers (active 1958–present) began by performing barbershop quartets (and later quintets) as regulars on *The Andy Williams Show* throughout the 1960s. At the end of the decade, with younger brother Donny (1957–), the brothers opted to perform more pop-oriented music. After revamping the band's image to appeal to the modern pop audience, The Osmonds earned new success. Donny, viewed as the "cute" member of the group, was often promoted as the lead singer. In 1976 Donny and younger sister Marie (1959–) starred in *The Donny and Marie Show,* a variety program featuring comedy sketches and musical numbers. The other Osmond brothers worked behind the scenes on the show, which ran until 1979. After some career ups and downs, Donny and Marie still make regular television appearances. Along with their older brothers, they also regularly perform on the oldies circuit.

Boy bands enjoyed continued popularity among young fans in the 1980s. Producer Maurice Starr (1953–), who had some limited success with the all-black quintet New Edition (active 1978–1997, 2003–present), started New Kids on the Block (active 1984–1994, 2007–present) as a white counterpart. Recruiting local adolescent singers and aspiring musicians through an audition process, Starr branded the quintet in ways similar to how Joseph Jackson and Berry Gordy had promoted Jackson 5. Starr found ways to get the group's music videos into heavy rotation on MTV, and he had the band star in its own Saturday morning cartoon.

After a scandal involving the European pop duo Milli Vanilli (active 1988–1998), whose Grammy was revoked when it was revealed the band's "singers" did not sing any of their songs, New Kids on the Block faced similar allegations in the media. Although untrue, the rumors, paired with a shift toward rap and grunge, led to the group's dissolution in 1995.

The story of Starr and New Kids on the Block is a template for the story of nearly every boy band, in which an impresario capitalizes on young talent for his own gain. The late 1990s saw another boom of boy bands that contrasted with the success of the Spice Girls (active 1994–2000, 2007–2008), Sheryl Crow (1962–), Sarah McLachlan (1968–), and countless other female pop and rock singers. Two of the biggest bands were the Backstreet Boys (active 1993–2002, 2005–present) and 'N Sync (active 1995–2002), both of which were managed by Lou Pearlman (1954–), an Orlando-based businessman who had no previous experience with music before starting a record label to mimic the success of New Kids on the Block. Although the Backstreet Boys had greater commercial success, 'N Sync featured singer Justin Timberlake (1981–), who has achieved a great level of fame as a solo artist and film actor. Pearlman's shady dealings in the business world caught up with him in 2006, when he was arrested for running a Ponzi scheme; he is currently in prison, with an expected release in 2029.

Boy bands have become solidified as part of the musical lexicon as a fabricated group of young boys, often under the auspices of a manager more interested in profit than music, who sing catchy pop music that has great appeal to young listeners. This technique of creating music and making stars in a calculated manner has expanded beyond the United States, the United Kingdom, and Australia to many non-English-speaking countries; entire genres have grown up around J-pop (Japan) and K-pop (South Korea).

See also: Crow, Sheryl; Disco; Jackson Family; Jackson, Michael; Jones, Quincy; Motown; Music Television; Pop Music; Zappa, Frank

Further Reading

Gray, Tyler. 2008. *The Hit Charade: Lou Pearlman, Boy Bands, and the Biggest Ponzi Scheme in U.S. History.* New York: HarperCollins.

Lefcowitz, Eric. 2011. *Monkee Business: The Revolutionary Made-for-TV Band.* Port Washington, NY: RetroFuture.

Osmond, Donny. 2006. *Life Is Just What You Make It: My Story So Far.* New York: Hyperion.

Vogel, Joseph. 2011. *Man in the Music: The Creative Life and Work of Michael Jackson.* New York: Sterling.

Alex DiBlasi

British Influences on American Rock Music

Although rock 'n' roll music had its origin in American R&B, British bands energized the medium in profound ways throughout the 1960s and beyond, exerting a remarkable influence on their American musical counterparts throughout rock's storied history. From its beat music roots, British rock 'n' roll flowered into a number of different genres, resulting in the British blues boom; the British invasion; and such subgenres as psychedelic rock, progressive rock, glam rock, heavy metal, punk rock, new wave, and synth rock, among a variety of others. In so doing, British musicians created a wide array of innovations, especially in the growth of the album as a creative form, as well as in approaches to instrumentation and songwriting.

The exportation of American rock 'n' roll to Great Britain largely occurred via the emergence of Elvis Presley (1935–1977) as an international phenomenon. His musical prowess and global fame exerted a powerful influence on British youth, who looked toward American R&B as their musical touchstones, as well as such American rock "musicals" as *Blackboard Jungle* (1955) and *Rock Around the Clock* (1955). This is especially true of the skiffle craze, which captured the imaginations of British teenagers during the 1960s, largely due to its lack of exclusivity. Given its improvised and makeshift instrumentation—often involving washboards and tea-chest basses, in addition to conventional instruments such as banjos and guitars—skiffle could be played by virtually anyone in any economic class or with any level of musical ability. Led by Lonnie Donegan, whose "Rock Island Line" (a song taken from an African American folksong popularized by Lead Belly, the iconic American folk and blues guitarist) emerged as the movement's unofficial anthem, skiffle energized a generation of British young people, inspiring them to form beat music groups across the United Kingdom.

In Great Britain, beat music blossomed in the wake of the skiffle craze, with bands such as The Beatles (active 1960–1970), The Searchers (active 1959–present), Herman's Hermits (active 1963–present), and Gerry and the Pacemakers (active 1959–1966), among others, merging American rock 'n' roll with R&B, doo-wop, and soul music. In the UK, beat music was seen as a clear departure from the crooners and balladeers who were dominating British music during the late 1950s and early 1960s, including such artists as Cliff Richard (1940–), Tommy Steele (1936–), and Marty Wilde (1939–). The result was a peculiar brand of beat music—so named for the backbeat rhythms at its core—that propelled the so-called British invasion onto the American musical and cultural scene in the early to mid-1960s. As with beat combos in the United States and UK alike, beat music—or the Merseybeat, as it was known in conjunction with Liverpool and North Country bands, with their proximity to Liverpool's River Mersey—worked from a basic instrumentation that featured vocals, lead, rhythm, and bass guitars, and drums.

The British blues boom evolved during this same era, led by such acts as The Rolling Stones (active 1962–present), The Kinks (active 1964–1966), The Who (active 1964–1982, 1985, 1988–1989, 1996–present), and The Yardbirds (active 1963–1968, 1992–present)—and later, Cream (active 1966–1968, 1993, 2005), Fleetwood Mac (active 1967–present), and Led Zeppelin (active 1968–1980). The British blues boom developed in the late 1950s, drawing its inspiration from American blues and jazz—most notably the work of Lead Belly (1888–1949), the iconic American folk and blues guitarist. The British importation of Chicago blues and Delta blues exerted a marked influence on the direction of this strain of British musical culture, heralded by key visits to English shores by Big Bill Broonzy (1903–1958) and Muddy Waters (1913–1983). Their forms of amplified, electric blues influenced legions of British musicians, including The Rolling Stones' Mick Jagger (1943–) and Keith Richards (1943–), as well as virtuoso blues guitarist Eric Clapton (1945–) and his Cream bandmates Jack Bruce (1943–) and Ginger Baker (1939–). Top-flight blues guitar masters such as Jeff Beck (1944–) and Jimmy Page (1944–) also found their mettle through the British blues boom.

The apex of the UK's emergent rock and blues influence occurred in the early 1960s, when British acts finally succeeded in turning the tide. Commonly known as the British invasion, this recalibration of the U.S.–UK intercreative influence was led by The Beatles, whose impact on popular music continues to resound and reverberate even five decades after their landmark first visit to the United States in early 1964. Coming in the wake of the assassination of President John F. Kennedy in Dallas in November 1963, The Beatles' timing simply couldn't have been more propitious. As esteemed rock critic Lester Bangs observed:

> America—perhaps young America in particular—had just lost a president who had seemed a godlike

The New Wave of British Heavy Metal

Black Sabbath's power and punk's speed combined in the mid-1970s to early 1980s in the new wave of British heavy metal (NWOBHM), spearheaded by Judas Priest (1969–present), Motörhead (1975–present), Diamond Head (1976–1985, 1991–1994, 2002–present), and Iron Maiden (1975–present). These bands tended to write songs about deviance and destruction at paces, volumes, and with attitudes matched only by punk bands like the Sex Pistols. Lars Ulrich (1963–) and James Hetfield (1963–), of America's most popular metal band, Metallica, cite the NWOBHM bands as their immediate ancestors and greatest inspirations. They included covers of Diamond Head's "Am I Evil?" and Holocaust's (1977–present) "The Small Hours" on their 1987 EP *Garage Days Re-Revisited.*

Peter Buckland

> embodiment of national ideals, who had been a youth-cult superstar himself. We were down, we needed a shot of cultural speed, something high, fast, loud, and superficial to fill the gap: we needed a fling after the wake. It was no accident that the Beatles had their overwhelmingly successful *Ed Sullivan Show* debut shortly after JFK was shot (the date was February 9th, 1964). (Bangs 1976, 169)

The superficiality of incipient Beatlemania was short-lived, as The Beatles consolidated both their fame and their creative energies in short order. Indeed, there is little argument among musicologists and cultural critics alike that The Beatles had a remarkable and sustained influence on rock music.

Their songs—like our greatest works of art and literature—almost exclusively concern themselves with the human condition and the dilemmas that confront us regarding our interpersonal relationships. Through the incomparable songbook of John Lennon (1940–1980) and Paul McCartney (1942–), The Beatles' albums offer a range of decidedly literary characters, from Mean Mr. Mustard, Eleanor Rigby, and Polythene Pam to Billy Shears, Bungalow Bill, and Rocky Raccoon. These personages, in addition to the psychological dimensions of the band members' personalities themselves, imbue their works with a particularly literary texture. "The Beatles treated the album as a journey from one place to another," Tim Riley observes. "They built cornerstones into their records by positioning their songs in relation to one another: beginnings and endings of sides can sum up, contradict, qualify, or cast a shadow over the songs they introduce or follow" (Riley 1988, 29–30).

For this reason, one can hardly imagine hearing the final a cappella chords of "Because" without anticipating "You Never Give Me Your Money" and the bittersweet nostalgia of the symphonic suite that punctuates the end of the band's career on *Abbey Road* (1969). Similarly, the manner in which "Drive My Car" and "Taxman" introduce *Rubber Soul* (1965) and *Revolver* (1966), respectively, not only signals us about the musical direction of various stages of the band's development, but also becomes inextricably bound up in our successive "listenings" to those recordings. Hence the positioning of The Beatles' songs on their albums underscores the ways the band intended us to receive—indeed, to interpret—their artistic output. Who could conceive, for example, of listening to the beginning of the *White Album* (1968) and not hearing the soaring jet engines that announce the familiar opening strains of "Back in the USSR"?

Perhaps it is the band's abiding self-consciousness about the overall production, design, and presentation of its art that invites us to *read* (and re-read) The Beatles in the first place. From their heyday as recording artists from 1962 through 1969, The Beatles made a staggering musical and lyrical leap from their first album, *Please Please Me* (1963), which they recorded in a mere ten hours, to *Sgt. Pepper's Lonely Hearts Club Band* (1967), the *White Album,* and *Abbey Road,* which took literally thousands of hours to complete. McCartney astutely recognized the artistic integrity of the band's musical oeuvre when he referred to its albums as a singular and sacrosanct "body of work." When considered in this fashion, The Beatles' corpus reveals itself to be a collection of musical and lyrical impressions evolving toward an aesthetic unity that appears to have reached its artistic height during the late 1960s and the band's studio years. A number of music critics echo McCartney's sentiments, including Ian MacDonald, who notes that "so obviously dazzling was the Beatles' achievement that few have questioned it." Their recordings, he adds, comprise "not only an outstanding repository of popular art but a cultural document of permanent significance" (MacDonald 1994, 1, 33). Riley similarly describes their canon as a "very intricate art. . . . The Beatles are our first recording *artists,* and they remain our best" (Riley 1988, 9, 26; italics added).

Perhaps most significant is that in the wake of The Beatles' spectacular cultural impact, musicians the world over rethought their notions of artistry. Quite suddenly,

In one of the most defining moments in music and television history, The Beatles perform on *The Ed Sullivan Show* in New York City on February 9, 1964. (AP Photo)

rock musicians reimagined themselves as full-fledged creative talents who would "author" coherent bodies of aesthetic output in the form of long-playing record albums. They were no different than their counterparts in the literary and fine arts, whose latest output would be considered in terms of its capacity for engendering widespread cultural sway.

But The Beatles' influence was far greater than merely being a rock 'n' roll touchstone. As cultural critic Greil Marcus remarks, the group's massive and sustained impact exists as a fully formed "pop explosion"—the second and latest such intercultural upheaval after the ascent of Elvis Presley. "A pop explosion is an irresistible cultural explosion that cuts across lines of class and race," Marcus writes, "and, most crucially, divides society itself by age. The surface of daily life (walk, talk, dress, symbolism, heroes, family affairs) is affected with such force that deep and substantive changes in the way large numbers of people think and act take place" (Marcus 1976a, 181). In spite of the band's own, relatively brief fusion as a working ensemble—it recorded almost the entirety of its output between September 1962 and August 1969—The Beatles erased and remade our conceptions of a pop-music phenomenon, impacting almost every segment and demographic of contemporary culture. It also influenced the direction of most, if not all, of rock music's subgenera in nearly the same instant, including folk and rock music, as well as the psychedelic rock, heavy metal, and progressive rock of the late 1960s and early 1970s.

While The Beatles' musical influence was indeed wide-ranging, the band's earliest impact in the years following its demise can be most clearly seen in the advent of the singer-songwriter era. The notion of rock music as artistry loomed large in The Beatles' wake—most especially in terms of the ways in which popular musicians sought to share their music as a form of personal expression. In the well-honed tradition of Lennon and McCartney, numerous American songwriters emerged on the East Coast in the late 1960s and early 1970s, including Simon and Garfunkel, former Apple recording artist James Taylor, Carly Simon, Bruce Springsteen, and Billy Joel. The American West Coast saw a similar emergence throughout the 1970s, including the California-oriented rock of the Eagles and Jackson Browne. In many ways the Eagles' landmark *Hotel California* album can be interpreted as a 1970s-era counterpart to *Sgt. Pepper,* given the latter album's penetrating social and cultural critique of American appetites for consumerism and excess. In addition to the title track's acerbic criticism of American cults of personality and identity politics, in the album's anthemic concluding track, "The Last Resort," the Eagles traced the brute interpersonal and environmental costs of manifest destiny's devastating march to the Pacific. In similar fashion, the apotheosis of Fleetwood Mac—made possible after British musicians Mick Fleetwood, Christine McVie, and John McVie began their innovative collaboration with American songwriters Lindsey Buckingham and Stevie Nicks—offers a remarkably successful case in point about the ways in which The Beatles' creative model (lush melodies and a rich, insightful lyricism) continues to resonate with listeners. As did *Hotel California,* Fleetwood Mac's *Rumours* captured the imagination of a generation desperately searching for meaning within the post-Vietnam, post-Watergate malaise of the 1970s.

For many rock 'n' roll aficionados, The Rolling Stones is The Beatles' British musical heir. After all, the members were not only contemporaries, but genuine friends and colleagues. Yet unlike The Beatles, The Rolling Stones was a deeper, more ingrained purveyor of a growing British blues tradition. As did so many British bands, as the 1960s rolled into the 1970s the Stones benefited from an emergent and highly influential paradigm shift as American AM radio gave way to the album-oriented fare of FM, its more clearly modulated and robust successor. The Rolling Stones' British invasion years were punctuated by a host of charming vignettes, including "Time Is on My Side," "The Last Time," and "Ruby Tuesday." But it was hit records like "(I Can't Get No) Satisfaction" and "Jumping Jack Flash" that redefined the band as the Fab Four's eminently raucous and more vulgar musical cousins. This was especially true of the Stones' vastly influential 1970s-era masterworks, *Sticky Fingers* (1971) and *Exile on Main Street* (1972). Within the span of a single year, The Rolling Stones (and later The Who) left an indelible mark on nascent 1970s rock culture, pushing the boundaries of the genre, chipping away relentlessly at the clean lines and undeniable charm of 1960s British pop—The Beatles included—and exploding them in the ensuing grunge. In terms of rock music as a creative medium, rock critic Robert Christgau describes The Rolling Stones as "the proof of the form. When the guitars and the drums and the voice come together in those elementary patters that no one else has ever quite managed to simulate, the most undeniable excitement is a virtually automatic result. To insist that this excitement doesn't reach you is not to articulate an aesthetic judgment but to assert a rather uninteresting crotchet of taste. It is to boast that you don't like rock and roll itself" (Christgau 1976, 200).

With his admitted and unbridled obsession with American blues, Eric Clapton gave new generations of music fans an appetite for the blues in his own right, clearly innovating the form in his own image. Performing with The Yardbirds, John Mayall and the Bluesbreakers (active 1963–1969, 1982–2008), Cream, Derek and the Dominos (active 1970–1971), and Blind Faith (active 1968–1969), and in a wide-ranging solo career, he transformed the notion of the electric guitar as the fount of rock's musical genius and expression. As rock critic Dave Marsh notes, "Eric Clapton was the focal point of the cult that formed around the electric guitar and guitarists during the sixties. Until the advent of Jimi Hendrix (1942–1970), Clapton was the unchallenged master of white rock-blues guitar playing. 'CLAPTON IS GOD,' read the graffiti in London; plenty of aspiring guitarists believed it" (Marsh 1976, 293). With American FM radio giving pervasive voice to his art, Clapton redefined rock guitar and the blues through one classic after another, including the bravura blues of "Crossroads" with Cream, the soul-baring "Layla" with Derek and the Dominos, and his solo, reggae-infused cover of "I Shot the Sheriff," (by Jamaican icon Bob Marley), among other gems.

The post-Beatles world of British music also saw considerable influence in the so-called art rock (or progressive rock) movement, which sprang almost directly from the residual psychedelia emanating from the near-global success of *Sgt. Pepper's Lonely Hearts Club Band.* A wide variety of British bands flowered in the album's expansive wake, including such acts as The Moody Blues (active 1964–1974, 1977–present), the Strawbs (active 1964–present), King Crimson (active 1969–1974, 1981–1984, 1994–2009), Yes (active 1968–1981, 1982–2004, 2008–present), Genesis (active 1967–1999, 2006–present), and perhaps most notably, Pink Floyd (active 1968–1996, 2005). Critic John Rockwell describes art rock as one of rock's most wide-ranging and eclectic genres, with its overt sense of creative detachment, classical music pretensions, and experimental, avant-garde proclivities.

Sgt. Pepper's most obvious cultural signpost is the "Summer of Love" that emerged in American and British culture in 1967. In the United States, many historians consider ground zero for the "Summer of Love" San Francisco's Haight-Ashbury district, where the counterculture flourished freely and enjoyed international media acclaim. A number of American bands originated during the post–*Sgt. Pepper* era, including Grateful Dead, Country Joe and the Fish, and Jefferson Airplane. The Beatles also exerted a considerable influence on virtuoso American guitarist Jimi Hendrix, who found his mettle as a musician in British nightclubs frequented by the group, particularly McCartney. Within days of the album's release, Hendrix performed a breathtaking, myth-making version of *Sgt. Pepper*'s title track at London's Saville Theatre. For Beatle Paul, Hendrix's performance was "the single biggest tribute" to *Sgt. Pepper* (Badman 2001, 289).

Although Pink Floyd found its own origins in the psychedelic rock of the late 1960s—most notably in *The Piper at the Gates of Dawn* (1967) and *A Saucerful of Secrets* (1968)—the band distinguished itself as art rock's most commercially successful and artistically influential stalwarts. The band's visionary art rock status was cemented with *The Dark Side of the Moon* (1973), the iconic album that spent nearly 850 weeks on the *Billboard* charts and sold in excess of forty-five million copies. In many ways *The Dark Side of the Moon* is the sum of its highly orchestrated parts, offering listeners an elongated and cogent critical attack on the mounting interpersonal pressures of contemporary life.

In addition to the album's innovative lyrics and music, *The Dark Side of the Moon*'s cover art—designed by Storm Thorgerson and Aubrey Powell of Hipgnosis fame—contextualizes the song cycle by affording the listener (or reader) a visual concatenation of the album's tracks. The cover itself depicts a ray of light as it enters a prism, producing a rainbow spectrum that continues onto the album's back cover, which features an inverted prism through which the rainbow is transmogrified once more into a ray of light. This complex of visual imagery can be read in terms of the ray of light's alteration into a rainbow of virtual otherness. The prism, with its attendant electrocardiogram, also evokes the sound of a beating heart, which both begins and concludes the album. "The heartbeat alludes to the human condition and sets the mood for the music," lead guitarist David Gilmour (1946–) observed, "which describes the emotions experienced during a lifetime" (quoted in Schaffner 1991, 176). The album's interior artwork includes a ghostly photograph of the ancient pyramids of Giza. In themselves the pyramids represent humankind's incredible penchant for erecting monuments to our own vanity and boundless ambition. The album's title denotes the seemingly inescapable madness that exists just beyond our ken: "I'll see you on the dark side of the moon," bassist Roger Waters (1943–) sings on "Brain Damage," referring to the paranoia and psychosis that threaten to overwhelm us. Simply put, the pressures of modern life, coupled with our insatiable desires for financial reward and interpersonal dominion, set us on a collision course with insanity. With *The Dark Side of the Moon,* Pink Floyd took The Beatles' efforts on *Sgt. Pepper's Lonely Hearts Club Band* a step further, creating a fully realized concept album that influenced rock music's approach to the album as cultural mouthpiece for years to come. A vast range of American acts have cited Pink Floyd as an influence, including the Foo Fighters, My Chemical Romance, Queensryche, Nine Inch Nails, and Canadian progressive rock band Rush.

The hard rock sounds of heavy metal underwent an apotheosis via the enduring work of Led Zeppelin, the band that challenged the boundaries of guitar-oriented rock with the chilling, bone-crunching thunder of its sound from 1969 until the untimely demise of its members in 1979. As rock critic Jim Miller noted, "In its time, Led Zeppelin was what the 'heavy' in heavy metal was all about. They were the innovators, they practically invented this sluggish, lumbering hybrid of highly amplified distortion. And during their moment—from 1969 to 1973, roughly—there was simply no one better at making their kind of music, a stately staggering, somnolent wake for the battered pleasures of the first psychedelic era" (Miller 1976, 329). Led Zeppelin was joined by a host of metal-oriented bands like Black Sabbath (active 1969–2006, 2011–present) and Deep Purple (active 1968–1976, 1984–present), but in its own right, Zeppelin redefined not only its medium but an era—most notably, the bombast and excess of the massive stadium rock tours that it pioneered during the 1970s. Yet in spite of its hard-rocking aspirations, Led Zeppelin exploited its metallic sound to propel such visionary, poetic, and aural landscapes as "Stairway to Heaven" and "Kashmir" into being—influencing generations of budding guitarists and songwriters in the process. Led Zeppelin's musical influence resounded with such American heavy metal acts as Megadeth, Velvet Revolver, Tool, and Dream Theater. Its impact reached across decades, influencing the direction and sound of such artists as The Smashing Pumpkins and Soundgarden, not to mention the grunge-oriented rock of Nirvana and Pearl Jam.

In the 1970s British rock also made pointed and lasting forays into glam rock (or glitter rock), through such masterworks as David Bowie's (1947–) concept album *The Rise and Fall of Ziggy Stardust and the Spiders from Mars* (1972), *Aladdin Sane* (1973), and *Diamond Dogs* (1974). In its fundamental manifestations, glam rock embraced rock as a form of intimidation through visual expression. At the same time, it exploited the medium as an intentionally destabilizing force, both socially and politically. As critic Tom Carson notes, "When David Bowie first appeared in America in 1972—orange-haired, glitter-clad, androgynous, metallic, and shrill—what was most shocking and radical about him wasn't the moon-age decadence he so glibly insinuated; it was the blatant theatricality with which he presented it." Yet in spite of his in-your-face persona, Bowie's faux glamorous look was explicitly designed to both divide and conquer his would-be audience. "It was easy either to embrace him as the wave of the future," Carson adds, "or to reject him as a soulless poseur" (Carson 1976, 386). Through his overt theatricality, Bowie reshaped the genre, with such timeless classics as "Suffragette City," "Ziggy Stardust," and "Life on Mars?" He enlivened rock as musical form, forcing listeners to not only consume the sonic contents of his wares, but also contend with the expressly visual qualities of his purposefully vexing physical form. American manifestations of glam rock were numerous and abiding, including the outlandish stage personae fashioned by KISS, as well as such later acts as Quiet Riot, Twisted Sister, and Mötley Crüe.

The punk and new wave movements of British music during the late 1970s and early 1980s challenged the aural and visual senses in an intentionally stultifying fashion as well. Led by the Sex Pistols (1975–1978), punk rock assaulted listeners' faculties in nearly every conceivable way, particularly through the high-energy violence of its mode. As Marcus observes, "The Pistols accomplished an interesting feat: they broke the story of rock and roll in half." The notion of "breaking" rock music's hold on generations of youths is integral to understanding the punk movement. As Marcus adds, "Punk rock was an aesthetic and political revolt based in a mass of contradictions that sustained it aesthetically and doomed it politically" (1976b, 451). The inherent violence of punk's representations of youth's desires for sex and fashion was likewise doomed to burn itself out with the changing times, just as any passing fancy. But it did so with a raw and lasting power, as evidenced by such punk anthems as the Sex Pistols' "God Save the Queen" and "Anarchy in the UK." New wave music worked from similar, albeit far less overt, manifestations, employing guitar and synth rock as tools of satire and parody. As Ken Tucker remarks about New Wave pioneer Nick Lowe (1949–): "Even at his most parodic, Lowe acknowledges both the pain and elation of even the most superficial infatuations. This is where his trashy, low-culture instincts illuminate his irony: he's eager to describe the base emotions—lust, unwarranted pride, mean jealousy—with some special degree of understanding" (Tucker 1976, 438). Tucker's words about Lowe could easily describe the aspirations of such new wave and new romantic auteurs as Adam Ant (1954–), ABC (active 1980–present), The Vapors (active 1979–1981), and Bow Wow Wow (active 1980–1983, 1997–1998, 2003–2006), among a wide range of others.

In many ways British rock had come full circle by the early 1980s. Originally emerging on the heels of Elvis Presley, the form had now returned to the rebellious, socially iconoclastic elements of its American progenitors. Having strayed from the brilliant, game-changing master texts of The Beatles and The Rolling Stones, rock in the UK had journeyed back to its early manifestations as an artistically and politically destabilizing mechanism. The same can easily be said for the synth rock of Depeche Mode (active 1980–present) and Tears for Fears (active 1981–present), not to mention the post-punk, alternative rock of U2 (active 1976–present) and the indie rock of Oasis (active 1991–2009) and others in the latter years of the twentieth century. The twenty-first century has proven to be every bit as fecund, with British bands such as Coldplay and Keane enjoying international renown. In Coldplay's case, front man Chris Martin's collaborations with American hip-hop artists—namely Jay-Z and Kanye West, as well as American vocalist Rihanna—demonstrate the British invasion turning back on itself some forty years later and creating vastly new musical fusions in its place.

In their own way, bands from The Beatles to Coldplay have refined their craft to invigorate the very same medium that gave us Chuck Berry (1926–), Little Richard (1932–), Buddy Holly (1936–1959), and a wide array of American practitioners. And in so doing, they have shared in its continuing evolution and expression.

See also: Album Art; Avant-garde in American Music, The Banjo; Berry, Chuck; Blues; Fleetwood Mac; Folk Music; Glam Rock; Guitar; Hendrix, Jimi; Holly, Buddy; Lead Belly; Little Richard; Metal; New Wave; Presley, Elvis; Progressive Rock; Psychedelic Music; Punk Rock; Radio; Rock 'n' Roll (Rock)

Further Reading

Badman, Keith. 2001. *The Beatles Off the Record: Outrageous Opinions and Unrehearsed Interviews.* London: Omnibus.

Bangs, Lester. 1976. "The British Invasion." In *The Rolling Stone Illustrated History of Rock and Roll,* edited by Jim Miller. New York: Random House.

Carson, Tom. 1976. "David Bowie." In *The Rolling Stone Illustrated History of Rock and Roll,* edited by Jim Miller, 386–389. New York: Random House.

Christgau, Robert. 1976. "The Rolling Stones." In *The Rolling Stone Illustrated History of Rock and Roll,* edited by Jim Miller, 190–200. New York: Random House.

Clayson, Alan. 1996. *Beat Merchants: The Origins, History, Impact, and Rock Legacy of the 1960s British Pop Groups.* London: Sterling.

Foster, Mo. 2011. *British Rock Guitar: The First 50 Years, the Musicians, and Their Stories.* Newcastle: Northumbria University Press.

MacDonald, Ian. 1994. *Revolution in the Head: The Beatles' Records and the Sixties.* New York: Holt.

Marcus, Greil. 1976a. "Anarchy in the UK." In *The Rolling Stone Illustrated History of Rock and Roll,* edited by Jim Miller, 451–463. New York: Random House.

Marcus, Greil. 1976b. "The Beatles." In *The Rolling Stone Illustrated History of Rock and Roll,* edited by Jim Miller, 177–189. New York: Random House.

Marsh, Dave. 1976. "Eric Clapton." *The Rolling Stone Illustrated History of Rock and Roll,* edited by Jim Miller, 293–296. New York: Random House.

Miles, Barry. 2009. *The British Invasion: The Music, the Times, the Era.* London: Sterling.

Miller, Jim, ed. 1976. *The Rolling Stone Illustrated History of Rock and Roll.* New York: Random House.

Riley, Tim. 1988. *Tell Me Why: A Beatles Commentary.* New York: Knopf.

Schaffner, Nicholas. 1991. *Saucerful of Secrets: The Pink Floyd Odyssey.* New York: Harmony Books.

Tucker, Ken. 1976. "New Wave: Britain." In *The Rolling Stone Illustrated History of Rock and Roll,* edited by Jim Miller, 435–439. New York: Random House.

Kenneth Womack

Broadway

For much of the twentieth century the Broadway musical hit song was so fully integrated into the mainstream of American popular music that many people upon first hearing a hit show tune might have had no idea that the song originated in a Broadway musical. Whether they first heard a local marching band play the patriotic rouser "[You're a] Grand Old Flag" from George M. Cohan's musical *George Washington, Jr.* (Broadway opening, 1906), caught a stunning 1960s television appearance by Paul Robeson singing his signature "Old Man River" from the Jerome Kern-Oscar Hammerstein II classic *Show Boat* (1927), or broke it down in a 1999 hip-hop club to Jay-Z's "Ghetto Anthem" remix of "Hard Knock Life" from the musical *Annie* (1977), Americans' love of Broadway music has been grounded chiefly in the hit show tune that broke away from the original show's song list to shine on its own in the galaxy of American popular music. Yet the popular show tune is still the child of a Broadway musical, and as such, the Broadway hit single is a pop song of a unique cultural order and stripe.

What Is "a Broadway Musical"?

As a subgenre of American music and theater, the "American Broadway musical" of today is a relatively

Original Broadway Cast Albums

Decca Records' original cast album of *Oklahoma!* in 1943 was so successful that it led to the creation of "the original Broadway cast album" as a viable commercial record genre for much of the mid- to late twentieth century. Although there had been a handful of Broadway cast recordings released sporadically prior to 1943, this album initiated the now standard industry practice of releasing a cast album for virtually any Broadway show that can sustain a reasonable run (Hischak 2007). Noting Decca's success with *Oklahoma!* (the album sold an astonishing one million copies in its first year), record company rivals Columbia, RCA Victor, and Capitol quickly joined the chase and secured their own recording rights to new Broadway shows (Malet 2010). The phenomenon of the Broadway cast album brought new, increased attention to whole scores of particularly well crafted or musically innovative shows and provided an additional platform for launching individual songs as hits. Lerner and Loewe's *My Fair Lady* (1956); McDermott, Ragno, and Rado's *Hair* (1968), Sondheim's *Company* (1970), Webber and Rice's *Jesus Christ Superstar* (1971), and more recently Larson's *Rent* (1996) and Andersson and Ulvaeus's *Mamma Mia!* (2001) are among numerous musicals that have drawn special critical and/or audience attention to their entire scores (as did other shows by Rodgers and Hammerstein, including *South Pacific* [1949] and *The Sound of Music* [1959]).

The cast album, invariably recorded in a studio and not during an actual onstage performance or rehearsal, rarely replicates precisely what the audience hears during a performance. Songs are often cut, trimmed, or rearranged to meet the restrictions of the recording process (Maslon 2004). However, audiences and record buyers have either not known or not cared about these variances and since the days of *Oklahoma!* have embraced the Broadway cast album as a bona fide representation of their favorite shows. Today "the cast album" category is often expanded or renamed (generally as "sound track") to include not only Broadway cast albums but also film and television sound tracks and other cast albums. The cast album is no longer as popular as in the mid-twentieth century, however.

References

Hischak, Thomas S. 2007. *The Rodgers and Hammerstein Encyclopedia.* Westport, CT: Greenwood Press.

Off-Broadway

Smaller theaters in New York that hold 100 to 499 seats are considered "off-Broadway." Plays, musicals, and revues may be produced and performed in these smaller spaces, then if they are successful, move to a larger Broadway theater. Some off-Broadway shows that later had runs on Broadway include the rock musical *Hair, A Chorus Line, Godspell, Spring Awakening,* and *Little Shop of Horrors.*

Off-off-Broadway shows, also called indie theater or independent theater, are performed in spaces with fewer than 100 seats.

Jacqueline Edmondson

self-limited, unambiguous term. A Broadway show, by definition and contract, opens in one of forty official Broadway theaters, so designated by the Broadway League (the New York–based professional association of American commercial theater producers and presenters, self-described as "the national trade association for the Broadway industry"). Thirty-nine of these theaters are located in the Times Square theater district of midtown Manhattan; one, the Vivian Beaumont Theatre, is housed in Lincoln Center in Manhattan's Upper West Side. No matter how good, popular, or "Broadway-like" an original American musical might be, if it never opens in one of these forty theaters, it is not a Broadway musical. Historians generally identify the "American-ness" of any Broadway show and its music through the nationality of its principal creative team. Typically, but not always, a musical assumes the national identity of its composer and lyricist, although few would contest the status of Disney Theatrical Productions' *The Lion King* (1997) as a major American musical despite the fact that composer Elton John and lyricist Tim Rice are English.

In general, Americans think of the Broadway musical as a twentieth-century cultural phenomenon, more or less contemporaneous with the rise of such distinctly American art forms as jazz and commercial film. To be sure, today's musical had a whirlwind adolescence during the era of Tin Pan Alley (roughly 1890s–1930s); matured in the midcentury golden age of the Rodgers and Hammerstein–inspired "book" or "integrated" musicals; smashed traditions in the 1970s and 1980s with the avant-garde sensibilities of Stephen Sondheim and groundbreaking "rock musicals"; and ushered in an era of spectacle-driven megamusicals at the end of the century, led by London's Andrew Lloyd Webber (*Cats; Phantom of the Opera,* 1988) and American media giant Walt Disney Company (*Beauty and the Beast,* 1994; *The Lion King*).

However, musical theater historians generally agree that the *first* original American Broadway musical was the 1866 garish spectacle *The Black Crook,* by the now long-forgotten composer George Bickwell, lyricist Theodore Kinnick, and author Charles M. Barras. More favorably embraced by history is *The Black Crook*'s producer/director William Wheatley. As theater manager for the prestigious Manhattan opera house Niblo's Garden, Wheatley hoped to open his fall 1866 season with something genuinely remarkable. Claiming to have spent an unprecedented $250,000 to produce the show, Wheatley endowed his extravaganza with lavish sets and backdrops exceeding even the most costly European-style operetta productions of the time, several incongruous appearances by a suggestively attired troupe of young French ballerinas, and a melodramatic love story of European intrigue (*The Black Crook* refers to the occult practices of the show's Germanic villain)—all with songs interspersed within scenes creating the rhythm of a vaudeville or minstrel show rather than a formally scored operetta.

With a running time of five hours, the show was longer, brasher, and more scandalous (owing to the ballerina leg show numbers, familiar at the time in lowbrow burlesque halls but not "legitimate" opera houses) than anything previously seen on New York stages. For all these reasons, it was unparalleled as a commercial success. It ran for sixteen months, three to four times longer than many hit musicals of the day. Wheatley claimed quite credibly that the show grossed over $1 million, making it the first New York show ever to have done so. *The Black Crook* now stands firmly in Broadway history as the first genuine long-running Broadway hit. Although none of the show's songs survived as American song classics, *The Black Crook* gave the American musical a historical reference point: a landmark for something new, wildly popular, and truly indigenous to American theater and music.

By the turn of the century New York commercial theater was made up of several diverse genres. Dominated in prestige and commercial investment by European and European-inspired American operettas and operas, early Broadway was also home to various minstrel shows, music hall revues, burlesques, and

The Golden Age of Musicals

Title	Date	Composer	Lyricist
Oklahoma!	1943	Richard Rodgers	Oscar Hammerstein II
One Touch of Venus	1943	Kurt Weill	Ogden Nash
Carousel	1945	Richard Rodgers	Oscar Hammerstein II
Annie Get Your Gun	1946	Irving Berlin	Irving Berlin
Street Scene	1947	Kurt Weill	Langston Hughes
Finian's Rainbow	1947	Burton Lane	E. Y. Harburg
Brigadoon	1947	Frederick Loewe	Alan Jay Lerner
Kiss Me, Kate	1948	Cole Porter	Cole Porter
Where's Charley	1948	Frank Loesser	Frank Loesser
South Pacific	1949	Richard Rodgers	Oscar Hammerstein II
Guys and Dolls	1950	Frank Loesser	Frank Loesser
The King and I	1951	Richard Rodgers	Oscar Hammerstein II
Paint Your Wagon	1951	Frederick Loewe	Alan Jay Lerner
Wonderful Town	1953	Leonard Bernstein	Betty Comden, Adolph Green
Kismet	1953	Alexandr Borodin	George Forrest, Robert Wright
The Pajama Game	1954	Richard Adler	Jerry Ross
Peter Pan	1954	Mark Charlap, Jule Styne	Carolyn Leigh, Betty Comden, Adolph Green
Damn Yankees	1955	Richard Adler	Jerry Ross
Fanny	1954	Harold Rome	Harold Rome
The Most Happy Fella	1956	Frank Loesser	Frank Loesser
My Fair Lady	1956	Frederick Loewe	Alan Jay Lerner
Candide	1956	Leonard Bernstein	various
West Side Story	1957	Leonard Bernstein	Stephen Sondheim
The Music Man	1957	Meredith Willson	Meredith Willson
The Flower Drum Song	1958	Richard Rodgers	Oscar Hammerstein II
The Sound of Music	1959	Richard Rodgers	Oscar Hammerstein II
Fiorello!	1959	Jerry Bock	Sheldon Harnick
Gypsy	1959	Jule Styne	Stephen Sondheim
Camelot	1960	Frederick Loewe	Alan Jay Lerner
How to Succeed in Business Without Really Trying	1961	Frank Loesser	Frank Loesser
A Funny Thing Happened on the Way to the Forum	1962	Stephen Sondheim	Stephen Sondheim
Hello Dolly!	1963	Jerry Herman	Jerry Herman
Fiddler on the Roof	1964	Jerry Bock	Sheldon Harnick

From Joseph P. Swain, "Musicals," in *Broadway: An Encyclopedia of Theater and American Culture,* ed. Thomas A. Greenfield (Santa Barbara, CA: ABC-Clio, 2010), 377–391.

vaudevilles—all more or less original American theatrical forms by comparison to opera or operetta. Although not yet a major source of American popular songs, Broadway at the turn of the century did provide some grist for the rapidly growing sheet music publishing industry housed in lower Manhattan's Tin Pan Alley—principally, although not exclusively, through vaudeville shows and music hall revues. By 1900 Englishmen W. S. Gilbert and Arthur Sullivan's operettas *HMS Pinafore* and *The Pirates of Penzance* had been hits in America for twenty years. Notable songs from these shows, such as "We Sail the Ocean Blue" (*Pinafore*) and "Poor Wandering One" (*Pirates*), were already well known to a generation of Americans. Moreover, American opera ensembles had seized upon published and bootlegged scores of Gilbert and Sullivan shows to mount their own productions of these surefire audience pleasers. In 1903 Victor Herbert, a classical musician, composed the artful musical *Babes in Toyland,* whose signature song "Toyland" remains a popular holiday classic to this day. In 1904 the aforementioned George M. Cohan, a hardscrabble road vaudevillian from Providence, Rhode Island, composed, wrote, and starred on Broadway in the musical *Little Johnny Jones.* The original production ran only six weeks, but it produced for all eternity *the* definitive Broadway anthem, "Give My Regards to Broadway," and Cohan's career signature song, "Yankee Doodle Boy." Impresario Flo Ziegfeld launched numerous American classic songs from his vaudeville/burlesque-influenced *Follies,* which ran almost annually on Broadway from 1907 to 1931. Ziegfeld's *Follies* quickly became a greenhouse for American pop songs. The second edition of the *Follies* in 1908 produced the still-popular "Shine on, Harvest Moon." Later editions of the *Follies* introduced or launched into popularity "If You Were the Only Girl in the World," "A Pretty Girl Is Like a Melody," and "Second Hand Rose."

Good Neighbors: Broadway Musicals, Tin Pan Alley, and the Birth of Modern Broadway

Tin Pan Alley, the ever-hustling songwriting and publishing business on West 28th Street between Fifth and Sixth Avenues, was located within walking distance of many of New York's most active theaters. Tin Pan Alley had been flourishing since the late nineteenth century, generating hit songs of the day through publication of sheet music to satisfy Americans' intense demand to have pianos in their homes and a steady stream of new popular songs to play on them (Furia 1992). Musicians known as song pluggers were employed by Tin Pan Alley producers to travel to stores, restaurants, beaches, parks, and street corners, performing the newest songs in hopes of attracting the attention of New York listeners and, eventually, the American public at large. The neighborhood theaters of Broadway provided a logical and eventually lucrative venue for finding new audiences for new songs. But despite the geographical proximity between Broadway and Tin Pan Alley, a full cross-fertilization between the two was slow in coming. With the exception of New York vaudeville houses and lower-class variety theaters, during the first decade of the new century Tin Pan Alley neither placed many of its own original songs in the musicals and operettas of Broadway nor culled many songs from New York's legitimate theaters to market as sheet music hits. Unlike the songs from operettas or musicals written in the operetta tradition, Tin Pan Alley songs of the early 1900s were based on straightforward formulas. Melodies were almost invariably built on a strict thirty-two-bar chorus—the hook or "money part" of the song that would draw family and friends around the living room piano for an evening of celebration and sing-a-long home entertainment (Furia 1992). Lyrical themes of Tin Pin Alley tunes were no less restrictive than their chorus structures and thus of little use to operetta, with its multiple characters, varying moods, and intersecting plotlines.

Nonetheless, the physical proximity of the two song-based industries, the number of New York musicians carving out their livings with jobs in both Tin Pan Alley and New York theater, and the enormous success of the sheet music industry itself would have eventually led to what later became the robust commercial relationship between Broadway and Tin Pan Alley. But it took World War I to bring about a genuine rapprochement between these two neighbors. By the end of World War I America had become somewhat disenchanted with its earlier worship of European culture in general and operetta in particular—often mocking the genre and its signature waltz numbers as "Viennese schmaltz" (Furia 2010). More important, the American musical stage began developing themes and plots that reflected the lyrical content of popular Tin Pan Alley tunes, while Tin Pan Alley tunesmiths began to enlarge upon the lyric and melody formulas of the pre–World War I Tin Pan Alley era.

It was in this period between the mid-1910s and the 1930s that, for the first time, some of the most successful composers and lyricists working in Tin Pan Alley also became famous for the songs that were finding their way into Broadway revues and musicals. Notwithstanding the remarkable accomplishments of such predecessors as the aforementioned Cohan and Herbert, the luminaries of this new generation have since become consecrated as the inventors of modern Broadway, who married the American popular song to the Broadway show tune: George Gershwin and Ira Gershwin ("Let's Call the Whole Thing Off"), Richard Rodgers and Lorenz Hart ("The Lady Is a Tramp"), Irving Berlin ("Puttin' on the

Ritz"), Cole Porter ("I Get a Kick Out of You"), and Jerome Kern and Oscar Hammerstein II ("Can't Help Lovin' Dat Man") (Starr and Waterman 2008).

These artists not only developed the Broadway musical into a wellspring of popular songs, they also expanded the artistic complexity of the musical form, increasingly drawing on American musical and lyrical idioms as well as themes and plots—effectively "Americanizing the American musical" (Furia 1992, 37). Landmark productions in this surging adolescent period of the American musical included The Princess Theatre Musicals from 1915 to 1920. Largely the experimental product of composer Jerome Kern and a handful of lyricists, this series of small shows represented an early self-conscious attempt to make of the American musical an integrated piece of work—with music, lyrics, and dialogue composed as a unified whole. The result was an increasingly thoughtful approach to developing characters and themes in musicals that would influence the composition of Broadway musicals for the next quarter of a century. Many of these Tin Pan Alley veterans would go on to create the first generation of modern Broadway musical masterpieces. In 1927 Kern teamed with Oscar Hammerstein II to create *Show Boat,* for many historians the show that launched the era of the modern American musical. Its masterful score and serious-minded treatment of race relations and class prejudice in America have made it one of Broadway's most revered works, musical or otherwise. The Gershwins contributed two landmark works during this period. *Of Thee I Sing* (1931), a modern love story as well as a biting satire on American politics, helped the politically shy American musical step boldly into the realm of contemporary satire. It was the first musical to win the Pulitzer Prize for drama. The Gershwins' *Porgy and Bess* (1935), apart from producing one of the most enduring American show tunes in history ("Summertime"), enjoys wide critical acclaim as one of the best American operas ever written. Cole Porter imbued both his lyrics and music with enough sophistication and wit to match the legacy of Gilbert and Sullivan without being in any way derivative of the English giants. Porter's *Anything Goes* (1934) not only hatched a nest of hit songs ("I Get a Kick Out of You," "You're the Top," "It's De-Lovely," and the title song "Anything Goes") but also gave flight to the career of Ethel Merman, the first post–World War I era major Broadway musical star (and later critically ordained as the quintessential Broadway "diva"). Richard Rodgers and Lorenz Hart's hit musical *Pal Joey* (1940) took the daring step of making the male lead a dishonest, cruel, despicable human being who nonetheless held the sympathies of the audience. The show's lasting popularity was aided considerably by its show-stopping torch song classic, "Betwitched, Bothered, and Bewildered."

These and many other inventive, sophisticated new musicals came into being under circumstances that seemed decidedly ill-suited to a renaissance of creative innovation in commercial musical theater. The decade of the Great Depression dealt a hard blow to Broadway theater and a fatal one to Tin Pan Alley. Many theaters and theater production companies closed down for good. Broadway not only fought for its survival against the general poverty gripping the nation, but also contended against loss of creative talent to the newly emerging radio industry across town and the burgeoning film industry across the country. Broadway theatergoers, accustomed to having two hundred or more new plays and musicals opening every season in the late 1920s, saw those numbers fall precipitously year by year in the decade that followed. Vaudeville shows and burlesques were becoming passé, and neither survived the Depression. Sheet music producers of Tin Pan Alley discovered initially that radio and the commercial recording industry both enhanced and rivaled their own business interests. But by the end of the Depression, sheet music had begun to surrender to radio, recordings, and phonographs its position of prominence as the means by which Americans heard, learned, and purchased their new favorite tunes.

The artistic boldness and range of the musical grew steadily throughout the 1930s and the 1940s, with the national trauma accompanying World War II scarcely impeding the musical's artistic progress any more than did the Depression. In fact, America's all-encompassing military, economic, and psychological involvement in World War II raised the roiling question of the country's changing national identity and its emerging place on the world stage—an oddly fortuitous circumstance for the development of the Broadway musical. Not unlike the country itself, the American musical would discover in the World War II era an entirely new self-identity: a new aesthetic, a new sophistication, and new status throughout the nation and beyond—having found them in Oklahoma, of all places.

The Rodgers and Hammerstein Era: Book Musicals, Cast Albums, and a Golden Age for Broadway.

The first collaboration by Broadway veterans Richard Rodgers and Oscar Hammerstein II, *Oklahoma!* (1943), arguably had more impact on the way musicals were subsequently written, composed, choreographed, staged, written about, marketed, and viewed by the public than any other musical in history (Greenfield and Brainard 2010). Commercially, *Oklahoma!* ran for a then-unprecedented two thousand plus performances and five years, redefining what a hit show could be. To the earlier Princess Musicals tradition of integrating song, story,

Performance of Rodgers and Hammerstein's musical *Oklahoma!* on Broadway 1943–1948, directed by Rouben Mamoulian. The musical epitomizes the development of the "book musical" and Rodgers and Hammerstein were awarded a special Pulitzer Prize for it in 1944. (Photofest)

and dialogue, *Oklahoma!* added new depth of character, including modern psychology and expressionistic-inspired dream staging. The show used the "book" of the musical as the anchor for all other aspects of the production, giving new prominence to the term "the book musical" and establishing literary coherence as the dominating aesthetic for writing and staging Broadway musicals for the next twenty years. With modern dance visionary Agnes de Mille as choreographer, *Oklahoma!* generated new ideas for integrating dance into Broadway musicals that influenced choreographers for decades to come. Instead of opening with the conventional grand attention-grabbing ensemble number, *Oklahoma!* opened quietly with the male lead (Alfred Drake as Curly) casually walking across the stage singing the solo, "Oh What a Beautiful Morning," one of half a dozen hit songs from the show. *Oklahoma!*'s original cast album was the first big-selling American recording of its kind and virtually launched the original Broadway cast album as a standard record industry genre (see sidebar).

The artistic achievements Rodgers and Hammerstein established with *Oklahoma!* set new standards for the Broadway musical in the postwar era. Broadway now entered a twenty-year-period that has become known variously as the golden age of the American musical, the era of "the book musical," and the era of the "Rodgers and Hammerstein–type" musical. This period, starting with *Oklahoma!* in 1943 and running through *Fiddler on the Roof* in 1966, brought forth an extraordinary pool of talent and an explosion of productivity in Broadway musical composition, lyric writing, dance, and theatrical direction, combined with "a heightened consciousness of the aesthetics of music, drama and, above all, a rich and popular musical language suited perfectly to such aims" (Swain 2010, 379). Along with Rodgers and Hammerstein, the golden age ushered in the composers and lyricists whose work has come to define the twentieth-century American Broadway musical: Alan Jay Lerner and Frederic Loewe (*Brigadoon,* 1947; *My Fair Lady,* 1956); Leonard Bernstein (*On the Town,* 1944; *West Side Story,* 1957); Frank Loesser (*Guys and Dolls,* 1950; *How to Succeed in Business Without Really Trying,* 1961); Jerry Herman (*Hello Dolly!* 1964); Meredith Willson (*The Music Man,* 1957); and Jerry Bock and Sheldon Harnick (*Fiddler on the Roof,* 1964). Of course, subsequent works by Rodgers and Hammerstein, such as *Carousel* (1945), *South Pacific* (1949), *The King and I* (1951), and *The Sound of Music* (1959), kept resetting the artistic standards for the competition and sustained the duo's prominence among their peers until Hammerstein's death in 1960 (see sidebar).

The richness of these golden age musicals and the songs they produced served both as the source of their commercial strength and ultimately the cause of their later decline in popularity. The book musical era coincided with the rise of rock 'n' roll in the 1950s and 1960s, as a newly affluent, predominantly white, middle-class youth population evolved into a powerful music-buying consumer demographic. The great hit songs of the golden age musicals, though popular with their parents and grandparents, found little favor among America's quick-spending, jitterbug-dancing postwar teenagers. Broadway shows were, in the parlance of the day, "totally square." What chance did "Some Enchanted Evening" from *South Pacific,* "Somewhere" from *West Side Story,* "I Could Have Danced All Night" from *My Fair Lady,* or "Sunrise, Sunset" from *Fiddler on the Roof* have against Elvis Presley's "Hound Dog" (1956), Ricky Nelson's "Poor Little Fool" (1958), The Beatles' "I Want to Hold Your Hand" (1964) or The Supremes' "Stop! In the Name of Love" (1965)? Rock 'n' roll in all its variant forms eventually drove show tunes and adult-oriented popular music off mainstream AM radio and relegated cast albums to the backrow bins of record stores. By the mid- to late 1960s, the aging audience for Rodgers and Hammerstein–type musicals was loyal but diminishing as a consumer force in the music industry. Rock music and Broadway musicals were still, as they had been since the beginning of the rock 'n' roll era, far apart. But that would change abruptly.

So Long, Farewell, Auf Wiedersehen to Book Musicals: Rock and Roll Is Here to Stay . . . on Broadway

Just as the bridge between Tin Pan Alley and mainstream Broadway musicals had been built by composers and lyricists working in both industries, the advent of rock music as a powerful force on Broadway was born of young New York artists piecing together a living in mainstream Broadway shows, rock and jazz clubs, Off-Broadway, and other gigs as they could get them. In the late 1960s composer Galt McDermott was a Canadian jazz and funk musician living in New York when he was approached by authors and lyricists Gerome Ragni and James Rado to write songs for what would become *Hair: The American Tribal Love Rock Musical.* Rado was a New York musician, actor, and aspiring writer of musicals, performing and recording with his own pop band and taking acting jobs in both Broadway and Off-Broadway productions. Ragni was an actor with a background in New York's radical experimental theater movements, whose open disdain for Broadway's tame commercialism was something of a brand trademark. Ragni and Rado brought the idea for *Hair* to Shakespeare in the Park producer Joseph Papp in 1967. Papp produced *Hair* that year in a limited six-week run to help launch his new nonprofit Public Theater. The Off-Broadway *Hair* drew favorable reviews and terrific word of mouth response. Rado and company picked up enough financial backing to enlarge the production and mount a Broadway opening in 1968.

Hair on Broadway was a sensation. It shocked audiences, especially older audiences, even as it somehow intrigued and charmed them. The show heralded new rules for Broadway musicals, including the advent of rock 'n' roll–based hit show tunes; nudity; deemphasizing the conventional book musical leading man–leading woman love story in favor of loosely connected, ensemble-based multiple plotlines; unabashed sexuality; interracial sex; drug use; antiestablishment politics; and a laying out of Broadway's welcome mat for America's youth and counterculture. Original cast and cover versions of songs from *Hair* soon charted high on *Billboard*'s Hot 100 singles listings. For the first time ever, songs from a Broadway show were being played in rotation on rock 'n' roll radio stations across the country, including "Easy to be Hard," "Aquarius/Let the Sunshine In," and the title song, "Hair."

With *Hair* demolishing the barrier between rock music and Broadway (to the considerable dismay of Rodgers and Hammerstein–era traditionalists), Broadway producers were emboldened to infuse rock music and other youth culture influences into new shows to lure young audiences to the theaters and get their shows' hit songs played on the radio. Among the more noteworthy endeavors in this vein have been *Jesus Christ Superstar* (1971), *Grease* (1972), *The Wiz* (1975), and *Godspell* (1976), and later, *The Who's Tommy* (1993), *Rent* (1996; the longest-running musical in this genre) and popular "jukebox musicals"—based on a score of preestablished popular songs rather than new songs written for an original show—like *Mamma Mia!* (2001), *Movin' Out* (2002), *Jersey Boys* (2005), and *Rock of Ages* (2009).

The market for the Rodgers and Hammerstein–type book musical was bound to fade into the background at some point owing to its aging fan base, but *Hair* is largely credited with (or vilified for) having boisterously accelerated the book musical's fall from prominence. The more venerated golden age book musicals and even earlier hit shows would continue to make their presence felt on Broadway through periodic revivals aimed at die-hard traditionalists and even younger audiences eager to see current popular stars in "old" shows (such as *Dukes of Hazard* TV star Tom Wopat in a 1992 revival of *Guys and Dolls,* country singer Reba McEntire in a 1999 revival of *Annie Get Your Gun,* or *Harry Potter* star Daniel Radcliffe in a 2011 revival of *How to Succeed in Business Without Really Trying*). Nonetheless, other new talents, influences, and trends were developing on Broadway at the close of the golden age and were no less important than *Hair* in pointing the American musical toward new horizons.

The new, younger Broadway audiences were not only interested in rock culture but generally more open to new musical styles and dramatic ideas than were their older counterparts. Composer and lyricist Stephen Sondheim, a protégé of Oscar Hammerstein II and a lyricist for several golden age musicals early in his career (*Gypsy, West Side Story*), rose to prominence as a composer and lyricist in the 1970s and 1980s by experimenting with avant-garde dissonant musical scores and nontraditional story formats. His 1970 musical *Company* recounts in quasi-anecdotal form a single man's anxieties about whether to marry or stay single. The show proved to be a breakthrough in what has come to be known as the "concept musical": a show whose plot consists of an episodic exploration of a theme rather than a linear story line. *Company* found a loyal following among young adults educated during the 1960s feminist and gay rights movements and fully prepared to accept ambivalence about matrimony and heterosexuality as a perfectly sensible resolution to a romantic musical comedy. A favorite of professional vocalists for the challenging melodic and lyrical structures of his songs, Sondheim has written very few radio-friendly, "easy listening" or pop commercial hit singles ("Send in the Clowns" from *A Little Night Music* [1973] being a rare exception). Even his most commercially popular musicals after 1973, including *Sweeney Todd* (1979), *Sunday in the Park with George* (1984), and *Into the Woods* (1987), produced no blockbuster hit singles.

Arguably the most extraordinary concept musical to emerge in this period was *A Chorus Line* (1975), choreographer-director Michael Bennett's stark re-creation of a Broadway dance audition in all its nerve-wracking brutality. The cast of dancers emerge onto a barren wasteland of an audition hall, their identities hidden behind their audition "head shots." The director's disembodied voice calls upon them to dance and tell their stories, rendering his judgments upon them as the show progresses. Their tales unfold in a broad swath of pained and wistful stories drawn or adapted from interviews Bennett had taped with real Broadway dancers. The show broke all previous longevity Broadway records, playing 6,137 performances in fifteen years. While currently the fourth-longest-running show in Broadway history, it remains the longest-running American musical. Significantly, the show gave new visibility and prestige to Broadway dancers, enhancing the status of top choreographer-directors for decades to come. The long-running, choreography-rich 1996 revival of *Chicago* and choreographer/director Susan Stromann's storytelling-through-dance *Contact* (2000) are among the numerous dance-driven shows that owe their "legs" to *A Chorus Line.*

Sounds and Fury: European Megamusicals, Disney, and Downloads

If rock music, Stephen Sondheim, and *A Chorus Line* brought to Broadway the most artistically significant musical, lyrical, and structural innovations of the post–Rodgers and Hammerstein era, it was some big-thinking Europeans and the Walt Disney Company that would set the new standards in musical staging, spectacle, and marketing. In 1982 England's Andrew Lloyd Webber, then in is mid-thirties, had been a highly respected musical composer for over a decade. He had earned a Tony Award for the musical score of *Evita* (1979) and Tony nominations for the scores of *Jesus Christ Superstar* (1971) and *Joseph and the Amazing Technicolor Dreamcoat* (1982). Furthermore, *Jesus Christ Superstar* had carved out a special place in musical theater history as a momentum-generating successor to *Hair* in the early development of the rock musical and for the unprecedented release of its original cast album in London and New York in advance of the show's having opened in either city. (The album was a hit on both sides of the Atlantic, producing singles on the American charts: "I Don't Know How to Love Him" and "Superstar.") But none of this background prepared Broadway for what was to become of *Cats* (1982), Webber's unlikely musical adaptation of T. S. Eliot's 1930 light verse book *Old Possum's Book of Practical Cats.* The first European megamusical "imported" from London to Broadway, *Cats* was beloved by American audiences for its spectacular junkyard set that overflowed the stage, outlandish costumes and makeup, athletic, innovative choreography, and the technological climax wherein a steaming hydraulic tire lifts two cats/actors toward a metaphoric heaven ("the Heaviside layer"). The simple episodic plot of *Cats* reflected the now-familiar "concept musical" and made the show accessible to children as well as adults—a rarity on Broadway at the time. Between its enormous fan base and an extravagant marketing campaign conceived by Webber's producing partner, fellow Brit Cameron Mackintosh, *Cats* eventually surpassed *A Chorus Line* as the longest-running musical ever on Broadway. (*Cats* closed in 2000 after 7,845 performances.) The show's most famous song, "Memory," became a hit recording and a concert standard for numerous singers, but it was the visual spectacle of the production itself that made the show phenomenally successful.

When it became clear that *Cats* was not merely a novelty show but a trendsetting phenomenon, Mackintosh and Webber were regularly vilified by American critics and theater professionals for pandering to the public with artistically shallow spectacle and technical effects rather than rich lyrics or genuinely original music. But the two Brits would have none of it, and neither would their worldwide audiences, whom they masterfully had learned to cultivate and please. In 1987 Mackintosh produced *Les Misérables* by French composer Claude-Michel Schönberg and lyricist Alain Boublil. This adaptation of Victor Hugo's nineteenth-century novel focuses on the plight of several displaced French peasants, specifically charismatic ex-prisoner Jean Valjean's flight from the law. The production was loud, gaudy, and in what was becoming a Mackintosh trademark, highlighted by a breathtaking technical stage effect: a rotating barricade that takes up most of the stage space and seems to rival the dimensions of a two- or three-story house. Like *Cats* before it, *Les Mis* (as it is popularly known) originated in Europe and transferred to Broadway. It, too, eclipsed the run of the top American musical *A Chorus Line* and settled behind *Cats* as the then second-longest-running musical of all time.

In 1988 the American professional theater community was still reeling from the commercial and creative impact of this "British invasion" of Broadway when Mackintosh transferred Webber's visually magnificent *Phantom of the Opera*—with its flying one-ton chandelier and splendid lake of candlelight—from London for its Broadway opening. Twenty-three years later *Phantom* is still running on Broadway, having become by far Broadway's longest-running show ever and a marketing phenomenon in its own league. With worldwide ticket revenue of all productions and authorized merchandise and licensing estimated in excess of $5 billion, *Phantom* is the single most lucrative enterprise in the history of the entertainment industry, even surpassing worldwide grosses of top movies.

Adding to the woes of American detractors of visually extravagant musicals was media giant The Walt Disney Company's foray into Broadway theater production. Disney was inspired by the success of Webber and Mackintosh's family-friendly, mass appeal, spectacle-driven megamusicals. In 1994 the company formed its own subsidiary, Disney Theatrical Productions (known commonly as Disney Theatricals), "to bring the Disney brand to Broadway" (Abrams 2010, 165). Disney had a propitious beginning on Broadway with *Beauty and the Beast* (1994). The show ran for thirteen years and ranks among the top 10 longest-running Broadway shows of all time. An adaptation of Disney's popular 1991 animated film of the same name, *Beauty* as a musical actually grew out of a short mini-show staged in Disney theme parks. Hit songs "Be Our Guest" and the show's title song, already popular from the film, would appear again in the Broadway musical. In 1997 Disney followed up *Beauty* with a stage adaptation of its 1994 animated film *The Lion King,* which by then was already on its way to becoming the most successful animated feature film in history. Julie Taymor, a novice on Broadway but a well-known director and puppeteer in experimental and international theater circles, designed and directed the Broadway show. *The Lion King* on Broadway eclipsed the extraordinary success of *Beauty and the Beast.* As they did with *Beauty, The Lion King* audiences thrilled to the imaginative staging of familiar hit songs from the film, including "Circle of Life," "Hakuna Matata," and "Can You Feel the Love Tonight," all written for Disney by British pop legend Elton John and *Jesus Christ Superstar* lyricist Tim Rice. Disney Theatricals has enjoyed other successes with less visually extravagant productions, including *Aida* (2000), *Tarzan* (2006), and an adaptation of the beloved 1964 film *Mary Poppins* (2006), with the forty-plus-year-old hit film songs "A Spoonful of Sugar" and "Supercalifragilistic-expialidocious" stopping the show every night.

Disney's corporate influence on Broadway extended beyond theater production into property purchase and theater restoration as well as corporate leadership in the now famous cleanup of Times Square in the late 1980s and 1990s. Although Disney was only one of several private and public entities involved in the project, it became the corporation most closely associated with Times Square's transformation from a haven for pornography, prostitution, and drug trafficking into a clean, safe, family-friendly entertainment district. Although widely hailed as a welcome transformation, "some New Yorkers lament that the theater district has taken on the pointedly non–New York appearance and feel of a Disney theme park" (Abrams 2010, 165).

In the last quarter of the twentieth century Disney Theatricals and European megamusicals had indeed brought forth the major new production values and marketing strategies to Broadway shows. As for the hit Broadway song, however, the most obvious changes came in the form of new applications of technology in music production and marketing that radically altered the music and recording industries as a whole. Digital downloads, online videos, and even cell phone ringtones all accompanied a seismic expansion of commercial music genres and markets.

For the last forty years, good songs from new Broadway shows—and even some old shows—have continued to find audiences, often initially by the traditional means of becoming a hit single whose release coincides with the show's opening. But increasingly producers and artists have been enhancing record or cast album sales through heretofore inconceivable ways of moving into new technology or adapting to newly emerging musical styles. In the 1970s, for example, producers introduced the practice of turning show tunes into dance mixes for clubs and dance track recordings. "Don't Cry for Me Argentina" from Andrew Lloyd Webber's *Evita* (1979) became the most popular song from the Broadway cast recording (sung by the star of the American production, Patti LuPone). Several other cover versions, including one by pop singer Olivia Newton-John, were reasonably successful as well. But the song became a worldwide dance hit when Madonna recorded a disco version after starring in the 1996 film adaptation of the musical. "Hard Knock Life," a hit children's chorus number from the traditional-style book musical *Annie* (1977), made the charts in 1999 when hip-hop artist Jay-Z remixed it as a dance record and retitled it "Ghetto Anthem." Jay-Z's version spent fifty-six weeks on the *Billboard* hip-hop charts. In 1983 *La Cage Aux Folles,* a breakthrough musical by Jerry Herman that poignantly addressed prejudice against gays as it reveled in its campy celebrations of gender "confusion," launched the show-stopping number "I Am What I Am." Herman had intended the song to serve as an anthem and inspiration for gays and lesbians in the theater audience and beyond. He succeeded. Popular disco singer Gloria Gaynor, a particular favorite artist in gay and lesbian dance clubs, covered the song in 1983. Her version spent ten weeks on the Hot R&B/hip-hop charts. In 2003 Linda Eder did a remake of the song, which became a hit again through digital download sales (see Greenfield and Brainard 2010, passim).

YouTube, which was founded in 2005, has become a critical element in enhancing recognition and sales of new and old music, and Broadway songs are no exception. *Hairspray* (2002), adapted from avant-garde filmmaker John Waters's nonmusical film homage to his Baltimore upbringing in the early 1960s, produced a surprisingly strong-selling Broadway cast album. A 2007 film adaptation of the musical yielded an even stronger sound track that peaked at number two during its thirty-five-week run on the *Billboard* 200 top album chart. The film sound track made hits of two songs from the original show, "You Can't Stop the Beat" and "Without You," with considerable assistance from download sales and popular YouTube clips from the film and stage cast performances. Similarly, composer Stephen Schwartz's *Wicked* (2003) featured the hit song "Defying Gravity," which was released as a single by the show's costar, Idina Menzel, within a year after the show opened. Eight years later, *Wicked* is still running on Broadway and has blanketed the United States with several successful touring productions. Clips of "Defying Gravity" remain a YouTube staple, with some five million hits on Menzel singing the song in character or in concert.

Curtain Call

For all its many distinct evolutionary phases, the Broadway musical relies more heavily for its survival on naturally selecting its own strongest characteristics rather than driving earlier versions of itself into extinction. In any Broadway season lineup, one can readily find the iconoclastic trendsetters breaking new boundaries, the contemporary mainstays holding down the cultural and commercial base, and traditionalists revisiting or revising Broadway's storied past. Broadway's 2010–2011 season, for example, found *The Lion King*'s director Julie Taymor reinventing the concept and the budget for the visually spectacular megamusical with *Spider-Man: Turn Off the Dark* (2011). Commonplace, grandma-friendly rock/jukebox musicals such as the long-running *Mamma Mia!* and the firmly established *Jersey Boys* contended with a noisy new neighbor, *American Idiot* (2010), a self-consciously loud, angry youth fable based on punk rockers' Green Day's best-selling album of the same name. Landmark productions *Phantom of the Opera, The Lion King,* and *Chicago* (which have a combined fifty-two years running on Broadway among them) surrendered the mantle of history to two major revivals mounted in 2011: Frank Loesser's golden age mainstay from 1961, *How to Succeed in Business Without Really Trying,* and Cole Porter's late Tin Pan Alley–era classic *Anything Goes.*

"Revivals are nice, but revel in the new," advised *New York Times* chief theater critic Ben Brantley in 2011, chiding Broadway producers, artists, and audiences to keep looking forward not backward for inspiration and joy in theater. The history of the Broadway musical suggests that Mr. Brantley might be preaching to the chorus if not the choir. Persistently seeking the new while never entirely discarding its traditions, the Broadway musical has developed the endearing habit of reveling where it may.

See also: Avant-garde in American Music, The; Bernstein, Leonard; British Influences on American Rock Music; Disney Music; Gershwin, George; Gershwin, Ira; Green Day; Hip-Hop; Kern, Jerome; Lyricists; Opera in America; Porter, Cole; Presley, Elvis; Radio; Robeson, Paul; Rock Musicals; Rodgers and Hammerstein; Schwartz, Stephen; Sondheim, Stephen; Supremes, The; Tin Pan Alley; Theater; Vaudeville and Burlesque

Further Reading

Abrams, Steve. 2010. "Disney Theatrical Productions." In *Broadway: An Encyclopedia of Theater and American Culture,* edited by Thomas A. Greenfield, 164–166. Santa Barbara, CA: ABC-Clio.

Brantley, Ben. 2011. "Revivals Are Nice but Revel in the New." *New York Times Online,* February 16. http://theater.nytimes.com/2011/02/20/theater/20brantley.html?_r=0.

The Broadway League. n.d. "About the League." www.broadwayleague.com.

Furia, Philip. 1992. *The Poets of Tin Pan Alley: A History of America's Great Lyricists.* Oxford: Oxford University Press.

Furia, Philip. 2010. "Show Tunes: From Tin Pan Alley to Pop Radio." In *Broadway: An Encyclopedia of Theater and American Culture,* edited by Thomas A. Greenfield, 572–578. Santa Barbara, CA: ABC-Clio.

Greenfield, Thomas A. 2010. "*Oklahoma!*" In *Broadway: An Encyclopedia of Theater and American Culture,* edited by Thomas A. Greenfield, 430–434. Santa Barbara, CA: ABC-Clio.

Greenfield, Thomas A., and Sue Ann Brainard. 2010. "Show Tunes: The Rock Era, Disney, and Downloads." In *Broadway: An Encyclopedia of Theater and American Culture,* edited by Thomas A. Greenfield, 578–586. Santa Barbara, CA: ABC-Clio.

Hischak, Thomas S. 2007. *The Rodgers and Hammerstein Encyclopedia.* Westport, CT: Greenwood Press.

Knapp, Raymond. 2005. *The American Musical and the Formation of National Identity.* Princeton, NJ: Princeton University Press, 2005.

Malet, Jeff. 2010. "*Oklahoma!* A [sic] Historical Perspective." *Georgetowner Online.* www.georgetowner.com.

Maslon, Laurence. 2004. *Broadway: The American Musical.* New York: Bulfinch Press.

Patinkin, Sheldon. 2008. "*No Legs, No Jokes, No Chance*"*: A History of the American Musical.* Evanston: Northwestern University Press

Simon, Paul. 2010. "Isn't It Rich?" *New York Times Online,* October 27. http://www.nytimes.com/2010/10/31/books/review/Simon-t.html?pagewanted=all.

Starr, Larry, and Christopher Waterman. 2008. "Giants of Tin Pan Alley." *America.gov: Engaging the World.* http://iipdigital.usembassy.gov/st/english/publication/2008/08/20080818103820eaifas0.4545252.html#axzz2KQQtKKe9.

Stempel, Larry. 2010. *Showtime: A History of the Broadway Musical Theater.* New York: W. W. Norton & Company.

Swain, Joseph P. 2010. "Musicals." In *Broadway: An Encyclopedia of Theater and American Culture,* edited by Thomas A. Greenfield, 377–391. Santa Barbara, CA: ABC-Clio.

Walsh, David, and Len Platt. 2003. *Musical Theater and American Culture.* Westport, CT: Praeger.

Thomas A. Greenfield and Kaitlyn C. Allen

Brooks, Garth (1962–)

Garth Brooks is a country singer-songwriter whose crossover appeal made him the best-selling solo artist in history. His fusion of traditional country with pop influences and the live performances that rivaled rock shows in drama and energy moved him to a level of achievement previously reserved for rock stars. In an image-conscious culture, Brooks, with his receding hairline and paunch, is an unlikely idol, but his ability to communicate with audiences has led to comparisons to musical legends such as Hank Williams (1923–1953) and Elvis Presley (1935–1977). Although his achievements remain unique, his success shattered boundaries that had limited country music largely to a niche audience.

Born Troyal Garth Brooks in Tulsa, Oklahoma, in 1962, Brooks's early musical influences included traditional country stars George Jones (1931–) and Merle Haggard (1937–); the neotraditional king George Strait (1952–); singer-songwriters Billy Joel (1949–), James Taylor (1948–), and Dan Fogelberg; and rock groups Boston, Journey, and Queen. Arriving in Nashville with the ambition to become the next George Strait, Brooks soon captured the attention of a Capitol Records talent scout and within a year was working on his first album. Released in 1989, the self-titled album generated four hits. "If Tomorrow Never Comes," cowritten by Brooks, became his first number one, and "The Dance" (1990), which also reached number one, became an international hit. Both songs, with their carpe diem theme, became signature tunes for Brooks.

No Fences (1990) generated four number one hits that showcase the combination of boisterous and message-driven songs that characterize Brooks's albums. "Friends in Low Places" captured the top spot on Country Music Television's best drinking songs, and "The Thunder Rolls" (1991), a song about an abusive philanderer shot by his wife, had shelters for battered women praising the video for raising awareness of domestic violence. *No Fences* became the biggest-selling country music album of all time. His third album, *Ropin' the Wind,* was even bigger, becoming the first album in history to debut at number one on both country and pop charts.

Brooks had moved into a position never before reached by a country star. He was outselling not only his country peers but also such pop headliners as Michael Jackson (1958–2009) and Bruce Springsteen (1949–). His concerts were also placing him in rock star ranks. Drawing stadium-sized crowds and selling out concerts, sometimes in under an hour, he treated fans to performances that included an elaborate light show, explosions, and the star himself swinging via a harness above the crowd. In 1997 a concert in New York City's Central Park drew a crowd of 250,000.

Named Artist of the Decade (1990s) by the Academy of Country Music and the American Music Awards and the Greatest Artist of the Century by *Radio & Records,* Brooks began the twenty-first-century making major changes. He and his wife divorced in 2000, and Brooks announced his retirement to spend more time with his three daughters. He spent the next nine years in Oklahoma, surfacing briefly for benefit performances. In 2005 he released "Good Ride, Cowboy," a tribute to Chris LeDoux (1948–2005), country music singer-songwriter

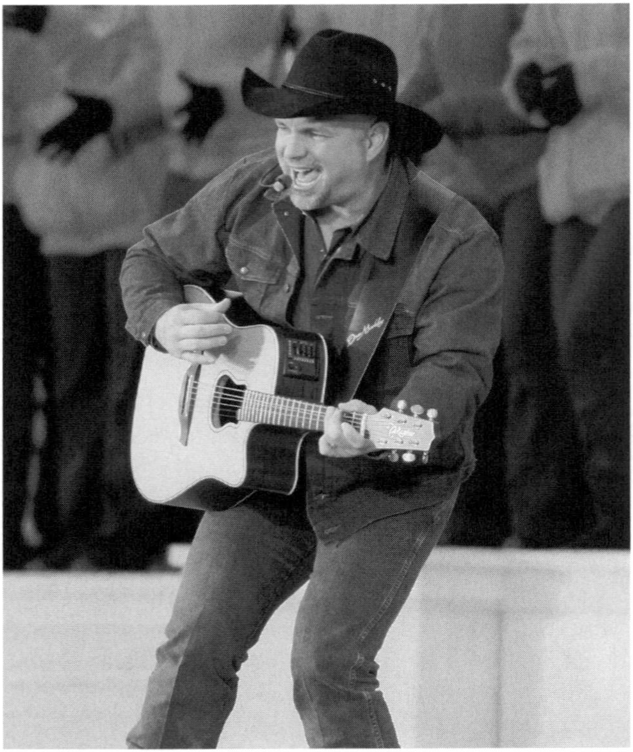

Garth Brooks performs at Barack Obama's inaugural celebration at the Lincoln Memorial in Washington, D.C., January 18, 2009. (Mark Wilson/iStockphoto.com)

and rodeo champion who died of cancer. He also married country singer Trisha Yearwood (1964–) in 2005. In 2009 Brooks began performing to sold-out crowds on the Las Vegas Strip. His album sales have now surpassed the 128 million mark, and he continues to shape country music through his influence on younger artists such as Miranda Lambert (1983–) and *American Idol* winner Scotty McCreery (1993–).

See also: Awards and Prizes for Music; Crossovers; Country Music; Jackson, Michael; Joel, Billy; Music Television; Pop Music; Presley, Elvis; Springsteen, Bruce; Strait, George; Taylor, James; Williams, Hank

Official Web Site: http://www.garthbrooks.com

Further Reading

Cox, Patsi Bale. 2009. *The Garth Factor: The Career Behind Country's Big Boom.* New York: Center Street.

Garth Brooks. n.d. http://www.garthbrooks.com/dialup/index.cfm?id=1 (accessed July 10, 2011).

Schoemer, Karen. 1998. "The World According to Garth." *Newsweek* 131, no. 11: 66. *Academic Search Premier,* EBSCO*host* (accessed July 11, 2011).

Wylene Rholetter

Brothers in American Music

As long as there has been American music, there have been brothers making it. Most of these siblings are now unknown to us: they sang together in church choirs, played at barn dances, or just entertained those around their front porches. But since the early twentieth century, when recording and radio performers emerged from their local areas and music styles proliferated, brothers were everywhere, making music together.

We can find brothers in every genre, from the swing jazz of Tommy Dorsey and Jimmy Dorsey, to the musical comedies written by George Gershwin and Ira Gershwin, to a variety of country music styles—especially the Appalachian-folk-inflected duos like the Stanley Brothers and the Louvin Brothers—to pop music like the Ames Brothers and Jonas Brothers, among others. And that isn't the half of it. In African American–focused music, there are doo-wop stars The Platters with Gaynel and Alex Hodge, soulsters The Isley Brothers, Motown's Jackson 5, the Neville Brothers (Art, Charles, Aaron, and Cyril) playing New Orleans R&B, and Malice and Pusha T, brothers in the rap group Clipse. Most of the groups with brothers are, however, in rock bands, in part because they are the most numerous type of commercial musical group. And we should note here that one of the major labels that parented rock, Chicago-based Chess Records, was run by brothers, Phil Chess and Leonard Chess.

Some siblings only worked with one another, while others were members of groups along with people unrelated to them; in either case most were two brothers. The Allman Brothers, a southern rock band formed in 1969, began when brothers Duane Allman and Greg Allman started a band with friends Dickey Bettes, Berry Oakley, Butch Trucks, and Jaimoe Johanson. The band continued after the tragic death of Duane Allman in 1971. Similarly, The Statler Brothers, a country music group, consists of two brothers, Don Reid and Harold Reid. Interestingly enough, no member of the band had the name "Statler." Some brother bands, such as Good Charlotte, are twins; The National has two sets of twins. There are groups with three brothers, like the Jonas Brothers; four, like the Ames Brothers; five, like Jackson 5; and even six, like The Osmonds, who began as a barbershop quartet before being joined by younger siblings.

For most of the music-making brothers, their parents' significance went beyond transmitting any musically relevant genes or merely buying their instruments. Especially in country music, parents played a crucial role. Ralph Stanley relates how his mother played the banjo in the claw-hammer style and taught him how to play (Gates 2001). Both parents were essential to the Louvin

The Everly Brothers

Don and Phil Everly connected many of the strains of the most popular forms of American music in the late 1950s and exemplified the strengths and strains among brothers. Both played acoustic guitar with a modified rockabilly rhythm, but it was their singing, the keening, high bluegrass style harmonies, influenced by the earlier Appalachian folk singing, that attracted fans, some of whom would become music makers themselves. Starting out as kids singing with their professional country music parents, Ike and Margaret, especially as regulars on *The Singing Everly Family* radio show, the brothers had their own act when rock 'n' roll went mainstream.

Their debut, "Bye Bye Love," reached number two on the *Billboard* chart in 1957, and over the next five years they had twenty-three singles in the top 30, four of which reached number one, such as "Wake Up Little Susie." The Everlys were the most successful brothers in music, judged by their number of hit songs, but their position in American music was secured by more than just hits. Influenced by older country acts, especially the Louvin Brothers, their impact, especially bringing harmony into rock 'n' roll, has been crucial, affecting a wide range of rock bands, including, The Beach Boys, The Beatles, The Hollies, and Eagles, along with individual performers such as Buddy Holly and Linda Ronstadt.

And, yes, the brothers fought. Their relationship became increasingly acrimonious, and their fights came to a head when Phil smashed his guitar on stage in California in 1973 and then stalked off. His brother could do nothing but tell the audience that they had broken up. A decade later, when they had reunited, Don said that the two "hadn't really been apart, since we were around six years old. It kept us immature, in a way, kept us from developing any individuality. Now it's difficult to remember what we were fighting about" (Palmer 1984).

Resources

Fricke, David. 2006. "The Everly Brothers." *Rolling Stone* no. 993 (February 9): 68.

Palmer, Robert. 1984. "The Pop Life: New Record by Everlys." *New York Times*, February 29.

Simons, David. "Rock Foundation: How the Everly Brothers Helped Pave the Way for the '60s Musical Revolution," *Acoustic Guitar* 11:2 (August 2000): 54ff.

Brothers. They began singing together when Ira was eleven and Charlie was eight. "My mama was an extremely good 4 note singer," Charlie said. (This is known as the sacred harp singing style.) "There was probably 100 songs in this book she had, and she knew every one of 'em, by heart. She would sing the notes, the fah soh lahs, and then she'd sing the words. Of course, she sang while cookin' dinner, cookin' supper, or washin' the dishes. Whatever she was doin', she was singin' an old song" ("Country Music Hall of Famer" 2009). Their father played a five-string banjo, and Ira learned to play it, but then switched to guitar. As children the brothers were too shy to show their faces when they sang. They would often get under their parents' bed, lying back to back, to sing. "That's how we learned to phrase together without lookin' at each other, without steppin' on each other's toes, or winking at each other" ("Country Music Hall of Famer" 2009).

Many of the brothers' parents were musicians themselves, including the father of Alex and Eddie Van Halen of the hard rock band Van Halen. The father of Luther Dickinson and Cody Dickinson of the North Mississippi Allstars, a blues southern rock group, was a musician and record producer, as was the father of Darrell (Dimebag) Abbott and Vinnie Paul (Abbott) of the thrash metal band Pantera.

Of course some parents are a bit more than encouraging, bordering on being abusive. Brian Wilson of The Beach Boys has written about how his father, Murray, a frustrated songwriter who played piano at home, bullied his children as he passed along his musical obsessions (Wilson 1991). Murray was responsible for The Beach Boys' (brothers Brian, Carl, and Dennis Wilson, and cousin Mike Love) early career, including getting them a contract with Capitol Records. Two years after that, following a blowup in the recording studio, Brian ousted his dad. Joe Jackson, father of Marlon, Jackie, Tito, Jermain, and Michael, rather harshly led his sons to become the chart-dominating pop phenomenon Jackson 5.

It was a complete family affair for some brothers, who when they were youngsters performed with their parents' musical acts and continued to work together independently when they grew up. The parents of The Everly Brothers played older folk music of the Appalachian

The Jonas Brothers at the world premiere of their movie *Jonas Brothers: The 3D Concert Experience*, at the El Capitan Theatre in Hollywood, California, February 24, 2009. Pictured from left are Kevin, Joe, and Nick. (Featureflash/Dreamstime.com)

area and country music, and their sons, Don and Phil, performed with them. The four Maines brothers (Lloyd, Donnie, Kenny, and Steve) began as The Little Maines Brothers Band to distinguish them from their dad's and uncle's group, whose name they took over in the mid-1970s.

Some brothers composed together, rather than perform. Two of the most prolific were Robert Sherman and Richard Sherman. This duo wrote the film scores for popular movies like *Mary Poppins, The Jungle Book, Chitty Chitty Bang Bang,* and *Charlotte's Web.* They have written perhaps more film music than any other songwriting team. Other brothers have teamed as producers, including the award-winning Berman brothers. Frank Berman and Chris Berman have worked with artists like Cher and the Baha Men (who won a Grammy for the 2001 song "Who Let the Dogs Out"). They are considered to be among the most successful producers in the United States today.

Brothers share a more similar culture with one another than they do with their parents, especially in popular, as opposed to folk and classical, music. And there is a sense of trust just because of this shared background. Nonetheless, differences are inevitable. A musical group, be it a country duo or a rock band, needs several kinds of leadership, especially in musical and commercial decisions. And if there is a leader, others need to be, more or less, followers. Research on siblings indicates that "first borns of both sexes tend to be 'alpha males'" (Sulloway 1996, 170), and when the eldest brother is in a group with a younger sibling (who since he was born has been used to following his older brother), the elder tends to take leadership. If there are others in the group, the younger brother's example of acquiescing to his older sibling sets a model for the rest.

First-borns, according to research, are those most likely to "lead fashionable reforms, populist revolutions, . . . innovations that do not threaten the status quo" (Sulloway 1996, 351). Thus one would expect the older brother to be the main songwriter for a group, at least initially creating the group's signature sound. And in groups like The Beach Boys, the Perkins Brothers, and the Flaming Lips, among so many others, that was the case. But there are numerous exceptions, and when the pattern is reversed, it creates a possible source of friction. Take, for example, Credence Clearwater Revival. John Fogerty and his school friends Stu and Doug formed a band, then got the older Fogerty brother, Tom, a multi-instrumentalist, to join them. It was Tom who got them signed by Fantasy Records. But the group's songwriter, front man, and producer was John. Writing songs means telling the instrumentalists what notes to play, which is a form of power. As producer, John was like an orchestra conductor, telling the others how to play their parts and adjusting the levels of each of their sounds in the mix. John recalls that each of the others, especially Tom, kept complaining that he wanted to have his part louder in the mix. "So it was a go around I had with Tom for the whole three years we were Credence, he kept saying 'my part's not loud enough'" (Levitin 188). Tom quit.

Siblings also tend to differentiate themselves from one another. One might play guitar, the other drums, as did "Dimebag" and Vinnie Paul in Pantera, or one plays guitar and the other plays bass, as did Dean DeLeo and Robert DeLeo in the Stone Temple Pilots and Bob Stinson and Tommy Stinson in the Replacements. Although Tommy Dorsey and Jimmy Dorsey both began by playing the trumpet, they soon changed instruments—Tommy taking up the trombone and Jimmy the saxophone. Ira Gershwin wasn't interested in playing the piano that his parents had bought for him, but his younger brother George took to it famously. When George needed a lyricist for the musical comedies he wrote, brother Ira was just perfect: one of their collaborations, *Of Thee I Sing,* in 1931, won the Pulitzer prize.

Alex Van Halen and Eddie Van Halen began their musical studies as classical pianists, but then took up rock instruments, Alex the guitar and Eddie the drums. But Alex messed around with Eddie's drums, and Eddie was so irritated that his brother played better than he did that he switched instruments with his older brother and spent infinite hours practicing in his room, like so many great electric guitarists.

There are definite advantages to collaborating with one's brother in a musical group. Coordinating is both difficult and crucial in many types of music; to have an established social relationship on which to build a musical one and get to construct it at an earlier age than others in the convenience of one's home provides a substantial head start. The numerous country harmony-singing duos like the Stanley Brothers are a case in point.

The advantages for brothers in rock bands are marked. As Rosemary Clawson argues, "[n]etworks of sociability provide the infrastructure for band formation," since, in rock bands, "friendship rather than skill or adult initiative is the basis of their earliest formation" (2008, 106). Brothers, especially when they are not too far apart in age, are already networked. Further, learning one's instrument is not enough; one needs to learn how to interact, musically and otherwise, with other musicians. Unlike in many other styles of music, especially classical, adults as instructors or supervisors, are absent from rock.

The notion of brotherhood in music goes beyond genetically related siblings. Metaphorical brothers like The Righteous Brothers and The Doobie Brothers play on the aura of kinship, and unrelated band members often speak of their relationships with each other in terms of brotherhood. Mike Campbell of Tom Petty's Heartbreakers says, "Groups are a very complicated thing. It's like a family, it's like a business relationship, it's a very emotional thing. You care about each other, and you tug just like brothers; you're jealous, and then you love each other. It's a very complicated monster" (Schruers 1995, 49). Metallica's drummer Lars Ulrich discussed his reaction to his front man James Hetfield's highly inebriated state: "That was rock bottom, when I was wondering what the future held. I mean, the brother in me wanted to run over and give him a big f****n' hug and say, like, 'You Okay?' But the member of Metallica [in me] wanted to go over and kick his f****n' ass" (Norris 2003, 76). Here, as in so many other uses of the word *brother,* it means caring and compassion for the other. But there is a special understanding of the word in musical groups. When Nick Oliveri was discussing why Josh Homme kicked him out of their band, stoner rockers Queens of the Stone Age, he described a specific altercation the two had: "We've known each other long enough and that's what happens, a brother fight, you know?" ("Josh Is Making a Mistake" 2004). Patrick Monahan says of his Train bandmates: "You become a family. You get along like brothers sometimes, where you fucking hate each other" (Bozza 2002, 36). Let's call this the Cain and Abel version of brotherhood. And the music press loves to focus on that angle.

So when we learn about the relationships of brothers in bands, it is usually about their fights. Tom Smothers and Dick Smothers, a folk duo, made a career out of this trope, with Tom endlessly repeating the sibling rivalry line, "Mom always liked you best!"

The press has no problem finding lack of brotherly love. Brothers know one another too well and have learned how to press each other's buttons, although they also know how to avoid doing so. The coverage of the blues rock band Black Crowes is an example. Their feuds constitute much of the fodder for their profiles. Both singer Chris Robinson and his guitarist brother Rich Robinson, three years younger, are not shy about their bickering:

> "You should write this down," Chris says, cackling, when Rich stumbles at the start of the song, trying to recall a guitar part. "The one who doesn't smoke weed doesn't remember anything!" Chris turns to Rich and pats him on the shoulder. "That was just a little witticism at your expense, little brother." Rich stares down at his guitar as if he hasn't heard or felt a thing. "Outside of music, we probably would never speak to each other," Rich says, laughing, something he does a lot when Chris is not around."

Brothers are ubiquitous across the gamut of musical styles. Their familial bonds give them a boost and can also bring them down.

See also: Beach Boys, The; Dorsey, Jimmy, and Dorsey, Tommy; Gershwin, George; Gershwin, Ira; Jackson Family; Metallica; Sisters in Music; Van Halen, Eddie; Wilson, Brian

Further Reading

Bozza, Anthony. 2002. "Train: The Little Band That Could." *Rolling Stone,* March 28, 35–36.

Clawson, Mary Ann. 2008. "Masculinity and Skill Acquisition in the Adolescent Rock Band." *Popular Music* 18, no. 1: 99–114.

"Country Music Hall of Famer, Charlie Louvin, Takes Us from 1927 to 2010." 2009. *Raised Country!* December 26. http://raisedcountry.com/charlie_louvin/

Fricke, David. 2008. "War of the Crowes." *Rolling Stone* March 20, 44ff.

Gates, David. 2001. "Annals of Bluegrass Constant Sorrow: The long road of Ralph Stanley." *New Yorker,* August 20 and 27, 88–94.

"Josh Is Making a Mistake." 2004. *Kerrang!* February 28.

Levitin, Daniel J. 1988. "John Fogerty Interview." *Audio Magazine* (January). http://www.psych.mcgill.ca/levitin/fogerty.html.

Norris, Chris. 2003. "Lars Attacks." *Spin* 19, no. 7: 76.

Schruers, Fred. 1995. "Tom Petty: On the Road." *Rolling Stone,* May 4, 49ff

Sulloway, Frank J. 1996. *Born to Rebel: Birth Order, Family Dynamics, and Creative Lives.* New York: Pantheon.

Wilson, Brian, with Todd Gold. 1991. *Wouldn't It Be Nice: My Own Story.* New York: HarperCollins.

Deena Weinstein

Brown, James (1933–2006)

James Brown was one of the most important figures in soul and funk music. His vocals, often erupting into nerve-shredding screams, brought the fire of gospel into R&B with more force than any other singer. The tight yet jagged rhythms of his arrangements, executed with earthy finesse by a host of talented sidemen, were crucial to soul's evolution into funk. The frenetic, gymnastic athleticism of his concerts made Brown one of popular music's most exciting stage acts.

Born into poverty in South Carolina on May 3, 1933, Brown weathered a stint in reform school as a teenager to begin performing on the R&B circuit in the mid-1950s. His 1956 debut single, "Please, Please, Please," was a top 10 R&B hit. But he was on the verge of being dropped by his label, King Records, before establishing himself as a consistent R&B chart act with a series of hits in the late 1950s and early 1960s. Brown's urgent, pleading vocals helped make his records among the earthiest R&B discs around, making him well equipped to make the transition to soul music as he brought more sophisticated horn arrangements and a yet grittier approach into his sound.

Although his 1963 album *Live at the Apollo* made number two on the pop charts, Brown truly crossed over to the pop audience with his electrifying appearance in the 1964 concert movie *The T.A.M.I. Show,* as well as his mid-1960s hits "Out of Sight," "Papa's Got a Brand New Bag," and "I Feel Good." The irregular, galvanizing tempos, nearly hysterical singing, and stripped-down melodies were the blueprint for funk, epitomized by the 1967 hit "Cold Sweat."

By the late 1960s Brown had become a figure of political importance as well. His 1968 hit "Say It Loud—I'm Black and I'm Proud" became an anthem of pride for the African American community. In Boston that

James Brown, known as the Godfather of Soul, performs in 1964. (Photofest)

same year, shortly after the assassination of Martin Luther King Jr., he helped defuse potential rioting by performing a televised concert and diplomatically cooling down overexcited youngsters in the audience when the show threatened to erupt into chaos. As an entrepreneur with numerous business interests within and outside of music, he also advocated African American economic self-empowerment, gaining the ear of numerous politicians along the way.

Though remaining a popular performer, Brown's influence and record sales declined from the 1970s onward; but the combination of hard, insinuating beats and skeletal melodic frameworks continued to form a bedrock of the funk catalog. He ran into grave personal troubles near the end of the 1980s, serving three years in prison on various charges relating to drugs, firearms, driving, and interactions with the police. Other brushes with the law hounded him until his death in Atlanta on December 25, 2006. By that time, however, he was firmly ensconced as a musical legend. His influence has endured long past the peak of his popularity, in part due to the numerous samples of his vintage recordings on countless tracks, especially rap discs.

See also: African American Influences on American Music; Funk and Postpsychedelic Funk; R&B

Further Reading

Brown, Geoff. 1996. *James Brown: Doin' It to Death.* London: Omnibus Press, 1996.

Brown, James, with Bruce Tucker.1986. *James Brown: The Godfather of Soul.* New York: Macmillan.

Brown, James, with Marc Eliot. 2005. *I Feel Good: A Memoir of a Life of Soul.* New York: New American Library.

Danielsen, Anne. 2006. *Presence and Pleasure: The Funk Grooves of James Brown and Parliament.* Middletown, CT: Wesleyan University Press.

Sullivan, James. 2008. *Hardest Working Man: How James Brown Saved the Soul of America.* New York: Penguin.

Richie Unterberger

Browne, Jackson (1948–)

Jackson Browne is a singer-songwriter who has reached millions of Americans and others worldwide with both his music and his humanitarian actions. Growing up in Los Angeles, he developed his songwriting skills in Laurel Canyon, a suburb that served as a haven for musicians and other artists in the late 1960s. His influences from this era include many much more famous songwriters, such as Neil Young (1945–), Joni Mitchell (1943–), Crosby, Stills & Nash (active 1968–1970; 1974; 1977–present), and James Taylor (1948–), all of whom lived within a few blocks of each other in the canyon (Hoskyns 2005). Early on, Browne was best known for helping to advance the careers of other musicians. He did this primarily by writing songs that became big hits for other artists, such as "These Days," which he wrote for one-time girlfriend Nico (1938–1988), and "Take It Easy," which launched the career of the Eagles (active 1971–1980, 1994–present), who were all good friends with Browne. The success of the Eagles in turn gave rise to another important figure, producer David Geffen (1943–). Geffen had launched Asylum Records, and the Eagles were its first big product. Geffen went on to form Geffen Records and has since become a major record and film producer (Hoskyns 2005). Browne also served as producer for other artists, most notably Warren Zevon (1947–2003), whose hit "Werewolves of London" was produced by Browne.

By the mid-1970s Browne had become a major star in his own right. He is perhaps best known for his hit song "Running on Empty," a folk-rock classic about life on the road and moving forward regardless of circumstances. Browne famously sued the 2008 John McCain campaign for U.S. president for using this song at rallies without his permission. In other songs, such as "The Pretender" and "For Everyman," Browne uses straightforward and earnest lyrics to tap into some of the most basic human yearnings and emotions. In the early 1980s Browne turned to more hook-based pop tunes for hits like "Lawyers in Love" and "Somebody's Baby," a song he wrote for the film *Fast Times at Ridgemont High.* Around this time he also became very active in several different social causes he felt passionate about. He formed Musicians United for Safe Energy (MUSE) to raise awareness about the dangers of nuclear power, a concern of many Americans after a nuclear accident on Three Mile Island in 1979. This group of musicians, which includes David Crosby (1941–), Graham Nash (1942–), and Bonnie Raitt (1949–), would reunite in 2011 in the wake of a tsunami that damaged several nuclear reactors in Japan (MUSE 2011). He has made frequent appearances at benefit concerts on behalf of such causes as Farm Aid and the victims of a 2011 shooting incident in Tucson, Arizona. In recognition of his contributions to both music and society, Browne has received several awards and honors, including his 2004 induction into the Rock and Roll Hall of Fame, an honorary doctorate in music from Occidental College in Los Angeles, and several

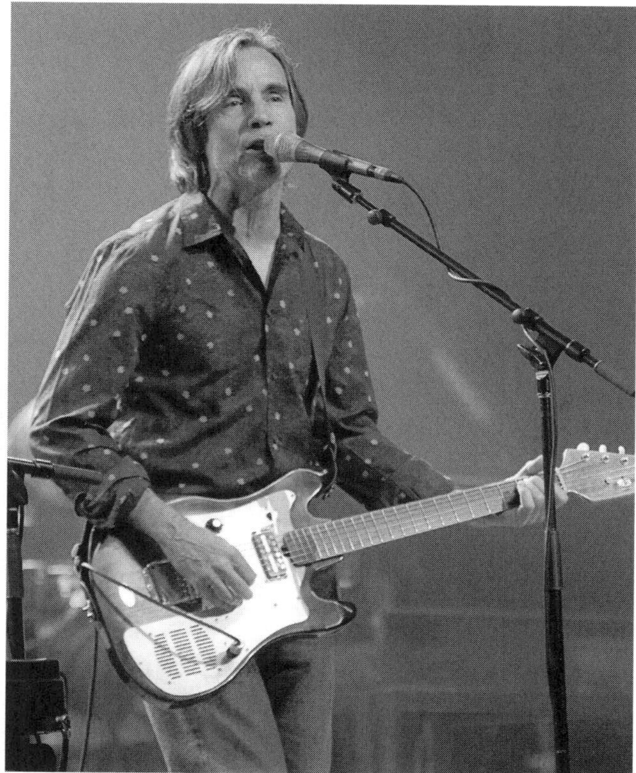

Jackson Browne performs at the 2010 Montreal Jazz Festival. (Mario Beauregard/Dreamstime.com)

other distinctions from humanitarian and environmental groups.

See also: Crosby, Stills & Nash; Producers; Raitt; Bonnie; Singer-Songwriters; Social Causes of Musicians; Taylor, James; Young, Neil

Official Web Site: http://www.jacksonbrowne.com

Further Reading

DeCurtis, Anthony. 2007. "Jackson Browne." *Rolling Stone Magazine* 1025/1026, 134–137.

Hoskyns, Barney. 2005. *Hotel California: Singer-Songwriters and Cocaine Cowboys in the LA Canyons, 1967–1976.* London: Fourth Estate.

MUSE. 2011. http://www.musiciansunited4safeenergy.com.

Don Traut

Brubeck, Dave (1920–2012)

Pianist and composer Dave Brubeck is considered to be one of jazz music's first pop stars, and he is credited with bringing jazz to new audiences in the 1950s and 1960s. With the Dave Brubeck Quartet (active 1951–1967 originally, and then continued with new members through 2012), Brubeck recorded original jazz music, including pieces like "Take Five," "Time Out," and "Blue Rondo a la Turk," and he reinvented jazz standards like "Pennies from Heaven." Brubeck is also known for introducing the 5/4 time signature into jazz music.

David Warren Brubeck was born in Concord, California, and grew up in the Sierra foothills town of Ione, the youngest of three sons born to Pete and Elizabeth Brubeck. Elizabeth, a church choir director and classically trained pianist, believed her sons should learn to play music rather than just listen to it, so she forbade them to listen to music on the radio. Young Brubeck played the piano by ear, primarily because his poor eyesight made it difficult for him to read music, and he composed original music while riding horses on his father's cattle ranch. He attended College of the Pacific, originally planning to study ranching. After a year he switched to music. He graduated and married his college sweetheart Iola in 1942, then was drafted into military service. While stationed as an infantry soldier in France in World War II, Brubeck was about to go on the front lines when he was recruited to play the piano in an army band. He created one of the first racially integrated military bands, called the Wolfpack Band. While serving in the military, Brubeck met saxophonist Paul Desmond (1924–1977), and the two began their long-time musical collaboration.

When Brubeck completed his military service, he studied music with modernist French composer Darius Milhaud (1892–1974) at Mills College in California. Milhaud's interest in polytonality influenced Brubeck, who became well known in the years that followed for experimenting with sound and time signatures. Milhaud encouraged Brubeck to pursue his interests in jazz, and Brubeck soon formed the Dave Brubeck Quartet. The group enjoyed a long-term residency in San Francisco and gained widespread popularity performing for college students across the country. With Eugene Wright as the bass player, the racially integrated band was a concern to some college deans and club owners, and the group's performances were sometimes canceled as a result.

Brubeck continued to compose and perform until just weeks before his death, recording more than one hundred albums across his lifetime. In 2008, Secretary of State Condoleezza Rice awarded Brubeck the Benjamin Franklin Award for Public Diplomacy. She told Brubeck that she grew up on his music, and her father was his greatest fan. In 2009 Brubeck was recognized as a Kennedy Center Honoree. In 2010 he was awarded the Miles Davis Award at the Montreal International Jazz Festival. He received honorary doctorates from Eastman School of Music, Berklee College of Music, and George Washington University.

See also: Jazz

Official Web Site: http://www.davebrubeck.com/live/

Further Reading

Jarenwattananon, Patrick. 2012. "Dave Brubeck: Beyond Take Five." http://www.npr.org/blogs/ablogsupreme/2012/12/05/166591728/dave-brubeck-beyond-take-five (accessed December 6, 2012).

"Music: The Man on Cloud No. 7." 1954. *Time* 64, no. 19: 76.

Ratliff, Ben. 2012. "Dave Brubeck: Jazz Musician, Dies at 91." http://www.nytimes.com/2012/12/06/arts/music/dave-brubeck-jazz-musician-dies-at-91.html?pagewanted=all&_r=0 (accessed December 6, 2012).

Jacqueline Edmondson

Bubblegum Pop

In the late 1960s, while America was convulsed with violent street protests, riots, the Vietnam War, and assassinations, bubblegum music improbably popped into being. A new generation of preteen music fans emerged who didn't care for the long, psychedelic jams of the San Francisco sound, the sophisticated lyrics of

Bob Dylan, the blistering hard rock of the MC5, or the increasing social consciousness of Motown acts like The Temptations. They wanted fun, catchy songs that they could dance to. Two enterprising young music promoters, Jerry Kasenetz and Jeff Katz (known as K&K), recognized this new market and captured it with the perfect name: bubblegum. It was cheap, sweet, and completely disposable.

The Roots of Bubblegum

Bubblegum drew on a long tradition of novelty songs, the Brill Building, garage rock, soul music, and the West Coast sound. By the mid-1960s all the ingredients for bubblegum were in place, and records that were bubblegum in everything but name were already becoming hits. In 1966 Tommy James and the Shondells recorded a two-year-old B-side by The Raindrops, the studio recording name of Brill Building songwriting team Jeff Barry and Ellie Greenwich. That simple, catchy song, "Hanky Panky," had disappeared along with The Raindrops, but this time around it launched the career of Tommy James and the Shondells.

On the West Coast the television show *The Monkees* exploited the success and formula of The Beatles' movies by creating a fake band and supplying it with hit singles written by Brill Building songwriters. Jeff Barry produced the band's biggest hit, "I'm a Believer." These examples point out the recurring elements in the development of bubblegum: Brill Building songwriting, interchangeable band names used by producers to front for studio musicians, music created for television instead of the radio, and the overwhelming influence on the genre of Jeff Barry.

Kasenetz and Katz

The earliest bubblegum bands in the K&K stable were originally regional garage rock groups. Because K&K owned the name for each group, they could put any musicians they wanted on those recordings. Records labeled "Ohio Express" fronted recordings for Sir Timothy and the Royals, Rare Breed, The Measles (featuring the young Joe Walsh), the singer Joey Levine backed by studio musicians, and even the nascent 10cc (when it was a studio conglomeration under Graham Gouldman). The Lemon Pipers were the first Kasenetz and Katz creation to soar up the charts, reaching number one in early 1968 with "Green Tambourine" on Buddah Records. Kasenetz and Katz quickly followed with hits by Ohio Express, "Yummy Yummy Yummy," and 1910 Fruitgum Company's "Simon Says."

The Era of Cartoon Rock

The Kasenetz and Katz bands ruled the bubblegum scene in 1968 and into the following year, racking up multiple gold records. But the biggest bubblegum record ever came from a cartoon act, The Archies, created by Don Kirshner. Like so many bubblegum impresarios, Kirshner's career ran for decades before and after bubblegum's golden era. He initially achieved success as the most significant music publisher out of the Brill Building, where he first worked with Jeff Barry and Ellie Greenwich. Kirshner went on to assemble the musical team behind The Monkees, controlling every aspect of the group's earliest hit recordings. When The Monkees fired Kirshner, he responded by creating The Archies

The Archies' second single "Sugar Sugar," outsold every other single in 1969, a success that spawned several trends. Throughout the remainder of the 1970s Saturday morning kids shows featured cartoon bands and kid show pop songs. The most significant of these kid show groups were Josie and the Pussycats and The Banana Splits. The Pussycats featured lead vocals by Patrice Holloway, the younger sister of soul legend Brenda Holloway, and backup vocals by Cherie Moor (née Cheryl Ladd), who would go on to star on the television show *Charlie's Angels*. The Banana Splits' show wasn't a cartoon, but live actors in full-body costumes bumbling about, backed by a song list written by such rock and soul luminaries as Barry White and Al Kooper. Saturday morning kids' shows produced albums for groups such as The Bugaloos, the Harlem Globetrotters, Kaptain Kool and the Kongs, Lancelot Link and the Evolution Revolution, the Hardy Boys, the Groovie Goolies, and Mission Magic. This was the heyday of bubblegum.

Bubblegum into the 1970s

The classic bubblegum era only lasted from 1968 to roughly 1973, but its influence on music in the 1970s extended in all directions. The British songwriting team Nicky Chinn and Mike Chapman modeled the early glam singles of The Sweet, Suzi Quatro, and Mud on the bubblegum template. Pioneering disco producer Giorgio Moroder's first hit "Looky Looky" and Abba's early single "Ring Ring" both copied the structure and even the repeated title of "Sugar Sugar." Early Jackson 5 singles like "ABC" were Berry Gordy's attempt to move Motown into that preteen market. By the mid-1970s the Bay City Rollers were combining elements of bubblegum, glam rock, and boy band appeal into one tartan-clad pop phenomenon.

But it was behind the scenes, rather than on the charts, that bubblegum held its greatest sway. The most important record company of the disco era, Casablanca, was created and run by a bubblegum veteran, Neil Bogart. Another Buddah Records exec, Marty Thau, went on to manage the proto punk band the New York Dolls and then founded the independent punk label Red Star, which put out seminal singles by Television and Suicide. Sire Records, which signed the Ramones, Talking Heads, and the Pretenders, was founded by longtime record executives Richard Gottehrer, who had gotten his start with the 1960s bubblegum band The Strangeloves, and Seymour Stein.

Bubblegum's Influence on Punk and New Wave

Many of the early punk and new wave bands acknowledged the influence of bubblegum on their work: the Talking Heads covered 1910 Fruitgum Co.'s "1-2-3 Red Light" in concert, the Ramones specifically cited the Bay City Rollers' bubblegum hit "Saturday Night" as the inspiration for "Blitzkrieg Bop," and The Cars simply stole the opening riff of "Yummy Yummy Yummy" for their first hit record, "Just What I Needed." Richard Gotterhrer and Mike Chapman both went on to produce key records of the new wave era, with Gotterhrer working with Blondie, the Go-Go's, and Marshall Crenshaw, while Chapman took The Knack and Blondie to the top of the charts.

Bubblegum into the 1980s

Jackson 5 deserves special note in the history of bubblegum, as the group proved to be especially influential in the history of the boy band, a subgenre closely related to bubblegum. In the early 1980s the songwriter-producer Maurice Starr decided to create an updated version of Jackson 5, and scouting a local talent show in Boston, he assembled New Edition. When that group proved successful, he decided that he could penetrate the pop charts with a similar group of white teenagers (New Edition was African American) and recruited more local kids to form New Kids on the Block, by far the biggest bubblegum group of the decade. (It's worth noting that this tactic of "whitewashing" or having white artists cover or emulate R&B is inextricably wound into the entire history of American pop music. What was unique about this instance was that Maurice Starr was himself black.) Two pop princesses were often pitted against each other in the media, as both Tiffany and Debbie Gibson went on to score bubblegum hits. Like the Jonas Brothers and Hanson, Debbie Gibson wasn't just a teenaged performer but also a songwriter and musician. Menudo also established itself as the preeminent teen act for the Latin market.

Boy Bands and Spice Girls

In Britain the boy bands never went away, and groups such as Take That were major pop stars throughout the 1980s. But in the United States boy bands fell out of style after New Edition and New Kids, and did not reemerge until the late 1990s. The single "Mmmbop" by Hanson in 1997 sparked a rebirth in the bubblegum market, followed quickly by the Spice Girls, who were a true pop phenomenon, generating gold records and even a movie. A new slate of boy bands exploded at the end of the century, led by the Backstreet Boys and 'N Sync, both of which were closely modeled on New Kids on the Block, though styling their vocals after Boyz II Men.

These groups came out of Orlando, Florida, under the control of Lou Pearlman. It was no coincidence that Orlando was also the home of Disney World Productions, which became a key incubator of young talent. Britney Spears, Christina Aguilera, JC Chaaez, and Justin Timberlake all started their careers on *The All New Mickey Mouse Club* (later *MMC*).

Breaking Down Bubblegum

It is important to remember that the phrase "bubblegum music" means different things depending on whether one is talking about its market (preteens), the age of its performers (often teenagers themselves), its method of production (assembly line studio bands with songwriter-producers), its sound (simple, danceable pop songs), its original historical context (the late 1960s and early 1970s canonical bands: The Archies, The Ohio Express, and others), or its relationship with media (designed for television instead of radio). This intersection of crass commercialism and pop music, the cross-media pollination, the influence of the psychedelic era on a preteen audience, and the ascendance of the songwriter-producer over the performers makes bubblegum a complex and intriguing subject. But those aspects of bubblegum challenged the assumptions of rock criticism at every level.

Critical writing about rock music evolved with the late 1960s counterculture, and bubblegum represented everything the counterculture hated. The first generation of rock critics valued albums over singles, autonomous bands, lyrical complexity, a folk-music-derived notion of musical authenticity (personal expression, music created without commercial interest, instrumental prowess), political engagement, "heavy" music, and sophisticated structures. Bubblegum was commercially designed, "plastic," singles-oriented, producer-driven studio music with simple lyrics and accessible pop sounds. In the late 1960s and early 1970s there was no greater insult in the critic's arsenal than to label a group bubblegum.

It was the rock critic Lester Bangs who first defended bubblegum, arguing that early rock 'n' roll was no less vital because it was lyrically unsophisticated, that a song like Little Richard's "Tutti Frutti" was both silly and revolutionary. It seemed puritanical and dishonest to dismiss music designed for pleasure and dancing, and the folkie notion of authenticity was both problematic (because folk music has never been pure, but always a vital mixture of commercial cross-influences) and often an impediment to musical innovation.

Further, whole genres of music (Motown, stax, reggae, disco, and country music out of both Nashville and Bakersfield) owed more to studio musicians and the writer-producer model than the autonomous band ideal, and a great pop single could be just as valid and often had more impact than entire albums. As postmodern critical theory began filtering into music writing, bubblegum proved a focal point for the idea of creating a pop persona, the complex intersection of media, how to understand culture as commercial product. In retrospect, the critical dismissal of bubblegum also contained an element of sexism, as the predominantly male rock critics of the era dismissed a genre aimed primarily at preteen girls.

As pop music rolls into the twenty-first century, the fact that bubblegum music still exists and continues to influence mainstream pop nearly fifty years after its arrival is not the most interesting thing about it. Certainly bubblegum exists, as it always did, spicing up cartoons on the Disney Channel, Cartoon Network, and Nickelodeon, or catering to a preteen audience with acts like the Jonas Brothers, Justin Bieber, or Miley Cyrus. But when Damon Albarn felt constrained by the success of his Brit pop group Blur, he formed Gorillaz, a completely imaginary band that existed primarily in cartoon form and turned out irresistibly catchy dance pop. He used the methods of bubblegum to create a new creative space for himself and his collaborators. And although pop provocateurs like Lady Gaga, Pink, Katy Perry, and Nikki Minaj aren't bubblegum acts, they know how to exploit the tools of bubblegum, using broadly cartoonish visual imagery and upbeat dance pop to upend the pop charts. Ultimately, the very things that made bubblegum so objectionable to its earliest critics—the mutable pop personas, the studio culture, the pleasure-seeking dance pop, the blatant commerciality, the strangeness of catering to a preteen market—have turned out to be the most useful strategies for musicians to critique pop music itself.

See also: B-Side, The Boy Bands; British Influences on American Rock Music; Disco; Disney Music; Dylan, Bob; Lady Gaga Glam Rock; Jackson Family; Motown; New Wave; New York Dolls; Pop Music; Richard, Little; Singer-Songwriters; Soul; Spears, Britney; Television Theme Songs

Further Reading

Brownlee, Nick. 2003. *Bubblegum: The History of Plastic Pop.* London: Sanctuary Publishing.

Cooper, Kim, and David Smay. 2001. *Bubblegum Music Is the Naked Truth: The Dark History of Prepubescent Pop, from the Banana Splits to Britney Spears.* Los Angeles: Feral House Publishing.

David Smay and Kim Cooper

Buffett, Jimmy (1946–)

Born in Pascagoula, Mississippi, on Christmas Day, 1946, and raised on the shores of the Gulf of Mexico, singer-songwriter Jimmy Buffett moved to Nashville in the late 1960s but failed to break into country music. Introduced to Key West, Florida, by fellow country musician Jerry Jeff Walker (1942–), he settled there in 1972 and began to invent the fun-loving-beach-bum persona that would become—through steady productivity and savvy marketing—the foundation of a successful four-decade career.

A White Sport Coat and a Pink Crustacean (1973) and *Living and Dying in ¾ Time* (1974), Buffett's first Florida-based albums, mixed delicate character-study ballads like "He Went to Paris" and "Death of an Unpopular Poet" with country tunes like "Why Don't We Get Drunk and Screw?" which reveled in their defiance of Nashville conventions. It was *A1A*—his second album of 1974, named for a coastal highway in Florida—that marked the emergence of Buffett's signature style, with five songs specifically *about* life on

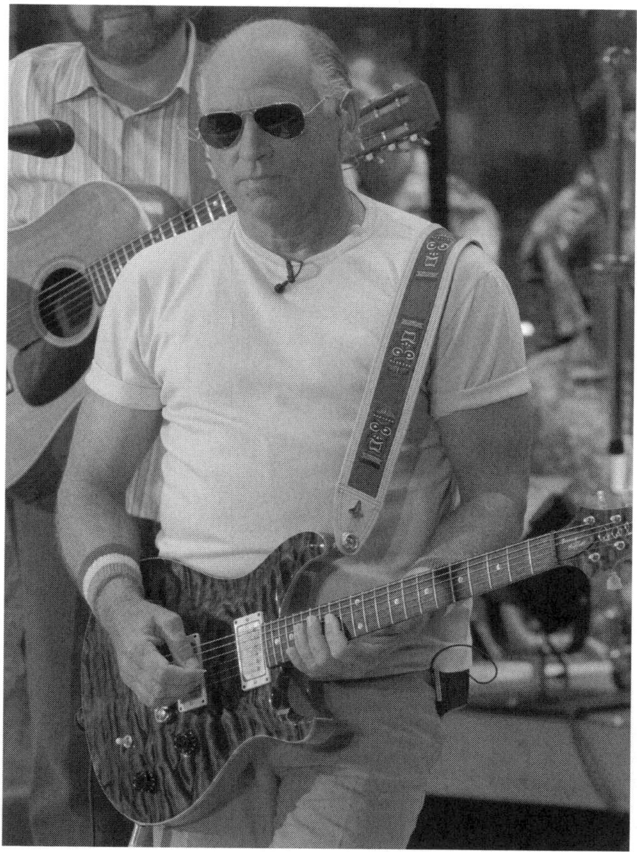

Jimmy Buffett's style has been described as country, folk, or even rock and roll. His most famous and popular songs concern Key West, Florida, and have a Caribbean influence. (Mychal Watts/WireImage)

Key West, including "A Pirate Looks at Forty" and "Trying to Reason with Hurricane Season." Refined in *Havana Daydreamin'* (1976) and perfected in *Changes in Latitudes, Changes in Attitudes* (1977), it blended country and Caribbean musical influences with subtle, complex lyrics. "Margaritaville," from *Changes in Latitudes,* was typical: an upbeat song about drinking the day away in a tropical bar counterpointed by the singer's growing ambivalence about his life. It became Buffett's biggest hit (surpassing the wistful love song "Come Monday") and for decades his only number one single.

The middling-but-steady sales of Buffett's singles and albums from the mid-1970s onward reflected the emergence of a burgeoning community of fans, who called themselves "Parrotheads." Drawn both to the music and to the fantasy lifestyle it symbolized, the Parrotheads enthusiastically supported annual concert tours; live albums; a chain of "Margaritaville" restaurants and gift shops; and a burgeoning line of licensed merchandise ranging from T-shirts and sandals to food, beer (Landshark Lager, brewed under license by Anheuser-Busch), and Margaritaville-brand rum. They also formed the core audience for Buffett's literary ventures: a collection of short stories based on his songs, several novels, a memoir, and two children's books coauthored with his daughter. A stable fan base and steady sales of his back-catalog albums to new fans enabled Buffett to pursue less commercial ventures, such as a musical based on Herman Wouk's 1965 novel *Don't Stop the Carnival* and campaigns for the preservation of Florida's endangered manatee population.

Buffett's music, absent from the country charts after the mid-1980s, reemerged there in 2003–2004 with *License to Chill,* an album featuring duets sung by Buffett and country stars such as Alan Jackson (1958–). The album reached number one on the *Billboard* country album chart (as did its successor, 2006's *Take the Weather with You*), and "It's Five O'Clock Somewhere," a Buffett-Jackson tune about tropical drinks and fantasies of the beach, topped the country singles chart. "Knee Deep," a collaboration with the Zac Brown Band (2002–), reached number one in the summer of 2011, strengthening ties between Jimmy Buffett and Nashville forty years after they had parted company.

See also: Audiences; Comedy and Satire in American Music; Country Music

Official Web Site: http://www.margaritaville.com/jimmybuffett.html

Further Reading

Buffett, Jimmy. 1998. *A Pirate Looks at Fifty.* New York: Random House.

McKenna, Erin, and Scott L. Pratt, eds. 1999. *Jimmy Buffett and Philosophy: The Porpoise-Driven Life.* New York: Open Court Publishing.

Ryan, Thomas F. 1998. *The Parrot Head Companion: An Insider's Guide to Jimmy Buffett.* New York: Kensington Publishing Corporation.

A. Bowdoin Van Riper

Cage, John (1912–1992)

John Cage was a composer, performer, writer, and visual artist. A pioneer of experimental music, he became a central figure in the avant-garde art of the 1960s. His influence was central to artists pursuing new approaches in music, dance, and theater, and his celebration of diverse, simultaneous styles in art characterizes today's culture.

Born in Los Angeles, Cage became interested in modern art, music, and literature while living in Paris in his twenties. Once he returned to America, he focused principally on composition, attending classes taught by Arnold Schoenberg (1874–1954) at University of Southern California and University of California at Los Angeles. His earliest works accepted all sounds as potentially useful for music; they were often scored for percussion. In 1935 he married the Russian American artist Xenia Kashevaroff.

After professional experiences on the West Coast and in Chicago, Cage and Xenia moved to New York; there he began an intense period of composition for the prepared piano, a grand piano into which had been inserted mutes of rubber, metal, and other materials that transformed its sound to resemble a gamelan orchestra. He divorced his wife in 1945, having left her to embark on a lifelong personal and artistic partnership with the choreographer Merce Cunningham (1919–2009). Along with Cunningham, he began to explore a new conception of music, dance, and other theatrical elements; sharing only a total time duration, each creative component would coexist, independent and equally worthy of attention on its own. His 1952 theatrical event at North Carolina's Black Mountain College included simultaneous performances

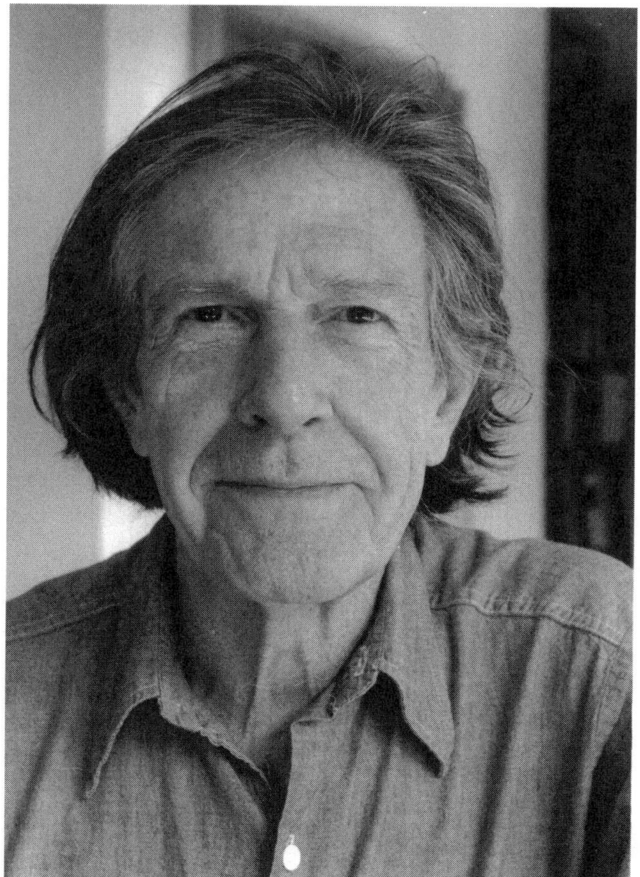

Avant-garde composer John Cage's revolutionary concepts questioned centuries of disciplined musical development and established new musical freedom during the 20th century. (HultonArchive/Getty Images)

of music, dance, and recited poetry as well as the exhibition of visual art; it became known as the first happening and was immeasurably decisive for the development of multimedia art in the 1960s.

Cage's music from 1950 onward involved the use of chance in the compositional process, which generally involved an ancient Chinese text, the I Ching (Book of Changes), and its method of tossing three coins six times to obtain a number corresponding to one of sixty-four symbols denoting the fluid, ever-changing state of the universe. He decided in advance a number of possibilities for each stage of the work, from the most general to the most specific; he then associated one or a range of the sixty-four I Ching numbers to correspond to these precompositional choices. The results of I Ching coin tosses—which he called chance operations—determined most aspects of the finished composition.

By reducing the composer's personality in the making of compositions, Cage exemplified his sustained interest in Eastern spirituality, especially Zen Buddhism, which stressed the importance of interconnectedness of all substance in the universe and the need to de-emphasize the ego so that it allowed for a continuous flow between experiences gathered from the senses and those from dreams. The extreme of his Zen influence manifests itself in *4'33"* (1952), a work that comprises only the unintended sounds of the space in which the work is heard. Some of his compositions gave his performers much more agency in the performance and sometimes the design of the music, while in others the results of Cage's chance operations were transcribed into a score that was learned by musicians as they would any music. A prolific writer, Cage employed similar techniques in writing and, from 1978 until his death, also employed chance operations in the visual arts of printmaking and painting.

Cage believed that music and art generally could be useful in society by demonstrating ways to live that stressed individual creativity over traditional forms of government. A few of his many important works include the musical compositions *Sonatas and Interludes for Prepared Piano* (1946–1948), *Concerto for Prepared Piano and Chamber Orchestra* (1950–1951), *Atlas Eclipticalis* for orchestra (1962), *Song Books* (1970), *Roaratorio: An Irish Circus on "Finnegans Wake"* (1979), and *Europeras 3 & 4* (1990); the text pieces *Empty Words* (1973–1974), *Diary: How to Improve the World (You Will Only Make Matters Worse)* (1965–1982), and *I–VI* (1988); and the visual works *Déreau* (1982) and *Smoke Weather Stone Weather* (1991).

See also: Avant-garde in Music, The; Composers, Progressive

Official Web Site: http://johncage.org/

Further Reading

Blofeld, John, trans. 1958. *The Zen Teaching of Huang Po on the Transmission of Mind.* New York: Grove Press.

Cage, John. 1961. *Silence: Lectures and Writings.* Middletown, CT: Wesleyan University Press.

Cage, John, and Joan Retallack. 1996. *Musicage: Cage Muses on Words, Music, Art; John Cage in Conversation with Joan Retallack.* Hanover, NH: University Press of New Hampshire.

Haskins, Rob. 2012. *John Cage.* London: Reaktion Books.

Kostelanetz, Richard, ed. 2002. *Conversing with Cage.* 2nd ed. New York: Routledge.

Millar, Jeremy. 2010. *Every Day Is a Good Day: The Visual Art of John Cage.* London: Hayward Publishing.

Pritchett, James. 1993. *The Music of John Cage.* Cambridge, UK: Cambridge University Press.

Rob Haskins

Cajun and Creole Music

Southern music historically has reflected the feelings, longings, and realities of working-class people who reside in the American South. Some have produced and consumed creations of melodious content. Yet when one thinks of southern musical manifestations, styles associated with opera, classical, or fine art traditions do not initially come to mind. For fans the world over, the South signifies sounds that echo sentiments summarized in genres such as the blues, country, gospel, jazz, R&B, honky-tonk, rockabilly, and soul. Recent efforts to distill these song types into a romanticized "roots music" phenomenon frequently overlook the less-than-ideal socioeconomic conditions responsible for the music's emergence. Confronting daily a hierarchical and status-conscious social structure that marginalized the majority of its population, working-class people utilized music as a means to transcend their marginalization.

No people in Dixie have experienced greater marginalization than the French-speaking black and white inhabitants of south Louisiana. They have occupied a twenty-two-parish (county) swath (Acadiana) that extends nearly 250 miles along the Gulf of Mexico (expanding northward approximately 100 miles inland) from just west of New Orleans to the Texas border. It is a geographical pocket of ethnic diversity that has affected (and in turn been affected by) southern culture. Two demographic fragments have been prominent. The first were exiled Acadians who settled in Louisiana beginning in 1764. Driven out of British-controlled Nova Scotia in 1755 because of their uncertain fidelity during hostilities between Great Britain and France, Acadians eventually disembarked along the bayous around present-day St. Martinville. The cultural and physical baggage they carried into their new environs included a love of ballads, a cappella singing, fiddles, and a propensity for dancing. Not long after they arrived, the Cajun outcasts began to expand their repertoire by incorporating the sounds and songs of surrounding Native Americans, Spaniards, African Americans, and Anglo-Americans. Indeed, this French-speaking and -singing community of whites served as a constant reminder that southern music represented a complex combination of many sources. Like the culture from which it evolved, Cajun music was never pure and unadulterated.

In addition to Cajuns, south Louisiana could boast of another French-singing community. This one was comprised of African Americans, whose culture conveyed many of the same characteristics exhibited by their displaced Canadian neighbors. In fact, despite formal and informal racial restrictions that kept them apart, the two groups, one white and the other black, paralleled and influenced each other constantly. French-speaking blacks were known as "Creoles." The term is a contested one that elicits as many definitions as sources consulted. The appellation has referred to people of mixed French and Spanish descent; it also denoted colonists born in Louisiana as opposed to those indigenous to France. It likewise has been applied to individuals of mixed racial heritage connected to the upper class. These "free people of color" began calling themselves "Creoles of color" to separate themselves from former slaves who gained their freedom following the Civil War. Here, the term "Creole" refers to French-speaking African Americans who have resided in rural south Louisiana. Although the designation recognizes the class/status distinctions that distinguished blacks within the region, it places greater emphasis on the racial similarities that united them.

Descendants of slaves or free people of color, Creoles in the late nineteenth century were sharecroppers and tenant farmers. Like their Cajun counterparts, many of whom also were economically disfranchised and dependent, Creoles were influenced by other cultures: Spanish, Native American, Anglo-American, and Caribbean sources contributed to the creation of their distinctive religious, culinary, folkloric, and artistic lifestyles. They, too, utilized music and dance as a means to express and entertain themselves, not in symphony halls and musical conservatories, but in family gatherings and house parties. Both Creoles and Cajuns established a tradition of hosting dances that lasted all night—the *bals de maison*. Participants would clear all of the furniture from the largest rooms of the house to make a space for dancing. Such Saturday night get-togethers also became known as the *fais-do-do* (pronounced dough). In a separate room set aside for infants, mothers rocked their children, encouraging them to "do do bebe"—"go to sleep baby"—so that they could return to dancing. This practice lingered well into the twentieth century.

Interestingly, the traditions shared by black and white inhabitants of south Louisiana both crossed and did not cross the color line. Musical festivities could be the same, but they also were separate. Contact between the groups occurred, but only within prescribed conditions. Such racial dynamics were as old as the music itself. Fiddles had been fixtures at *fais-do-dos* since the very beginning of mid-eighteenth-century French settlement. Black and white musicians became conversant in performing Anglo-inspired jigs, hoedowns, and Virginia reels to go along with the *valses à deux temps*. African American fiddlers frequently were summoned to play at dances attended by whites, thus creating a medium of exchange that followed socially acceptable racial parameters. The fiddle was compact and easy to transport. Creole and Cajun musicians had no difficulty adapting it to engage and entertain revelers.

In the late nineteenth century German settlers and merchants from Texas disseminated affordable accordions into south Louisiana. At least one scholar has maintained that African American musicians pressed the squeezebox into the region's consciousness. There is little doubt that the accordion transformed the musical culture. A loud and sturdy instrument with a limited number of notes, the accordion was particularly functional in providing music for dancing. Paired with fiddlers, accordionists dominated through their volume alone. As historians have noted, however, the accordion was unsophisticated in its melodic range and actually tended to simplify much of the Cajun and Creole repertoire. Nevertheless, the accordion quickly evolved into the instrument utilized for large and crowded venues, especially as dancers did variations of the two-step. It became the instrument most associated with Cajun and Creole music. The accordion contributed to the old-time sound, which for many alleviated the tensions that accompanied social change and modernity; for those with middle-class aspirations who sought to move up by looking down on rustic reminders of their recent past, however, the "chanky-chank" of the accordion was an abrasive symbol of estrangement.

The wider world's initial exposure to accordion-style Cajun music occurred in the late 1920s. In 1928 Joe Falcon and Cleoma Breaux recorded in New Orleans the first Cajun commercial recording ("*Allons à Lafayette*"). Falcon played accordion; Breaux played guitar and sang. The two would marry four years later. Cleoma's father, Auguste, had been a legendary accordionist; her three brothers also were musicians. In addition to guitar, Cleoma played a variety of instruments, including the accordion and fiddle. She and her husband performed throughout south Louisiana. Cleoma's appearances in rowdy dance halls challenged her society's gender rules, and in her adherence to Hollywood fashion, helped break down her community's rural isolation. The Falcons recorded over forty sides between 1928 and 1940, and their recording success opened the door for numerous contemporaries, such as Sady Courvillle, Mayus Lafleur, Leo Soileau, and Angelas Lejeune. Yet by the time of her untimely death at age thirty-five in 1941, the accordion had gone out of fashion with south Louisiana bands. A new generation of Cajun stylists was emulating country music and western swing heard on radio and records. Accordions were stored in the closet. Their exodus, however, would be temporary.

One final note on the racial aspects of the accordion; Amèdè Ardoin, a Creole accordionist who brought elements of jazz and blues into his performance style, became one of the area's most popular entertainers. In New Orleans in 1929, he and Dennis McGee recorded six Creole/Cajun songs for Columbia Records. Ardoin later recorded at least twenty-eight more songs (several of them in New York City) and continued to perform throughout south Louisiana and neighboring Texas. legend has it that while Ardoin was playing at a farmhouse in Eunice, Louisiana, in the late 1930s, during a break in the music a young white woman offered him a handkerchief to wipe sweat from his brow. Two white men became so enraged at this violation of racial etiquette that they followed Ardoin out of the farmhouse and beat him before running over him with their truck. They then threw his broken body into a ditch. Although Ardoin did not die from the injuries, he never recovered, and apparently died in the state's mental institution a few years later.

Ardoin's fate is a reminder that shared musical traditions during the Jim Crow era were not necessarily powerful enough to overcome racial prejudice and discrimination. Despite the cross-fertilization that occurred between Creole and Cajun musicians in south Louisiana, two different and separate traditions coexisted alongside each other. This tendency persisted in the years leading up to and following World War II. As Cajun music gravitated toward country forms, Creole drifted toward blues and R&B, eventually evolving into zydeco. The term is derived from a dance tune known in both Cajun and Creole circles, "*Les Haricots Sont Pas Salès* (The Snap Beans Are Not Salted)." Clifton Chenier, born in 1925, the son of sharecroppers, emerged as the music's greatest early practitioner. An accordionist, he teamed with his brother, who played the washboard (also called a *frottoir*—a metal rubbing board worn as a vest; it replaced the fiddle in zydeco bands), to perform in clubs surrounding the Texas oil fields and refineries where they worked. The music they made echoed the La-La (one-step dance) music they had heard while growing up in St. Landry Parish. The Cheniers also had absorbed other available musical influences, including the blues, jazz, Cajun, Afro-Caribbean rhythms, and Ardoin's Creole songs. Synthesizing it all, Clifton created a music that swept African American rural and urban dance halls from south Louisiana to east Texas. Like jazz earlier in the century, zydeco accompanied black migrants on their postwar great migration to California. In the early 1950s Chenier recorded in Los Angeles, and he had a ready-made audience for his ramped-up renditions of Creole music. Others, such as John Delafose, Boozoo Chavis, Rockin, Doopsey, Queen Ida, and Buckwheat Zydeco, spread the good news first proclaimed by Chenier.

Cajun music in the post–World War II era also underwent a transformation. While many younger musicians continued to follow the latest trends in country music, including honky-tonk, rockabilly, and later rock 'n' roll (Hackberry Ramblers, Harry Choates, and the "Swamp Pop" phenomenon), accordion-toting artists such as Iry Lejeune, Lawrence Walker, Aldus Roger, D. L. Menard, and Nathan Abshire led Cajun music back to its roots and away from its inclination toward Americanization. This revival reached unprecedented heights in 1964, when the Newport Folk Festival invited to perform on its stage traditional Louisiana musicians Gladius Thibodeaux, Louis "Vinesse" LeJeune, and Dewey Balfa. Later in the decade Louisiana established the Council for the Development of French in Louisiana (CODOFIL); in 1974 the organization established a "Tribute to Cajun Music Festival" in Lafayette, an annual gathering that eventually became *Festivals Acadiens.* Combined with its appearances at national festivals and the continued popularity into the new millennium of indigenous artists such as Zachary Richard, BeauSoleil, Nathan Williams, Marc Savoy, and C. J. Chenier, Cajun and Creole music was accorded a high regard that Amèdè Ardoin and Cleoma Breaux Falcon would have found astonishing, if not incomprehensible.

For a people who often had felt stigmatized because of their French heritage—a cultural inheritance that upwardly mobile residents equated with poverty, ignorance, and ethnic depravity (as a means to eradicate its cultural influence, state and local school boards in 1916 initiated a policy that banned French from the classroom)—such accolades surely were welcomed. But they also seemed ironic. Their music finally was perceived not as a liability, but as a strength. Cajuns and Creoles, of course, had understood this from the beginning.

BeauSoleil with Michael Doucet performs at the 2010 New Orleans Jazz & Heritage Festival in New Orleans, Louisiana, May 1, 2010. (Rick Diamond/Getty Images)

Historically, Cajun and Creole music represented a local art form to which nearly all had access. The music that natives produced and consumed at house parties as well as in dance halls and juke joints generally did not require formal education and training to be appreciated or replicated. It originated with ordinary people who sang in styles or played instruments (fiddles, harmonicas, triangles, spoons) that likewise could be mastered by others of similar socioeconomic and educational backgrounds and circumstances. Most important, perhaps, the music's lyrical content addressed themes and issues that corresponded to the daily experiences and needs of its people. Whether they represented joy or sorrow or were a response to freedom or oppression, the sounds of music seemed always to accompany work, play, and worship. Indeed, music was a constant presence in situations where people loved, laughed, cried, celebrated, mourned, lived, and died.

The majority of Cajuns and Creoles were a musical people. This circumstance was due to several factors. Demographically, the Native Americans, Europeans, and West Africans who came into contact in south Louisiana all claimed age-old musical traditions. Such ancient practices were not identical, but they nevertheless demonstrated that music was central to each group. Native Americans believed music (and dance) possessed magical qualities that could be summoned to benefit those who participated in its creation and reception. It was a major component of public celebrations and religious rituals and also maintained an importance in quarters that were more private and personal. Moreover, music served as the transmitter of an indigenous people's history, keeping alive earlier stories and legends.

Music, particularly ballads, functioned in a similar fashion for Acadian migrants, the large majority of whom were not literate. In the absence of a written literature, ballads provided a journalistic perspective on past as well as more recent events. In addition, they offered guides for morality, often producing narratives that described in graphic (and frequently superstitious) detail the harmful consequences of waywardness. Yet ballads, like other forms of French music brought to south Louisiana, also furnished entertainment, whether performed in the home or in areas of public amusement. Dancing to fiddle tunes during celebrations such as weddings and community gatherings was standard practice on the prairies of south Louisiana.

As for West Africans forcibly relocated and enslaved in south Louisiana, their engagement with music was even more pronounced. Music was a significant connection to another world, perhaps a spiritual realm. With its deep-seated emphasis on polyphonic and polyrhythmic tendencies, it also connected enslaved people to each other. Through the melodic sounds of voices and the rhythmic swinging and swaying of bodies, West African exiles (many of whom also had come under the influence of Caribbean religious and musical sources) were able to converge present with past and one to all in a manner that helped deny slavery's power to nullify a people and a culture.

The legacies established by these original inhabitants, especially those from West Africa and Nova Scotia, cannot be overstated. They were central to the evolution of music in south Louisiana. Yet neither can one take too lightly the rural and agricultural milieu from which the music emerged. Working behind a mule and plow, often separated by long distances from neighbors, farmers frequently sang out or hollered simply to hear a human voice, even if it was only their own. Those within earshot might respond, making for an enlivened exchange. If nothing else, such activities helped break the monotony of rural seclusion. The work songs and field hollers of slave laborers, in addition to establishing a regimented pace, likewise relieved the boredom that ensued from isolation and repetitious toil. Characterized by improvisation and the give and take of call and response between leader and chorus, the songs could reflect either a spiritual or secular bent, referencing concerns or topics that all understood. In a rural folk society that relied almost exclusively on agriculture, the emphasis on such verbal expression reiterated the importance of oral communication. Inhabitants relied on the spoken rather than the written word for their information, inspiration, and entertainment. It is no coincidence, then, that music flowed from an environment in which public oratory, whether in the form of political posturing, commodity auctioneering, or the aural art form of front porch storytelling, played a prominent role. Indeed, south Louisiana's musical heritage has rested heavily on a long-standing and pervasive oral culture.

Most important to the evolution of Cajun and Creole music, however, has been the relationship of people to power. Put simply, the large majority of French-speaking people in south Louisiana have possessed little real access to social, economic, or political authority and security. In a semifeudal province legendary for sustaining a rigid hierarchical structure that favored the few while ignoring the many, both black and white, the masses were marginalized. And the ramifications of systemic discrimination along racial, class, and gender lines have been horrendous. For generations, Louisiana seemingly has reserved a permanent place at the bottom of national economic and social indices (GNP per capita, education, age expectancy, health, and safety).

Yet the trials and tribulations that its citizens have endured set in motion a musical surge that has yet to subside. Enjoying little satisfaction associated with material acquisition, political prerogative, or social status, ordinary Louisianians turned to music, a cost-effective and seemingly apolitical means of enjoyment, release, creative sustenance, and self-expression. Unable to connect personal worth and integrity to work (labor-intensive jobs that promised little material or monetary reward), politics (a history of suffrage restrictions, voter intimidation, government corruption, and questionable electoral maneuvering that led to feelings of political powerlessness), or social status (formal and informal rules that informed everyone of their "place" in the community), they created an alternative space that privileged music as a means to articulate who they were and why they mattered.

While Creoles and Cajuns have demonstrated that music can provide a functional antidote to the oppression and dehumanization of daily life, they also have revealed that "leisure activities" in themselves have rarely cured the structural and societal conditions that made the music necessary. Still, music certainly has made life more tolerable. This may be one of history's more enduring lessons. *Laissez les bons temps rouler!*

See also: A Cappella; Accordion; African American Gospel Music; African American Influences on American Music; Blues; Country Music; Honky-Tonk Music; Improvisation; Intercultural and Interracial Music; Jazz; Native American Music; R&B; Rockabilly; Roots Music; Slave Songs; Soul; Zydeco

Further Reading

Ancelet, Barry Jean. 1989. *Cajun Music: Its Origins and Development.* Lafayette: The Center for Louisiana Studies, University of Louisiana.

Ancelet, Barry Jean, with photographs by Elemore Morgan Jr. 1999. *Cajun and Creole Music Makers.* Jackson: University Press of Mississippi.

Ancelet, Barry Jean, Jay Edwards, and Glen Pitre. 1991. *Cajun Country.* Jackson: University Press of Mississippi.

Bernard, Shane K. 1996. *Swamp Pop: Cajun and Creole Rhythm and Blues.* Jackson: University Press of Mississippi.

Bernard, Shane K. 2003. *The Cajuns: Americanization of a People.* Jackson: University Press of Mississippi.

Brasseaux, Ryan A. 2009. *Cajun Breakdown: The Emergence of an American-Made Music.* New York: Oxford University Press.

Brasseaux, Ryan A., and Kevin S. Fontenot. 2006. *Accordions, Fiddles, Two-Step & Swing: A Cajun Music Reader.* Lafayette: The Center for Louisiana Studies, University of Louisiana.

Broven, John. 1983. *South to Louisiana: The Music of the Cajun Bayous.* New Orleans: Pelican Publishing.

Faragher, John Mack. 2006. *A Great and Noble Scheme: The Tragic Story of the Expulsion of the French Acadians from Their American Homeland.* New York: W.W. Norton and Company.

Gould, Philip. 1992. *Cajun and Zydeco Music.* Baton Rouge: Louisiana State University Press.

Joyner, Charles. 1999. *Shared Traditions: Southern History and Folk Culture.* Urbana: University of Illinois Press.

Koster, Rick. 2002. *Louisiana Music: A Journey from R&B to Zydeco, Jazz to Country, Blues to Gospel, Cajun Music to Swamp Pop to Carnival Music and Beyond.* Cambridge, MA: Da Capo Press.

Levine, Lawrence. 1977. *Black Culture and Black Consciousness: Afro-American Folk Thought from Slavery to Freedom.* New York: Oxford University Press.

Malone, Bill, with Dave Stricklin. 2003. *Southern Music, American Music.* 2nd rev. ed. Lexington: University Press of Kentucky.

Sandmel, Ben. 1999. *Zydeco!* Jackson: University Press of Mississippi.

Savoy, Ann Allen. 1984. *Cajun Music: A Reflection of a People.* Eunice, LA: Bluebird Press.

Tisserand, Michael. 1998. *The Kingdom of Zydeco.* New York: Arcade Publishing.

Michael T. Bertrand

Campaign Music

Political campaign songs are not unique to the United States of America. Music has always been a tool for expression, which intertwines with both the personal and the political. However, the United States developed a political culture unlike any other in the nineteenth century. Through a combination of political ideology, culture, and technology the United States developed a mode of political expression that was distinct and served a variety of purposes. Not only were songs used to gather crowds and rouse excitement, but they were also a tool for political organizers and voters to communicate with each other to develop correct political messaging. Therefore the themes of political songs represented the sentiments and desires of the American population.

American political culture evolved dramatically from its early incarnation in the late eighteenth century. The political change and move toward "universal manhood suffrage" allowed voters to have more influence on national presidential elections. Thus, earlier songs, such as "Jefferson and Liberty," written by Robert Tree Paine as a protest against the Alien and Sedition Acts, were high-minded and more sophisticated. America did not develop its own brand of music until the rise of minstrelsy in the 1830s. The democratization of the political culture coincided with the creation of unique American music. Although many lyrics were still set to the tunes of English, Scottish, and Irish songs, America now had its own unique style, which was more relatable to the daily experiences of most Americans.

Andrew Jackson's campaign song, "The Hunters of Kentucky" was the perfect representation of the dramatic change in political music. The tune, written by Samuel Woodworth for the song "The Unfortunate Miss Bailey," was uniquely American and identified Jackson and his troops in a common cause. Politicians would quickly adopt this strategy, which culminated in the first modern campaign of William Henry Harrison in 1840. Harrison's campaign introduced a catchy slogan and song, "Tippecanoe and Tyler Too." With banners, parades, multiple song books, pins, and ribbons, Harrison was marketed as a hard-cider-drinking war hero. The message was not entirely accurate, but Harrison was able to ride it to the White House.

The next twenty years of presidential campaigns followed the same patterns. Every candidate used the same popular minstrel song tunes, many of which became American standards, such as "Oh Susannah," "Old Dan Tucker," "Dandy Jim of Caroline," "Uncle Ned," and "Boatman's Dance." The tastes of voters were very similar when it came to popular music. In fact, campaigns continued to use the same Irish, Scottish, and English tunes, such as "Yankee Doodle," "Rosin the Beau," and "John Anderson My Jo John." Even stranger, the messages started to sound quite similar. Most candidates had a song touting their great military experience, even if their accomplishments were minimal. This manly part of campaign songs was also expressed in the vulgarity that was used. Van Buren "deserved the lowest place in hell," Abraham Lincoln was ugly, Lewis Cass was "Cass without the C," and Stephen Douglas was too short. In one campaign song, "The Short and Long of It," Lincoln "splits a rail" through Douglas's coat tail and "quickly thrust(s) the prong of it." Such imagery was popular among the new political culture and occasionally was balanced by the use of women in songs. The "Clay Girl's Song" in 1844 was written from the female perspective; she would not give her hand in marriage to any man who did not vote for Henry Clay. John C. Fremont used his wife Jessie in a variety of songs during the 1856 campaign. Republican songsters often noted that women should be at political gatherings and noted at which points in a song women should join in singing.

After the Civil War campaign songs often took up on the rhetoric of the war. Republicans especially tried to "wave the bloody shirt" to get votes from the new freedmen and ex-soldiers. The 1876 campaign in particular took on many old war themes. Rutherford B. Hayes ironically brought about the official end of Reconstruction to secure the presidency despite his campaign songs. James Garfield's campaign used the tune "When Jonny Comes Marching Home" for the song "If the Johnnies Get into Power Again," which aimed to scare voters about the impact of a Democratic administration. The strategy changed in four years by simply taking advantage of Grover Cleveland fathering an illegitimate child, with the song "Ma Ma Where's My Pa?" Benjamin Harrison also used songs about his relationship to Tippecanoe and his record doing the Civil War, not to mention Cleveland chickening out of the war by hiring a substitute, as expressed in the song "There Are No Flies on Harrison." Cleveland shot back with "His Grandfather's Hat," put to the tune of his "Grandfather's Clock"; the song argued that Harrison was not ready to fill his grandfather's shoes.

The twentieth century brought in political songs that were written by professional songwriters, as the old methods of political mobilization and advertising began to change. "Wilson That's All" in 1912 proved to be a witty take an a popular brand of whisky that happened to share the name of the Democratic nominee. Most songs, however, were not as distinctive, such as the 1908 song "Get on a Raft with Taft." Al Jolson contributed to a song for Warren G. Harding in 1920, and his successor won the day with "Keep Cool and Keep Coolidge" in 1924. By the 1930s generic popular songs had become more important. Although Franklin D. Roosevelt had original songs, it was "Happy Days Are Here Again" that remained most associated with his campaign; the song expressed hope for better times, yet it was not written with FDR in mind. The last year that original campaign songs played a critical role in a campaign was in 1948, when a third-party progressive candidate, Henry Wallace, had at least a dozen songs, with one pleading with Americans to get off "The Same Merry Go-Round."

Most candidates after that would use campaign songs as novelties, but they would never be the centerpiece of a campaign. Even so, Irving Berlin's "I Like Ike" and Frank Sinatra's special recoding of "High Hopes" for John F. Kennedy proved to be memorable parts of successful campaigns. Politicians usually pick a popular song to represent a campaign, as Bill Clinton did with Fleetwood Mac's "Don't Stop Thinking about Tomorrow" in 1992. There is little relationship between this type of song and the historical roots of the campaign song, but the latter's modern version is more likely to be seen in Internet video parodies on social networking Web sites. This is the future of political expression for the twenty-first century. The Internet also plays a role in allowing followers to vote for campaign songs. President Obama in 2012 asked for suggestions for campaign songs to be added to his account on Spotify, the online music streaming service; he had no one song as his theme, nor did his opponent, Mitt Romney.

See also: Berlin, Irving; Sinatra, Frank

Further Reading

Abraham Lincoln Historical Digitization Project. 2000. Northern Illinois University. http://lincoln.lib.niu.edu/ (accessed January 9, 2011).

Silber, Irwin. 1971. *Songs America Voted By.* Harrisburg, PA: Stackpole.

Stuart Schimler

Capricorn Records

Brothers Phil Walden and Allen Walden's Capricorn Records, the de facto record label for the southern rock genre during the 1970s, would become the home of the Allman Brothers Band, Marshall Tucker Band, Sea Level, Grinderswitch, Wet Willie, and Elvin Bishop. In 1967 Phil Walden approached Jerry Wexler, the vice president of Atlantic Records, to secure funding to build a studio in his hometown of Macon, Georgia. Wexler suggested that Walden not only build a studio, but start an independent record label that would be distributed by Atlantic. Walden and Wexler had a successful working relationship, as Walden had been the manager of R&B artists Otis Redding, Sam and Dave, and Percy Sledge, all of whom had recorded hit records released on Atlantic Records. The goal was to create a studio that would rival Fame Studios in Muscle Shoals, Alabama, and Stax Studio in Memphis, Tennessee.

The first artist signed to Capricorn Records was Duane Allman. Walden would build a house band around drummer Johnny Sandlin and keyboardist Paul Hornsby, both of whom had been members of one of Duane Allman and Greg Allman's earlier bands, The Allman Joys & Hour Glass. In addition to playing in Capricorn's rhythm section, Hornsby and Sandlin would produce a wide range of Capricorn acts, as well as play in the band Cowboy. Capricorn experienced severe financial problems and eventually went out of business in 1979. The Capricorn label was reactivated in the early 1990s and became the home of country star Kenny Chesney and southern rock jam band Widespread Panic.

See also: Allman Brothers; Redding, Otis

Further Reading

Brant, Marley. 1999. *Southern Rockers.* New York: Billboard Books.

Freeman, Scott. 1995. *Midnight Riders: The Story of the Allman Brothers.* Boston: Little, Brown.

Ralph Wood

Carey, Mariah (1969–)

A native of Long Island, New York, Mariah Carey is the multiracial daughter of an Irish American opera singer and an Afro-Venezuelan American aeronautical engineer. Discovered by Columbia Records executive Tommy Mottola, she found overnight success with her self-titled debut CD in 1990. Carey won many fans with her catchy pop songs (half of which she cowrote), but it was her wide-ranging voice that garnered the greatest attention. In addition to a strong chest voice and the ability to belt melismatic gospel lines, she sang in the high-lying whistle register like 1970s singer Minnie Riperton. Exaggerated claims repeatedly reported Carey's range as seven octaves (nearly that of a piano), but her vocal range is closer to five octaves. Her first album earned two Grammy Awards (Best New Artist and Best Female Pop Vocal Performance) and had five number one hits. With *Emotions* (1991) and *Music Box* (1993), Carey firmly established her commercial credibility and went on to become the top-selling recording artist of the 1990s. In addition to her marriage to Tommy Mottola (1993), the decade brought the integration of hip-hop and R&B elements into her songwriting and musical collaboration for *Daydream* (1995). After divorcing Mottola, Carey continued to revamp her image from pop power-ballad songstress to sexy soulful singer with *Butterfly* (1997) and *Rainbow* (1999), working with guest artists such as rappers Jay-Z and Snoop Dogg. Her album sales dropped despite her winning the World Music Award for Best-Selling Female Artist of the Millennium. Critics found fault with the sameness of her songs and her increasingly sexualized video persona. She parted ways with Columbia and signed a deal with Virgin Records in 2001 for a reported $80 million. The same year her acting in the semiautobiographical film *Glitter* (2001) was disparaged; she won the Golden Razzberry for Worst Actress. Reportedly Carey had something of an emotional breakdown due to overwork and the demise of her romance with singer Luis Miguel. In 2002 she faced more challenges: Virgin bought out her contract, and her father succumbed to cancer. Her first release for Def Jam/Island Records, *Charmbracelet,* revealed some vocal deterioration, with increased raspiness and decreased range and agility. Yet Carey rediscovered commercial success with *The Emancipation of Mimi* (2005). The top-selling album of the year, it won her three more Grammy Awards. In 2008 she married *America's Got Talent* host/comedian Nick Cannon, eleven years her junior. Carey regained her reputation as an actress with her supporting role (sans makeup) in the critically touted *Precious* (2009). Her second Christmas album was released in 2010. As a songwriter, she has been criticized for her overly sentimental, simplistic lyrics and predictable hip-hop dance tunes. Her voice has not retained the impressive range and flexibility of her stunning first single, "Vision of Love." But Mariah Carey remains an influential recording artist who successfully integrated gospel, R&B, and hip-hop influences into mainstream popular music, justifying her current spot at number six on *Billboard*'s 100 Top All-Time Artists (behind The Beatles, Madonna, Elton John, Elvis Presley, and Stevie Wonder).

Mariah Carey performs at Samsung AT&T Summer Krush concert series in Los Angeles, July 31, 2008. (AP Photo/Matt Sayles)

See also: Actors as Composers, Songwriters, or Performers; Hip-Hop; Pop Music; R&B; Singer-Songwriters; Women in American Music

Further Reading

Sapet, Kerrily. 2009. *Mariah Carey: Singer, Songwriter, Record Producer, and Actress.* Transcending Race in America: Biographies of Biracial Achievers. Broomall, PA: Mason Crest.

Shapiro, Marc. 2001. *Mariah Carey: The Unauthorized Biography.* Toronto: ECW Press.

Linda Lister

The Carter Family (Active 1927–1944)

The Carter Family made over three hundred recordings and was the first popular county music vocal group. They formulated the country song as it is known today.

In the early years of the twentieth century a rather tall and lanky young man crossed Clinch Mountain in southwest Virginia seeking to sell fruit trees from a catalog. His name was Alvin Pleasant Delaney Carter, or simply "A. P." or "Doc." He walked the dirt roads, going from door to door, until he rounded a bend and heard beautiful singing echoing down the hollows. There, on the front porch of a farmhouse, was the most stunning girl he had ever seen. Legend has it she was singing a song called "Engine One-Forty-Three" and playing an autoharp. He approached her timidly. After she finished her song, he asked if she would be interested in purchasing his wares and offered her the catalog. This young girl was Sara Elizabeth Dougherty. Theirs was a short courtship, and in 1915 they were married. Thus was born what was to become The Carter Family, or the "Original Carter Family."

A. P.'s brother Ezra, or "Eck," married Sara's cousin Maybelle, and the two girls moved to Maces Springs, Virginia, on the south side of the "Clinch" where the brothers lived. A. P. loved music and was a great student of it. He learned to play the fiddle and dance, although choral music was his great love. He encouraged Sara to keep singing, and she and her cousin Maybelle refined their style and methods. Early on A. P. was gathering songs and bringing them to the cousins. He had a strong baritone harmony and headed up each and every rehearsal, bringing original songs to them along with his own arrangements of those he "discovered." He was often gone from home, seeking out new music.

In the late summer of 1927 A. P. read an advertisement placed by producer and publisher Ralph Peer in the Bristol, Virginia, newspaper seeking talent. It promised a free recording session should the artist be chosen; each song the producer chose to record would earn the performer $50. And so A. P., Sara, and a very pregnant Maybelle climbed into their car and drove a very rough twenty-five miles to Bristol.

On August 2, 1927, The Carter Family recorded six songs, including "Single Girl, Married Girl" and "Bury Me Beneath the Willow." With Sara singing the lead vocal and accompanying herself on autoharp, they greatly impressed Peer, who signed them to a record deal and in time would publish A. P.'s compositions. Talent came from near and far that week to record with Peer, including The Stoneman Family and "The Singing Brakeman" Jimmie Rogers. Due to the resounding influence these artists had on the formation of country music, many historians believe this was the most important week in country music history.

Prior to the 1930s "hillbilly music" was mainly regarded as instrumental, but the Carters changed that with their vocal recordings. A. P. was a master editor, taking long and rambling songs and condensing them into shorter, two-and-one-half-minute versions, usually with verses and choruses. The songs were about everyday life, lost love, and faith. Many of these songs, including "Can the Circle Be Unbroken," "Wildwood Flower," and "Wabash Cannonball," were recorded by numerous artists over the following decades and have become an important part of the country songbook.

Maybelle Carter created a guitar playing style known as the "Carter Scratch." For many years this was the dominant guitar style in country music. This simple method of playing the rhythm on the high strings of the guitar at the same time as playing the melody on the lower strings may be heard in all styles of music today. Musicians from all genres credit her as a major influence, from Chet Atkins, who was a longtime friend and bandmate, to Keith Richards and Jerry Garcia.

In the late 1930s the Carters moved to Del Rio, Texas, and signed a contract with the radio station XERA. This station and a few others like it just across the border in Mexico did not follow the U.S. laws and could broadcast at much higher levels, hence sending their radio programs to a much greater audience. It was said that the signal could be heard on barbed wire or even on metal teeth fillings. Whether or not these claims are true, *The Carter Family Hour* was heard over much of the United States, and their popularity grew. Unfortunately, A. P. and Sara's marriage was in dire straits, and the couple divorced in 1939, although the group continued to perform for a few years. In 1943 Sara retired from music and moved to California with her new husband, Coy Bayes. A. P. returned to Maces Springs and ran a country store, recording again with Sara, and their children Janette and Joe, in the late 1950s.

Through the 1940s and 1950s Maybelle, along with her daughters Helen, June, and Anita, continued to make music, performing on many live radio shows and in 1950 joining WSM's *Grand Ole Opry* in Nashville, Tennessee.

A. P. died in 1960. It is unfortunate that he may not have been aware of the great influence he had on music, for in the following years The Carter Family records were re-released, and Maybelle and her daughters Helen, June, and Anita went on the road with Johnny Cash and brought the songs to a new audience. In 1968 Johnny Cash and June Carter were married.

Maybelle and Sara reunited briefly during the late 1960s and performed together at the Newport Folk Festival and other occasions. In 1970 The Carter Family became the first musical group inducted into the Country Music Hall of Fame, a fitting honor for this first family of country music.

Maybelle passed away on October 23, 1978, and Sara followed her on January 8, 1979, but their legacy lives on. The music of The Carter Family is sung by hundreds of artists in venues all around the world. Guitar teachers everywhere teach Maybelle's methods, some not even aware of the origins of the style. And each and every country song that is written owes at least some of its style to A. P. Carter.

See also: Cash, Johnny; Country Music; Country Music, Women In; Garcia, Jerry; Grand Ole Opry; Guitar; Halls of Fame

Official Web Site: http://www.carterfamilyfold.org/

Further Reading

Cash, John. 2007. *June Carter Cash: Anchored in Love.* New York: Thomas Nelson Publishers.

Zwonitzer, Mark, and Charles Hirshberg. 2004. *Will You Miss Me When I'm Gone? The Carter Family and Their Legacy in American Music.* New York: Simon & Schuster.

John Carter Cash

Cash, Johnny (1932–2003)

Born February 26, 1932, near Kingsland, Arkansas, singer-songwriter Johnny Cash became one of America's most enduring musical figures and cultural icons. His image and art molded thinking about politics, history, religion, and the American outlaw.

After serving in the U.S. Air Force, Cash spent the early years of his recording career in Memphis, Tennessee, where in the mid-1950s young white musicians infused country music with R&B to form what became known as rockabilly. Elvis Presley stepped to the forefront of the new genre in 1955, but Carl Perkins, Jerry Lee Lewis, and Johnny Cash soon followed. Cash debuted on Sun Records in 1955, and over the next two years he minted hits such as "Folsom Prison Blues," "I Walk the Line," and "Get Rhythm."

"Folsom Prison Blues," which borrowed heavily from bandleader Gordon Jenkins's "Crescent City Blues," became strongly associated with Cash and planted the seeds of his involvement in the hotly political issue of prison reform. Recorded in 1955, its imagery of murder and lonely train whistles in the distance became so closely identified with Cash that many thought he had actually spent time in prison. In 1968 Cash did the next best thing, recording a concert at the California penitentiary that resulted in the album *At Folsom Prison.* It lifted Cash's profile to international levels and placed him in the vortex of prison reform. For the next four years he rarely went long without commenting on eroding prison conditions and irrational penal laws. Advocates cited Cash's remarks, and politicians invited him to endorse their reform legislation. Indeed, for a time he symbolized the movement.

At Folsom Prison also solidified Cash's role as an American troubadour. Over the years, in addition to telling stories of prisoners, he had sung about historical and mythical figures such as Davy Crockett, Crazy Horse, John Henry, and John Wesley Hardin and about the rural experience, in classics such as "Five Feet High and Rising" (1959) and "Pickin' Time" (1959). Ironically, the *Folsom* album also promoted his image as an American outlaw, a cloak he readily wore, mostly because it helped sell records. Cash had spent a night in jail here and there on drunk and disorderly charges and had weathered a highly publicized arrest on drug charges in 1965. These events, as well as the brooding delivery of dark themes in "Give My Love to Rose" (1957), "Don't Take Your Guns to Town" (1959), "The Ballad of Ira Hayes" (1964), and other songs, contributed to his outlaw persona. Cash attempted to distance himself from that persona in the 1970s, as he toured with the celebrated Carter Family of country singers, and he married June Carter in 1968. Together they had a son, John Carter Cash (born 1970), and Carter and Cash each had children from previous marriages, some of whom have had successful careers as performers and songwriters, including Johnny's daughter Rosanne Cash (1955–), June's daughter Carlene Carter (1955–), and John Carter Cash (1970–), who is also a music producer. Although Johnny Cash portrayed a patriotic appearance in the 1970s and later and had a highly visible association with evangelist Billy Graham, he did not succeed in escaping his outlaw associations. In fact, it was the mysterious Cash of Folsom Prison that hip-hop

Johnny Cash, pictured here in 1970, is widely considered one of the most influential musicians of the 20th century. (Photofest)

and metal producer Rick Rubin tapped when he began recording the aging star in the 1990s. Rubin produced four albums with Cash before the singer's death in 2003, all featuring grim, black-and-white cover shots of Cash and songs such as the old murder ballad "Delia's Gone" (1994) and Trent Reznor's "Hurt" (2003). On the strength of such material and the recasting of his outlaw image, Cash captured young audiences who sought darkness in their music.

Cash combined authentic ballad songwriting with formidable powers of expression to become one of the greatest artists and cultural forces America ever produced. His work and his image embody varied aspects of our national experience. He died outside Nashville on September 12, 2003. A tribute recording, *We Walk the Line,* was released in August 2012, featuring performances by Willie Nelson and Kris Kristofferson, Shelby Lynne, Lucinda Williams, Shooter Jennings, and the Chocolate Drops, among others.

See also: Country Music; Lewis, Jerry Lee; Perkins, Carl; Presley, Elvis; Prison Music; R&B; Rockabilly

Official Web Site: http://www.johnnycash.com

Further Reading

Cash, Johnny, with Patrick Carr. 2003. *Cash: The Autobiography.* New York: HarperCollins.

Neimark, Anne. 2009. *Up Close: Johnny Cash.* Charlotte, NC: Baker & Taylor.

Streissguth, Michael. 2006. *Johnny Cash: The Biography.* Philadelphia, PA: Da Capo Press.

Michael Streissguth

Celtic Music in America

Celtic music is a catchall, and thus convenient, phrase, which refers to the indigenous music of the Celtic lands—namely, Scotland, Ireland, Wales, Cornwall, the Isle of Man, and Brittany—as well as the music of the broader Celtic diaspora. *Celtic* can apply to traditional and modern music—both instrumental and song—that is rooted in the tradition, including songs of the English-speaking and Gaelic-speaking Celtic worlds. This entry concentrates primarily on the music of the Irish and Scots, since those two emigrant groups have had the most impact on the development of music in the United States.

The music was brought over to America by Irish, Scots-Irish, and Scots emigrants in the seventeenth, eighteenth, and nineteenth centuries and played a major role in the development of bluegrass, old timey, and country music. The urban folk revival of the late 1950s and 1960s, as well as a new wave of emigration, primarily from Ireland in the 1950s, brought traditional Celtic musicians to the attention of a broader, and appreciative, audience. Thus, until fairly recently traditional Celtic music was considered a largely immigrant tradition. Starting in the mid-twentieth century, however, and especially by the 1970s and 1980s, American-born musicians, especially but not exclusively Irish Americans, began to contribute greatly to the tradition. Consequently, the sound of Celtic music in America is similar but different from its native roots. It is a combination of immigrant impulses, rural custom, and urban grit.

Generally speaking, the indigenous music of the Celtic lands shares some common characteristics. In brief, Celtic music can be described as circular, melodic, and ornamental. The practice of ornamentation, which refers to varying the notes in a song or tune, is a defining feature of the music. There are three types of ornamentation: a musician can decorate a tune by trills or grace notes, change the order of the melody, or make slight variations in the rhythm or meter. Such characteristics allow for an endless variety within a set framework. In fact, variation, embellishment, and ornamentation form the heart of the music.

Several musical forms are unique to a specific Celtic country, such as the Welsh choir in Wales, the Hebridean *waulking* song in the Scottish Highlands, and the *sean-nos* style of Gaelic singing in Ireland. For the most part, these traditions did not play a prominent role in the Celtic music tradition in America.

Most traditional Irish and Scottish music is dance music, even though today it is played primarily for listening, with the bulk of the tunes dating from the eighteenth century. The majority of tunes are reels, jigs, hornpipes, polkas, slides, and airs. The uniquely Scottish strathspey is played in a slow, staccato-like manner. Celtic music in America also includes a rich and robust singing tradition, from ancient balladry to Irish rebel songs and street ballads, and should be differentiated from the faux Irish American songs manufactured by the commercial American Tin Pan Alley tradition.

The types of instruments played in the Celtic lands and subsequently in Celtic America include the bagpipes (including the softer sounding Irish uilleann pipes and the louder Scottish Great Highland Pipes), the fiddle, the flute, the tin whistle, the accordion, the concertina, the harp (called the clarsach in Scotland), and various stringed instruments. Unique to the Irish tradition is the bodhrán, a one-sided drum typically but not inclusively made of goatskin.

A major feature of Celtic music is the session, a loose collection of musicians who typically but not always meet in a pub to play music. The session is among the primary means of keeping the tradition alive as well as of passing on knowledge while attracting both new blood and seasoned veterans. At sessions the musicians express their technical skill, stamping each tune indelibly with their own personality. Essentially, the melody functions as a framework, a musical skeleton that the tune hangs on. For this reason, a tune is never played quite the same way twice; that is, the tune will be different each time it is played but still recognizable. A typical repertoire during a session consists mostly of dance tunes, but slow airs and the occasional song can also be heard. Ultimately the aim of a session is to get the maximum number of musicians playing together on the maximum number of tunes. Sessions are more than just musical events, though. They also serve as social gatherings and help to build community.

A pioneering figure in the history of Celtic music in America was Francis O'Neill. Born in County Cork in 1849, O'Neill immigrated to Chicago in 1873. Although he later became the city's police superintendent, he is best remembered as an indefatigable collector of Irish music. His works include *O'Neill's Music of Ireland* (1903), which contains 1,850 pieces of music and became known as "the Book" and even today is considered the Bible of Irish music; *The Dance Music of Ireland: 1001 Gems* (1907); *Irish Folk Music: A Fascinating Hobby* (1910); and *Irish Minstrels and Musicians* (1913).

The rise of the recording industry in the first few decades of the twentieth century changed the course of Celtic music. In particular, the recordings of two fiddle players from County Sligo, Michael Coleman and James Morrison, made a huge impact on Irish and Irish American musicians. Both immigrants to the United States, Coleman and Morrison played in a fluid, fast, and highly ornamented—and hence very popular—style. Their techniques were imitated to such an extent that their styles superseded virtually all other regional styles. Subsequent generations of musicians emulated their styles, which led to the standardization of Irish music on both sides of the Atlantic, as musicians began to learn tunes from recordings rather than from other players.

Hundreds of recordings of traditional musicians were released during the early decades of the twentieth century. Among the recording companies that specialized in Irish music were Emerald, M & C New Republic Record Company, Keltic Records, Copley Records, and the Gaelic Phonograph Record Company. As the market for Irish music grew, the big record companies, such as Columbia, Decca, and Victor, began recording Irish musicians. Today Shanachie, established in 1975, and Green Linnet, established the following year, are among the most prominent labels that continue to release the work of Irish and other Celtic musicians.

Until the advent of the recording industry, traditional music was an insular affair, performed mostly in private houses and at parties, weddings, and wakes, as well as in the dance halls that played such an important role, especially among Irish Americans. The dance hall was an important social institution. It was the place to make new friends, line up jobs, and court potential sweethearts.

While the popularity of traditional music was waning in the Old World, the late 1950s and early 1960s saw a revival of interest in America. In the early 1970s the primary market for Celtic music in the United States was mostly a college-educated, middle-class audience, and though the repertoire may have been largely the same as in the homeland, the arrangements, attitude, and approach in the New World were different from the more conservative mindset of earlier generations of musicians. During the 1970s in particular, various traditional music societies and schools of music instruction were active. Increasingly, Celtic musicians began performing for predominantly non-Celtic audiences, at folk festivals, in coffeehouses, and on the college concert circuit across the country. What's more, economic distress during the 1980s in Ireland precipitated a new wave of young men and women, many of whom were musicians, immigrating to American shores. Their presence led to a further revitalization of the music.

Marching and pipe bands are also an important part of the Celtic music tradition in America. To this day,

The Columbus Shamrock Club Pipe and Drum Corps march in the annual Memorial Day parade in Worthington, Ohio, May 30, 2011. (Thomas Arbour/iStockphoto.com)

many major American cities have Irish and Scottish marching and pipe bands. In addition, various musician groups, clubs, music and dance competitions, and organizations as well as formal and informal céilís (also spelled ceilidhs) have played a major role in the revival of interest in the music and help to perpetuate the tradition. In addition, interaction with fellow musicians—both Celtic and non-Celtic—in America and in the Celtic lands themselves has led to a vigorous cross-fertilization of various styles.

Among the liveliest centers of Celtic music in America today are New York, Boston, Philadelphia, Chicago, and San Francisco. Several major institutions in the United States house significant collections of Celtic music, including the Irish Music Center of the John J. Burns Library at Boston College and the O'Neill Irish Music Collection, housed at the Hesburgh Library at the University of Notre Dame in Indiana.

Celtic music in America remains a living, vibrant part of the ongoing ethnic fabric, as the music passes from generation to generation and new songs and tunes enter the tradition. At this juncture, the music should continue to have a long and healthy future.

See also: Accordion; Immigrant Music; Tin Pan Alley

Further Reading

Carolan, Nicholas. 1997. *A Harvest Saved: Francis O'Neill and Irish Music in Chicago.* Cork, Ireland: Ossian Publications

Carson, Ciaran. 1986. *Irish Traditional Music.* Belfast: Appletree.

Gedutis, Susan. 2004. *See You at the Hall: Boston's Golden Era of Irish Music and Dance.* Boston: Northeastern University Press.

Moloney, Mick. 2002. *Far from the Shamrock Shore: The Story of Irish American Immigration Through Song.* New York: Crown.

O'Connor, Nuala. 1991. *Bringing It All Back Home: The Influence of Irish Music.* London: BBC Books.

Sawyers, June Skinner. 2001. *Celtic Music: A Complete Guide.* New York: Da Capo Press.

Skerrett, Ellen, and Mary Lesch, eds. 2008. *Francis O'Neill: Chief O'Neill's Sketchy Recollections of an Eventful Life in Chicago.* Evanston, IL: Northwestern University Press.

Wood, Nicola. 1991. *Scottish Traditional Music.* Edinburgh: Chambers.

June Sawyers

Ceremonial Music

Music plays an integral role in the ceremonies of American public life. Sociologist Emile Durkheim first identified the important role of secular rituals in reaffirming community ties, and scholars like Christopher Small have noted that music can serve a powerful ritual function. In some cases, music has come to define the ritual—like the playing of "Hail to the Chief" for the president. In others, it is the act of singing together that provides what Benedict Anderson has called *unisonance,* or the physical manifestation of a community. Over time the meaning of these songs becomes inextricably linked to the ceremonies in which they play a role, and these associations are strengthened with each repetition of the musical ritual.

Many subcultures coexist within American culture, and a thorough survey of all kinds of ceremonial music found in the United States would be impossible. Here we examine several aspects of secular ceremonial music in select areas of American culture: rites of passage, political and military functions, civic meetings, sports rituals, parades, and Native American powwows.

Weddings

The music used at weddings is often determined by the religious practices and cultural tastes of the individuals involved. However, two songs from the nineteenth-century European classical music tradition have become standard at many Christian weddings in the United States, reinforced by their appearance in films and on television. The processional is Richard Wagner's "Bridal Chorus" from the 1850 opera *Lohengrin* (often referred to as "Here Comes the Bride"), and the recessional is Felix Mendelssohn's "Wedding March," taken from incidental music that he wrote for *A Midsummer Night's Dream* in 1842.

Graduations

American universities have used Sir Edward Elgar's "Pomp and Circumstance" for graduations since the beginning of the twentieth century. Originally composed for the coronation of King Edward VII, it began its life as a graduation accompaniment in 1905 when it was played at the commencement ceremonies at Yale University at which Sir Elgar received an honorary degree.

Political Ceremonies

The song "Hail to the Chief" has been played to announce the arrival of the president of the United States at ceremonial events since the 1840s. The song is an adaptation of a traditional Scottish tune, which appeared in a nineteenth-century production of the musical play *The Lady of the Lake.* Its ceremonial use dates back to President Tyler, whose wife instructed the U.S. Marine Band to play the song at the president's official appearances. The Marine Band is called "The President's Own" for its exclusive role in providing ceremonial music for the president at inaugurations and other events.

The national anthem is also a fixture in public and political ceremonies. Famously penned by Francis Scott Key in 1814 and set to the drinking song "Anacreon of Heaven," "The Star-Spangled Banner" became the official U.S. national anthem by an act of Congress in 1931.

Military Ceremonies

Within each branch of the U.S. military, bands and other ensembles have their own protocol for ceremonial songs and bugle calls played for specific functions and specific dignitaries. One ceremonial song common across military branches is "Taps," a bugle call played at the end of each day and at military funerals. Bagpipes are also often present at military funerals, as well as those of fallen police officers or firefighters, often performing the hymn "Amazing Grace."

Civic Meetings

Many civic organizations use songs to demarcate the beginning and end of their meetings. These often include the national anthem and other patriotic songs, as well as songs specific to the organization's mission. For example, the song "Lift Ev'ry Voice and Sing," composed by brothers James Weldon Johnson and John Rosamond Johnson in 1900, was adopted as the "Negro national anthem" by the NAACP in 1920 and is now often sung at meetings of African American civic groups. "Solidarity Forever," a pro-union song composed by Ralph Chaplin in 1915, has become a common anthem at labor union meetings.

Sports Events

Sports events are often powerful sites for secular ceremonies, as sports arenas offer enormous spaces for public gatherings. All professional sports include a performance of the national anthem before the game, a ceremony that began just after the U.S. entry into World War II and has become a lasting part of the ceremony of sports. The anthem is often performed by a well-known or local performer, thus providing a means of connecting the game to either the local community or national popular culture. In baseball, singing "Take Me Out to the Ball Game" has become common during the seventh-inning stretch. The song is a Tin Pan Alley hit from 1908, but singing it didn't become a ritualized part of professional baseball until the early 1980s, when Harry Caray's famous performances with the Chicago Cubs were televised nationally.

Parades

The ceremonies of parades command the power of public space. Parades on national holidays often feature patriotic songs performed by marching bands. Ethnic parades serve as a platform for traditionally marginalized groups to be heard and seen in public spaces. Commemorating holidays such as St. Patrick's Day or Columbus Day, Mardi Gras/Carnival, or independence day celebrations for immigrant communities, such parades often feature traditional music and dance alongside American patriotic songs that affirm a sense of belonging to American culture as well.

Native American Powwows

Music plays an integral role in the ceremonies of the pan-tribal Native American powwows. These events, which feature singing and drumming as accompaniment to a diverse array of competitive dances, have become somewhat standardized across the country, though regional differences exist between the North and South. Music at Native American powwows features a large horizontal "host drum," played by a group of drummers who also sing in a call and response pattern. Lyrics often rely heavily on vocables so that songs can be shared across tribal groups and languages.

See also: Musical Preferences, Cultural Identities, and Demographics; Native American Music; Powwow Music and Dance; Sports and Music; Tin Pan Alley

Further Reading

Anderson, Benedict. 1991. *Imagined Communities: Reflections on the Origins and Spread of Nationalism.* New York: Verso.

Bohlman, Philip V. 1998. "Immigrant, Folk, and Regional Musics in the Twentieth Century." In *The Cambridge History of American Music,* edited by David Nicholls, 276–308. Cambridge, UK: Cambridge University Press.

Browner, Tara. 2004. *The Heartbeat of the People: Music and Dance of the Northern Pow-wow.* Urbana: University of Illinois Press.

Crepeau, Richard. 2002. "Sport and the National Anthem (March 21, 1996)." *Aethlon: The Journal of Sports Literature* 20, no. 1: 69–71.

Diamond, Beverley. 2008. *Native American Music in Eastern North America.* New York: Oxford University Press.

Durkheim, Emile. 1995. *The Elementary Forms of Religious Life.* Translated by Karen E. Fields. New York: The Free Press.

Kirk, Elise K. 1997. "'Hail to the Chief': The Origins and Legacies of an American Ceremonial Tune." *American Music* 15, no. 2: 123–136.

Slobin, Mark. 1993. *Subcultural Sounds: Micromusics of the West.* Middletown, CT: Wesleyan University Press.

Small, Christopher. 1998. *Musicking: The Meanings of Performing and Listening.* Middletown, CT: Wesleyan University Press.

Turino, Thomas. 2008. *Music as Social Life: The Politics of Participation.* Chicago: University of Chicago Press.

Sheryl Kaskowitz

Chamber Music

Chamber music is a vital part of American music and culture. Musicians continue to play it in their homes for pleasure, and audiences continue to go to concert and recital halls to hear amateur and professional chamber groups perform. Ensemble musicians develop close relationships as they share these musical experiences; the philosopher Johann Goethe described it as four rational people conversing. Numerous societies exist to promote chamber music in the United States, and the number of chamber music concerts increased at the end of the twentieth century, in part because popular chamber groups engage in crossover styles that combine classical music with jazz and other genres.

At the beginning of the twentieth century, the chamber music genre had changed little since the nineteenth century and generally constituted works that were meant to be performed in a small, intimate space or room by two to ten performers with one person on a part, without the need for a conductor. Public concerts, concert halls, and opera in American culture were still relatively young, and European music was still the model. Music making in the American home remained a popular pastime, as recreational music making had been for many generations. Most middle- and upper-class families owned some version of a keyboard instrument, whether it was a piano, spinet, harmonium, or concertina. Chamber music in the home often included piano sonatas by Haydn, Mozart, and Beethoven as well as keyboard arrangements of symphonies, operas, and opera arias for piano or piano duos (piano four hands).

At the turn of the century the string quartet genre remained authentic to its eighteenth-century beginnings, but a noticeable change emerged as the century progressed: the technical expectations of the string quartet began to move beyond the musical capabilities of most amateurs, and thus a distinctive difference emerged between amateur and professional musicians. Nevertheless, amateur musicians demanded music for occasions that fit their everyday American lives, including functional music for religion, instruction, recreation, and entertainment (Crawford 2001, 495). Most recreational singing in the middle-class home included the parlor song, and the most fashionable parlor songs featured texts of courtship, loyalty to country, or even social issues and evoked nostalgia and familiarity with a catchy and memorable tune accompanied by piano. Parlor songs were easily accessible to the public and were published in mass quantities as a result of the burgeoning music publishing business in America.

Most American composers working in the first half of the twentieth century were trained by European immigrants or by Americans who were educated in Europe (mainly Austria and Germany). Music reflected the European classical structures, genres, and styles that dominated throughout the nineteenth century, and the string quartet remained one of the most popular chamber music genres. As experimentation fostered many composers' need to expand beyond the language of the nineteenth century, composers varied the instrumentation of chamber music to include nontraditional combinations of instruments, including percussion and voice. This was no doubt influenced by the European models of nontraditional chamber music in the early twentieth century, which included Igor Stravinsky's *L'histoire du soldat* (*The Soldier's Tale*), Claude Debussy's *Sonata for Flute, Viola, and Harp,* and Arnold Schoenberg's *Pierrot Lunaire.*

Most of the influential composers at the turn of that century were associated with New England universities from Boston to New York, and they are often categorized as the Second New England School (the First New England School being the Yankee tunesmiths who wrote sacred hymns and psalters in the New England colonies) (Hitchcock 1999, 150). The so-called leader of the Second New England School of composers was John Knowles Paine (1839–1906); his followers included George Chadwick (1854–1931), Horatio Parker (1863–1919), Edward MacDowell (1860–1908), and Amy Cheney Beach (1867–1944).

Although the American composers of the New England School who followed Paine were mostly trained by non-Americans, the next generation was more interested in incorporating an American sound in their music, although just what constituted that sound would become a topic of great debate.

When Antonín Dvořák (1841–1904) traveled to America between 1892 and 1895 he ignited a debate among American composers when he suggested they use the melodies and rhythms of African songs and the indigenous Indian peoples as a basis of a national musical style. The irony of a foreigner asking American composers to develop an American sound was not lost on those American composers. Edward MacDowell (1860–1908) was the most popular and visible American composer when Dvořák visited America. Although one of MacDowell's most famous works was his program symphony *Indian Suite* (1896), in which he based each movement on a Native melody, he believed quoting or paraphrasing Negro and Native American melodies and rhythms as a basis for art to be shallow. MacDowell was not opposed to writing music that characterized an American landscape or a historical past, which is revealed in his piano chamber music *Woodland Sketches* (1896). Inspired by the New England countryside and reflective of his own aesthetic experiences, each movement of *Woodland Sketches* has a descriptive title; the most famous movements are "To a Wild Rose" and "To a Water Lily." Two other similar collections of piano cycles followed, including *Sea Pieces* (1886–1888) and *New England Idylls* (1901–1903). In addition to these character pieces for piano, MacDowell also wrote forty-two songs in the Germanic lieder tradition, in which the piano serves as a part of the poetic and musical character.

Like MacDowell, Amy Cheney Beach (1867–1944) disagreed with Dvořák's infamous prescription for American music. Although she agreed that American composers should adopt a sense of nationalism in their music, she noted that as a Caucasian Irish American from New England, she knew little of the Negro culture, songs, or music. Her roots lay in the tradition of Irish and Gaelic melodies, which became her musical representation of nationalism by reflecting the plight of the Irish people in America. Beach's chamber music includes her short character pieces for piano, 120 songs, a sonata for violin and piano, and a set of variations for flute and strings, which was commissioned for the San Francisco Chamber Music Society.

Charles Ives (1874–1954) was the last of the Second New England School composers, and his music straddles the European tradition and the new modernism at the beginning of the twentieth century. Ives was educated at Yale and studied with Horatio Parker. His style is known for his use of American folk and familiar tunes, but not because he aspired to be a part of the American composers' dialogue on what made music American. Ives used familiar tunes as inspiration and to create a musical image of an experience for the audience—he created a personal style, rather than subscribing to one particular idiom (Tawa, Block, and Burkholder 1996, 55). As a musical transcendentalist, Ives subscribed to the philosophical doctrines of Ralph Waldo Emerson and Henry David Thoreau and the spirituality of nature. His second Piano Sonata, the "Concord Sonata" (1909–1915), has four movements, and each is given a title of a transcendentalist author. Ives's connection to tradition is evident as an extension of Parker, Chadwick, and Paine, especially with his penchant for portraying New England sites and principles in his music; however, he remained receptive to new sounds and possibilities (Tawa, Block, and Burkholder 1996, 52). Ives used his traditional knowledge of harmony and counterpoint to combine layers of sound and dissonant tone clusters (learned from his own father, who was a bandmaster) and familiar tunes to create a sound all his own, independent from his peers at the time.

Ives interrupts the historical timeline of twentieth-century composers. Chronologically he was an extension of the New England composers at the end of the nineteenth century, but musically he employed a myriad of compositional styles, including tonality, atonality, tone clusters, polytonality, and traditional techniques mixed with experimentation. Furthermore, it is remarkable that most of Ives's music was composed outside of the contemporary music scene in the first half of the twentieth century. Since he was primarily a composer in his free time, as he was employed as an insurance salesman, he was isolated in Connecticut (even though he worked in New York) and was not regularly influenced by the significant composers of the time. After his retirement from the insurance business, Ives sought to publish more of his music, and the first real public interest in his music began at that time. Ives's chamber works include 114 songs, piano sonatas, violin sonatas, and string quartets. He also wrote programmatic chamber music and works that include nontraditional instrumentation, such as *All the Way Around and Back* for piano, violin, flute, bugle, and bells.

Between 1920 and 1945 a true reaction against the classical/romantic tradition began as many composers strove to achieve an antiromantic and unsentimental style by using compositional techniques like extreme chromaticism, polytonality, whole tone scales, and serialism, which deliberately displaced the expectation of a tonal center. During these years composers and critics begin to discuss music within these boundaries as modern (Hitchcock 1999, 202). Chamber music remained a significant genre for modern composers in the years before 1945, and by this time professional musicians, who combined technical excellence with a penchant for modernism and experimentation, predominantly performed the genre. Reaction against the grandiose music of the nineteenth century inspired composers to write in smaller chamber styles, and a variety of instrumental and vocal combinations emerged that reflected the diverse possibilities of modern music. By the end of the twentieth century numerous professional chamber ensembles had been established, some focused solely on modern music and others encompassing a variety of traditional and modern music in their repertory. Although the string quartet continued to be an important ensemble for twentieth-century composers, a variety of other instrumental and vocal combinations were recognized in chamber music, including percussion and music with tape. In addition, an interest in writing for homogeneous instruments in chamber music emerged, including the brass quintet; woodwind quintet; saxophone quartet; flute quartet/quintet; and various combinations of mallet, auxiliary, and battery percussion.

During the years following the First World War a quest began to compose, perform, and market modern music. Music in American concert halls consisted of the classical/romantic repertory of those American composers (discussed previously) who were rooted in tradition while experimenting with adapting folk and popular tunes to characterize an American style. In the 1920s and 1930s a new generation of American composers emerged who view the European tradition as one to revere for inspiration, but not as a paradigm to follow strictly. This group, which included Aaron Copland (1900–1990), Walter Piston (1894–1976), Roy Harris (1898–1979), and Virgil Thomson (1896–1989), traveled to France to study with the composer-teacher, Nadia Boulanger (1887–1979), who encouraged her American students to be innovative and to cultivate their American distinctiveness by not subscribing to just one compositional style (Hitchcock 1999, 203). In 1954 Copland wrote in *Music and Imagination* about this promising group of American students who studied with Boulanger: their quest was to be universal within their American style, far away from a popular idiom (Morgan 1991, 285).

In 1921 the first of many musical associations devoted to promoting new music was organized. Edgard Varèse (1883–1965), a French composer who immigrated to America, established the International Composers' Guild (ICG) in New York, which presented works by modern composers who represented a definite spirit of the current time (Lott 1983, 268). Approximately two-thirds of the works presented in these concerts from 1921 to 1927 were by European composers (Schoenberg's *Pierrot Lunaire* received its American premiere by the ICG in 1923), but many were by modern and experimental American composers like Carl Ruggles, Henry Cowell, Leo Ornstein, and William Grant Still. Varèse and the ICG board employed professional instrumentalists, vocalists, and composers for these concerts; thus the series was known for the high quality of musicianship and respectable performances (Lott 1983, 270). The ICG became an important part of the New York music scene and an important thread for new music in America. Significant chamber works performed at the ICG concerts included *Of Men and Mountains* and *Angles* for six trumpets by Carl Ruggles and *Ensemble* by Henry Cowell. Varèse also premiered many of his first works for winds (including *Density 21.5* for solo flute) and percussion ensemble in the ICG programs,

Edgard Varèse reorganized music's structural components to emphasize masses of sound rather than linear elements. His influential experiments of the 1920s broke with traditional concepts and forms. He later manipulated technological advances in post–World War II electronics to construct major works from sounds on tape. (Library of Congress)

which would greatly influence the variety of chamber ensemble writing in the later twentieth century. Although the ICG was discontinued in 1927, the series began a trend of showcasing modern music in America and helped gain critical and audience respect for the contemporary composer. Its sister organization in California was the New Music Society, founded in 1925 by Henry Cowell, and many of works premiered in New York with the ICG received their second performance in California.

Former members of the ICG who were disenchanted with Varèse's strict rule, which only allowed first performances of a new work, founded the League of Composers (LOC) in 1923, a quasi-rival to the ICG. The LOC was pivotal in jump-starting the careers of American composers like Aaron Copland, Roger Sessions, Marc Blitzstein, and Ruth Crawford, who performed many of their chamber works at these concerts. Although Copland's music was performed regularly by the LOC, he envisioned an organization whose efforts focused solely on American music, specifically promising young Americans. In 1928 Copland paired with Roger Sessions (1896–1985) to form the Copland-Sessions Concert Series. Both Copland and Sessions were young, up-and-coming composers who emerged on the scene from very different educational backgrounds. Copland was a student of Nadia Boulanger (1887–1979) in France; Sessions studied with Horatio Parker at Yale and then privately with Ernest Bloch. Most of the music in the Copland-Sessions Concert Series was instrumental and vocal chamber music, although some programs included music from the stage or theater. Two facets of an obvious thread in American compositional style were revealed in these concerts: those composers who were French influenced (mainly former students of Nadia Boulanger) and those who were relatively self-taught, like Henry Cowell, Ruth Crawford, Adolff Weiss, and Dane Rudhyar (Oja 1979, 216). Copland was dedicated to showcasing young American composers, regardless of their education or training.

In 1928 Varèse organized the Pan-American Association of Composers (PAAC), dedicated to composers from both North and South America. Chamber music continued to be important at PAAC concerts, including Copland's *As It Fell upon a Day* for soprano, flute, and clarinet and string quartets by both Ruth Crawford and Walter Piston. On the West Coast, Henry Cowell's New Music Society also performed works by up-and-coming American composers, although he remained closely connected to the New York scene, as many of his own works were performed by the ICG and the PAAC. Cowell published many of the works from these concert organizations in the *New Music Quarterly,* which was dedicated to publishing works for the modern composer until 1958. Cowell's music was associated with a group of composers known as "ultramodern" and included the innovative use of tone clusters, nontraditional use of timbre, banging on the keys of the piano, and strumming the strings on the inside of the piano—the primary technique used in his solo piano piece *The Banshee.* Cowell's most interesting experimentations were with rhythm, which he stated was connected intervallicly to harmony. He even devised a new rhythmic notational system to explain his discovery. After explaining this theory in his treatise *New Musical Resources* (published in 1930), he wrote two chamber compositions that reflect his compositional process: the *Quartet Romantic* (1917) for two flutes, violin, and viola, and the *Quartet Euphometric* (1919). Much of Cowell's later chamber music incorporated his interest in non-Western music, especially Irish or Asian folk material. In 1940 he composed *The Universal Flute* for shakuhachi, inspired by a Japanese shakuhachi player Cowell knew in California.

A significant era of American chamber music in the twentieth century was piloted at the Library of Congress through the patroness Elizabeth Sprague Coolidge

(1864–1953). Mrs. Coolidge established a foundation for the support of chamber music in 1925, "to make possible, through the Library of Congress, the composition and performance of music in ways which might otherwise be considered too unique or too expensive to be ordinarily undertaken. Not this alone, of course, nor with a view to extravagance for its own sake; but as an occasional possibility of giving precedence to considerations of quality over those of quantity; to artistic rather than to economic values; and to opportunity rather than to expediency" ("Elizabeth Sprague Coolidge Foundation Collection" 2011). Chamber concerts were organized and American composers were commissioned to write works that would be performed in the series and archived in the Library of Congress holdings.

After World War II composers were inspired to initiate a musical revolution—new sounds with a new medium that equaled a new kind of music. Some composers would find that newness in modern formulas like tonality, atonality, and neoclassicalism, but others would find originality in electronic music, minimalism, and other techniques that do not fit within a classified genre. Elliot Carter (1908–) was a student of Nadia Boulanger whose early compositions were in the neoclassical style, comparable to his peers Copland, Piston, and Thomson. His String Quartet no. 1 reveals a new approach, in which each instrument acts as a character (also typical in his other string quartets), which is fitting since it was influenced by Jean Cocteau's dreamlike film *Le sang d'un poète* (Gann 1997, 701).

Much of America's musical innovation after 1945 occurred in New York and its surrounding areas, and much of the experimentation in sound took place in chamber music, as it remained a medium for an intimate conversation of ideas from the composer among the performers. Two monumental events changed the course of modern music after 1950: the development of electronic music with the possibilities of recorded sound and John Cage.

Varèse explored unusual combinations of instruments and sonorities, and he avoided strings in his works because they were too closely associated with the tradition of the nineteenth century. The first composer to write for percussion ensemble (*Ionisation* in 1929–1931), his writing foreshadowed the possibilities of unusual sounds he would later find in electronic music. Sound influenced all of Varèse's music, and he formally stated that he refused to use sounds that already existed; furthermore, he was uniquely inspired by music and sound that replicated urban sounds, landscapes, and industrial technology (Morgan 1991, 307–308). His dream was realized when he used a combination of winds, percussion, and two-track tapes in *Déserts* (1954) and recorded sounds in *Poèm électronique* (1957–1958).

Milton Babbitt (1916–) was greatly influenced by Arnold Schoenberg, and as a result he conceived serial composition as a direct extension of the principles of "classical" twelve-tone music. His chamber work *Three Compositions for Piano* (1947) was one of his first works to serialize both pitch and nonpitch elements. Babbitt wrote five string quartets and a variety of other chamber works using serial counterpoint. When the electronic synthesizer was invented in the late 1950s, sound was easier to record, contrary to using two-track tapes, which required manually splicing sections of the tape together to create the final product. To Babbitt, the synthesizer realized the possibility of totally organized music with regard to pitch, rhythm, dynamics, and timbre. Babbitt was director at the Columbia-Princeton Electronic Music Center, where the Mark II electronic sound synthesizer was used. He wrote two pieces for the Mark II, but also used it combined with live instruments, in *Vision and Prayer* (1961) and *Philomel* (1964). Electronic sound would further influence almost every composer throughout the twentieth century up to the modern day, as recording, composition, and performance are greatly affected by the innovations of electronic media.

John Cage (1912–1992) was the first American to compose a piece for tape, *Imaginary Landscape No. 5,* in 1952 (Crawford 2001, 706). Cage's career, however, was defined by his philosophy on sound, noise, and the elements of music. In 1953 he composed *4′33″,* which quickly became the piece that defined Cage and his music. *4′33″* is technically a chamber work for solo piano, but the performer is instructed by the composer to sit at the piano for four minutes and thirty-three seconds without playing a note. The performer is also instructed to open and close the piano lid three times to denote the three separate movements. Although the immediate impression was a work of silence, Cage envisioned anything but silence; *4′33″* is a composition of sound with unintentional and ambient sounds from the audience and the surrounding performance area.

Percussive sounds fascinated Cage, and he experimented with placing bolts, screws, nails, rubber bands, and other objects between the strings of the piano to create nontraditional sounds in the "prepared piano." This is represented in *Sonatas and Interludes,* which was also heavily influenced by Cage's philosophical interest in ancient religions. Each movement, in binary form, expresses the nine emotions acknowledged by Indian aesthetics: the heroic, the erotic, the mirthful, the wondrous, fear, anger, sorrow, disgust, and tranquility (Gann 1997, 131). Cage's later works employed the composition of chance operations. For Cage, anything could determine the chance procedure of the composition: dice, coins, or the numbers of the I Ching made the decisions of pitches, duration, and dynamics by chance.

When Cage experimented with indeterminacy, even his strongest supporters were outraged, because the notation itself is ambiguous; therefore, the performance can evolve to many different outcomes.

Cage was one of the most important American composers of the second half of the twentieth century. He proved that silence was just as important as sound. He influenced the next generation of American composers with the concept that individualism is as important as is the freedom of expression. Unfortunately for audiences, however, he contributed to the gap between composers and audiences. Cage was ridiculed and critics were fascinated, not by his music, but by the spectacle that was involved in performing his music—so anti-European and antitraditional.

In minimalism, the gap was lessened, as audiences were drawn to music with minimal properties. The four most significant minimalists who emerged in the 1960s were Terry Riley (1935–), Steve Reich (1936–), John Adams (1947–), and Philip Glass (1937–). Their music used traditional instruments combined with synthesizers and amplified sound with the repetition loops as in electronic music. In a sense, minimalism became the new generation of chamber music, using a small number of performers with a simple repetition of melody, harmony, and rhythm (Gann 1997, 199).

Since the 1960s chamber music in America has encompassed a wide range of compositional styles, including jazz, non-Western elements, and even spiritual overtures. In addition, twentieth-century composers embraced traditional and electronic instrumentation in their chamber works. There are many opportunities for chamber music, including organizations whose mission is to promote the variety of repertoire in this genre, such as Chamber Music America, the Associated Chamber Music Players, the Chamber Music Society of Lincoln Center, and the Fischoff National Chamber Music Association.

See also: Adams, John C.; Cage, John; Classical Music in America; Copland, Aaron; Electronic and Computer Music; Glass, Philip; Ives, Charles; Minimalism; Music Patrons and Supporters; Opera in America; Reich, Steve; Seeger Family; Silence in Music

Further Reading

Chamber Music America. n.d. http://www.chambermusic.org/.

Crawford, Richard. 2001. *America's Musical Life: A History.* New York: W.W. Norton & Co.

"Elizabeth Sprague Coolidge Foundation Collection." 2011. *Performing Arts Encyclopedia.* Library of Congress. http://memory.loc.gov/diglib/ihas/loc.natlib.scdb.200033839/default.html.

Gann, Kyle. 1997. *American Music in the Twentieth Century.* Belmont, CA: Wadsworth/Thomson.

Hitchcock, H. Wiley, ed. 1999. *Music in the United States: A Historical Introduction.* Upper Saddle River, NJ: Prentice Hall.

Lott, R. Allen. 1983. "'New Music for New Ears': The International Composers' Guild." *Journal of the American Musicological Society* 36, no. 2 (Summer): 266–286.

McCalla, James. 2003. *Twentieth-Century Chamber Music.* New York: Schirmer.

Morgan, Robert P. 1991. *Twentieth Century Music.* New York: W.W. Norton & Co.

Oja, Carol J. 1979. "The Copland-Sessions Concerts and Their Reception in the Contemporary Press." *The Musical Quarterly* 65, no. 2 (April): 212–229.

Root, Deane L. 1972. "The Pan American Association of Composers (1928–1934)." *Anuario Interamericano de Investigacion Musical* 8: 49–72.

Tawa, Nicholas E., Geoffrey Block, and J. Peter Burkholder, eds.1996. *Charles Ives and the Classical Tradition.* New Haven, CT: Yale University Press.

Amy Tully

Chapin, Harry (1942–1981)

Harry Chapin was one of America's most authentic, creative, and intellectual songwriters in the 1970s. Attuned to Americans' frustrations, estrangement, and loneliness, Chapin's lyrics explore the decade via grotesque individuals seeking a personal, societal, or national anchor to believe in.

Chapin was born in 1942 in New York City. His family environment encouraged him to explore music as an escape from boredom and as a means of intellectual communication, with the guitar as his primary musical instrument. Like many of his later lyrical creations, Chapin was disillusioned and searching for direction. He attended the Air Force Academy for three months, dropped out of Cornell University twice, and was nominated for an Academy Award in 1969 for *Legendary Champions,* a boxing feature documentary. His cinematic success did not quench his desire to explore and compose and later record, his "Story Songs," which were often five to ten minutes long. Inspired by a musical tradition established by Woody Guthrie, Pete Seeger, and Bob Dylan, Chapin's folk rock and folk music addressed love, sex, violence, and loss.

Driven by the song "Taxi," which rose to number twenty-four on *Billboard,* Chapin's debut album *Heads & Tales* (1972) climbed to number sixty. Electra Records,

Singer-songwriter Harry Chapin performs at Avery Fischer Hall in New York City, 1976. (AP Photo)

a small record company, signed Chapin to a nine-album contract that included free studio time, which was unprecedented at the time. *Sniper and Other Love Songs* (1972) followed, containing such notable songs as "Better Place to Be," which Chapin described as his most romantic song; "Sniper"; and "Circle," which was a hit in Europe for The Seekers. Whereas *Short Stories* (1973), which included "W*O*L*D" and the haunting "Mr. Tanner," had only average album sales, *Verities & Balderdash* (1974) became his first gold album; it included "Cat's in the Cradle," which was a poem written by Sandy Chapin, his wife. "Cat's in the Cradle" went gold, stayed number one for two weeks, and remained on *Billboard*'s top 40 for nineteen consecutive weeks. Ironically, Chapin's band did not record with him on that album. His other Electra Record albums included *Portrait Gallery* (1975), *Greatest Stories Live* (1976), *On the Road to Kingdom Come* (1976), *Dance Band on the* Titanic (1977), *Living Room Suite* (1978), and *Legends of Lost and Found* (1979). Boardwalk Records released *Sequel* in 1982, and *The Last Protest Singer* (1988), his twelfth and last album, was released after his death.

Being cognizant of social causes spurred Chapin to try to help others. Believing that cynicism was the biggest bore, Chapin and Father Bill Ayers founded World Hunger Year (WHY) in 1973. Both men wanted to eliminate world hunger; Chapin, who raised over $5 million, lobbied Congress, donated sales of merchandise at concerts, and waived his performance fee at benefit events. Posthumously he was awarded the Congressional Gold Medal (1987) for his leadership to eliminate world hunger; he also served on President Jimmy Carter's Presidential Commission on World Hunger.

Chapin died in a car accident in 1981. Nine senators and thirty congressmen eulogized him for his humanitarian efforts. Chapin's music and activism revealed the best of America.

See also: Dylan, Bob; Guthrie, Woody; Seeger, Pete; Singer-songwriters; Social Causes of Musicians

Michael K. Schoenecke

Charles, Ray (1930–2004)

Of all the African American musicians crucial to the origination of soul music, Ray Charles may have been the most important. By combining blues, gospel, and jazz with his searing vocals, he helped invent a new form of musical expression. Peaking in popularity in the first half of the 1960s, he also ventured into country and western sounds, helping to pave the way for greater crossover acceptance of African American entertainers as a whole.

Born in Albany, Georgia, on September 23, 1930, Ray Charles Robinson lost his sight to glaucoma as a young boy and was sent to the Florida School for the Deaf and Blind for his education. In his teens he worked in Florida as a professional pianist, singer, and arranger. Eager to expand his professional and personal horizons by moving as far away as possible, he relocated to Seattle in 1948. There he quickly established himself in the city's jazz community, making his first recordings for the Downbeat and Swingtime labels in the late 1940s and early 1950s.

Charles had some success in the R&B market with his early singles, combining jazz, pop, and blues in a smooth manner reminiscent of Nat King Cole and Charles Brown. It wasn't until he moved to Atlantic Records in 1952, however, that he truly found his artistic voice. With earthier vocals, superior material (often penned by Charles himself), and tighter arrangements, his sound toughened considerably. The 1954 R&B chart-topper "I Got a Woman" was a landmark recording in both his career and African American popular music, marrying gospel and R&B with unprecedented fire. Throughout the rest of the 1950s he issued numerous classic singles, throwing in some early rock 'n' roll and, on his albums and at live concerts, sophisticated jazz.

It wasn't until 1959's top 10 hit "What'd I Say," however, that Charles made a big dent in the pop market. Already a huge star to African American audiences, he

Ray Charles

Artists Who Influenced Ray Charles	**Artists Whom Ray Charles Influenced**
Charles Brown	Aretha Franklin
Lowell Fulson	The Beatles
Nat King Cole	Joe Cocker
Percy Mayfield	Steve Winwood
Quincy Jones	Wilson Pickett

became one of the world's most popular entertainers when he moved to ABC-Paramount Records at the end of the decade. Leavening his R&B with some pop-jazz, he topped the pop charts in the early 1960s with "Hit the Road Jack" and "Georgia on My Mind." Though radical, his turn toward country and western paid big artistic and commercial dividends when both "I Can't Stop Loving You" and the *Modern Sounds in Country and Western* album went to number one in 1962.

An arrest for heroin possession in 1965 threatened to derail his career, and though he kicked his addiction, he passed both his artistic and commercial peaks after the mid-1960s. He continued to be an extremely popular and beloved performer and concert attraction, however, singing at the presidential inaugurations of both Ronald Reagan and Bill Clinton. He also gained enormous respect as a role model for both Americans with disabilities and creative artists of all kinds, as he retained an unusual degree of control over his recordings and other musical business interests. He died of liver cancer in Beverly Hills, California, on June 10, 2004, two months before the release of his final album, *Genius Loves Company,* which included songs recorded with Norah Jones, James Taylor, Elton John, Willie Nelson, Bonnie Raitt, Natalie Cole, Van Morrison, and others. A few months after his death the biographical movie *Ray,* directed by Taylor Hackford and starring Jamie Foxx (who won an Academy Award for Best Actor in the role), premiered; it was both a critical and a box office success.

See also: African American Gospel Music; African American Influences on American Music; Blues; Country Music; Disabilities and Music; Jazz; R&B

Further Reading

Charles, Ray, and David Ritz. 2004. *Brother Ray: Ray Charles' Own Story.* Cambridge, MA: Da Capo Press.

Lydon, Michael. 1998. *Ray Charles.* New York: Penguin.

Robinson, Ray Charles, Jr., and Mary Jane Ross. 2010. *You Don't Know Me: Reflections of My Father, Ray Charles.* New York: Crown.

Richie Unterberger

Blues singer Ray Charles performs at the 25th annual Easter Seal fundraiser in Pasadena, California, March 3, 1996. (AP Photo/John Hayes)

Checker, Chubby (1941–)

Singer Chubby Checker (born Ernest Evans) greatly influenced music and how people dance to it. He is best known for popularizing the dance move "the twist" with his hit song of the same name. The twist encouraged couples to dance separately from one another, something new at the time. Young people twisted their hips and swung their arms and legs as they enjoyed the upbeat songs that became popular in dance halls. Soon after "The Twist" was released in 1959, other artists incorporated the dance into song titles, including "Twist and Shout" (which was recorded by The Beatles) and "Twistin' the Night Away." The dance move also influenced several dance crazes that followed, including the pony, the fly, and the hucklebuck. "The Twist" was the only single to hit the *Billboard* Hot 100 two separate times, and it was named the biggest chart hit of all time by *Billboard Magazine* in 2008.

Ernest Evans was born in South Carolina and grew up in South Philadelphia, Pennsylvania. While he was in high school, the owner of a meat market where he worked arranged for him to have an audition with Dick Clark for the *American Bandstand* show, which was recorded in Philadelphia. After the audition Dick Clark's wife asked Evans his name. He told her that his friends called him Chubby, and she reportedly inquired "Like in Checker?" (a play off the fact that he did an imitation of Fats Domino during the audition). The name stuck.

Chubby Checker, America's King of the Twist, demonstrates how it's done during a visit to London, England, September 3, 1962. (AP Photo)

Checker went on to sign with Cameo-Parkway in 1959, where he recorded "The Twist," a song originally released by Hank Ballard (1927–2003). When Checker performed the song on *American Bandstand,* it soared to number one.

Checker went on to have a number of hit singles, although none was as popular as "The Twist." Young people flocked to dance halls, where Checker's songs were all the rage. His hits included "The Hucklebuck" (1960), "Pony Time" (1961), "Limbo Rock" (1962), and "Birdland" (1963). In 1961 Checker earned a Grammy for Best Rock Performance for his single "Let's Twist Again."

After 1965 Checker's popularity waned when the British invasion took hold in the United States. His influence on dance continued, however, and people on dance floors around the world can be found twisting.

In 2008 Checker had a number one single on the *Billboard* dance chart with his song "Knock Down the Walls." He continues to perform and has recorded a public service announcement for the Social Security Administration.

He has his own product line in the snack food industry, including chocolate bars, beef jerky, hot dogs, steaks, and popcorn. He also continues to tour and perform for audiences around the world.

See also: African American Influences on American Music; B-Side, The Rock 'n' Roll (Rock); Television Advertisements and Music

Official Web Site: http://chubbychecker.com/

Further Reading

Bronson, Fred. 2003. *The Billboard Book of Number One Hits.* New York: Billboard Books.

Jackson, John. 1997. *"American Bandstand": Dick Clark and the Making of a Rock 'n' Roll Empire.* New York: Oxford University Press.

Jacqueline Edmondson

Cheerleading Music

Competitive cheerleading, an offshoot of American traditional cheerleading, is an athletic activity that integrates music, dance, tumbling, and stunts. Whereas traditional cheerleading focuses on guiding crowd spirit at sports events, competitive cheerleading is a recent development whose primary focus is on competitive performance. Starting in the early 1980s, coaches and organizations such as the NCA (National Cheerleaders Association) and the UCA (United Cheerleaders Association) wanted to legitimize cheerleading; to that end, they began sponsoring competitions. Since then the growth and increasing complexity of the cheerleading industry have brought it to near-professional status. Rules and regulations with an emphasis on safety continue to develop under the guidance of regional and national cheerleading organizations.

Where does music fit in this overtly visual performance? As one cheerleading administrator says, "Cheerleading is a visual and aural sensation." Competitive cheerleading coaches agree that the music plays a much more significant role than in the past. More than ever, they believe that the music can make or break a routine, and this means that coaches must constantly rethink the relationship between music and cheerleading. As competition increases, coaches experiment with new ways of creating a catchy and effective music track. The music not only enhances the visual; it is the voice of the squad and its communicator, the element that transforms this genre from being just an athletic curiosity to a conveyer of complex cultural messages. Each sound track for a competitive cheerleading routine must show a squad's personality and individuality. It is not enough to use a song for the song's sake.

Traditional cheerleading consists of chants and rhymes. Taped, popular music was introduced to cheerleading in the mid-1970s, accompanying some very basic and rudimentary routines. As competitive cheerleading branched off and evolved, so did the music. Since 1995 the music in competitive cheerleading has settled into a "cut-and-paste" style, in which song clips, usually popular, are spliced together, changing rapidly from one to the next, punctuated with sound effects and blips of text. A song clip within the routine can vary in length from two to thirty seconds. Most are within a three- to ten-second duration.

There are numerous categories or divisions in competitive cheerleading. One category, All-Stars, pushes the boundaries more than the others, because an All-Star routine consists entirely of song clips, effects, and text. There is no break as in a "cheer" routine (the squad breaks momentarily to do a traditional cheer). An All-Star routine is the most distantly removed category from traditional cheerleading. Here, the sound track has no connection to cheerleading history whatsoever.

Two factors enabled music to blossom in competitive cheerleading. First, the major cheerleading organizations like the NCA and the UCA pay blanket licensing fees for the use of popular music clips. This blanket policy may be the key to understanding the creative freedom of the genre. It gives a squad carte blanche to select any song it wishes for its competitive routine. The second factor is technology. Editing a song into snippets or song clips facilitates creating in the cut-and-paste style. With the personal computer, coaches, DJs, and amateurs have been able to create their own individualistic sound tracks with relative ease. In addition, music technology can speed up or slow down songs to fit a general tempo or speed, allowing consistent tempi between songs (the average cheerleading music track is around 140 bpm). "Variety is what makes different teams and their routines special. Flexibility with music is a must," says one coach. This statement reflects the importance and influence of technology in realizing these goals and needs in competitive cheerleading. In addition to the song clips, a cheerleading routine is enhanced with the addition of blips of text, either from a song or something created specifically for the routine. Like sound effects, blips of text punctuate the action of a tumbling segment or a stunt, or add a message.

To the outside viewer, a cheerleading performance is a spectacle and sensory bombardment. However, in the cheerleading world it is a form of expression, demonstrating the tight relationship between music and choreography. In this sense competitive cheerleading is very insular, relying on more subtle messages relayed between squad and judges. This cheerleading language relies heavily on language that evolved as the genre did. How does a viewer decode all this? For example, a typical competitive cheerleading All-Star routine is a sequence of stunts, dance, tumbling, and transitions. Song clips can be categorized into two areas: "direct music association" and "indirect music association." Direct music association means that a music clip is self-referential, or that the song clip or words are used to draw attention directly to the cheerleaders. For example, Roy Orbison's "Pretty Woman," when used in a dance segment, signals to the audience that the cheerleaders are pretty women. With indirect music association, an Ozzy Osbourne guitar riff may suggest something in a tumbling section, but the message is not as clear, because it has no direct connection to the choreography. Sometimes in a routine, several things are occurring at the same time (e.g., a tumbling segment in the foreground, stunts in the background). The music will fit one of these, which requires the viewer to quickly analyze the reference. Because of the cut-and-paste style, these references are fleeting, and the overall effect is dizzying. But this is where the creativity lies. The rapid-fire editing, the barrage of references, the competitive aspect, and spectacular nature of the music and choreography make competitive cheerleading an exciting experience, particularly within the All-Star division.

Competitive cheerleading's function in American culture is ambiguous; it presents itself as a sport or athletic activity, but has developed into a genre intimately structured around music, sound, message, and movement. As the sport develops, the relationship and communication between audience and squad becomes more sophisticated, which has placed the genre in a league of its own. Oddly enough, competitive cheerleading may be a forerunner to the creation of a multimedia spectacle and language based purely on the appropriation of mainstream musical iconography. As profound as this concept is, it is too early to know how this will ultimately play out in competitive cheerleading.

See also: Dance Instruction and Music; Technology and Music

Further Reading

Hanson, Mary Ellen. 1995. *Go! Fight! Win!* Bowling Green, OH: Bowling Green State University Popular Press.

Kracauer, Siegfried. 1995. *The Mass Ornament.* Cambridge, MA: Harvard University Press.

Wright, Mary Catherine. 2002. "Fly Flip Music Clip: The Music of Competitive Cheerleading." PhD diss., Princeton University.

Mary C. Wright

Cher performs at the 2010 MTV Video Music Awards in Los Angeles, September 12, 2010. (Kevin Winter/Getty Images)

Cher (1946–)

Cher is an internationally recognized singer, performer, and actress whose career has spanned over fifty years. She became famous with her husband Sonny Bono (1935–1998) as a member of the pop duo Sonny & Cher (active 1964–1977), before going on to achieve successes as a solo artist and actress. Cher has sold more than one hundred million records worldwide and earned many awards and recognitions, including an Academy Award, a Grammy Award, an Emmy Award, three Golden Globes, and a Cannes Film Festival Award. She had at least one number one hit on the *Billboard* charts in each of six decades, an accomplishment no other artist can claim. Cher has consistently performed to sold-out audiences at Caesars Palace in Las Vegas and on her world tours.

Born Cherilyn Sarkisian in El Centro, California, to an Armenian American father and a mother who was part Cherokee, Cher left high school when she was sixteen years of age. She soon met Sonny Bono, who was eleven years her senior, and became a backup singer on several albums that producer Phil Spector (1939–) released. Sonny and Cher began to perform as a duo in 1964, and their first album as Sonny & Cher (1965) contained the single "I've Got You Babe," which catapulted the couple to fame. They continued to release music into the early 1970s, including the hit song "The Beat Goes On," accumulating eleven *Billboard* top 40 hits. The pair performed on numerous television shows, including the *Ed Sullivan Show* and *American Bandstand,* before launching their own television variety show, *The Sonny and Cher Comedy Hour* (1971). The show, which combined comedic segments and live music, garnered fifteen Emmy nominations and featured guests such as Tina Turner (1939–), Chuck Berry (1926–), the Jackson 5 (active 1964–1990), and other popular artists and actors. By the time the show was in its third season, Sonny and Cher's marriage ended in a very public and unpleasant divorce. Cher launched her own television show, *The Cher Show,* which broadcast from 1975 to 1976.

Cher launched her solo career with the album *All I Really Want to Do* (1965). She had a string of unsuccessful albums in the 1970s until she joined the disco craze and released *Take Me Home* in 1979. The album went gold and included the number one single "Take Me Home."

In the 1980s Cher became more involved with acting, both on Broadway, in *Come Back to the Five and Dime, Jimmy Dean, Jimmy Dean,* and in films like *Silkwood* (1983), *Mask* (1985), *Witches of Eastwick* (1987), *Suspect* (1987), and *Moonstruck* (1987), for which she won an Academy Award for Best Actress. She also returned to the recording studio in 1987 and released the hit album *Cher,* which was followed by the top-selling albums *Heart of Stone* (1989) and *Love Hurts* (1991). She toured internationally to promote the albums and appeared in several music videos, perhaps most famously in the video for "If I Could Turn Back Time," in which she wore a thong and see-through outfit as she performed on a U.S. Navy ship.

Cher's album *Believe* (1998) was considered the best album of the year, and the title track is perhaps her top hit of all time. She continued to perform tirelessly throughout the 2000s, including a 2003 "Farewell Tour," a three-year, two-hundred-show commitment at Caesars Palace in Las Vegas, and performances on television and film, including the 2010 movie *Burlesque.*

Even into her sixties, Cher was known as an exotic beauty who donned elaborate and sometimes daring costumes for her performances. She was also recognized for her perseverance and for overcoming difficulties in her personal life and career. She continues to enjoy a large and devoted international fan base, particularly among the gay community, and she has influenced many famous artists, including Lady Gaga (1986–), Britney

Spears (1981–), and Tracy Chapman (1964–). Cher has a star on the Hollywood Walk of Fame with her first husband, Sonny Bono.

See also: Awards and Prizes for Music; Berry, Chuck; Disco; Jackson Family; Music Television; Musicians as Actors; Television Variety Shows; Turner, Tina

Official Web Site: http://www.cher.com

Further Reading

Bego, Mark, and Mary Wilson. 2004. *Cher: If You Believe.* New York: Taylor Trade Publishing.

Cassata, Mary Ann. 2002. *The Cher Scrapbook.* New York: Citadel.

Coplon, Jeff, and Cher. 1999. *The First Time.* New York: Pocket Books.

Jacqueline Edmondson

Children's Film Music

Music is found in almost all children's films. What, however, is the function of this music? How does it achieve this? Do the ways in which music is used in children's films differ from those in which it is aimed at other age groups? This entry offers ways of understanding the effects of music in children's films, and it also questions the notion that the understanding of these gestures changes with respect to different age groups. Children's responses to music in film are marked by their own previous interactions with it. From these formative encounters emerge strongly conditioned responses to musical references in film. This is an important function of the musical underscore in cinema, because it enables or provides a context for children (or indeed, any spectator) to understand film scenes. Music might be used to instill concepts or to promote approaches to understanding moral situations in film, and children may navigate the emotional and moral aspects of a film scene or a character's identity through the music used.

There are questions about how musical spectatorship might feasibly be understood. The widespread use of music in children's films is evidence of its important function, but a problem emerges in defining exactly what a children's film is. This entry argues that the dominant ideological positions that the music helps to configure are those developed and inculcated within children and thus remain broadly similar into adulthood. In other words, the basic tenets of the sound track in mass-entertainment cinema apply from childhood into adulthood. Moreover, the nuanced and "undercover" means by which music works within the overall film narrative allow it to configure scenes without being overly intrusive and without requiring close attention to be paid to it. For children (and indeed, for adults), this does not really enhance understanding of a scene, since this would imply a predetermined and singular narrative, present in an imaginary existence before music's involvement; rather, it determines and constructs *how* a scene or a character should be understood. It can be argued, therefore, that for children the use of music in film, and repeated uses of similar musical gestures with certain character types or situations, might contribute to the nascent construction, consolidation, or entrenchment of ideological values, whereas in the case of adults, whose values are more established, the music feeds these attitudes and values and reinforces *pre*determined ideological positions.

Context and Question

Writing about music in children's films (or films for children) brings up several issues about the identity, not only of music in film generally, but more pertinently, about the extent to which it is possible to isolate differences between music that is "designed" for children (and even what this might suggest) and how this music is to be understood by adults. Does it follow, for example, that adults' reading of the music in a film scene aimed at children is different, deeper, or more nuanced? To suggest that it is presupposes that music in film offers specific details rather than a more generalized emotional or psychological (even moral) casting of a scene; that it locates specific details of the narrative or that it is able to "speak" in a singularly clear way. It also suggests that music is understood innately, providing a clear descriptive supplement to a scene or character. That such music cannot do this, however—that the way in which film music frames subjectivities is broad—suggests that it is understood variously and that these varieties and hermeneutic "levels" are as much to do with spectator-listeners' cultural awareness as they are to do with innate specific musical communication.

The paradox that emerges, therefore, goes something like this: if responses to film music are individual and differ depending on a spectator's association, familiarity with, or committedness to the music, then in what way does film music help to shape the viewing experience? A succinct answer to this "problem" might suggest that although there are varieties and levels of commitment to the ways in which the music could be read, there are also broader culturally bound associations that often-repeated musical gestures suggest—what are sometimes termed "referential clichés." These widely recognized musical tropes, though loose, also possess (through their prior association with certain identities or archetypes) the potential for strong ideological referencing.

In particular, the capacity of music in film to imply a further psychological substrate of a character's identity suggests this process is at least partly governed by dominant ideological positions. The film musicologist Anahid Kassabian (2001) has argued that understanding film music in these terms is crucial for a clearer sense of how and why its effect is so strong. She suggests that a central reason for the deployment of music in film is to forge (or not) an identification with the spectator-listener. The extent and quality of this identification depends, to a large degree, on the spectator's familiarity with the referential codes of the music. The result, for Kassabian, is the construction of two types of identity-relations—"affiliating" and "assimilating"—depending, importantly, on the type of music used. Broadly, these two types refer to the direction, scope, and function of the identification created:

> Composed scores, most often associated with classical Hollywood scoring traditions, condition what I call *assimilating identifications.* Such paths are structured to draw perceivers into socially and historically unfamiliar positions, as do larger scale processes of assimilation. . . . [C]ompiled scores [however] offer what I call *affiliating identifications,* and they operate quite differently from composed scores. These ties depend on histories forged outside the film scene, and they allow for a fair bit of mobility within it. If offers of assimilating identifications try to narrow the psychic field, then offers of affiliating identifications open it wide. This difference is, to my mind, at the heart of filmgoers' relationships to contemporary film music. (2001, 2–3)

Although Kassabian's theory has been widely critiqued, refined, and modified over the last ten years, her fundamental claim holds true and helps to offer a point from which one might conceptualize the function of music in children's films. Such positions of assimilation might include a distinction between good and evil or between fictional truth and, what the music suggests to an audience, a deceit covered up from other characters and otherwise unknowable without the "help" of the music. The wider and more distinct the binary, the clearer can be music's framing of it.

Mass-entertainment cinema has generally functioned in this way because it was seen to have to meet the needs of a broader audience, whose familiarity with the archetypes was more expected. It is partly for this reason that this approach to scoring films was previously criticized for its manipulative and coercive role. Such a position is not confined to music, however. Lawrence Kramer (1995) has written about the ideological force of the "logic of alterity," in which a powerful binary of self and other exists to provide some form of cultural and social hierarchy. In music, Kramer claimed, this binary lay in the ways in which its academic study differed from the sensuality and experience of listening to it. One might be tempted to extend these propositions and to state that the "use" of music in film, because it lacks descriptive focus and a specific referential ability, is to forge (or even to force) some kind of differentiated meaning, even some kind of supplemental meaning. It will always have this effect, but the differences rest in the degree and subtlety with which this is read into the scene by the spectator. Therefore, the clearer and more strongly associated the referential cliché suggested by the music is with an event or an idea, the more likely it is that it will be understood in a similar way.

Kathryn Kalinak (1992) has written of how music in film scenes of women sometimes attempted to frame their moral identity through the use of instrumentation, dissonance, or lack thereof into a binary she termed "fallen woman" and "virtuous wife." She argued that

> [v]isual displays of female sexuality were accompanied by a nucleus of musical practices which carried implications of indecency and promiscuity through their association with so-called decadent forms such as jazz, the blues, and ragtime. These included a predilection for woodwind and brass instrumentation, particularly saxophones and muted horns; a dependence upon unusual harmonies, including chromaticism and dissonance; the use of dotted rhythms and syncopation; and the incorporation of portamento . . . and blues notes. (120)

By contrast, the virtuous wife, in this case exemplified by the character of Mary McPhilip in the 1935 film *The Informer,*

> embodies none of these pejorative musical conventions. Played initially by violins, and in one memorable reiteration a harp, her leitmotif is accompanied by simple triadic harmonies. Various musical markings used in conjunction with her motif suggest its intent: "dolcissimo" (very sweetly); "poco appassionata" (a little impassioned); "legato" (smoothly); and "Heaven Music." Interestingly, this final marking appears in the music which accompanies Katie's confrontation with Mary. Despite the fact that Mary inadvertently prevents her brother's escape from the British death squad and seems to do little else in an emergency than wring her hands, she is ennobled by her leitmotif rather than censured by it. (122)

It is clear, therefore, that ideological framing is a key function of the musical sound track and although posited along gender lines by Kalinak, the same processes can be observed (heard) in films for children, where the very concept is established.

"Mickey Mousing"

An important approach in the process of how these musical associations in film are accrued by children at an early stage can be found in the ways that some early cartoons followed the physical action of a character with similar musical movements. This process—known as "Mickey Mousing"—enabled the music to be seen to "participate" in the action and for it to be quickly and formatively interpreted along lines that are readily accessible to a child and also intensify the experience of the scene for the spectator.

A familiar enough example of this occurs in the music by Scott Bradley for the MGM cartoon series *Tom and Jerry* (1940), in which a character is seen walking or, more usually, tip-toeing quietly up or down the stairs. Alongside his footsteps is a musical "equivalent" of this movement, either up or down the scale and usually in semitones. The effect is twofold: first it reinforces the importance of this particular on-screen action and suggests that it is crucial to that part of the narrative. (Maybe a character is attempting to escape or move away without being noticed.) Second, it identifies a moment of tension or increasing tension in the narrative at that point. This moment and action is both understood as important and also encourages a deeper connection with the ramifications of these actions. To deploy Kassabian's concept, Mickey Mousing is a more direct, but no less effective, form of assimilation: the child spectator is invited (even coerced), without much room for avoiding this, into reading the music of the scene as imbuing it with much greater narrative significance. The tension mounts (as it must), and the scene and its anticipated outcome are concatenated as a result, encouraging a displacing of the artifices of cinema and promoting the (learned) inevitability of the learned outcome. Spectators find themselves unable to escape this narrative outcome that the music has helped to set up, and its effect is remembered (bodily, as most musical memories are rooted this way) for the next time.

To be sure, at this stage Mickey Mousing depends on a musical *and* visual symbiosis to function successfully. The semitonal movement by Tom or Jerry only works if we see as well as hear its presentation. However, the music's reference is more removed from the specific action (climbing or descending the stairs) that we see, and this enables it both to amplify the action itself and to stress the importance of this action in terms of the narrative outcome.

Similarly, in the Warner Brothers' cartoon *Rhapsody Rabbit* (1946), in which Bugs Bunny performs Franz Liszt's Hungarian Rhapsody No. 2, the use of Mickey Mousing dovetails into and out of what we see on screen. The performance foregrounds the music, since we see the main character performing as a concert pianist. However, as well as performing the work as it is known, the cartoon plays with principles of Mickey Mousing to create a distinction between what we see as plausible and the comedic implausibility of other moments, in which Bugs simultaneously attempts to continue playing the piece as well as battling with the mouse (who is trying to thwart his efforts). The interplay of these two narratives (performance and battle) introduces an opportunity for the music to develop along the binary lines described and for children to become acculturated into the ways in which musical gestures circumscribe ideological positions. The frustrations of Bugs Bunny as the mouse sabotages strings and notes and cheekily intervenes in Bugs's performance are evident, and the music changes to mark these effects. It is also the case that the music begins, though only in a nascent form, to mark out the subject positions of characters, identifying the mouse's mischievousness over and above Bugs's attempts to capture and stop him. The audience therefore is gently, but firmly, aligned with the character of the mouse; through this kind of positioning, children learn to read film music along binary lines, in the first instance, but from then to interpret character and moral situations using the same approach. In short, they accept the persuasive "invitation" that much film music offers.

The comedic tone of this cartoon short is obvious, and its audience is made to understand this through the strongly foregrounded use of referential clichés in terms of both music and visuals. Just before Bugs starts to perform he is interrupted by an audience member coughing loudly; his demeanor clearly belies his feelings about the matter.

Such a clear way of exaggerating feelings and reactions is also evident in the ways in which music is to be understood here. There is, of course, the likelihood that prior familiarity with the musical gestures will allow for a more nuanced interpretation, but nonetheless, the widespread use of Mickey Mousing techniques, together with the foregrounding of music as a central component of the narrative of this short, helps to engage an audience of children more easily. From here, subsequent repetitions of this type of music engender clearer and faster reading of scenes. The specific deployment of classical music (something that Hollywood cinema more generally used during this period as a way of affording prestige to its mass-entertainment product), in this case by using Wagner as the curtains to Bugs Bunny's performance opens, sets up the idea of using music as a conveyance of the details of characters and actions, but also instills its cultural value as something of artistic importance. This is to a certain extent parodied by Bugs Bunny in this short. Nonetheless, it is only through the recognition of music and its cultural value that an undercutting of these values can be carried off to comic effect.

Ideological/Psychological Specificity

The idea that gender is strongly encoded from an early stage in musical terms in cinema supports the suggestion that a primary role of the orchestral underscore was to offer an ideological (for was gender not ever so?) sense of how the scene should be underscored—how the political, moral, or ideological undercurrent was to be interpreted. Such forms of sexualization or political positioning are less present in films aimed at children specifically, but the ideological binary offered by the music is very much in evidence. Its clear use from an early stage allows for gender subsequently to be understood along the very same binary and valorizing terms when it does emerge. To return to Kramer's idea of the logic of alterity that is a prominent aspect of music's role in film (and culture more widely), one finds that as previously identified, this most often takes the form of a presentation of right and wrong (the good and the evil) in films for children. How notions of right and wrong are framed is also important for how the types and musical gestures deployed are then understood thereafter. The process is both cyclical and cumulative. The requirement of familiarity with the musical gestures is central to the extent and ways in which music in children's films can operate and manipulate. With this in mind, it is worth noting how music in films whose audience may contain children, but whose ideological framework differs from that of mainstream Hollywood cinema, is liable to effect different responses, conditioned by music with which that audience is familiar. The now global renown of Japanese film director Hayao Miyazaki, however, is not matched by a musical style that is quickly interpreted. Children in particular, whose musical readings are prompted by prior association with musical gestures, may be apt to make an interpretation of the music in *Spirited Away* (2001) or *Princess Mononoke* (1997) in general, or even "othered" contexts, drawing on experiences of music's use in the Hollywood domain. Of course the same can be said of adult audiences, and it is this that complicates the problems of defining the differences between the reception of film music by children and adults. Adults' reception is based first on how they were "taught" or experienced music used as children. Although these modes of reception and stylistic nuance change, they rarely change much. It is for this reason that at the outset of this entry the idea of film music, its ideological values, and those of the society that produced it (and thus consume it) are seen as central in how children come to understand music in films. The differences between adults' and children's reading of music in American cinema are broadly similar. Indeed, this must be so, because the processes of ideological conveyance are the same, learned from childhood. The ways in which these musical "positions" are later interpreted offers a rich perspective on the values and attitudes of the society from which they emerged.

See also: Children's Musical Lives; Film Music

Further Reading

Adorno, Theodor W., and Hanns Eisler. 1994. *Composing for the Films.* London: Athlone.

Franklin, Peter. 2011. *Seeing Through Music: Gender and Modernism in Classic Hollywood Film Scores.* Oxford: Oxford University Press.

Gorbman, Claudia. 1987. *Unheard Melodies: Narrative Film Music.* Bloomington: BFI/University of Indiana Press.

Kalinak, Kathryn. 1992. *Settling the Score: Music and the Classical Hollywood Film.* Madison: University of Wisconsin Press.

Kassabian, Anahid. 2001. *Hearing Film: Tracking Identifications in Contemporary Hollywood Film Music.* London: Routledge.

Kramer, Lawrence. 1995. *Classical Music and Postmodern Knowledge.* Berkeley: University of California Press.

Koizumi, Kyoko. 2010. "An Animated Partnership: Joe Hisaishi's Musical Contributions to Hayao Miyazaki's Films." In *Drawn to Sound: Animation, Film Music and Sonicity,* edited by Rebecca Coyle, 60–74. London: Equinox Press.

Alexander Binns

Children's Musical Lives

Music dwells within children; it is something they all engage because they are driven instinctively to do so. It is intricately woven into the tapestry of childhood experience and identity development through a wide variety of encounters involving many different influences and settings. Musical engagement throughout a person's lifetime is a highly individual endeavor, much like the uniqueness of fingerprints. This entry discusses the musical lives of children in the settings of home, school, and play as a means to both explore and celebrate the many and varied ways in which children are musical, acknowledging that children's musical lives are complex and multifaceted.

Children's Musical Lives at Home

Naturally, children's musical lives begin in the home with parents and caregivers. Their primary interaction and socialization occur in the home, and music is most certainly a part of these processes. Many of us may fondly recall engaging with music in our homes, with our families. Perhaps we played "Patty-cake" handclapping games with our mothers, sang at the piano with our grandparents, or listened to rock 'n' roll in the car with dad. Perhaps we belted out favorite folk songs during long family car rides, sang a sweet lullaby to a baby cousin, or serenaded our loved ones with "Happy Birthday" each year. Regardless of the form or function, children have rich musical encounters in the home setting.

It may be surprising to learn that children's musical lives in the home actually begin before they are born. Unborn fetuses have a developed sense of hearing by twenty weeks of gestation. After that mark they can hear all the very same sounds as their mother, including the contours of the mother's voice and every musical sound that she herself takes in. Once born, infants have the important task of continuing to make sense out of the sounds they hear, a task they can accomplish with more sophistication than might be expected. Infants can demonstrate musical preferences and can remember bits of music for several days (Trehub 2006). Their musical worlds may involve lullabies, bouncing on a caregiver's knee, or perhaps most important, the undulating vocal patterns we use when communicating with babies.

With regard to children's music in the home, Ruth Crawford Seeger (1948), composer and preserver of children's folk music, remarked that "many of us open a savings account at the bank when a child is born, and add layer after layer of small deposits which he can later draw on for a college education. Perhaps a fund of songs might be begun as early, and added to layer after layer—an ever-growing wealth of materials which he can draw on at will" (21). As children grow from infants into toddlers and eventually to school age, their musical encounters in the home and with family may illustrate Seeger's layering of musical experiences and knowledge. The following are just a few practical examples of this layering occurring in the home.

When asked what he liked about music, seven-year-old Billy exclaimed; "I like it because it's on every single day and you don't have to worry about having no music at home" (Crafts, Cavicchi, and Keil 1993, 17), indicating his recognition of and desire to have music in this very intimate and important of spaces. Similarly, five-year-old Johnny declared his engagement with music in the home in the form of lullabies: "you have to have a lullaby before you sleep . . . that's what lullabies means" (Crafts, Cavicchi, and Keil 1993, 11). In her exploration of music in children's lives, Patricia Shehan Campbell (2010) observed the Anderson family and the many ways that music occurred in their home, everything from playful chants and singing along with the television to more formal facilitation and encouragement of private instrumental study. Watts (2009) discussed childhood musical engagement with individuals of varying ages and found that musical experiences in the home provided foundations for future musical engagement. For example, Christine explained that as a child growing up on the Hawaiian island of Oahu, "I only listened to Hawaiian music" due to the influence of her father, who "loved beautiful, Old School music . . . he liked really deep meanings," and this influence has led her to become "a traditionalist when it comes to music" (125). These brief snippets provide a window into the important musical happenings in the home.

Children's Musical Lives at School

Children's musical encounters in the school setting may be what we first think of when considering music in the lives of young people, as school music carries with it a certain visibility and orientation toward public performance. Perhaps many of us can reflect on school music encounters, a holiday pageant, or a helpful tune that aided in recalling important academic information. Perhaps we participated in instrumental or choral music ensembles, naturally gravitating toward the flute or the trombone or the human voice as a means to express ourselves. Music is embedded within the school setting in many different ways and for many different purposes, creating yet another interesting and important component of children's musical lives.

Although variations are bound to exist due to funding issues, community interest, and available resources, children's musical lives in school feature commonalities. Many school music encounters for children and youth involve general classroom music for all students, as well as choral music and instrumental music (band and orchestral instruments). Nontraditional musical opportunities may also assume a place in this musical landscape, with such ensembles as Caribbean steel pan groups, mariachi bands, African drumming ensembles, or even bucket bands, utilizing found objects to create percussive sounds as in the popular Broadway show *Stomp*. Although these experiences are typically facilitated by a trained music educator, children also engage with music in their regular classrooms, learning songs, rhymes, and other tuneful mnemonic devices to help them recall a wide variety of important information.

Regardless of the format of children's music making in the school setting, several commonalities occur in this formal music education endeavor. MENC: The National Association for Music Education supports music in the schools, providing resources to music educators of all types. Among MENC's efforts toward the proliferation of music in the schools has been the creation and implementation of National Standards for Music Education.

Children take part in a music class at the Mott Haven Academy Charter School, in the Bronx borough of New York City, April 13, 2011. (AP Photo/Mary Altaffer)

These nine benchmarks set forth goals and guidelines for student achievement in school music programs and include singing, playing instruments, improvisation, composition, engaging with notation, listening to music, evaluating music, understanding how music relates to other art forms, and understanding music in its historical and cultural contexts (MENC 1994). Although each standard might not be met in each performance or educational setting in music, this list provides a sound overview of the types of activities children and youths can and should encounter in their school music settings.

Music in the schools provides an essential and vital outlet for children to create, express themselves, or just find a safe social space in which to exist. Six-year-old Carley remarked; "Music's my favorite thing in school. The reason I don't like gym the most is because sometimes we go in with older kids and we get called names . . . no one does any of those things in music" (Crafts, Cavicchi, and Keil 1993, 15). Music in school means so much to ten-year-old Alan that he explained: "I wish we had more music time" (Campbell 2010, 180). Watts (2009) tapped into the voices of individuals of varying generations who fondly described their formal musical encounters in school, participating in school-wide musical performances, playing instruments in the band, or singing with choral ensembles. Even in her sixties, Jean tenderly described a meaningful school music encounter involving the Blessed Mother's May Altar in her Catholic elementary school: "[T]he day it was your turn, you got to pick out the song . . . and mine was always 'Immaculate Mary'" (Watts 2009, 43).

Children's Musical Lives at Play

Although children have very rich musical lives in the home and at school, they also possess a fascinating musical culture of their very own while at play. We might recall music filtering into our own play, whether through rhythmic chants used to select who will perform the role of "it" in a game of tag or the sing-songy tunes that accompany jump rope. Perhaps we sang and chanted as we performed complex handclapping maneuvers or even made up our own songs in service of our play activities. Children's musical play represents a facet of their musicking that is all their own—it is carried out by children and passed on by children, largely without the interference of adults.

Digging a bit deeper into the meanings, forms, and functions of children's musical play, Marsh and Young

(2006) defined these behaviors as musical "activities that children initiate of their own accord and in which they may choose to participate with others voluntarily" (289). The term *musical play* has come to encompass a broad range of play activities that often take on different forms concurrent with varying stages of childhood development. According to Campbell (1998), musical play may take on the form of songs (occasionally accompanied by handclapping), chants, games, or dances. In addition, "rhythmicking," that is, creating patterns of sound through various means, and children's many minute musical "utterances" may contribute to musical play (Campbell 1998, 65–67). Playgrounds, backyards, and bus stops across the globe are home to these child-created musical moments, a multitude of jump rope chants, handclapping songs, singing games, and radio jingles all serving as musical training grounds for children and youth. Marsh (1992) asserted that children's musical play is characterized by the "spontaneous and fleeting nature of naturally occurring performances" (136). She further set forth three central characteristics that are featured in children's singing games: music, text, and movement (Marsh 1999). Campbell (1991) explained that music of children's own making often has a limited tessitura, involves much repetition, includes chantlike/rhythmic aspects, is often complex in nature, and features movement.

This rich and fascinating world of children's self-initiated and transmitted playful engagement with music is bounded only by imagination and creativity. Looking back on her youth, Jennifer recalled her girlhood musical play as a vital and substantive aspect of her childhood social life. An avid enjoyer of handclapping games, jump rope songs, and various other forms of musical play, Jennifer shared that "[musical play] was just entertainment in its rawest form, it was right there all the time" (Watts 2009, 72). Ten-year-old Samantha discussed her musical play in the form of jump rope songs on the playground, but also her playful engagement with the mediated music she shares with her friends. She laughed and said, "I like the sound of music because sometimes . . . when you're hyper and listening to music, sometimes you bounce off the walls!" (Watts 2009, 79).

It may be easy to overlook the remarkable sophistication and depth found in children's musical lives. This entry merely scratches the surface of what young people know and can do in music, the artistic choices they make, their transmission practices, and their natural inclination to behave musically. The ubiquitous settings of home, school, and play provide limitless opportunities for children to engage with music, whether through listening and consumption, critique and evaluation, or active participation and doing. Reflecting on children's multifaceted musical lives provides inspiration to appreciate our own musical beginnings while imagining the possibilities for our musical future.

See also: Education and Music; Music Making at Home; Music Teachers; National Music Organizations; Seeger Family

Further Reading

Campbell, P. S. 1991. "The Child-Song-Genre: A Comparison of Songs by and for Children." *International Journal of Music Education* 17: 14–23.

Campbell, P. S. 1998. *Songs in Their Heads: Music and Its Meaning in Children's Lives.* New York: Oxford University Press.

Campbell, P. S. 2010. *Songs in Their Heads: Music and Its Meaning in Children's Lives.* 2nd ed. New York: Oxford University Press.

Crafts, S. D., D. Cavicchi, and C. Keil. 1993. *My Music: Explorations of Music in Daily Life.* Middletown, CT: Wesleyan University Press.

Marsh, K. 1992. "An Ethical Framework for the Study and Pedagogical Use of Australian Children's Playground Singing Games." In *ISME Yearbook,* 133–139. Dublin, Ireland: Ashville Media Group.

Marsh, K. 1999. "Mediated Orality: The Role of Popular Music in the Changing Tradition of Children's Musical Play." *Research Studies in Music Education* 13: 2–12.

Marsh, K., and S. Young. 2006. "Musical Play." In *The Child as Musician: A Handbook of Musical Development,* edited by G. E. McPherson, 289–310. New York: Oxford University Press.

MENC. 1994. *National Standards for Arts Education.* Lanham, MD: Rowman & Littlefield Education.

Seeger, R. C. 1948. *American Folk Songs for Children.* New York: Oak Publications.

Trehub, S. 2006. "Infants as Musical Connoisseurs." In *The Child as Musician: A Handbook of Musical Development,* edited by G. E. McPherson, 33–49. New York: Oxford University Press.

Watts, S. H. 2009. "Transgenerational Musical Play: Oral History Accounts of Girls' Musical Engagement." PhD diss., University of Washington, Seattle.

Sarah Watts

Children's Television Music

Exposure and access to television and media sources that allow us to record and replay material is an everyday occurrence and is thus deeply embedded in the human culture on an international scale. This access to

Alison Krauss and The Union Station join the Count in a number-counting jamboree on Sesame Street, December 14, 2004. (Theo Wargo/WireImage for Sesame Workshop)

media is increasing exponentially each day, providing people around the world with the opportunity to engage with a wide range of music-based entertainment. Among this type of programming, children's television is also increasing in types (and scope) of shows that are available to young children and are aimed not only at entertainment but also at education. Though born from American culture, children's television shows have been adapted to meet the needs and cultural norms of societies around the world. Likewise, the range of shows and musical styles within those shows has expanded significantly in the last twenty years. Music plays an important role in enhancing the appeal and distinction of children's television shows as well as characterizing a number of aspects of the shows. The appeal and inclusiveness of music, regardless of an individual's age or ability level, is also a key element of selecting or composing music to accompany a show.

Beginnings

Since it first aired on November 10, 1969, *Sesame Street* has set the stage for educational children's television as a medium for learning. This engaging show is comprised of vignettes with puppets, people, and cartoons and punctuated with catchy tunes that convey both academic information and social messages. More than forty years after its creation, the deeply rooted education and research that continue to ground the show have made it one of the most recognized children's television programs worldwide. Central to the charm, appeal, and impact of this long-standing program is its music.

Because musical meaning is embedded in rich social and personal contexts, the songs of *Sesame Street* provide a structure for remembering and applying various types of information in the context of a vignette with the characters. Not only do these songs provide a framework for the information, they also have the capacity to establish an emotional response or meaning as well. In a show segment in which famed character Cookie Monster is singing about cookies, he is focusing on the letter and sound- recognition for "C". The musical elements of rhythm and melody support this simple, easily replicated melody that becomes very memorable when paired with antics of Cookie Monster's affection for cookies.

In addition to the social-emotional benefits, music has the capacity to increase arousal and engagement for the listener, which makes "catchy" music an essential piece of a successful show. The multisensory (i.e., something can hear, move to, see) nature of music in television is able to captivate an audience and entice participation. The songs of a particular show are something that children are likely to replicate. These examples of positive social behavior that are demonstrated in the context of a musical context or song provide a memorable way for children to learn quickly and easily, allowing them to replicate the song and the complementary behaviors so that they can practice the concepts in the context of other social situations. For example, a repetitive melody that is simple, with limited pitch range that repeats a phrase like "I can be your friend" and is paired with visual images of children engaging in positive social behaviors, can transfer to an individual child's social experience. The child might sing the melodic phrase as a way to cue, describe, or teach other children to model the desired behaviors.

This function of music, to facilitate communication, self-regulation, and attachment with others, is the catalyst for describing music as an effective means of communicating with children and facilitating learning. Coupled with visual representation and symbols, music and television provide developmental building blocks for communication, cultural references, and norms and help children begin to interpret the world around them.

From literal messages and communication to metaphorical ones, music supports the capacity for interaction and fantasy or pretend-play, which is central to the development of young children and their ability to understand and function within social norms as well as their ability to self-regulate. Beginning in 1968, *Mr. Rogers' Neighborhood* paired very distinct aspects or elements of music such as melody and timbre with predictable elements that occurred in each show to help children discern a predictable sequence of events and to establish both character and form. For example, each show began with Fred Rogers arriving at his home, changing his jacket for a sweater, and changing his shoes, all while singing the show's theme. Each show had a sequence of pretend-play prompted by the trolley, whose "voice" was the distinct, high sound of a glockenspiel. This "voice" is a quintessential example of providing a symbolic representation using a musical stimulus.

Research on Music in Children's Television

Although there are numerous examples of the various functions of music in music and children's television, the role of media in the acquisition of musical heritage and skill, including what influence the media have on a group or individual's repertoire, is not well documented. Published literature consists primarily of anecdotal accounts of relationships between musical aspects or non-musical outcomes of children's shows. A few studies have investigated sociocultural aspects, explicit and implicit learning, as well as acquisition and retention of various developmental skills.

In 1995 Wolfe and Jellison interviewed preschool children about various aspects of music video excerpts from *Sesame Street* that were identified by a panel of adults as intending to teach a particular message. Messages were both explicit and implicit. Although children were able to identify explicit messages, they had more difficulty transferring or generalizing a message. Recommendations based on the results of this article indicate that children's television designed for a specific educational purpose must utilize high repetition, and that shows with an educational purpose provide a comfortable environment for follow-up discussion as opposed to the assumption that children simply watch and glean the desired information.

In a follow-up study, Jellison and Wolfe (1999) compared the opinions of fifth graders and adults about the messages for preschool children in the video *Songs from Sesame Street.* Outcomes of this study indicated that adults listed significantly more implicit messages than did fifth graders, which was consistent with findings from the previously mentioned study. Data show that preschoolers report explicit messages, as did the fifth graders in this study. Significant differences were also found between fifth graders and adults concerning importance, learning, and liking. The implications of each of these studies for adults who use music segments from children's television as educational experiences for young children is that in order for children to learn and retain the information embedded in music of a children's television show, the music must be explicitly taught or followed up on if there is an expectation that children will be able to utilize the lessons contained in the video.

In an effort to examine the relationship between live music experiences and music experiences imbedded in a children's television show, Register (2004) measured early literacy outcomes of kindergarten students who engaged in various treatment conditions to learn literacy skills. Of the two groups who watched the children's television show, the group that experienced live music groups as well had a higher percentage of on-task behavior. Early literacy skill measure test scores, however, were similar in both groups, suggesting that children were learning in both groups, although the live music experiences were more engaging. Perhaps the function of music in both conditions was to present desired material in a medium that children were able to retain.

In contrast to the previous studies, which examined the relationship between the music in children's shows for non-music outcomes, some researchers are interested in the impact that children's television has on music learning for children. For example, McGuire (2001) observed the relationship between the availability of a children's television program and song recognition to investigate the relationship and association between a child's ability to recognize songs from the television show *Barney & Friends* and self-reported frequency of watching the show. Results indicated that there was not a positive relationship between these two variables, and that while children remembered songs from the show that had general popularity in the American culture, they did not remember the versions of those songs altered by creators of the show.

Similarly, Cassidy and Gerringer (1999) investigated the effects of children's videos on music development and preference. Although children did listen longer when both audio and video stimuli were present, their data indicated that children had a preference for more child-directed, modern genres of music when compared with classical music. Data from this study pose an interesting question about the effect and influence of music genres on children's interest and engagement in a particular television show as a result of the music that accompanies the program. The children's television show *Little Einsteins* is an example of a cartoon with purposeful, explicit messages to teach young children about classical music and works of art in the context of a thirty-minute adventure episode.

Although these topics are not well explored, there are interesting findings that warrant further investigation of the roles and effects that music can have on children in the context of a television show. In addition, related fields such as neurological, perception, and cognition research indicate that music is stored in a variety of areas in the brain, and exposure and active engagement in music indicates increased growth patterns and responsiveness in brain activity. These comprehensive effects of music, developmentally speaking, are believed to be numerous and distributed across all developmental domains. Further investigation of how both aural and visual input are processed, stored, and utilized by children is certainly warranted.

Shifts in Diversity of Music Offered to Young Children

Buller (2003) writes about music in children's television in a more informal, anecdotal way that notes the changes in music over time for use in children's television programming. Both music composed specifically for a particular show and precomposed selections utilize familiarity, influenced by the ease with which we access music of all types and varieties. In the last five to seven years, children's television has employed new techniques, and the topics and intended (and directly stated) goals of the shows are quite specific about what they are designed to provide for young children. This new breed of show is specifically targeted at highlighting skills such as early literacy, pretend-play, and science-based information. In addition to using music as a way to help children identify and remember information, greater attention is paid to the genre of music used to deliver the information and greater inclusion of the various styles of music that families listen to at home. The show, *The Backyardigans,* utilizes a specific genre of music for each show and frequently uses recognizable tunes with new lyrics to describe and advance the story line. In addition, the specific musical genre of each show seeks to expose children to a wide variety of music and to perhaps dispel stereotypes about personality or culture associated with a specific genre. For example, an episode that is set in space might utilize country or reggae music as opposed to a more predictable choice of electronic or synthesized music.

There are also some children's shows that either focus solely on music or have music as a central part of delivery. *Jack's Big Music Show* incorporates the puppets and vignettes seen in many other children's shows, and its story lines unfold with the music of various artists and genres. The *Imagination Movers* is another example of a show that is very music dependent. Built around the *Imagination Movers* band, this show focuses on problem solving and deductive reasoning and is rich with musical interludes that are easily marketed as their own CD and utilized as part of a live concert touring show. Both of these shows are examples of how embedded music is in our culture and the primary role that music assumes in entertainment. The focus on music for music's sake and growth in this industry continues to parallel that of developmentally appropriate practice in early childhood education. Music is part of the multisensory approach to learning.

See also: Children's Musical Lives; Electronic and Computer Music; Psychology of Music

Further Reading

Buller, Jennifer. 2003. "Music in Children's Television." *Canadian Music Educator* 44, no. 3: 32–36.

Cassidy, Jane, and John Gerringer. 1999. "Effects of Animated Videos on Children's Music Development." *Update: Applications of Research in Music Education* 17: 3–7.

Jellison, Judith, and David Wolfe. 1999. "Video Songs from *Sesame Street*: A Comparison of Fifth Graders' and Adults' Opinions Regarding Messages for Preschool Children." *Journal of Research in Music Education* 47: 64–77.

McGuire, Ken M. 2001. "The Relationship Between the Availability of a Children's Television Program and Song Recognition." *Journal of Research in Music Education* 50: 227–244.

Register, Dena. 2004. "The Effects of Live Music Groups Versus an Educational Children's Television Program on the Emerging Literacy of Young Children." *Journal of Music Therapy* 41: 2–27.

Wolfe, David, and Judith Jellison. 1995. "Interviews with Preschool Children about Music Videos." *Journal of Music Therapy* 32: 265–285.

Dena Register

Choruses, Men's

The emergence and organization of community and collegiate male choruses in the United States dates to around the mid-nineteenth century. While American male choruses and glee clubs have flourished for more than 150 years, their roots are embedded in the Western European male singing societies. Their historical lineage can be traced back as far as the mid-eighteenth century to the English catch, glee, and part-song traditions, as well as the German *Männerchor* tradition, which emerged shortly thereafter in the early nineteenth century. A general historical awareness of these Western European traditions is fundamental to understanding the establishment of American male singing societies.

Historical Perspective: The Western European Traditions

Although many of the early male singing societies in England embraced the socially elite, they eventually grew in membership to include the middle class, sharing a commonality of fellowship in song. These groups were often considered to be informal singing societies, but they began to encourage a more advanced level of artistic merit inherent within the compositions they performed. The first male singing society to formally be called a "glee club," in 1787, had a membership "not drawn exclusively from the ranks of nobility and gentry, but . . . from the rising middle class and London's body of professional musicians" (Rubin 2003, 102). The first male singing society in Germany was established in 1809 by Carl Zelter (1758–1832). The group was referred to as the Berlin *Liedertafel* and was comprised of twenty-five men. Although selective, its mission was analogous to that of groups found in England, embracing original compositions of lasting musical value. As the male singing tradition began to proliferate across Germany, these groups also began to accept a more inclusive membership, promoting affable friendship while advancing German song and poetry. By the mid-nineteenth century male glee clubs began appearing at many German universities. "Almost all academic fraternities of the universities maintained glee clubs, and professors sang as well as students. It is interesting to note that most students continued to sing with these organizations long after graduation. This swelled the memberships of many clubs, and in some instances organizations had more than two hundred members on their rolls" (Thomas 1962). The rapid growth and expansion of male singing societies in England and Germany significantly influenced the male choral traditions that began to develop across the ever-expanding American nation.

Male Singing Societies in America: The Influence of German Immigrants

As the population of immigrants increased throughout the first half of the nineteenth century, many communities in America's cities began to exhibit some of the same societal traditions of music making that had been so important in Europe. The first recognized male singing society in America is credited to a group of German immigrants, who established a *Gesangverein* in Philadelphia in 1835. Another important German American male singing society during this period was the *Liederkranz* of New York City, which was founded in 1847. Amazingly, by 1860, the organization boasted a membership of over five hundred men, which quickly expanded to more than fifteen hundred by 1894. "Apparently the group flourished under the leadership of piano maker William Steinway, who served as its president for much of the time from 1867 until his death in 1896" (Osborne 1994, 6). Among the other German- influenced male singing societies in America, the *Columbus Maennerchor* of Ohio, founded in 1848, is one of the oldest American *Männerchore* still thriving today.

The Rise of American Male Choral Societies

The formation of male singing societies among native-born American citizens closely followed the organized structure and mission of the earlier German American singing societies. Founded in New York City in 1866, the Mendelssohn Glee Club is the oldest noncollegiate male singing society in America and lays claim to be the second oldest American musical organization, after the New York Philharmonic, founded in 1842. In an effort to promote and advance the male choral art in America, the Glee Club programmed many concerts that featured only American composers during the early- to mid-twentieth century, including Horatio Parker (1863–1919), Harry T. Burleigh (1866–1949), Archibald T. Davison (1883–1961), and Randall Thompson (1899–1984). The group sponsored composition contests in a manner analogous to the traditions of England and Germany to promote and encourage the composition of new male choral music of artistic value among American composers.

The University Glee Club of New York City was founded in 1894 and was organized to provide choral music experiences for men of all ages, like the Mendelssohn Glee Club. Still in existence, the group boasts a membership of over 150 singers. Male singing societies continued to rise throughout the late nineteenth century and into the first decades of the twentieth. Other representative male singing societies that were established during this time include the Orpheus Club of Philadelphia (1872); the Singer's Club of Cleveland (1891); the Mendelssohn Club of Kingston, New York (1903); the Choral Club of Hartford in West Hartford, Connecticut (1907); the Orpheus Club of Ridgewood, New Jersey (1909); and the Mendelssohn Club of Albany, New York (1909). An inclusive membership of men from all professions has continually been embraced throughout the rise of male singing societies in America, including professional and amateur musicians, who share a common interest in the camaraderie and fellowship that is innate in singing great choral music for men's voices.

Collegiate Male Glee Clubs

The development of collegiate male glee clubs in America began in 1858 with the organization of the Harvard Glee Club, followed by the University of Michigan Glee Club in 1859 and the Yale Glee Club in 1861. While the organization of early collegiate male glee clubs paralleled the formation of community male groups, collegiate clubs experienced rapid growth in the years following the Civil War (1861–1865). Singing was often a recreational activity enjoyed by many soldiers, and when they returned home at the conclusion of the war, many pursued a college education, carrying with them a continuing interest in singing. As a result, many collegiate glee clubs began as self-directed student organizations prior to officially being recognized as academic organizations. Often considered among the oldest student groups on campus, collegiate glee clubs' membership generally reflects an all-encompassing group of students representing all academic disciplines. Although many of the community-based male singing societies embraced a more serious form of music, the repertoire of early collegiate glee clubs often consisted of lighthearted and humorous songs, embodying school spirit and pride. Among the first faculty-appointed conductors of a collegiate glee club was Archibald T. Davison, who became conductor of the Harvard Glee Club in 1919. Under his leadership the Harvard Glee Club began to embrace higher musical standards, performing repertoire of lasting artistic merit, ranging from simple folksongs to more complex works of the master composers of Western art music. Many collegiate glee clubs followed this model while still honoring the beloved traditions of school spirit and camaraderie. Additional collegiate glee clubs founded across the United States were very similar to those first established on the campuses of Harvard, Michigan, and Yale. Although collegiate glee clubs are now often included in the academic community and uphold higher artistic missions, they continue to embody a sense of school spirit and pride.

Advocacy of the Male Choral Movement

While community and collegiate male choruses continued to prosper throughout the twentieth century, professional service organizations were created in an effort to support the advancement of male choruses across the nation. Among the foremost organizations of this kind are the Intercollegiate Men's Choruses (IMC), Associated Male Choruses of America (AMCA), Barbershop Harmony Society, American Choral Directors Association (ACDA), Chorus America, and the Gay and Lesbian Association of Choruses (GALA). The oldest professional service organization to support the male choral art was IMC, founded in 1914. It quickly instituted collegiate glee club competitions in an effort to support interest and growth in collegiate singing, which occurred at the same time that many collegiate glee clubs were striving to achieve higher artistic standards. Continuing to advance and nurture the male choral art in the twenty-first century, IMC instituted a Male Chorus Commissioning Consortium in 2006 to supplement the existing male choral repertoire.

A Continuing Increase in Community Male Choruses

Male choral singing increased across the United States during the latter part of the twentieth century with the organization of numerous community male choruses. Among these were the Turtle Creek Chorale (1980), the Washington Men's Camerata (1984), and the Naperville Men's Glee Club (1988).The Turtle Creek Chorale, based in Dallas, Texas, is one of the best-known community gay male choruses in America and has a membership of over 150. The Washington Men's Camerata, based in Washington, D.C., has made an immeasurable contribution to the male choral art. In 1998, with the assistance of the National Endowment for the Arts, the Camerata created the National Library of Men's Choral Music.

Community and collegiate male choruses in America continue to encourage and foster an inclusive membership regardless of age, race, creed, sexual orientation, profession, or academic discipline. The brotherhood and spirit inherent in male singing societies draws men together into a common bond, sharing a passion for music that often evolves into lifelong friendships. The encouragement and acceptance of men into a musical

Members of the Harvard Glee Club pose with President Herbert Hoover (center), April 8, 1929. (Library of Congress)

community has positively impacted the musical advancement of the male choral art across the nation.

See also: Choruses, Women's; European Music in America

Further Reading

Osborne, William. 1994. *American Singing Societies and Their Partsongs: Ten Prominent American Composers of the Genre (1860–1940) and the Seminal Singing Societies That Performed the Repertory.* Monograph no. 8. Lawton, OK: American Choral Directors Association.

Rubin, Emanuel. 2003. *The English Glee in the Reign of George III: Participatory Art Music for an Urban Society.* Warren, MI: Harmonie Press.

Thomas, Arnold Ray. 1962. "The Development of Male Glee Clubs in American Colleges and Universities." PhD diss., Columbia University.

Jeremy D. Jones

Choruses, Women's

The women's community choir has a significant history. Its history in American music is fairly recent. The female voice choir had an interesting emancipation. Almost emerging out of boredom and isolation, women's "song" was largely ignored except in hymnody or parlor settings, until it established itself in middle-class culture. Singing societies, both male and female, flourished in the late 1800s and early 1900s. Women organized and ran their own women's music clubs beginning in the 1870s, such as the St. Cecilia Society of New York. Composers—many of them women—responded to the increased demand for music for women's voices, building up a substantial repertoire that was issued by publishers in special series (Hubbard 1996; Block 1991).

In the early 1930s large choruses for women began to surface. Sophie Drinker (1995) cites Margaret Dessoff's Adesdi Choir of fifty women. This choir was unique for its time because it only performed music written originally for women's voices. Drinker recalls a 1940 concert in Philadelphia presented by girls from a Catholic school in New York, led by Mother Georgia Stevens. Three thousand people attended and heard an exceptional program of quality music written by women, presented by talented female singers who were trained and led by a woman. In Drinker's opinion, the performance of these young students was better than the more mature choir led by Margaret Dessoff (Hubbard 1996; Drinker 1995).

American Classical Orchestra Women's Chorus performs Brahms's Vier Gesange at Alice Tully Hall in New York City, October 15, 2012. (Hiroyuki Ito/Getty Images)

Still another women's choral movement began sometime in the late 1920s. Called Mothersingers, these choruses were officially organized through local Parent Teacher Associations (PTAs) in 1932. A few are still in existence across the country today, performing in schools, churches, and communities. In 1954 the *Music Educators National Journal* published an article noting that a highlight of the state music educators convention was the performance of the seven-hundred-member Mothersingers chorus under the direction of the supervisor of music in Los Angeles. In California in the 1960s the Mothersingers reorganized into an umbrella organization called California Women's Chorus, Inc. This organization is still in existence, with a mission to promote women's choral music and grant awards to high school and college students to help further their musical education.

Catherine Roma, whose work serves as a model for bringing the choral arts to a wide community for more than thirty-five years, became one of the founding mothers of the women's choral movement when she started Anna Crusis Women's Choir in her native Philadelphia in 1975. Anna Crusis was the first women's chorus to become a member of the Gay and Lesbian Association of Choruses (GALA), begun in 1982. GALA fosters the growth and development of women's community choirs. Today more than thirty women's community choirs belong to GALA. Bernice Johnson Reagon, founder of Sweet Honey in the Rock, was the first female composer to have a work commissioned for women's voices, for the 1989 GALA festival.

The Sister Singers Network, a cooperative web of feminist choruses who support and enrich the women's choral movement, now encompasses more than ninety-five women's choirs throughout the fifty states. Member choruses regularly commission new works and perform not only the "classic" concert repertoire for women's voices, but music that they feel is more reflective of the varied lives and concerns of all women. The membership of the Sweet Adelines, a worldwide organization of women singers committed to advancing the art form of barbershop harmony, is more than five hundred choruses and twelve hundred quartets on five continents.

In large numbers over a wide area, women have been singing together for a long time and have obtained and provided considerable pleasure in the process. Women's community choirs, such as Mirinesse Women's Choir and Vox Femina Los Angeles, bring critical listeners to their feet at the American Choral Directors Association and

Chorus America conferences. The World Choral Symposium features some of the finest international women's choruses, such as Elektra, Cantoría Alberto Grau, and Lady Cove Women's Chorus. The world-renowned Tokyo's Ladies' Consort, SAYAKA, has demonstrated its prowess at international festivals. Professional women's choruses such as Anonymous 4, Sweet Honey in the Rock, KITKA, and many others perform regularly throughout the United States and abroad. Over the last two centuries, women's choral music has grown steadily, generating interest on all continents, promoting strong self-images for women, and showcasing artistic excellence. The women's community choir movement is alive and well. It has a vivid history and a bright future.

See also: Choruses, Men's; Women in American Music

Further Reading

Drinker, Sophie. 1995. *Music and Women: The Story of Women and their Relation to Music.* New York: The Feminist Press.

Sharp, Avery T., and James Floyd. 2002. *Choral Music: A Research and Information Guide.* New York: Routledge.

Iris Levine

Christian Rock

The American counterculture of the 1960s and 1970s served as a cultural flashpoint that contributed to how youths were perceived, ideas were processed, and art was expressed. The Jesus movement, a Christian revival among hippies, radically remapped evangelical Christianity, creating urgency for evangelicals to focus on youth culture. The result was the birth of Christian rock music. Although the official Jesus movement faded, the spirit of the original movement continues to surface in various forms, redefining boundaries and reorienting the faithful to new, emerging ways of signifying the sacred.

As the Jesus movement began to dissolve in the late 1970s, the religious Right adopted the tools of popular culture to further its own cause. Post–Jesus movement evangelicals used music, books, and film to engage in the culture war, arguing that social issues such as abortion, feminism, gay rights, and secular humanism were all signs of a declining Christian nation. Among the tools used to engage in the culture war was music.

While the use of the popular vernacular was nothing new for evangelicals, the Jesus movement provided a template for cultural engagement that elevated evangelicals to new status. American Protestant ministers have often used entertainment to attract a crowd. Early revivalists such as Billy Sunday (1862–1935) "turned to the techniques of modern show business as a means of drumming up support" (Marsden 2001). Political scientist Duane Oldfield (1996) also iterates the ongoing connections between popular culture and evangelicalism, emphasizing the "populist, democratic character of American popular religion."

As an outflow of this post-hippie revival, the Jesus movement's message was artistically communicated

Christian Rock: The Short Life of Keith Green

Keith Green (1953–1982) is considered one of the quintessential singer-songwriters of the contemporary Christian music (CCM) genre. Though versatile as a pianist and singer, Green's primary skill was as a songsmith, always seeking to craft songs that offered deep theological reflection. His musical style was similar to Billy Joel's. After spending his early years in New York, Green's family relocated to the San Fernando Valley in California, which would prove to be important in his development as a musician. Green began singing and writing his own songs at the age of six, then signed a recording contract with Decca Records at the age of eleven, becoming the youngest person ever signed to the American Society of Composers, Authors, and Publishers (ASCAP). He enjoyed minor successes as a young pop star, but sought something deeper. After exploring drugs, Eastern mysticism, and "free love," Green converted to Christianity at the age of twenty-one. The Greens became friends with the newly converted Bob Dylan (1941–), who attended their church. As a sort of "John the Baptist" of music, Green's confrontational style earned him respect among those who believed the Christian music industry had become too materialistic. Living what he preached, in 1979 Green asked to be released from his recording contract after he decided that selling his music was wrong because it was essentially "selling" the gospel. He wanted his fans to be allowed to pay what they could afford for his records. Although he was one of CCM's biggest stars at the time, Green continued to resist the establishment. On July 28, 1982, Green was killed in a plane crash, along with his three-year-old son, Josiah, and two-year-old daughter, Bethany. Two other daughters, Rebekah and Rachel, and his wife, Melody, survive him. Melody continues to oversee Last Days Ministries, his Christian organization. His death affected the CCM community in much the same way John Lennon's (1940–1980) death affected the general market.

through multiple media. "Jesus music" evolved, becoming Christian rock and contemporary Christian music (CCM). Early Jesus rockers such as Children of the Day (active 1971–1979), Love Song (active 1970–1976), Andraé Crouch (1942–), Randy Stonehill (1952–), Barry McGuire (1935–), and Larry Norman (1947–2008) laid the foundation for artists who would play a role in the creation of a new industry: the "parallel universe" of popular evangelical music. These singers and groups included Keith Green (1953–1982), Rich Mullins (1955–1997), Michael Card (1957–), Amy Grant (1960–), Michael W. Smith (1957–), Petra (active 1972–2006, 2010–present), Stryper (active 1983–1992, 2003–present), the Resurrection Band (active 1972–2000), Whitecross (active 1985–present), dc Talk (1987–2001), DeGarmo & Key (active 1978–2006), and Jars of Clay (active 1993–present).

Perhaps the three most influential artists in CCM (in terms of laying a foundation for broad social appeal) have been Amy Grant, Michael W. Smith, and Larry Norman. Fascinated with the countercultural youth movements of the 1960s, Norman chose to adopt the cultural vernacular, hoping to share his belief with hippies. Along with his long blond hair, Norman's unique mix of Christianity and rock 'n' roll made him the perfect icon for Christian rock.

Norman is widely regarded as the "father of Christian rock." Founder of the band People! (active 1965–1971, 1974, 2006–2007), he released an album that featured a remake of "I Love You," formerly recorded by The Zombies (active 1961–1968, 1991, 1997, 2001–present). The version recorded by People! appeared on an album Norman hoped to title *We Need a Whole Lot More Jesus and a Lot Less Rock and Roll.* Capitol Records rejected the title, choosing to release the work as *I Love You* in 1968. In 1970 Norman and Capitol Records released *Upon This Rock,* widely considered to be the world's first Christian rock album. Considered too Christian for the secular market and too rock 'n' roll for the church, Norman found himself rejected by both industries. Despite health problems and isolation from the official Christian music industry, during the 1980s Norman launched his own record label, Solid Rock.

With the grit, authenticity, and shocking lyrics of *Street Level* (One Way Records, 1970) and *Bootleg* (One Way Records, 1972), Norman's public persona earned him respect among numerous general market rock stars. *Only Visiting This Planet* (which included arrangements by Beatles producer George Martin, 1926–) was chosen as the best Christian album of all time in 1988, only to be ranked number two the following year in the wake of Amy Grant's *Lead Me On.* Norman's music has influenced artists such as John Mellencamp (1951–) and U2 (active 1976–present), a group that is often viewed as Christian in both music and mission.

Starting in the 1970s, Amy Grant's voice earned her a place of respect among the gatekeepers of CCM. *Lead Me On* (1988) is considered the number one Christian album of all time. *Age to Age* (1982) demonstrated a staying power that helped launch the careers of co-collaborators such as Rich Mullins, Michael Card, and Michael W. Smith, three widely regarded luminaries among CCM consumers.

Grant's impact on the general market extends well beyond the cloistered world of popular Christian music. The Recording Industry Association of America compiled a list of the 365 "most significant songs of the twentieth century" and placed Grant's version of Michael W. Smith's song "Friends" at number 326, behind Elton John's (1947–) "Candle in the Wind." After going platinum, her career took a turn as she found herself appearing on *The Tonight Show,* rather than *The 700 Club.* In 1985 Amy Grant released *Unguarded,* which became a commercial breakthrough on the *Billboard* charts. "Find a Way" became Grant's first top 40 single, after which her duet with Peter Cetera (1944–), former singer of the group Chicago (active 1967–present), thrust Grant into the limelight. "The Next Time I Fall" rose to number one on the charts, making Grant a mainstream celebrity. The world of Christian music "had long awaited such general-market validation," writes journalist Andrew Beaujon (2006).

Now featured in *Life* and *Rolling Stone,* Grant was launched into the general "secular" market. After the 1988 release of *Lead Me On,* her music took on a playful feel, sending a message to Christian consumers—persons of faith can have fun. Then *Heart in Motion* (Myrrh, 1994) brought with it the lighthearted "Baby, Baby," and "Every Heartbeat" (written by Wayne Kirkpatrick and Charlie Peacock). *Heart in Motion* reached blockbuster status. Selling almost six million copies, the album created a buzz among consumers with such force that Grant's fame in many ways rivaled Madonna's (1958–). Grant's current contract with A&M Records underscores her ability to remain relevant within the cultural mainstream. As the wife of country music star Vince Gill (1957–), she is no stranger to the secular limelight. Grant has received various Grammy and Dove Awards, as well as a star on the Hollywood Walk of Fame.

A Christian pop sensation, singer-songwriter Michael W. Smith is among the pantheon of top-selling artists in CCM. His career began in 1982 after he accepted an invitation to play keyboards for Amy Grant. In 1983 he released *The Michael W. Smith Project* on Reunion Records, debuting the now classic "Friends," a song that would be named by critics in 1998 as the "best contemporary Christian song of all time." Following Amy Grant, Smith attempted to cross over into the general market. *The Big Picture* was pitched to A&M Records.

Christian rockers Amy Grant and Michael W. Smith perform in Redlands, California, February 4, 2011. (Pixelite/Dreamstime.com)

Although Smith never fully achieved crossover success, he is still a presence in mainstream media. Over the years he has appeared on *Good Morning America, The Tonight Show, Live with Regis and Kathy Lee, Entertainment Tonight, CBS This Morning,* and *The Arsenio Hall Show.* Despite his status as an artist who caters to a largely niche genre, Smith's charismatic appeal earned him the distinction of being named one of "The Fifty Most Beautiful People in the World" by *People* magazine (not to mention an honorary doctorate from Alderson-Broadus College, West Virginia). A recipient of numerous awards, Smith's albums have earned him both gold and platinum status.

The social influence of CCM is far-reaching. It has become "a major component of the financial underpinnings of American evangelicalism's mass media and bookstore infrastructure, as well as a significant aspect of everyday life and devotion in the evangelical subculture, spawning radio station formats, summer festivals, websites and the like" (Eskridge 1998). Although this niche genre was once relatively inconsequential, the respectability of contemporary Christian music (or Christians making popular music) increased as songs crossed over from niche genres to mainstream markets.

Historically there has been a struggle among Christian musicians, the general market, and local churches. Larry Norman was accused of being too Christian for the general market and too rock 'n' roll for the church. When the Resurrection Band (REZ) attempted to engage the market, their topics did not endear them to either world. Much like Norman, REZ was, according to Beaujon (2006), considered "too hard for the Christian market and too Christian for the general market." However, StarSong Records signed REZ and released what became a "classic of Christian rock." *Awaiting Your Reply* (1978) was one of the first truly Christian hard rock albums. The album created a template for the emergence of new "types" of Christian rock.

REZ (along with its Christian commune, Jesus People USA) founded the edgy, enigmatic Cornerstone Festival in 1984, which would influence the rise of countless "indie" rockers and various crossover bands. Although the festival has its roots in the Jesus music of the early 1970s, its tolerant position on theology and music has in many ways challenged the way popular "Christian" music is defined and marketed. The result has been a groundswell of "crossover" groups, such as P.O.D. (active 1992–present), Switchfoot (active 1996–present),

Jars of Clay, and Sixpence None the Richer (active 1992–2004, 2008–present). A landmark achievement for evangelical popular music, Sixpence None the Richer appeared on the *Late Show with David Letterman* and has made licensing deals with network television. P.O.D. shocked and inspired adoring fans by touring with Ozzy Osbourne's Ozz Fest, as well as other general market groups. However, the idea of a Christian group performing in secular, rock music venues was (at one time) anathema to the evangelical edict to be in the world, but not of it. That Christian music groups found it difficult to find employment in secular venues only exacerbated the problem, making it difficult for subcultural, evangelical pop music groups to gain exposure. In response, Cornerstone provided a venue in which fringe groups were accepted and those who sought to "cross over" into the general market were accepted and encouraged.

Much of the debate about CCM has been due to disagreements about how Christian musicians should interact with "the world." Sociologists Jay R. Howard and John M. Streck (1999) offer three different approaches to CCM that categorize the genre based on how the Christian music industry has historically dealt with tensions among faith, art, business, entertainment, and culture. "Separational" CCM is used to glorify God and spread the Christian message. "Integrational" CCM strives to cross over into the general market. These artists are entertainers who are vocal about their faith. "Transformational" Christian musicians view art as a valuable means to enter the world as agents of God. These musicians do not view music as merely a tool for religious worship or evangelism, but as something to be valued and enjoyed, regardless of the message; any Christian message is merely incidental to what is believed to be a result of God's presence in the world.

In the late 1990s the transformational model began to take hold as various musician-producers such as Charlie Peacock (1956–) began to redefine popular Christian music. In recent years CCM has evolved into a form that has lost historical connections to gospel music. While it maintains traces of evangelical themes, CCM has developed into a different genre entirely.

The evangelical subculture has always been somewhat culturally pliable. Philip Goff and Alan Heimert (1998) have argued that religious history continues to "shape and be shaped by larger cultural forces" uncovering "today's strange bedfellows, evangelicals and postmodernists, who together have launched a forceful objection to longstanding assumptions and paradigms." The fabric of U.S. culture is such that there is an almost symbiotic relationship between religious belief and religious expression. Contemporary Christian music is not immune to the forces of pluralism, nor is it immune to the evolution of human taste. Thus it is not surprising that this particular genre of American music both influences and reflects the changing landscape of American society and culture.

See also: Awards and Prizes in Music; Counterculture in American Music; Crossovers; Madonna; Psychedelic Music; Recording Industry Association of America; Rock 'n' Roll (Rock)

Further Reading

Balmer, Randall. 2006. *Thy Kingdom Come: An Evangelical's Lament: How the Religious Right Distorts the Faith and Threatens America.* New York: Basic Books.

Beaujon, Andrew. 2006. *Body Piercing Saved My Life: Inside the Phenomenon of Christian Rock.* Cambridge: Da Capo Press.

Bivens, Jason. 2008. *Religion of Fear: The Politics of Horror in Conservative Evangelicalism.* New York: Oxford University Press.

Eskridge, Larry. 1998 "'One Way': Billy Graham, the Jesus Generation, and the Idea of an Evangelical Youth Culture." *Church History* 67, no. 1: 106.

Gitlin, Todd. 1993. *The Sixties: Years of Hope, Days of Rage.* New York: Bantam Books.

Glanzer, Perry L. 2003. "Christ and the Heavy Metal Subculture: Applying Qualitative Analysis to the Contemporary Debate about H. Richard Niebuhr's *Christ and Culture.*" *Journal of Religion and Society* 5: 1–16.

Goff, Philip, and Alan Heimert. 1998 "Revivals and Revolution: Historiographic Turns Since Alan Heimert's 'Religion and the American Mind'." *Church History* 67, no. 4: 695–721.

Howard, Jay R., and John M. Streck. 1999. *Apostles of Rock: The Splintered World of Contemporary Christian Music.* Lexington: University Press of Kentucky.

Luhr, Eileen. 2009. *Witnessing Suburbia: Conservative and Christian Youth Culture.* Berkeley: University of California Press.

Marini, Stephen A. 2003. *Sacred Song in America: Religion, Music, and Public Culture.* Chicago: University of Illinois Press.

Marsden, George M. 2001. *Religion and American Culture.* 2nd ed. Belmont, CA: Wadsworth.

Miller, Donald E. 1999. *Reinventing American Protestantism: Christianity in the New Millennium.* Berkeley: University of California Press.

Oldfield, Duane Murray. 1996. *The Right and the Righteous: The Christian Right Confronts the Republican Party.* Lanham, MD: Rowman & Littlefield Publishers.

Peacock, Charlie. 2004. *At the Crossroads: Inside the Past, Present, and Future of Contemporary Christian Music.* Colorado Springs, CO: WaterBrook Press.

Powell, Mark, Allan. 2002. *The Encyclopedia of Contemporary Christian Music*. Peabody, MA: Hendrickson Publishers.

Stowe, David W. 2011. *No Sympathy for the Devil: Christian Pop Music and the Transformation of American Evangelicalism*. Chapel Hill: University of North Carolina Press.

Shawn David Young

Christmas Music, Contemporary

Enduring hymns like "Adeste Fideles (Oh, Come All Ye Faithful)," "Ave Maria," and "Silent Night" and endearing holiday hits like "The Christmas Song" (1946); "Hello, Mr. Kringle" (1939); and "White Christmas" (1942) ruled America's December airwaves during the first half of the twentieth century. Only a few novelty numbers, such as "Here Comes Santa Claus (Down Santa Claus Lane)" (1947) and "Santa Claus Is Comin' to Town" (1934) provided audio diversions from traditional tinsel-time tunes. Of course everything—including Christmas recordings—changed with the emergence of rock 'n' roll. Holiday hits were no longer just pop crooning or gospel choir releases. A manic menagerie of mistletoe melodies suddenly appeared on vinyl, on the radio, and on turntables throughout the United States. These rocking rhythms and madcap lyrics were generated by young recording artists with backgrounds in blues, country, doo-wop, rockabilly, R&B, and soul music. Bing Crosby (1903–1977), Perry Como (1912–2001), The Andrews Sisters (active 1925–1967), Nat King Cole (1919–1965), and Gene Autry (1907–1998) were forced to yield their monopoly on holiday hit territory. Elvis Presley (1935–1977), Bobby Helms (1933–1997), Charles Brown (1922–1999), Brenda Lee (1944–), and even The Chipmunks (active 1958–1972, 1979–present) opened the doors to future holiday hits by Otis Redding (1941–1967), Bruce Springsteen (1949–), King Curtis (1934–1971), Kathy Mattea (1958–), and Elmo and Patsy (active 1974–present). Between 1950 and 2010 a startling number of innovative and zany Christmas recordings were recorded and released.

The most dramatic changes in post-1950 Christmas lyrics occurred with the introduction of sexually suggestive comments and an increased emphasis on depictions of holiday loneliness. Recordings that illustrate the sensual nature of mistletoe-influenced celebrations include "(All I Want for Christmas Is to) Lay Around and Love on You" (1991); "Baby, It's Cold Outside" (1949); "Back Door Santa" (1968); "I'll Be Your Santa, Baby" (1973); "I'm Your Santa" (1992); "Santa Claus Is Back in Town" (1957); "Santa Claus Wants Some Lovin'" (1974); and "Shimmy Down My Chimney (Fill Up My Stocking)" (2004). These slightly ribald ditties were not performed by underground artists, either. They were holiday hits for Clarence Carter (1936–), Alison Krauss (1971–), Elvis Presley, Vanessa Williams (1963–), and others. A more common refrain, especially among lonely male singers, is the malaise experienced by those who have been abandoned by loved ones just before Christmas Day. This sad situation is articulated again and again in tunes like "Blue Christmas" (1957), "Blues for Christmas" (1960), "A Bluesman's Christmas" (2003), "Christmas Blues" (1968), "Christmas (Comes But Once a Year)" (1960), "Christmas Tears" (1961), "Christmas Time Blues" (1950), "Empty Stocking Blues" (1950), "Far Away Blues (Xmas Blues)" (1950), "Just a Lonely Christmas" (1953), "Lonely Christmas" (1950), "Merry Merry Christmas Baby" (1988), and "Spending Christmas with the Blues" (1996). A huge hit for Darlene Love (1941–) was "Christmas (Baby Please Come Home)" (1963) by Jeff Barry, Ellie Greenwich, and Phil Spector, which Love rousingly sings every year with Paul Shaffer and the CBS Orchestra on a *Late Night with David Letterman* Christmas show.

Lighthearted lyrics that rejoice in the happy feelings of holiday well-being far outnumber laments about Christmas loneliness. Christmas continues to be portrayed as a time of joyous family gatherings, friendly greetings among shoppers and old friends, and exchanges of festively wrapped gifts. Both new holiday songs and revivals of earlier Yuletide hits populate the airwaves throughout December. The list of contemporary artists saluting traditional values ranges from Detroit Junior (1931–2005), Marcia Ball (1949–), and Titus Turner (1933–) to Natalie Cole (1950–), Vince Guaraldi (1928–1976), and Jose Feliciano (1945–). These family-oriented recordings include "Christmas Day" (1960), "Christmas Fais Do Do" (2003), "Christmas Morning" (1952), "The Christmas Song (Chestnuts Roasting on an Open Fire)" (1946), "Christmas Time Is Here" (the song from the annually televised *A Charlie Brown Christmas*) (1967), "Deck the Halls with Boogie Woogie" (1992), "Duke's Christmas" (2000), "Feliz Navidad" (1970), "A Holly Jolly Christmas" (1964), "Jingle Bell Jamboree" (2003), "Jingle Bell Rock" (1957), "Let's Make Every Day a Christmas Day" (1961), "Merry Christmas Baby" (1986), "Rock and Roll Christmas" (1995), "Rockabilly Christmas" (2004), "Rockin' Around The Christmas Tree" (1960), "White Christmas" (1942), and "Winter Wonderland" (1934).

Singers desiring special gifts are also quite vocal about their preferences. Specific requests include "A Five Pound Box of Money" (1995); "I Want a Hippopotamus for Christmas" (1953); "(I Want a) Rock and Roll

Guitar" (1960); "I Want Elvis for Christmas" (1956); "I Want My Baby for Christmas" (1950); and "Santa, I Want a Stratocaster" (1997). Confessions are also offered about the appropriateness or inappropriateness of pre-Christmas demeanor. One singer claims that she has "Really Been Good This Year" (2003), but another sadly acknowledges that he won't be getting "Nuttin' for Christmas" (1955) because of his bad behavior throughout the year.

While images of the babe of Bethlehem dominated early-twentieth-century Christmas recordings, tales about the jolly old elf from the North Pole have been far more frequent over the past sixty years. Santa Claus is variously depicted as a fatherly gift-giver, a party-oriented dancer and reveler, a lecherous womanizer, and the driver of a "Hot Rod Sleigh" (1995). The only consistent element among these diverse illustrations of Santa is his attire: a red suit with white cuffs and collar, black boots, and a red cap perched on his white-bearded head. Recordings that regale listeners with the antics of Kris Kringle include "Boogie Woogie Santa Claus" (1990); "Check It Out, Santa" (2002); "Dig That Crazy Santa Claus" (2005); "Donde Esta Santa Claus" (1958); "(Everybody's Waitin' for) the Man with the Bag" (2008); "Hey Santa Claus" (1953); "I Saw Mommy Kissing Santa Claus" (1952); "I'm Gonna Tell Santa Claus on You" (1953); "(It Must've Been Ol') Santa Claus" (1993); "Little Saint Nick" (1963); "The Man with All the Toys" (1964); "Mr. Santa" (1955); "Rockin' 'N' Rollin' with Santa Claus" (1955); "Rockin' Santa Claus" (1959); "A Roly Poly (Rockin' Rollin' Santa Claus)" (1960); "A Rootin' Tootin' Santa Claus" (1951); "Santa Ain't Jivin'" (1997); "Santa Baby" (1953); "The Santa Claus Boogie" (1994); "Santa Claus Got Stuck (In My Chimney)" (1950); "Santa Claus Is Comin' (In a Boogie Woogie Choo Choo Train)" (1995); "Santa Claus Is Comin' to Town" (1934); "Santa Claus Is Watching You" (1962); "Santa Claus, Santa Claus" (1968); "Santa, Don't Let Me Down" (1995); "Santa Looked a Lot Like Daddy" (1965); "Santa on His 1990 Harley" (1989); "Santa's a Fat Bitch" (1997); "Santa's Got a Brand New Bag" (1965); "Santa's Messin' with the Kid" (1977); "Stay a Little Longer, Santa" (2003); "There's Trouble Brewin'" (1963); and "This Year's Santa Baby" (1954).

Beyond the North Pole's most famous imaginary figure, contemporary songwriters have created a fascinating menagerie of creatures who inhabit the Christmas audio landscape. For example, Alvin, Theodore, and Simon are key holiday performers in "The Chipmunk Song" (1968), "The Chipmunk Song (Christmas Don't Be Late)" (1958), and "Christmas Boogie" (1968). Of course the often frustrated David Seville serves as the ringmaster for the singing circus of chipmunks. Cowboy film star Gene Autry is associated with two other holiday figures:"Frosty the Snowman" (1951) and "Rudolph the Red Nosed Reindeer" (1950). The latter sleigh-puller has also been lauded in "Rudolph the Red-Nosed Reindeer" (1957) by The Cadillacs; "Run, Rudolph, Run" (1958) by Chuck Berry; and "They Shined up Rudolph's Nose" (1959) by Johnny Horton. Other fictional Christmas creatures include The Singing Dogs, who bark "Jingle Bells" (1975), as well as "Leroy the Redneck Reindeer" (1996); "Snoopy's Christmas" (1968); and "You're a Mean One, Mr. Grinch" (1966). Anthropomorphic humor aside, numerous Christmas novelty records portray human behavior as even more comical than most animal antics. From Spike Jones (1911–1965), Homer and Jethro (active 1936–1972), and Stan Freberg (1926–) to Pearl Bailey (1918–1990), Elmo and Patsy, and Yogi Yorgesson (1908–1956), novelty artists use linguistic tricks, TV and radio show parodies, and images drawn from an array of popular culture personalities to manufacture merry holiday madness. Recordings that tickle the Yuletide funny bone are "All I Want for Christmas (Is My Two Front Teeth)" (1950); "All I Want for Christmas (Is My Upper Plate)" (1953); "Christmas Dragnet—Parts 1 & 2" (1953); "Five Pound Box of Money" (1959); "Grandma Got Run Over by a Reindeer" (1981); "Green Chritma" (1958); "I Farted on Santa's Lap (Now Christmas Is Gonna Stink for Me)" (2002); "I Saw Mommy Kissing Santa Claus" (1952); "I Saw Mommy Smoochin' Santy Claus" (1953); "I Was a Bad Boy This Year" (2002); "I Yust Go Nuts at Christmas" (1950); "Merry Christmas in the N.F.L." (1980); "Monster's Holiday" (1962); "Please Daddy (Don't Get Drunk This Christmas)" (1973); "Santa and the Satellite—Parts 1 & 2" (1957); "The Twelve Blue Days of Christmas" (2002); "The Twelve Gifts of Christmas" (1963); "Yingle Bells" (1950); and "Yulesville" (1959).

Has there been any public backlash to the shifting themes presented in contemporary Christmas recordings? That is, do those who support family-centered values and traditional Christmas imagery object to the sexual innuendoes, drunken revelry, and comedic characters featured in modern holiday melodies? Do churchgoing listeners find the elevation of Santa Claus and commercialism over the Christ child and evangelism to be outrageous? The answer to all three questions is affirmative. Early on, Red Foley pleaded "Put Christ Back into Christmas" (1953). Among the contemporary recordings that continue to exhibit traditional holiday imagery are "The Little Drummer Boy" (1941); "Mary, Did You Know" (1993); "Mary's Boy Child" (1956); "Peace on Earth/Little Drummer Boy" (1982); "Do You Hear What I Hear?" (1962); "There's a New Kid in Town" (1993); "'Twas the Night Before Christmas" (1942); as well as modern recordings of traditional songs such as "Silent Night," "O Holy Night," "The Twelve Days of Christmas," and many, many more. Beyond those seeking more traditional audio fare at Christmastime, more radical songsmiths have utilized the season of peace and love to launch holiday anthems that decry the existence of poverty, international warfare, famine, homelessness, racial injustice, and political inequality. Social consciousness is displayed in Bob Geldof's and Band Aid's "Do They Know It's Christmas?" (1984); John Lennon and Yoko Ono's "Happy Xmas (War Is Over)" (1971); Roy Orbison's "Pretty Paper" (1963); James Brown's "Santa Claus Go Straight to the Ghetto" (1968); Simon and Garfunkel's "7 O'Clock News/Silent Night" (1966); and "Some Children See Him" (by Wihla Hudson and Alfred Burt, 1951), recorded by many singers, including James Taylor and Harry Connick Jr. with Wynton Marsalis.

Clearly, contemporary Christmas recordings are more diverse, more spicy, more politically motivated, more comedic, and more oriented toward Santa Claus and materialism than the pop and gospel discs of the 1920s, 1930s, and 1940s. Yet there is also ample audio evidence that traditional tunes—from "Silent Night" to "White Christmas"—and other songs that promote values of peace, love, and charity were composed, recorded, and released between 1950 and 2012.

See also: Autry, Gene; Blues; Cole, Nat King; Comedy and Satire in American Music; Crosby, Bing; Presley, Elvis; R&B

Further Reading

Collins, Ace. 2001. *Stories Behind the Best-Loved Songs of Christmas.* Grand Rapids, MI: Zondervan Press.

Cooper, B. Lee. 1991. "Christmas." In *Popular Music Perspectives: Ideas, Themes, and Patterns in Contemporary Lyrics,* 68–81. Bowling Green, OH: Bowling Green State University Press.

Cooper, B. Lee. 1990. "Christmas Songs as American Cultural History: Audio Resources for Classroom Investigation, 1940–1990." *Social Education* 54: 374–379.

Cooper, B. Lee. 1999–2000. "Holly Jolly Rock, Rhythm, and Blues: Christmas Recordings on Compact Disc." *Rock and Blues News* 7: 29–30.

Doggett, Peter. 1981. "Rockin' Around the Christmas Tree." *Record Collector* 28: 44–51.

Dr. Demento. 1977. "Santa and the Hot 100: The History of Holiday Hit-Making. *Waxpaper* 2: 18–20, 36.

Marling, Karla Ann. 2000. *Merry Christmas! Celebrating America's Greatest Holiday.* Cambridge, MA: Harvard University Press.

Marsh, Dave, and Steve Propes.1993. *Merry Christmas, Baby: Holiday Music from Bing to Sting.* Boston: Little, Brown.

Studwell, William. 1995. *The Christmas Carol Reader.* Binghamton, NY: Harrington Park Press.

B. Lee Cooper

Classical Music in America

Classical music is a term devised in the nineteenth and twentieth centuries to distinguish "art" music from folk music or popular music. In the United States it has often denoted music by composers who are familiar with or trained in the styles of European concert music from the eighteenth and nineteenth centuries. Although this has become less true in recent decades, in the early and mid-twentieth century classical music was often strenuously opposed to jazz and rock. Many saw classical music as a high or pure art form that needed to be preserved (in the manner of anything classic). More controversially, some felt the need to protect classical music from commercialism or other economic pressures and to keep it as free as possible from what they believed to be questionable or ephemeral social content.

The history of classical music in the United States is thus a history of importing and exporting (of music, musicians, and stylistic trends) and of changing ideas about education and social class. It is also a history populated by thousands upon thousands of individuals, most of whom were involved in more than one of the many aspects of musical life: performing, teaching, composing, and writing reviews or preconcert publicity. While this story is typically told by focusing on just a few composers and styles, it is important to remember that every composer reflects the preoccupations of his or her time, and that every piece can be seen as evidence of ideas not just about musical style, but also about larger cultural concerns.

The earliest institutions devoted to classical or art music in North America were, of course, colonial institutions: the churches of New England and the missions and cathedrals of New Spain. Although these institutions were devoted to religious music rather than secular or concert music, they were nonetheless the primary sites where one could find trained musicians, European-style instruments like the organ, and a healthy interest in matters of musical quality and style. In Puritan New England, debates centered on the proper performance practice for relatively simple settings of the biblical psalms, or psalmody, by composers such as William Billings (1746–1800), Daniel Read (1757–1836), and Timothy Swan (1758–1842). In the early eighteenth century, to enhance congregational participation, some communities hired an itinerant singing schoolteacher, who assembled men and women together for a short course in reading and singing from musical notation. A uniquely Anglo-American system of notation was devised to facilitate singing by those who had very little training. Using shaped noteheads to indicate where each note falls in the scale, this method persists today in groups of Sacred Harp singers, who take their name from the mid-nineteenth-century publications that shaped their repertoire, *The Southern Harmony* (1835) and *The Sacred Harp* (1844).

By contrast, the Catholic music performed in the eighteenth-century cathedrals of major cities in Mexico and South America could be quite elaborate, involving not just an organ but also orchestral accompaniment for choral music in the latest European styles of W. A. Mozart (1756–1792) and F. J. Haydn (1732–1809). Music in the frontier communities of California and the Spanish Catholic Southwest (New Mexico, Texas) was more austere and varied considerably from mission to mission, depending on the availability of instruments, the other demands of mission life, and the musical inclinations of the presiding padre. Mission music ranged from hymn tunes and simple choral settings to more intricate contrapuntal music. The mission community also witnessed performances of contemporary dramatic works called *tonadillas* and *zarzuelas,* imported directly from the metropolitan centers of Spain and Latin America.

With the significant exception of the Moravian communities who settled in Pennsylvania and North Carolina, secular or art music in the colonies usually involved solo songs and keyboard music performed in the home, by amateurs or by musicians who were employed in part by the church. Politicians like Thomas Jefferson (1743–1826) and Benjamin Franklin (1706–1790) were avid amateur musicians. Their associate Francis Hopkinson (1737–1791) was an accomplished harpsichord player, familiar with European operatic and instrumental music. In addition to writing patriotic songs and compiling them into short dramatic works, he wrote what is believed to be the first published composition by an American, his *Seven Songs for the Harpsichord or Forte Piano* (1788; dedicated to George Washington).

Because of its strong presence in eighteenth-century churches and its importance in Great Britain, choral music was the first to flourish in the northeastern United States. Choral societies quickly expanded their repertoire to include both sacred and secular music. Chief among these was the venerable Handel and Haydn Society. It was founded in Boston in 1815 and developed quickly under the leadership of Lowell Mason (1792–1872), a composer, conductor, music publisher, and key figure in nineteenth-century music education. Alongside the choral society, the wind band was perhaps the most important vehicle for secular music in most American towns and cities. Having outlasted its functional, military origins, the band became a regular ensemble, featuring marches and dance music, but also arrangements of European classical music, including opera overtures and works by Ludwig van Beethoven (1770–1827), Felix Mendelssohn (1809–1847), Richard Wagner (1813–1883), and Johann Strauss II (1825–1899). John Philip Sousa (1854–1932) later standardized an American band repertory of marches, first through his direction of the U. S. Marine Corps Band and then with his own professional ensemble.

Building on the success of traveling European singers, especially Swedish soprano Jenny Lind (1820–1887), opera companies, and virtuoso instrumentalists, American singers and ensembles gradually gained a foothold in the concert world, giving performances for a paying public. Pianist Louis Moreau Gottschalk (1829–1869), for example, toured the world performing his own compositions, often with allusions to Caribbean or Creole dance music that reflected his origins in New Orleans. Though organized, institutional performances would never fully replace free or ad hoc concert giving, many nineteenth-century ensembles, especially symphony orchestras and opera companies, began to adopt habits of classical concert life that are still familiar to us today: socially stratified seating based on tickets of different prices, concerts organized into a preplanned season, summer festivals, tours to outlying areas, and so forth. Another significant change in nineteenth-century classical concert life involved programming. Early concerts typically featured a potpourri of selections, interspersing arias for solo singer and orchestra, light dance music, and choral selections, with concert overtures and individual movements excerpted from symphonies. Bandmaster Patrick S. Gilmore (1829–1892) organized a massive Peace Jubilee in 1869, featuring more than ten thousand musicians and singers performing excerpts from symphonies, oratories, and other, shorter works. Influential conductors like Theodore Thomas (1835–1905) attempted to use the symphony orchestra to make "good music" popular. Over the course of the nineteenth century, however, orchestral concerts became less varied and more "serious," with strict expectations for dignified audience behavior and a reverent attitude toward the orchestral masterworks that has inspired cultural historian Lawrence Levine (1990) to call this a "sacralization" of musical culture. Whether this sacralization is seen as a beneficial reform movement or the repressive effect of cultural elitism, the attitudes it represented fall right in line with widespread ideas about classical music as a tool for personal improvement and social uplift.

For those who believed that the goal of classical music was social uplift, the best possible programming featured the recognized masterpieces of European music: Bach,

Beethoven, and Brahms, the emblematic figures of the classical repertory or canon. Yet from the start advocates like George Frederick Bristow (1825–1898) and William Henry Fry (1813–1864) argued for more frequent performances of works by American composers. The earliest of these composers were widely scattered and worked in relative isolation; for example, Anthony Philip Heinrich (1781–1861) immigrated from Central Europe to Kentucky, where he wrote several orchestral pieces before moving east to Boston in the 1820s and later to New York, where he played viola in the New York Philharmonic (founded 1841–1842). As the nineteenth century wore on, the status of American composers gradually rose in tandem with the establishment of American musical institutions (symphony orchestras, chamber music groups, opera companies, and music departments in universities). Around the turn of the century, growing up with this institutional infrastructure, a generation of American composers came of age who were interested not just in emulating European composers but also in creating a uniquely American sound.

Their efforts gained publicity and support when Jeanette Thurber invited Czech composer Antonín Dvořák (1841–1904) to direct the National Conservatory of Music in New York City. Dvořák's years at the Conservatory (1891–1895) also saw the composition of his famous Symphony in E Minor ("From the New World"), which, together with articles that the composer wrote for prominent American journals, sparked intense debate about whether Native American music and African American spirituals were the appropriate or even the best source material for American classical music. In fact, many American composers at the turn of the century chose to incorporate Native American melodies into their compositions, a practice known as Indianism and advocated especially by Arthur Farwell (1872–1952). The underlying assumption of Indianism was drawn from earlier European assumptions about musical nationalism: that to create a national-sounding classical music, one should incorporate indigenous or "native" folk music. While this worked reasonably well for European nations, it caused all sorts of controversy in the United States, a multiethnic nation of many immigrant groups. Many Indianist scores ended up sounding exotic to their audiences rather than national or familiar. Nonetheless, a handful of works like Edward MacDowell's (1860–1908) "Indian" Suite (1897) became relatively popular in the concert hall.

The "Indian" Suite was something of an exception for MacDowell, who generally distanced himself from prevalent ideas about nationalism. Like most American composers of the time, he found it necessary to study in Europe, and the influence of Franz Liszt (1811–1886) can be heard in his symphonic poems and virtuosic piano concertos. He also wrote numerous piano miniatures well known for their delicate harmonies and suitable for performance in the home, including the popular "To a Wild Rose" (1896). MacDowell was the first professor of music at Columbia University, and after his death his wife Marian founded an important artists' retreat in his memory. His contemporaries also became founding figures at institutions of higher learning as American composers began to seek training not just in Europe but also at home. These figures included John Knowles Paine (1836–1909) at Harvard University, Horatio Parker (1863–1919) at Yale, and George Whitefield Chadwick (1854–1931) at the New England Conservatory of Music. Chadwick had a pronounced American accent, frequently making use of melodies that sound like Anglo-American hymns or folk tunes in his symphonies, chamber music, and his opera *The Padrone* (1912), which is set in an Italian immigrant community. Standing somewhat apart from these Yankee gentlemen was Amy Beach (1867–1944)—known in her lifetime as Mrs. H. H. A. Beach—whose harmonic language was more adventurous and whose career path was shaped by the fact that she was an upper-class woman. She was not allowed to study abroad or to meet

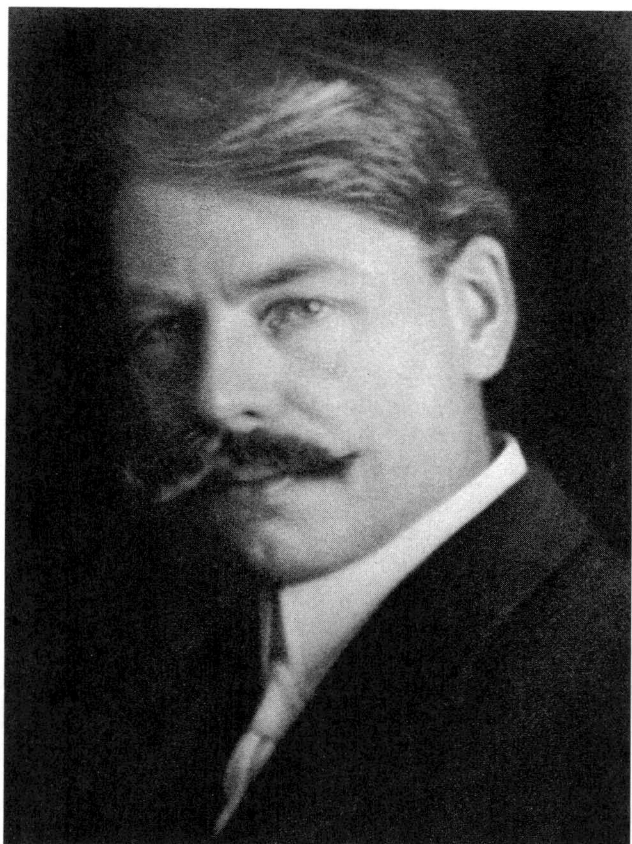

American composer and pianist Edward MacDowell, 1937. (Library of Congress)

informally with the male composers of her generation in Boston's social clubs. She was a child prodigy on the piano and taught herself composition and orchestration by careful study of published scores and by attending the rehearsals of the Boston Symphony Orchestra (founded in 1881), for whom she composed her "Gaelic" Symphony (1896) and a Piano Concerto (1900). She also wrote many highly acclaimed songs. Though her marriage curtailed her career as a performer—it was considered inappropriate for her to appear too often or too prominently on the stage—it gave her the financial security to devote herself to composition.

In terms of lasting influence and stylistic change, the most important American composer of the early twentieth century was Charles Ives (1874–1954). Like Beach, he did not need to make a living through music; he gained financial independence as a successful insurance salesman. Outside of business hours, he composed highly imaginative and sometimes erratic or unfinished scores. Though he worked for a time as a church organist and studied at Yale with the relatively conservative Horatio Parker, Ives preferred to cite his inventive bandmaster father as his chief musical influence. In "Putnam's Camp" from *Three Places in New England* (1914, rev. 1929), he captured a child's excitement at a Fourth of July picnic by drawing upon the musical resources of band music, ragtime, and patriotic song. In typical Ivesian fashion, however, he placed these familiar tunes or styles in a context that makes them sound strange: unpredictable juxtapositions, surprising key changes, innovative harmonies, and even a passage that imitates the sound of two bands marching at two different tempos. Many of his string quartets and symphonies also make extensive use of quotations from hymn tunes and patriotic or popular songs.

While some of Ives's music displays complex textures and a humorous or boisterous spirit, other works are more contemplative. One of Ives's most frequently performed scores is *The Unanswered Question* (1906), in which a solo trumpet interjects its angular and searching melody into a nearly static background of slow-moving and consonant string parts, sparking a series of increasingly aggressive responses from a group of flutes. This work is characteristic of Ives's in its unusual performing forces and its aim to push listeners out of their complacent listening habits. In this goal, Ives was influenced by the New England philosophical and literary movement of transcendentalism, which involved such writers as Ralph Waldo Emerson and Henry David Thoreau. Ives memorialized these men, along with Nathaniel Hawthorne and the Alcott family, in his impressive and intricate *Concord* Sonata for solo piano, which incorporates Beethoven, hymn tunes, ragtime, and other material in a web of musical forms and motivic allusions.

Many of Ives's scores exist in multiple versions; he did not always prepare his manuscripts fully for publication and performance. The *Concord* Sonata, for example, was composed between 1909 and 1915, first published in 1920, and most frequently performed in a much later edition prepared by John Kirkpatrick (1892–1915). Ives's unwillingness to finalize his scores and his purposeful alienation from the conventional musical institutions of his day meant that most of his music was relatively unknown until long after it had been written. Apart from the *Concord* Sonata, Ives's music was chiefly circulated through a volume called *114 Songs,* which he published and disseminated himself. Here one can find some of the composer's best-loved songs, including "The Housatonic at Stockbridge" (depicting a walk by a misty river), "Majority" (featuring cluster chords), "Charlie Rutlage" (based on a cowboy song), and a number of evocations of World War I, which had a shattering effect on the composer and his creativity.

Though Ives stopped composing around 1920, it was not until the 1930s and 1940s that other composers discovered his music, usually through the *114 Songs.* Among his early champions were Henry Cowell (1897–1965), Aaron Copland (1900–1990), and Elliott Carter (1908–2012). Cowell was a child prodigy and quickly gained notoriety because of his iconoclastic keyboard techniques. In pieces like "Tides of Manaunaun" (ca. 1917) he exploited what he called "tone clusters," in which the player's entire fist or forearm is used to depress large spans of adjacent keys at once; in "The Banshee" (1925) and "Aeolian Harp" (1923), Cowell instructs the performer to strum and pluck the interior strings of the piano, creating ethereal and eerie sound pictures. Cowell was extremely influential on later composers, especially John Cage (1912–1992), because of his iconoclastic use of the piano, the new types of musical notation his music required, and his attention to non-Western or "world" music as a resource for contemporary composition. In similar fashion, the emigré composer Edgard Varèse (1883–1965) drew upon percussion instruments from around the world and increased the ratio of allowable "noise" in American classical music by including sirens and other mechanical sounds; later in the 1950s, Varèse was also a pioneer in electronic music.

While Cowell's and Varèse's music seemed eccentric to many audiences—they were sometimes known as "ultramodern" composers—both were great organizers and promoters of music by their contemporaries. During the 1910s and 1920s many organizations were founded to support "new music" in urban centers like New York City. The International Composers Guild, founded by Varèse and Carlos Salzedo (1885–1961); the League of Composers (which broke away from the Guild in 1923); and Cowell's own New Music Society (founded in 1925) commissioned and performed new American works that were often excluded from conservative concert halls and sponsored the U.S. premieres of important European scores by Schoenberg, Stravinsky, and others. Many of these organizations also published journals full of reviews and essays on contemporary music, often written by the composers themselves. These "composer-critics" helped explain new music to audiences who sometimes needed their help to understand new trends in musical style and technology.

Among these composer-critics were Virgil Thomson (1896–1989), Roger Sessions (1896–1989), Copland, and Carter. Like American composers of previous generations, these men traveled to Europe to hone their compositional skills, but in the aftermath of World War I they gravitated to France and Italy rather than Germany. Thomson in particular maintained a French address for decades and was deeply influenced by the French composer Erik Satie (1866–1925). Even after he returned to the United States to become chief music critic for the *New York Herald Tribune,* he maintained close ties to the other expatriate Americans he had met in Paris, particularly Gertrude Stein (1874–1946), who wrote the texts for his Americana operas *Four Saints in Three Acts* (which featured an all-black cast) and *The Mother of Us All* (about Susan B. Anthony and women's suffrage). Like Thomson, George Antheil (1900–1959) also gained fame in Paris before returning to the States. Taking the riotous premiere of Igor Stravinsky's (1882–1971) *Rite of Spring* as a benchmark, his noisy *Ballet Méchanique* (1924) earned him a reputation as the "bad boy" of American music and overshadowed his more serious, later scores.

Many who went to Paris chose to study with Nadia Boulanger (1887–1979), a composer and conductor in her own right, but best known as a teacher. On the one hand, Boulanger helped generations of American composers find their own "voices," sometimes embracing the sounds of jazz, which was very popular in Paris during and after the war. On the other hand, Boulanger acted as a surrogate for Stravinsky (who had few students of his own), propagating his ideas about neoclassicism: a supposedly "objective" reaction to the emotional excesses of German romantic music, emphasizing instead clarity of form, careful control of phrasing, and sometimes lighthearted references to the music of pre-romantic composers like Mozart and J. S. Bach.

Boulanger's most famous pupil was Aaron Copland. When he returned to the United States in 1924, he was gripped by the desire to bring art music into contact with life around him. In the 1920s, especially in his native New York City, this meant experimenting with fusions between classical music and jazz. In 1924 audiences at New York's Aeolian Hall had experienced a watershed work in George Gershwin's *Rhapsody in Blue,* commissioned by swing bandleader Paul Whiteman. Building on his experiences with the New York sheet music industry (Tin Pan Alley), George Gershwin (1898–1937) created a tuneful, appealing score that still carried some of the colorful components of jazz and blues. *Rhapsody in Blue* was advertised as an "experiment in modern music" and was widely seen as an "elevation" of jazz to a level of greater social respectability. Gershwin's opera *Porgy and Bess* (1935) remains one of the few American operas to secure a place in the international repertory, and its most famous number, the lullaby "Summertime," has been adopted as the basis for many jazz improvisations. By contrast, Copland's jazziest scores, *Music for the Theatre* (1925) and the Piano Concerto of 1926, preserved the more dissonant harmonies and aggressive rhythms typical of Stravinsky and other modernists. Dissonance, austerity, and tight motivic construction also characterize what many consider Copland's most important early work: the *Piano Variations* (1930). Though these works were less well received by the general public, they still helped Copland make a name for himself as the leading classical composer of his generation.

Although jazz rhythms and instrumentation remained part of his compositional language, Copland's appreciation for the improvisatory character and emotional variety of jazz music was somewhat limited, and he subsequently turned to other types of folklore (Latin and Anglo-American). By contrast, African American composer William Grant Still (1895–1978) worked extensively as a jazz arranger in addition to studying with Chadwick and Varèse. He produced a wide range of neoclassical and African American–inspired scores such as *From the Land of Dreams* (1924) and the *Afro-American Symphony* (1930), as well as numerous dramatic works, including the opera *Troubled Island* (1937–1949) and the cantata *And They Lynched Him on a Tree* (1940). Edward Kennedy "Duke" Ellington (1899–1974) went still further in blurring the boundaries between jazz arranging and classical composition. In 1943 he wrote the epic *Black, Brown, and Beige* for jazz orchestra (1943), which premiered at Carnegie Hall and was devoted to depicting episodes in African American history; later in life he composed a number of equally ambitious suites and sacred works.

During the Great Depression many composers and other intellectuals felt the pull of leftist politics, including socialism and communism. The capitalist system seemed to have failed, and in the midst of this economic crisis, it seemed appropriate to reach out to the largest possible audience. Copland was a lifelong leftist, and in the 1930s this was reflected in his more accessible, populist scores. First among these was *El Salón México*

(1932–1936), written after composer Carlos Chávez (1899–1978) invited him to visit Mexico. Of equal importance were the three Americana ballets Copland wrote for famous American choreographers: *Billy the Kid* (1938, for Eugene Loring and Lincoln Kirstein), *Rodeo* (1942, for Agnes de Mille), and *Appalachian Spring* (1946, for Martha Graham). Other composers who had previously espoused modernist techniques, including Marc Blitzstein (1905–1964), Elie Siegmeister (1909–1991), and Ruth Crawford Seeger (1901–1953), turned instead toward simpler music and folk-song arranging.

World War II inspired many composers to write patriotic scores. Roy Harris's Third Symphony (1939), commissioned by Serge Koussevitzky (1874–1951) and the Boston Symphony Orchestra, became one of the most frequently performed American symphonies during the war, and he followed this with *Folksong Symphony* (1940) and many other works reflecting the American scene. Harris's pupil William Schuman (1910–1992) also composed a number of significant works for orchestra and band. Copland's own massive Third Symphony (1942–1946) alternates military and pastoral passages, while also incorporating the music of his famous *Fanfare for the Common Man* (1942). This latter score, with its reference to the "common man," carries special significance for a composer like Copland, who reached national fame but could easily have been marginalized because of his Russian Jewish heritage, his leftist politics, or his homosexuality. More than many other composers, Copland was comfortable with his sexuality, and he served as an inspiration to younger gay or bisexual composers, including the neotonal composer Samuel Barber (1910–1981) and his partner, the opera composer Gian Carlo Menotti (1911–2007), the songwriter Ned Rorem (1923–), and the famous conductor-composer Leonard Bernstein (1918–1990), whose scores range from fervent symphonies, to an eclectic mass, to the iconic show *West Side Story* (1957).

Even during wartime, not all American composers of Copland's generation were keen to borrow folk songs or rouse patriotic fervor. Some found the union of music and politics distasteful and strove instead for ever greater clarity and ever more intricate structures. These trends were bolstered by the emigration to the United States of many of Europe's most famous composers, fleeing the racial policies of the Nazi regime and the general disruption of concert life across the continent. Among Americans, Sessions and Walter Piston were especially successful in combining widely held neoclassical ideals with their own individual idioms. Elliott Carter, slightly younger than Sessions or Walter Piston (1894–1976), infused neoclassical genres like the string quartet with a new and pressing sense of dramatic action. Carter is most famous for his treatment of time and tempo, especially for the technique of "metric modulation," in which subdivisions of the beat are regrouped to effect a smooth change from one meter to another. He remained an active composer even after turning one hundred years old, and some of his more recent works are large-scale and vocal, including the song cycle *Tempo e Tempi* (1998–1999, for soprano and chamber ensemble) and the opera *What Next?* (2008).

Carter's attention to fine nuances of musical gesture and structure were typical of American classical music in the postwar and Cold War years, decades devoted to the exploration of musical freedom and control. Reacting against the intense patriotism of the war years, and in marked contrast to the government-imposed populism forced upon composers working on the Soviet side of the Iron Curtain, composers in the United States and Western Europe embraced a more abstract musical language. The desire to elevate musical structure above easily recognizable content is best exemplified by the development and intensification of the "serial" or twelve-tone techniques of Arnold Schoenberg (1874–1951) and his students, especially Alban Berg (1885–1935) and Anton Webern (1883–1945). After much trial and error, Schoenberg had departed radically from the conventional major or minor scales, which gave rise to relatively predictable points of harmonic tension and release. Instead he aimed to "emancipate dissonance," by organizing all twelve pitches of the chromatic scale into a row or "series" and using the properties of this row to generate new kinds of melody and harmony. In the 1940s and 1950s, inspired by a desire for mathematical purity and "scientific" progress, composers extended these same principles to organize not just pitches but also rhythms, dynamics, and even instrumentation. This method was known as "total serialism"; among Americans, Milton Babbitt (1916–2011) was its most famous proponent.

There were many American precedents for serial composers' preoccupation with musical structure. Copland's *Piano Variations,* for example, had the tight motivic organization, spiky dissonances, and angularity of much serial music. And Ruth Crawford Seeger's String Quartet (1931) had effectively serialized aspects of duration and dynamics. In the postwar West, efforts to increase the rigor and complexity of musical utterance found a natural home in universities and research institutes, as the career of Milton Babbitt makes clear. Except for his service during World War II, he spent his student years and most of his adult career at Princeton University. Though he was a fan of Broadway musicals, Babbitt believed that as a composer it was his job to "advance" the art of music, rather than entertaining audiences. He encapsulated these views in an essay called "The

Composer as Specialist," but better known under the more provocative title that an editor provided for it: "Who Cares If You Listen?" Here Babbitt argued that composers, like scientists, did not need to cater to the common man, but should answer instead to the higher ideals of progress and rigorous investigation, for which university music departments offered an appropriate laboratory environment. Indeed, the cultural prestige of serial composition at major U.S. universities was such that even a populist composer like Copland felt compelled to try his hand at composing in this radically unpopulist style during the 1960s and 1970s.

While serial composers of the postwar period responded to a desire for greater control and precision of musical language, other composers sought instead to transform the way music is defined and perceived. No one was more influential than John Cage in articulating the philosophy of what is commonly called experimental music, but might better be called experiential music. Cage was particularly interested in blurring the boundaries between music and noise. In his early years, working with Lou Harrison (1917–2003), he favored the percussion ensemble; building on Cowell's earlier work, he invented the prepared piano by inserting objects (screws, erasers, etc.) into the piano strings to make the sound more varied and more percussive. Cage considered all sound to be worthy of our attention. More radically, he wanted listeners to hear and value each sound independently, without recourse to the conventional relationships between sounds suggested by scales, chord progressions, or regular meters. Cage's most infamous creation, the "silent" piece called *4′33″*, takes its title from the total duration of its three movements and consists of all the atmospheric sounds that happen to occur in the room during that time period.

4′33″ reflects many of Cage's most important aesthetic principles: the sounds will be different at every performance, the meaning of the piece depends primarily on the listener, and the old habits of concert behavior are called into question. By setting a temporal or durational "frame," Cage found a way to create music without intentionally specifying what sounds would occur. In the later decades of his career, he explored ever more inventive ways of distancing the music he wrote from his own personal preferences. Cage is associated with "indeterminacy," "chance music," or "aleatory music," in which certain compositional decisions are delegated to such random processes as flipping coins, throwing dice, or using the Chinese book of changes, the I Ching. He wrote pieces for unusual sound sources (including radio, cactus needles, and flower pots), dictating with great precision how and when the performer should move, but leaving to chance the sounds that might result.

Cage influenced a very broad spectrum of composers on both sides of the Atlantic. In his attempt to remove artistic intention from the creative process, his ideas were shaped by Eastern philosophy, seeking to "quiet the mind" and open it to "divine influences." A similar impulse animates the scores of Morton Feldman (1926–1987), which are often exquisitely delicate, pointillistic in nature, and meditative in scope, but without relying on "chance" procedures. Cage's close associates Christian Wolff (1934–) and Earle Brown (1926–2002) are best known for their graphic scores, which challenge performers to give their own musical interpretation of geometric patterns and other visual stimuli. Some members of Cage's generation made independent innovations in the realms of rhythm, pitch, and tuning. Harry Partch (1901–1974) created entirely new instruments designed in accordance with the mathematically perfect ratios of "just intonation," rather than the imperfect ones of the well-tempered keyboard. Inspired by the technology of the player piano, Conlon Nancarrow (1912–1997) wrote pieces that require a superhuman rhythmic virtuosity and velocity. Many other composers in later years have taken Cage's embrace of noise and his questioning of concert hall decorum to new heights and depths. Among these may be counted performance artists Meredith Monk (1942–) and Laurie Anderson (1947–), whose work gained an enormous crossover following in the 1980s. From the late 1960s to the present, Pauline Oliveros (1932–) has explored the ideas of "deep listening" and "sonic meditation," using her own keen ear and a vision of the psychological and spiritual power of music to create powerful and often collaborative musical experiences.

From the start, the emphasis in experimental music on percussion and unusual sound sources reflects a much broader feeling of dissatisfaction with the resources and tone colors of conventional orchestral instruments and techniques. Throughout the second half of the twentieth century, composers demanded more elaborate and more challenging special effects, known as "extended techniques," from instrumentalists and vocalists dedicated to the performance of contemporary music. This trend arose hand in hand with the invention of new instruments and the new sonic possibilities provided by amplification and electronics. The development of magnetic tape in the 1940s allowed composers to record and manipulate everyday sounds, creating collages known as *musique concrète.* Electronically generated sounds and the earliest synthesizers allowed for wholly novel sounds, which could be manipulated with far greater precision than a live performer might achieve.

These developments were especially satisfying to Varèse, whose compositional life reached a virtual standstill in the 1930s and 1940s as he waited for technology to catch up with his visions of "sound masses" and instruments "obedient" to every nuance of his fertile imagination. When such instruments finally became available, he produced two of his latest and best known works: *Déserts* (1950–1954), which alternates passages for acoustic instruments with episodes of *musique concrète,* and *Poème Electronique,* written to be projected from speakers installed inside a pavilion designed by the Swiss architect Le Corbusier for the Brussels World's Fair in 1959. For decades before the advent of the personal computer, electronic music had to be written at electronic music studios specially equipped for the purpose. Babbitt produced his best known electronic piece, *Philomel* (1964), at the Columbia-Princeton Electronic Music Center in New York City. Based on John Hollander's poetic retelling of a Greek myth, it features a soprano who performs live and a tape part made up of electronic sounds, including the prerecorded voice of soprano Bethany Beardslee (1927–). Like many electronic works, *Philomel* invites questions about the act of performance, the placement of sound sources (speakers) on stage, and the impact of technology both to enhance and to restrict the freedom of composers and performers. Mario Davidovsky (1934–) has grappled with these issues in his impressive series of pieces called *Synchronisms* (1962–present), and composers continue to respond individually and collectively to successive waves of music technology: new computer algorithms, digital sampling, and multisite performance opportunities made possible by the Internet.

The most widely acknowledged union of music and technology came not from the rarified realms of the electronic music studio, but rather as a reaction against the dissonant strictures of serialism and the distance that many modernist works maintained from the average listener. By analogy to a movement in the visual arts and architecture, this trend is typically called minimalism, whether the composers like it or not. LaMonte Young (1935–) composed scores consisting of single tones, chords, or other radically simple material sustained for minutes at a time. In San Francisco in 1964, Terry Riley (1935–) wrote the pioneering *In C* for any combination of instruments. *In C* consists of fifty-three short fragments, firmly suggesting C as a consonant tonal center. Each player repeats each fragment as many times as he or she wishes before moving on to the next one. The result is an overlapping but rhythmically steady collage.

The best known minimalists are Steve Reich (1936–) and Philip Glass (1937–). Both were trained in twelve-tone composition; both became fascinated by the rhythmic patterning of non-Western music; and both founded their own performing ensembles, devoted to tonal, repetitive, highly patterned, and high-energy music, often incorporating references to modern rock, either in instrumentation or in rhythm. Reich came to prominence with his ideas about "process music," wherein a piece is shaped by the unfolding of a single, gradual, audible process. Initially, Reich was enabled by the techniques of electronic music: recording the same sound music on two loops of magnetic tape and allowing these loops to move gradually out of sync with one another during playback. This gave rise to his purely electronic *It's Gonna Rain* (1965) and *Come Out* (1966), but also laid the groundwork for acoustic scores like *Violin Phase* and *Piano Phase,* both written in 1967. More recently Reich has used musical processes with greater flexibility in such scores as *Music for 18 Musicians* (1974–1976) and *Different Trains* (1988), which uses recorded voices to reflect on the transport trains of the Holocaust, contrasting them with the railroad cars Reich himself rode as a child in the United States.

While Reich was influenced by the interlocking patterns of African drumming, Philip Glass incorporated the additive and subtractive rhythmic patterning of South Indian tala structures in his scores. He made a specialty of multimedia works, beginning with the hypnotic operatic blockbuster *Einstein on the Beach* (1976), a five-hour, nearly textless "portrait" of Einstein, staged by Robert Wilson. Glass's later operas and especially his film scores have made him probably the most often heard "classical" composer of the twentieth century. More properly considered a postminimalist, John Adams (1947–) is also best known for his dramatic works, although he has written in many genres. *Nixon in China* (1985–1987) was the first of several operas focused on recent history or current events, the newest of which, *Doctor Atomic* (2004–2005), treats Robert Oppenheimer and the team that created the atom bomb. Adams has also written popular concert works, such as *Short Ride in a Fast Machine* (1986) and the more meditative *On the Transmigration of Souls* (2002), a response to the attacks of September 11, 2001.

If one had to choose a single, overarching trend to represent American classical music in the later twentieth and early twenty-first centuries (minimalism included), that trend would probably involve the fusion of sound sources and styles from diverse times and places. In pointed reaction to the ideal of unrelenting artistic "progress" espoused by many serial composers, George Rochberg (1918–2005) in the 1970s began writing string quartets whose sounding surface is practically indistinguishable from Beethoven or Bela Bartók (1881–1948), but whose real meaning depends on a uniquely twentieth-century feeling of retrospect. Unlike the earlier neoclassical impulse, which sought to achieve a kind of "purity" or "objectivity," many of these latter-day fusions call attention in an Ivesian way to the significance of borrowed material and point up the incongruity of this material within its new surroundings. George Crumb's (1929–) *Black Angels* (1970), for amplified string quartet, incorporates quotations from Schubert, Saint-Saens, and Renaissance composer John Dowland (1563–1626) in a haunting response to the Vietnam War. The San Francisco–based Kronos Quartet was formed in part because of the inspiring example of this piece, exemplifying the close and often symbiotic relationship between composers and performing ensembles devoted to new music. William Bolcom (1938–), John Corigliano (1938–), John Harbison (1938–), and many others have also made imaginative use of the classical tradition to create new and compelling scores.

Another type of fusion involves the combination of classical with popular music or world music. This habit is as old as classical music itself, but it has been intensified and accelerated by today's nearly instant availability of sound recordings and digital sound files from what Cowell once called "the whole world of music." Like the attempts in the 1920s to fuse classical music and jazz (given further impetus in the 1960s by conductor-composer Gunther Schuller [1925–] and his idea of "third stream" music), new fusions by David Lang (1957–), Steven Mackey (1957–), Michael Torke (1961–), and John Zorn (1953–), among many others, have disrupted older stories about classical music as an elite phenomenon, capable of transcending the messy imperfections of modern life. Though sometimes criticized as careless or "eclectic," these fusions across geographical boundaries or perceived class or ethnic lines continue to have an enormous vitalizing effect on contemporary classical music and its social significance in the United States.

See also: Adams, John Coolidge; Art Music (Mainstream); Bernstein, Leonard; Cage, John; Cajun and Creole Music; Copland, Aaron; Distortion and Feedback; Electronic and Computer Music; Ellington, Duke; Expatriate Musicians in the United States; Folk Music; Gershwin, George; Glass, Phillip; Ives, Charles; Jazz; Latin Music in the United States; Minimalism; Native American Music; Partch, Harry; Pop Music; Reich, Steve; Sacred Music; Seeger Family; Shape Note Singing; Silence in Music; Sousa, John Philip; Technology and Music; Tin Pan Alley; World Music

Further Reading

Alexander, J. Heywood. 2002. *To Stretch Our Ears: A Documentary History of America's Music.* New York: W. W. Norton.

Chase, Gilbert. 1987. *America's Music, from the Pilgrims to the Present.* Rev. 3rd ed. Urbana: University of Illinois Press.

Crawford, Richard. 1993. *The American Musical Landscape.* Berkeley and Los Angeles: University of California Press.

Crawford, Richard. 2001. *America's Musical Life: A History.* New York: W. W. Norton.

Gann, Kyle. 1997. *American Music in the Twentieth Century.* New York: Schirmer Books.

Hamm, Charles. 1983. *Music in the New World.* New York: W. W. Norton.

Hitchcock, H. Wiley. 1969. *Music in the United States: A Historical Introduction.* Englewood Cliffs, NJ: Prentice-Hall.

Horowitz, Joseph. 2005. *Classical Music in America: A History of Its Rise and Fall.* New York: W. W. Norton.

Levine, Lawrence. 1990. *Highbrow/Lowbrow: The Emergence of Cultural Hierarchy in America.* Cambridge, MA: Harvard University Press.

Nicholls, David, ed. 1998. *The Cambridge History of American Music.* New York: Cambridge University Press.

Oja, Carol. 2000. *Making Music Modern: New York in the 1920s.* New York: Oxford University Press.

Struble, John Warthen. 1995. *The History of American Classical Music: MacDowell through Minimalism.* New York: Facts on File.

Tick, Judith. 2008. *Music in the USA: A Documentary Companion.* New York: Oxford University Press.

Beth E. Levy

Classical Music, Women in

Art music in the United States has historically provided the same opportunities and challenges for women's participation as in other professions. Although doors have gradually opened in the world of music as they have in other arenas, just like in business and politics, lower and mid-level doors are more easily accessed than higher positions. At the beginning of the second decade of the twenty-first century, highly successful singers and instrumental soloists abound, and women comprise about one-third of the performers in the major symphonies, but the repertoire played is still overwhelmingly male. Female musicians are beginning to win major artistic awards, yet only one woman has become the music director of a major American symphony orchestra. What has facilitated the growth of women's professional success in music is the same as in all professions: women forging new paths individually coupled with broader social changes. As goes the nation, so goes the symphony.

The United States inherited its elite culture and social mores from Europe. Women received musical training as they received lessons in all of the feminine accomplishments, so that they could entertain prospective

Violinist Maud Powell, ca. 1919. (Library of Congress)

suitors as teenagers and create a gracious domestic atmosphere as married adults. They learned to sing, dance, and play properly feminine instruments such as the piano, guitar, and harp to skill levels commensurate with their musical abilities and household educational budget. Since in the upper classes women's sphere was the home, respectable women were expected to perform in the home as much as they were forbidden to perform publicly. This social requirement gave women with musical abilities and ambitions both the opportunity to study music seriously and a private venue for musical performance.

The first professional musicians in the United States came from Europe, and because opera needs female performers for female roles, the earliest women touring came with theatrical companies. Mary Ann Pownall (1751–1796) came to America from England in 1792, Maria Malibran (1808–1836) began performing in Italian opera in the United States in 1825, and Swedish singer Jenny Lind (1820–1867) started concertizing in 1850.

The city of Boston seemed to be a nurturing place for women, and throughout the nineteenth century many of the women who succeeded in public performance originated there. One of the first paid female instrumentalists was Sophia Hewitt (1799–1845), who was hired as the organist for the Handel and Haydn society in Boston in 1820 (Ammer 2001, 17). Although she only accompanied the society for a decade, she taught and performed professionally throughout her life. Her daughter, Eliza Ostinelli Biscaccianti (1824–1896), became one of the first American-born professional concert singers. Classically trained vocalists who followed her include Clara Louise Kellog (1842–1916), Emma Abbot (1850–1891), Annie Louise Cary (1841–1931), Minnie Hauk (1851–1925), and Alma Gluck (1884–1938). Elizabeth Taylor Greenfield (ca. 1817–1876) was the first African American female classical concert singer; Sissieretta Jones (1869–1933) followed in her wake, as did Anna Madah Hyers (1853–1934) and Emma Louise Hyers (1855–1904), who even ran their own theatrical company for a few years.

During the second half of the nineteenth century a fashion for virtuosi coincided with growing awareness and interests in women's rights, and music conservatories began accepting women, making the highest level of musical education available to them. The number of women who made money through music increased to the point where it is impossible to include a complete list in this short entry. Pianists included Teresa Carreño (1853–1917), Julie Rivé-King (1854–1937), and Fannie Bloomfield Zeisler (1863–1927). Camilla Urso (1842–1902), a child prodigy, was the first female professional violinist, and Maud Powell (1867–1920) was possibly the most famous nineteenth-century female American violinist.

Although women were mostly barred from playing in professional orchestras with men, in the 1870s, after a visit from the Vienna Ladies Orchestra, which toured to great success in the United States in 1871, all-women's instrumental ensembles began to form. Toward the end of the century there were a number of all-female bands and orchestras playing locally as well as occasionally touring. Most groups played both classical and popular music, but an increasing number of women's symphony orchestras were established to perform serious art music.

Traditionally both men and women growing up in musical families were trained in composition as they were trained on their instruments and voices, and a public performance was not complete without a composition written by the performer. Mary Ann Pownall's concert repertoire included her own songs, as did those of Faustine Hasses Hodges (1822–1895), church organist Susan Parkhurst (1846–1918), pianist Teresa Carreño, Augusta Browne (1821–1882), and Carrie Jacobs-Bond (1861–1946).

Because parlor music—light music for home entertainment—was the domestic purview of women, some of the published parlor music of the nineteenth century was by women. By the end of the century the conservatory training necessary to write large and complex art works was available to women in New England, and a small group of women composers of art music emerged. Helen Hopekirk (1856–1945) and Margaret Ruthven Lang (1867–1971) wrote primarily chamber music; Amy Beach (1867–1944), the most successful and famous of these early women composers, was the first American woman to write both a symphony and a large-scale mass.

As the twentieth century saw the expansion of women's political rights into the right to vote and hold office as well as some economic success on corporate ladders, so female musicians gained continuing support and success. Vocal music continued to be considered the most feminine, so solo and choral singers succeeded in greater numbers and with greater equity than in other areas. Instrumentalists began to gain entry into professional male-dominated symphony orchestras in 1903, when the musicians union began to accept women. After World War I more women were able to join professional as well as community orchestras, but until the 1980s women comprised less than 10 percent of professional orchestral performers. In the 1970s and 1980s, when blind auditions began to replace the typical network-based hiring process, the proportion of women in major symphony orchestras grew, and it stands today at around 35 percent (Goldin and Rouse 2000). As women gained more access to major symphony orchestras, all-female ensembles began to dwindle. While most of the earlier ensembles stopped operating, both the Women Composers Orchestra of Baltimore/Maryland Women's Symphony (1985–1996) and the Bay Area Women's Philharmonic/Women's Philharmonic (1991–2004) were established toward the end of the twentieth century, not only to support female orchestral musicians, but also to play compositions by women, which continue to be programmed in disproportionately low numbers.

The twentieth century brought multiple compositional styles to play in art music, and a complete list of composers is impractical. Marion Bauer (1887–1955) worked with impressionistic idioms; Elinor Remick Warren (1906–1991) wrote in a neoromantic style, and both Louise Talma (1906–1996) and Dika Newlin (1923–2006) explored twelve-tone compositions. American nationalist composers employed regional and ethnically based sounds. In the 1920s the Harlem Renaissance had expanded opportunities for African Americans; Florence Price (1887–1953), Margaret Bonds (1913–1972), and Undine Smith Moore (1904–1989) incorporated styles from their rich musical traditions into their compositions, as did succeeding black composers such as Julia Perry (1924–1979), Evelyn La Rue Pittman (1910–), and Lena McLin (1929–). Alice Parker (1925–) used southern idioms and American subjects. Julia Frances Smith (1911–1989) and Radie Britain (1903–1994) incorporated the American musical idioms of the rural West and Southwest into their compositions.

Marga Richter (1926–) included non-Western instruments in standard Western ensembles; Barbara Kolb (1939–) used prerecorded instruments and other electronically generated sounds with live performance. Some of Pauline Oliveros's (1932–) work employs computer-generated sounds, as well as improvisation. Meredith Monk (1942–) works with dance and movement as much as voice, and Laurie Anderson (1947–) works with mixed and multimedia.

The creation of compositions determines only part of the composer's success; for works to be recognized they must be performed. Amy Beach was the first woman to have large works performed. Her *Mass in E-flat,* though a critical success, was only performed once in her lifetime. Her *Gaelic Symphony* premiered in 1896 and was played a number of times after that before World War I. Harriet Ware's (1877–1962) symphonic poem *The Artisan* was programmed in 1929 by the New York Symphony Orchestra. George Barrère's Little Symphony in New York programmed several works by Mary Howe (1882–1964), as did the Society of American Women Composers, and in 1954 the Vienna Symphony Orchestra in Austria programmed three of her symphonies. Florence Price's Symphony in E Minor was the first symphony by an African American woman to be performed by a major symphony orchestra when played by the Chicago Symphony in 1933. Several orchestras, including the Los Angeles Philharmonic, the New York Philharmonic, and the Detroit Symphony, programmed Elinor Remick Warren's works. These early examples of programming have not proved as effective to opening more doors to more female composers, as might be expected, and women's compositions today comprise less than 10 percent of the music played by American symphony orchestras.

Perhaps the most difficult performing role that a woman might pursue is conducting, because this is the job demanding the most power and status. Even many of the early all-women ensembles had male conductors. Possibly because women were in choirs long before they were accepted in orchestras, women choral conductors have been more prevalent than women orchestral conductors. Hermine Rudersdorff (1822–1882) conducted the Handel and Haydn Society of Boston in parts of Mendelsson's *Elijah* in 1872, and Selma Borg conducted one performance of it at Boston's Music Hall in June 1879. By the turn of the century two women, Caroline

Nichols (1864–1939) and Emma Steiner (1852–1929), were conducting regularly, the former a woman's ensemble, and the latter working primarily in light opera.

In the twentieth century a few women, like Ethel Leginska (1886–1970) and Antonia Brico (1902–1989), founded all-women's orchestras to conduct in the absence of regular work with male-dominated orchestras, because opportunities for women were still scarce in the second half of the century. After Sarah Caldwell (1924–2006) broke ground in the 1970s as a guest conductor with major orchestras, including the Metropolitan Opera and the New York Philharmonic, JoAnn Falleta (1954–) was appointed the music director of the Long Beach Symphony in 1989, the Virginia Symphony Orchestra in 1991, and the Buffalo Philharmonic Orchestra in 1998. Then in 2007 Marin Alsop became the music director for the Baltimore Symphony Orchestra, the first woman to be appointed music director of a top-tier orchestra.

With increased programming and performing success has come increasing recognition of artistic merit and success in the form of awards. Ruth Crawford Seeger (1901–1953) was the first woman to win a Guggenheim Fellowship, in 1930. Florence Price won two Wanamaker Foundation Awards in the 1930s. Radie Britain won the Hollywood Bowl Prize in 1930 and Juilliard Publication Award in 1945. Julia Perry won the Boulanger Grand Prix in 1952, and Barbara Kolb became the first American woman to win the Prix de Rome in 1969. In the 1970s the National Endowment for the Arts Medal of Honor recognized an important set of opera singers, including Marion Anderson (1897–1993), Beverly Sills (1929–2007), Roberta Peters (1930–), Marylyn Horne (1934–), and Leontyne Price (1927–). In 1983 Ellen Taafe Zwilich (1939–) became the first woman to win a Pulitzer Prize for music; Shulamit Ran (1949–), Melinda Wagner (1957–), and Jennifer Higdon (b. 1962–) have received it since then. In 1988 Joan Tower (1938–) won the Kennedy Center Friedheim Award, and in 1990 she became the first woman to win the Grawemeyer Award. Meredith Monk, Marin Alsop, violinists Regina Carter (1966–) and Liela Josefowiz (1977–), as well as singer Dawn Upshaw (1960–) have all received MacArthur Fellowships.

Women throughout American history have struggled in all fields to gain respect and parity with men. In music, women have entered singly and exceptionally, then in greater numbers, until the exceptions became accepted and expected and in enough time, changed the rules. The first singers accepted on stage led the way to instrumentalists performing professionally, who brought in their wake composers and conductors. These jobs have led the way to greater recognition and awards. This same pattern of individuals paving roads so others may follow can be seen in all musical and nonmusical fields, business, and politics. Yet as in these other fields, true representative equality has not yet been reached; in 2013 women do not earn as much as men and are not employed in orchestras as often as men, compositions by women are played at only 10 percent of the rate of men's, and women attain leadership positions far less often then men do. But enough change has occurred to look positively toward the future, where equality is within our reach. As goes the nation, so goes our music.

See also: Art Music (Mainstream); Classical Music in America; Composers, Women; Harlem Renaissance; Improvisation; Music Making at Home; Opera in America; Orchestras

Further Reading

Ammer, Christine. 2001. *Unsung: A History of Women in American Music.* 2nd ed. Portland, OR: Amadeus Press.

Edwards, J. Michele, and Leslie Lassetter. 2001 "North America since 1920." In *Women and Music: A History,* 2nd ed., edited by Karin Pendle, 314–386. Bloomington: Indiana University Press.

Gertig, Suzanne L. 2002. "Classical Music." In *Women and Music in America since 1900: An Encyclopedia,* edited by Kristine H. Burns, 1: 99–104. 2 vols. Westport, CT: Greenwood Press.

Goldin, Claudia, and Cecilia Rouse. 2000. "Orchestrating Impartiality: The Impact of 'Blind' Auditions on Female Musicians." *The American Economic Review* 90: 715–741.

Tick, Judith. 1983. *American Women Composers before 1870.* Ann Arbor and London: UMI Research Press.

Robin Armstrong

Cline, Patsy (1932–1963)

Patsy Cline, with her rich contralto voice and glamorous style, remains one of the most influential and popular female singers in American music history.

Virginia Patterson Hensley was born on September 8, 1932, in Winchester, Virginia, the oldest of three children born to Hilda and Sam Patterson Hensley. Her father left the family when she was fifteen years of age, and Ginny, as she was called during her childhood, dropped out of school to find work to help support her family. In spite of her family's hardships, Ginny believed she would be famous one day. She began to sing at an early age, attributing her booming voice to a childhood illness and throat infection. As a teenager Ginny sang in local talent shows and clubs. In her early twenties she began to perform regularly on radio stations and

Artists Influenced by Patsy Cline

Faith Hill	Loretta Lynn
k. d. lang	Reba McIntyre
LeAnn Rimes	Trisha Yearwood
Linda Ronstadt	Wynonna Judd

attracted a good following. She was briefly married to Gerald Cline and adopted the stage name Patsy Cline (the name Patsy was derived from her middle name). The marriage soon dissolved, in part because of Patsy's ambitions to become a professional singer, but she retained the stage name. Cline later married Charlie Dick and had two children with him, Julia (1958) and Randy (1961).

Cline's network television debut was on January 7, 1956, on ABC's *Grand Ole Opry* (she later joined the Opry in 1960). Her big break followed in 1957, when she won the Arthur Godfrey Talent program, which led to the release of her hit single "Walkin' After Midnight." The song reached number two on the country music chart and number twelve on the pop chart, making her one of the first female crossover stars. Her arrangements often included strings and other instruments not typical in country music at the time.

She was known as a tough negotiator who performed on her own terms, which was uncommon for women in her day. During an era when women in country music were expected to wear calico and frills, she donned elegant gowns and pearls, opening up possibilities for women to have a different image. Cline was the first female country music singer to perform at Carnegie Hall in New York City and to headline her own show in Las Vegas. She was known for encouraging other women who were starting out in country music, including Loretta Lynn, Dottie West, and Brenda Lee. She helped other women musicians financially and emotionally when they went through difficult times.

Patsy Cline died in a plane crash in March 1963 when she was just thirty years old, yet her music remains timeless. Her hits, such as "I Fall to Pieces," "Crazy," and "Walkin' After Midnight," remain popular among audiences of all ages and musical tastes. Her legacy has had a lasting influence. She broadened the audience and appeal of country music and made tremendous strides for women in the music industry. Cline was the first female solo artist inducted into the Country Music Hall of Fame, ten years after her death. Accolades continued in the decades after her death: she was awarded the Grammy Lifetime Achievement Award (1995); she was voted number eleven in the VH1 list of the 100 Greatest Women in Rock and Roll (1999), was voted number one in the list of 40 Greatest Women of Country Music (CMT 2002) by artists and country music industry members, and was ranked number forty-six in *Rolling Stone*'s list of 100 Greatest Singers of All Time.

Patsy Cline was one of the first country and western entertainers to become successful in both country and popular music, and her influence is seen on nearly all of the female singers in both genres who came after her. (AP Photo)

See also: Crossovers; Lynn, Loretta; Women in American Music

Further Reading

CMT. 2002. *40 Greatest Women of Country Music.* Nashville, TN: Tangible Vision Productions.

Hazen, Cindy, and Mike Freeman. 1999. *Love Always, Patsy: Patsy Cline's Letters to a Friend.* New York: Berkley Books.

Jones, Margaret. 1999. *Patsy: The Life and Times of Patsy Cline.* New York: Da Capo Press.

Nassour, Ellis. 2008. *Honky Tonk Angel: The Intimate Story of Patsy Cline.* Chicago: Chicago Review Press.

Jacqueline Edmondson

Clinton, George (1941–)

George Clinton is a bandleader, singer, songwriter, producer, and most important, pioneering and iconic figure in the history of funk music. Indeed, if James Brown was the "Godfather of Soul," then George Clinton is the "Godfather of Funk," or perhaps better, "Dr. Funkenstein"—a name he coined to describe the mad-scientist experimentalism with which he approached the bluesy and soulful roots of funk music. By adding futuristic electronic instrumental elements, extraterrestrial lyrics, and science fiction stage shows to the music that he made with the collective known as Parliament-Funkadelic, he propelled blues, soul, and funk into the 1970s and beyond.

Clinton was born in Kannapolis, North Carolina, in 1941 and raised in Plainfield, New Jersey, where he founded the five-member doo-wop group The Parliaments in the late 1950s. In the mid-1960s Clinton gained notoriety for his work with Detroit's famed Motown Records as a songwriter and producer. Around the same time Clinton scored his first hit for The Parliaments, "(I Wanna) Testify." The song is an early example of Clinton's move from the doo-wop tradition to the soul, rock, and funk genres. Clinton's vocals in particular feature the bluesy contours typical of soul and rock music, with a focus on a solo singer rather than the multivoiced close harmonies of doo-wop. In addition, the track shows the instrumental influences of James Brown's band in its punchy horn arrangements, funky syncopated guitar accompaniments, and active bass part—stylistic elements that Clinton would take to a new level in developing his own signature sound over the next decade.

Because of contractual disputes, Clinton and his band began performing under the name Funkadelic shortly after their initial successes. Though the group still featured all five original members of The Parliaments, as Funkadelic Clinton's group was now a band rather than a vocal group, featuring guitarist Eddie Hazel, bassist Billy Bass Nelson, and later keyboardist Bernie Worrell, among others. As the name indicates, Funkadelic developed a unique style of bluesy, guitar-driven funk that was also informed by the psychedelic rock of the late 1960s. The group gained popularity with the release of their first three albums—*Funkadelic, Free Your Mind . . . And Your Ass Will Follow,* and *Maggot Brain*—in the period 1970–1971. These early free-form albums established Clinton's reputation as a creative and experimental bandleader as well as an irreverent and sometimes controversial iconoclast.

After Funkadelic's initial successes, many of the musicians who had performed with Brown's band in the 1960s joined Clinton's growing collective, most notably bassist Bootsy Collins; guitarist Catfish Collins; and Brown's famed horn section, The Horny Horns, led by trombonist

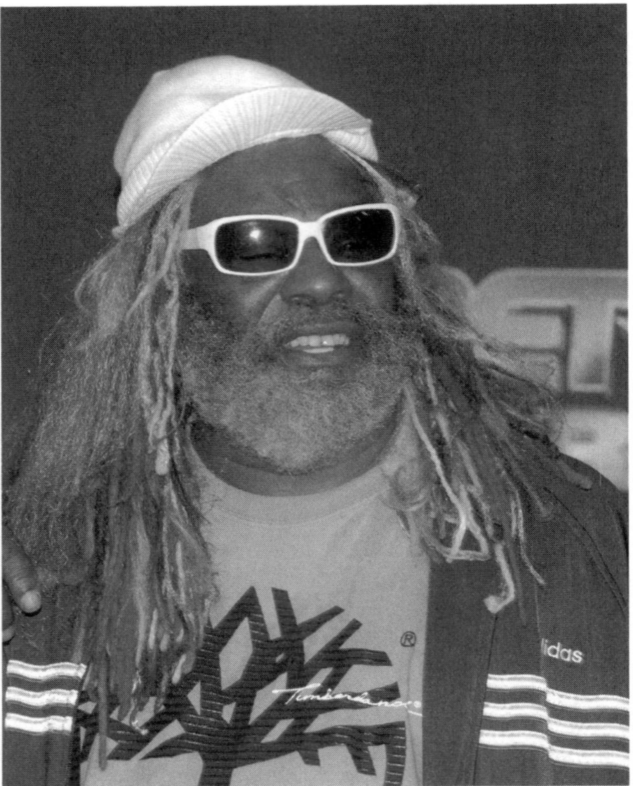

George Clinton of Parliament-Funkadelic at BET's 25th Anniversary, November 1, 2005. (John Sciulli/iStockphoto.com)

Fred Wesley and saxophonist Maceo Parker. In 1974 Clinton revived the name "Parliament" to feature the horn section and another side of the band's creative abilities. While Funkadelic would continue to record free-form and album-oriented funk-rock, Parliament would record in a futuristic, yet more mainstream disco-funk style and release a steady stream of chart-topping singles. Clinton's two interrelated bands are commonly referred to as Parliament-Funkadelic (or simply P-Funk) today.

Following the creative and commercial successes of the Parliament albums *Up for the Down Stroke* and *Chocolate City,* Clinton and his wildly inventive bandmates began to develop a playful but detailed mythological narrative, drawing on black nationalist movements and claiming that funk music was of extraterrestrial origins. The lyrics and stage shows featured pyramids side by side with space ships, thus rewriting the history of the future to include black people. The best examples of this mythology, which also coincide with P-Funk's golden age of 1975–1978, can be found on the albums *The Mothership Connection, The Clones of Dr. Funkenstein,* and *Funkentelechy vs. The Placebo Syndrome.*

Clinton continues to lead, write, arrange, produce, and perform with P-Funk All-Stars, the contemporary incarnation of his collective. In 1997 Clinton and fifteen members of Parliament-Funkadelic were inducted into the Rock and Roll Hall of Fame. Today his influence can be felt most prominently in the realm of hip-hop, where countless artists have sampled his intricate and funky sound, from Dr. Dre and the Beastie Boys to LL Cool J and Common. His work was also foundational to the genre of funk-rock and the music of bands like Fishbone and The Red Hot Chili Peppers, a band that he worked with as a producer in 1985. Finally, his P-Funk mythology is the most notable example from the 1970s of Afrofuturism, an antiracist creative and intellectual tradition that works to reimagine the future of black cultural production.

See also: African American Influences on American Music; Brown, James; Funk and Postpsychedelic Funk; Halls of Fame; Hip-Hop; Motown

Official Web Site: http://www.georgeclinton.com/

Further Reading

Mills, David. 1998. *George Clinton and P-Funk: An Oral History (For the Record).* New York: Avon Books.

Vincent, Ricky. 1996. *Funk: The Music, the People, and the Rhythm of the One.* New York: St. Martin's Griffin Publishing.

Griff Rollefson

Clothing and Appearance in Song

Songwriters and singers treat men and women as musical mannequins. They adorn their human subjects with "Buttons and Bows" (1948), "A Zoot Suit (For My Sunday Gal)" (1942), "Brass Buttons" (1961), "Handbags and Gladrags" (1972), or "Just a Blue Serge Suit" (1945). No one ever wants to be seen naked. This includes the shy "Lady Godiva" (1966), as well as the royal fool sporting "The Emperor's New Clothes" (1990). From the "Material Girl" (1985) to "Dapper Dan" (1922), lyrical ladies and gentlemen delight in being "Dressed for Success" (1989). Of course not all attire is either comfortable or classy. The occupational wardrobes of factory workers and assembly line employees are depicted in "Blue Collar" (1973), "Blue Collar Blues" (1981), and "Blue Collar Man (Long Nights)" (1978). Far fewer clothing alternatives await convicted felons. Johnny Cash describes a prisoner's garb in "I Got Stripes" (1959).

From zoot suits to black leather jackets and motorcycle boots, from Bermuda shorts to tie-dyed T-shirts and red blue jeans, popular songs frequently focus on clothing fads to depict smartly attired hipsters and coolly clad artists. As ZZ Top reflected, every girl they have ever encountered was crazy about a "Sharp Dressed Man" (1983). In the late 1950s nothing made a better impression on a prom date, according to Marty Robbins, than a young man decked out in "A White Sport Coat (And a Pink Carnation)" (1957). What female fashions are likely to attract attention since the mid-twentieth century? An "Itsy Bitsy Teenie Weenie Yellow Polkadot Bikini" (1960) or a "One Piece Topless Bathing Suit" (1964) are sure attention grabbers on the beach. Other lyrically acclaimed women's outfits are noted in "Big Leg Woman (With a Short Short Mini Skirt)" (1970), a "Country Girl with Hot Pants" (1970), and "Short Shorts" (1958). Universal dating apparel among young rockers of both genders consists of tight jeans and fancy footwear. Songs that salute products produced by Wrangler, Levi Strauss, and even Calvin Klein include "Baby Makes Her Blue Jeans Talk" (1982), "Jeans On" (1977), and "Tight Fittin' Jeans" (1981). Fascinating shoe imagery appears in "Betty Lou Got a New Pair of Shoes" (1958), "Boogie Woogie Dancin' Shoes" (1979), "Cowboy Boots" (1963), and "White Bucks and Saddle Shoes" (1958).

Beyond clothing and footwear, the human body is an audio palette awaiting colorful creativity. A stylish auburn wig can cover a "Bald Head" (1950), Professor Longhair's (a.k.a. Roy Byrd) only national commercial hit, and eliminate the "Cleanhead Blues" (1946). Songs about bald heads remain popular, from the Kinks' "Bald Headed Woman" (1964) and Bob Marley's "Crazy Baldhead" (1976) to the three-woman blues ensemble Saffire-The Uppity Blues Women (active 1987–2009) and their recording of "Bald-Headed Blues" (2009).

For those blessed with abundant hair, like "My Boy—Flat Top" (1955) and "The Girl with the Golden Braids" (1957), other personalized head adornments are reasonable. Some might select "Scarlet Ribbons (For Her Hair)" (1959); others may travel west to "San Francisco (Be Sure to Wear Flowers in Your Hair)" (1967); and a few might simply say "Kookie, Kookie, Lend Me Your Comb" (1959) while they arrange a distinctive "Ducktail" (1956). Just ask "Lydia, the Tattooed Lady" (1939). Many men and women eschew emphasis on cover-up clothing in favor of "Half a Heart Tattoo" (2003), "The Rose Tattoo" (1955), or a "Texas Tattoo" (1993).

Not unlike the idiosyncrasy of "Your Tattoo" (1995), the frequent use of "Sun Glasses" (1958) can also become a fashion statement. Shades worn during the evening hours in dance clubs or at uptown restaurants—"Sunglasses After Dark" (1958) and "Sunglasses at Night" (1984) and "The Future's So Bright, I Gotta Wear Shades" (1986)—may seem overly ostentatious, though.

For every recording that addresses the quality of male attire, there are a dozen songs commenting on some aspect of female clothing. Fashions designed specifically for professional men are depicted in "Black Suits Comin' (Nod Ya Head)" (2002), "Brother Bill (The Last Clean Shirt)" (1964), and "Button Up Your Overcoat" (1929).

Humorous observations about men's trousers are delivered in "Sam, You Made the Pants Too Long" (1966) and "Donald Where's Your Troosers?" (1961). At one time, Western garb for males was always a popular topic, whether commenting on "Cowboy Boots" (1963) or "This Cowboy's Hat" (1983). The abandonment of traditional cowhand virtues and Western simplicity in style is also explored lyrically in "The Cowboy in the Continental Suit" (1964), "Cowboy in a Three Piece Business Suit" (1982), and "Rhinestone Cowboy" (1975). Rodeo star Chris LeDoux sang about "This Cowboy's Hat" (1991), and Garth Brooks's "Good Ride Cowboy" (2005), a tribute to his friend LeDoux, described how the rodeo rider always wore his hat down tight.

There is a great deal of diversity in songs treating women's apparel. Color options for women range from "Pink Chiffon" (1960), "Blue Velvet" (1955), and a "Red Sweater" (1957) to "A Long Cool Woman (In a Black Dress)" (1972) and "White on White" (1964). There are varying lengths and cuts of women's clothing. This fact is lyrically illustrated in "Bermuda Shorts" (1957), "Big Legs, Tight Skirt" (1965), "Blue Skirt Waltz" (1949), "Boppin' in a Sack" (1958), "Country Girl in Hot Pants" (1971), "Long Skirt Baby Blues" (1948), "My First Formal Gown" (1956), "No Chemise, Please" (1958), "Pink Pedal Pushers" (1958), "Pretty Plaid Skirt (And Long Black Sox)" (1959), "Straight Skirt" (1958), "Tight Capris" (1958), and "Tight Skirt and Sweater" (1958). Even in the realm of blue jeans, a decidedly unisex leisure apparel, a woman is more frequently identified as a "Dungaree Doll" (1955), a beautiful vision in "Tight Fittin' Jeans" (1981), or a "Venus in Blue Jeans" (1962). Other recordings that laud the female figure in jeans include "Blue Jeans and a Boy's Shirt" (1958), "Forever in Blue Jeans" (1979), "Pigtails and Blue Jeans" (1958), "Red Blue Jeans and a Pony Tail" (1957), "Too Much Butt" (2009), and "T-Shirts 'n' Jeans" (1972).

There is a similar gender imbalance in songs dealing with shoes and socks. That is, there are many more recordings that examine female footwear than there are tunes about male shoes, boots, or brogans. Songs devoted to socks are "Bobby Sox Blues" (1947), "Bobby Sox to Stockings" (1959), "Fishnet" (1988), "A Fool for Your Stockings" (1994), "Knee Socks" (1959), and "Your Socks Don't Match" (1943). Foot attire may be distinctive in respect to color, style, or function. Obviously, dancing is the dominant concern for those wearing "Blue Suede Shoes" (1956) or "Boogie Shoes" (1978). Other recordings that acknowledge the centrality of stylish shoes include "Boogie Woogie Dancin' Shoes" (1979), "Dig Them Squeaky Shoes" (1955), "The Gal with the Yaller Shoes" (1956), "Hang Up My Rock 'n' Roll Shoes" (1958), "Hi-Heel Sneakers" (1964), "New Shoes" (1957), "One, Two, Button My Shoe" (1936), "Penny Loafers and Bobby Sox" (1957), "Pink Shoe Laces" (1959), "Pointed Toe Shoes" (1959), "Rockin' Shoes" (1957), "Slip-In Mules (No High Heel Sneakers)" (1964), "Travelin' Shoes" (1974), "White Buckskin Sneakers and Checkerboard Socks" (1959), "Who Wears These Shoes?" (1984), and "Yellow Pants and Blue Suede Shoes" (1959).

To be a genuinely "Dedicated Follower of Fashion" (1966), one must devote a considerable amount of personal time to "Shoppin' for Clothes" (1960). The Coasters will attest to this fact. Or as Boogaloo and His Gallant Crew have observed, a fashionista can locate the perfect "Clothes Line (Wrap It Up)" (1956). Lyrically, a woman may be stunning either as "The Girl in the Little Green Hat" (1933) or as a cool chick of the 1960s in a "Leopard-Skin Pill-Box Hat" (1967). But the vast majority of clothing-related popular recordings are focused on providing "Music to Watch Girls By" (1966). Whether it's "Betty in Bermudas" (1963) or a young "Tie-Dye Princess" (1971), singers use clothing styles in their descriptions of women in song. When seeking dates for the "Bluejean Bop" (1956), men may be attracted by "Chantilly Lace" (1958), "A Gal in Calico" (1947), a "Devil with a Blue Dress" (1976), or a "Long Legged Girl (With the Short Dress On)" (1967). In assessing the frequency and variety of sound recordings that address issues of personal appearance, fashion statements, or particular clothing styles, one must acknowledge that dapper ditties are immensely popular. From "Black Slacks" (1956) to "Petticoats of Portugal" (1956), male and female attire dominates song titles and lyrics alike.

See also: Clothing Styles and Musicians

Further Reading

Carr, Roy, Brian Case, and Fred Dellar. 1986. *The Hip: Hipsters, Jazz, and the Beat.* London: Faber and Faber.

Corrigan, Peter. 2008. *The Dressed Society: Clothing, the Body, and Some Meanings of the World.* London: SAGE Publications.

Heard, Gary Lee, with David Cultrara. 2003. *Body Art: The Human Canvas—Ink and Steel.* Portland, OR: Collectors Press.

Jones, Mablen. 1987. *Getting It On: The Clothing of Rock 'n' Roll.* New York: Abbeville Press.

McRobbie, Angela, ed. 1999. *Zoot Suits and Second-Hand Dresses: An Anthology of Fashion and Music.* Boston: Unwin Hyman.

Planer, John H. 1990. "Function in the Country Song 'Tight Fittin' Jeans'." *Popular Music and Society* 14: 27–50.

Polhemus, Ted, and Lynn Proctor. 1984. *Pop Styles.* London: Vermilion Press.

Sculatti, Gene, ed. 1982. *The Catalog of Cool.* New York: Warner Book.

Stewart, Tony, ed. 1982. *Cool Cats: 25 Years of Rock 'n' Roll Style.* New York: Delilah Books.

B. Lee Cooper

Clothing Styles and Musicians

Early Traditions

Even before the arrival of the Europeans in the Americas, clothing was an integral part of music and dance for the approximately two million people living in what later became the United States. There is little information about early clothing, but natives used materials such as leather, fur, and cotton to create items ranging from loincloths and leggings to vests and robes. Face and body paint, tattooing, and elaborate hairstyles were part of rituals in which music was essential. Some elements are in use in current tribal ceremonies such as the Ghost Dance, a ritual performed among several native groups in which men wear ghost shirts with spirit world imagery. Powwow ceremonies are known for their regalia or cultural dress, including lower back adornments or bustles made with large feathered disks and bundles of ribbon or yarn.

During the eighteenth and nineteenth centuries enslaved Africans worked on plantations under excruciating circumstances. The spiritual developed as the work song for slaves in the fields. Themes reflected the tribulations of physical labor and a yearning to return to Africa. Owners provided slaves with used clothes and garments made from coarse materials or "negro cloth." Minstrel shows, popular after the 1820s, explored the slave experience, with musical performances requiring costumes for stock characters such as the dandy and the mammy. Minstrel shows performed by white actors required blackface makeup, which accentuated—in a cartoonish and racist manner—the facial features of African slaves. After the Civil War black actors performed in blackface or whiteface in minstrel and burlesque shows. The costumes worn on stage were a reflection of prevalent fashions of the period. Women wore gowns, aprons, and head coverings; men donned trousers, shirts, and three-piece suits.

Ragtime, a variation of marching music infused with African rhythms, boomed from the late 1890s to the late 1910s. Famed composers and performers include Scott Joplin, James Scott, and Joseph Lamb. Nowadays ragtime is associated with clothing worn at the turn of the twentieth century: for men, three-piece suits, fedora hats, and white plantation suits; for women, shirtwaist separates or lightweight white or pastel tea and garden gowns. Other nineteenth and early twentieth-century forms of entertainment—including vaudeville and burlesque—are also associated with period fashion. Burlesque shows included a variety of acts such as puppets, comedy, dancers, and striptease. Lavish and somewhat body-revealing costumes worn by burlesque female acts evolved into the feathered and sequined pieces worn by performers for revues such as the Ziegfeld Follies in the early 1900s and outfits worn by Las Vegas showgirls.

Blues, Jazz, Country, and the Dance Craze

Blues music appeared initially among African American communities in the late 1880s, particularly around the Mississippi Delta, but gained widespread fame with celebrated blues performers from the early part of the twentieth century, including Bessie Smith and "Ma" Rainey. Heavily embellished 1920s gowns, jeweled caps, and exotic headdresses are forever associated with blues female interpreters, as are the elegant formal suits worn by male musicians.

Jazz music began in the early twentieth century in New Orleans, spreading fast to cities such as Chicago and New York in the 1920s, a decade known as the Jazz Age due to the crucial role music played during the time of flappers and Prohibition. The "liberated" women of the period obtained the right to vote when Congress passed the Nineteenth Amendment on June 4, 1919. Knee-length dresses in boxy silhouettes, bobbed hair, and headbands afforded comfort and style on the dance floor. The Charleston was executed with heel kicks and knee-bending movements enhanced by fringed skirts, sequined dresses, and feather boas.

Swing was popular from the 1920s to the 1940s. Big band performers dressed formally, but comfortably, with slightly oversized three-piece suits and fedora or panama hats. Louis Jordan—the father of R&B—wore easy fitting-suits in light colors matched to white shoes and bold ties. Those on the dance floor wore fashionable clothes for ease of movement. In some areas of New York and California, African American and Latino youths embraced the zoot suit, which consisted of high-waisted pants, broad-shouldered jackets with wide lapels, a large bow tie, and a long watch chain. Swing and jazz performers played a significant role entertaining American troops during World War II. Hollywood perpetuated the image of World War II service men dancing in their uniforms or simply wearing short-sleeved undershirts or Hawaiian print shirts.

Louis Jordan, "The King of the Jukebox," and his orchestra in 1944. His over-sized three-piece suit was typical of the swing era. (Bettmann/Corbis)

Country or western music originated in the Appalachian mountains, with influences from folk, gospel, and blues. In the 1930s it gained popularity through radio transmissions—particularly from the Grand Ole Opry in Nashville, Tennessee. Stetson hats, jeans, denim pieces, and fitted Western or cowboy shirts with crescent-shaped front pockets were part of the attire for country musicians from the outset. Gene Autry was crucial in popularizing these items, with his persona of the Singing Cowboy. He wore Western shirts with intricate embroidery, colorful ascots, and embellished leather gun holsters. Hank Williams—a 1950s country superstar—wore two-piece white suits, Stetson hats, and Western shirts with decorative embroidery and piping. Williams was among the first country musicians to wear lavishly embellished suits. The Nudie Suit, introduced by Ukrainian American tailor Nudie Cohn and singer Porter Wagoner, became an identifiable element of country music. It featured European folk designs and cowboy imagery embroidered with rhinestones and beads. Country clothing adapted to changing styles of the twentieth century, at times incorporating leather vests, oversized belt buckles, Wrangler jeans, and rhinestone-encrusted pieces. Certain fashion statements are associated with specific celebrities, such as Kitty Wells's gingham dresses, Dolly Parton's big hair and revealing, low-cut tops, Billy Ray Cyrus's mullet, and Willie Nelson's bandana.

The 1950s: Rock 'n' Roll

Casual wear became increasingly popular during the suburban growth of the postwar period. Teenage life during the 1950s revolved around diners and jukeboxes as rock 'n' roll music gained popularity. Teenagers defined themselves as independent from older generations and used clothing to express this new identity, arising as a consumer market crucial to both the music and fashion industries. They wore versatile clothes, including wide circle skirts, capri pants, sport ankle socks, and large loose pullovers or Sloppy Joes. Young men embraced casual styles, including easy-fitting pants and letterman sweaters. Influences on fashion also came from Hollywood movies, which portrayed a "rebel look" for young men, including jeans, visible white undershirts, and leather jackets. These items became the stereotypical look of 1950s rockers.

Beat generation poets and their followers—often seen in the company of jazz and bebop musicians such as Charlie Parker, Dizzy Gillespie, and Miles Davis—wore black outfits and dirty sneakers. Beat women wore peasant blouses and long ponytails. Influences in clothing also came from the British Teddy Boys, a group of working-class London men who dressed in Edwardian-inspired styles, including fitted, narrow trousers, pointed-toe shoes, and elaborate hairstyles. Early rock 'n' roll and rockabilly performers such as Little Richard and Ike Turner were famous for their conk hairstyles, in which their hair was greased and combed up.

Television programs, such as *The Ed Sullivan Show* (1948–1971), allowed audiences to see the way musicians dressed. The show famously aired performances by Jerry Lee Lewis, The Beatles, and Elvis Presley. Fans admired and copied Presley's fashion style, particularly his sculpted hair. The ducktail haircut became popular among rock 'n' roll fans of the period. Presley wore slender dress shirts and trousers with boxy jackets. Later his style incorporated colorful, shiny suits with high collars, pink sports coats, and white shoes. In the 1970s he adopted a more theatrical style, wearing white jumpsuits, capes, and heavily embellished suits.

The 1960s: Motown, Psychedelia, Hippies, and Mods

In 1959 Chubby Checker ushered in the most popular dance of the 1960s: the twist. Based on twisting the hips back and forth, the dance was enhanced by full skirts and fringed outfits. It was later featured in the series of beach party movies starring Annette Funicello and Frankie Avalon, in which trendy bikini swimsuits were also highlighted. Surf music—coming mostly from California—enjoyed great popularity. The quintessential surf band, The Beach Boys, wore easy-fitting, colorful suits, striped short-sleeved shirts, baggy shorts, Hawaiian prints, and deck shoes.

In 1960 the Motown Record Corporation in Detroit, Michigan, became the first record label owned by African Americans. It supported the crossover careers of several acts, including Jackson 5, The Four Tops, The Supremes, and Martha and the Vandellas. Most of these acts—particularly during the early part of their careers—performed wearing mainstream fashion. Female groups wore sequined gowns, feather and fur accessories or trims, high-heeled, stylish shoes, and wigs or high pompadour hairdos. Fish tail and baby doll dresses, lavish pant suits, and low décolleté, sleeveless gowns worn with opera gloves were occasionally part of the wardrobe. Male bands wore suits in bright colors featuring decorative piping or dinner jackets with dark trousers and white shoes. During the civil rights movement—which brought attention to inequality issues affecting African Americans—clothing was used as a form of self-identification. Some black performers left behind fashionable mainstream looks in favor of African-inspired outfits such as dashikis and caftans. Full-shape, curled "Afro" hair was adopted by musicians, including Jackson 5. The band also wore shirts with bold prints, colorful vests, and bell-bottom pants, all fashionable clothing elements at the time.

The Vietnam War provided a background for the hippie movement of the late 1960s and early 1970s. Haight-Ashbury Streets in San Francisco was one of the first places where hippie fashion and long hair were seen. As a style tribe, the hippies were strongly defined by both music and dress. Their peace-seeking lifestyle used clothing as a protest tool in solidarity with the working classes. Hippie fashion was a mix and match of psychedelic and peasant looks, with a preference for natural fabrics. Hippies sported long hair and wore denim jeans with patches or other alterations, along with sandals made of hemp or leather. Men wore colorful prints, and women favored long, loose dresses inspired by Native American, Asian, and Latin American cultures. A number of musical acts of the period identified themselves with the hippie lifestyle or were embraced by the movement. Janis Joplin wore bell bottom pants, loose tops in loud prints and colors, and large amounts of inexpensive costume jewelry. She was also famous for not wearing undergarments. Jimi Hendrix's wardrobe incorporated gypsy-like items including ruffled shirts, headscarves, neckerchiefs, and elaborate vests. Creedence Clearwater Revival and Bob Dylan—among other acts—sported less bold looks, wearing jeans, peasant tops, and ethnic-inspired pieces. Hippie fashion reached mainstream via the 1965 Broadway musical *Hair* and the 1969 Woodstock music festival and subsequent documentary movie.

Psychedelic rock featured complex structures and exotic instrumentation led by electric guitars, such as the music of the Grateful Dead, Jefferson Airplane, and The Moody Blues. Psychedelic imagery—inspired in part by acid trips and hallucinations—appeared widely in poster, album cover, and T-shirt designs for these bands. Psychedelic prints were used for men's pants and nearly every garment worn by women. Influences also came from The Beatles' Indian- and Moroccan-inspired clothing, including paisley shirts, floral pattern pants, and beaded or embroidered tunics.

Certainly The Beatles were also influential in bringing mod styles to the United States. They wore straight-cut, collarless Nehru jackets, brocade vests, and narrow trousers tapered at the leg. Mod fashion spawned from "the swinging city" of London, particularly Carnaby Street, where fashion designers, musicians, and their youthful followers were experimenting with an eclectic mix of styles, such as peasant garments, historical pieces, and elements of dress from worldwide cultures. The name mod or modernist derived from the group's taste for modern jazz, but they also favored soul, ska, R&B, and pop. Fashion associated with mod subculture and its favorite performers faced negative reactions in the United States. Among those styles were miniskirts, minidresses, and hot pants. Midi- (mid-length) and maxi- (full-length) skirts were seen as alternatives. Hair was either long and loose or in built-up beehives. Males wore a variety of colors and patterns, including bell bottom flared pants, turtlenecks, and pullovers.

The 1970s: Disco, Glam, Punk, and Heavy Metal

The "Peacock Revolution" of the 1970s brought color variety to men's clothes. Casual wear shirts fit the body closely and came with a variety of closures. Colorful leisure suits—with shirtlike jackets—enjoyed great popularity among fans of disco dance music. Celebrated disco artists included Donna Summer, The Village People, KC & the Sunshine Band, and Gloria Gaynor. The 1977 movie *Saturday Night Fever* made John Travolta an international sensation and disco a mainstream trend. Disco fashion involved loud, clashing colors. Men wore tight pants with wide legs or bell bottoms, matching jackets, and solid color, unbuttoned shirts. Hair chest and gold chains were often an integral part of the look. Women wore hot pants, spandex tops, lamé dresses, and satin jumpsuits. Polyester outfits and platform shoes were part of the wardrobe for both males and females.

Other popular music styles of the 1970s included reggae, funk, and glam rock. The Jamaican band Bob Marley and the Wailers was the most successful act. Reggae fashion—grounded on the Rastafarian movement—included beads, dreadlocks, turbans, and marijuana leaf motifs. Red, gold, and green—the colors of the Ethiopian flag—were commonly used. Funk acts such as Sly & the Family Stone in the 1960s and bands fronted by George Clinton in the 1970s wore dramatic makeup, satin jumpsuits, sequined outfits, large jewelry, and platform shoes. The epic staging of funk was also seen in glam rock, where flashy, gender-bending clothing was the norm. British acts including Garry Glitter, Slade, T-Rex, and particularly David Bowie, influenced American glam musicians. The New York Dolls, a proto-punk band, introduced elements of glam rock into the American garage band scene. They performed in drag, including ballet tutus, spandex trousers, strapless dresses, and full makeup. Suzi Quatro wore tight black leather pants and jumpsuits. She often opened for Alice Cooper, a singer known for epic stage shows. His act—considered heavy metal music—included a variety of costume changes with androgynous sequined pieces. Cooper's dark stage persona wore striking black and white makeup, leather or lycra pieces, and fake blood. Mötley Crüe, Ratt, and other heavy metal bands of the 1980s wore heavy stage makeup, big hair, and revealing pieces of clothing in loud colors, animal prints, or bold patterns. Thrash metal bands like Megadeth, Slayer, and Metallica performed wearing denim and leather. Some acts were also known as "hair bands" or "hair metal" due to their long and feathered hairstyles.

Punk music derived from late 1960s American garage rock and was later injected with some British flare and a penchant for outrageous and experimental fashion. The sense of pessimism, irony, and rebellion in the lyrics and music was also projected onto the clothes worn by punk acts. British punk was particularly inclined to ideas of anarchy and sedition—often expressed through liberal attitudes toward sex. Punk attire was also about promoting a do-it-yourself aesthetic and a thrift store look, with torn clothes and deconstructed garments. Leather jackets, bondage pieces, dog collars, jumpsuits, and gender-bending outfits were among a myriad of possibilities. By the 1980s a mainstream version of punk was almost solely associated with tattoos, body piercing, and Mohawks.

The 1980s: Pop, Urban Styling, and the Business of Fashion

The obsession during the 1980s with consumption and affluence translated in fashion into an interest in labels, particularly designer jeans. The "Me" generation enjoyed expensive products based almost solely on brand reputation. Nike, Adidas, Members Only, and Z'Cavaricci were among the brands that enjoyed an additional push after being embraced by musicians. Musicians became more concerned with their personal presentation as music television grew. MTV aired for the first time in 1981 and was followed by other television music channels, with CMT debuting in 1983 and VH1 in 1985. Corporate design became essential for musicians working tirelessly to build brand recognition.

Yuppies—young affluent professionals—dressed in elegant clothes, including Italian double-breasted suits. The "power suit" became the ultimate tool in the dress-for-success environment of the 1980s. Musical acts incorporating this formal aesthetic included Robert Palmer and Huey Lewis & the News. Preppies—those soon to be yuppies—wore blazers, sweaters, formal trousers, and loafer shoes. The look was best embraced by the Go-Gos; new wave bands such as The Cars; and

Psychedelic soul group Sly and the Family Stone pose for a portrait in 1968. Pictured from left are Rosie Stone, Larry Graham, Sly Stone, Freddie Stone, Gregg Errico, Jerry Martini, Cynthia Robinson. (Michael Ochs Archives/Getty Images)

counterpart acts from the United Kingdom such as Orchestral Manoeuvres in the Dark (OMD), Duran Duran, and Simple Minds.

Pastel or neon colors, skirted suits with oversized shoulder pads, and leather miniskirts demarcated fashion for women and appeared in the wardrobes of artists such as Debbie Gibson and Tiffany. The fitness craze of the late 1970s and early 1980s made workout clothes a new wardrobe necessity. The 1983 musical movie *Flashdance* made gray, off-the-shoulder sweatshirts, leg warmers, and other gym clothes trendy. Denim was popular not only for jeans but also skirts, jackets, and vests. Treatments for denim included acid wash or embroidered, slashed, and torn pieces, as seen in the wardrobes of acts like Salt-N-Pepa and the Australian band INXS. The quintessential album cover for *Born in the USA* (1984) famously featured Bruce Springsteen's derriere in a pair of jeans.

Other 1980s artists experimented with bold fashion statements. Prince—known for purple clothing—wore fitted pants, revealing shirts with flounces, animal prints, cravats, and vintage trench coats. Cindy Lauper enjoyed large jewelry, asymmetrical haircuts, and neon-colored clothes. Madonna introduced a number of fashion trends. Her early eighties thrift-store look incorporated ripped-up mesh shirts, distressed jeans, leggings, and jewelry pieces with crucifixes and rosary beads. She wore dominatrix-inspired costumes for some videos, as well as corsets and pointy bustiers, as part of an underwear-as-outerwear trend in the early 1990s. As her career progressed, Madonna portrayed a changing fashion persona, at times wearing elegant formal clothes, androgynous pieces, goth fashion, and Jewish Kabbalah bracelets. A thrift-store look was also the dominant aesthetic of new wave group The B-52s, who dressed with items inspired by rockabilly and early rock, including beehive up-dos for the women. Costume was essential in Michael Jackson's performance and video work. He used a number of recognizable clothing items, such as the sequined jacket for the *Billie Jean* video, sequined gloves, sparkling socks, and a variety of military style jackets. Also recognizable were his fedora hats, pants with zipper and buckle detailing, white undershirts, and the red leather, zippered jacket from the *Thriller* video.

The Sugarhill Gang is credited with introducing rap music to the American mainstream. The members' simple wardrobe consisted of T-shirts, jeans, tracksuits, tank tops, and fedora hats. Hip-hop evolved predominantly in the Bronx, New York, during the early 1970s in the hands of amateur DJs. As hip-hop rose on the American and global scenes, the apparel associated with the genre became essential to the success of its performers. Their clothing choices included oversized garments (marked XXXL), Kangol hats, baseball caps, and white sneakers with untied shoelaces. Jewelry, conspicuous in quantity and size, was worn by males and females. During the 1980s and 1990s the fashion choices of certain acts gathered nearly as much notice as their music. The trio RUN-D.M.C. wore black garments and large gold chains. Flavor Flav of Public Enemy wore a large clock on his chest. LL Cool J and members of the Wu-Tan Clan made the tracksuit a trademark. The duo Kriss-Kross wore reversed pants, and MC Hammer used low-crotch, baggy parachute pants. Christopher "Kid" Reid from Kid 'N Play, Big Daddy Kane, and others wore the hi-top fade hairstyle, with sharp edges and high tops, while loose and glossy "Jheri" curls were seen on rappers Eazy-E and Kurtis Blow.

Breakdancing—a style of dance incorporating fast acrobatic moves—took the American streets by storm in the 1980s. B-boys wore padded tracksuits in bright colors, while B-girls dressed in hip-snug trousers and fitted tops, including sleeveless muscle T-shirts. Rap female artists of the early 1980s, including members of the groups Sequence and Funky Four Plus One, wore tight jeans, bold makeup, and high-heeled shoes. Women in hip-hop also donned sequined miniskirts and Kente prints or African-inspired jewelry. Ice-T and Tupac Shakur, among others, popularized "gangsta" style, influenced by prison clothing and gang members. During the late 1990s male musicians in "ghetto-fabulous" fashion showcased luxurious, oversized designer coats and alligator or snakeskin shoes. Females wore brightly colored tube dresses, fur wraps, and luxurious accessories. "Bling-bling," a term used to describe over-the-top jewelry, was introduced in a 1999 song by Baby Gangsta. Grills—jewelry encrusted metal teeth coverings—were also part of the trend.

The 1990s: Grunge, Raves, and Goth

By the 1990s an increasingly global popular culture was susceptible to fashion influences from around the world. The Internet facilitated global communications, while trade agreements made it easier for companies to take their manufacturing plants from one country to another. The Internet made selling and buying clothing products easier than before. American musicians developed a strong presence on the World Wide Web, where they promoted events and sold not just music but also apparel such as T-shirts and hats.

Guitar-based grunge music spun out of Seattle, Washington. Bands like Soundgarden, Pearl Jam, and Nirvana achieved great success in the early 1990s. Grunge icons like Kurt Cobain popularized a thrift-store fashion aesthetic based on old jeans, flannel plaid button-down shirts layered with a T-shirt, army surplus garments, and vintage cardigans. Also popular were ripped and torn baggy jeans and corduroys occasionally worn below the waistline, exposing boxer shorts. Grunge females followed Courtney Love's style, consisting of baby doll and vintage dresses, fishnet stockings, hair scrunchies, and Mary Jane shoes. Hair was unkempt for men and women. Grunge musicians were also in part responsible for the great popularity of vintage clothing and bohemian or boho-chic. Designers such as Marc Jacobs and Anna Sui incorporated grunge elements in their collections.

Those attending electronic and house music dance parties or "raves" wore bright clothes with glow-in-the-dark embellishments. Platform shoes, legwarmers, baggy pants, hairpieces, and light toys were part of the look. Rave fashion was also associated with cyber fashion or cybergoth style, which relied on technology and futuristic elements. Cybergoth was inspired by science fiction and incorporated fishnet, glossy materials, metallic fabrics, and novelty prints. In general, goth style was inspired by nineteenth-century gothic romanticism. Goths wore dark colors—predominantly black—along with lace and netting embellishments and accessories such as spiked dog collars and wallet chains. White face makeup with black eyeliner, sculptural hairstyles, and platform shoes completed the look. Jewelry included religious and spiritual symbols used without specific reference to their original meaning. Black was dominant as a color elsewhere in 1990s fashion, particularly due to a trend toward minimalism in the work of fashion designers such as Calvin Klein and Donna Karan. The look was embraced by crossover Latin music stars such as Ricky Martin, Enrique Iglesias, and Marc Anthony.

During the 1990s and early 2000s fashion designers became more involved in the practice of dressing musicians for videos, live concerts, and red carpet events. A fashion designer could get a great business push simply because a musician wore his or her brand at a public appearance. A 1994 *Saturday Night Live* episode with Snoop Doggy Dogg dressed in Tommy Hilfiger started a craze among other urban acts and fans of hip-hop music for Hilfiger clothes. By the 2000s rock stars had become bona fide fashion figures, and some ventured into fashion design themselves. Successful lines by performers included Sean John by Sean Combs, Russell Simmons's Phat Farm, Gwen Stefani's L.A.M.B.,

Jennifer Lopez's Sweetface, Justin Timberlake's William Rast, and the Jessica Simpson collection.

The 2000s: Experimentation and Postmodernism

Fashion and music intermingled more than ever in the late 1990s and early 2000s. Both industries marketed in each other's media, on the assumption that fans of a certain type of music would be interested in following fashion trends set by musical acts in that genre. With musicians constantly in the public and social media, fans were always aware of their sartorial choices.

Experimentation and antidesign tendencies in fashion were often labeled postmodernism; a concept that implies the end of grand narratives in art, literature, and design. In fashion, postmodernism is defined by a mix of design elements. A sense of irony and wit was invested in new creations, praising antifunctionalism and alternative design. Lady Gaga was known for her outrageous fashion choices, including a 2010 dress designed by Franc Fernandez made entirely of raw meat. Postmodern fashion also translated into practices of deconstruction and recycling, as seen in the wardrobes of musicians such as Toni Braxton, Pink, Lil' Kim, and Christina Aguilera. Also noticeable was a tendency to self-production and self-distribution of unique pieces incorporating unusual materials. Wearable art and experimental fashion pieces were often created by musicians themselves or in collaboration with designers. In 2004 Jon Fishman of Phish wore a dress made of audiotapes playable with audiotape-head gloves. He collaborated on the project with Alyce Santora, the inventor of "sonic fabric." The band OK GO was known for incorporating media technology in its live shows. Moritz Waldemeyer designed performance costumes for OK GO featuring LED lights spelling the band's name.

Postmodern fashion was also marked by historical and ethnic dress influences. Bands MGMT and Panic at the Disco wore a variety of 1960s, 1970s, and nineteenth-century inspired pieces. Female acts, including Katy Perry and Beyoncé Knowles, wore vintage dresses and accessories. Gwen Stefani explored several influences, including Indian dress and fashionable looks from Harajuku Station in Japan. Erykah Badu and India Arie incorporated African and Rastafarian clothing elements in their wardrobes. Madonna, Britney Spears, and other celebrities wore red strings from Jewish Kabbalah mysticism. By 2011 hip-hop, pop, and dance music dominated American airwaves. Rising fashion icons among the music community included Ke$ha, Nicki Minaj, Adam Lambert, and Bruno Mars.

See also: African American Influences on American Music; B-52s, The; Badu, Erykah; Beyoncé; Big Band Music; Blues; Cobain, Kurt; Cooper, Alice; Disco; Folk Music; Funk and Postpsychedelic Funk; Glam Rock; Goth; *Grand Ole Opry*; Hendrix, Jimi; Jackson, Michael; Jazz; Joplin, Janis; Lady Gaga; Madonna; Metal; Motown; Music Television; Native American Music; Nirvana; Parton, Dolly; Pearl Jam; Pop Music; Presley, Elvis; Prince; Psychedelic Music; Punk Rock; R&B; Ragtime; Rap and Rappers; Rock 'n' Roll (Rock); *Saturday Night Live*; Ska; Slave Songs; Soul; Spears, Britney; Swing Music

Further Reading

Buxbaun, Gerda, ed. 2005. *Icons of Fashion: The 20th Century.* New York: Prestel.

English, Bonnie. 2007. *A Cultural History of Fashion in the 20th Century: From the Catwalk to the Sidewalk.* Oxford: Berg.

Gorman, Paul. 2006. *The Look: Adventures in Rock and Pop Fashion.* London: Adelita Ltd.

Heatly, Michael, ed. 2006. *The Definitive Illustrated Encyclopedia of Rock.* London: Flame Tree Publishing.

Peterson, Amy T., ed. 2008. *The Greenwood Encyclopedia of Clothing Through American History: 1900 to the Present,* Vol. 1. Westport, CT: Greenwood.

Sims, Josh. 2002. *Rock Fashion.* London: Omnibus Press.

José Blanco F.

Club Venues

Live music has been performed everywhere from stadiums and amphitheaters to basements and high school gymnasiums, but the environment of a club venue is distinctive in several respects. The smaller club venues bring musicians and audiences together and create a reciprocal energy that can intensify the sonic and physical experience of a live performance. The nightclub atmosphere—the "dim lights, thick smoke, and loud, loud music," as Gram Parsons and the Flying Burrito Brothers sang—becomes a player and an instrument in the total live music experience. Thousands of these venues have opened and closed their doors to live music across America, but a number were able to endure and achieve a legendary status that makes them synonymous with the history of popular music.

Historically, honky-tonks and juke joints were the main places for live music in the rural regions of the United States. Scattered throughout the Deep South, Midwest, and Southwest, juke joints and honky-tonks were typically small, dusty, ramshackle buildings that agricultural laborers would frequent for a night of drinking and dancing. Juke joints proved to be vital in the development of the blues, as a circuit developed for traveling musicians like Son House (1902–1988) and Robert Johnson (1911–1938). Honky-tonks were similarly crucial in the growth of what was called "hillbilly" music, made by and for white working-class people across the American countryside.

In the first half of the twentieth century nightclubs in several American cities were host to some extraordinary musical innovations. With the two world wars and growing demand for industrial labor, millions of Americans moved to cities from more rural regions of the country, and as a result cities from Chicago and Detroit in the North, to New Orleans and Memphis in the South, became focal points in the development of popular music. In New Orleans jazz flourished as the music performed at bars and brothels in the red-light district. Meanwhile, blues musicians began recording in Chicago, and a cluster of nightclubs—Silvio's, the Gatewood Tavern, the Flame Club, and the 708—eventually sprang up on Indiana Avenue on the city's South Side and Lake Street on the West Side.

In New York's neighborhood of Harlem, nightclubs and ballrooms provided the setting for the city's legendary jazz scene after World War I. After Prohibition took effect in 1920, the Harlem nightlife began attracting some of the city's affluent and more adventurous whites, who were in search of a night of music, drink, and dance. On 141st Street and Lenox Ave., the Cotton Club maintained a "whites-only" attendance policy for its audiences, but it helped launch the careers of jazz legends like Fletcher Henderson, Duke Ellington (1899–1974), and Cab Calloway (1907–1994). One block away the Savoy Ballroom emerged as the Cotton Club's racially integrated counterpart after opening its doors in 1926, and it was here that the Lindy hop and several other dances synonymous with the Jazz Age were invented. The Apollo Theater began hosting "Amateur Night" in 1934, with the competition's first winner, Ella Fitzgerald (1917–1996), moving on to sing for Chick Webb's house band at the Savoy. At roughly the same time, another young female vocalist named Billie Holiday (1915–1959) had been discovered by producer John Hammond while singing at a Harlem club called Covan's, and she then moved on to become the resident vocalist at another vital club venue, Monroe's Uptown House.

During the 1940s and 1950s New York nightclubs were an essential part of the development of bebop and other bold innovations in jazz music. In Harlem, Minton's Playhouse emerged as a key venue for Dizzie Gillespie (1917–1993), Charlie Parker (1920–1955), and Thelonious Monk (1917–1982), where they developed their faster and more freewheeling styles of jazz music. However, following the repeal of Prohibition in 1933 and the Harlem race riot of 1935, the nucleus of New York's jazz scene relocated from Harlem to New York's midtown and downtown neighborhoods. The blocks of 52nd Street between 5th and 7th Avenues became New York's new home for jazz, in nightclubs such as the Yacht Club, the Spotlite, the Three Deuces, Tondelayo's, and Birdland. Meanwhile, as bebop and then "cool jazz" grew in popularity among New York's artists, bohemians, and political radicals, a number of nightclubs also emerged in Greenwich Village and lower Manhattan, including the Village Vanguard, which opened in 1935 and adopted an all-jazz format in 1957; Arthur's Tavern, which opened in adjoining Sheridan Square in 1937; and the Five Spot Café in Cooper Square, where Thelonious Monk recorded some groundbreaking live performances, and Ornette Coleman created a new form of "free jazz" in a series of improvisational performances.

Los Angeles also hosted a vibrant jazz and R&B scene during the 1930s and 1940s on Central Avenue, a major thoroughfare that runs through the city's predominantly African American neighborhoods. The hub of the scene was the Dunbar Hotel, which included a nightclub where the greatest jazz musicians of the time performed, and an adjacent club called the Showboat that was owned by former heavyweight champion Jack Johnson. After World War II the scene moved, along with the black community, to the Watts district, where the focal point was the Barrelhouse Club, which was owned by the musician, producer, and songwriter Johnny Otis (1921–2012) and became a vital spot for the evolution of swing and R&B.

In the 1940s and 1950s the American music business had begun drifting west, with Hollywood becoming home to Capitol Records and several of the smaller but crucially significant independents like Dot Records and Specialty Records. A one-and-a-half-mile area of Hollywood's Sunset Boulevard, commonly known as the Sunset Strip, had also hosted a vibrant night life since the 1920s, especially for the city's newly minted movie stars. From then on there were close links between musicians and movie stars on Hollywood's Sunset Strip, with the Chateau Marmont Hotel and nightclubs like Ciro's, the Trocadero, and the El Mocambo creating an environment of decadence and debauchery for the celebrity elite.

A different kind of scene was developing by the end of the 1950s in Los Angeles at Venice Beach, where beat poetry, jazz, and folk music had become the core elements in an emerging counterculture that questioned the conformity and materialism of American society. Across the country the main venue for the performance of jazz and folk music within this Beat culture was the coffeehouse, a place where music could intermingle with conservation. The Venice West Café and the Gas House were the central gathering places for beatniks on Venice

Beach, and farther south, Hermosa Beach was host to the Lighthouse Jazz Café and the Insomniac Café. In New York the counterculture of Beats was linked to a longer tradition of bohemianism and radicalism that has been centered in Greenwich Village since the 1920s. MacDougal Street was the center of New York's Beat culture, where writers, musicians, and assorted ne'er-do-wells congregated to talk, drink, and listen to music at the Gaslight Cafe, the San Remo Café, and Café Wha?

The Beats and an emerging counterculture also found a welcoming environment in the city of San Francisco. A culture of diversity and dissent had already developed in San Francisco, owing to the collision of a great number of immigrant groups in the relatively small city, a breathtaking cityscape and quirky geography that attracted artists of all sorts, and a radical history that crested in 1934 with a general strike of workers throughout the city. San Francisco's thriving jazz scene being centered in the Fillmore District during the 1940s and 1950s led some to call it the "Harlem of the West." In the second half of the 1950s the Beats established an oasis for poetry and jazz in the North Beach neighborhood, immersed in the red-light district of the city's infamous Barbary Coast and wedged between its Chinese and Italian populations. In North Beach the poet Lawrence Ferlinghetti established City Lights bookstore and an accompanying publishing company, and the Beats congregated not only in the many coffeehouses and bars nearby but also in the Co-existence Bagel Shop, where San Francisco police often came just to harass the patrons who had beards and sandals.

In the 1960s the Beats begat a younger cohort of "hippies," and the center of the counterculture shifted to a neighborhood adjacent to Golden Gate Park known for the intersection of two of its main streets, Haight and Ashbury. Before the 1967 "Summer of Love" made San Francisco into the hippie capital of the world, musicians, artists, and a radical community action troupe known as the Diggers had begun moving into the Haight-Ashbury, a declining neighborhood whose large Victorian houses could be rented for cheap. The psychedelic rock scene developed in this neighborhood, whose residents famously included Janis Joplin (1943–1970) and the Grateful Dead (active 1965–1995). The primary venue for the San Francisco scene was located back in the city's historically black and Japanese neighborhood, the Fillmore, where Bill Graham began hosting rock shows in 1966. With its strobe lights, flashes of color, and projection of amorphous images, the Fillmore and its smaller rival, the Avalon Ballroom, created a total psychedelic atmosphere while bands like the Jefferson Airplane (active 1965–1974, 1989), Big Brother and the Holding Company (active 1965–1968, 1969–1972, 1987–present), and the Grateful Dead undertook their musical experimentations onstage. As the San Francisco scene expanded in the late 1960s and early 1970s, Bill Graham moved the Fillmore to a new location and renamed it the Fillmore West (distinguishing it from his Fillmore East in New York), and he also began regularly hosting concerts in a former ice-skating rink called Winterland, where *The Last Waltz* was filmed and the Sex Pistols (active 1975–1978) played their infamous final concert in 1978.

Down in Los Angeles, the folk music revival at the beginning of the 1960s had transformed into a modern form of folk-rock by the middle of the decade, and young people began frequenting nightclubs on the Sunset Strip, where this new crop of musicians performed. As the hippie subculture was emerging and moral panics about youth, music, and drugs had begun to spread, police sought to enforce a 10 PM curfew and announced plans to demolish a club called Pandora's Box, a hot spot for folk-rock. The conflict between youth and police came to a head in the so-called Sunset Strip Riots in late 1966. The series of demonstrations, melees, and arrests inspired Buffalo Springfield (active 1966–1968, 2010–2012) to write the anthem "For What It's Worth." The Whisky a Go Go, a discotheque where go-go dancers danced in cages, opened on Sunset Blvd. in 1964, and it immediately assumed the central place in the Hollywood scene. Just a little farther west on Sunset was another club, called the London Fog, which in 1966 employed a house band from Venice Beach called The Doors (active 1965–1973). As they gained a local following, The Doors were hired to become the house band at the Whisky, until one night when their singer, Jim Morrison, outraged the club's management by adding a profane, Oedipal section to the epic song "The End."

Whereas the musicians in San Francisco were largely suspicious of the major record labels, the links between the Sunset Strip scene and Hollywood's neighboring culture industry were much friendlier, and by the 1970s Los Angeles had solidified its position as the world's capital of the music business. The folk-rock movement that began in the mid-1960s grew exponentially over the next ten years, but in the process the local music community also splintered into a collection of singer-songwriters. The Troubador, a nightclub just off Sunset Blvd., was a crucial starting point for many of these singer-songwriter stars of the 1970s, including Joni Mitchell (1943–), Jackson Browne (1948–), and James Taylor (1948–). The Roxy Theater also became a vital spot on the Sunset Strip after it opened in 1973, with Neil Young (1945–) performing during the club's inaugural week. The Strip also became a notorious destination for arena rock megastars like Led Zeppelin (active 1968–1980), David Bowie (1947–), and The Rolling Stones (active 1962–), who were treated like princes when they came to West Hollywood to eat and drink at Rodney Binginheimer's English Disco or trash the hotel rooms of the Continental "Riot House."

During the 1970s rock music was big business, rock stars formed a new kind of elite, and rock concerts had become enormous spectacles typically held in sports arenas or stadiums. The burgeoning reaction against these commercial trends would come to be known as punk, and its initial salvo against the rock establishment was fired from New York. In the late 1960s and early 1970s the main hangout in lower Manhattan for musicians and artists was Max's Kansas City, a nightclub and restaurant that was a favorite of Andy Warhol and his entourage, and where The Velvet Underground (active 1964–1973, 1990, 1992–1994, 1996) played regularly until 1970. By 1974 a burgeoning punk scene was based in a small club in the Bowery, a traditionally rough neighborhood that had become even more derelict as New York City teetered on the verge of bankruptcy. The club's owner originally intended it to host country, bluegrass, and blues music, and thus he gave it the acronym CBGB, but almost immediately the club was overtaken by an eclectic crowd with a darker sensibility that was searching for an alternative to what rock music had become. A succession of eclectic performers—The Patti Smith Group, the Ramones, Television, Blondie, the Talking Heads—emerged from CBGB, which would become enshrined as the birthplace of punk rock until it closed in 2006.

Punk had a democratizing effect on live music, as punk's "do-it-yourself" (DIY) ethic championed expressiveness over musical competency, mocked and ridiculed rock stars, and sought to close the distance between musicians and audiences in an era of stadium rock. The venues for punk music were small and generally makeshift, usually forged out of underused places in any particular city's more dilapidated neighborhoods. In Los Angeles, one of the primary venues for the local punk scene, the Masque, was built in a dingy basement, while another central place for punk shows was the city's declining Chinatown neighborhood, where a fierce rivalry developed between the Hong Kong Café and Madame Wong's. Meanwhile, in East LA a Chicano punk scene developed, with performances at the Self-Help Graphic & Arts community center in a venue called the Vex. In San Francisco the punk scene was centered back in the old Beat stomping grounds of North Beach, where the key venue was a former Filipino restaurant and nightclub called the Mabuhay Gardens, better known to local punks simply as the Mab.

Across the country punk helped create a network of club venues that allowed local music scenes to develop, where local bands could build an audience and where prominent acts like Black Flag or the Dead Kennedys came to perform on tour. The DIY ethic, initially articulated by punk and then advanced by its hardcore successors during the 1980s, made it possible for shows to be held in any number of provisional spaces, from abandoned movie theaters to community youth centers to church basements.

For example, outside of the college town of Lawrence, Kansas, punk shows were regularly held in a cinderblock building surrounded by cornfields, known as the Outhouse. In Berkeley, California, a collective of people involved with the hardcore fanzine *Maximumrocknroll* created a volunteer-run, all-ages, and not-for-profit venue at 924 Gilman Street, where it subsisted as a leading venue in the punk scene for over twenty years.

Many small venues arose and flourished as regional punk scenes began developing. In Boston the Rathskeller, more commonly known as the Rat, a small and dimly lit establishment, opened its doors in 1974 in Kenmore Square, where local punks frequently fought with Red Sox fans outside the subway stop for Fenway Park. In Minneapolis, First Avenue and its smaller annex, the 7th Street Entry, nurtured the emergence of a midwestern punk scene and provided the setting for the live recording of Hüsker Dü's debut album, *Land Speed Record.* The Washington, D.C., hardcore scene initially found a home in the basement of a community center called the Wilson Center, at least until bands like Bad Brains and Minor Threat amassed a following large enough for them to fill bigger local venues like the 9:30 Club.

Strong local music scenes have also developed as they intersected with DIY punk in American college towns. In Austin, Texas, a city with a renowned history of live music that spills out of a long stretch of bars and clubs near the University of Texas, a club called Raul's emerged as the focal point of Austin's punk scene. In Athens, Georgia, a local musician and art student began hosting shows at his loft in 1978, naming it the 40 Watt Club in a joking reference to the sole lightbulb that swung from the ceiling. The 40 Watt Club relocated across the street before moving to its third and final location, where it has since helped launch the careers of R.E.M. (active 1990–2011) and many other Athens bands while becoming a revered venue for independent rock that has survived for over thirty years.

Venues for live music have continued to proliferate during the past few decades. As the bigger concerts are dominated by monopolistic corporate interests, the smaller club venues continue to provide a cheaper alternative with a more intimate atmosphere. Meanwhile, for musicians live performance is more important than ever, because digital reproduction and file-sharing make it almost impossible to earn a living from recorded music. Great numbers of club venues have opened in cities where gentrification has transformed urban neighborhoods from ethnic enclaves and centers of industry into playgrounds of consumption and style for the young and hip. Some of these clubs specialize in re-creating a nostalgic environment for consumers in search of authenticity, while others recycle the imagery and icons of the past with a more playful sense of irony and camp. Club venues will probably continue to thrive, because they serve as a meeting point for audiences in search of authenticity and an exciting atmosphere, musicians who must perform live if they are going to play music, and cities that can prosper as young members of the "creative class" revitalize neighborhoods with live music.

See also: Browne, Jackson; Ellington, Duke; Fitzgerald, Ella; Gillespie, Dizzie; Grateful Dead; Harlem Renaissance; Holiday, Billie; House, Son; Jazz; Jefferson Airplane; Johnson, Robert; Joplin, Janis; Monk, Thelonius; Otis, Johnny; Parker, Charlie; Punk; R.E.M.; Rock 'n' Roll (Rock); Taylor, James; Young, Neil

Further Reading

Buckland, Gail. 2000. *Who Shot Rock and Roll: A Photographic History, 1955–Present.* New York: Knopf.

Epting, Chris. 2007. *Led Zeppelin Crashed Here: The Rock and Roll Landmarks of North America.* Santa Monica, CA: Santa Monica Press.

Waggoner, Susan. 2001. *Nightclub Nights: Art, Legend, Style 1920–1960.* New York: Rizzoli.

Ryan Moore

Nirvana lead singer and guitarist Kurt Cobain performing on stage. (AP Photo)

Cobain, Kurt (1967–1994)

Kurt Cobain was the singer, guitarist, and main songwriter for Seattle-based grunge band Nirvana (active 1987–1994). His music combined a punk sound with melodic riffs, and his lyrics spoke to disaffected youth across the world. His band is often credited with helping to break down the boundaries between "independent" and "mainstream" music, paving the way for the success of a variety of bands that would once have remained on the musical margins. Since his suicide at age twenty-seven he has become an iconic figure in the rock canon.

Born in the small town of Aberdeen in Washington State, Cobain was reportedly deeply affected by the divorce of his parents when he was seven. This, in combination with taking prescription behavior-modifying drugs such as ritalin from an early age, has been cited as a major contributory factor to the anger, disillusionment, and cynicism expressed in Cobain's music. Cobain's childhood after the divorce was full of upheaval and illness; conflict with his parents and their partners eventually left him homeless at the age of seventeen.

However, after receiving the gift of a guitar on his fourteenth birthday, Cobain became dedicated to learning how to play the instrument. Inspired by punk and new wave bands, as well as by more melodic groups such as The Beatles, in the mid-1980s he began playing with other musicians, including members of the Melvins (active 1983–present) and Krist Novoselic (1965–), who would go on to play bass with Cobain. By March 1988 Cobain and Novoselic had recorded a demo and were performing under the name Nirvana, and in January 1989 they recorded their first album, *Bleach,* for Seattle's Sub Pop label, with drummer Chad Channing.

The album was met with critical acclaim, and the band was hailed as a star of the newly emerging Seattle scene. As Thurston Moore, leader of Sonic Youth, remarked in a 2009 interview:

> They were a band that represented what was going on with the demographic that was out there, more so than Guns N' Roses, who were the kings of rock at that point. Any Midwestern kid who was pimply-faced with a bad haircut could look at Nirvana and go, "Oh, that's me." As opposed to looking at Guns N' Roses [and thinking], "Oh, I wish I was that." They didn't have to wish they were Kurt Cobain, they were Kurt Cobain. ("Paper Guru" 2009)

This star status was more than confirmed with the release of the band's next album, *Nevermind* (with Dave Grohl replacing Channing on drums) in September 1991, on the major label Geffen. *Nevermind* achieved gold status and reached number one on the U.S. album charts in early 1992 and the band was adopted as the "voice of their generation."

Despite the way Cobain actively sought commercial success for his band, the scale of the fame achieved seems to have caused problems for him. His long-standing health issues and problems with drug abuse were exacerbated during periods of intense touring and publicity. His personal life suffered also. In 1992 Cobain married and had a daughter with Courtney Love (1964–), front woman of the band Hole (active 1989–2002, 2009–present). Their relationship was under constant scrutiny, to the extent that the couple's newly born daughter was (briefly) taken from their custody following reports that they had been taking drugs. Cobain became increasingly depressed. In March 1994 he overdosed on prescription pills in Rome, but was resuscitated. A month later he was found dead in his home from a self-inflicted gunshot wound to the head. A suicide note was found nearby. Since this time his life has been the subject of a number of documentaries, books, and films, including the 2006 documentary *About a Son* and Gus Van Sant's *Last Days* (2005).

See also: Grunge; Guitar; New Wave; Nirvana; Punk Rock

Further Reading

Azerrad, Michael. *About a Son.* 2007. Directed by A. J. Schnack. Shout! Factory. DVD.

Cross, Charles R. 2001. *Heavier Than Heaven: The Biography of Kurt Cobain.* London: Sceptre.

"The Paper Guru Interview: Thurston Moore." 2009. *Paper Magazine* (July 2009). http://www.papermag.com/arts_and_style/2009/07/the-paper-guru-interview.php.

Prato, Greg. 2009. *Grunge Is Dead: The Oral History of Seattle Rock Music.* Toronto: ECW Press.

True, Everett. 2007. *Nirvana: The Biography.* New York: Da Capo Press.

Catherine Strong

Coffee Shops and American Music

Coffee shops and bookstores are popular sites for music and social interaction in cities and towns across the United States. People gather in these spaces to talk, read, write, play games, and pass time. The aroma of coffee and lure of interesting texts and conversations create an atmosphere that is enhanced by music, whether it is background music or live performance. Indeed, over time music has become integral to these spaces.

Coffeehouses have been part of communities since the fifteenth and sixteenth centuries. Some of the earliest shops documented were in Istanbul, Cairo, Damascus, and Persian cities. Coffee made its way to Europe as trade through the British East India Company and Dutch East India Company increased, and coffeehouses soon followed. The first coffeehouse in England was established in Oxford in 1650 in a building that is now known as the Grand Café. Intellectuals like Voltaire and Jean Jacques Rousseau frequented the Café Procope in Paris, a site considered to be integral to the French Enlightenment. Coffeehouses were often exclusive, reflecting the politics of those who gathered in them, and women were sometimes not permitted to frequent these spaces, particularly in England and France. At times various rulers, including Charles II, tried to suppress gatherings at coffeehouses because of the political nature of the discussions and the perceived threat they posed to their leadership.

The first coffee shop in the United States was established in Boston in 1676. The shops often reflected the cultural heritage of the neighborhoods where they were located, particularly through the pastries and light fare served alongside the varieties of coffees, teas, and espressos, which were found in Italian neighborhoods. Beginning in the late 1950s coffeehouses became an entertainment venue as musicians, usually folk performers, were drawn to these intimate spaces that easily accommodated a single musician and a guitar. The Beats, a group of post–World War II writers and other people who identified with them, were connected with coffeehouses in neighborhoods like Greenwich Village in New York City and North Beach in San Francisco. These writers, including Jack Kerouac, William Burroughs, and Allen Ginsberg, inspired changes in attitudes and norms that embraced experimentation with drugs, sex, Eastern religion, and open forms of expression.

Elements of the Beat culture influenced the hippie culture of the 1960s, and coffeehouses became hubs for folk musicians and activists who sought social change. Bob Dylan performed folk music at the 10 O'Clock Scholar, a coffee shop in Minneapolis near the University of Minnesota campus. Joan Baez, who experienced coffee shop culture when she was seventeen years old and her Harvard professor father took her to Tulla's Coffee Grinder in Boston, began to perform regularly in coffee shops in the Boston area. Jerry Garcia was known to play guitar and write poems while hanging out at Kepler's Books in Palo Alto, California. Songs were also written about the coffee shop culture, such as "The Coffee House Blues" by Lightnin' Hopkins.

In 1967 the Last Exit on Broadway coffee shop opened in Seattle near the University of Washington campus, beginning the city's reputation for coffee shops and counterculture. In 1971 the Starbucks coffee shop chain began in Seattle and in time expanded to cities across the United States and more than fifty-five countries. These coffee shops host live musicians, play recorded music throughout the store, and sell music on CDs and over the Internet to customers. Starbucks Coffee Shops' Web site claims the company is just as passionate about music as about coffee, and that all music played in the stores is handpicked. In 1995 Starbucks sold *Blue Note Blend,* its first of many CDs. Hear Music, which began in 1990 as a catalog company before Starbucks purchased it in 1999, is the company's retail music concept and record label. In 2007 the Hear Music record label was launched as a joint venture between Starbucks and Concord Music Group, and Paul McCartney became the first artist to sign with the new label, followed by Joni Mitchell, Carly Simon, James Taylor, John Mellencamp, and others. Starbucks is one of the top 40 music-oriented retailers, promoting a range of genres and artists from the Bee Gees to Taylor Swift, Elton John, the Kings of Leon, and John Legend and the Roots. Its top-selling CD was Ray Charles's *Genius Loves Company.* Hear Music often features world music, the traditional or cultural music of indigenous peoples around the world. As scholar Anahid Kassabian (2004) has observed, the world music sold at Starbucks often coincides with countries associated with growing coffee, like Brazil and Cuba. This lends itself to a form of musical tourism that vicariously allows listeners to experience other cultures.

Music in the style found in coffeehouses can be enjoyed at any time if listeners tune in to the Sirius XM music channel The Coffee House, which broadcasts music by singer-songwriters and acoustic rock musicians, similar to the music one might hear in a local coffee shop or bookstore café.

Although music, food and beverages, and means of social interaction evolve and change over time and cultures, it seems clear that music will always be integral to the social spaces people inhabit. Currently, as both chain and independent bookstores close or struggle to stay in business in the e-book age, there are fewer bookstores with coffee bars or cafés. Nonetheless, coffeehouses have been an important site for these interactions between music and people, and they have influenced American music and culture across the centuries.

See also: Food and Music; Mellencamp, John; Mitchell, Joni; Satellite Radio; Simon, Carly; Taylor, James; World Music

Further Reading

Cowan, Brian. 2005. *The Social Life of Coffee: The Emergence of the British Coffeehouse.* New Haven, CT: Yale University Press.

Ellis, Markman. 2004. *The Coffee House: A Cultural History.* London: Weidenfeld & Nicolson.

Kassabian, Anahid. 2004. "Would You Like Some World Music with Your Latte? Starbucks, Putumayo, and Distributed Tourism." *Twentieth-century Music* 1: 209–223.

Jacqueline Edmondson

Cole, Nat King (1919–1965)

Born in Montgomery, Alabama, Nathaniel Adams Cole was one of the most influential African American singers, pianists, songwriters, and actors of the twentieth century. He released more than forty albums and one hundred singles. His most prominent contributions are his successful crossing over from jazz to popular music and introducing "race music" to the larger American musical scene.

Cole's year of birth is subject to dispute; it was either 1915, 1916, or 1919. His parents heavily influenced his musical career even in his childhood. Cole's mother, Perlina Adames Coles, was a pianist and choir director at the church where her husband, Edward James Coles, was a Baptist minister. Cole started playing organ and singing in his father's church at the age of twelve.

Cole's musical career blossomed after the family moved to Chicago. Wendell Philips High School nurtured his passion for jazz music. He established and led a band called Rogues of Rhythm and a quintet called Nat Coles and His Royal Dukes. At sixteen Nat joined one of his brothers, Eddie, to become the pianist for Eddie's quintet, the Solid Swingers (1930s). In 1936 both Eddie and Nat left Chicago after joining the revival of the all black musical comedy *Shuffle Along* (1921). When the show ended suddenly in Long Beach, California, Nat and his wife, Nadine Robinson (divorced in 1948), remained in California. Once he found a job as a pianist at the Century Club in Santa Monica, he soon became a regular performer, well recognized by other jazz musicians.

The name Nat King Cole originated in either 1937 or 1938. Nat organized a small group to play at the Sewanee Inn, a nightclub in Los Angeles. Its owner nicknamed him "King Cole," and the group was soon known as the King Cole Trio. The trio also included Oscar Moore (1916–1981) and Wesley Prince (1907–1980). They signed with Capitol Records in 1943 and produced the hit song, "Straighten Up and Fly Right" in 1944. The trio's success continued in the 1940s with "Get Your Kicks on Route 66" (1944), "For Sentimental Reasons" (1946), and others. The trio also appeared in movies such as *The Stork Club* (1945), *See My Lawyer* (1945),

Jazz pianist and singer Nat King Cole in New York, ca. 1947. (William P. Gottlieb/Ira and Leonore S. Gershwin Fund Collection, Music Division, Library of Congress)

and *Breakfast in Hollywood* (1946). "The Christmas Song" (1946) was a turning point for Cole, realizing the crossover from the R&B and jazz markets to the popular market. From this period on he shifted away from the trio and focused on his work as a vocalist. "Nature Boy" (1948), "Mona Lisa" (1950), "Too Young" (1951), "Send for Me" (1957), and other hit songs reflected Cole's new style.

Despite his success, Cole faced racism. His white neighbors collectively protested when he purchased a house in Los Angeles in 1949. The NAACP and its chief counsel, Thurgood Marshall, criticized him for playing for segregated audiences. In 1956 NBC offered Cole his own television show, which maintained high ratings but failed to secure many advertisers. Few companies at the time considered shows for African Americans to be worthy of their investment.

A lifetime heavy smoker, Cole was diagnosed with lung cancer in 1964. Despite receiving medical treatment, he died on February 15, 1965, in Santa Monica, California. His daughter, Natalie Cole (1950–), has become a successful Grammy Award–winning singer in her own right. In 1991 she had a hit with her album *Unforgettable,* which featured her singing American standards, including a duet with her father, made by recording her singing with a recording by her father. At the 1992 Grammy Awards, *Unforgettable* won Record of the Year, Song of the Year, and Album of the Year, among others. Natalie Cole continues to record and perform.

See also: African American Influences on American Music; Jazz; Pop Music

Further Reading

Epstein, Daniel Mark. 2000. *Nat King Cole.* Boston: Northeastern University Press.

Haskins, James, and Kathleen Benson. 1984. *Nat King Cole.* New York: Stein and Day.

Yuya Kiuchi

Collaborations in Music

Collaborations between musicians have always been a way for them to cross genre lines and expose others to different sounds and sonic structures. Music in any form is collaboration and has always been about how musicians and artists work together to create something for the audience. Through the combination of writers and performers across genres, audiences have been exposed to newer forms of music that they may not have previously experienced. Collaborations have continuously been a beneficial part of American musical culture.

Musical collaboration occurs on all levels, within bands and between musicians. Working together in a group or with a songwriter is the major key to success in music. Examples of groups coming together to collaborate can be found in some of the earliest music on Earth. The earliest written forms of music are suggested to be from the Hurrians, ca. 1400 BC, and these hymns, or chants, could constitute the earliest form of pure musical collaboration between humans (Buccellati 2003). Music throughout history has revolved around partnerships and how people work together to inspire, motivate, move, or influence the audience. This has not changed and continues to be the focal point of musical collaborations. The importance of exposing people to different sounds is key to the development of music and to advancing music in the future.

The history of Western music contains many examples of people working together to get a certain pitch, tenor, or sound, but it is the way in which individuals collaborate that has pushed the boundaries of music and allowed audiences to be exposed to newer sounds. Even within the sanctity of the church, musical collaboration was highly discussed, praised, and vilified. In the sixteenth century Christian church music was directly linked to the Word and focused on collaboration among voices. "All 16th–century music measures itself by its relation to the word and its intelligibility, adopting the technique of imitative polyphony and placing enormous and unbearable strains on the traditional" (Randel 2003, 178). One of the most innovative collaborations within the church occurred on June 21, 1836, in England at a Freemasons' hall. Tallis's "Song of Forty Parts" was sung by about one hundred singers with no instrumentation; it stands as one of the largest collaborations from that time (Gould 1853). This strict formula began to break down over time, but the voice and organ collaboration is still found in many forms of church music. Perhaps the largest musical collaborations occurred in the church, and the audience's relationship to the song was always paramount.

In America the Puritan view of musical collaboration was that it was inherently evil and needed to be controlled. *Confession of the Puritans* (1571) contains the following about the singing of psalms: "We allow the people to join in one voice in a psalm-tune, but not in tossing the psalm from one side to the other, with the intermingling of organs" (Gould 1853). Although this attitude would eventually change, the important point is that voices were still allowed to come together in praise. Through this type of collaboration the Word of God was still sacred. The audience was central to the development of the scripture, and the song format focused on delivering, through collaboration, the foundations of the faith. As society progressed, music changed, and collaborations among musicians and vocalists began to take on an extremely different slant, as entertainment.

Some early forms of American popular music were based on vocal collaborations in folk music. This type of music focused on how the musician's voice worked with a banjo or guitar and how two vocalists could motivate listeners. Robert Winslow Gordon (1888–1961) was the first director at the Archive of American Folk-Song, which was established by the Library of Congress on July 1, 1928. This archive began the official collections of folk music in America, and Gordon was influential in obtaining songs from rural performers and street musicians throughout the country. He was succeeded by Alan Lomax (1915–2002), who focused on the outsider status of folk music and musicians who were not influenced by modernization. This allowed for the voice to take precedence over the music and the collaboration between singer and audience to be at the forefront (Cohen 2002). Friendships between musicians who were not influenced by modernization formed the framework of American music. These songs encouraged many people who heard them to "get back" to a time that they thought lost to the modern world.

The history of jazz and Western swing music in America is also full of musical collaboration. The Original Dixieland Jass Band, which would later change the spelling of its name to Jazz, was the first jazz band to record, and its "Livery Stable Blues" (1917) was the first jazz recording. Other groups playing in a similar style existed before this band, but this was the first example of recorded jazz. The way that the musicians worked together in New Orleans/Dixieland swing music also reflects some of the first forms of musical collaboration between artists. This style of playing music together inspired many more musicians to work together to expose audiences to different forms of sound. Jazz continued to dominate American popular music, and in the 1950s collaboration pushed music forward again.

Artists such as Miles Davis (1926–1991) and John Coltrane (1926–1967) were among the first popular musicians to succeed in crossing styles to expose others to newer sounds. The smoother trumpet sound of Davis mixed with the harsher sounds of Coltrane's saxophone on many Columbia recordings and showed audiences the diversity of sound inherent in jazz and American music. From 1955 to 1959 the two artists worked together for Columbia, and Miles Davis brought in many other musicians to record during these sessions. By bringing together musicians like John Coltrane and Cannonball Adderley (1928–1975) on saxophone; Red Garland (1923–1984), Bill Evans (1929–1980), and Wynton Kelly (1931–1971) on piano; Paul Chambers (1935–1969) on bass; and Philly Joe Jones (1923–1985) and Jimmy Cobb (1929–) on drums, Davis created a set of recordings that would change the way jazz sounded and was received. These recordings inspired many musicians to branch out and collaborate with different-sounding players and encouraged record labels to take risks on music that was not completely straightforward.

Collaborations between musicians were also influential in early folk songs. Folk music in America formed the framework of musical collaboration and produced songs that have inspired many. Collaborating artists such as Woody Guthrie (1912–1967) and Cisco Huston (1918–1961) and Simon & Garfunkel (active 1957–1970, 1981–1983, 2003–2004, 2009) gave audiences two voices working in unison. Paul Simon (1941–) and Art Garfunkel (1941–), using the stage name Tom & Jerry, recorded their hit song "Hey Schoolgirl" in 1957 and demonstrated a sound that showcased the era. They became extremely successful artists on Columbia Records. Cisco Huston and Woody Guthrie, whose voices blended extremely well, also allowed people to hear two completely different styles of voice in collaboration.

In 1944 Guthrie began re-recording old folk songs with new lyrics that he had written. These early recordings for Asch Records showcased the importance of different voices working together to inspire and push music forward. The way that Guthrie used friends and fellow musicians to construct songs was extremely important in developing and establishing a sound of folk and American music. Through these recordings he developed a sound that inspires many today. Songs like "Pretty Boy Floyd" and "Bury Me Beneath the Willow" became the focal point of American musical collaboration in voice.

In the 1950s the friendships and stage presence of a group of singers garnered great attention throughout America with shows in Las Vegas and around the country. Singers like Cab Calloway (1907–1994); Louis Prima (1910–1978); and the Rat Pack of Frank Sinatra (1915–1998), Dean Martin (1917–1995), Sammy Davis Jr. (1925–1990), Peter Lawford (1923–1984), and Joey Bishop (1918–2007) all gave friendship and musical collaboration a boost into the world of popular music. These singers succeeded based on how they worked together, in different pitch and sound, to expose audiences to the big band swing and lounge music that had been popular in earlier decades.

Louis Prima worked closely with the New Orleans saxophonist Sam Butera (1927–2009) and the vocalist who would later become his wife, Keely Smith (1932–), to reproduce and create the sounds that he had grown up listening to and performing. His musical career began in the 1930s. He was one of the first acts to appear and be successful in Las Vegas. At the outset of his career he played trumpet in New Orleans and then moved to New York to perform with big bands and a small jazz combo called Louis Prima and his New Orleans Gang. They recorded many famous tracks, including "Sing, Sing, Sing," which would later be covered by Benny Goodman's band (active 1926–1986) and become an iconic representation of America. As the first big band era of the 1920s and 1930s drew to a close, he found himself looking for work, and that is when the Vegas shows began. His career was emblematic of what collaboration and friendship between musicians can do. Singing together, he and his future wife showed the musical world how working extremely close can bring magic to the stage.

The Rat Pack was a group of on-again, off-again friends who worked extremely well together on stage; whether they did so off stage is another topic. They started as a group of friends who gathered to drink at Humphrey Bogart's house and were originally called the Holmby Hills Rat Pack. After Bogart's death they came back together in the 1960s and became one of the most recognized groups of singers in America. Each member was successful individually, but the way that they worked together enhanced the group's fame. The differences in vocal expression and sound among this group were the key to their success. While their showmanship gained them fans, their insistence on maintaining their individuality kept their careers strong. Each member brought his own sound, attitude, demeanor, and musical focus to the group, and this is what made them famous. They helped define American music through their many recordings and movie appearances, culminating in the hit movie *Ocean's Eleven* in 1960. This movie and their many performances demonstrated what friendship and collaboration can do within music. They had a falling out during the 1960s, but they had already set the stage for how entertainers would work together in the future.

Popularity and awards are often considered signifiers of the importance of working together as musicians, and the Recording Academy has recently begun to honor direct collaboration between musicians. The Recording Academy did not have a category for collaboration until its thirty-first awards presentation in 1988. Beginning with the award for Best Country Vocal Collaboration for Roy Orbison (1936–1988) and k. d. lang (1961–), the award system finally gave credit to musicians who had come together to experience different sonic tones. The next collaboration category was added in 1994; the award for Best Pop Vocal Collaboration went to Al Green (1946–) and Lyle Lovett (1957–). The final award category for collaboration to be added was Best Rap/Sung Collaboration, which went to Eve (1978–) and Gwen Stefani (1969–) in 2001. The genre that started off as pure collaboration between singer and turntable was the last to receive a nomination from the Academy.

Many other genres that use musical collaboration have won awards. Classical music and vocal performance have always had more than one person as the focus of the award. During the first Grammy Awards in 1958, the award for Best Performance by an Orchestra went to Billy May's Big Fat Brass, and the award for Best Performance by a Vocal Group or Chorus went to Keely Smith and Louis Prima for "That Old Black Magic." These are only some of the categories of the Grammys that focused on how people worked together to make music.

In the 1980s collaboration took on a new feel and sound, with hip-hop and rap changing the world. Hip-hop and rap have always been about singers/MCs working with nothing more than a beat to create sonic structures and song frameworks. One of the most important collaborations in hip-hop and rock was Run-D.M.C. (active 1981–2002) and Aerosmith (active 1970–present) performing the song "Walk this Way." In 1986 this pairing of two completely different genres inspired countless future collaborations. Run-D.M.C. took a great risk in pairing its hip-hop vocals with a rock feel and beat. This risk paid off by exposing many people, in both genres, to a different sound and experience. This was the main point of the musical collaboration, and the song was a success, leading to a wider variety of music enthusiasts listening to hip-hop and rock music.

Many other examples exist of rap and hip-hop crossing with rock, and an entire new genre was created, called rap-rock for its collaboration of sound. The first bands in the mainstream to try this new genre were Anthrax (active 1981–present) and Ice-T's Bodycount (active 1990–2006, 2009–present). The genre was further developed by groups like Rage Against the Machine (active 1991–2000, 2007–present), Korn (active 1993–present), Limp Bizkit (active 1994–2005, 2009–present), and Linkin Park (active 1996–present). All of these groups blended sonic structures and combined with different artists to expose audiences to new sounds. By adding a DJ or MC to rock sounds, these groups both challenged audiences to pay attention and gained immense success. Although not the first groups to do this, they pushed the boundaries of both genres by incorporating rap's lyrical structure with rock's song format.

This crossing of genres is the major way for musical collaboration to inspire and push the boundaries of sound and audience. While doing so, pairings have given older artists new life and have resurrected careers that were dormant for long periods of time. Many examples exist of newer bands "finding" older artists and recording with them in an attempt to revive a feeling or sound that has been lost. Some of the most successful examples of this are Jack White (1975–) and Loretta Lynn (1935–), and the American Recording series with Johnny Cash (1932–2003) and many other contemporary musicians. Through the use of newer writers and artists, these "classic" performers have been exposed to a new generation of fans and gained a new life through collaboration.

One of the greatest examples of consistent collaboration is Johnny Cash and his album entitled *American Recordings.* In 1994 Rick Rubin (1963–) decided to record Cash in his living room with only a guitar. On this album Cash recorded his own songs and performed songs by Tom Waits (1949–) and Glenn Danzig (1955–). The songs penned by Waits and Danzig helped the album gain new audiences and propelled Cash into a new status among younger listeners. The album won the Grammy Award for "Best Contemporary Folk Album" and led to a series of recordings based on collaborations.

The American Recordings series continued for four more albums and is one of the last collections of music that Cash recorded. Through this collection of records, entitled *American II: Unchained*; *American III: Solitary Man*; *American IV: The Man Comes Around*; *American V: A Hundred Highways*; and *American VI: Ain't No Grave,* Cash worked with many different artists and exposed countless listeners to his sound. On *American IV* Cash recorded the song "Hurt," written by Trent Reznor (1965–) and his band Nine Inch Nails (active 1988–present). This song became a huge hit and drove Cash's resurgence into the mainstream. Throughout the series of albums Cash recorded songs by Tom Petty (1950–), Chris Cornell (1964–), Beck (1970–), Sting (1951–), Bruce Springsteen (1949–), Paul Simon, John Lennon (1940–1980), and Paul McCartney (1942–), and others that crossed many different genres. This series of collaborations remains one of the deepest and most resonating sets of recording in recent times. Cash's last recording, before his death in September 2003, was captured during these sessions and appears on *American VI: Ain't No Grave.* "I Corinthians: 15:55" is said to be the last song that Cash wrote during his life, and although it is not a collaboration, it appears alongside songs by Sheryl Crow (1962–) and Kris Kristofferson (1936–).

In 2004 Jack White recorded Loretta Lynn's album *Van Lear Rose.* The song "Portland, Oregon" won the Grammy Award for "Best Country Collaboration with Vocals." This album was well received critically, and many people found for the first time or rediscovered Loretta Lynn's vocal prowess. These types of collaborations are often cited as mere attempts to make a profit, but in this case, White's love for Lynn's music and desire to keep her voice and spirit young gave the record a new sound. "It's interesting to see how this album will be taken by [rock] fans," White said. "I think a lot of White Stripes fans are already into it. Even if it's just because I'm involved that they check it out, that's all it takes. I wish somebody would've put a Loretta Lynn album in front of me when I was 10 years old" (DeAngelo, Gottlieb, and Conge 2004). This statement makes clear why musical collaboration is so vital for exposing new people to older and different sounds.

Another recent effective collaboration was between Rhianna (1983–) and Jennifer Nettles (1974–) and the 2011 Country Music Awards. This performance was beneficial to both artists and audiences in country and R&B. The song "California King Bed" resonated with the audience in a way that captured the feel and soul of both genres. The risk that was taken paid off, as the song was very successful. Rhianna, who is known for reggae-influenced soul and R&B, gave the Country Music Awards a new sonic structure and focal point throughout the song's performance. In an interview with *The Daily Mail* in England, Nettles stated: "It [the performance] is such a moment. And I think what it shows us is that good music is good and good performance is good, and as long as you like it, who cares what you call it. Get out there and have fun with each other" (Johnson 2011). This concept of having fun regardless of genre is one of the most basic goals of musical collaboration. Throughout the performance, the crowd was awed and impressed by the vocal display of both women, and this allowed both genres to gain new fans and supporters.

Collaboration and friendship have played one of the most important roles in music in defining sound, pushing boundaries, and challenging audiences throughout the world. Without people coming together to sing, write, perform, and entertain, the way we hear and think of music would not be the same. From the first instances of music through the way music was shaped by the church to modern-day performances and recordings, collaboration has remained at the forefront in musical history. It remains to be seen what the newest or latest collaboration will be, but it will always be about artists creating sound that is different. It is this difference and the way that musicians work together to create that is paramount within American music and the world's.

See also: Aerosmith; Awards and Prizes for Music; Big Band Music; Cash, Johnny; Coltrane, John; Crossovers; Crow, Sheryl; Davis, Miles; Folk Music; Garfunkel, Art; Goodman, Benny; Guthrie, Woody; Hip-Hop; Jazz; Kristofferson, Kris; Lynn, Loretta; Orbison, Roy; Petty, Tom; R&B; Rage Against the Machine; Rap and Rappers; Rock 'n' Roll (Rock); Rubin, Rick; Simon, Paul; Springsteen, Bruce; Swing; White, Jack

Further Reading

Buccellati, G. 2003. "Hurrian Music." *IIMAS.* http://128.97.6.202/urkeshpublic/music.htm.

Cohen, Ronald D. 2002. *Rainbow Quest: The Folk Music Revival and American Society, 1940–1970.* Amherst and Boston: University of Massachusetts Press.

D'Angelo, Joe, Meridith Gottlieb, and Bill Conge. 2004. "Jack White Surprises Loretta Lynn by Cranking Up the Country: Stripes Singer Produced, Performed on *Van Lear Rose.*" *MTV.com.* http://www.mtv.com/news/articles/1486953/jack-white-cranks-up-country-loretta.jhtml.

Gould, Nathaniel Duren.1853. *Church Music in America.* Boston: A.N. Johnson.

"Jazz Milestones." n.d. *A Passion for Jazz!* http://www.apassion4jazz.net/milestones.html (accessed July 28, 2009).

Johnson, Chris. 2011. "Flame-haired Rihanna Sets the Stage Alight at Academy of Country Music Awards." *Associated Newspapers Ltd.,* April 4. http://www.dailymail.co.uk/tvshowbiz/article-1373094/Academy-Country-Music-Awards-2011-Flame-haired-Rihanna-sets-stage-alight.html#ixzz1RzniUgZh.

Randel, Don Michael, ed. 2003. *The Harvard Dictionary of Music.* Cambridge, MA: Harvard University Press.

Eric James Abbey and Maggie Lin

Coltrane, John (1926–1967)

Few in the jazz community can claim to have influenced as many musicians as John Coltrane has. His reach not only among musicians but in other artistic endeavors is still felt today, decades after his death. His contribution to American culture is twofold: he helped to establish jazz as a uniquely American art style and also established the credibility of the avant-garde scene in jazz, which has ties to the civil rights movement.

Coltrane was born in 1926 in North Carolina and cut his teeth playing in a navy jazz band after he enlisted in 1945. He also played as a sideman in Dizzy Gillespie's (1917–1993) Big Band. Through his collaborations with Miles Davis (1926–1991) and later Thelonious Monk (1917–1982) he solidified himself as a jazz virtuoso and began to cultivate, as critic Ira Gitler surmised (1958), his sheets of sound. He later established a quartet that became synonymous with his name, including McCoy Tyner (1938–), Elvin Jones (1927–2004), and Jimmy Garrison (1934–1976). He became one of the few jazz musicians to score a number one hit, with his rendition of "My Favorite Things," which became a staple of his repertoire.

What is supremely unique about Coltrane was his drive to expand his music. He overcame an addiction to heroin and soon began channeling his newfound spirituality into his music. His composition, *A Love Supreme,* is his love note to spirituality itself and has been one of his best-selling albums. During the mid-1960s, he began to transition into the avant-garde music scene. Coltrane's music during this era was described by some as antijazz; they criticized his penchant for playing long, extended solos in his set that would carry on for upwards of an hour and reach into the extended range of the horn, which many decried as howls and screams (Kofsky 1998). He became a figurehead of the jazz scene, an established superstar who gave credibility to a fledgling style of music.

His music during this time was championed by specific counterculture groups, many of which had ties to the civil rights movement of the 1960s. When asked if his music was meant to reflect the anger of the oppressed, Coltrane simply stated he was only angry at himself for not achieving the goals he had set for himself (Kofsky 1998).

His personal vision outweighed his need for financial or critical success; he was true to this vision and therefore truly an inspiration to those who had the same needs.

See also: African American Influences on American Music; Avant-garde in American Music, The; Davis, Miles; Drugs and Music; Jazz; Monk, Thelonius

Official Web Site: http://www.johncoltrane.com/

Further Reading

Backus, R. 1976. *Fire Music: A Political History of Jazz.* New York: Vanguard Press.

Jazz saxophonist John Coltrane, ca. 1962. (Michael Ochs Archives/Getty Images)

Gerard, C. 1998. *Jazz in Black and White.* Westport, CT: Praeger Publishing.

Gitler, Ira. 1958. "Trane on the Track." *Downbeat,* October 16. http://www.downbeat.com/default.asp?sect=stories&subsect=story_detail&sid=355.

Jones, L. 2001. *Blues People.* New York: Perennial Publishing.

Kofsky, F. 1998. *John Coltrane and the Jazz Revolution of the 1960s.* New York: Pathfinder Press.

Mathieson, K. *Giant Steps: Bebop and the Creators of Modern Jazz.* Edinburgh: Payback Press, 1999.

Greg Dedrick

Combs, Sean (1969–) (a.k.a. Sean "Puffy" Combs; "Puff Daddy," 1997–2001; Sean "P Diddy" Combs, 2001–2005; "Diddy," 2005–Present)

Sean Combs is one of the most important figures in hip-hop. A savvy businessman, Combs has been successful in the music industry as a performer and producer. He has starred in several television shows, created a clothing line, and organized political movements. He has also been involved in his share of controversy and is almost as well known for his nonmusical activities.

Combs was born in Harlem, New York, in 1969. He spent most of his early life in Mount Vernon, New York. His business acumen was apparent even when he was very young: he lied about his age and identity to acquire and manage multiple newspaper delivery routes. He moved to Washington, D.C., to attend Howard University and took an internship at Uptown Records. This internship led to a job offer, and he dropped out of Howard. He became an A&R (artists and repertoire) agent for Uptown and produced albums for Father MC, Mary J. Blige, and Heavy D and the Boyz. He aspired to be a vice president in the company but was fired in 1993; some say he may have been a bit too ambitious for his own good.

He started Bad Boy Records in his apartment later that year and soon signed Craig Mack and Notorious B.I.G. (Christopher Wallace) to his label. In 1994 Mack's single "Flava in Your Ear" made it into the top 10 and achieved platinum status (one million copies shipped) from the Recording Industry Association of America (RIAA). Notorious B.I.G.'s "Big Poppa" also made it into the top 10 and was certified double platinum. In 2002 Arista Records stopped distributing Bad Boy's lineup, signing Faith Evans away from Diddy's label. Bad Boy Records returned in 2006 with a new roster of artists. Diddy's most recent project, Diddy Dirty Money, debuted in late 2010.

Diddy has had his share of controversy, most notably as a result of his involvement in the Death Row/Bad Boy Records feud, which resulted in the shooting deaths of Tupac Shakur (1996) and Notorious B.I.G. (1997). One of Diddy's best-known songs, "I'll Be Missing You," was written to honor B.I.G. In 1999 he was charged with possession of a weapon following a shooting at a New York City nightclub. He was acquitted of the criminal charge and settled out of court in a related civil lawsuit.

Diddy has met with success outside of the music industry as well. In 2004 he teamed up with MTV to spearhead the "Vote or Die" campaign, which encouraged young people to get out and vote. He has starred in a number of reality television shows, including seasons two through four of *Making the Band* and *I Want to Work for Diddy,* both of which aired in the mid-2000s. He also started an acclaimed, successful clothing company, Sean John, which has won numerous design awards around the world. In 2003, with little preparation, he ran the New York City Marathon. He also raised nearly $2 million to benefit inner-city schools.

Sean Combs at a pre-Grammy party at the Beverly Hilton Hotel in Beverly Hills, February 11, 2007. (Feature Flash/ Dreamstime.com)

See also: African American Influences on American Music; Hip-Hop; Hip-Hop Nation; Notorious Musicians; Rap and Rappers; Shakur, Tupac; Social Causes of Musicians

Further Reading

Cable, Andrew. 1998. *A Family Affair: The Unauthorized Sean "Puffy" Combs Story.* New York: Ballantine.

Ro, Ronin. 2001. *Bad Boy: The Influence of Sean "Puffy" Combs on the Music Industry.* New York: Pocket Books.

Michael Berry

Comedy and Satire in American Music

Wherever there is seriousness in music, there is an opportunity for comedy. Although the use of comedy and satire in music has a long history, it can truly be said to have flourished since 1945. In an age when mass media and the relative ease of travel provided far wider accessibility than ever before, musical humorists in the United States found ample opportunities to ply their craft and have a significant impact on American culture more widely (as opposed to merely locally or regionally) and even to reach audiences around the world. Comedy in music can take several forms. We might find it in the title of a work, such as "humoresque" or "scherzo," as well as such examples as the1952 hit novelty song "I Saw Mommy Kissing Santa Claus," or Peter Schickele's "Schleptet," instead of "Septet." Comedy can also appear within the musical structure of a piece itself, such as contrasting musical styles, clichés, parodies of common melodies or rhythms, or unusual instrumentation. Finally—and most commonly—comedy can arise through actual performance, such as singing serious lyrics in a lighthearted manner, or playing or conducting music in a comic fashion. In the fields of both popular and classical music, several performers have drawn on one or more of these approaches with the goal of making people laugh.

Popular Music

Spike Jones (Lindley Armstrong Jones; 1911–1965) was a pioneer in parodying popular music in the modern era. With his band, Spike Jones & His City Slickers, he specialized in using unusual instruments for aural effects, including cowbells, washboards, and even pistols. The group's first major hit, "Der Fuehrer's Face," was featured in a Disney cartoon of the same title that earned an Academy Award in 1942. The song provided the foundation for Jones's later work in musical comedy. Capitalizing on their growing popularity, the band launched the Musical Depreciation Revue in 1947, an ensemble of more than twenty male and female musicians, singers, and comedians, which toured the country regularly for a decade. The group added original "instruments," such as a goat that could bleat in the key of C, or a "latrinophone" that used a toilet seat and a harp made of catgut. Top hits during this period, among others, were "Cocktails for Two" (with hiccups) and "All I Want for Christmas Is My Two Front Teeth."

Born in Long Beach, Jones became involved in show business at a young age as a jazz drummer and then bandleader. He first led a dance band, drawing on ragtime, swing, and other styles, working in part with Bing Crosby, before discovering he could make people laugh with silly or humorous arrangements. Spike Jones & His City Slickers was one of the only groups at the time that parodied popular songs as well as performing other humorous pieces, many of which Jones orchestrated, which demanded absolute precision and able musicianship. With a well-earned reputation as the "King of Corn," he appealed to both children and adults, although he once commented that he was "too corny for the elite and too elite for the corny." Jones also parodied classical music and opera, thereby in his words "murdering the classics"; Leoncavello's *Pagliacci* became "Pal-Yat-Chee," Offenbach's *Orpheus* became "Morpheus," and Liszt's *Hungarian Rhapsody* became "Rhapsody from Hunger(y)." Jones's work in musical comedy provided an inspiration for many artists who followed, including Stan Freberg and "Weird Al" Yankovic. Writing the introduction to a book on Spike Jones, Peter Schickele of P. D. Q. Bach fame stated that for him, the bandleader "was not just a door to musical humor, but a door to music itself."

Tom Lehrer (1928–) took a very different route. What made Lehrer's form of comedy distinctive was the often biting social commentary that characterized his music. Coming of age with a host of comedians who reinvented political humor during the Cold War (such as Mort Sahl) or challenged social and cultural mores (such as Lenny Bruce), Lehrer forced his audience to reevaluate the society in which they lived; he was no mere entertainer. As one of the only contemporary comedians with a training in mathematics, his erudite lyrics were set to tunes he wrote or at times borrowed, accompanied by his very capable piano playing in the music hall style of ragtime, waltz, and other genres. A master of different accents, his subjects varied widely, including urban life ("The Old Dope Peddler," "Pollution," and "Poisoning Pigeons in the Park"), the Cold War ("So Long, Mom (A Song for World War III)," "MLF Lullaby," and "Wernher von Braun"), religion ("The Vatican Rag"), and even mathematics ("Lobachevsky" and "New Math").

Lehrer's comedy lay mainly in his deadpan, wry style, which belied the often dark humor of the lyrics, further contrasting at times starkly with upbeat, almost joyful melodies. Inspired by the singing style of entertainer Danny Kaye and the lyrics of Kaye's wife Sylvia Fine, Lehrer began performing in nightclubs while studying mathematics at Harvard, then put mathematics on hold to tour the country, serve in the army, and go on an international tour in 1959–1960. After recording several albums, he abandoned touring to return to academia, teaching first at MIT (1962–1971) and then at UC Santa Cruz, although he continued to perform occasionally in public. A revue of his songs appeared as a musical, entitled *Tomfoolery,* in 1980.

Even more than Tom Lehrer, Steve Martin (1945–) is part of a generation of comedians with an antiestablishment bent. Satirizing social mores, especially about drugs and sex, became commonplace in his stand-up routine in the 1960s and 1970s. Like Peter Schickele in classical music, Martin specialized in the buffoon character who could never quite "get it right." The comedy came from the sheer zaniness of his portrayals, using the banjo at times as a prop or as the centerpiece, inviting the audience to sing along: "Now this two-fifths of the room, now this three-fifths." When the act appeared to be failing, he provoked his audience mockingly: "What's the matter, you people uptight or something?"

Throughout his stand-up career, music remained an essential element of Martin's comedy. He began learning the banjo as a teenager and picked up some pointers from John McEuen of the Nitty Gritty Dirt Band, with whom he toured as an opening act. As his comic routines became more physical over time, he also added singing and dancing; as he noted: "It was true I couldn't sing or dance, but singing *funny* and dancing *funny* were another matter." A song that he wrote, "King Tut," which mocked the popularity of a traveling Tutankhamen exhibit, sold over a million copies and reached number seventeen in 1978 on the U.S. *Billboard* chart. It was backed by the group "Toot Uncommons," which consisted of members of the Nitty Gritty Dirt Band. Placing ever more emphasis on the banjo, Martin recorded an all-instrumental piece, "Drop Thumb Medley," for one comedy album, and on his final album, *The Steve Martin Brothers* (1981), an entire side was devoted to bluegrass music. Even as he moved away from stand-up comedy during the 1980s, he continued to perform the banjo with humorous overtones on stage, and in 2011 with a bluegrass ensemble, Steep Canyon Rangers, he recorded "King Tut" with an extended banjo solo.

"Weird Al" Yankovic (1959–) claims as influences Spike Jones and Tom Lehrer, as well as comedians Stan Freberg (1926–) and Allan Sherman (1924–1973; who wrote "Hello Muddah, Hello Faddah"), and he shared the almost manic zaniness of Steve Martin. He began performing as a college student at Cal State San Luis Obispo in the 1970s, singing "My Bologna" while playing accordion, from lyrics he wrote based on a phenomenally popular song by a pop group, the Knack, called "My Sharona." Yankovic's song was played on Dr. Demento's radio show, and favorable audience response led to another single, "Another One Rides the Bus," based on the melody to the rock group Queen's "Another One Bites the Dust." Yankovic soon began lampooning the self-seriousness of many pop, rock, and hip-hop performers, including Michael Jackson, Madonna, and the rapper Chamillionaire. It is significant that he got approval from the artists he parodied before he released a song; only a few musicians evidently refused that approval, among them R&B artist Prince and rapper Eminem.

Essential to Yankovic's comedy was its flamboyant, visual nature. He began including videos with all of his albums after 1983, such as "Eat It," a parody of Michael Jackson's "Beat It," and "Smells Like Nirvana," which parodied Nirvana's "Smells Like Teen Spirit," thereby benefiting markedly from the growing popularity of MTV during the 1980s. Further songs included "Fat," a parody of Michael Jackson's "Bad," and "White and

Weird Al Yankovic at Village Theater in Westwood, California, April 27, 2011. (Carrie Nelson/Dreamstime.com)

Nerdy," which parodied Chamillionaire's "Ridin' Dirty"; Madonna's "Like a Virgin" became "Like a Surgeon," a title that Madonna herself apparently suggested to Yankovic. Popular among performers and audiences alike, Yankovic continued his parodies and special brand of humor into the twenty-first century.

Another important source of comedy in popular music is the television program *Saturday Night Live* (SNL), which has featured numerous artists who used music in a comic fashion, among them John Belushi (1949–1982) and Dan Akroyd (1952–), who formed the Blues Brothers, and guest hosts like Steve Martin and Dudley Moore (1935–2002). More recently, Adam Sandler (1966–) targeted popular culture figures and other subjects with such pieces as "The Hannukah Song," about famous stars who are Jewish or part-Jewish, and "Lunchlady Land," based on an employee at a university dining hall. He also created a character on SNL, "Operaman," who took the persona of an operatic tenor and sang pseudo-Italian, bawdy lyrics with subtitles.

Finally, performers in the field of political satire, inspired by contemporary events in Washington, D.C., included Mark Russell (Mark Ruslander; 1932–), who began performing in nightclubs and bars in the early 1960s, and the comedy troupe Capitol Steps, which began in 1981. Russell's lyrics and piano playing recalled the wry humor of Tom Lehrer, and Capitol Steps built their irreverent, sharp lyrics on tunes from popular songs, relying heavily on double entendres and innuendo. No erring politician was safe from their gleeful attacks. The extensive touring schedules, albums, and devoted followers of both Russell and Capitol Steps demonstrated the vitality that popular music and political satire continued to enjoy among Americans in the twenty-first century.

Classical Music

Comedy in modern American classical music is represented by the beloved Victor Borge (Borge Rosenbaum; 1909–2000), a highly trained concert pianist before he ever began performing comedy. Borge's humor arose chiefly from parodying the self-seriousness of classical music artists. He often began playing a piece with absolute earnestness, then dropped in musical quotations from other works or even other genres (jazz, ragtime, etc.). He could play a piano concerto that drew on well-known passages of several different piano concertos, thereby amusing the music connoisseurs as well as the general public. His comic patter between playing became legendary, such as: "And now, in honor of the 150th anniversary of Beethoven's death, I would like to play 'Clear the Saloon,' er, 'Clair de Lune,' by Debussy. I don't play Beethoven so well, but I play Debussy very badly, and Beethoven would have liked that."

Born in Denmark, he studied piano and performance in Berlin under teachers who had studied with Liszt and Busoni. Beginning as a classical pianist and then performing in musical reviews, he began satirizing Hitler in the 1930s and so was forced to flee Denmark after the Nazi invasion in 1940. Arriving almost penniless in America, Borge performed on Bing Crosby's radio program *Kraft Music Hall* and soon transformed himself from a virtuoso musician, with the name of Borge Rosenbaum, into a comic performer named Victor Borge. When he discovered that American audiences enjoyed the combination of classical music and satire, he created a one-man show called "Comedy in Music" in 1953, which ran for an extraordinary 849 performances. Soon earning the nickname of the "Great Dane," his career lasted into his eighties.

Borge had broken an important barrier in postwar American music and proved that a highly trained classical music artist could also be funny. His dapper dress and suave, European accent were a perfect foil to his antics on stage. His humor included slapstick, such as falling off the piano stool when a mezzo-soprano he was accompanying sang a high note, and he further developed the uncanny ability to mimic singers, from bass singers up to coloratura sopranos. Extending his comic reach into conducting when in his sixties, Borge began leading the Amsterdam Concertgebouw and the New York Philharmonic Orchestra and conducted numerous operettas and light operas, such as Johann Strauss's *Die Fledermaus* and Wolfgang Mozart's *The Magic Flute.*

Although he did not have the extensive classical training of Borge, longtime comedian and entertainer Jack Benny (Benjamin Kubelsky; 1894–1974), began making waves in classical music during the 1940s. He may well have started doing this at the Hollywood Bowl in 1944, when he appeared in a concert to raise funds for Greek war relief during World War II. He played "Love in Bloom," the theme song from his then highly popular radio show, to the accompaniment of the Los Angeles Philharmonic, with conductor Alfred Wallenstein. According to Benny, he performed the piece like a serious violinist, complete with white tie and tails. With no hint of comedy, he walked offstage without smiling and got a standing ovation from the audience and even the orchestra. Benny had often used music in his radio and stand-up routines, but almost never classical music. That all changed after this performance, when he began parodying the self-importance of the concert violinist in benefit concerts around the country as well as on his television program during the 1950s and 1960s, *The Jack Benny Show.*

Benny's goals in combining classical music with comedy were twofold: not only to aid symphony orchestras and pension funds through philanthropic concerts, but also to make classical music accessible to audiences across age and class. Following his Bowl performance, Benny's standard approach was to appear in white tie and tails with a symphony orchestra. He would emulate the movements or manner of a classical violinist, yet without the required skill. As virtuoso violinist Isaac Stern, with whom Benny helped save Carnegie Hall, once remarked: "Jack, when you walk out on that stage in your white tie and tails, holding the fiddle like an emperor, you look like the greatest violinist in the world. It's a shame you have to play" (Hughes 2002, 169).

The humor, however, lay in the fact that Benny *could* play well (he had studied violin as a child and had played since his earliest vaudeville performances), yet he always presented himself as the bumbler on stage. In one common routine, he would walk proudly onstage to a thunderous ovation, nod to the conductor, raise his violin to his chin as if to play, and say, "Oops, I forgot my bow," before walking offstage to retrieve it. At other times, such as while accompanying Isaac Stern playing Bach's Concerto for Two Violins in D Minor, Benny might interject with "Show off," or "Don't fool around with me, buster," to the delight of audiences, who paid a lot of money to watch him in such performances. Favorite pieces in Benny's repertoire were Rimsky-Korsakov's *Capriccio espagnol,* Sarasate's *Zigeunerweisen* ("Gypsy Airs"), Saint-Saëns' *Introduction and Rondo Capriccioso,* and excerpts from Mendelssohn's Violin Concerto; he performed with more than twenty orchestras in America and abroad from 1944 until shortly before his death in 1974. Benny also invited classical music artists to appear on his television show, such as Stern and pianist Liberace, and even had a dream sequence, "The Sixty Piece Orchestra Skit," in which he performed onstage as a professional violinist. Significantly, Benny never made fun of classical music itself, but only of the seriousness of the classical musician.

Like Benny, Danny Kaye (David Daniel Kaminsky; 1913–1987) applied his enormous comedic talents to the field of classical music. Although a singer and popular film actor since his debut in the 1930s, he moved into classical music during the 1950s by mocking the iconic figure of the symphony orchestra conductor. Kaye was an expert mimic and studied various conductors' every gesture, receiving pointers from such luminaries (and admirers) as conductors Eugene Ormandy (who first invited him to a guest performance in 1954), Leonard Bernstein, and Dmitri Mitropoulos. Like Spike Jones, Kaye's humor relied on sight gags and props (flyswatters, guns with blank cartridges, and a series of batons that he threw around during his act). Common routines were to sing or shout along with the orchestra or to begin a fight with the concertmaster and force him to leave the stage, whereupon Kaye would then "shoot" him and return to continue conducting the orchestra.

Although he relied strongly on slapstick, a key aspect of his comedy was his actual knowledge of the music and above all, timing. Before conducting a work, he would apparently listen to recordings of it many times to memorize it (he could not read music), thus learning the "cues" when various instruments came in; as a result he earned the respect of the musicians he conducted. His agility and natural grace further made him *look* like a conductor. His repertoire included mainly nineteenth-century orchestral classics such as excerpts from Beethoven's Symphony No. 5, Ravel's *Bolero,* and Tchaikovsky's *Nutcracker Suite,* as well as operatic excerpts, including Rossini's *La Gazza Ladra,* Verdi's *Aida,* and Wagner's *Lohengrin.* Kaye performed entirely for benefit concerts, as Benny had done, conducting more than thirty American orchestras as well as more than twenty orchestras abroad during a conducting career that spanned thirty-one years (1954 to 1985).

Peter Schickele (1935–), the founder of the fictitious son of Johann Sebastian Bach, called "P. D. Q. Bach," shared several traits with other comedians described here. Like Borge, Schickele had received serious training in music, having studied at Swarthmore and subsequently with composers Roy Harris (1954) and Darius Milhaud (1959). He further taught at Julliard, where he cofounded a group that played its members' serious compositions. With the invention of P. D. Q. Bach in 1965 at a concert at New York's Town Hall, Schickele developed a persona unique in musical comedy; as he stated, P. D. Q. Bach was the "last, and by all means the least," of Bach's children (Schickele 1976, 4). Presenting a kind of drunken buffoon who could never achieve success even if he tried, Schickele combined a wide musical knowledge with humorous antics and props. Inspired in part by the "slapstick burlesque" of Spike Jones, Schickele used a variety of musical "instruments," including a bicycle and a "left-handed sewer-flute."

Schickele's compositions largely parodied works from the classical and baroque periods, readily apparent in the titles, such as *Gross Concerto for Divers Flutes* (which included a nose flute), Concerto for Piano vs. Orchestra, and *Fuga Meshuga.* Like Borge, he often integrated different genres in his pieces, such as jazz, blues, or ragtime, as well as common folk tunes, notably Stephen Foster's "Old Black Joe" in *The Seasonings* (1965), and "Shave and a Haircut" in the fifth movement of *The Short-Tempered Clavier* (1993). Also similar to Borge, one of Schickele's skills was to provide humor for music connoisseurs as well as the general public; for example, he added a particularly long harpsichord cadenza in *Iphigenia in Brooklyn* (1963), or used wrong notes, dissonance, or "accidents" in *Schleptet in E♭ Major* (1967), based on Beethoven's Septet for woodwinds, horn, and strings. Although a serious composer as well as a humorist, Schickele will perhaps always be remembered as an expert in musical parody who taught his audience not to take classical music too seriously.

Comedy and satire will remain an important part of music in American life, adding to audience enjoyment.

See also: Audiences; Banjo; Bernstein, Leonard; Big Band Music; Classical Music in America; Crosby, Bing; Hip-Hop; Jackson, Michael; Madonna; Mathematics and Music; Opera in America; Pop Music; Prince; R&B; Ragtime; Rock 'n' Roll (Rock); *Saturday Night Live*; Swing Music; Unusual Techniques and Uses of Musical Instruments

Further Reading

Borge, Victor. 1994. *My Favorite Comedies in Music.* New York: M. Evans & Company.

Giddens, Gary. 2006. *Natural Selection: Gary Giddins on Comedy, Film, Music, and Books.* New York: Oxford University Press.

Hughes, Carlton. 2002. *Moments for Music: 175 Short Stories About Music and Brief Glimpses into the Lives of Musicians Past and Present.* Lincoln, NE: Writer's Club Press.

Schickele, Peter. 1976. *The Definitive Biography of P.D.Q. Bach.* New York: Random House.

Kenneth Marcus

Commercial Successes in the Music Industry

Commercial success in the music industry is obviously related to one's ability to use musical artisanship as a basis for generating profits and to accumulate substantial wealth. That may seem fairly straightforward, but commercial success is an elusive concept that is continuously negotiated within the industry to determine both what should be considered "success" as well as how it should be measured. This entry discusses commercial success in the popular music industry and strategies used to achieve it. It also explains how the notion of commercial success is affected by the digitization of the music world.

Risk and Reward

Popular music industry professionals often explain that their business is riskier than most other businesses. One of the main reasons for this claim is that a considerable part of their costs is incurred at the very beginning of project—before it is possible to determine its commercial potential. Even when the artist is established and when critics agree the production is fantastic, there are still too many unknowns to be able to accurately predict if the project will be commercially successful and generate enough revenues to cover its costs.

It is interesting to note that it is not only difficult to predict commercial success, it is also a bit thorny to evaluate whether a completed project actually has been commercially successful or not. A project may be very profitable for one party involved, but a major loss for another. This kind of tension primarily exists between the artist and the record label. Artists often claim to have been cheated and exploited by their record labels, and that they have not been given a fair share of a project's commercial success. On the other hand, record labels' assessment of an artist's commercial potential is often flawed, which means that the label never is able to recoup the advances that have been paid when the contract was signed.

Charts and Certifications

Rather than using a project's profitability as a measure of commercial success, a somewhat less disputed method is to disregard the costs and focus on the revenues, or simply identify the most "popular" compositions, recordings, or artists during a particular period. *Billboard* magazine created one of the first such charts, the "Hit Parade," in 1936, inspired by a radio show by the same name that was launched the previous year. The Hit Parade listed those songs that during a week had been given the most airplay by a number of selected radio stations. This information provided market intelligence to record labels, a continuous and predictable flow of news to radio stations and entertainment media, and an update on what was considered to be popular at the moment to the mainstream music audience. Eventually the Hit Parade bifurcated into charts focused on different genres, geographical areas, ethnic groups, and other distinguishing features.

As music distribution technologies have developed over the past several decades, various data sources considered to be relevant at the time have been used to create the charts. In 2011 *Billboard* magazine regularly published seventy charts focused on different genres, territories, and media technologies. Although it certainly was and still is possible to manipulate these charts, they have emerged as the most accepted measure of what is considered to be commercial success in the popular music industry.

The charts fulfill a crucial role in the music industry system, providing feedback from the market to the record labels about what kind of artist and what kind of music are commercially successful at the moment. This feedback constitutes an important part of the structure that generates the fundamental dynamics of the industry. The charts allow a record label to monitor the rise and fall of its own artists in relation to other labels' artists. If an artist is moving up the chart, the label will try to work with the positive momentum and spend more promotion money on that artist, which in turn will propel the artist even further up the chart. Conversely, if an artist is moving down the chart toward a lower position, the label reads that movement as a signal that it should save its promotion money from being wasted on that song or artist. This decision will accelerate the speed of the artist's fall. In other words, the charts close a reinforcing feedback loop linking record labels, media outlets, and music audiences together. This feedback loop constitutes the "engine" that drives an artist toward greater commercial success but also pushes a falling artist off the charts.

Another structure for recognizing commercial success is the "gold," "platinum," and "diamond" certification, issued by the Recording Industry Association of America (RIAA). A record label can request that RIAA certifies the label has shipped a certain number of albums to retailers and other channels. It should be noted that the RIAA certifications are not linked to consumer sales, but to the label's net shipments after returns. This means that a record label with deep pockets may use the certifications as part of an album's marketing campaign. By shipping a large number of units to retailers and then requesting a certification from the RIAA, it is possible to claim the record "has certified platinum" in the promotional materials, even though only a limited number have been sold to consumers.

In summary, commercial success in the American popular music industry has traditionally been measured and recognized by the use of mechanisms such as *Billboard* charts and RIAA certifications. The evolution of a project's commercial success is often presented via references to certifications and chart movements.

The Traditional Notion of Commercial Success Is Challenged

The structures presented above were all shaped during the music industry's predigital era, when commercial success was linked to an artist's ability to sell a lot of records. As the sales of recorded music continue to fall and the industry moves away from this model, the concept of commercial success is challenged. This transformation can be noticed in a number of ways. One example is how organizations, which award the aforementioned gold and platinum certifications, have reduced their requirements so that the shipment of albums and singles can be certified even when they no longer sell as well as during the old days.

As the link between record sales and commercial success becomes weaker, the role of charts as measures of commercial success is being eroded. For instance, the number of units sold to reach the charts' top positions is currently significantly smaller than a few years ago. This also means that an increasing number of albums and singles might be able to reach those top positions, even if only for a single week. Once at the top, the titles are quickly being pushed down by the flickering hit, which is next in line. This volatility significantly reduces the usefulness of the chart, both as a market research tool for record labels and as a source of news for entertainment reporters. One reporter reflected on this development: "We stopped posting weekly recaps of the country's best-selling albums around the end of 2010 because, frankly, it was hard to find news in the same story week after week. A new album would top the chart despite lackluster sales, then slip out of the number 1 spot the following week. Rinse, repeat" (Ganz 2011). Because there still is a demand for an agreed upon measure of commercial success, entrepreneurs have tried to create new mechanisms that can capture the signs of popularity in the digital age. These mechanisms have primarily been focused on monitoring music listeners' behavior on a number of well-established social media services. By factoring in data such as the number of new fans added to an artist's Facebook page, the number of times a video has been played on YouTube, and the number of times a track has been "scrobbled" by Last.fm, an online music recommendation service, it is possible to create measures of an artist's online popularity at a certain point in time. These measures have not yet reached the level of perceived legitimacy that was previously

Scouting Potential Talent on Social Media Networks

British singers Adele Adkins (1988–), also known as Adele, and Lily Allen (1985–), as well as Canadian Justin Bieber (1994–), are examples of artists with very successful careers that partly or entirely originated online. Adkins and Allen posted their recordings on MySpace, and Bieber posted his videos on YouTube. Their careers have taken very different trajectories, but they all started through one person spreading the word to another person that there was a song that he or she liked. As this unpredictable communication process from person to person continued, the song eventually went "viral" and reached the consciousness of mainstream media and record labels' A&R departments. All three artists are now signed to traditional record labels, selling millions of records, and are counted among the popular music industry's biggest commercial successes.

held by traditional measures. For these measures to serve as a reasonably comprehensive image of commercial success in the digital age, additional data probably need to be added to the measures. For instance, usage data might be added from cloud-based music services such as MOG, Rdio, Spotify, etc., as well as traditional sales data from online and offline retailers.

The measures of commercial success discussed so far have all been focused on recorded music. However, in the contemporary music industry, the importance of recorded music in relation to the other parts of the music industry, such as publishing and live performance, is diminishing. In the predigital age, performances were primarily used to promote the main product, that is, recording and commercial success could very well be achieved without being a very successful live artist. In the digital age this is no longer the case. It is increasingly difficult to make money by selling recorded music to consumers, and artists have increasingly come to rely on revenues from concerts and tours.

To create a comprehensive representation of an artist's commercial success that takes this changing balance into consideration, it is necessary to factor in the artist's ability to attract a live audience. This is, however, fairly problematic. The live music sector is very diverse and ranges from small shows in local pubs and clubs, to Las Vegas residencies, to music festivals, to global arena tours. The agreements between the parties involved in these events differ from case to case and are most often not publicly available. This makes it difficult to both find and use financial data or ticket sales data as the basis for a reliable measure of commercial success in the live music sector.

Creating Commercial Success in the Digital Age

Because of the processes presented above, it is increasingly difficult to measure commercial success in the popular music industry. Regardless of this growing difficulty, commercial success and mainstream popularity are still the elusive goal for most artists in the industry. So how does an artist reach this goal, and what are the strategies used by record labels to propel their artists' careers toward commercial success? In the music industry's predigital era, the path to commercial success was not easy, but it was fairly straightforward. A number of gates had to be passed to reach that goal, including the A&R agent, the label executive, the programmer at the radio station, and eventually the unpredictable audience. Radio airplay created audience awareness, and if the song resonated with the audience, there was a hit.

In the early days of digitization, it was commonly expected that the intermediators, such as radio stations and record label executives, simply would be short-circuited and disappear. Artists would be able to reach across the Internet to meet directly with their fans, and they would be able to create their own success without interference from record labels. However, as time went by it became evident that this "disintermediation" did not happen. Some of the intermediators certainly did lose their influence, but on the other hand, new intermediators took their place. Someone has to sponsor the marketing and distribution of a production even in the digital age, and this someone is the same organization as during the predigital days: the record label.

No doubt there are instances when artists and their music have been able to build a considerable fan base via social media services and without the support of a traditional record label. While such success stories are useful fodder for entertainment news media, it is generally not viable to build a long-term strategy based on the unlikely event of breaking through via Facebook, MySpace, or YouTube. The communication patterns on social media networks are chaotic and unpredictable, and it is primarily pure chance that decides which one of all the hopeful teenagers who publish their songs on YouTube eventually will be invited to be on *The Tonight Show with Jay Leno*. Those songs and artists that do break through via these channels fairly soon find themselves associated with a traditional record label, which can help them take their careers to the next level.

The Role of Broadcast Media in Creating Commercial Success

Broadcast media and the popular music industry have had a symbiotic relationship more or less since their respective beginnings. This relationship has evolved over several decades, and currently it appears that traditional broadcast media have lost some of their influence in shaping taste among the mainstream audience. However, a number of broadcast media phenomena still have the necessary reach and power to repeatedly create commercial success. Television shows such as *Glee* have sent more songs up the *Billboard* Hot 100 chart than has any artist, including the Beatles (1960–1970) and Elvis Presley (1935–1977). Another TV series that has generated musical commercial success is Disney's *Hannah Montana,* which has sold twenty-one million albums to date. In addition to these TV fictional series, the reality television genre has established a number of talent shows, such as *American Idol* and *America's Got Talent,* among the most successful shows on national television. The amount of exposure given to the artists who stay on these shows for an entire season is sufficient to launch more or less every winning artist into stardom. Most of these careers have been short lived and have ended as soon as a new season of the show has started, but a few winners have been able to build sustainable international careers. Two of the brightest shining stars are Kelly Clarkson (1982–) and Susan Boyle (1961–). Clarkson, who won on *American Idol* in 2002, has maintained her career for almost a decade and has more or less been able to leave her *Idol* legacy behind. She has been certified multiple platinum for two of her albums and received two Grammy awards. The Susan Boyle fairy tale differs radically from Clarkson's. When Boyle won on *Britain's Got Talent* in 2009 she was forty-eight years old, unemployed, and living alone in her childhood home in Blackburn, Scotland. Her extraordinary voice, combined with her personal story, made her debut album (appropriately titled *I Dreamed a Dream*) the biggest selling album worldwide in 2009.

These examples illustrate an increasingly common practice among the risk-aversive record labels in the contemporary music industry. Traditionally a record label often signed artists that did not have any previous commercial success or recording experience but were simply perceived by A&R agents and record label executives to have some kind of potential. The potential talents were then held on a tight leash and were groomed and developed to one day become commercially successful. Motown Records in Detroit during the 1960s was perhaps the best-known implementation of this operational model. Today this kind of artist development procedures is not as common. Artists are generally signed later in their careers, when they have been able to prove that they already have the ability to perform on stage and attract millions of viewers on YouTube. This practice considerably lowers the record label's risk as well as its cost of establishing the artist's brand among its target audience.

Another example of the music companies' growing risk aversion is the increased focus on established artists, for both live performances and studio recordings. A concert tour production with an established artist such as Madonna (1958–), Metallica (active 1981–), or Paul Simon (1941–) is a fairly low-risk venture because the artist's brand is already well established among the audience. As a consequence of this strategy, the average age of the highest earning musician increased from thirty-six in the early 1990s to forty-four twenty years later. This trend can for obvious reasons not go on forever, but it should nevertheless be noted that some of the world's highest earning artists are no longer part of this earthly world. Michael Jackson's (1958–2009) estate made far more money during the year after his death than the two most profitable living acts (U2 [active 1976–] and AC/DC [active 1973–]) combined did during that year. John Lennon (1940–1980) and Elvis Presley are two examples of other celebrities who continue to be among the world's most commercially successful music brands many years after their deaths.

50 Cent's (1975–) 2003 album was titled *Get Rich or Die Trying,* and even though the motivational drivers certainly differ from one artist to another, the prospect of commercial success is likely to continue to be one of the main motivations for artists in the popular music industry. However, as the industry evolves, this dream seems to become ever more elusive. Digitization allows an increasing number of artists to share the limelight, but the amount of commercial success each artist is able to enjoy is becoming smaller and smaller. Andy Warhol's prediction that everyone would have (only) fifteen minutes of fame seems to be truer than ever.

See also: Disney Music; Jackson, Michael; Madonna; Metallica; Motown; Pop Music; Presley, Elvis; Radio; Simon, Paul; Television and Music

Further Reading

Ganz, Jacob. 2011. "2011's Chart-Toppers: Disaster, Narrowly Avoided." *NPR Music—the Record,* April 1. http://goo.gl/NmmRH.

IFPI. 2010. *Investing in Music.* London: International Federation of the Phonographic Industry.

IFPI. 2009–2011. *Recording Industry in Numbers.* London: International Federation of the Phonographic Industry.

King, Mike. 2009. *Music Marketing—Press Promotion Distribution and Retail.* Boston: Berklee Press.

Mjos, Ole J. 2011. *Music, Social Media and Global Mobility: MySpace, Facebook, YouTube.* New York: Routledge.

Smith, Kathleen E. R. 2003. *God Bless America: Tin Pan Alley Goes to War.* Lexington: University Press of Kentucky

Tyler, Don. 2008. *Music of the Postwar Era.* Westport, CT: Greenwood Press.

Whitburn, Joel. 2010. *The Billboard Book of Top 40 Hits.* 9th ed. New York: Crown Publishing.

White, Adam. 1990. *The Billboard Book of Gold & Platinum Records.* New York: Billboard Books.

Wikström, Patrik. 2009. *The Music Industry: Music in the Cloud.* Cambridge, UK: Polity Press.

Patrik Wikström

Commercials and Advertisements

Music was used in various forms to sell products through commercials and advertisements throughout the twentieth century, even before the inception of broadcast media like radio and television. As Timothy Taylor (2010) describes, street cries—tonal vocalizations from individuals standing on the street to sell products—preceded the use of music as we commonly understand it; the practice originated long before America's founding.

For Taylor (2010), more important to the rise of music in advertising, and certainly more directly related to the practice, is the use of verse, a practice that emerged in the late nineteenth century. Verse pitches essentially involved jingles without music: performers would say rhythmic poetry that mentioned and described a product. Those verses became immensely popular among consumers, so much so that a manufacturer produced a play that incorporated verses and music. The show's financial success spawned other shows, which similarly included advertising verses.

Live musical performances were not the only way that companies got the word out about their products. Some companies would also produce sheet music with advertisements directly on the page. Still others would commission and promote songs that mentioned their products in a favorable light or would actively change song lyrics so that they might mention a product they'd like to sell. All of these practices happened before the creation and proliferation of radio technology.

Before World War II companies would spend more money on print advertisements than on radio broadcasts, but several entities did begin their foray into broadcasted advertisements in the 1930s (Taylor 2010). This took the form of sponsorship, rather than creating a separate, short commercial as we know advertisements today (though some of these programs did include short, jingle-like theme songs).

During the Great Depression a sluggish economy meant that advertisers wanted to create better, more effective commercials inexpensively. This meant first improving their songs. These advertisers did not simply alter existing popular songs; they composed original themes. By composing an original advertising theme, advertisers could create a more effective piece of music (at least in terms of exposing a product to the market) and could have complete ownership of that song. Nevertheless, songs were still woven into the narrative of a program and could not stand alone as independent jingles.

According to Taylor (2010), the first stand-alone jingle—though he is careful to note that locating the original jingle is a difficult task—was in a 1926 Wheaties commercial, sung by the Wheaties barbershop quartet. Yet the jingle was not used more broadly until Pepsi released a "national broadcast standalone singing commercial" in 1939 (Taylor 2010). Well into the 1940s, the jingle became immensely popular, which was a double-edged sword: as memorable as the jingles were, they also bothered audiences, so much so that some radio stations banned singing commercials by 1944. Although jingles are still used in contemporary commercials, popular songs or complementary scores are often played beneath a narrative.

Tasks for Music in Commercials

Considering the historical trajectory of music in commercials, however it manifests itself, requires some examination of how music functions as a persuasive mechanism. After all, the goal of a commercial is to persuade a consumer to buy a product, so what about music makes it persuasive? David Huron (1989) provides a helpful taxonomy of six ways that music can work within a broadcast advertisement to persuade audiences.

The first way is entertainment: music can make an advertisement seem more attractive. This does not necessarily mean an audience member must find pleasure in the music or the advertisement; rather, it simply draws attention to the advertisement or to the product. In this case, the music in the advertisement does not necessarily need to have anything to do with the product.

The second way is structure/continuity. Music can join together disparate elements of a commercial, like images, voice-over, or a vocalized list of product appeals. This practice first emerged in film, in which music was used as a means to link together scene changes or edits that otherwise might create a disjointed narrative. In this capacity, music can also heighten the drama of a narrative, as would a film score. Contrary to commercials in which music entertains or draws attention, the music here is closely linked to the content of the advertisement.

The third way is memorability. Simply put, being able to recognize a product means a consumer is more likely to buy it. Jingles fall into this category, given their short, catchy structure, which often mimics the spoken word.

The fourth way is lyrical language. If a message is simply vocalized or uttered in normal speech, Huron (1989) contends, it is more likely to be critiqued. Vocal music, on the contrary, sounds more poetic and emotional and may invite less criticism. It also invites more emotional connection to the product being sold or the company selling the product.

The fifth way is targeting. Targeted advertising involves reaching a particular niche market, a more cost-effective mode of advertising that does not require a company to waste time or money communicating a message to people who are not likely to buy a product. The difficult task, then, is how to use media to reach that target group—which may involve music. Using a particular musical style, such as country music, would reach a different audience than would using electronica.

The sixth way is authority establishment. Music can be used to increase the credibility and authority of the product or the company. One means of accomplishing this is through endorsement, by showing that certain groups might use a particular product. Here again, using a particular musical style may communicate this.

Huron (1989) notes, however, that consumers are quick to become savvy to advertisers' tried and true techniques. This requires advertisers to reinvent the strategies they use to persuade audiences in order to stay ahead of the curve. This means that music may be used in constantly changing ways so that a company may avoid being labeled inauthentic or as making a contrived effort to sell. Drawing on different genres or sounds is one way that a company might avoid being written off like this. Timothy Taylor argues that the increased use of electronica music in commercials is the result of musicians in that genre being unable to find audiences broadly. They shop their music around to television commercials, and demographic shifts in who selects music for commercials means that alternative, underground songs are more often used. They thus appear as tastemakers and arbiters, as cool: "Advertisers also realized that if they made an obscure band into a hit, their taste and perspicacity would make them look good to their potential customers" (Taylor 2007, 241).

Meaning of Commercials

How, then, does music actually affect meaning? Linda Scott (1990) notes that music's persuasive power in commercials lies not within the sound itself, but in the interaction among sound, image, and narrative content. The meaning that emerges from this relationship among these elements is also culturally contingent: the act of interpreting music is rooted, fundamentally, in cultural context and shared experience. Like Huron, Scott provides a list of several ways that music can have meaning in a commercial, all of which link music directly to the narrative: using dissonance and consonance to resolve tension, representing motion, using rhythm and repetition, turning music into a narrative, using music to call to mind a common location or shared space, structuring time, forging identifications with groups, or creating an ethos that a song can point to.

Nicholas Cook is also skeptical about music in itself having meaning, even in the context of a commercial. He notes "a lack of consensus as to what kind of communication music is, or indeed whether it can properly be called communication at all" (Cook 1994, 27). Given that a commercial is a form of media whose purpose is known—to sell a particular product—advertisements become perfect tools to analyze the meaning of music. He notes that music can be associated with a product being sold (e.g., a sound might be understood as lively, comforting, foreboding, etc.) and can also suggest deeper meanings about more abstract ideas. In either case, though—as for Scott—context matters. An advertisement's music must interact with the structure of the commercial to have meaning.

Cook also explains how music affects audiences. First, because commercials are short and expensive, advertisers use particular styles to persuade rather than the lyrics of a song. Moreover, he notes that listeners are rarely conscious of music in commercials even when they are affected by it, the exception being the always memorable jingle. Here, then, lies a flaw of analysis, for Cook: the mode of analysis we employ in exploring how music is effective in commercials does not reflect the way we encounter music in commercials naturally. Finally, Cook sees the role of music as being primarily emotional: while the narrative of the commercial deals with "the specific, with the objective," music involves responses: "values, emotions, and attitudes" (Cook 1994, 38). That connection is crucial for companies seeking to sell products.

See also: Country Music; Electronica

Further Reading

Christian, Elizabeth Barfoot. 2010. *Rock Brands: Selling Sound in a Media Saturated Culture.* Lanham, MD: Rowman and Littlefield Publishing.

Cook, Nicholas. 1994. "Music and Meaning in Commercials." *Popular Music* 13, no. 1: 27–40.

Gorn, Gerald J. 1982. "The Effects of Music in Advertising on Choice Behavior: A Classical Conditioning Approach." *The Journal of Marketing* 46, no. 1: 94–101.

Huron, David. 1989. "Music in Advertising: An Analytic Paradigm." *The Music Quarterly* 73, no. 4: 557–574.

Karmen, Steve. 2005. *Who Killed the Jingle? How a Unique American Art Form Disappeared.* Milwaukee, WI: Hal Leonard.

Kellaris, James J., and Anthony D. Cox. 1989. "The Effects of Background Music in Advertising: A Reassessment." *Journal of Consumer Research* 16, no. 1: 113–118.

Klein, Bethany. 2008. "In Perfect Harmony: Popular Music and Cola Advertising." *Popular Music and Society* 31, no. 1: 1–20.

Scott, Linda M. 1990. "Understanding Jingles and Needledrop: A Rhetorical Approach to Music in Advertising." *Journal of Consumer Research* 17, no. 2: 223–236.

Taylor, Timothy D. 2007. "The Changing Shape of the Culture Industry; or, How Did Electronica Music Get into Television Commercials?" *Television and New Media* 8, no. 3: 235–258.

Taylor, Timothy D. 2010. "The Rise of the Jingle." *Advertising and Society Review* 11, no. 2.

Carrie Andersen

Community Bands

Community bands have evolved and flourished throughout the history of the United States, but it is difficult to pinpoint when they were first formed. Until the 1800s, much of the music that made up the programs of community bands was of European origin. It is also difficult to identify when the repertoire of music created for performances first showed distinctive American traits. Community bands frequently reflected social and political changes in the United States as it experienced wars, the transition from an agricultural economy to an industrial revolution, large-scale immigration, and many other significant dynamics. The emerging forms of community band music reflected the larger society and the types of music that were sought by various groups in the population. Military music was important, as was patriotic music. Community bands expanded in response to people or groups wanting to sponsor or be associated with them, including athletic teams, large corporations, factories, churches, religious groups, schools, the Salvation Army, marching groups, drum and bugle corps, and other local community organizations. These bands provided education, entertainment, loyalty, cohesiveness, identity, and camaraderie as they interacted with the musical content that each played for its town or city (Hartz 2003).

Many American bandmasters originally used musical compositions written by Europeans. These compositions were often symphonic, larger in musical content and longer in performance than the typical community band usually played. Subsequently, more bandmasters and composers began to perform programs with an American flavor and an identity that separated the musical work done in the United States from that of other nations. As American music became more indigenous, it also became more mature, and American composers and band performers began to write music for particular niches, such as musical theater, patriotic events, and civil observances. For example, the American Civil War generated many patriotic, religious, and romantic songs from 1861 to 1865, with a decreasing output of community band material following the war. By the late 1800s and early 1900s, American musicians created or adapted songs known for their growing popularity that would fit with their community bands. As the U.S. population moved westward, community band content spread outward across the country. Many community bands contributed to a growing library of popular tunes. It was a time when community bands were increasing in their productivity and provision of popular music. Hartz (2003) notes that some band scholars believe community bands experienced a revival at the end of the twentieth century, a period of new band development, new music, and an increase in music education.

Size and Elements of Community Bands

There are currently about 2,500 to 3,000 community bands in the United States, although that number fluctuates, in part because of the names, criteria, and variety of approaches used to count community bands. One estimate is that there were 10,000 bands in the United States in 1889. At least 100 of these bands are still active (http://www.bloomingdalecornetband.org/bands/us19th.php).

In general, community bands are flexible and generic (Rehrig 1991), although they share important elements. Specifically, community band structure is built on a concert band ensemble, which typically has a specific number of instruments, of specific types. The number of players in a community band depends on the size of the

Hinsdale Brass Band, from Hinsdale, New Hampshire, ca. 1906. (Library of Congress)

town or city in which it is located. A community band is a group of wind and percussion players, generally sponsored by the town or city in which it is located. It is primarily made up of amateur performers, usually holds regular rehearsals, and performs at least one to three times per year, although as many as eight or nine indoor and outdoor concerts may be performed by particular bands. The concert band ensemble was the origin of the community orchestra and community band. The word "ensemble" came to mean a group of no fixed size or instrumentation, except when a composer chose to call for a specific number and type of instruments (Reed 1991, ix).

Sprinkled among the players in such bands are often several players who have retired from military bands. Most adult bands outside of college or military institutions are community bands. Some of the players in the band may actually be music educators who teach elementary and secondary school students how to appreciate, march, and play music. Thus, players in a community band may have diverse reasons for participating. Some players want to keep their musical skills alive, others seek fellowship and camaraderie, still others simply enjoy playing interesting and well-performed music, and yet others have learned to play a musical instrument while they were in high school or college but did not follow music as a career and now seek an opportunity to pursue their musical abilities.

As the nineteenth and twentieth centuries unfolded, community bands increasingly became the musical context for patriotism stemming from the wars in which the United States was involved (e.g., the war of 1812, the Civil War, World Wars I and II, Vietnam, Iraq, and Afghanistan). These community bands, traveling from town to town or city to city performing, became popular and spawned more community bands to reinforce the stirring music of the day. However, by the end of World War I community bands were decreasing as many new forms of entertainment and cultural shifts (e.g., automobiles, radio) began to replace them.

Although some community bands receive some form of performer remuneration, most do not. These bands may receive grants from local philanthropists or community recreation funds, or donations may be used to pay soloists or band directors but not performers.

Community bands have many names. Some carry the name of the town or city in which they are located, but many bands have names that describe the musical instruments used (e.g., brass band) or other particular features. Some bands are also marching bands, performing in parades or patriotic events. Other community bands have a myriad of names.

Some community bands are small and limited in the instrumentation they have available to play certain songs. Other bands may have sixty to one hundred or even more players, with instrumentation to perform virtually any music requested.

History of Community Bands

The names and history of community bands are often a function of when and where their members arrived in the United States. Some immigrants brought the band tradition with them to the United States. In other cases, particular immigrant groups developed bands in the towns where they lived. Although woodwind instruments were used by some bands, most community bands emphasized brass instruments. Community bands can represent a large range of entities; they can be town, citizen, or civic bands; military bands; concert bands; wind bands; brass bands; reed bands; police bands; symphonic bands; dance bands; rock bands; and so forth.

By the middle of the 1800s, when brass instruments with valves came into wide use, the music played by community bands began to change to melodies that were shorter in length than the earlier European music. Audiences became familiar with marches, polkas, and patriotic performances, and instrumental solos with band accompaniment, as well as brief adaptations of operettas, operas, and other master works, became more available.

Developments in community bands contnued during the first couple of decades after the Civil War, including a large amount of music written and published specifically for them, as well as the inclusion of woodwinds, where brass and percussion instruments had previously predominated. Community band music was being brought to towns and cities that could not financially support other types of outstanding traveling music. At that time there were fewer than ten symphony orchestras in the United States. Thus, community bands were filling an entertainment void with music accessible to the American public.

Among the important community bands that stood out and served as models for other community bands in the United States were those provided by the Salvation Army. These British-style brass and religious community bands spread throughout continental Europe and the United States. The Salvation Army, as a part of the Christian church, has had brass bands (a.k.a. community bands) since 1878. These bands are integral to the church (the Salvation Army). They vary widely in size, complement, quality, and location, and like other community bands, they depend on the musicianship of available local personnel.

Contributions of the Community Band

Composers, scholars, bandmasters, and other important figures in the history, creation, and performance of music in America have suggested that two types of music are played by community bands: (1) music composed expressly for bands and (2) music first composed for other instrumentation and later adapted for bands (Rehrig 1991). These two perspectives essentially divide in half the roughly four centuries of community band history.

During the nineteenth and twentieth centuries composers imitated, transcribed, and increasingly wrote music, in some cases using European models but more and more with distinctive American structure and melodies. If American music is understood to be music with a recognizable American character, then it began in the nineteenth century, and has grown since then. During that same period, community bands have evolved and increased in number and range.

Almost in parallel with the growing volume of music being written for various musical purposes, community bands have evolved and increased in quality and in variety of musical programs. A community band may also be called a "brass band" or some other term. Typically, a "community band" is sponsored or supported by a particular town or city, whereas "brass band" means that this particular community band plays brass instruments, not strings or woodwinds.

Thus the vocabulary and context used to name individual bands and their instruments is important. For example, it can be argued that any band that plays most of the music for a local community is a community band. Further, a band, whatever its name or title, is not rigidly defined or prone to standardization.

From the early 1900s to the present day, musical classics have increased, among other popular emphases, that were seen as excellent examples of American expressions of its dreams, patriotism, and diversity. Many individual tunes included depictions of American themes that were aspects of musical theater and community bands. Examples are tunes from musicals such as *Oklahoma!* (Richard Rodgers); *Guys and Dolls* (Frank Loessor); *Porgy and Bess, The Rhapsody in Blue,* and *An American in Paris* (George Gershwin); *West Side Story* (Leonard Bernstein); and *The Music Man* (Meredith Willson).

By the early 1900s, American musicians were writing and playing music related to the increasingly popular patriotic songs that were being played across the United States and by invitation in other nations. "The March King," John Philip Sousa (1854–1932), was one of the best known and creative composers and a bandmaster who traveled to other nations and served as a strong advocate of contemporary American music, particularly classic marches and community band pieces.

In addition to community bands, nearly every public and private school district has a band. Given the worldwide economic crisis, it is possible that some school music programs will be removed from the schools where they are currently located. School music programs, whether in jeopardy or not, typically use instrumentation that is not standardized, but can still be used in music education. As necessary, bandmasters are typically able to depart from guidelines and create their own content.

School bands, though not usually considered community-based bands, can fall into that category. Students either take lessons for free or pay for individual or private lessons beginning around fifth or sixth grade. As their ability as musicians increases, they move through the academic and extracurricular ranks. School band members tend to participate in upper elementary, junior high school, and senior high school. School bands vary in size and execution, the number of students in the band, and the ability of the players. Some school bands follow a set curriculum that lays out particular styles standard in music education programs. The high school band program is similar to a community band in ability and repertoire.

Conclusion

Community bands are mainstays in music in the United States. Many local bands in the United States may not think of themselves as community bands. The term is used to describe a particular community band and often its unique characteristics. Also, important organizations support community bands.

Finally, community bands often compete with their peers and are represented in music societies. Notable examples include the Association of Concert Bands, National Concert Bands of America, and the Honor Band of America. These musical organizations vary in their purposes, but typically reflect standards of achievement, collect information about individual bands or soloists, make music available to member community bands, attend national conventions of musicians, have instruments for sale, and provide many musical accessories for members. For example, in its mission statement the Association of Concert Bands encourages and fosters adult concerts as well as community, municipal, and civic activities to ensure that all musicians have an opportunity to participate in music with other adults. The Association of Concert Bands, at its convention in 2011, used a theme of the many colors of community bands. Community bands come in many sizes and shapes, with a diverse blending of instrument combinations. The Honor Band of America selects outstanding high school students to play in an annual honor concert every year. The ensemble is formed entirely of high school students.

See also: Bernstein, Leonard; Gershwin, George; Military Bands and Songs; Musical Theater; National Music Organizations; Patriotic Music; Sousa, John Philip

Further Reading

Carson, William S. 2003. *On the Path to Excellence: The Northshore Concert Band.* Galesville, MD: Meredith Music.

Hartz, M. J. 2003. "The American Community Band: History and Development." Master's thesis, Marshall University.

Hindley, Geoffrey, ed. 1976. *The Larousse Encyclopedia of Music.* Secaucus, NJ: Chartwell Books.

The Instrumental Company. 1982. *Band Music Guide.* 8th ed. Evanston, IL: The Instrumental Company.

Marvin, A. 1997. "Facing the Music: The Turn of the Century Hometown Band." *Kansas Heritage* 5, no. 4: 4–8.

Mattern, Mark. 1998. *Acting in Concert: Music, Community, and Political Action.* New Brunswick, NJ: Rutgers University Press.

Neidig, K. 1975. "A Survey of Community Bands in the U.S." *The Instrumentalist* 30: 40–47.

Reed, A. 1991. Preface to *The Heritage Encyclopedia of Band Music, Composers and Their Music.* Westernville, OH: Integrity Press.

Rehrig, W. H. and R. Hoe, eds. 1991. *The Heritage Encyclopedia of Band Music, Composers and Their Music,* Vol. 1, A–N. Westernville, OH: Integrity Press.

Rothrock, D. 1991. "The Perpetuation of the Moravian Instrumental Music Tradition: Bernard Jacob Phof and the Salem North Carolina Bands (1979–1960)." EdD diss., University of North Carolina at Greensboro.

Edwin Herr

Composers, Progressive

Progressive American composition in 1960 was dominated by two approaches: the school of so-called twelve-tone composition, located principally in American colleges, universities, and music schools, and an experimental tradition famously represented by the chance composition of John Cage (1912–1992), who maintained that then-current notions of music needed thorough reevaluation. Since that time, these two tendencies have more or less persisted alongside such other styles

Progressive Music for Bands and Choirs: Beginnings

Although the words "classical music" usually conjure up the exalted sounds of opera, chamber music, and the symphony orchestra, many Americans came of age without ready access to these ensembles except through radio and television broadcasts and recordings. However, a great many students had direct access to performed music through the long-standing educational musical ensembles of choirs and wind bands. Of the two, chorus has the longer history; it originated in the singing school tradition of New England and was as much an outlet for social interaction as for musical performance. Bands, which emerged from the military band tradition, blossomed into an important source of musical entertainment nationwide; toward the close of the nineteenth century, professional bands began to tour the country, including the New York 22nd Regiment Band under the direction of Patrick S. Gilmore (1829–1892). Other important band conductors include John Philip Sousa (1854–1932), Edwin Franko Goldman (1878–1956), and his son Richard Franko Goldman (1910–1980); all three wrote extensively for the ensemble.

Both bands and choirs are somewhat tainted by their social aspects; needlessly so, because prominent composers have produced works for both. In particular, a number of internationally known twentieth-century composers, including Vincent Persichetti (1915–1987), Karel Husa (1921–), Warren Benson (1924–2005), and Joseph Schwantner (b. 1943), contributed some of the best-known works for the standard band (containing multiples of reeds and brass instruments) as well as the more recent wind ensemble. The latter is a small group with more flexible instrumentation that usually assigns one player to each separate part, conceptualized in 1952 by Frederick Fennell (1914–2004), a professor at the Eastman School of Music in Rochester, New York.

as minimalism and postminimalism; electronic music; performance art; a somewhat more conservative, "centrist" tradition; and a host of other styles that borrow in varying degrees from both classical and vernacular traditions. New forms of technology for music that have come of age in the first decade of the twenty-first century now make possible an even further fragmentation of styles and the genuine possibility of important compositional activity outside large cities, independent of traditional mechanisms for music production. The variety of musical styles and modes of expression pose important new questions for listeners and music historians.

The Historical Background

American composition since 1960 has been as complex, contentious, and varied as American life generally, and has been shaped by many of the same historical and cultural events that have made the last half century so memorable. After the assassination of President John F. Kennedy (1917–1963), the country was immersed in grief and turmoil. Kennedy's successor, Lyndon B. Johnson (1908–1973), promised to fulfill Kennedy's dreams, and Johnson's "Great Society" introduced more social programs than had ever been in place before. He also, however, plunged the country into one of the most unpopular wars in the country's history, Vietnam's civil war (1963–1974); the national wounds from that conflict remained long after the war was over, borne in large part by the returning veterans, who found themselves vilified and eventually largely forgotten by large swathes of the American people.

The Vietnam War occurred in concert with, and no doubt helped to fuel, an unprecedented uprising among students and other young adults who felt increasingly disenfranchised by the repressive atmosphere of the 1950s: the tendency to inculcate unquestioning obedience to governmental authority. College campuses including the University of California at Berkeley, and others demanded free speech and agitated vigorously against the war, while other marginalized groups—African Americans, women, and gays—demanded the dignity that they deserved under the U.S. Constitution. An atmosphere of experimentation and extreme license prevailed in Berkeley, San Francisco, and other cities, as people began a Dionysian sojourn into the worlds of premarital sex and drug use, designed to shake up conventions and open the mind to new possibilities. Such excesses often led to tragic results, none more memorable than the shocking series of murderers masterminded by Charles Manson (1934–) or the deadly riots at Kent State University in 1970.

In 1968 a new president was elected—Richard M. Nixon (1913–1994)—who promised to end the war in Vietnam and quell unrest at home. America, weary of violence and uncertainty, seemed wholeheartedly to embrace Nixon's path back from the precipice. Eventually the war ended and the country prospered—indeed, its international prestige grew with the president's historic visit to China in 1972—but Nixon's own anxieties about the continuing divide between Left and Right led him to maintain political advantage at any cost, and ultimately his efforts to obstruct the prosecution of crimes

Recent Art Music for Band Ensembles and Choruses

The educational aspect of much band or wind ensemble music has contributed to its less exalted status as a medium of art music, even though many works with simpler technical demands display compositional ingenuity, craft, and aesthetic beauty, such as the *Elegy* (1972) by John Barnes Chance (1932–1972), Eric Whitacre's (1970–) *October* (2000), and a *Fantasy on a Theme by Sousa* (2003) by Andrew Boysen Jr. (1968–). Recent compositions have been created by composers with solid credentials in concert music for other media—such as David Del Tredici's (1937–) *In Wartime* (2005) and *Circus Maximus* (2004) by John Corigliano (1938–)—as well as a growing number of works by other composers born after 1940, who have contributed significantly to the medium, including *Symphony No. 4* by David Maslanka (1943–), *Redline Tango* (2004) by John Mackey (b. 1973), and Frank Ticheli's (b. 1958) *Symphony No. 2* (2003).

The natural euphony of a chorus has likewise led to a renewed interest in music for the medium that garnered an extraordinarily wide appeal. Whitacre's *Sleep* (2000) was recently recorded by a "virtual choir" of 2,052 singers under the composer's direction and is widely available on the Internet. A number of choral works by Morten Lauridsen (1943–), including the *Chansons de Roses* (1994), are performed by amateur and professional choruses alike. The simplicity and near-instant accessibility of this music calls into question many assumptions about twentieth-century aesthetics more radically than the minimalists ever did. The challenges of creating such music without descending into outright kitsch are many, and time will tell whether such works remain an enduring part of the repertoire. At present, however, this music constitutes a welcome and important part of American musical life.

he himself had sanctioned led to his resignation and a nadir in civic faith.

National prosperity weakened, too, under the next two presidents—Gerald R. Ford (1913–2006) and Jimmy Carter (1924–)—until 1980, when Ronald Reagan (1911–2004) was elected and initiated a view of America that stressed economic recovery and a resurgence of conservatism, questioning the wisdom of the social advances that had swept the nation only twenty years previously. Since that time, the multiple cultures that compose America—including Latinos, Asians, Muslims, bisexuals, transgenders, and the disabled—increasingly have made their presence known. The country is beset by an almost hopeless ideological divide between Left and Right as well as threats from within and without—most notoriously, the destruction of the World Trade Center on September 11, 2001. The complexity and paradox of this time have engendered a new sense of urgency, and musical composition has not been unaffected by the growing fragmentation and confusion of this historical moment.

This entry charts the main lines of American composition as they developed from around 1960 to the present. The account is not comprehensive, nor is every historically significant composer or work mentioned; rather, it attempts to give a snapshot of the variety of compositional expression, type of venue, and geographic locale that has characterized American composition in the last fifty years. In particular, this approach reflects the rapid expansion of technology during the period, which obligates historians to consider both highly touted and little-known composers and their modes of expression.

The Musical Scene in America, 1960 to 1965

Although composers in the United States had ample opportunities to practice their art from the early decades of the twentieth century through World War II, the ascendance of university music departments after the war had a profound impact on composition in America. Obligated to make significant contributions to teaching, scholarship, and committee service and outreach, composition professors found that universities acted as patrons for new music every bit as effectively as the aristocrats and state or religious institutions that had sustained composers in previous centuries.

The academic spirit also fostered the discipline of music theory, which proposes various analytical methods to study structural aspects of sounding music as well as new models for composition; many theorists worked to reveal the structure of music by such composers as Arnold Schoenberg (1874–1953), who rejected a key center in favor of a constant circulation of the chromatic scale's twelve tones, often ordered in a particular way. Milton Babbitt (1916–2011), at the very forefront of this effort, drew upon this research to create a music offering vastly new possibilities, from the general sound to the gesture and overall form. His revelatory approach bore fruit in such works as *Philomel* (1965, for voice and electronic sounds) and *Concerti for Orchestra* (2004), but the challenges of addressing his music remain formidable.

American Composition to 1960

From its beginnings, the American tradition of classical music relied heavily on European models. The first music schools appeared by the mid-nineteenth century, including the Peabody Conservatory of Music (1853) and the Oberlin College Conservatory (1865). Even then, most composers felt obliged to complete their training in Europe. Visiting in 1892, Antonín Dvořák (1841–1904) encouraged American composers to draw on the folk music resources of their country as a wellspring for a uniquely nationalistic music while still maintaining the stylistic assumptions of European models.

A certain independent attitude always characterized American culture, however; the self-taught William Billings (1746–1800) took licenses with the rules of European harmony whenever his imagination suggested he should. This pioneering spirit asserted itself even more forcefully in the early twentieth century, when modernity inspired composers all over the world to introduce radical new sounds into music. Charles Ives (1874–1954) made his living selling insurance while devoting himself to composition whenever he could; often the complex harmonies, rhythms, and textures of his music eerily prefigured comparable achievements in Europe, even though he had very little idea of developments there. On the West Coast Henry Cowell (1897–1965) developed an array of novel approaches in his *New Musical Resources* (1930), assisted in part by his work with the musicologist and composer Charles Seeger (1886–1979).

The influx of émigrés resulting from the horrors of World War II helped increase the presence of music education in conservatories and universities. Paul Hindemith (1895–1963) taught at Yale, Arnold Schoenberg (1874–1951) at USC and UCLA. In the mid-1930s a so-called American sound in composition began to take shape with the open harmonies and propulsive rhythms of Roy Harris (1895–1979) and Aaron Copland (1900–1990); younger students working with these composers or with composers who had long and distinguished pedagogical careers, such as Walter Piston (1895–1976) and Vincent Persichetti (1915–1987), developed this particular strain of the American style. Still others, influenced by Schoenberg's interest in a constant circulation of all twelve tones in the chromatic scale, pursued his goals—sometimes in vastly modified form—with far-reaching consequences.

Not so doctrinaire as Babbitt, Elliott Carter (1908–2012) employed a richly dissonant idiom and unremittingly complex textures in his music as a reflection of the flux, unpredictability, and density of modern life. The image of dialogue—sometimes civilized, sometimes not—informs his music, and just as the pace of conversation rarely marches along in an even rhythm, Carter's rhythms shift and change like colors in a kaleidoscope, projecting infinite shades and patterns. His early String Quartet no. 2 (1959), which earned him the Pulitzer Prize the following year, is one of his best-known works, but later scores such as *A Mirror on Which to Dwell* (1975) and *Three Illusions for Orchestra* (2004) attest to the sonic beauty and lyric potential of his music.

Both Carter and Babbitt taught in university settings and worked within established musical institutions. An important alternative was offered through the work of John Cage (1912–1992). Born in Los Angeles, Cage worked briefly with Henry Cowell (1895–1963) and Schoenberg. His music was for some time better known to artists and dancers than to musicians. (He worked for over forty years with the dance company begun by his life partner, Merce Cunningham [1919–2009].) Cage's first important works (1936–1948) included percussion and the prepared piano—an extension of one of Cowell's ideas in which bolts, rubber, and other materials were inserted between the strings to modify the sound of the instrument; they were made by precompositional creation of a "rhythmic structure" or abstract number of beats that could be filled with any kind of content (sounding or silent), and that content could either articulate the structure or not.

From 1950 Cage cultivated the use of chance operations in his composition as a principle to allow sounds to be themselves rather than to express the mind of a composer; he imagined a number of variable possibilities for each separate aspect of a musical composition, from the most general to the most specific. These he assigned to one or to a range of the sixty-four numbers in the I Ching, one of the Chinese classics; by tossing three coins six times to obtain one of these numbers, he knew which variable to choose. Compositions made in this way entailed extremely laborious work; *Music of Changes* (1951) took nine months to complete. Once it was finished, however, musicians learned the music just as they did any other traditional composition. Cage later extended his principles to create what he called indeterminacy, in which performers had considerably more choice in interpreting his notations and in making such important decisions as how long a performance would last. His final works, such as the piano duet *Two*[2]

Composer Elliott Carter poses at the piano in his New York City apartment, May 2, 1960. (AP Photo/John Lent)

(pronounced "two two," 1989) aim for more of a reconciliation between chance composition and indeterminacy. But his lifelong goal of remaining open to all kinds of sounds makes his music utterly different in character from Babbitt's or Carter's.

Responses to Cage's Legacy: 1965 to 1976

Cage's influence on those around him was legendary. By the mid-1950s he had established what was often called a New York School of composition, including Morton Feldman (1926–1987), Earle Brown (1926–2002), and Christian Wolff (1934–). None of these men used Cage's chance methods (Feldman composed intuitively, while some of Brown's best-known works employ novel images rather than conventional notation), but all three embraced his idea that music should challenge previously held assumptions. At this moment the most highly regarded of the group is Feldman. His unerring sense for tone color (one of his works, *Why Patterns?* [1978], is scored for alto flute, piano, and glockenspiel), tendency to avoid musical development in favor of presenting a succession of ideas that recur in many guises, and explorations of extremely long durations as a source for new ideas about musical form (his second string quartet [1983] lasts between five and six hours), make him a composer's composer.

Meanwhile, Cage's openness to the world around him resulted in a profound reaction from artists of every stamp. He felt that the notion of a musical mainstream had been replaced by a situation more akin to an ocean containing myriad stylistic approaches. In particular, many composers felt that they now had unlimited possibilities for directions to be taken in composition, though not a few of them reacted by embracing styles that were designed to be a critique of Cage's example. Alvin Lucier (1931–), inspired by Cage's idea that sounds should be valued for themselves, irrespective of whatever compositional design they might be placed in, pursued a long career characterized by one amazing sonic discovery after another. He is perhaps best known for *I Am Sitting in a Room* (1971), in which he records and re-records himself speaking a short text so that the recording gradually reinforces the resonant characteristics of the room's architecture, turning the speech into the musical tones of that architecture. Later works, such as *947* (for flute and sine tones [2001]), ingeniously continue these concerns: the flutist plays tones close or identical to combinations of sine tones to create various kinds of acoustical beating.

Cage had always heralded electronic music as the most natural future for music, but aside from a handful of pieces including *Williams Mix* (1952) and *Sculptures Musicales* (1985), he did not devote sustained attention to the medium. Important work that continued the lines he himself espoused has been done by composers associated with the San Francisco Tape Music Center (1961 to 1967), a group that included Ramon Sender (1934–), Morton Subotnick (1933–), and Pauline Oliveros (1932–). Oliveros's *Bye Bye Butterfly* (1965), which involves extremely modest technology (two oscillators, two tape recorders, and a phonograph playing excerpts from Puccini's *Madame Butterfly*), presents a haunting tapestry in which the sounds echo, repeat again and again, and gradually combine into complex layers resembling waves crashing against the shore; it is a classic of electronic music. David Tudor (1926–1996), who began his career as a pianist associated with Cage and other avant-garde composers, soon pioneered live electro-acoustic music; one of his best-known works, *Rainforest II* (1972), constitutes an environment of continuous and diverse electronic sounds—most of which result from technology of Tudor's own design—constantly varying in density and timbre. Alvin Curran (1938–), who has lived for many years in Rome and performed with the live-electronic ensemble Musica Elettronica Viva, combines a variety of sounds in his early music; *Fiori Chiari Fiori Oscuri* ("Light Flowers, Dark Flowers," 1974), for example, comprises ambient textures; bare, childlike keyboard improvisations; a child counting in Italian; and hectic passagework for what sounds like an ensemble of ancient recorders. It builds to a glittering and almost painful climax with a fragment of a child's call and layers of birdsong. A very different approach appears in the work of Wendy Carlos (1938–); most famous for her best-selling album of Bach transcriptions for the Moog synthesizer, *Switched-On Bach* (1968), Carlos used the medium of electronics to emulate and extend traditional ideas of orchestration. Such works as *Timesteps* (1971) ingeniously unite electronic technology with musical ideas that never depart far from the idea of a tonal center with recognizable rhythms and form.

Beginning in 1965, another group of composers offered an even more radical interpretation of Cage's dictum, "Permission granted. But not to do whatever you want" (Cage 1967, 28). Many figures in the artistic community called Fluxus, some of whom studied with Cage during his short tenure at the New School for Music Research, thought of their works as music, but of a very special kind. For instance, *Proposition* (1962), by Alison Knowles (1933–), consists only of the single sentence, "Make a salad." La Monte Young (1934–) contributed similar works to the Fluxus group, but his later works, such as *The Tortoise: His Dreams and Journeys* (from 1964), explore a very restricted number of pitches for extremely long durations. This concept was allied with the techniques of a steady pulse, a pared down pitch language, and the repetition of small modules in Terry Riley's (1935–) *In C,* which was composed and premiered in San Francisco in 1964; the resulting style, best known as minimalism, initially demonstrated some affinities with the reductionist visual art of the period, but shortly afterward proved capable of more dramatic effects.

Meanwhile, another composer who participated in the *In C* premiere, Steve Reich (1936–), sought to extend Riley's ideas in a more rigorous and personal manner. Fortuitously lining up two identical tape loops of speech and manipulating them so that one would move slowly out of phase with the other, synchronize with the original (now exactly one note ahead), and repeat the process again and again (*It's Gonna Rain* [1965]), Reich found a path forward. He eventually moved to New York and transferred the so-called phasing technique to instruments in such works as *Piano Phase* (1967) and *Drumming* (1971). Shortly after renewing his acquaintance with Reich, Philip Glass (1937–), who had been exploring similar ideas in his own music, began to produce a series of works in which short, repeating modules of music are varied by the semisystematic addition or subtraction of one or a related group of notes. A series of such works culminated in the masterly *Music in Similar Motion* (1969).

Cage's interest in collage as a fundamental component of composition (which he exploited in such works as *Imaginary Landscape no. 5* [1952]), as well as his long-standing interest in the theatrical potential of new music, also manifests itself in many works by George Crumb (1929–). In such works as *Makrokosmos III,* for two amplified pianos and percussion (1974), Crumb's own modernistic style merges effortlessly with quotations by other composers (in this work, Bach). The quotation of previous music influenced other composers, including George Rochberg (1918–2005); both he and David Del Tredici (1937–) unabashedly returned to compositional techniques and predilections that could have appeared a century earlier. The first movement of Rochberg's fifth string quartet (1979) begins with a sonata-form movement that strongly resembles Beethoven, while Del Tredici's *Child Alice* (1977–1981) is a sustained large work for voice and orchestra that, in its loving references to the melodies and harmonies of nineteenth-century music and lush orchestration, exemplifies a trend of the late 1970s and 1980s known as the new romanticism.

Reactions and Divergences: 1976 to 1992

Both Reich and Glass became increasingly interested in the possibilities of tonal movement, more rapid musical development, and timbral variety (even sonic beauty) in their works of the later 1970s. Reich's *Music for Eighteen Musicians* (1974–1976), arguably his most important work, led to increased visibility worldwide through its recording on ECM; Glass's first opera, *Einstein on the Beach* (1975, premiered 1976) inaugurated his own sustained interest in large-scale music-theater works as well as a fruitful engagement with the harmonic and melodic gestures of music from the nineteenth-century tradition. The two composers were given a number of prominent commissions (Glass for opera and film scores and Reich for orchestral works), and the style of the music permeated advertising and an electronic-instrument-heavy style of popular music known as technopop.

The style also proved adaptable to a wide range of expression outside of minimalism's originally austere reductionism. An interest in a kind of modular counterpoint underpins *The Continuing Story of Counterpoint* (1976–1987) by David Borden (1938–), whose Mother Mallard Ensemble was the first musical group to use portable synthesizers; the harmonic variety and lengthy, intricate canons of part 11 (1986)—scored for two pianos—show how easily the minimalist style can be adapted to the creative inclinations of very different aesthetic sensibilities. William Duckworth's (1943–) *Time Curve Preludes* (1977–1978) combines the pulse-driven and repetitive tendencies of classic minimalism with a host of other influences, including Indian music and the incisive rhythms of American bluegrass. Each of the twenty-four preludes in the set unfolds in a time scale more typical of classical music, and the relatively faster speed of musical change results in a richer and more emotionally expressive brand of minimalism, dubbed by many "postminimalism."

Both Borden and Duckworth were East Coast composers supported by academia (Borden at Cornell University and Duckworth at Bucknell). On the West Coast, John Adams (1947–) initiated a series of compositions influenced by minimalism while teaching at San Francisco Conservatory; his later work as composer-in-residence with the San Francisco Symphony led to a series of richly orchestrated and dramatic works—including *Harmonium* (1981) and *Harmonielehre* (1984)—that completed minimalism's transferral to the concert hall. Adams's growing acclaim allowed him to leave his teaching position around 1982, and his later works abandon minimalism's preference for unrelieved tonal-sounding music in favor of a rich palette of styles and gestures that span the entire history of the twentieth century; in the main, he has remained a composer resolutely committed to the orchestra.

Although the wide presence of minimalism superficially suggested the arrival of a new common practice that could rescue classical music from what some viewed as the untenable complexity practiced by such composers as Babbitt, quite a few composers in succeeding generations were inspired by Babbitt's scholarship, teaching, and self-professed commitment to "question that morality which suggests that it is more virtuous to stoop to attempt to conquer the masses than to attempt to create a standard to which they might aspire" (Babbitt 2003, 433). Many of these composers continued vigorous activity in composition, making use of ideas pioneered in his work; like him, many, including Charles Wuorinen (b. 1938) and Andrew Mead (1952–), are or have been affiliated with colleges, universities, or conservatories. The label often applied to their work, "maximalism," is ultimately as misleading as the term "minimalism" is for Reich and Glass.

One of the most important in this group, Robert Morris (1943–), maintains, as Babbitt did before him, an active career as a composer and music theorist; his scholarship and other intellectual pursuits have had a profound impact on his compositional thinking. The early work *Varnam* (1972), for instance, bears a superficial relationship to minimalism in its reduced pitch content and steady pulse, while the choice of material (from the scales found of South Indian Carnatic music) suggests the then-current vogue for Eastern musical cultures. But Morris's union of Western and Eastern compositional models is comprehensive and thoughtful, intended to preserve the best aspects of both rather than simply to exoticize the non-Western materials. By contrast, the intricate polyphony of *MA* (1992), for computer-generated sounds, is intended to reflect Morris's deep interest in Buddhist philosophy, in that the separate melodic strands—differentiated as much by timbre as by pitch and duration—suggest a wide variety of structural interpretations rather than the single trajectory characteristic of much Western music. More recent work, such as *SOUND/PATH/FIELD* (2006), extends this metaphor both sonically, through the employment of multiple ensembles of varying size, and geographically, by separating the ensembles in a large outdoor environment within which both musicians and the audience may move.

Another group of composers capitalized on a variety of influences from the more experimental wing of American composition—in particular, Cage and the minimalists—in their work, which was decidedly interdisciplinary in spirit and frankly geared toward theater. Robert Ashley (1930–) collaborated early on with an experimental filmmaker, George Manupelli (1931–). Ashley came of age

American avant-garde musician and singer Meredith Monk chants at Dar Al-Assad Center for the Arts in Damascus, Syria, April 21, 2008. (AP Photo/Bassem Tellawi)

in the heady decade of the 1960s, during which time he cofounded the important ONCE Festival in Ann Arbor, Michigan (1958–1969); at ONCE, a haven for the most provocative new art and music, he performed his controversial *Wolfman* (1964), a notorious piece for tape and performer, both of which are amplified to such high levels that the sound is frequently colored with harsh feedback. A later work, *Perfect Lives* (first broadcast 1984)—described as "an opera for television"—comprises seven episodes of twenty-some minutes each (like an American television series). The decidedly atypical plot concerns a singer and pianist performing in a Midwest lounge, who decide to collaborate with the captain of a high school football team and his older sister in a bank robbery. Its visual content includes state-of-the-art computer graphics, numerous shots of Midwest Americana, and the oblique editing style soon to be popularized in the music videos of MTV. The music consists of Ashley's unusual narration (which alternates between the sound of an avuncular storyteller and an avant-garde singer) along with his own music and contributions from a variety of other musicians, including the improvising pianist "Blue" Gene Tyranny (1945–).

Although women were increasingly visible in all styles of American composition during this period (see Composers, Women), many were drawn to the new interdisciplinary musical forms. Trained primarily in visual art, the performance artist Laurie Anderson (1947–) combines the deadpan delivery reminiscent of television newscasters with simple accompaniments produced by elaborate electronic devices to deliver a series of her own poetic observations on the foibles of modern life in the seven-hour work *United States,* premiered at the Brooklyn Academy of Music in 1983. Meanwhile, composers such as Joan La Barbara (1947–) and Meredith Monk (1942–) developed an elaborate vocal music for solo or ensemble performance, often used in connection with theater or dance. Monk's *Atlas* (1991) is an evening-length opera loosely inspired by the life of Alexandra David-Neel, a scientist who was the first Western woman to travel in Tibet. (In the opera, a character named Alexandra appears at various ages throughout the opera and makes journeys both on and beyond Earth.) The vocal writing involves a great number of the techniques that Monk discovered in her own performances (often further developed and altered in collaboration with her performers), and the story unfolds largely through pure and surprisingly expressive vocalizing rather than through a conventional text. Often the elaborate rhythms and pitches of the singers generate a noticeable tension with the simpler, repetitive accompaniments, as in "Agricultural Community," the first number from part two. All these composers use a variety of musical styles, many of which stress reduced pitch collections and repetition as a structural device.

Major advances in technology during the 1980s made it increasingly possible for composers to work productively, efficiently, and economically with electronic music. The large synthesizers of the 1960s and 1970s were prohibitively expensive and difficult to maintain. Toward the end of that decade, however, portable instruments became more readily available (as demonstrated by Borden's Mother Mallard Ensemble, above). The technology was vastly improved in 1983 by the introduction of MIDI (Musical Instrument Digital Interface), a universal standard for all electronic instruments that enabled them to be connected together and controlled remotely—most often via a personal computer—allowing new implications for composition and performance. Improvements in sound synthesis through digital technology also made it possible to create much more nuanced electronic timbres that could approach, often very closely, the variety of tonal variation available through virtuoso performers of conventional instruments. Computer music could generate sounds anew, or composers could sample preexisting sound sources (such as speech), encode the audio information of the signal as digital information, edit the digital information in any way they chose, and reconvert the digital information into an audio signal once again. Pioneers in this form of composition include Paul Lansky (1944–), whose *Six Fantasies on a Poem of Thomas Campion* (1978–1979) uses various kinds of digital technology to process a single reading of the poem so as to reveal different musical elements implicit in the original reading.

Composers and performers sought ever more spontaneous methods of creating electronic music in real time throughout the 1980s, developing both new kinds of digital interfaces to control electronic instruments (e.g., sensors attached to their bodies and programmed to respond to various kinds of movement) and software such as Max, which allows the composer to send input to an instrument, which the software then reinterprets or reacts to in either highly controlled or variable ways. Atau Tanaka (1963–) is one of many composers intimately involved with these innovations. Such technology has had immeasurable impact on the worlds of both classical and popular music, obligating audiences and critics to seriously reevaluate the traditional definitions of musical instruments and musical performance.

The principal institutions and ensembles long associated with classical music—in particular, the symphony orchestra—continue to attract a host of composers, who seem to aim for a kind of centrist mode of expression: their melodies and harmonies acknowledge the variety of twentieth-century style, but remain more or less committed to a complex and dissonant language; older forms such as symphony and concerto remain pertinent to them (just as the programs of the symphony orchestra continue to follow the familiar pattern of programming symphonies and concertos as their main fare). The result, as in Christopher Rouse's (1949–) second symphony (conceived in the mid-1980s but completed in 1994), heralds a vital new repertoire of attractive, multimovement concert works that nicely complement the great symphonic works of the past without overshadowing them entirely. (The heritage of the nineteenth century guarantees that the classic symphonies of Beethoven, Brahms, and others will likely remain the cornerstone of the symphonic repertoire for the foreseeable future.) Other symphonic composers of this generation include John Harbison (1938–), Ellen Taaffe Zwilich (1939–), and John Corigliano (1938–).

Although jazz is treated in a separate entry in this encyclopedia, it would be foolish not to acknowledge its important impact on American composition, which has taken many forms. In addition to older attempts to make use of the rhythms and manners of jazz in a somewhat exploitative form—for instance, Aaron Copland's (1900–1990) clarinet concerto of 1949, or as a more thoroughgoing attempt to unite the traditions of jazz and classical music to create a new hybrid representing the best of both, as in the so-called Third Stream movement of Gunther Schuller (1925–)—the interaction between jazz and the complex classical music of the 1960s was strongly represented by the free jazz movement, and increasingly composers conversant in improvisation have incorporated it as a source for creative material no less important than notated music. Anthony Braxton (1945–) has enjoyed an extensive career as a jazz performer, and his works (each titled only with the word "composition" and an Arabic number to indicate chronology) are an important inspiration to a generation of younger composers. His Composition no. 193 (1996), made two years after Braxton received the prestigious Genius Grant from the MacArthur Foundation, counterpoints a dissonant and complex ostinato for a number of instruments, resembling a walking bass line, with improvisations of ever-increasing density (some performed by the avant-garde trombonist Roland Dahinden [1962–]). The music of John Zorn (1950–) also relies heavily on improvisation as well as the ability, in such works as *Cobra* (1984), to perform in a dizzying array of styles in quick succession. Younger composers such as Vijay Iver (1971–) and David Crowell (1980–) have strong backgrounds in jazz, but also make use of the fluency in many musical styles typical of composers in younger generations (see below).

Overwhelming Abundance: 1992 to 2010

Since the time of Cage's death in 1992, the variety that he predicted would occur has grown even larger and more diverse than it was during the late 1970s and 1980s, and America's composers contribute with music for every imaginable institution and venue. Although economic downturns and declining audiences continue to threaten the well-being of the symphony orchestra, the most prestigious ensembles continue with full seasons, and many regularly patronize living composers. Augusta Read Thomas (1964–) held the position of composer-in-residence with the Chicago Symphony Orchestra from 1996 to 2007; such works as *Astral Canticle* (2005) take advantage of the coloristic potential of the orchestra alongside piquant harmony and melody. The violin concerto (2009) of Jennifer Higdon (1962–), which won the 2010 Pulitzer Prize for music, was commissioned by a consortium of four orchestras; its idiom, somewhat more conservative than Thomas's, displays a clear sense of harmonic direction and rhythmic drive, balanced by an elegant gift for melody and colorful orchestration.

Other works designed for the concert hall or operatic stage exemplify both the multicultural attitude of this time and also a renewed importance in addressing overtly social themes. The *Pasión según San Marco* ("Passion According to St. Mark," 2000) by Osvaldo

Golijov (1960–) draws from a wide range of different translations—some exalted, some harshly vernacular—as the text for the work, allying it with a wide variety of music, including Latino dance styles, to stress the earthy and physical tradition of the Passion in South American cultures. A similar variety of music—from lush new romanticism to unrelieved dissonance—can be found in the opera *Margaret Garner* (2005) by Richard Danielpour (1951–). Toni Morrison's (1931–) libretto, adapted from her own novel *Beloved* (1987), tells the complex story of Garner, a runaway slave from Kentucky who murdered her own daughter rather than allow her to return to a life of slavery. During her trial, the lawyers and jury debated whether Garner had committed murder or simply destroyed the property of her owner without legal permission to do so.

Many younger composers eagerly embrace traditional concert works and venues as the best media for their gifts. The prodigy Jay Greenberg (1991–) composed his fifth symphony at the age of thirteen; the work, richly orchestrated and imaginative, offers a glimpse of Greenberg's promise alongside his unabashed love for Shostakovich and Bartók. Likewise, the two-piano sonata (2004) of Conrad Tao (1995–) bristles with unrefined references to Prokofiev, but shows an enviable compositional technique. By contrast, Conrad Winslow's (1985–) *Chariot* (2010)—a ballet scored for an unusual ensemble of oboe, trumpet, amplified harpsichord, and tuba—both stretches and exploits the instruments' characteristic identities, remains tautly controlled and coherent, but bursts with variety both harmonic and gestural. A final young composer, Nico Muhly (1981–), can trace much of his musical style to the minimalists and such Europeans as György Ligeti (1923–2006), but works such as *I Drink the Air Before Me* (2009) remain resolutely and somewhat awkwardly wedded to the classical music tradition.

Despite this age in which it is increasingly difficult to imagine anything truly new, various composers continue to push the boundaries of what music can be in order to carve out space for a renewed, and decidedly pluralistic, avant-garde. Mikel Rouse (1957–) combines complex but visceral rock-music-like rhythms with an elaborate skein of simultaneously spoken or chanted texts that he dubs "counterpoetry"; in his opera *Dennis Cleveland* (1996), a work whose dramaturgy is drawn from talk-show television, Rouse himself performs the title role.

John Luther Adams (1953–), after studying at Wesleyan and the California Institute of the Arts, migrated northward to Alaska, where he still lives. His music manifests what he calls "sonic geography": not so much a poetic evocation of a particular place as a translation of a specific location into sound—in his case, the vast expanse and serenity of a largely undeveloped terrain. Chief among his works are two evening-length pieces—*Strange and Sacred Noise* (1991–1997) for percussion quartet and *In the White Silence* (1998) for harp, celesta, string quartet, and string orchestra—and the shorter *Dark Waves* (2007), for orchestra and electronic sounds. Although the music seems static on an initial hearing, repeated listenings repay attention with an unexpected variety of detail. A similar sensibility appears in the music of Cenk Ergün (1978–); no matter the tempo of his music, he explores a limited range of material to reveal the powerful variety of sonic difference within them. Like Feldman and Ryan Vigil (1978–), he is also interested in compositions that explore extremely long durations.

Not a few composers have become interested in alternate tuning systems, following important work by such earlier figures as Harry Partch (1901–1974) and Ben Johnston (1926–). Kyle Gann's (1955–) *Custer and Sitting Bull* (1995), a kind of solo cantata for speaking voice and electronics, sets a series of texts by or attributed to the two protagonists in order to expose the inherent complexity in this historic conflict of cultures. The final movement, "Custer's Ghost to Sitting Bull," is unforgettable for the tragic text (beautifully declaimed by Gann himself) and a somber musical accompaniment based on a scale of thirty-one tones to an octave rather than the twelve common in the conventional tuning system of equal temperament. A more recent example of music in so-called just intonation is the haunting score for a production of Sarah Ruhl's (1974–) play *Eurydice,* composed by Toby Twining (1958–), who was awarded a Guggenheim Fellowship in 2011; the music, scored for Twining's own ensemble of singers and cello, requires throat singing and other particularized techniques in addition to mastering the difficult tuning. Jim Altieri (1978–) continues the tradition with a growing body of works employing just intonation; he is also active in the design of software for various musical installations of John Luther Adams and similar projects.

Two other younger composers—both of whom studied with Roger Reynolds (1934–) at the University of California at San Diego—display in their work an interest in complexity that allies it to a sensibility more familiar in postwar Europe. Steven Kazuo Takasugi's (1960–) *Letters from Prison* (2009), inspired by work of the German playwright Ernst Toller, offers a densely complex and satisfying environment of processed sounds performed by Takasugi, including vocalizations, koto, and other ad hoc instruments he created. Ben Hackbarth (1982–) explores the relationship between electronic instruments and acoustic ones in a multitude of ways in order to respond to and enlarge the musical predilections and shared experiences of his audiences. *Crumbling Walls and Wandering Rocks* (2009), for chamber orchestra and electronic sounds, takes as its point of departure the separate journeys of characters in the tenth episode of James Joyce's (1882–1941) *Ulysses* (1922); just as the characters are sometimes unaware of each other and sometimes encounter each other unexpectedly, so too do the complex streams of sound in Hackbarth's score appear sometimes stratified and separate and at others colliding and evolving together.

Distinct responses to concerns of the late twentieth century are manifested in two composers of Asian ethnicity. Inspired by the musical possibilities suggested by the X-ray of an injured friend, Ken Ueno (1970–) created a viola concerto, *Talus* (2007), in which certain sounds and their transformations were derived from spectrographic analysis of the X-ray. By contrast, an abiding interest in intertextuality and the thorough reconfiguration of musical sources from the past is a continuing concern in the music of Singaporean Marc Chan (1975–), who makes his home in New York. Chan's *J's Box* (2006) is a collection of works whose musical material all derives from the pitches in the first prelude of J. S. Bach's *Well-Tempered Clavier.*

The world and modes of visual art have always stimulated the minds of composers, and more recently the domains of music and art have intersected ever more closely. Several prominent young composers have strong ties to visual arts and, in many cases, dual careers in that field. Christian Marclay (1955–) divides his time equally between art and music, and though his recent artistic work (such as the twenty-four-hour film *The Clock* [2010]) has brought him more attention than his music, he is a pioneer in the creation of performance involving turntables; his work commenced independently of hip-hop artists, but both partake in the same attitude toward performance, multiculturalism, and the rich semantic associations of past music. Like theirs, Marclay's work can be meticulously edited or improvised; his musical ear is superb and his taste for creating works with this medium unparalleled. Pamela Z (1956–) is situated squarely in the world of performance art, but musical sound is a cornerstone of her work, usually supplied by her own singing with electronic processing. Recent works such as *Baggage Allowance* (2010) include a sophisticated component of video and movement in addition to the sounds of her voice; the work is a surprisingly profound meditation on traveling in today's world. Tristan Perich (1982–), like Marclay, is equally active in visual art, composition, and performance. He is probably best-known for *1-Bit Symphony* (2009–2010), which presents a handmade, programmed microchip equipped with a battery-operated power supply and headphone jack; the circuit produces the music in real time. Recent works such as *interference logic* (2011) combine the one-bit electronics with performing musicians (in this case, a quartet of electric guitars). Although the 1-bit electronics create a dense (usually tonal) landscape not unlike early minimal music, the rhythmic layers and psychoacoustic variety of the music frequently surpass the earlier models.

Many young composers have matured during a time in which the former stylistic allegiances—minimalism versus serialism, jazz versus classical—no longer apply, because they have steeped themselves in all sorts of music and often distinguish themselves as expert performers in a variety of repertories. The work of DJ Spooky (a.k.a. Paul D. Miller, 1970–), Daniel Bernard Roumain (DBR) (1970–), Joan Jeanrenaud (1956–), and Mason Bates (1977–) all depend on extremely close interactions with hip-hop or electronic dance music as the core of its aesthetic, together with the various kinds of techniques of mixing and collage upon which those musics depend.

Caleb Burhans (1980–) boasts a wide range of activities as a performer (including voice, guitar, and violin) as well as absolutely insatiable musical interests that consider no musical style or national tradition as off limits. In spite of his frequent forays into the world of indie pop music, his work retains a certain melancholy that frequently goes against the grain of the musical styles he adopts in his own work. Corey Dargel (1977–) is best-known for art songs that superficially resemble popular music, but which, on closer listening, deliver complex and often disturbing dividends both poetically and musically. *Last Words from Texas* (2011), for instance, uses the final words of death-row inmates; the final song, "Date of Execution June 26, 2007," counterpoints a playful, tonal musical accompaniment (the simplest cadential progression in A major) with such unexpectedly poignant lines as "I know I was going to tell a joke. / Death has set me free" in an off-kilter declamation and with pitch choices that point out the absurdity of the accompaniment without excessive ado. Like Burhans, Carla Kihlstedt (1971–) is a violinist and singer in addition to being a composer, and her *Necessary Monsters* (2010) takes as its point of departure the strange creatures in Jorge Luis Borges's (1899–1986) *Book of Imaginary Beings* (1957). Choosing nine of the animals, Kihlstedt set a series of poems about them by Rafael Osés (1968–) for an unwieldy but compelling instrumental ensemble, voice, and narrator, which has been enjoying an enhanced life as a staged performance. The music is an indefinable amalgam of pop and classical influences, neither fish nor fowl.

Envoi: Looking toward the Future

If the extraordinary variety exemplified in this small cross-section of composers and composers active in the United States continues to develop along its current course, the future promises to offer countless opportunities for audiences and many new kinds of composition. The technology of electronic music becomes ever more flexible and responsive to real-time performance, which is one of the most important desiderata of the medium; indeed, the extraordinary versatility of Ableton Live, a software package universally hailed by today's popular electronic artists, is already beginning to prove itself useful to current and anticipated needs in so-called classical electronic music composition and performance. The situation for some symphony orchestras is precarious, and opera remains a costly venture that promises few revivals for opera composers past an initial run. Nevertheless, those ensembles and opera companies that do continue to flourish make excellent efforts to perpetuate the work for new composers. Indeed, a recent triple bill of one-act operas staged by the New York City Opera—John Zorn's *La Machine de l'être* (2011), Morton Feldman's *Neither* (1977), and Arnold Schoenberg's *Erwartung* (1909)—proved one of the highlights of the season. Mainstream soloists and chamber ensembles seem less wary about commissioning and performing new works, while such specialist ensembles as the Kronos Quartet, Ensemble Dal Niente, Earplay, S? Percussion, eighth blackbird, the JACK Quartet and ETHEL (both string quartets), Ensemble Signal, and Alarm Will Sound suggest a healthier performance situation for new music than ever before. Important musical institutions of high schools, colleges, and universities continue to supply an important demand for new music, and some of that music is beginning to make its mark on the larger musical scene (see sidebar, "Recent Art Music for Band Ensembles and Choruses"). And of course, composers such as Philip Glass, Meredith Monk, and Toby Twining have created rich bodies of work for their own performer-specific ensembles; a host of other younger composers, such as David Crowell, have followed their example.

As always, the major cities of America—in particular, New York, San Francisco, Houston, and Chicago—have all proved long-standing centers of interest in new music. Composers who are not regularly performed in these cities have little chance of garnering the widest possible critical attention. Nevertheless, advances in music engraving software; recording engineering, mastering, and production; and music distribution in both digital and physical formats via SoundCloud, iTunes, Bandcamp, CD Baby, and a host of other sources have made it possible for composers in smaller cities and more remote areas to advertise and sell their music, as well as to make contact with presenting organizations that might commission new works or perform current ones. Even composers as well known as Philip Glass have turned to such methods. Glass long ago established his own artists' representative group and self-published his music, leaving rentals and distributions to other companies; more recently he has established his own record label, Orange Mountain Music, which has made it possible to release much more of his extensive output than would likely be possible through larger companies, such as Nonesuch, that have long been committed to new music.

At the same time, social networking Internet sites such as MySpace, Facebook, and others make it possible for these composers to generate worldwide audiences without venturing very far from home. Three composers who use social networking are Joshua Carro (1982–), a West Coast–based sound artist interested in simple materials, complex sound processing, and long durations; Scott Pender (1959–) of Washington, D.C., whose alliance of repetitive, postminimal music with a persuasive feeling for form and classical phrase structures has breathed welcome new life into the style; and R. A. Moulds (1958–) of Baltimore, Maryland, whose music is so resolutely conservative in form, harmony, melody, and rhythm that its very presence suggests a singular kind of artistic subversion in today's pluralistic time. It is not impossible to imagine a future in which new music becomes more regional, as it was, for example, during much of the seventeenth and early eighteenth centuries.

See also: Adams, John Coolidge; Analog versus Digital Recordings; Art Music (Experimental); Art Music (Mainstream); Avant-garde in American Music, The; Bluegrass; Broadway; Cage, John; Classical Music; Composers, Women; Conservatories and Music Schools; Copland, Aaron; Glass, Philip; Ives, Charles; Jazz; Minimalism; Music Television; Reich, Steven; Seeger Family; Sousa, John Philip; Technology and Music; Tichelli, Frank; Whitacre, Eric

Further Reading

American Music Center. http://www.amc.net/ (accessed August 7, 2011).

Babbitt, Milton. 2003. *Collected Essays of Milton Babbitt.* Princeton, NJ: Princeton University Press.

Bernstein, David W. 2008. *The San Francisco Tape Music Center: 1960s Counterculture and the Avant-Garde.* Berkeley: University of California Press.

Cage, John. 1961. *Silence: Lectures and Writings.* Middletown, CT: Wesleyan University Press.

Cage, John. 1967. *A Year from Monday: New Lectures and Writings.* Middletown, CT: Wesleyan University Press.

Cage, John. 1996. *Musicage: Cage Muses on Words, Art, Music; John Cage in Conversation with Joan Retallack.* Hanover: University Press of New Hampshire.

Crawford, Richard. 2000. *America's Musical Life: A History.* New York: Norton.

Gagne, Cole, and Tracy Caras. 1982. *Soundpieces: Interviews with American Composers.* Metuchen, NJ: Scarecrow Press.

Gann, Kyle. 1997. *American Music in the Twentieth Century.* New York: Schirmer Books.

Gann, Kyle. 2003. *Post-classic: Kyle Gann on Music after the Fact.* http://www.artsjournal.com/postclassic/ (accessed August 3, 2012).

Hitchcock, H. Wiley, and Kyle Gann. *Music in the United States: A Historical Introduction.* 4th ed. Englewood Cliffs, NJ: Prentice-Hall.

Kelly, Caleb. 2009. *Cracked Media: The Sound of Malfunction.* Cambridge, MA: MIT Press.

"Meet the Composer" (Part of New Music USA). 2012. http://www.meetthecomposer.org/ (accessed August 3, 2012).

Nicholls, David. 1998. *The Cambridge History of American Music.* New York: Cambridge University Press.

Potter, Keith. 2000. *Four Musical Minimalists: La Monte Young, Terry Riley, Steve Reich, Philip Glass.* New York: Cambridge University Press.

Reeves, Thomas C. 2000. *Twentieth-Century America: A Brief History.* New York: Oxford University Press.

Straus, Joseph N. 2009. *Twelve-Tone Music in America.* New York: Cambridge University Press.

Strickland, Edward. 1991. *American Composers: Dialogues on Contemporary Music.* Bloomington: Indiana University Press.

Rob Haskins

Composers, Women

Two important events in American history illustrate exactly how recently the nation began to consider the importance of women: the Nineteenth Amendment (1920) to the U.S. Constitution, which declared that the right to vote "shall not be denied or abridged . . . on account of sex," and efforts to pass the Equal Rights Amendment (first proposed as the constitution's twenty-eighth amendment in 1972, reintroduced many times thereafter, and still three states short of the required ratification by thirty-eight states), which would guarantee that "equality of rights under the law shall not be denied or abridged by the United States or by any other state on account of sex." In American music, women have had little trouble entering into the field as performers and teachers; but women with active careers in composition and conducting were rare until after 1960. Although the imbalance has noticeably lessened for women composers in recent years (see Composers, Progressive), it is worthwhile to consider the broader achievements of women in the field.

Earlier in the twentieth century, a woman's social class usually helped facilitate study in music. Amy

American pianist and composer Amy Cheney Beach. (Library of Congress)

Cheney Beach (1867–1944) hailed from an important New Hampshire family who had the cultural background and financial means to further her considerable talents, demonstrated already in her first year. Beach's European training helped shape her relatively conservative compositional style. Nevertheless, composers of her generation were not restricted in their stylistic interests: both Johanna Beyer (1888–1944), a German émigré, and Ruth Crawford (1901–1953, later Ruth Crawford Seeger) were committed to the so-called ultramodernist style of the 1920s represented by Henry Cowell (1895–1963) and others; the music of both women, especially Beyer, remains far too little known.

After 1960 a number of American-trained composers made substantial inroads into a largely male-dominated world. Jean Eichelberger Ivey (1923–2010) was an important figure in the development of electronic music, while Judith Lang Zaimont's (1945–) considerable skills as a pianist resulted in a number of earlier works for the instrument (or for voice and piano) and, more recently, a more diversified output emphasizing instrumental music. Both women participated actively in university life, and indeed academic positions have helped to support a number of women composers who have explored a variety of musical styles, including Pauline Oliveros

(1932–), Elaine Barkin (1932–), Faye-Ellen Silverman (1947–), Chen Yi (1953–), and Lori Dobbins (1959–).

Other women have been able to sustain distinguished compositional careers largely outside of academia and, like their male counterparts, their compositional interests reflect the extraordinary diversity that has developed over the past fifty years. Tania León (1943–) is a professor at the City College of New York, but her career also includes music-theater work for the Dance Theater of Harlem and others, ranging from Broadway to the avant-garde director Robert Wilson (1947–) as well as an active career as a conductor; her later music includes African and Cuban styles allied with more traditional modernistic techniques. Laurie Spiegel (1945–), employed the personal computer to develop what is known as algorithmic composition (composition in which some of the decisions regarding the development of the music are made through the assistance of software), while Bernadette Speech (1948–) combines a number of wide-ranging interests in her music, including a concern for small collections of notes that recur without literal repetition—recalling the work of her teacher, Morton Feldman (1926–1987)—as well as the incorporation of improvisation following her interest in the free jazz of the 1960s. A more centrist tendency manifests itself in the work of Joan Tower (1938–) and Melinda Wagner (1957–), while such composers as Julia Wolfe (1958–) and Caroline Mallonée (1975–) draw on a diverse range of stylistic options.

See also: Art Music (Experimental); Art Music (Mainstream); Avant-garde in American Music, The; Composers, Progressive

Further Reading

Glickman, Sylvia, and Martha Furman Schleifer. 2003. *From Convent to Concert Hall:* A *Guide to Women Composers.* Westport, CT: Greenwood Press.

Jezic, Diane Peacock. 1994. *Women Composers: The Lost Tradition Found.* 2nd ed. New York: CUNY Press.

Sadie, Julie Anne, and Rhian Samuel. 1995. *The Norton/Grove Dictionary of Women Composers.* New York: W.W. Norton & Company.

Rob Haskins

Concerts for Social Causes

Concerts for social causes have become a commonplace part of society's response to humanitarian crises. While music and musicians have a long history of social, cultural, and political commentary—including participation in such events as the 1963 March on Washington—the staging of a large-scale concert to draw attention to specific societal needs or ideas began with ex-Beatle George Harrison's 1971 Concert for Bangladesh, with its inspiration and success spawning numerous other concerts in support of all manner of social needs and political voice.

Today we are quite attuned to superstar musicians like Wyclef Jean (1969–) or U2's Bono (1960–) lending their voices and popularity to social causes like helping to feed starving people in Darfur or raising money for Haitian earthquake relief. Concerts like those expressing solidarity with New Yorkers after the World Trade Center attacks and the victims of Hurricane Katrina's devastation, for example, have become commonplace. Musicians from all genres, countries, cultures, and political perspectives continually offer their music to ask for our support and engage our collective humane spirit. But music has long been a vehicle for social commentary (consider the songs and concerts of folk and "protest" pioneers like Woody Guthrie [1912–1967] or Pete Seeger [1919–]). It was an important part of the 1963 civil rights March on Washington for Jobs and Freedom. The program at the Lincoln Memorial was, of course, most famous for Martin Luther King Jr's "I Have a Dream" speech, in which he asked people not to judge one another "on the color of their skin, but on the content of their character," but it also included Marian Anderson (1897–1993)—the African American opera singer who earlier in her career had been denied access to sing at Constitution Hall in Washington, D.C., because of her race—leading the assembled thousands in the U.S. national anthem, as well as performances by Mahalia Jackson (1911–1972), Peter, Paul and Mary (active 1961–1970, 1978–2009), Joan Baez (1941–), and Bob Dylan (1941–).

The seminal large-scale, festival concert for the "social cause" of peace and togetherness was, of course, the original Woodstock (1969), three days of concerts attended by an estimated 500,000 people on Yasgur's farm in Bethel, New York. This festival, billed as "3 Days of Peace & Music," included folk and rock performers like Janis Joplin (1943–1970), The Who (active 1964–1982, 1985, 1988–1989, 1996–present), Sly & the Family Stone (active 1966–1983, 2006), Crosby, Stills, Nash & Young (active 1968–1970, 1974, 1977–present), the Band (active 1964 (1964)–1976, 1983–1999), and Jimi Hendrix (1942–1970), whose message of peace and community was immortalized in the song "Woodstock" by Joni Mitchell (1943–) (who ironically did not appear at the show): "By the time we got to Woodstock,/ We were half a million strong / And everywhere there was song and celebration / And I dreamed I saw bombers / Riding shotgun in the sky / And they were turning into butterflies / Above our nation."

But large-scale concerts—attempting to reach globally across cultures, classes, and ethnicities—to draw attention to or raise money for specific social causes or humanitarian aid really began with ex-Beatle George Harrison's Concert for Bangladesh (1971), which brought together such musical legends and performers as Eric Clapton (1945–), Bob Dylan, Billy Preston (1946–2006), Leon Russell (1942–), and Ringo Starr (1940–), as well as Ravi Shankar (1920–), the Indian sitar virtuoso (who had first approached Harrison and others to help the hundreds of thousands of people devastated by a natural disaster and caught between governments refusing to do something about their plight). The result was two sold-out Madison Square Garden shows, a Grammy Award–winning album, and film *Concert for Bangledesh,* all of which raised money for UNICEF, for millions of Pakistani refugees fleeing persecution by crossing the border into India. As numerous people have remarked, George Harrison's efforts were substantial—inspirational and effective—and showed how music and musicians with a conscience could serve the greater good. Writing in 1972, rock historian Jon Landau (1972) noted that through this concert "George Harrison emerges . . . as a man with a sense of his own role in the place of things, and as a man prepared to face reality openly and with a judgment and maturity with few parallels among his peers. From the personal point of view, *Concert for Bangladesh* was George's moment. He put it together; and he pulled it off, and for that he deserves the admiration of all of us." Many years later, the admiration for Harrison and what he accomplished is still palpable. As Kofi Annan, the former United Nations Secretary-General, acknowledged: "George and his friends were pioneers" (Concert for Bangladesh Web site). On the occasion of the fortieth anniversary of the concert, Ravi Shankar reminded us that "an enormous amount of money was collected and this never could have been achieved without the help of George. What happened is now history. . . . [O]vernight the name of the country Bangladesh came to be known all over the world. Millions of dollars were raised and given to UNICEF who distributed milk, blankets, and clothes to refugees" (Concert for Bangladesh Web site).

At the end of the 1970s Jackson Browne (1948–), Graham Nash (1942–), and Bonnie Raitt (1949–) led the group Musicians United for Safe Energy (MUSE) in staging the No Nukes Concerts (1979) and protest rally (five shows at Madison Square Garden and a gathering in Battery Park City New York) to draw attention to the dangers of nuclear power. Organized in response to the Three Mile Island nuclear accident, the No Nukes shows included performances by Browne, Raitt, Crosby, Stills & Nash, as well as Tom Petty and the Heartbreakers (active 1976–present), The Doobie Brothers (active 1970–1982, 1987–present), James Taylor (1948–), Carly Simon (1945–), and Bruce Springsteen (1949–) and the E Street Band (active 1972–present). Thirty-two years later, in response to the tsunami devastation and subsequent nuclear reactor leaks in Japan, the leaders of the original concerts came together again for a concert to raise money for Japanese victims' relief, remind people of the dangers of nuclear power, and advocate for safer forms of energy production.

The Secret Policeman's Balls (1976, 1979, 1981, and following) were a series of concerts originally conceived of and led by the British comedian John Cleese (1939–), of Monty Python fame, in support of the human rights group Amnesty International. The first shows—which did not use the "policeman" title—consisted mostly of comedic acts, other Python players as well as popular British comics like Rowan Atkinson (1955–), Stephen Fry (1957–), and Hugh Laurie (1959–). Later shows, most notably the 1981 concert, included musicians like Pete Townshend (1945–), Eric Clapton, Jeff Beck (1944–), and Sting (1951–). The shows have had a long, successful run of raising awareness and support for Amnesty International and have been recognized by other famous musicians, including Bob Geldof (1951–) of The Boomtown Rats (active 1975–1986) and U2's Bono, as the inspiration for their own efforts to organize concerts for social causes or needs.

In the 1980s the MTV age saw perhaps the most famous and immediately far-reaching musicians for social awareness project, led by Quincy Jones (1933–) and Michael Jackson (1958–2009) and inspired by Harry Belafonte (1927–): the "We Are the World" record and video of 1985, which sold more than twenty million copies. Again, a huge mix of talent, across ages and styles—Lionel Ritchie (1949–), Bruce Springsteen, Ray Charles (1930–2004), Stevie Wonder (1950–), Paul Simon (1941–), Bob Dylan, Billy Joel (1949–), Tina Turner (1939–), Diana Ross (1944–), Cyndi Lauper (1953–), and Willie Nelson (1933–), among others—came together to bring attention to people in severe need. Through the USA for Africa organization, millions of dollars were raised for relief aid, and today the organization remains a potent force for raising awareness and providing support. As Denise Dalaimo noted in a piece on the USA for Africa Web site, the amazing collaboration and ultimate global popularity of the "We Are The World" song and video demonstrated how "popular music forced a level of cross-cultural communication that governments had resisted for years" (USA for Africa Web site), which resulted in tangible awareness and support for those less fortunate.

The next concerts to generate widespread publicity and mobilize global efforts were the Live Aid shows in 1985, organized by Bob Geldof of The Boomtown Rats,

Willie Nelson sings before a crowd of over 50,000 people at the 10th annual Farm Aid concert held at Cardinal Stadium in Louisville, Kentucky, October 1, 1995. Farm Aid was created to raise money for legal assistance and financial counseling for family farmers. (AP Photo/Timothy D. Easley)

initially for Ethiopian famine relief (and following on the heels of Geldof and others' Band Aid, "Do They Know Its Christmas?" music album project). Main concerts in England included acts like Queen (active 1971–present), David Bowie (1947–), Elton John, and Paul McCartney (1942–present), and in the United States, Neil Young (1945–), Tom Petty, The Cars, and Mick Jagger. The concerts were coordinated at venues all around the world and broadcast globally. Some $67 million was raised, and the concerts were said to have reached 1.4 billion people. Later that same year, Willie Nelson, Neil Young, and John Mellencamp (1951–) organized the Farm Aid concert. Said to have been motivated by a comment Bob Dylan made during his Live Aid performance that perhaps some of the money being raised could go to help farmers "right here in America," Farm Aid's goal was to draw attention to the plight of the small farmer. Unlike other one-off "concerts for social causes" (including the Live Aid efforts), Farm Aid has had a run of concerts over more than twenty years, parlaying the initial success of the original concerts into an ongoing educational, awareness, and support program. Musicians like Willie Nelson and Neil Young have been joined by a newer generation of artists like Dave Matthews (1967–) to continue, in the words of the organization "to keep family farmers on their land."

Recent concerts have taken on more overtly political tones and included participation by both celebrity activists and politicians. Perhaps not surprisingly, the Concert for New York City, organized by Paul McCartney and held only six weeks after the attacks on the World Trade Center, included appearances by New York City mayor Rudolph Guiliani as well as then New York senator Hillary Clinton and former U.S. president Bill Clinton. The emphasis was on honoring the "first responders": the police, firefighting, and emergency personnel who risked, and many of whom lost, their lives, in the Twin Towers destruction. The music very much became the message as an all-star lineup including McCartney, Elton John, Billy Joel, Jay-Z (1969–), Kid Rock (1971–), and The Who performed (with The Who's "Won't Get Fooled Again" receiving one of the biggest ovations).

The 2005 Live 8 concerts are also important to understand in regard to the increasing political activism connected to such shows and their organizers and participants. Bob Geldof and others organized Live 8 to coincide with the G-8 economic summit then being held in Scotland (where political leaders from the largest First World economies were meeting to set policies, etc.) to call attention to the need to support African and other Third World countries with not just "relief" aid, but real integration into the global economy and a voice in the political system that controls it.

Like Live 8, the 2007 Live Earth: Concerts for a Climate in Crisis—held on 07/07/07—made explicit the link between promoting a social cause and political activism, in this case, drawing people's attention to the effects of climate change and global warming on the environment and our lives. Organized in conjunction with former U.S, vice president Al Gore, Live Earth "was built upon the belief that entertainment has the power to transcend social and cultural barriers to move the world community to action" (Live Earth Web site). These initial shows were held on seven continents and broadcast to 132 countries. Live Earth was also one of the first large-scale events to utilize Internet video streaming—in partnership with MSN—to broadcast its show to millions of viewers worldwide.

Arriving at a moment when a musician like Bono has the ear of presidents and prime ministers and is acknowledged by many for his thorough understanding of the issues surrounding aiding countries or peoples, as opposed to simply helping a cause by organizing or performing at a fund-raising show, has not happened without criticism. Many humanitarian activists and aid workers view such "celebrity" involvement as obscuring the real long-term issues and needs facing countries and people like those in Africa in favor of a "feel good" or patronizing narcissism, with one critic, Naomi Klein, describing this as "the Bono-ization" of activism. She worries that when such celebrities "engage in talks with world leaders at forums such as Davos they are legitimizing the structures in place, and the inequalities that arise from these structures, rather than promoting any radical change" (quoted in Delaney 2007).

Such criticism notwithstanding, it is clear that the music industry and many of its most famous activist and socially conscious voices—from Woody Gurthrie, Bob Dylan, and George Harrison, to Bob Geldof, Michael Jackson, and Bono—have played a large and valuable role in making people aware of issues and needs both in their individual communities and across the globe. Each of the individual concerts described raised substantial money and considerable awareness and support. It is perhaps fitting to end where most people recognize that the popularity and success of "music for social causes" began: by acknowledging how one of the members of the first truly superstar, truly global group, The Beatles, lent his fame and commitment to support the needs of people without voice—George Harrison's Concert for Bangladesh. As Anthony DeCurtis wrote in *Rolling Stone* in 2005: "The Concert for Bangladesh is rightly enshrined in rock history as the model for Band Aid, Live Aid, Live 8 and every other superstar benefit concert. . . . When his friend and teacher, Ravi Shankar, told [Harrison] about a massive humanitarian crisis taking place in East Pakistan and asked if the former Beatle could do anything to help," he, of course, did, and the rest, as they say, is musical—and perhaps more important, human and humane—history.

See also: Baez, Joan; Browne, Jackson; Charles, Ray; Crosby, Stills & Nash; Dave Matthews Band; Dylan, Bob; Environmental Activism in Music; Guthrie Family; Hendrix, Jimi; Hurricane Katrina and Music; Jackson, Michael; Jay-Z; Joel, Billy; Jones, Quincy; Joplin, Janis; Mellencamp, John; Nelson, Willie; Raitt, Bonnie; September 11th Commemorations; Seeger, Pete; Simon, Paul; Social Causes of Musicians; Springsteen Bruce; Taylor, James; Turner, Tina

Official Web Sites:

Concert for Bangladesh: http://theconcertforbangladesh.com/theconcert/

Farm Aid: http://www.farmaid.org

Live Earth: http://liveearth.org

Live 8: http://www.live8live.com/

USA for Africa: http://www.usaforafrica.org/legacy_popculture.html

Further Reading

Delaney, Brigid. 2007. "The Bono-ization of Activism." *CNN World Weekly,* October 12. http://edition.cnn.com/2007/WORLD/europe/10/12/ww.klein/index.html (accessed April 4, 2013).

DeCurtis, Anthony. 2005. "George Harrison: Concert for Bangladesh (Reissue)." *Rolling Stone,* October 20. http://www.rollingstone.com/music/albumreviews/concert-for-bangladesh-reissue-20051020 (accessed February 13, 2013).

Landau, Jon. 1972. "George Harrison: Concert for Bangladesh." *Rolling Stone,* February 3. http://www.rollingstone.com/music/albumreviews/concert-for-bangladesh-19720203 (accessed February 13, 2013).

Lisa O'Neill and Paul Almonte

Conjunto

The word *conjunto* means *group* in Spanish and is commonly referred to as a small musical ensemble that is

Santiago Jimenez, Jr. plays the button accordion, accompanied by Rigo Garza, left, on el bajo sexto and Joe Perez, right, on el tololoche, at the Narciso Marinez Cultural Arts Center in San Benito, Texas, July 14, 2004. (AP Photo/Joe Hermosa)

associated with Mexican music. Conjunto is also a musical genre that originated in the borderlands of south Texas and is one of the few musical genres that originated in the United States. This folk music shares common characteristics with *conjunto norteño* from northern Mexico. Even though these two genres may sound similar to an unfamiliar listener, each has its own unique characteristics. Today, conjunto music can be heard on car stereos, in concert and dance halls, at weddings, at quinceañeras, at community festivals, at Hispanic holiday celebrations, in bars, at music festivals, and at community music schools. It has become a symbol of pride and cultural identity for *Tejanos* (Spanish for Texas Mexicans).

The rise of conjunto began when the diatonic accordion made its way into south Texas with the Polish, German, and Czech immigrants who settled around San Antonio sometime after 1850 (Perez 1985). The heart of the conjunto is the accordion and its brother, the *bajo sexto,* which is a twelve-string rhythm-bass guitar that traditionally provided the dual rhythm and harmony, until the drum set was introduced, allowing it to play lead lines and offbeat strums (Hernández 2001). The *tololoche,* the upright bass, was added to the pair in the 1940s and then later was replaced by the electric bass. Vocals also became standard in the 1940s. The drum set and the public-address system were added in the 1950s, thus solidifying the standard instrumentation of the conjunto.

Conjunto became commercialized in the 1920s when record labels such as RCA Victor (Bluebird), Decca, and Columbia (Okeh) took an interest in recording it, hoping to reach the same success with African American music in the early 1920s (Peña 1985). Radio enabled conjunto to grow in popularity and made it a musical staple in the lives of Tejanos and of people across the country and the globe. As a young and emerging genre of music, conjunto has evolved through a variety of stages to become what is heard today. Conjunto song styles include a mixture of Mexican, European, and American music and include polkas, schottisches, canción rancheras, boleros, cumbias, huapangos, corridos, waltzes, rock, jazz, and popular music.

Once called the music of the working class, conjunto is a traditional folk music that was once played by the people of the rural or working class and could even be heard in the fields when the field laborers took their breaks or ended their workdays. Conjunto scholar Manual Peña (2001) believes that conjunto music became a reflection of the societal and economic conflicts between the different generations of working and middle-class Mexican Americans that stemmed from the growing disparity of cultural assimilation into mainstream American society. Furthermore, conjunto has been a primarily male-dominated genre that reflects the traditional gender roles of male dominance or this notion of machismo within Hispanic culture. Women have been a minority in conjunto because of the prominent male themes in the songs, the physical locations of performances, the physical size of the accordion and bajo sexto, and the tradition of transmission (Harnish 2009). Lydia Mendoza paved the way for women like Eva Ybarra and Laura Canales to knock down the societal and musical barriers to become prominent conjunto musicians and active participants in the performance of this vibrant music.

Other musical genres and cultural groups have influenced and been influenced by conjunto music and musicians. Musicians of this genre often played rock, pop, blues, jazz, country, and R&B in other performing groups. Leonardo "Flaco" Jiménez, one of the most prominent musicians of the conjunto genre, has spread the music to other parts of the world and has incorporated it into other musical genres. He has recorded with Ry Cooder, Emmy Lou Harris, Dwight Yoakam, Stephen Stills, and The Rolling Stones (Reyna 2000). Esteban Jordán, another musician who crossed several musical boundaries, was a child prodigy of conjunto music. In addition to conjunto, he played pop music, jazz, rock, blues, and a variety of Latin music. He incorporated modern chord progressions and jazz riffs into the traditional conjunto repertoire (Reyna 2000). Marcus Riojas Jr., known as "Marky Lee," who was inducted into the Tejano music hall of fame in 1999, has incorporated R&B into his traditional conjunto sound with his new group, Marky Lee y Hache Tres. Born in the birthplace of conjunto (San Benito, Texas), Baldemar Garza Huerta, also known as Freddy Fender, was a famous Mexican American musician who played in the group Texas Tornados in the early 1990s; that group combined conjunto, country, rock 'n' roll, and the blues. The Texmaniacs is another well-established conjunto group that has revived the genre today and has made it more appealing to the younger generation, incorporating Texas rock, blues, and R&B into conjunto songs while still being grounded in the traditional folk music (Los Texmaniacs n.d.).

The common accordion riffs heard in conjunto gave birth to the popular organ hook in the 1966 hit "96 Tears" by Question Mark and the Mysterians who were of Mexican American descent (*American Sabor* 2007). Founder Juan Tejeda of the Tejano Conjunto Festival in San Antonio explained that nonconjunto bands that played rock, blues, Cajun, and zydeco music were allowed into the festival because conjunto was beginning to show influences of these other musical genres. Furthermore, conjunto music has contributed to and borrowed from German music to this day, being an active participant in the German heritage festivals and events that take place in central Texas (Adams 2010).

Conjunto is a traditional folk music with deep, embedded roots within the Mexican American society that remains a vibrant part of musical culture in today's mainstream American society. As it has traveled around the world, it continues to inspire other musical genres and is open to new musical intersections. It mirrors the migration of Mexican Americans, their assimilation into American society, and their acknowledgment and preservation of their cultural roots, which is why conjunto will remain an influential, interactive participant in the American culture and music scene.

See also: Accordion; Blues; Folk Music; Immigrant Music; Harris, Emmy Lou; Jazz; Pop Music; Radio; R&B; Rock 'n' Roll (Rock); Women in American Music; Zydeco

Further Reading

Adams, Joy K. 2010. "Conjunto Culture: Celebration and Racialization in the German-Texan 'Borderlands'." *GeoJournal* 75, no. 3: 303–314.

American Sabor: Latinos in U.S. Popular Music. 2007. Experience Music Project/Science Fiction Museum and Hall of Fame.

Harnish, David. 2009. "Tejano Music in the Urbanizing Midwest: The Musical Story of Conjunto Master Jesse Ponce." *Journal of the Society for American Music* 3, no. (2: 195–219.

Hernández, Ramón, Jr. 2001. "An Informal History of the *Bajo Sexto.*" In *Puro Conjunto: An Album in Words and Pictures: Writings, Posters, and Photographs from the Tejano Conjunto Festival en San Antonio, 1982–1998,* edited by Juan Tejeda and Avelardo Valdez. Austin, TX: CMAS Books.

Peña, Manuel. 1985. *The Texas-Mexican Conjunto: History of a Working-Class Music.* Austin, TX: University of Texas Press.

Peña, Manuel. 2001. "From *Ranchero* to *Jaitón:* Ethnicity and Class in Texas-Mexican Music." In *Puro Conjunto: An Album in Words and Pictures: Writings, Posters, and Photographs from the Tejano Conjunto Festival en San Antonio, 1982–1998,* edited by Juan Tejeda and Avelardo Valdez. Austin, TX: CMAS Books.

Pérez, Carlota. 1986. "Las Nuevas Tecnologias: Una Vision De Conjunto." *Estudios Internacionales* 19: 76; *La Tercera Revolución Industrial* (Octubre–Diciembre): 420–459.

Reyna, José R. 2000. "Tejano Music." In *Garland Encyclopedia of World Music. Volume 3: The United States and Canada,* 1390. New York: Routledge.

Riojas, Yvette J. A. n.d. "Growing Up 'Tejano': A Tale of Tejano Music Influence." Hispanic Culture Online. http://www.hispanic-culture-online.com/tejano-music.html.

Los Texmaniacs. n.d. "Bio." http://www.texmaniacs.com/bio.html.

Amanda Soto

Conservatories and Music Schools

Conservatories of music and college- and university-based music schools have had a profound influence and impact on the cultural landscape of America since the last third of the nineteenth century. These schools have collectively educated the millions of people who have taught in our public schools, performed in our symphony orchestras, sung in our opera companies and on our musical theater stages, and composed music for films. These graduates have also become administrators of arts institutions and music therapists. They have worked in the music publishing and production business and served on boards of music institutions. Wherever one finds music in America, one will find a graduate of one of these institutions.

College and University Music Schools and Independent Conservatories of Music: The Beginnings

The first professional conservatories and music schools in the United States were founded in the 1860s. These conservatories and music schools came into existence as the country was maturing, industrialization was the word of the day, and an arts culture with deep European roots was beginning to develop in East Coast cities and a few cities beyond. Music was one of the powerful symbols of culture, refinement, education, and wealth, and the Eurocentric aesthetics of the educated and wealthy helped lay the foundation for these fledgling, non-degree-granting schools, which later became some of the best professional, degree-granting music schools in the world.

American conservatories were patterned in great part after the first great European conservatories (also called conservatoires), including the Paris Conservatoire (1795), England's Royal Academy of Music (1822), and Germany's Leipzig Conservatory (1847). But the American versions of conservatories were quite different from the European ones. These schools were not supported by the U.S. government, like their counterparts in Europe, and relied only on tuition and gifts to operate. These schools also added non-music coursework to the curriculum, some from their beginning, in direct contrast to those in Europe, which had no such requirements; with few exceptions, this remains true in both America and Europe today.

As in much of society in the nineteenth century, early study of music was divided between genders and with few exceptions was not open to people of color. Men participated in small numbers and tended to study music to become professional performers and teachers, whereas women, the vast majority of those who studied music in these schools, became teachers or studied to become more "refined" and educated in the arts.

The first four conservatories all began operating in the same year, 1867. They were the New England Conservatory of Music and Boston Conservatory of Music, both in Boston; the Cincinnati Conservatory of Music (Cincinnati Conservatory of Music merged with the Cincinnati College of Music, and then merged again with the University of Cincinnati); and the Chicago Musical College (now part of Roosevelt University). Other conservatories opened their doors to students during the following two decades, including the Philadelphia Academy of Music (now part of The University of the Arts); California Conservatory of Music and the Arts (now a part of the California Institute of the Arts); and two conservatories in Milwaukee, the Milwaukee Institute of Music and the Leuning Conservatory of Music. Others were founded during this time but did not survive much longer than the turn of the twentieth century.

Music schools and departments within colleges and universities came into existence about the same time as independent conservatories. One of the first was the Oberlin Conservatory (1865), which was and is part of Oberlin College (founded 1833). The Lawrence College (now University) Conservatory of Music was founded in 1894, and Northwestern University's School of Music began in 1895.

Music education is and always has been far more expensive than almost any other subject because of the high cost of private instruction. It was in part due to those elevated costs that all but seven of the independent conservatories failed to survive the twentieth century. Some went out of business. Others merged with colleges and universities (Kansas City Conservatory became part of the University of Missouri–Kansas City), while others became non-degree-granting community music schools (Wisconsin Conservatory of Music—formerly the Milwaukee Institute of Music). Those that survived the twentieth century and are still in operation are The Juilliard School (founded 1905) and Manhattan School of Music (founded 1917) in New York City, New England Conservatory of Music and The Boston Conservatory, The Curtis Institute of Music (founded 1924) in Philadelphia, The Cleveland Institute of Music (founded 1920), and San Francisco Conservatory of Music (founded 1917).

Conservatories and Music Schools: Their Influence and Impact on Society

As they had in the nineteenth century, conservatories and music schools had a major impact on American culture, onstage but also offstage, in such areas as public school education, private teaching, and music therapy, but also in related fields like vaudeville during the first part of the twentieth century, then in musical theater, and ultimately in film and popular music.

Onstage, the most obvious impact is where it would be expected, in orchestras and opera houses. Here the impact was almost universal. In the earliest days of orchestras in America, many players came from Europe, where they had been educated. As American higher education music training grew in quality and stature, it began to produce graduates who were increasingly able to compete with Europeans and were ultimately appointed to orchestras; this change gradually brought an end to the imperative to import musicians from Europe. By the mid-twentieth century the majority of musicians in the professional orchestras of the country came from American music schools and conservatories, primarily the latter. By the end of the twentieth century nearly all of the musicians in American orchestras, whether American or from other countries, had been trained in American institutions. However, by this time the nearly exclusive supremacy of conservatory training had waned, and there were musicians from conservatories and music schools throughout the nation in orchestras of all sizes and reputation. American instrumental musicians are members of orchestras in nearly every country and on every continent as well, so America's influence beyond its borders is also significant.

Similar patterns developed among opera singers, although later. Today American singers are some of the best trained in the world. Unlike instrumentalists, who tend to work for one orchestra or one or more in the same region, world-class singers perform on the world's stages, and as a consequence they are far more scattered throughout the globe than are their instrumental counterparts.

Musical theater and film are other arenas in which one sees the immense impact of training at conservatories and music schools. Jerry Herman (1931–), the composer of *La Cage aux Folles, Hello, Dolly!,* and *Mame,* graduated from the University of Miami's School of Music. Leonard Bernstein (1918–1990), the pianist, conductor, and composer of classical, popular, and theater music (*Candide, West Side Story*) graduated from the world-renowned Curtis Institute of Music (as well as Harvard University). Stephen Schwartz (1948–) attended The Juilliard School and Carnegie Mellon University and has composed works for both theater and film (*Wicked* and films such as Disney's *Pocahontas* and *Enchanted*) John Williams (1932–), perhaps the most famous movie composer of all time (*Harry Potter* and *Star Wars* films), attended The Juilliard School and the University of California, Los Angeles, and Elliot Goldenthal (1954–) (*Batman Forever, The Tempest, Public Enemies, Frida*) graduated with both a bachelor's and master's degrees from Manhattan School of Music, where he studied with the famous Pulitzer Prize– and Grammy Award–winning classical composer John Corigliano (1938–).

Nearly a century after the founding of the first conservatories and music schools, a new discipline was added to the curricula and degree offerings at a small number of institutions: jazz, the thoroughly American art form. As opposed to the beginnings of the country's musical institutions, founded on European musical tastes, this is an example of American culture changing music education and curriculum. Jazz had become a popular genre of music, mostly in large cities of the East Coast, mid-South region, and northern Midwest. As it became more and more popular and moved outside the African American communities where it was created, jazz gained entry into the music schools of the country. Jazz often started as an extracurricular study and later as a college "minor" of study. As it became more and more popular in those schools, some institutions decided to offer a college major in jazz.

One of the very first institutions to offer jazz studies was the Berklee College of Music in Boston. It opened its doors in 1945 and offered jazz lessons and classes. In the early 1960s it began offering degrees, as well as classes in rock music. Early on Berklee produced some of the greatest names in jazz and pop music, including Quincy Jones (1933–), Melissa Etheridge (1961–), Keith Jarrett (1945–), Branford Marsalis (1960–), and Pat Metheny (1954–).

Jazz has now become an integral part of virtually every music school and conservatory in the country, and most younger professional jazz musicians have had formal music training in a conservatory or music school. Interestingly, however, independent conservatories by and large took many more years to follow their university and college counterparts in embracing jazz as a field of study, either formally or informally. However, for the most part they, too, embraced jazz as a "legitimate" discipline, and by the 1980s most had some kind of program in jazz, informal or formal, as part of their institutions. Even the venerable and world-famous Juilliard began offering jazz as a major in the 1990s, one of the last institutions in the country to do so, with the great musician Wynton Marsalis (1961–) as its leader.

Perhaps more important than performance studies, whether classical or jazz based, is the study of music education and the preparation of students for careers as teachers in the nation's kindergarten through high school (K–12) education. This is where the majority of music majors in colleges and universities focus their aspirations, and these professionals then go out into communities to teach in elementary, middle, and high schools. Today there are tens of thousands of music teachers in both public and private K–12 schools. Virtually all of the public music teachers and many of the private music teachers have undergraduate degrees in music education.

These teachers, who serve the youth of America and their cultural education, have had an enormous effect on the lives of millions of individual students as well as society as a whole, providing entrée for many into the world of music beyond what is available on Web sites and popular radio stations. From teaching music in elementary school to exposing students to classical guitar, band and orchestral instruments, and other instruments such as the ukulele or harmonica, to providing ensemble experiences like choir, band, guitar ensembles, various types of jazz ensembles, and orchestra, these teachers provide the basis for the country's continuing engagement in "making music" and enjoying music.

Since the 1970s, when serious economic pressures caused schools throughout the country to cut back or eliminate music education in schools, school music programs have decreased in number. When economic times get better, some of these programs come back, but some have not. Since the onset of the economic downturn in 2008, the same patterns have been repeated across the country: Music and other arts programs in many sectors are experiencing significant cutbacks or elimination due to budget shortages. Many people fear that these cuts in arts programs will contribute to the reduction in cultural literacy among the nation's citizens. It should be noted here that many school districts, particularly those in major metropolitan cities and in many rural areas throughout the nation, have for decades not had appropriate funding to provide for education in some or all of the arts. These areas, where median income is often low among those who attend public schools, have been the hardest hit by cuts in arts funding during the past four decades.

The National Association for Music Education (http://www.menc.org), founded in 1907, is the national organization for music educators who teach primarily at the K–12 levels. It has more than seventy-five thousand members and sixty thousand honor students and supporters. The association not only provides resources to its members, but also serves as a national advocate for music education, with special focus on the public sector.

Pedagogy and Music Therapy

Two other areas of study in music schools that have gained much more legitimacy and grown significantly in the past several decades are pedagogy and music therapy. *Pedagogy* generally refers to one-on-one teaching or private lessons. Most often formal pedagogy degree programs are found in voice and piano, but they can also be found in strings. Students in these disciplines study, in addition to solo and ensemble performance, the art of teaching privately in the studio. These degree programs focus on the development of children from young childhood instrument study through the teenage years and beyond, including proper repertoire selection and technique training. Those studying pedagogy normally choose to become local, private music teachers, like the thousands found in nearly every town and city in the country.

Like the school music teachers, these teachers have a national organization that provides support and advocacy. The Music Teachers National Association (http://www.mtna.org/) was founded in 1876 by Theodore Presser, the great American music publisher, and has twenty-four thousand members. This organization also sponsors annual competitions for the students of its members, which take place at the local, regional, and national levels and include age levels from young children to young artists (college- and graduate-school-aged students). These competitions serve as a way for some of the most outstanding students of member teachers to display their talents and accomplishments as well as gain additional experience by preparing for such competitions and performing under very controlled circumstances, with competition "judges" evaluating each contestant.

In addition to training future private teachers for careers in their private studios, many conservatories and music schools also provide music lessons, chamber music and large ensemble experiences, as well as instruction in music theory and music history to precollege and adult students. The most famous institution to do so is The Juilliard School (http://juilliard.edu/youth-adult/pre-college/index.php). Its Pre-College Division provides intense study on Saturdays throughout the regular academic year. Many performers have received their earliest training there. Numerous other institutions, from Houston's Rice University to the San Francisco Conservatory of Music, to the Oberlin College Conservatory of Music, offer community music programs as well.

"Music Therapy is the clinical and evidence-based use of music interventions to accomplish individualized goals within a therapeutic relationship by a credentialed professional who has completed an approved music therapy program." This is the official definition of music therapy provided by the American Music Therapy Association (http://www.musictherapy.org/), founded in 1950. Music therapists assist their clients with a variety of issues, from general promotion of wellness; to physical rehabilitation; to combatting stress, improving memory, and laying the foundation for the alleviation of pain and the expression of feelings.

The effect that our music schools and conservatories have had on American culture goes well beyond the classroom and studio. At numerous institutions, concert series give communities, often too small to provide the financial support needed to present their own series, a rich array of performers, from classical music stars, to orchestral and chamber music series, to folk and world music offerings. These series can be found at large research universities, like the University of Michigan (http://www.ums.org/), and at small liberal arts colleges like Wisconsin's Lawrence University (http://www.lawrence.edu/news/performingartsseries/). Other institutions, like the regional State University of New York at Potsdam, serve their communities with a wide variety of performance opportunities, from concert series to music and musical theater performances in which the community is invited to audition and participate (http://www2.potsdam.edu/cps/). Through the variety of offerings for communities of all sizes, the nation's music schools and conservatories provide their communities with a rich array of performances and opportunities to participate in performances.

Professor Stephen Webber, top, watches his students practice their scratch skills in the Berklee College of Music's new class, "Turntable Techniques," Boston, February 12, 2004. (AP Photo/Adam Hunger)

Popular Music of the Late Twentieth and Early Twenty-first Centuries and Its Presence in Music Schools and Conservatories

As much as current popular music is finding its way into the curricula of various conservatories and music schools, it has yet to find a permanent or broad-based home there. It is not surprising that this is the case today, because this is how it has been for much, it not all, of the past century or more. During the first half of the twentieth century big band was extremely popular throughout America, yet there was probably not a single music school or conservatory that formally taught big band repertoire or studied it as an art form. As discussed previously, jazz was also a popular music form during music of the twentieth century, but it was not brought fully into most schools of music until the last third of that century. Rock 'n' roll in the second half of the twentieth century was also not studied formally until very recently, well after it was no longer current popular music. A few truly popular (current) forms of music (e.g., hip-hop, rap, heavy metal) have been adopted rather recently as part of postsecondary (college/university) training, and these have usually not been part of formal degree programs, but rather part of curricular enrichment. Other than occasional discussions in classes for non-music majors and some "world music" classes for music majors, formal study of these popular music forms, like their predecessors, is essentially absent from the vast majority of conservatories and music schools. This is especially true of those schools at which performance is the driving or most popular major.

Nonetheless, as noted previously, some schools, like Berklee College of Music, have explored popular music from their beginnings, so it is no surprise that Berklee added such subjects as rock, rap, and hip-hop as well as reggae, salsa, heavy metal, and bluegrass to its curriculum. Columbia College Chicago, another institution that has long been at the forefront of more popular forms of music, has expanded its curriculum to include many of these same genres. These, along with schools as different as the University of Wisconsin–Madison and Long Island University, have all begun to offer courses in these more recent popular musical forms. In 2009 McNally Smith College of Music in Minneapolis (founded 1985; http://www.mcnallysmith.edu/) announced a new diploma program in hip-hop, becoming the first accredited college to offer a diploma in this art form.

Interestingly, some of the most venerable institutions in the United States have invested time and resources in the study and/or support and promotion of hip-hop, putting them at the forefront of the study and preservation of this art form: Harvard University established the Hip Hop Archive in 2002 (http://dubois.fas.harvard.edu/hiphop-archive-harvard-university) and works in conjunction with Stanford University (http://www.stanford.edu/group/hiphoparchive/); Cornell's Hip Hop Collection catalogs the genre from its beginnings in the 1980s to the present (http://rmc.library.cornell.edu/hiphop/); New York City's Columbia University has its Hip Hop Society (http://welcometocush.tumblr.com/); Ohio University supports a chapter of the Hip Hop Collective (http://www.ohio.edu/orgs/hiphop/); and in 2011 Princeton University hosted Hip Hop Symposium, featuring DJ D.Scott.

It is interesting to note that although the vast majority of rap artists and hip-hop artists do not have formal music training, some did attend college (Ludacris [1977–] studied music management at Georgia State University; rapper MC Lars graduated from Stanford with a degree in English; Chuck D [1960–], front man for Public Enemy, earned his BA in graphic design from Adelphi University).

Conclusion

Formal music training began in America at the same time as or even before the founding of professional music organizations such as symphony orchestras and opera companies. These schools were launched in the last third of the nineteenth century, and their numbers—both of independent conservatories and music schools, which were part of larger colleges and universities—increased exponentially during the decades that followed. These schools began and evolved at much the same time as their European counterparts, but the European schools grew out of a centuries-long tradition of classical music, whereas the American schools developed in an environment where there were often few, if any, professional music organizations in the cities where they were located. In many cases these American schools were the catalysts for professional organizations (e.g., the faculty of the New England Conservatory created the Boston Symphony). These schools started as fledgling operations, employing European musicians as faculty, but many soon developed into some of the finest music schools in the world, and thousands of students from around the globe come to America to study at them. Indeed, most conservatories of music get 30–50 percent of their students from countries other than the United States.

Throughout the past century, music schools have had a tremendous impact on the culture of America. They have trained the vast majority of professional classical musicians who perform in and lead our arts organizations. They have educated nearly all of our teachers in public and private local school systems, and these teachers in turn have taught millions of students from ages five to eighteen in thousands of classrooms in every corner of the country.

College/university-level conservatories and schools of music have also expanded their scope of study since their beginnings in the 1860s, embracing a broader curriculum beyond performance and music education. They have included pedagogy (the study of private, one-on-one teaching), music therapy, and arts administration. Later they added jazz ensembles and then the jazz major. More recently, others have begun to study and promote truly current popular forms of music, although this has yet to become widespread or a part of the general music curriculum. In the end, the vast majority of institutions continue to focus on "classical" music and now jazz, maintaining and perfecting the traditions of the past for future generations.

See also: Art Music (Mainstream); Bernstein, Leonard; Big Band Music; Children's Musical Lives; Film Music; Hip-Hop; Jazz; Jones, Quincy; Marsalis, Wynton; Metal; Music Teachers; Musical Theater; Music Therapy; Pop Music; Professional Music Making; Rap and Rappers; Rock 'n' Roll (Rock); Schwartz, Stephen; Williams, John

Further Reading

Bennett, F. C. 1904. *History of Music and Art in Illinois.* Philadelphia: Historical Publications.

Burgwyn, D. 1999. "Seventy-five Years of The Curtis Institute of Music." Unpublished manuscript, The Curtis Institute of Music, Philadelphia.

Fitzpatrick, J. E. 1963. "The Music Conservatory in America." PhD diss., Boston University.

Gandre, James. 2001. "And Then There Were Seven: An Historical Case Study of the Seven Independent American Conservatories of Music That Survived the Twentieth Century." PhD diss., University of Nebraska–Lincoln.

Hays, T. O. 1999. "The Music Department in Higher Education: History, Connections, and Conflicts, 1865–1998." PhD diss., Loyola University, Chicago.

Hendrich, R. M. 1978. "The Future of Musical Performance Training: The Conservatory vs. the University." PhD diss., University of Massachusetts at Amherst.

Kingsbury, H. 1988. *Music, Talent, and Performance: A Conservatory Cultural System.* Philadelphia: Temple University Press.

Kogan, J. 1987. *Nothing But the Best.* New York: Random House.

Landes, Heather A. 2008. "On Being a Music Major." PhD diss., Loyola University, Chicago.

McPherson, B., and J. Klein. 1995. "Measure by Measure: A History of New England Conservatory from 1867." Unpublished manuscript, New England Conservatory of Music, Boston.

Olmstead, A. 1999. *Juilliard: A History.* Urbana: University of Illinois Press.

Plasket, D. J. 1992. "Training Musicians and Developing People: Can a Music Conservatory Do It All?" PhD diss., Harvard University, Cambridge, Massachusetts.

James C. Gandre

A Controversial Comparison

In August 1966 a comment made by John Lennon (1940–1980) to a British journalist that was published in the American teen magazine *Datebook* caused an immense controversy in the United States. Commenting on the popularity of The Beatles (1960–1970), Lennon stated that the band had become more popular than Jesus. Although the comment caused no controversy when initially published in Great Britain, upon its publication in *Datebook*, public protests broke out in America, including burning the band's albums in public and making threats against it. The uproar was so severe that the band's manager, Brian Epstein, considered canceling its upcoming U.S. tour. Indicative of the comment's lasting effects, the Vatican made a public announcement in 2008 that Lennon was forgiven for his comment, made more than forty years before.

Controversies in Music

As with all art forms and products of culture, controversies have been part of the culture of American music for ages. Whether one looks at the era of classical music or the twenty-first century, there have been many kinds of controversies related to popular music. Among the recurring themes in these controversies are the qualities and performances of the music and the behavior of the artists on and off the stage. Characteristic of the global culture of the late twentieth and early twenty-first centuries, the most common controversies arise from the contents of the lyrics, the social impact of music, and the fact that popular musicians in the twenty-first century live under nonstop media attention and public scrutiny.

When considering controversies in popular music in the twenty-first century, it is important to note that the birth of genres such as rock 'n' roll, and the mere existence of punk, hip-hop, and heavy metal, are controversial in and of themselves; in the traditional high culture versus low culture debate, the aforementioned genres break classical musical norms to such an extent that their strongest detractors question their cultural value completely. The controversies of the popular genres of the twenty-first century can be divided into some fairly broad and yet quite distinct topics: the political voice of musicians, profanity and "inappropriate" lyrical contents and their potential to influence fan behavior, issues of authenticity, and the musicians' controversial behavior.

Musicians and Sociopolitical Messages

Not unlike rock 'n' roll when it burst into contemporary culture in the 1950s, hip-hop, punk, and metal have all faced strong criticism since their first beats, chords, and growls hit the airwaves. Various groups of people, including politicians and musicologists, have tirelessly called into question the musical quality, morality, and propriety of these genres and suggested that not only is listening to them a waste of time, it is also demoralizing and a sign of immaturity. While the detractors of popular music have not quieted down, they are now facing a perhaps stronger opposition than ever before. Hip-hop, punk, and metal have gained global popularity as meaningful musical genres, representing global community among the fans and expressing the thoughts and sociopolitical concerns of artists and fans to an increasingly global audience. What is more, these genres can no longer be called youth music, because they involve participants and attract fans of all ages.

Even though hip-hop, punk, and metal are all explicitly sociopolitical and controversial in much of their lyrical themes, punk is the one that most encourages political activism in all forms. The antiestablishment music genre and movement that originated in the United States and the United Kingdom in the 1970s has evolved from a rebellious movement to a chart-topping, global voice of sociocriticism that has even reached Broadway in New York City. Legendary bands, such as The Clash (active 1976–1986), New York Dolls (active 1971–1976, 2004–present), Ramones (active 1974–1996), and the Sex Pistols (active 1975–1978), started a musical genre of short and fast melodies with three-chord tunes and often sociocritical and political lyrics that is now popular worldwide. Today, while voting percentages and public interest in partisan politics are low everywhere in the Western world, punk, with its youthful rebellion and often educated political viewpoints, voices the opinions of millions of global citizens and attracts a global audience with bands like Bad Religion (active 1979–present), Green Day (active 1987–present), Anti-Flag (active 1988–1989, 1993–present), Rise Against (active 1999–present), and Flogging Molly (active 1997–present) in the forefront. Descriptive of the new, more educated form of punk rebellion and the political voice of punk, often even the most popular punk bands encourage and inspire activism; take on environmental, religious, and political issues in their lyrics; and encourage their fans to register to vote. In its advocacy of the "do it yourself" ethos and critical thinking, punk remains

"Elvis the Pelvis"

One of the earliest controversies regarding musicians' performances on TV occurred in June 1956, when Elvis Presley appeared on *The Milton Berle Show* for the second time in his career. Elvis's hip-swiveling performing style when he sang "Hound Dog" caused an excited reaction among the studio audience. The day following the performance, the media nicknamed him "Elvis the Pelvis," referring to his suggestive movements during the performance, and the artist was publicly criticized by parents, religious groups, and the media. The artist himself was taken aback by the influence his performance was claimed to have, stating, "It's only music. . . . I've been blamed for just about everything wrong in this country." As is often the case, the controversy added fuel to the fire of Elvis's popularity, eventually leading to "the King's" booking three performances on *The Ed Sullivan Show,* although the popular host had previously denied any interest in having Presley perform on his show. Although the performances were a significant step in Elvis's career because of the prestige of *The Ed Sullivan Show,* they are significant in popular music history for other reasons. On his third appearance, the producers of the show decided to censor what the TV audience (reportedly almost sixty million viewers) would see, showing him only from the waist up.

controversial, because it always encourages its listeners and the participants in its culture to think and engage politicians and authorities in an open discourse of the values and priorities in a culture. At best, the result of the political activism of the music community is concerts in support of a cause (e.g., Rock Against Racism, Live Aid, the Haiti earthquake); at its worst, it leads to violent clashes between the public and the police.

Within these contemporary politically charged genres, there have been numerous incidents that caused controversy. Whether one looks at the queen of England or any sitting presidents of the United States, they have all faced direct and explicit criticism from popular musicians—hip-hop and punk artists in particular—in the late twentieth and early twenty-first centuries. From Green Day's album *American Idiot* to Kanye West's (1977–) comment that President Bush does not care about African Americans, political messages have been numerous in both the music and the public commentary of musicians. In a later interview, West admitted regretting his comments, made during A Concert for Hurricane Relief in 2005, explaining that he got carried away with his emotions regarding the devastation of Hurricane Katrina and didn't use right words to describe his frustration with the government's response to the natural disaster and its aftermath. The weight of West's words, however, seems to have been immense; despite the strong criticism he faced throughout his presidency, in his biography President Bush wrote that the worst moment of his presidency was when West called him a racist.

Contents of the Music and Their Potential Influence

One of the oldest controversies in contemporary music is the debate over the contents of lyrics and their potential to incite action. Since the earliest days of rock 'n' roll, explicit lyrics have caused controversy and aroused debate over censorship of music, revolving around the free speech rights of artists and public debates about "obscene" material. One of the victories for the detractors of explicit lyrics was the 1985 founding of Parents' Music Resource Center, which managed to institute a level of oversight for popular music. Consequently, terms such as "radio edit" and "Parental Advisory: Explicit Lyrics" stickers have become common vocabulary in the music industry. Immediately following its inception, PMRC took numerous artists, primarily metal musicians and hip-hop artists, to court, accusing them of using obscene lyrics. Although it seems logical that something concrete like the artists' explicit lyrics were scrutinized in court, the members of the metal band Judas Priest (active 1969–present), probably did not expect to be tried for subliminal messages in their songs. Nevertheless, the band faced trial to determine whether subliminal messages on their album *Stained Class* caused two young men to attempt suicide in 1985. The boys' parents' case depended on the existence and the instigative, pro-suicide nature of subliminal messages on the album, but District Judge Jerry Whitehead ruled that there was no conclusive evidence of subliminal messages and dismissed the case.

Although scientific research on subliminal messages contends that people's "hearing" subliminal messages is most likely a function of active construction on the part of listeners based on something they have been told to listen to, and there haven't been court cases about subliminal messages since the Judas Priest trial, musicians—especially rappers, punk rockers, and metal bands—continue to face strong public scrutiny and criticism of their lyrics and their potentially inciting contents. Despite the fact that already in the 1980s, lawsuits regarding a cause–effect relationship between lyrical contents of popular music and criminal behavior did not result in convictions, the genres continue to attract

Toward a New Era: Digital Access to Music

In April 2000 veteran metal band Metallica (1981–present) filed a lawsuit against a company called Napster. The suit was based on the band's argument that Napster encouraged piracy and violated copyright laws because its users could trade copyrighted songs through its servers, with no compensation paid to the artists. The case, which was settled in 2001, became controversial mainly because Metallica was seen as greedy by a vocal component of music fans who had become used to sharing music through peer networks online (from one computer to another) without any cost. The lawsuit resulted in the artists' victory, leaving them and their record labels with the final say over how their music could be accessed. Commenting on the case, Metallica's drummer, Lars Ulrich (1963–), said that the band never had a problem with the concept of sharing music over the Internet per se; instead, the band members saw the biggest problem with Napster being that it never expressed any interest in cooperating with artists or the Recording Industry Association of America in creating the terms for using its service. Once the case was settled, Metallica's statement said that in the band's view, the resolution addressed the best interests of the artists and fans alike. In hindsight, *Metallica et al. v. Napster, Inc.* and its settlement paved the way for how fans in the twenty-first century access music. Internet-based services such as Pandora Radio and Spotify now make music accessible to fans around the world in ways that keep the artists' rights intact.

sensational headlines, accusations, and negative stereotyping. One of the reasons that the accusations and speculations continue to resurface is that some academics who have done research on the potential influences of music on youth have expressed concerns about the possible effects of controversial music on listeners with previously diagnosed mental health issues or a disposition to emotional problems. Holistically—considering that punk bands continue to not only address sociopolitical concerns in song lyrics but also encourage their fans to take up action based on their lyrics, and that some members of the more extreme metal subgenres, such as Black Metal, have publicly encouraged their fans to attack institutionalized religion and Christianity—the continuity of the public debate over controversial lyrics is understandable.

One of the most notorious musicians in the United States at the turn of the millennium was Marilyn Manson (1969–), whose music was accused of inspiring the Columbine school shootings. In one of the earliest news reports on the shooting, the two high school shooters were stated to have been, among other things, social outcasts and fans of Marilyn Manson's music. Immediately Hilary Rosen, president and CEO of the Recording Industry Association of America, commented on the issue and stated what many people already knew: that it is difficult, if not impossible. to find one reason for such tragic events, and surely no artist's music puts guns in the hands of perpetrators. Manson himself responded to the accusations with his own discussion of music, its impact, and the values of American culture in *Rolling Stone* magazine, in an article entitled "Columbine: Whose Fault Is It?" Starting his essay with perhaps an expectedly provocative approach—a discussion of the contents and lessons of the Bible, including references to Cain killing his brother Abel—Manson basically reiterated Rosen's message about music being an easy target and a convenient scapegoat. Arguing that there is a "human disposition to violence," Manson noted that murder has been part of people's actions since long before the products of culture that often are accused of inciting violence were invented. Describing the publicity about him after Columbine as a witch hunt, he claimed, in an interestingly similar fashion to Elvis Presley (1935–1977) in June 1956 (see sidebar), that the speculations about the Columbine shooters' musical tastes had made him an enigma and embodiment of all society's ills. In the end, Manson was not put on trial for inspiring the Columbine shootings, and his career did not seem to be influenced by the publicity, but he remains a notorious and controversial artist, not the least because, as he said himself, he creates music that challenges people's worldviews and provokes questions and further thinking.

Finally, when examining the possible impact of music on its listeners, one of the most controversial and certainly one of the most unexpected aspects of popular music in the twenty-first century is using music as a form of torture. Although many musicians have publicly stated that they do not want their music played as torture, there are those who are not necessarily offended if their songs are used to torture POWs. Torture by music is used not only to create fear in its object but also to prolong capture shock; it takes over one's mind and is therefore less tolerable than physical pain and inescapable. It is also notable that the music used as torture is not always rock or anything even remotely aggressive, nor are the lyrics necessarily relevant to the use: "I Love You" by Barney the Purple Dinosaur is high on the list of the most popular songs used for torture.

Understandably, the recording industry does not wish to discuss the topic, and few artists have actually been reached to comment on the issue in detail. Of those who have publicly discussed the issue, some criticize it heavily; some seem to be indifferent about the matter; others are even for it, claiming that "any publicity is good publicity"; while yet others question whether playing music can actually be a serious form of torture. Whatever one's view on the matter, music as torture must work for those who use it—the continuity of the method speaks for itself. That musicians speak against it or question the effect of loud music as torture is understandable.

Issues of Authenticity

Broadly speaking, one continuing controversial topic in popular music is the artists' authenticity. In genres such as punk, hip-hop, and metal, questions of authenticity often surface as "selling out" artistic integrity for financial success; however, in pop music the discussion and debate often revolve around musical talent and lip-synching. Perhaps two of the most notorious incidents of lip-synching are Milli Vanilli's (active 1988–1998) admission of never singing on their Grammy-winning albums and the scandalous misleading of global TV audiences at the Opening Ceremonies of the 2008 Olympics in Beijing, China, when one Chinese little girl sang the country's national anthem backstage and another lip-synched it; the performance was shown to hundreds of millions of viewers around the world.

In 1989 the German duo Milli Vanilli were performing their hit "Girl You Know It's True" when their vocal track began to skip. Fans at the concert didn't seem to notice, or to care for that matter, but critics began questioning the duo's authenticity. Eventually the band's manager gave in to media pressure and revealed that the duo didn't actually sing on their award-winning records. Immediately after that, their Grammy for best new artist was withdrawn, their label dropped them, and the band's career quickly collapsed. Although Milli Vanilli are in a league of their own in the extent of their lack of authenticity, they are surely not alone regarding lip-synching. Among others, such major artists as Britney Spears (1981–), Luciano Pavarotti (1935–2007), and Madonna (1958–) have been accused of not singing on stage. As is the case with many controversies, the reliance on technology in a supposedly "live" performance is nothing new: reportedly, even the world famous TV show *American Bandstand* actually had no band. It seems that vocal tracks or even complete songs playing to a live audience when an artist is supposedly performing live has been part of the world of entertainment for as long as technology has made it possible.

Even if lip-synching is part of pop music and we should accept it as part of the "deal," the morality of the decision-making process of the Chinese officials responsible for the Opening Ceremonies at the Beijing Olympics in 2008 is still debatable. Explaining that they wanted the world to see a singer with a flawless image, the officials replaced the singer's image with that of another girl lip-synching the Chinese national anthem. The decision was made by a member of the Chinese politburo, who decided that Ms. Yang Peiyi, who had been selected to do the honors based on her voice, was not suitable for the visible role because of her buck teeth. So a prettier girl was shown while Ms. Yang sang backstage, all in an effort to make sure China would be seen at its best. After finding out about the scheme, the worldwide audience's opinion of the hosts was probably exactly the opposite.

Musicians' Behavior

The behavior of popular musicians has always been considered eccentric, if not rebellious. One of the best-known, unresolved controversies over musicians' behavior deals with the authenticity of the musicians' lifestyles in relation to the lyrical contents of their music. Since its birth in the 1970s, rap has been among the most provocative genres of popular music. Sadly, events that occurred in the late 1990s involving the East Coast versus West Coast rivalry in hip-hop left a permanent black mark in the history of popular music. Two major rap artists, 2PAC (Tupac Shakur, 1971–1996) and Notorious B.I.G. (Christopher Wallace, 1972–1997) were killed within six months. Representing the two sides of the conflict, the two artists of "Gangsta Rap" unfortunately became the victims of the street violence they sang about. The lyrics of the genre often tell stories of the violent life in inner-city neighborhoods, and since the birth of the genre, Gangsta Rap has increasingly attracted controversy and criticism for its violent lyrics. The peak of that criticism occurred in 1996–1997, when 2PAC and Notorious B.I.G. were killed. Both artists' murders remain unsolved, and although Gangsta Rap as a genre remains—at least thematically—closely connected to the violent reality of life on the streets, the murders of 2PAC and "Biggie Smalls" seem to have halted what was initially seen as a potentially persistent cycle of revenge. However, the controversies and theories surrounding both deaths—including theories that both are alive—do seem to proliferate, making the two rappers some of the most mythological artists of twentieth-century popular music.

Unfortunately, one recurring controversy about musicians is their violent behavior. From the tumultuous relationships between Ike Turner (1931–2007) and Tina Turner (1939–) and Bobby Brown (1969–) and Whitney Houston (1963–2012), to that between R&B singer Chris Brown (1989–) and his then girlfriend, pop/R&B singer Rihanna (1988–), domestic violence in particular has deservedly aroused media attention for decades. According to various sources, Brown had a history of abusing Rihanna, and the heavily publicized domestic violence incident that was reported right before the Grammy Awards show in 2009 was "the last straw." Brown was sentenced to five years of probation and fourteen hundred hours of community service. The couple have since broken up, and both artists have continued their careers—Rihanna more successfully than Brown.

A distinct characteristic of artists' behavior in late twentieth- and early twenty-first-century American culture is the complex relationship between the their sexuality and its public display, especially in the media. Although the line between inappropriate and appropriate bodily movements (see sidebar) and exposed parts of the human body has been a topic of public debate for decades, the complexity of the issue was perhaps best illustrated by the discourse following the 2004 Super Bowl XXXVIII "wardrobe malfunction" incident, when Justin Timberlake (1981–) accidentally exposed a part of Janet Jackson's (1966–) breast during their half-time show duet. An immense uproar of criticism and complaints immediately followed the incident. *Time* magazine called the event "The Hypocrisy Bowl," and the origins of the headline were clearly spelled out in the introductory paragraph, which mocked the "storm in a teacup" and the hypocrisy of the entire media spectacle. The Super Bowl is one of the world's most-watched sporting events and the nation's most-watched TV show, and football as a sport is very traditionally masculine, played by big, strong, and athletic men while beautiful, scantily clad women cheer them on. In addition, that all this happened on TV, at an event where corporations pay millions to run their ads—often targeted to an audience of "old school" masculinity—only highlighted the hypocrisy of the controversy; in the context in which it happened, Jackson's "wardrobe malfunction" was hardly more offensive than the dance teams' and cheerleaders' uniforms and body movements, or than many of the ads that ran throughout the spectacle. Similar to the audience reactions, the comments by all parties concerned and public authorities ranged over a wide spectrum. In the same *Time* article, journalist James Poniewozik summed up the complexity of "obscenity" and "sexuality" in media quite effectively, reminding us all that both words are subjective in connotation, and therefore their definitions depend on interpretation and context. In the wake of the incident, CBS was fined $550,000 by the FCC for airing the show, but a federal appeals court overturned the decision. In the end the only tangible thing that came out of the controversy was another interesting anecdote in the long history of controversial incidents involving musicians in the media.

Conclusion

Whether it is for the lyrics or the actions of the musicians, or any other topic discussed here, popular music has been and always will be controversial to at least some members of society. In some cases the controversy depends on the connotations and interpretations of "norm" and "appropriate," and therefore "controversial," too, is a matter of interpretation. In other cases, such as murder, reckless driving under the influence, and pedophilia, which some musicians have been guilty of, there is no room for interpretation. Furthermore, as long as the saying "any publicity is good publicity" remains even partially true, there will always be artists who seek controversy as a public ploy and others who are controversial by their mere existence and self-expression. In the postmodern, fragmented, twenty-first-century global culture, perhaps the irony is the acknowledgment of the constant existence of controversy in music and the realization that controversy is, in a way, part of the "norm."

See also: Antiestablishment Themes in American Songs; Copyright Laws; Green Day; Hip-Hop; Madonna; Metal; Metallica; Murder and Murderers; New York Dolls; Presley, Elvis; Punk Rock; Ramones; Recording Industry Association of America; Rock 'n' Roll (Rock); Sex and Sexuality in the Music Industry; Shakur, Tupac; Spears, Britney; Super Bowl Half-Time Shows; Torture and Punishment Through Music; Turner, Tina; West, Kanye

Further Reading

Atkins, Robert, and Svetlana Mintcheva. 2006. *Censoring Culture: Contemporary Threats to Free Expression.* New York: New Press.

Forman, Murray, and Mark Anthony Neal. *That's the Joint! The Hip-Hop Studies Reader.* New York: Routledge.

Hargrave, Andrea Millwood, and Sonia Livingstone. 2009. *Harm and Offense in Media Content: A Review of the Evidence.* Chicago: Intellect.

Manson, Marilyn. 1999. "Columbine: Whose Fault Is It?" *Rolling Stone* 815: 23.

Menn, Joseph. 2003. *All the Rave: The Rise and Fall of Shawn Fanning's Napster.* New York: Crown Business.

Roleff, Tamara L. 2001. *Censorship: Opposing Viewpoints.* San Diego, CA: Greenhaven.

Vokey, John R., and J. Don Read. 1985. "Subliminal Messages: Between the Devil and the Media." *American Psychologist* 40, no. 11: 1231–1239.

Mika Elovaara

Cooper, Alice (1948–)

"Alice Cooper" was originally a band collectively called Alice Cooper, but is better known as the stage name of Vincent Furnier, the lead singer. Alice Cooper is credited for starting the genre known as "shock rock," with an act featuring gore, mayhem, electrocutions, and once even a dead chicken. These led to both notoriety and praise for the band's music. Alice Cooper continues to tour with a heavily theatrical stage show and gore-drenched music that has influenced punk, heavy metal, and artists such as Lady Gaga. Alice Cooper is one of the best-selling artists of the last forty years and has sold more than sixty-five million albums. Cooper acts in films and currently hosts a radio show on Sirius radio, *Nights with Alice Cooper.* He is also a golf fanatic and wrote a book on the topic.

The band Alice Cooper originally formed in 1965 was called the Earwigs. He eventually settled on the linep of Glen Buxton (1947–1997; lead guitar), Michael Bruce (1948–; guitar and keyboards), Dennis Dunaway (1946–; bass) and Neal Smith (1947–; drums).

The band evolved into Alice Cooper in 1968 and was discovered by Frank Zappa (1940–1993), who singed the group to his label. Early on the band was featured on a compilation record, *Zapped,* on Bizarre records, which also included Wild Man Fischer (1944–2011), the GTO's (1969), and Lord Buckley (1906–1960). The original band released several acclaimed records, including *Pretties for You* (1969), *Killer* (1971), *School's Out* (1972), and *Billion Dollar Babies* (1973). Internal dissension led to the departure of most of the original band members, and by 1975 the band was just Alice Cooper and a constant string of new members. Starting in the early 1970s, elaborate stage shows and gruesome props were the norm (at one show a live chicken was thrown into the audience and torn apart by the crowd), leading to condemnation by critics but an ever-increasing audience. Cooper achieved even more popularity with the 1975 album *Welcome to My Nightmare,* which made him a superstar as well as a pop culture figure. Cooper hobnobbed with his idols, including Groucho Marx (1890–1977), Jack Benny (1894–1974), and George Burns (1896–1996), and even appeared on *The Muppet Show* in 1978. He had previously stated that what he did was really "vaudeville with a heavy metal beat."

Cooper continued to tour, reportedly drinking a case of beer or a bottle of whiskey every day. He gave up his heavy addiction to alcohol in 1983 and became a born-again Christian. Cooper's record sales eventually declined, until he embraced the new heavy metal scene of the 1980s and had a major hit with Poison in 1987.

Alice Cooper's legacy continues; his followers include Kiss (active 1973–present), White Zombie (active 1985–1998) Rob Zombie (1965–), Marilyn Manson (1969–), Gwar (active 1984–present), and even Lady Gaga (1986–). Joey Ramone (1951–2001) was an early fan, and after having trouble with obsessive compulsive disorder, he was heartened by the song, "The Ballad of Dwight Fry," from the band's second album, *Love It to Death.*

Alice Cooper in concert, ca. 1970. (Michael Ochs Archives/ Getty Images)

Cooper continues to tour and was inducted into the Rock and Roll Hall of Fame in 2010.

See also: Lady Gaga; Manson, Marilyn; Metal; Punk; Vaudeville and Burlesque; Zappa, Frank

Further Reading

Cooper, Alice. 2007. *Alice Cooper, Golf Monster: A Rock 'N' Roller's 12 Steps to Becoming a Golf Addict.* New York: Crown.

Leigh, Mickey, and Legs McNeil. 2009. *I Slept with Joey Ramone: A Family Memoir.* New York: Touchstone.

Roara, Phil. 2011. "Go Ask Alice." *New York Daily News,* August 7, 20–21.

Brian Cogan

Copland, Aaron (1900–1990)

Aaron Copland is a central figure of twentieth-century American music. As a composer, writer, and cultural historian, Copland viewed his work as an act of citizenship that required engagement in the issues and concerns of the day. He expected this engagement to inform his work as a musician because he believed that "you can't create music unless you are moved by events" (Pollack 1999, 271).

Born at the turn of the twentieth century to Lithuanian Jewish immigrants, Copland experienced the United States and the struggle for democracy through times of dramatic change and upheaval. He grew up in Brooklyn, New York, and spent three years as a composition student in Europe after World War I. This is where some of his interest in American music first developed, particularly as he listened with fresh ears to American jazz permeating the streets of Vienna. Copland admired composer Gabriel Fauré (1845–1924) and others who wrote music that reflected distinctly French styles, and he believed there should similarly be an identifiable American form of music.

When Copland returned to the United States, he befriended artists and musicians who were committed to capturing America through their work. This goal was not limited to an idealized view of America, but instead was directed toward the lived experiences and struggles people faced in the 1920s and 1930s, as evidenced in Walker Evans's photographs and James Agee's text in *Let Us Now Praise Famous Men* (1941), among others. Copland also hoped to engage young people in the complexities of life and art through his music, and he began to write for this age group in the 1930s. He befriended many important musicians of his time, including Leonard Bernstein (1918–1990) and Russian bassist and music director Serge Koussevitzky (1874–1951).

Copland became a very public figure through his composition, conducting, writing, and public advocacy for American music and musicians. He advocated for government support of the arts and was involved with the Federal Music Project during the Roosevelt administration. Copland never shied away from political engagement; for example, in 1959, during the height of the Cold War, he engaged several Russian composers in an interview for public broadcast. The House Un-American Activities Committee (HUAC) questioned Copland's political views in 1953, and he (along with Leonard Bernstein, Orson Welles, Pete Seeger, and 147 others) had been named in a 1951 pamphlet compiled by former FBI agents, called "Red Channels," listing artists believed to have communist interests.

The connection of social concerns to his music involved historical considerations as he worked to create a distinctly American form of music. Copland believed firmly that artists did not work in isolation; instead, he recognized that connections to the past were both a moral imperative and professional obligation. His compositions captured the uniqueness of the times in which he lived as well as the influences on those times, and he hoped to challenge audiences to see the world in new and different ways through his music. In addition to many piano and orchestral works, some of his most famous pieces are "Fanfare for the Common Man" (1942, brass and percussion), *Appalachian Spring* (1944, ballet), and *The Tender Land* (1954, opera).

American composer Aaron Copland at his home in Ossining, New York, June 28, 1956. (AP Photo)

See also: Bernstein, Leonard; Federal Music Project; Jazz; Jewish American Music and Musicians

Further Reading

Crist, Elizabeth B. 2005. *Music for the Common Man: Aaron Copland during the Depression and War.* London: Oxford University Press.

Kostelanetz, Richard. 2004. *Aaron Copland: A Reader; Selected Writings 1923–1972.* New York: Routledge.

Oja, Carol J., and Judith Tick. 2005. *Aaron Copland and His World.* Princeton, NJ: Princeton University Press.

Pollack, Howard. 1999. *Aaron Copland: The Life and Work of an Uncommon Man.* Chicago: University of Illinois Press.

Jacqueline Edmondson

Copyright Laws

There are two basic types of copyright that affect music in the United States: the copyright that covers the music itself (usually held by the composer and publisher) and a separate copyright that covers recordings of that music (usually held by the record company). In the past fifty years there has been significant expansion in the reach of these copyrights, while the last decade has seen increasing opposition to that expansion. The roots of this conflict go back to the basic purpose of modern copyright, which is to balance an incentive for creators to create with the need for society to be able to build on and improve those creations.

The first modern copyright law is generally said to have been the Statute of Anne, enacted by the British Parliament in 1710 in reaction to the king's practice of restricting the flow of information by granting perpetual "exclusive rights" to certain favored publishers. It provided that henceforth exclusive rights to a work would be granted for a limited period of time, after which that work would pass into the public domain and become available for anyone to build upon and disseminate for the good of all. Thus creators got a government-enforced monopoly for a limited time, during which they could exploit their work, after which the public got the work to feed future creativity. When the U.S. Constitution was enacted in the 1780s it incorporated this concept. Authors and inventors were granted exclusive rights to their writing and discoveries for "limited times," specifically to "promote the progress of science and useful arts" (U.S. Constitution, Article I, Section 8).

This basic trade-off between creators and the public endured in the United States for the next 180 years, although the term of protection was gradually lengthened and the types of creative works covered expanded. Beginning in the 1960s rights-holding entities, particularly large entertainment companies, began to lobby Congress aggressively to tilt the balance more toward their interests. In this they were largely successful. Copyright terms for corporate-held works ("works-for-hire") were increased from a maximum of fifty-six years to seventy-five years, and then ninety-five years. Personally held works became eligible for a new "life-plus" term, now set at the life of the creator plus seventy years. Virtually all registration and marking requirements were eliminated, making it easy for creators to get a copyright (today copyright is automatically conferred the moment a creation is "fixed," i.e., written down or recorded, with no action required by the creator). Simultaneously, litigation in the courts progressively narrowed traditional exceptions to copyright's reach, such as what constituted "fair use" of a copyrighted work.

Probably the high point of copyright expansion in the United States, at least to date, was a pair of bills enacted in 1998 and signed by President Clinton: the Copyright Term Extension Act, or CTEA (also known as the Sonny Bono Act, after one of its chief proponents) and the Digital Millennium Copyright Act, or DMCA. The former increased copyright terms by twenty years, ensuring that most works would not enter the public domain until approximately a century after their publication. For sound recordings, this was, and remains, the longest copyright term in the world. The DMCA brought U.S. copyright laws into conformity with two 1996 treaties with the World Intellectual Property Organization (WIPO), which had previously been lobbied by multinational entertainment companies to require tougher copyright laws of all its signatory nations. Among other things, the DMCA required equipment makers to install copyright "locks" (called digital rights management software) on their equipment, criminalized any attempt to defeat these locks even for noninfringing purposes, and introduced extremely high penalties for copyright infringement, regardless of whether or not it was for profit.

Impact on Music, Recording, and Preservation

The dramatic expansion of copyright via legislation and judicial rulings has been controversial in the arts. On the one hand, entertainment companies and many authors and composers feel that it is necessary to combat massive theft of creative works in the digital age, when easy copying and Internet distribution make controlling a work (much less profiting from it) difficult. Longer terms are necessary, they argue, because people are living longer and in some cases outliving their copyrights.

Archivists, scholars, and users argue that longer terms and more restrictive copyright laws have had a significant chilling effect on creativity; seriously endanger the preservation and accessibility of America's cultural heritage; and are basically a form of corporate welfare, because most of the benefits go to corporations and not to actual creators.

The chilling effect has been felt in several areas. Sampling, a modern musical art form in which snippets of prior recordings are used as part of a new one, has been severely constrained by judicial rulings that held that even the briefest or most subtle use of a prior recording requires the permission of (and payment to) the prior rights holder. A landmark sampling case was *Grand Upright Music, Ltd v. Warner Bros. Records Inc.* (1991), in which singer/songwriter Gilbert O'Sullivan's publisher sued rap artist Biz Markie for using a few seconds from O'Sullivan's recording "Alone Again (Naturally)" on Markie's album *I Need a Haircut.* Judge Kevin Thomas Duffy ruled emphatically in favor of the plaintiff, opening with the biblical admonition "thou shalt not steal," lambasting the defendants for "callous disregard for the law," and even recommending criminal prosecution. The strongly worded and somewhat one-sided decision was not appealed, and as a result labels immediately cut back sharply on sampling, requiring considerable expenditures by artists to secure permissions for any samples they did use. A "permissions" industry quickly grew up, negotiating for such permissions for even minor uses. The entire field was constrained, with newer, less well-funded artists disproportionately affected.

Film documentarians have also felt the chilling effect. They have been subjected to considerable expense and extensive entanglements for slight or incidental exposure of copyrighted works (e.g., a snippet of overheard music, or a picture on a TV screen in the background of a scene). A notorious example is *Eyes on the Prize,* the acclaimed 1987 documentary about the civil rights movement, which was withdrawn from circulation for more than a decade because the original producers had only been able to afford short-term licenses for the montage of music and visuals it contained. As the film's twentieth anniversary approached, a movement dubbed Eyes on the Screen was launched to protest the suppression of the iconic film by copyright law and to encourage mass, unauthorized screenings during Black History Month. Eventually the producers of the film obtained grants from the Ford Foundation and others enabling them to pay off rights holders and once again make the documentary legally available.

A broader concern for creativity in the arts is the way in which expansive copyright prevents creators from building on the past, without first securing permission from the "owners" of the past. It has been argued that jazz and blues, which evolved in the early twentieth century through an extensive process of borrowing and modifying of musical ideas, could never happen today. The lawyers would haul everybody into court. Author James Boyle points out that in the 1950s Ray Charles based his groundbreaking fusion of gospel and rhythm and blues, "I've Got a Woman," on the gospel song "I've Got a Savior" and based "This Little Girl of Mine" even more obviously on "This Little Light of Mine," to the dismay of its religiously inclined composer (Boyle 2008, 134–138). Today, with much more stringent copyright laws, Boyle maintains that Charles would probably be sued for both. Since copyright holders need no reason to deny permission, the right is absolute—the songs could be suppressed simply because the original author didn't like Charles's music. Thus the "old" can squelch the "new."

Expanded copyright law has also made it difficult for libraries and archives to legally preserve copyrighted recordings, including those that are very old or out-of-print. A section of the 1976 Copyright Act permits such preservation, but it has been outdated by changes in technology such as digital storage. Copyright holders have attempted to restrict digital preservation for fear that it will lead to digital dissemination. Many archives simply ignore the archaic rules and employ digital preservation anyway, but archivists protest that they should not be forced to choose between obeying the law or saving deteriorating recordings.

Probably the most serious impact of expanded copyright has been limiting access to historical materials. Access, especially digital access, is what rights holders are most worried about, and in the zealous efforts to protect current and profitable materials, much historical and out-of-print material has been swept into the net as well. Copyright law in the United States does not distinguish between a recording that was released last year and is economically valuable, and one made a century ago that has been unavailable for ninety-nine of those years.

A recent study, *Survey of Reissues of U.S. Recordings,* threw this problem into sharp relief (Brooks 2005). The first statistical study of the availability of older recordings from rights holders, it revealed that nearly all historical recordings (i.e., those listed in major academic discographies) made in the United States prior to 1965 were still under state or federal copyright. However, an average of only 14 percent were available from the rights holders. Moreover, the percent available declined sharply with age. Approximately 25 percent of the recordings made between 1940 and 1954 were available, but only 12 percent of those made between 1920 and 1939 were, and almost none of those made prior to 1920 were available. Far larger percentages were reissued by non-rights holders, for example labels in other countries where the same recordings were in the public domain. Clearly, a very large proportion of America's recorded history is being "locked up" in the United States by copyright law, legally available to no one.

Restricted availability has resulted in what is sometimes known as "dark archives" (where copyrighted material can be placed, but where it cannot be heard by the public at large). This undermines the very purpose of a public archive and makes it difficult to justify funding for preservation. Few institutions will devote scarce funds to preservation when the results cannot be disseminated. Donors are also reluctant to donate rare materials to archives that will then lock them away. In the view of most experts, preservation and access are intertwined. Neither is practical without the other.

Another effect of expanded copyright has been the creation of "orphan works." The elimination of registration and marking formalities in the 1970s made it easy to obtain a copyright, but hard for potential users to identify the owner. Combined with very long copyright terms, this has created a large body of older works that have been abandoned, but cannot be used because the owner is untraceable. If someone makes use of such a work, for example in a documentary or a performance, and the owner does later emerge, that owner can sue the user both for actual damages and for extremely high punitive damages. The fact that the user conducted a diligent search for the owner, or that the use was nonprofit (e.g., a museum exhibition), makes no difference. The result, of course, is that untraceable works, many of them historic, simply don't get used at all.

Related to orphan works is the problem of out-of-print works. In this case the owner is known but declines to make the work available, usually because it would not be sufficiently profitable. This is generally not a problem for printed works, which can be accessed in libraries or through the used-book market. However, older sound recordings are much harder to find and may be reproducible only by obsolete technologies (e.g., cylinders, 78s, wire recordings, etc.). Various proposals have been made to make copyright after a certain period subject to a "use it or lose it" provision (you retain copyright only if you make the work available) or subject to some form of compulsory licensing, but none of these has made much headway.

One of the least understood but most significant quirks in U.S. copyright law regarding recordings is an obscure provision that places sound recordings made before 1972 under state rather than federal copyright law. This applies only to sound recordings, not to other types of intellectual property. Since state copyright is almost always perpetual, and laws and court rulings vary widely from state to state, this has created a chaotic situation in which archives and users have thrown up their hands and treat *all* U.S. recordings as restricted. A court ruling in New York in 2005, *Capitol Records, Inc. v. Naxos of America,* solidified this view, stating that recording copyright there was absolute and perpetual, even extending to imported recordings that were in the public domain in their own country. As a result of the "state law" provision, the United States is the only country in the world in which there is effectively no public domain for sound recordings, no matter how old they are. (In theory this situation will change in the year 2067, when current legislation provides that the "pre-1972" state law provision will sunset. However, many believe that unless contested the date will eventually be pushed back.) In addition to creating a very confused legal status for pre-1972 recordings, the provision means that any changes in federal copyright law, for example to update the preservation exceptions or increase access, will not apply to older recordings.

Recent Developments in the Public Debate over Copyright

There were objections by library associations and scholars as copyright expanded in the late twentieth century, but they were largely ineffective against well-funded entertainment industry lobbyists. However, in the early 2000s a broader and more organized opposition began to take shape. So far the result has been primarily to slow copyright expansion rather than to reverse it, but a growing body of evidence is being assembled that suggests the laws need to be refined.

Fueling this movement has been a stream of books and articles documenting the negative effects of expanded copyright and articulating a vision of a better balance of public and private interests. Among the thought leaders in the copyright reform movement have been Lawrence Lessig (*The Future of Ideas,* 2001; *Free Culture,* 2004; *Remix: Making Art and Commerce Thrive in the Hybrid Economy,* 2008); Siva Vaidhyanathan (*Copyrights and Copywrongs,* 2001); Joanna Demers (*Steal This Music: How Intellectual Property Law Affects Musical Creativity,* 2006); and former National Endowment for the Arts chairman Bill Ivey (*Arts, Inc.: How Greed and Neglect Have Destroyed Our Cultural Rights,* 2008). A useful collection of essays on the subject is Simon Frith and Lee Marshall, eds., *Music and Copyright* (2nd ed., 2004).

At the same time, public advocacy groups have sprung up to support those accused of infringement and work to rein in what they perceive as overreaching laws. Among them are the Electronic Frontier Foundation (1990), Public Knowledge (2001), and more recently the Historical Recording Coalition for Access and Preservation (2008). The American Library Association, the Association of Research Libraries, and the Association of College and Research Libraries have formed The Library Copyright Alliance to work for copyright changes that allow libraries to better serve the public.

The Association for Recorded Sound Collections has set five goals for copyright reform regarding sound recordings:

1. Place all U.S. recordings under a single, understandable national law by repealing the provision that keeps recordings made before 1972 under state law.
2. Harmonize the term of coverage for U.S. recordings with that of most foreign countries, that is, a term of between fifty and seventy-five years rather than the current ninety-five years (for works-for-hire).
3. Legalize the use of orphan recordings, those for which no owner can be located.
4. Permit and encourage the reissue by third parties of recordings that remain out-of-print for

extended periods, with appropriate compensation to the copyright owners.

5. Change U.S. copyright laws to allow the use of current technology and best practices in the preservation of sound recordings by nonprofit institutions.

The first major twenty-first-century battle over copyright was *Eldred v. Ashcroft,* a legal challenge to the Copyright Term Extension Act that reached the U.S. Supreme Court in 2003. A broad coalition of archives, scholars, and economists argued that Congress had exceeded its constitutional authority by establishing copyright terms that exceeded any reasonable definition of "limited times" and thus had harmed the public domain. The Court ruled seven to two against the challenge, finding that it was up to Congress itself to define "limited times."

Although the CTEA challenge failed, the process of prosecuting the case brought together many entities that had not previously worked together or in some cases even been involved in copyright activism. Coordination and data sharing were newly facilitated by the Internet. This became apparent in the next major challenge to expanded copyright, which took place in the United Kingdom in 2005–2006 and had a very different outcome. The multinational recording companies had been pushing the British government to expand sound recording copyright there from the existing fifty years to the ninety-five-year term they had won in the United States. Ironically this would have shut down one of the few sources from which Americans could obtain historical U.S. recordings, because U.S. recordings more than fifty years old were in the public domain (and frequently reissued) in Europe, but under copyright (and seldom reissued) in the United States. The British government commissioned Andrew Gowers, former editor of the *Financial Times,* to conduct a wide-ranging review of intellectual property laws in the UK and make recommendations. When Gowers issued his report in 2006, he recommended many changes, broadly affecting enforcement and help for smaller rights holders, but came out firmly against any increase in the fifty-year recording copyright term, finding no economic justification for such a move. The government of Prime Minister Tony Blair, then under political attack on many fronts, refused to overrule Gowers's findings and left the term intact.

Furious over this first major defeat, the recording companies then shifted their efforts to Brussels in an attempt to persuade the European Union to mandate a ninety-five-year recording copyright term throughout Europe. They once again had the support of many politicians, but faced determined opposition from consumers, national archives, and several member countries. The issue is still unresolved.

The copyright battles in the United States and Europe produced many types of evidence documenting, often for the first time, the harmful effects of excessive copyright. This evidence did not exist when copyright was being expanded during the second half of the twentieth century. For example, several European academic studies examined the differences between sound recordings and other types of intellectual property and enunciated the philosophical basis for shorter terms for recordings. Some of these studies are referenced at the Web site http://soundcopyright.eu/learn (e.g., *The Gowers Review of Intellectual Property* [HM Treasury, 2006]; *Review of the Economic Evidence Relating to an Extension of the Term of Copyright in Sound Recordings* [Centre for Intellectual Property and Information Law, University of Cambridge, ca. 2006]; *The Recasting of Copyright & Related Rights for the Knowledge Economy* [Institute for Information Law, University of Amsterdam, The Netherlands, November 2006]). All of these studies addressed the proposal to extend European sound recording copyright from fifty to either seventy or ninety-five years and concluded that such an extension was not warranted. The Cambridge study concluded that extension would result in less than a 1 percent increase in rights holder revenues, while incurring substantial social cost. Gowers concluded that the optimal term for recording copyright was in fact *less* than fifty years (although his report did not recommend that).

In the United States the National Recording Preservation Act of 2000 established the National Recording Preservation Board at the Library of Congress and directed it to study the current state of sound recording preservation and access and report back with recommended changes in the law. This has led to a series of studies commissioned by the Library of Congress and published by the Council on Library and Information Resources, including *Survey of Reissues of U.S. Recordings* by Tim Brooks (2005); *Copyright Issues Relevant to Digital Preservation and Dissemination of Pre-1972 Commercial Sound Recordings by Libraries and Archives* by June M. Besek (2005); *Copyright and Related Issues Relevant to Digital Preservation and Dissemination of Unpublished Pre-1972 Sound Recordings by Libraries and Archives* by June M. Besek (2009); *Protection for Pre-1972 Sound Recordings under State Law and Its Impact on Use by Nonprofit Institutions: A 10-State Analysis* by Peter Jaszi (2009); and *The State of Recorded Sound Preservation in the United States: A National Legacy at Risk in the Digital Age* by Rob Bamberger and Sam Brylawski (2010).

In an attempt to deal with the orphan works issue, legislation was introduced in the U.S. Congress in 2003 and 2005 (The Public Domain Enhancement Act), but did not pass. The U.S. Copyright Office then conducted a study and in 2006 issued *Report on Orphan Works.* It recommended changes in the law to allow use of orphan works without penalty if a diligent search for the owner had been made and if rights could be recaptured by an owner who did later emerge. Although the recommendations had broad support, they were opposed by a vocal minority, principally photographers, who claimed it was a "license to steal" their work. Sloganeering won out, and though legislation based on the study was introduced in 2006 and 2008, it also did not pass.

A different—and controversial—model for making orphan works available that could eventually impact music and recordings is the Google Books Project. In 2004 Google, the Internet search giant, began scanning books housed in major libraries across the United States and internationally. This led to a lawsuit by publishers and authors, but in 2008 an agreement was reached, containing three components. Google could make public domain books freely available on the Internet and could display limited portions of copyrighted books with links to allow purchase of the book. Most controversial, it could make available orphan works, those whose owners did not register with a Google-established book registry. If it stands, this is essentially an end run around the frozen legislative attempts to address orphan works, at least for books.

Preservation issues have also begun to be addressed. In 2005 the Library of Congress convened the Section 108 Study Group, named after the section of U.S. copyright law that allows preservation and access to copyrighted materials in libraries and archives, to update outdated provisions of the law. Roundtables were held and comments solicited, and in 2008 *The Section 108 Study Group Report* was issued. However, rights-holder lawyers and lobbyists blocked many of the changes recommended by experts, particularly those related to access.

Even the long-standing pre-1972 "state law" provision finally received attention. In 2009, as a result of lobbying by the Association for Recorded Sound Collections, the Copyright Office was directed by Congress to study for the first time the "desirability and means" of bringing pre-1972 recordings under federal law. The outcome of the study remains to be seen; however, the fact that a study is taking place at all is another example of the recent trend to document and force public discussion of provisions of copyright law that have negatively affected the arts. Previously, most copyright decisions were made behind closed doors in Washington, D.C., with little if any public involvement.

Today the relationship of copyright and the creative arts is in flux. Ironically, the fact that the law has become so tilted toward the interests of rights holders has done little to benefit the recording industry, which has suffered substantial declines in revenue, and has led many people to simply ignore laws that are widely perceived to be unbalanced and unfair. Perhaps the mounting evidence that the current system serves no one very well will eventually result in a better balance between the interests of users and creators.

See also: Charles, Ray; Legal Issues and Legislation in Music

Further Reading

Boyle, James. 2008. *The Public Domain: Enclosing the Commons of the Mind.* New Haven, CT: Yale University Press, 134–138.

Brooks, Tim. 2005. *Survey of Reissues of U.S. Recordings.* Washington, DC: Library of Congress and Council on Library and Information Resources.

Sound Copyright. n.d. http://www.soundcopyright.eu/learn.html.

Timothy H. Brooks

Cotten, Elizabeth "Libba" (1895–1987)

Listen to the song "Freight Train," and you'll immediately hear the unique style and sound that blues and folk singer-songwriter Elizabeth Nevills Cotten contributed to American music and culture. A self-taught, left-handed guitarist who played the guitar upside down when compared to other guitarists, Cotten developed her own style of picking that uses the thumb for melodies and the fingers for bass lines. Her finger-picking style is a signature of her performances and among her legacies.

Born in Carrboro, North Carolina, in 1895, Elizabeth began to play her brother's banjo at eight years of age. She saved her money and bought her own guitar when she was eleven years old. Around the same time, she began to write songs, including "Freight Train," which would later become one of her most famous tunes.

Elizabeth married Frank Cotten when she was fifteen years old and had a daughter, Lillie, soon after. While she was raising her daughter, she stopped playing guitar except for occasional performances in church. After Lillie married, Cotten divorced her husband. She worked at various jobs until she became a maid for the Seeger family, caring for Charles and Ruth's children: Mike, Peggy, Barbara, and Penny. During this time she began to play the guitar again, and the musical Seeger family took notice.

Artists Who Have Covered Elizabeth Cotten's Songs

Bob Dylan	Peter, Paul and Mary
Jerry Garcia	Taj Mahal

In the 1950s Mike Seeger recorded Cotten for his *Folksongs and Instruments with Guitar* album. Cotten began to perform publicly with Seeger, and in the early 1960s she joined the folk revival, performing at the Philadelphia Folk Festival and Newport Folk Festival alongside artists such as John Lee Hooker, Muddy Waters, and Mississippi John Hurt. Cotten connected well with audiences, who loved her gentle yet feisty and spirited ways.

Cotten began to write more original songs and in 1967 recorded the album *Shake Sugaree* with her grandchildren. She continued to perform publicly and release albums well into her eighties. Cotten played the Philadelphia Folk Festival in 1986, and her final concert in Harlem in February 1987. She died a few months later at age ninety-two.

Elizabeth Cotten won a Grammy Award for Best Ethnic or Traditional Recording for her album *Elizabeth Cotten Live!* (1984), and a Grammy nomination in 1986 for Best Traditional Folk Recording. She was given the National Endowment for the Arts National Heritage Fellow Award (1984) and was listed among the seventy-five most influential African American women in the documentary *I Dream a World.*

See also: Folk Music; Guitar; Hooker, John Lee; Hurt, Mississippi John; Roots Music; Seeger, Mike; Seeger Family; Waters, Muddy.

Further Reading

Santelli, Robert. 2001. *American Roots Music.* New York: Harry N. Abrams.

Wenberg, Michael. 2002. *Elizabeth's Song.* Hillsboro, OR: Beyond Words Publishing.

Jacqueline Edmondson

Counterculture in American Music

When pressed to define the starting and ending points of the U.S. counterculture era, some activists and historians point to the February 1, 1960, sit-in at a racially segregated lunch counter by four black students in Greensboro, North Carolina, and the end of the Vietnam conflict in 1975, as the bookends. For example, activist Tom Hayden (1988) and historian Terry H. Anderson (1995) include in their books insightful discussion about the starting and ending dates of the counterculture. Throughout this period popular music played a prominent role in informing and reflecting the counterculture. In fact, one can reasonably argue that music was so fully integrated into the counterculture that one could not really study and understand the era without knowing its music. Although various aspects of the 1960–1975 counterculture overlap, it is convenient to consider the connections between music and the following components of the counterculture: 1) the antiwar movement, 2) support for the oppressed, 3) radical politics, 4) recreational drug use, 5) the hippie lifestyle, and 6) the sexual revolution. As one considers the relationships between the popular music of the era and the counterculture, it is important to consider an observation that numerous commentators have made: that, in the words of music writer Jon Landau (who later became Bruce Springsteen's manager and producer), "rock, the music of the Sixties, was a music of spontaneity. It was folk music" (1972, 40). In other words, despite the commercial nature of some of the music associated with the counterculture, this music—to an extent greater than in previous generations—became a shared communal experience, a music of the people, or at least of young people who shared certain beliefs about the relationship of their generation to the lifestyles, politics, policies, and values of their parents' generation. For example, the chorus of John Lennon's 1969 composition "Give Peace a Chance" became a folk-like anthem at antiwar rallies almost immediately after the release of Lennon's recording.

Although the United States was involved in the ongoing conflict between South Vietnam and North Vietnam at the start of the 1960s—by supplying trainers for and advisors to the South Vietnamese military—the American presence increased rapidly after the autumn 1964 Gulf of Tonkin Resolution. Prior to that time, there were antiwar songs, some of which became among the better known of the era. These songs, such as Pete Seeger's "Where Have All the Flowers Gone" and Bob Dylan's "Masters of War," dealt more with war in general terms or were understood as a reaction to concerns about the possibility of global thermonuclear war between the United States and the Soviet Union. Other, older songs also were used at antiwar rallies before and during the Vietnam conflict. These include "Down by the Riverside," with its "ain't gonna study war no more" refrain, and "We Shall Overcome," a song that was associated with civil rights rallies of the 1950s, but was adopted by antiwar activists in the 1960s.

As the Vietnam conflict unfolded, protest songwriters saw their work published in *Sing Out!* and *Broadside,* two magazines that included song lyrics, lead sheets, and articles about folk and protest music. In the realm of commercial music, it is important to consider that counterculture, antiwar music was more the exception than the rule. As evidence, historians Kenneth J. Bindas and Craig Houston (1989) studied commercial recordings of the 1965–1974 period and found that only approximately 1.5 percent of the records that made the pop charts had anything to do with the war. To the extent that Bindas and Houston were accurate in their assessment, though, popularity at the time and the continuing legacy of recordings such as Creedence Clearwater Revival's "Fortunate Son" and "Run Through the Jungle," Edwin Starr's recording of "War," The Doors' "The Unknown Soldier," Marvin Gaye's "What's Going On," Melanie's "Lay Down (Candles in the Rain)," and Cat Stevens's "Peace Train," among others, suggest that some of the antiwar chart singles may have impacted public consciousness to a greater extent than quantity alone might suggest. In addition, album cuts and recordings from non-chart-oriented genres such as blues protested the war (e.g., J. B. Lenoir's "Vietnam Blues" and Buffy Sainte-Marie's "Moratorium") and celebrated the era's draft resisters (e.g., Steppenwolf's "Draft Resister"), and some songs that may or may not have been meant to comment on the war were interpreted as antiwar statements (e.g., Bob Dylan's "It Ain't Me, Babe," which was recorded by a large number of artists during the mid-1960s and was a substantial hit for The Turtles). A few others, such as Country Joe (McDonald) & the Fish's "I-Feel-Like-I'm-Fixin'-to-Die Rag," achieved little commercial success, but were iconic works that reflected the sense of bitter irony and tension that marked the political debate of the period.

The various social movements of the era that found Americans protesting for racial, gender, ethnic, and other forms of equality—such as the civil rights movement, the women's movement, the American Indian movement, the black power movement, the Latino workers' movement of César Chávez, and others—also spawned popular music, used music in rallies, and generally opened up Americans' ears to new styles and genres. For example, Carole King's album, *Tapestry,* was embraced as an important coming-of-age work in the context of the women's movement, and Helen Reddy's song, "I Am Woman" provided a musically accessible, but more pointed lyrical edge that also reflected the movement. Black power statements such as James Brown's "Say It Loud (I'm Black and I'm Proud)" and several songs by Sly Stone (e.g., "Don't Call Me Nigger, Whitey" and "Thank You (Falletinme Be Mice Elf Agin)") either were commercially successful singles or were included on popular albums. Some artists, such as Stone, and John Lennon and Yoko Ono ("Woman Is the Nigger of the World"), were deliberately pointed and provocative in their titles and their lyrics; however, some songs that made no overt reference to any of the movements of the era were interpreted as social commentary because of who the performers were and the social context of the time. For example, Aretha Franklin's popular recording of Otis Redding's song "Respect" could be understood as a call for respect for African Americans, as a call for respect for women, or (as Redding apparently intended, based on a literal reading of the text) as a one-on-one relationship song.

The era was notable for Abbie Hoffman, Jerry Rubin, John Sinclair, and other proponents of radical politics. Again, music was tied to this aspect of the counterculture, with the New York–based group the Fugs aligned with Hoffman and Rubin and their brand of politics as street theater (e.g., the Fugs song "Kill for Peace"), and the Detroit-based proto-punk band, the MC5, serving as a vehicle for John Sinclair and the White Panther Party's calls to revolution. While the Fugs and the MC5 had relatively small audiences, revolutionary politics received a significant musical boost when big-name artists John Lennon and Yoko Ono released their 1972 album *Sometime in New York City.* This album included protest songs about prison conditions; expressed support for jailed activists Angela Davis and John Sinclair (both of whom are portrayed as victims of political oppression on the album); and took on racial and gender equality, the Vietnam conflict, and virtually every other political and social issue associated with the radical politics of the time.

One of the most iconic aspects of the counterculture era is its reputation for widespread recreational (as opposed to medicinal) drug use. By the mid-1960s young people were turning to psychedelic drugs such as marijuana and LSD, and musicians exhibited the influence of these drugs. In fact, musicians were an integral part of author Ken Kesey's early "acid tests"; an early incarnation of the Grateful Dead served as the house band for these experimentation sessions. Disjunct, impressionistic imagery and studio effects such as stereo panning, electronically manipulated vocals, and instrumental tone colors were all either associated with the use of psychedelic drugs or understood as simulations of drug "trips." Some of the music and musicians associated with this style were the Electric Prunes ("I Had Too Much to Dream Last Night"), The Beatles (particularly on the albums *Revolver* and *Sgt. Pepper's Lonely Hearts Club Band,* as well as in the song "Strawberry Fields Forever"), the Grateful Dead, Jimi Hendrix (e.g., Hendrix's arrangement of Bob Dylan's "All Along the Watchtower"), and Bob Dylan. By the end of the 1960s some songwriters were distinguishing between what they considered "good" illegal drugs (e.g., marijuana)

The American rock group Country Joe & the Fish perform in the rain at the Woodstock Music and Arts Fair in Bethel, New York, August 17, 1969. (Bill Eppridge/Time & Life Pictures/Getty Images)

and "bad" illegal drugs (e.g., addictive opiates such as heroin). Hoyt Axton's composition, "The Pusher," as popularized by Steppenwolf, presents this dichotomy.

In reaction to the traditional and more conservative values of their parents' generation, their displeasure with consumerism, and the war in Vietnam, some young people dropped out of conventional society. They grew their hair long, lived a communal lifestyle, engaged in "free love," used psychedelic drugs—in short, they became hippies. Eventually the hippie lifestyle morphed into the back-to-the-land movement, with its hippie communes, macrobiotic food, and the emergence of organic food co-ops. While a number of popular songs of the era reflect and affirm the various components of the hippie lifestyle, John Phillips's composition, "San Francisco (Be Sure to Wear Flowers in Your Hair)," which was popularized by singer Scott McKenzie, captured the spirit of San Francisco's 1967 hippie "Summer of Love" perhaps better than any other. The emergence of the back-to-the-land movement roughly coincided with the integration of country and rock by musicians such as Michael Nesmith, Bob Dylan, Rick Nelson and the Stone Canyon Band, and Gram Parsons. Some pop music festivals of the late 1960s and early 1970s—the time of the emergence of the back-to-the-land movement—included performances by older roots-music performers, such as Maybelle Carter and Doc Watson.

The communal nature of the hippie lifestyle lent itself to multiday rock festivals. The first major rock festival, the 1967 Monterey International Pop Music Festival, included performances by the Byrds, Eric Burdon and the Animals, Buffalo Springfield, the Jimi Hendrix Experience, Country Joe & the Fish, Big Brother and the Holding Company, Ravi Shankar, and Otis Redding. The most iconic musical hippie happening of the 1960s, however, was the Woodstock Music and Art Fair, which took place in August 1969. Perhaps as many as 400,000–500,000 young people attended the Woodstock festival, braving rain, lack of sanitation, and lack of food. They heard performances by a wide variety of acts, including Janis Joplin; The Who; Santana; the Grateful Dead; Melanie; Crosby, Stills & Nash; Jimi Hendrix; Jefferson Airplane; Joe Cocker; Joan Baez; Sha Na Na; and others. Jimi Hendrix's virtuosic, distorted, and at times highly dissonant performance of "The Star-Spangled Banner" on electric guitar near the conclusion of the festival typifies the contradictions of the counterculture era: it could be heard as patriotic, as antiwar, or as dismissive of tradition, depending on the listener's political leanings.

The counterculture movements of the 1960–1975 period also led to musical reactions from the right wing. Songs such as Harlan Howard's "Mr. Professor" and Pat Boone's "Wish You Were Here, Buddy" (to name just two of numerous examples) placed the blame for the hippie lifestyle and what the Right saw as an abandonment of the troops serving in Vietnam on radical ideas that were seen by conservatives as germinating on university campuses. Traditional family values, patriotism during an unpopular war, traditional religious values, and opposition to communism were all themes that found their way into the (almost exclusively) country songs that were written in reaction to the political views and lifestyle of members of the counterculture.

The complexities of the relationships between art and reality during the counterculture era might best be found in the musical *Hair.* Young, unemployed actors James Rado and Gerome Ragni developed the show and the lyrics for the songs in the mid-1960s. The Canadian composer Galt MacDermot was hired to write the music, which he based on the styles of popular music that were receiving radio airplay at the time. *Hair* is a particularly interesting musical because the show both 1) provided a stylized snapshot of the hippie lifestyle, concern for the environment, interest in non-Western religions, protest of war, and free love; and 2) to a certain extent *was* part of the counterculture, particularly in the original production's use of nudity and the smoking of marijuana onstage.

See also: Antiestablishment Themes in American Songs; Baez, Joan; Brown, James; Carter Family; Crosby, Stills & Nash; Drugs and Music; Dylan, Bob; Folk Music; Franklin, Aretha; Grateful Dead; Hendrix, Jimi; Joplin, Janis; Music Magazines and Journalism; Protest Music; Redding, Otis; Rock Musicals; Rock 'n Roll (Rock); Roots Music; Santana, Carlos; Seeger, Pete

Further Reading

Anderson, Terry H. 1995. *The Movement and the Sixties.* New York: Oxford University Press.

Bindas, Kenneth J., and Craig Houston. 1989. "'Takin' Care of Business': Rock Music, Vietnam and the Protest Myth." *Historian* 52 (November): 1–23.

Hayden, Tom. 1988. *Reunion: A Memoir.* New York: Random House.

Landau, Jon. 1972. *It's Too Late to Stop Now.* San Francisco: Straight Arrow Books.

Perone, James E. 2004. *Music of the Counterculture Era.* Westport, CT: Greenwood Press.

James E. Perone

Country Music

Country music is a form of commercial popular music that emerged in the early 1920s, with its roots in the folk music of the southern Appalachian and southwestern regions of the United States. This regional heritage is evident in the genre's name itself; beginning in 1949, the music industry called it "country and western," eventually dropping the latter designation in 1962 (Whitburn 2005, 9). It is interdependent on American culture, as Larry L. Naylor explains: "American culture exists by virtue of the ideas, behaviors, and products shared by all Americans, regardless of other cultural identities that may also characterize them" (1999, 1). The link between country music and American culture is evident throughout its history. For example, when the WSM *Barn Dance* was first broadcast from a Nashville radio studio in 1925, its initial success was meaningful to the regional audience who could hear it and enjoyed that kind of music. Only when the radio show was broadcast nationally over the NBC network in 1939 could the program (now renamed the *Grand Ole Opry*) become a part of American culture. From Roy Acuff, who emerged as the first superstar of country music as the host of the *Opry,* to Carrie Underwood, whose career in country music was boosted by winning the television talent show *American Idol* in 2005, there has been a long line of country music performers who have found success not only within the regions and cultures of America where country music is more likely to be popular, but have become national icons. In addition to the performers, country music songs have become part of the American cultural fabric, especially during times of conflict. Songs like Merle Haggard's "Okie from Muskogee" (1969) and "The Fighting Side of Me" (1970) are as much a part of our collective memory of the Vietnam era as Peter, Paul and Mary's "Where Have All the Flowers Gone?" (1962) or Edwin Starr's "War" (1970), and Toby Keith's "Courtesy of the Red, White, and Blue (The Angry American)" (2001) was a controversial anthem of the Second Gulf War. This entry highlights some of the points at which country music (as represented by its music and performers) emerged from its own subcultural context into the American mainstream.

In the 1920s and 1930s country music was primarily regional, and its popular reception was closely tied to perceptions of southern or western regionalisms. A number of radio shows featured the music, sometimes including performers who were either not from the South or were southerners who emphasized their "backwoodsy-ness" through exaggerated accents, wearing work clothes without shoes or with holes and patches, and using silly names and humor. Jimmie Rodgers and The Carter Family were the first stars of the genre, and while each would later be lauded as originators of country music, their contemporary success was limited due to the illness of the former (Rodgers died of tuberculosis in 1933) and the breakup of the latter (A. P. and Sara Carter divorced in 1939 after a long separation, ending what is now known as the "Original" Carter Family). It was not initially through recordings or radio but through film that country music was exposed to mainstream American audiences, in the figure of the "singing cowboy." Gene Autry signed his first film contract in 1934, and with his overwhelming popularity, "the myth of the singing cowboy simultaneously assumed a new dimension and gained the most potent forum yet for its widespread dissemination" (Malone 1993, 91). Autry, Roy Rogers, and Tex Ritter introduced millions of Americans to the music of the American West through their films and records. Autry and Rogers were also savvy businessmen who saw that their appeal was particularly strong to American children and marketed hats, lunchboxes, toy guitars, and cap guns with their names and pictures on them to the younger set. As mentioned previously, the *Grand Ole Opry* was first broadcast nationally in 1939, and it was Roy Acuff as program host, humorist, and entertainer who became most identified with the "country" side of music and, to some extent, with what the general public understood to be "American." The apocryphal story of Japanese soldiers shouting, "To hell with Roosevelt; to hell with Babe Ruth; to hell with Roy Acuff!" at American soldiers during the battle of Okinawa in 1945 (Malone 1985, 193) demonstrates that by the end of World War II, Acuff (and, consequently, the music that he sang) had gained iconic status as "all-American."

After the war there was an expanded interest in country music as American soldiers were exposed to it on Armed Forces Radio and southern veterans sought jobs in the industrial Midwest and throughout California, bringing their musical tastes with them. Record companies determined that it made more sense to set up their own recording studios in Nashville so that musicians who were congregating around the Grand Ole Opry would not have to travel to New York or Los Angeles to record. In turn, having high-quality studios with local producers like Chet Atkins, Owen Bradley, and Don Law, who could find the best studio musicians, meant that the studios could adapt to changing tastes, especially when rock 'n' roll (arguably an offshoot of country music, especially in the version dubbed "rockabilly") threatened the popularity of the genre in the 1950s. Nashville studios began using violins on their records to "sweeten" the perceived "twang" of the prevalent honky-tonk style of Ernest Tubb and Hank Williams, resulting in what was later derogatorily named "The Nashville Sound" (Jensen 1998, 76–81).

Hand in hand with the development of the studios was the rise of music publishing houses in Nashville; the major performance-rights organizations ASCAP and BMI quickly set up shop there. The biggest star of country music in the early postwar era was Hank Williams, who became better known in the wider popular world for his songs than for the versions he sang. Although hesitant at first, pop music stars such as Tony Bennett and Rosemary Clooney recorded million-selling versions of Williams's songs ("Cold, Cold Heart" [1951] and "Half as Much" [1952], respectively), much to the pleasure of the songwriter and his publishing company, Acuff-Rose. (Roy Acuff had partnered with songwriter Fred Rose in 1942 to create the first Nashville-based music publishing company.) Country music also got a boost in the 1950s from comedians like Andy Griffith and Tennessee Ernie Ford, who also sang country songs; Ford would have a number one record in 1955 with "Sixteen Tons," which was originally composed by Merle Travis, an extremely talented guitarist who could never have received the national attention that Ford could at that time.

Television in the 1960s had an enormous impact on the popularity of country music. For some country music hearkened back to a time before Vietnam and hippies; although Merle Haggard was ambivalent about his own political leanings, songs like "Workin' Man Blues," "Okie from Muskogee," and "The Fightin' Side of Me" were anthems for Nixon's Silent Majority. Network programmers gave Glen Campbell and Johnny Cash their own variety shows, while CBS seemed to specialize in "cornball comedy" series like *The Beverly Hillbillies, Petticoat Junction,* and *Green Acres,* as well as the variety program *Hee Haw,* prompting some to call the network the "Country Broadcasting System" (Hollis 2008, 191).

In the 1970s country music seemed to come apart as the industry pushed toward a more mainstream sound with mainstream acts. For example, although Willie Nelson and Waylon Jennings had some success in Nashville (particularly Nelson, as a songwriter), they decided to make Austin, Texas, their musical and spiritual home, becoming identified with an "outlaw" movement. Charlie Rich, one of the most iconoclastic artists of the 1960s, found professional success in the new "countrypolitan" sound, which relied even more heavily on string accompaniments than the "Nashville Sound" had. In 1974 Rich won the Entertainer of the Year award from the Country Music Association; when he had the duty of presenting the award the following year on national television to John Denver, a performer whose country "authenticity" was openly questioned by the music industry, Rich took the envelope and lit it on fire with his lighter. The "countrypolitan" movement reached its zenith with the film *Urban Cowboy* (1979), starring Debra Winger and John Travolta. Not only was the film a success, the sound track sold several million copies (as did the singles that were spun off the album) and created a craze for country-themed bars, line dancing, mechanical bulls, and Western clothing. Much of country music in the 1980s either continued in a "pop-country" vein or countered in the "New Traditionalist" style of George Strait, Randy Travis, and Dwight Yoakam.

As country moved into the 1990s, its newest star was an Oklahoma singer with an ambition to sell more records than Elvis Presley. Garth Brooks managed to do so (arguably), but more important, he expanded the possibilities for Nashville-centered artists to reach national audiences. While the "arena rock" era of KISS and Aerosmith had waned, Brooks created "arena country," selling out stadiums with shows that included pyrotechnics and stage trickery. His albums were always marketed to a country audience but his live shows had national appeal; his 1997 free concert in New York's Central Park was attended by over 980,000 people and attracted 14.6 million viewers on HBO (Cox 2009). In 1999 Brooks effectively killed his own career by making appearances as his pop star alter ego, Chris Gaines; ironically, Brooks lost his cultural icon status when he turned his attention away from country. Unable to maintain his audience, Brooks retired to become a house husband with his second wife, country singer Trisha Yearwood; he has since released several singles and has been performing in Las Vegas.

If Brooks kept it country while modeling his stage act for popular audiences, Shania Twain decided to make her brand of country nearly indistinguishable from pop music. A moderately successful recording act from Ontario, Twain caught the attention of heavy metal producer Mutt Lange, who decided he would produce her next record (and would eventually become her husband). The first single from the album, "Any Man of Mine," had a very country-sounding chorus, but the verses were delivered like a football cheer and the accompanying video brought more attention to Twain's exposed belly button than her music. Twain and Lange composed extremely catchy songs, and Lange's production mixed fiddles, electric guitars, and musical car horns (e.g., "Man! I Feel Like a Woman"). Twain successfully tapped into the broad market that Brooks had uncovered, but did not choose to lose her identity in order to court a pop audience; instead, she released her albums in separate pop and country versions. After releasing just three albums over seven years, Twain settled into domesticity with Lange in Switzerland until their divorce and, like Brooks, her retirement may be short-lived. Nevertheless, Twain opened the door to performers like Faith Hill, who also played the dual role of country chanteuse and pop "diva."

After the September 11, 2001, attacks, it was country music that provided an emotional salve to the country's sense of confusion, helplessness, and anger. Alan Jackson premiered his "Where Were You (When the World Stopped Turning)" at the Country Music Association awards show on November 7; the next day, radio stations were playing the broadcast version of the song. When the studio version of the song (recorded before the CMA broadcast) was released at the end of the month, it became a number one country song as well as a number twenty-eight pop hit and won the Grammy Award for Best Country Song in 2002. An unexpected result of the rise in patriotic feeling was the revival of Lee Greenwood's "God Bless the U.S.A." Originally recorded in 1984, the song reached number seven on the country charts and was played at the Republican National Convention in Dallas that year. There was renewed interest in the song during the first Gulf War of 1990–1991, but it became an anthem of the Second Gulf War, along with Irving Berlin's "God Bless America." The song was re-released in 2001 and became a hit a second time, reaching number sixteen on both the country and pop charts.

While Alan Jackson tapped into the uncertainty of the immediate aftermath of 9/11 and Greenwood's soaring patriotism (albeit with the unfortunate opening line to the chorus, "I'm proud to be an American where *at least I know* I'm free" [emphasis added]), there was also a jingoistic streak in the country that was captured by country artists. One of the least artful was Darryl Worley's "Have You Forgotten?" Inspired by having performed for U.S. troops in Afghanistan and Kuwait in December 2002, Worley and fellow musician Wynn Varble composed the song, which Worley premiered on the *Grand Ole Opry* on January 10, 2003. It received much criticism for its tying of the 9/11 tragedy to the Gulf War (the line "Some say this country's just out looking for a fight / Well, after 9/11, man, I'd have to say that's right" was particularly vilified), but that didn't prevent it from becoming a number one country song as well as a number twenty-two pop song. But unquestionably, the most talked-about song at this time was Toby Keith's "Courtesy of the Red, White, & Blue (The Angry American)." The song was originally written to be performed in front of military audiences, but Keith was encouraged by soldiers to record it. Released in May 2002, it became a number one country hit and was number twenty-five on the pop charts. Worley's song inspired grumbling mostly among music critics, but two incidents pushed Keith's song into the national spotlight. ABC had approached Keith to perform at its July 4, 2002, celebration broadcast, but Peter Jennings, who was hosting the show, requested that Keith change some of the lyrics ("we'll put a boot in your ass; it's the American way" may have been the most offensive) or sing another song. Keith

Toby Keith, center, performs "Courtesy of the Red, White & Blue" at the 37th Annual Academy of Country Music Awards in Los Angeles, May 22, 2002. (AP Photo/Kevork Djansezian)

refused to appear on the show at all and then mocked Jennings for his Canadian citizenship. (Jennings would become a naturalized citizen the following year.) The following month, in an interview with the *Los Angeles Daily News,* Natalie Maines, lead singer of the popular country trio the Dixie Chicks, said that she hated the song. "It's ignorant," she explained, "and it makes country music sound ignorant. . . . Anybody can write, 'We'll put a boot in your ass.'" In response, Keith displayed a doctored photo of Maines with Saddam Hussein at his concerts as a backdrop. This feud came to a head at the American Country Music award telecast of May 21, 2003, when Maines appeared with the Chicks wearing a FUTK T-shirt (Rudder 2005).

The second half of the 2000s was notable for two women who eschewed the traditional road through Nashville to become big stars. Country careers have been kicked off on national talent shows before—Patsy Cline on Arthur Godfrey's *Talent Scouts* (1957) and Sawyer Brown on *Star Search* (1983; hosted by Ed McMahon)—but Carrie Underwood's victory on the fourth season of *American Idol* (2005) was unique in that the format of *Idol* forces contestants to demonstrate their versatility, and Underwood proved that she could succeed in both country and pop. For example, her first single, "Inside Your Heaven," was written as her coronation song for *American Idol* and was pitched to pop radio, where it became a number one record, only reaching number fifty-two on the country chart. By contrast, the next single, "Jesus, Take the Wheel," was heavily promoted on country radio, reaching number one, while only reaching number twenty on the pop charts. Underwood records primarily in Nashville and has become a member of the Grand Ole Opry; on the other hand, she has become well known for her fashion sense and—until her marriage to hockey player Mike Fisher—her high-profile relationship with football player Tony Romo.

While Carrie Underwood's career took her through Hollywood to get to Nashville, Taylor Swift went through Nashville to get to Hollywood. A songwriting prodigy from Pennsylvania, Swift's family moved to Nashville when she was fourteen, where she was signed by Sony/ATV Tree publishing as a songwriter. At the age of sixteen, she released her eponymous first album (2006), which peaked at number one country and number five pop. Swift was not the first female teen idol in

Nashville—she was preceded by Brenda Lee in the 1950s and Tanya Tucker in the 1970s—but Lee and Tucker performed songs written by men without much consideration for their ages (and in Tucker's case, notoriously so). Swift wrote her songs with the sentiments of a teenager, and that's how her tunes were marketed. Her second album, *Fearless,* topped both the country and pop charts and became the first album to win the American Music Award, Academy of Country Music Award, Country Music Association Award, and Grammy Award for Album of the Year. Swift's fan base may mostly be young girls, but she became a national celebrity following the 2009 MTV Music Video Awards, when rapper Kanye West interrupted her acceptance speech for the Best Female Video Award to say that another nominated video was more deserving. Like Underwood, Swift has used her beauty sense to her advantage, becoming a model for CoverGirl cosmetics, and she has a line of clothing that is sold at Wal-Mart. Swift has also tried her hand at acting, appearing in an episode of the television series *CSI* and in the 2010 film *Valentine's Day.*

Almost since its inception, country music has influenced American culture in significant ways. The "singing cowboy" introduced Western songs and the iconic image of a male performer with a "ten-gallon" hat and guitar. The *Grand Ole Opry* radio program delivered the new music from the Southeast to millions of homes, making Nashville the locus for the genre, and the *Opry*'s cast of singers, instrumentalists, and comedians became the palate from which future entertainers borrowed. The country music industry that consolidated after World War II has always been interested in reaching out to the popular music audience, whether promoting the songs of Hank Williams to pop singers or through releasing pop and country versions of Shania Twain's albums. In the aftermath of the 9/11 attacks, country music songs spoke to and for Americans who were coping with the unspeakable acts of terrorism. The relationship between country music and American culture will continue to evolve in conjunction with the changing demographics of the country. Country music is no more uniquely "American" than jazz or gospel or hip-hop, but the genre's strong influence on American culture says much about how this music and its performers has been able to relate to so many Americans for nearly a century.

See also: Autry, Gene; Awards and Prizes for Music; Brooks, Garth; Carter Family, The; Cash, Johnny; Cline, Patsy; Denver, John; Dixie Chicks; Clothing and Appearance in Song; Folk Music; *Grand Ole Opry*; Haggard, Merle; Hill, Faith; Honky-Tonk Music; Nelson, Willie; Peter, Paul and Mary; Presley, Elvis; Radio; Rogers, Roy; September 11th Commemorations; Television Variety Shows; Toys and Music; Tucker, Tanya; War Music; West, Kanye; Williams, Hank

Further Reading

Cox, Patsi Bale. 2009. *The Garth Factor: The Career Behind Country's Big Boom.* New York: Center Street.

Green, Douglas B. 2002. *Singing in the Saddle: The History of the Singing Cowboy.* Nashville: Country Music Foundation Press & Vanderbilt University Press.

Hollis, Tim. 2008. *Ain't That a Knee-Slapper: Rural Comedy in the Twentieth Century.* Jackson: University Press of Mississippi.

Jensen, Joli. 1998. *The Nashville Sound: Authenticity, Commercialization, and Country Music.* Nashville, TN: Vanderbilt University Press.

Malone, Bill C. 1985. *Country Music, U.S.A.* Rev. ed. Austin: University of Texas Press.

Malone, Bill C. 1993. *Singing Cowboys and Musical Mountaineers: Southern Culture and the Roots of Country Music.* Athens: University of Georgia Press.

Naylor, Larry L. 1999. "Introduction to American Cultural Diversity: Unresolved Questions, Issues, and Problems." In *Problems and Issues of Diversity in the United States,* edited by Larry L. Naylor. Westport, CT: Bergin & Garvey.

Rudder, Randy. 2005. "In Whose Name?: Country Artists Speak Out on Gulf War II." In *Country Music Goes to War,* edited by Charles K. Wolfe and James E. Akenson. Lexington: University Press of Kentucky.

Whitburn, Joel. 1986. *Pop Memories 1890–1954.* Menomonee Falls, WI: Record Research.

Whitburn, Joel. 2005. *Top Country Songs 1944–2005.* 6th ed. Menomonee Falls, WI: Record Research.

Morris S. Levy

Country Music, Women In

Country music traces its roots to regional vernacular traditions: the songs of home and hearth found in the domestic music and fiddle tunes of Appalachia. It originated as the music of women, who in the nineteenth and early twentieth centuries made the music of the homestead. As the bearers of tradition and creators of community, they passed on the traditions of vernacular music to successive generations. Gender roles of the day dictated that women belonged in the home and typically equated public entertainment with prostitution, leaving space only for family musical groups.

The Carter Family (active 1927–1944)—America's "First Family of Country Music"—drew audiences, both northern and southern, urban and rural, to the genre, with their recording of "Single Girl, Married Girl"

(1927). Maybelle Carter (1909–1978), whose "scratch style" of picking has influenced generations of performers, male and female, performed with The Carter Family until 1941, and then with her daughters, Anita (1933–1999), Helen (1927–1998), and June (1929–2003; she later married Johnny Cash), as Mother Maybelle and the Carter Sisters, into the 1970s.

The 1930s and 1940s marked a high point for women in country music. Programming such as Rudy Vallee's national radio show, *The Fleischmann's Yeast Hour* (NBC), and the *WLS National Barn Dance* featured numerous female stars, such as Mary Ford (1924–1977; she later sold millions of records with her husband, guitarist Les Paul, 1915–2009). These women performed as solo acts and in bands, including at least a dozen sister acts, in keeping with country music's emphasis on promoting family values. Nashville's Grand Ole Opry also offered performance opportunities for numerous female performers of country music, showcasing singers such as Jean Shepard (1933–), Wilma Lee Cooper (1921–2011), and Loretta Lynn (1932–) among its earliest female performers. With its blending of well-known country, Western, honky-tonk, gospel, and bluegrass performers such as Dolly Parton (1946–), Emmylou Harris (1947–), and fiddler Alison Krauss (1971–), the Opry has played a significant role in highlighting the contributions of women in these interrelated genres and subgenres of music.

The 1930s and 1940s offered additional opportunities—and greater independence—for female country music performers. Radio contracts became available for women like Margaret Whiting (1924–2011), Jo Stafford (1917–2008), and Patti Page (1927–), and female country singers were hired to promote war bond sales and travel on morale-building USO tours. In addition, professional opportunities for women in country music emerged in promotion, booking, and publishing. By the end of the 1940s there were two female-owned country labels—Lois Nettles's Red Bird Records and Macey Henry's Macey Records. Women also launched country music journalism as fan magazines developed and became the lead writers for *Rural Radio* (1938–1939), *The Mountain Broadcast and Prairie Recorder* (1939–1947), and *Record Round-up* (1946–1949).

The 1950s and 1960s were decades of change in country music. The early years were presided over by singer Kitty Wells (1919–2012) as the "Queen of Country Music." Wells's controversial hit "It Wasn't God Who Made Honky Tonk Angels" (1952) was the first song recorded by a woman to reach number one on the *Billboard* country chart, but was also banned by radio stations and the Grand Ole Opry, alike. Later in the decade Wells's song would serve as an icon of country music ideology, as the genre was polarized by the emergence of two distinct sounds: one with the sheen of urban sophistication, the other with the rough edges of the working class. The "Nashville Sound" blended pop music elements with country, with smooth, highly structured components of 1950s pop music, creating a sophisticated sound that departed dramatically from the genre's origins among poor farmers and laborers. This new "countrypolitan" sound found its most enduring voices in singers Patsy Cline (1932–1963) and Brenda Lee (1944–). The two delivered songs that moved easily between country and pop audiences, such as "I Fall to Pieces" (1961), "Crazy" (1961), and "Break It to Me Gently" (1962), featuring languid rhythms, string orchestras, and smooth, harmonized background vocals.

Country singer Kitty Wells poses for a portrait, ca. 1954. (Michael Ochs Archives/Getty Images)

In response to this slick, overproduced version of country music, the "Bakersfield Sound" emerged on the West Coast. Raw, plainspoken, rock-influenced, and energetic, it was a highly masculine sound that took pride in staying true to its country roots. Female performers of the Bakersfield Sound, such as Rose Maddox (1925–1988), and Kitty Wells, sang about life and love gone bad, with songs like "Sing a Little Song of Heartache" (1962). The influence of these early country roots singers can be found in the songs of contemporary female country performers such as Loretta Lynn, Tanya Tucker (1958–), and Lucinda Williams (1953–).

These caste and class differences in country music began to resolve over the next two decades, as crossover performers and their songs continued to blur the boundaries of country music. Strong female figures with broad-spectrum appeal emerged on the country music scene. Award-winning Opry performers such as Dolly Parton and Loretta Lynn crossed over, not only into pop music, but into film, as well. Singers like Barbara Mandrell (1948–), Tammy Wynette (1942–1988), Reba McEntire (1955–), and Lynn Anderson (1947–) took women's share of the country music market from less than 10 to over 30 percent in a single decade. The country music industry itself followed similar trends, with female executives heading the majority of country music's trade associations, booking agencies, music publishers, public relations firms, radio stations, and recording companies.

As country music approached and entered the new millennium, the genre experienced a resurgence in popular culture, with its female performers at the forefront. Female country performers like Shania Twain (1965–) and Faith Hill (1967–) and multigenre performers like Bonnie Raitt (1949–) toured sell-out shows and garnered multiple Grammy Awards. Other multiple-award-winning performers such as Martina McBride (1966–), Trisha Yearwood (1964–), Carrie Underwood (1983–), and Taylor Swift (1989–), along with female-fronted bands like Little Big Town (active 1998–present), the Dixie Chicks (active 1989–present), and Sugarland (active 2003–present) also proved to be groundbreaking crossover artists, topping charts with songs such as "Independence Day" (1993), "Before He Cheats" (2005), and "Boondocks" (2005), which offered a uniquely female perspective and bridged the gap between urban and rural country by combining the pop-styled "Nashville Sound" with lyrics that harkened back to working-class honky-tonk roots.

Several women country artists were standouts in the second decade of the twenty-first century. Carrie Underwood continued to have number one hits with songs like "All American Girl" (2008), "Cowboy Cassanova" (2009), "Temporary Home" (2010), and "Good Girl" (2012). Miranda Lambert (1983–), who gained nationwide attention on *Nashville Stars,* was the Academy of Country Music's top new female vocalist in 2007, followed by top female vocalist or female vocalist of the year from 2008 to 2012. Taylor Swift's debut album *Taylor Swift* (2006) peaked at number one on the U.S. country charts, and her second album, *Fearless* (2008), topped the *Billboard* 200 for eleven nonconsecutive weeks, making Swift an international and commercial success. Her third album, *Speak Now* (2010), continued her success and fame.

Women will continue to make a mark on country music. The legacy of women in country music, which extends from The Carter Family through contemporary artists, will continue to inspire and promote the genre to new and returning artists.

See also: Bluegrass; Cash, Johnny; Cash, June Carter; Cline, Patsy; Crossovers; *Grand Olé Opry*; Krauss, Alison; Lynn, Loretta; McEntire, Reba; Music Magazines and Journalism; Carter Family, The; Parton, Dolly; Pop Music; Radio; Tucker, Tanya; Wynette, Tammy

Further Reading

Bufwack, Mary, and Robert Oermann. 2003. *Finding Her Voice: Women in Country Music, 1800–2000.* Nashville, TN: Vanderbilt University Press.

Green, Douglas. 1976. *Country Roots: The Origin of Country Music.* New York: Hawthorne Books.

Malone, Bill C. 1985. *Country Music USA.* Austin: University of Texas Press.

Cynthia J. Miller

Cover Songs

"Cover song" refers to the recording of a song generally identified with a singer or musical group by another group or singer. Schematically, Artist 1 performs/records song x; Artist 2 in turn performs/records song x, and is thus said to "cover" either song x or Artist 1's version of song x. The relationship between the original version and covers of that version is often ambiguous. Here the canonical recording of a song—the best-known or most popular version—will be referred to as the "base," whereas other recordings of that version will be referred to as the "cover."

At first glance the fundamental idea of an artist covering the work of another is straightforward. The temptation may be to identify the first recorded version of a given song as the original; all subsequent versions would thereby be considered covers. Indeed, this is often the case: the original song is widely known, popular, even canonical, and any other versions are understood to be renditions of that paradigmatic version. While this approach solves a number of problems that arise in understanding the relationship between a song and its cover, it does so by paying a substantial price. This approach 1) begs the question and simply defines what is and what is not the original song (and thus, by extension, its cover); 2) conflicts sharply with ordinary usage when certain later versions of songs become canonical; and 3) ignores the systematic ambiguity found in the relationship between a base song and its cover(s). Consequently, this relationship needs to be clarified, which both makes more explicit precisely how ambiguous the very notion of a "cover song" can be and provides a more satisfactory account of the relationship between the two versions in question.

Various kinds of covers have been recorded. Taking the term "cover song" as the genus, an understanding of its specific relationship to the song it covers—the base—is fundamental to providing an informative analysis of the cover song. Here a number of such species of cover songs are identified, along with a few representative examples. Such a list is not intended to be exhaustive, nor are the distinctions among the various kinds of cover songs always easily drawn.

One type of cover song is the *reduplication cover,* an attempt to generate an exact duplicate of a song or performance. Such an attempt lies at one extreme of the very idea of a cover song, in that a successful reproduction would make the cover and the base indistinguishable. These are most frequently found in live performances, such as the Dark Star Orchestra's re-creations of specific live shows of the Grateful Dead (active 1965–1995), including onstage talk, tuning, and other details. Todd Rundgren's 1976 "Faithful" is a studio album that attempts to reproduce exact copies of base material, leading to Steve Bailey's remark that such cover songs are "so 'faithful' as to be pointless" (2003).

The interpretive cover is generally what is taken to be the cover song *simpliciter,* in which an artist records or performs a version of a song standardly associated with another artist. However, even within this approach, there can be distinguished a *minor interpretative cover* and *major interpretive cover.* The former may be regarded as an homage to the "base" song; maintaining the tempo, melody, lyrics, and general instrumentation of the original. (One might offer Talking Heads' [active 1974–1991, 2002] recording of Al Green's "Take Me to the River," or The Beatles' [active 1960–1970] version of the Isley Brothers' "Twist and Shout" as examples.) A band may cover a given song in this fashion for many reasons, but doing so can establish its musical bona fides and indicate an important set of influences.

In contrast, a major interpretive cover presents a version that is sonically distinct, in various ways, from its base song. The base song will be recognizable in this type of cover, but it becomes fundamentally a new song. Lyrics may be altered, instrumentation changed, tempo sped up or slowed down; it may serve, at the extreme, as simply a reference point for those providing the new major interpretation. On occasion, such a cover version can be sufficiently successful that it replaces the base song as the canonical version, as in Aretha Franklin's (1942–) cover of "Respect." Similarly, some are surprised to discover that Jimi Hendrix's (1942–1970) "All Along the Watchtower" is a cover of Bob Dylan's (1941–) original. As this example indicates, different generations may identify different versions of songs as the base song and, consequently, as a cover of that base. In any case, this demonstrates that reducing the term "cover song" to such major interpretations neglects the term's systematic ambiguity.

Send-up covers share with major interpretive covers the result that a virtually new song emerges. Yet send-up covers subvert the base song in a distinct way, often by maintaining an ironic distance from it. The most memorable send-up covers require a rethinking of the base and offer a broader spectrum of available perspectives. Thus the Gourds (active 1994–present) use bluegrass instrumentation and a country sensibility for their send-up of Snoop Dogg's (1971–) "Gin and Juice," leading a rap about alcohol, marijuana, promiscuity, and questionable sexual politics to somewhat ridiculous observations of white country musicians. At the same time, it reveals that regardless of approach, some things (alcohol, marijuana, promiscuity, and questionable sexual politics) may be more universal than marketers sometimes seem to assume. Sid Vicious's (1957–1979) ironic cover of Frank Sinatra's "I Did It My Way" and Devo's (active 1972–1991, 1996–present) same approach to The Rolling Stones' "(I Can't Get No) Satisfaction" similarly can provide a subversive context and unanticipated meaning.

At one extreme of the term "cover song" is a reduplication that is so faithful it is indistinguishable from the base song. At the other extreme is the *parody cover,* where the relationship between the two songs is at its most tenuous. The parody takes the base song solely as a point of reference and has little if anything to do with it otherwise. There is as little risk that Homer and Jethro's (active 1936–1972) "Don't Let the Stars Get in Your Eyeballs" will be confused with Perry Como's (1912–2001) Don't Let the Stars Get in Your Eyes" as there is that any of "Weird Al" Yankovic's (1959–) versions of pop hits will be taken to be serious musical performances (like his version of Cyndi Lauper's [1953–] "Girls Just Want to Have Fun," "Girls Just Want to Have Lunch"). Some conceivably earnest covers are such inappropriate choices for the artist that they result in unintentional parodies or novelty songs, such as William Shatner's (1931–) cover of The Beatles' "Lucy in the Sky with Diamonds."

In sum, the term "cover song" is systematically ambiguous, and in any discussion of cover songs and their evaluation, it is crucial to make clear what specific kind of cover song is involved. Even so, peculiarities remain, and difficulties in determining what version, if any, is canonical. It is difficult to suggest that when Carole King (1942–) recorded a song she wrote, "(You Make Me Feel Like) A Natural Woman," she was covering her own song. At the same time, Aretha Franklin's version must be seen as canonical and would be identified by few as a standard cover song. A proper analysis of cover songs, consequently, must pay close attention to these and other semantic issues that arise in the context of discussing cover songs.

See also: Bluegrass; Comedy and Satire in American music; Dylan, Bob; Franklin, Aretha; Grateful Dead; Hendrix, Jimi; King, Carole; Rap and Rappers; Talking Heads

Further Reading

Bailey, Steve. 2003. "Faithful or Foolish: The Emergence of the 'Ironic Cover Album' and Rock Culture." *Popular Music and Society* 26: 141–159.

Butler, Mark. 2003. "Taking It Seriously: Intertextuality and Authenticity in Two Covers by the Pet Shop Boys." *Popular Music* 22: 1–19.

Coyle, Michael. 2002. "Hijacked Hits and Antic Authenticity: Cover Songs, Race, and Postwar Marketing." In *Rock Over the Edge: Transformations in Popular Music Culture,* edited by R. Beebe, D. Fulbrook, and B. Saunders, 133–157. Durham, N.C.: Duke University Press.

Cusic, Don. 2005. "In Defense of Cover Songs." *Popular Music and Society* 28: 171–175.

Davenport, Kimberly. 1995. "Impossible Liberties: Contemporary Artists on the Life of Their Work Over Time." *Art Journal* 54: 40–52.

Plastekes, George. 2005. "Re-flections on the Cover Age: A Collage of Continuous Coverage in Popular Music." *Popular Music and Society* 28: 137–161.

Kurt Mosser

Critics and Reviewers

Music critics and music reviewers comment on musical performances, recordings, and artists through a variety of media: magazines, blogs, zines, television, and radio. They bring attention to music because of its quality, or lack thereof. Some listeners may learn about different forms of music or performance through reviews they hear, although it is difficult to gauge the extent to which music and musicians are actually influenced by reviews.

In the nineteenth century Boston emerged as an important center of musical activity. The Handel and Haydn Society, founded in 1815; the establishment of the music department at Harvard University in 1862; and the development of the Boston Symphony Orchestra in 1880 helped shape the city's strong cultural life.

American music reviewers, working under strict deadlines, usually penned their articles immediately after performances, a marked contrast from the high-minded and more elaborate European essay-reviews of the nineteenth century.

The father of American musical criticism, John Sullivan Dwight (1813–1893), in reviews in his own journal, *Dwight's Journal of Music,* reflected Boston's conservative musical tastes. He favored the clarity and precision of Beethoven and Mozart rather than the dense romanticism of Wagner and Brahms.

William Foster Apthorp (1848–1913) wrote critical articles for Boston's *Evening Transcript* in a clear style that reflected his belief that reviews should do nothing more than express enlightened opinions. He also penned program notes for Boston Symphony concerts.

Contemporary music gained a firm footing with the writing of Philip Hale (1854–1934), who worked for a number of Boston newspapers, including the *Home Journal* and *The Herald.* Like Apthorp, Hale wrote program notes for the Boston Symphony performances. He often drew analogies from literature in his writing, using lines from William Blake and Walt Whitman to explain passages in Schubert's music, for example. Yet he equally covered the music of his generation, exploring the depths of works by Richard Strauss (1965–1949) and Claude Debussy (1862–1918).

Music criticism in New York City blossomed around 1880, due to industrial expansion. Wealthy patrons helped establish the Metropolitan Opera, which opened its doors in 1883. The city's newspapers, which gave more space to musical subjects, ran articles by the "Great Five": Henry Finck (1854–1926), Henry Krehbiel (1854–1923), William Henderson (1855–1937), Richard Aldrich (1863–1937), and James Gibbons Huneker (1860–1921). Krehbiel came to the New York *Tribune* as a music critic in 1880 after reporting on baseball and murder cases for the Cincinnati *Gazette.* A reviewer of a conservative stripe, he unpacked the music of Brahms and Tchaikovsky—two composers who would come to dominate American concert halls in the ensuing decades—for New York readers. Krehbiel also authored books on the New York Philharmonic, African American music, and Wagner.

But New York's brightest star among reviewers was James Gibbons Huneker, who wrote for the *Recorder, Times,* and *Sun* during the first decades of the twentieth century. As a writer, he drew on his experience as a novelist and lover of visual arts, citing passages from Ibsen, Whitman, Tolstoy, Yeats, and Goethe in his music criticism. Huneker admired the large-scale romantic works of Richard Strauss and commented on the difficult *Also Sprach Zarathustra,* a tone poem based on Nietzsche's novel, as "cathedral in tone, sublime, and fantastic, with its grotesque gargoyles, hideous flying abutments, exquisite traceries, prodigious arches, half Gothic, half infernal, huge and resounding spaces, gorgeous façades and heaven-splitting spires" (quoted in Graf 1946, 317). Wagner, he wrote, was the last of the great romantics.

Women began playing leading roles in music journalism by the mid-nineteenth century. The feminist Margaret Fuller (1810–1850) authored articles on classical music and served as editor of *The Dial* during the 1840s.

In 1926 the *New York Post* hired the celebrated concert pianist Olga Samaroff (1882–1948) (born Lucy Hickenlooper; she adopted the Russian stage name when her career took off) as its chief music critic. In her two years there she engendered controversy with other reviewers, especially Samuel Chotzinoff (1889–1964) of the *World,* over her refusal to review mediocre and poor performances. Indeed, her opinion stemmed from her background as a professional performer, and she knew that a bad review could possibly destroy the career of a new, young artist.

H. L. (Henry Louis) Mencken (1880–1956) approached music criticism from his role as a journalist. Like Dwight, he wrote favorably of the great masters, praising their contributions to the canon of symphonic music. He also wrote about contemporary musical developments. Serving as a reporter for the *Baltimore Herald* and as an editor of the *Morning Herald* and *Evening Sun* during his career, Mencken used his power as a reviewer to bolster what he viewed as purity in the musical arts. He trumpeted the virtues of Gilbert and Sullivan operettas but blasted American Broadway theater, praised the formal architecture of a Beethoven symphony but detested jazz as vulgar.

At the turn of the twentieth century, music reviewers in major metropolitan newspapers reflected European tastes in music and culture: the symphony orchestras of New York and Boston, for example, performed works by such luminaries as Franz Joseph Haydn (1732–1809), Wolfgang Amadeus Mozart (1756–1792), Ludwig van Beethoven (1770–1827), and Johannes Brahms (1833–1897), among others. Reviewers for American papers were journalists who obtained high levels of musical knowledge and, as some scholars have noted, were among some of the greatest writers in the nation.

Virgil Thomson (1896–1989) exemplified the composer-critic as a reviewer for the *New York Herald Tribune* from 1940 to 1954. He described the music he heard in great detail; his reviews served as listening guides for the reader.

In the 1960s newspapers such as the *New York Times* maintained strict boundaries between critics reviewing classical and popular music. That changed in 1972, when the *Times* hired John Rockwell (1940–), a writer well versed in both realms of American musical life. Rockwell established what in the industry became known as "crossover" criticism: an aesthetic whereby the reviewer covered popular and classical music and, moreover, viewed the two on an equal footing rather than as segregated. The idea spread to include other genres and subgenres of music as well. "I . . . came to believe that experimental music, vernacular music and non-Western music were important and enjoyable, too, and that a 'music critic' had no business excluding entire traditions that most of the world thought of as 'music' just because they didn't conform to his own cultural prejudices," he wrote in his 1983 book *All American Music* (quoted in Grant 1998, 308–309). The trend branched out into popular criticism. Writers such as Robert Christgau (1942–) of the *Village Voice* and Greil Marcus (1945–) of the *Rolling Stone* employed more high-minded prose when reviewing rock music, just as classical critics had done in previous decades. The quality and depth of much popular music by the end of the 1960s, as exemplified by The Beach Boys' (active 1961–present) *Pet Sounds* and The Beatles' (active 1960–1970) *Sgt. Pepper's* album, earned increasing attention among America's cultural elite.

As newspapers cut their budgets for arts critics in the 1990s and 2000s, Rockwell's totalist approach became the norm as much for economic purposes, perhaps, as aesthetic ones. Alex Ross (1960–), a stringer for the *New York Times,* became music critic at the *New Yorker,* where he is at home reviewing concerts of Wagner, Bruckner, British rock, and Bjork as well as writing analytical essays on literary topics. Anne Midgette, the classical music critic for the *Washington Post,* covers popular music and even fashion during the off-season on her blog, *The Classical Beat.*

The role of the music critic has indeed changed since the mid-nineteenth century. Then, critics were custodians of musical style and taste; currently, they represent only an informed professional opinion. Composer and critic Kyle Gann (1955–), who wrote for the *Village Voice,* stated, "When you first become a critic, you've got a million opinions that you feel determined to express or burst. But after the first 500 or so articles, you find that those opinions don't shake the world, that music cannot be steered from its destined course to any great extent, and that, in the end, there's not that much difference between one opinion and another—each one is a little burst of hot air" (quoted in Grant 1998, 328).

The rise of the blogosphere during the 2000s has leveled the metaphorical playing field, because the Internet serves as a valuable portal for the consumption and sharing of a myriad of musical styles and genres. Music criticism, then, has become a type of professional hobby for many writers. Writers on music of many stripes—historians, students, journalists, composers, performers, and listeners—contribute their thoughts in easily accessible blogs.

See also: Beach Boys, The; Classical Music in America; Pop Music

Further Reading

Graf, Max. 1946. *Composer and Critic: Two Hundred Years of Music Criticism.* New York: Norton.

Grant, Mark N. 1998. *Maestros of the Pen: A History of Classical Music Criticism in America.* Boston: Northeastern University Press.

Aaron C. Keebaugh

Croce, Jim (1943–1973)

With his nasal tenor vocals and easygoing acoustic guitar melodies, Jim Croce captured audiences with both poignant, deeply moving ballads, such as "Time in a Bottle" (1972) and upbeat, bluesy pop songs such as "Bad, Bad, Leroy Brown" (1973). Although his life was cut short by a plane crash in Natchitoches, Louisiana, in 1973, the fame and respect he worked so hard to achieve during his lifetime ultimately came after his death. Known for his pop hits about a cast of characters drawn straight from his own string of blue-collar jobs, Croce masterfully penned music that resonated with many working-class Americans, especially those who lived through the social and cultural upheavals of the late 1960s and early 1970s.

A gifted guitarist, songwriter, and vocalist, Jim Croce was born January 10, 1943, in Philadelphia, Pennsylvania. He learned the accordion at an early age in a childhood home that was often filled with the sounds of Bessie Smith (1894–1937), Fats Waller (1904–1943), and other jazz artists. During his time at Villanova University, he formed bands and played a Stella twelve-string guitar, a staple of the popular folk revival of the time. Croce even toured the Middle East and Africa on a State Department–sponsored mission promoting folk music. After college he worked various jobs, from welding to recording voice-overs to teaching special education students. A disc jockey gig introduced Croce to a number of blues legends, including Edward "Son" House (1902–1988). Despite once bashing his thumb with a sledgehammer, Croce developed a proficient finger-picking guitar style. In 1969 he and his wife Ingrid moved to New York City, but they were unsuccessful on the coffeehouse circuit and eventually returned to a farm in Lyndell, Pennsylvania. While driving trucks and doing excavating work, Croce struggled to make ends meet, even resorting to selling his small collection of instruments. Despite this, he continued to write and record until his six-song demo tape caught the attention of a producer. Croce traveled to New York to record his first successful LP, *You Don't Mess Around with Jim* (1972). Propelled by the title track and bolstered by the January 1973 single "Bad, Bad, Leroy Brown," he began a rigorous touring schedule that took him all over the country.

Jim Croce, ca. 1970. (Michael Ochs Archives/Getty Images)

Croce's lyrics drew heavily on the details of his life, and his voice, despite his tough-guy appearance, echoed his warm personality. In the winter of 1971, with his dream of performing slipping away, he composed one of his most popular and enduring songs. Written for his then-unborn son A. J., "Time in a Bottle" earnestly expresses what he cherished most in life in the midst of difficult times, a sentiment that connected with many audiences around the country. He recorded just two more albums, *Life and Times* (1973) and *I've Got a Name* (1973) before the tragic accident on September 20, 1973. After he performed at Northwestern State University, his plane crashed during takeoff, killing everyone on board, including his accompanist, fellow guitarist, and close friend Marty Muehleisen (1949–1973). Following his death, his album sales skyrocketed, and his songs, including the ballads "Operator (That's Not the Way It Feels)" (1972) and "I'll Just Have to Say I Love

You in a Song" (1973), became radio hits throughout the 1970s and 1980s.

See also: Folk Music; House, Edward "Son"; Jazz; Pop Music; Smith, Bessie

Official Web Site: http://www.jimcroce.com/

Further Reading

Croce, Ingrid. 2004. *Jim Croce: Time in a Bottle, A Photographic Memoir.* Milwaukee, WI: Hal Leonard.

Croce, Ingrid. 2007. "Jim Croce—The Official Site." http://www.jimcroce.com.

Croce, Jim. 1974. *Jim Croce: His Life and Music.* New York: Big 3 Music Corp.

Andrew D. A. Bozanic

Crosby, Bing (1903–1977)

An astute businessman, innovative thinker, and velvet-voiced crooner, Bing Crosby dominated the entertainment industry for decades. His performance style complemented emergent entertainment technology as his rich baritone voice, soothing melodic tones, and mellow casual manner conveyed by microphone an intimacy that radio audiences welcomed. His "everyman" persona translated well to the silver screen, helped to mainstream Catholicism, and influenced subsequent vocal artists. Further, his investments in technology revolutionized the recording industry and the way Americans prepared breakfast.

Born Harry Lillis Crosby on May 3, 1903, in Tacoma, Washington, he was the fourth of seven children in an Irish Catholic American family. Dubbed "Bing" by a neighbor when he was seven years old, Crosby grew up singing along with his father's phonograph; in school plays; and eventually in a band and on vaudeville, where he crooned a mix of jazz, Irish folk songs, and Tin Pan Alley hits. During his fifty-year career he recorded hundreds of songs (thirty-eight number one hits), contributed to more than one hundred films, and hosted and appeared in a number of televised musical variety shows. Crosby's version of Irving Berlin's "White Christmas" still holds the world record for the best-selling recording of all time.

Crosby's status as a cultural icon grew through memorable musical performances with entertainers such as Fred Astaire, Frank Sinatra, Danny Kaye, Rosemary Clooney, Louis Armstrong, and the Andrew Sisters. Often cast as half of a cinematic comedic duo, his series of "road" movies with Bob Hope successfully

Bing Crosby was a singer, radio performer, and movie star. By the time he died in 1977, he had become one of America's most popular entertainers. (Library of Congress)

incorporated vaudevillian slapstick humor with big screen plots. Popular and influential, many credit his portrayal of Catholic priests in *Going My Way* (1944), *The Bells of St. Mary's* (1945), and *Say One for Me* (1959) with mainstreaming Catholicism; the Protestant majority easily identified with his modern, patriotic characters. Crosby's soft and sensual crooning style influenced singers Roy Orbison, Elvis Presley, the Everly Brothers, and The Beatles, who themselves crooned rock ballads and even recorded many of Crosby's songs. Perhaps the best tribute to his influence was his 1977 duet with rocker David Bowie, who harmonized "Peace on Earth" with Crosby's "Little Drummer Boy."

A shrewd businessman, Crosby invested in burgeoning technology, real estate, the oil and entertainment industries, and food distribution companies. He established a number of corporations, including Bing Crosby Enterprises, Project Records, and Bing Crosby Productions. He had an ownership stake in the Pittsburgh Pirates major league baseball team, the Del Mar Racetrack, and the Blue Skies Trailer Park (a ritzy park in Palm Springs intended to draw affluent vacationers to palm-tree-shaded golf courses). His investments in recording innovation resulted in the magnetic recording tape, which he promoted as a replacement for live radio broadcasts. This technology revolutionized radio and television, as magnetic recording tape was the key component of audio and video cassettes. His investment in the Minute Maid company resulted in the development of "fast-freezing" technology, which gave America frozen orange juice. Crosby died suddenly of a heart attack on October 14, 1977, on a golf course in Madrid, Spain.

See also: Armstrong, Louis; Astaire, Fred; Berlin, Irving; Bowie, David; Jazz; Orbison, Roy; Presley, Elvis; Sinatra, Frank; Tin Pan Alley; Vaudeville and Burlesque

Official Web Site: http://www.bingcrosby.com

Further Reading

BCE, Inc. 2011. "The Official Home of Bing Crosby: The Place for All Things Bing." www.bingcrosby.com.

Giddons, Gary. 2001. *Bing Crosby: A Pocketful of Dreams; The Early Years, 1903–1940.* Boston: Little, Brown.

Prigozy, Ruth, and Walter Raubicheck, eds. 2007. *Going My Way: Bing Crosby and American Culture.* Rochester, NY: University of Rochester Press.

Jennifer Robin Terry

Crosby, Stills & Nash (Active 1968–1970, 1973, 1974, 1977–Present)

The year 1969 was a difficult one in many ways. The country was still reeling from the presidential election the previous year, violence only seemed to be spreading in the streets and on college campuses across the United States, and the Vietnam War raged on. The euphoria surrounding the three days of peace and love at Woodstock that summer was undone by a murder committed at Altamont in the middle of a Rolling Stones concert in December.

One notable bright spot in music at the time was a trio consisting of Americans David Crosby (1941–) and Stephen Stills (1945–), and Graham Nash (1942–), an Englishman. Each had come out of successful bands that had reached (or passed) their respective peaks: Crosby from the pioneering folk-rock band The Byrds; Stills from the similarly oriented but more virtuoso outfit Buffalo Springfield; and Nash out of the British pop-rock band the Hollies. From the outset their creative devices and collaborative synergies allowed them to achieve heights of musical creation that astounded fans of their previous endeavors. The trio mixed extraordinary three-part harmonies with a distinctive songwriting voice from each member: Crosby the brooding social observer and critic; Stills the guitar virtuoso (and multi-instrumentalist) fluent in country, folk, and hard rock; and Nash the pop-poet with a touch of the fantasist about him. For all the individuality of their voices, their work came off as a group effort. In their earlier bands, each had been obliged to compromise his musical sensibilities, but on the trio's self-titled debut album (issued in May 1969), in a manner reminiscent of The Beatles in their prime, each song seemed to display an odd mix of individuality and unity in equal measures. The freeing up of the members from the constraints of their previous musical surroundings emboldened each of them. On "Wooden Ships" and "Long Time Gone," David Crosby's writing and singing lofted into places, some poignant and some angry, and all of them laced with piercing lyrical and musical conceits, that he had scarcely touched with The Byrds. On the opener, "Suite: Judy Blue Eyes," Stephen Stills's composing and playing took him into realms of folk, country, and rock (and personal expression) that Buffalo Springfield had never shown the flexibility to approach. On "Marrakesh Express," "Pre-Road Downs," and "Lady of the Island," Graham Nash's work soared in gorgeous lyricism across realms alternatively playful and profoundly beautiful. With help from Neil Young, they could do this all on stage as well. With their second-ever public performance, in front of 500,000 people at Woodstock, their counterculture credibility was established and their future was made. Their influence was immediate: suddenly even the Grateful Dead were doing harmony vocals ("Uncle John's Band"), and a brace of would-be rivals, including Prelude and Marvin, Welch & Farrar, were springing up as well.

The trio, occasionally joined by Neil Young and known at times as Crosby, Stills, Nash & Young (active 1968–1970, 1973, 1974 with later reunions), has continued to delight audiences with their harmonies and energy for forty years, still carrying some of the glow of that beautiful beginning.

See also: Grateful Dead; Young, Neil

Official Web Site: http://www.csny.com/

Further Reading

Crosby, David, and Carl Gottlieb. 2006. *Since Then: How I Survived Everything and Lived to Tell About It.* New York: Putnam.

Rogan, Johnny. 1996. *Crosby, Stills, Nash & Young: The Visual Documentary.* New York: Omnibus Press.

Zimmer, Dave. 2008. *Crosby, Stills & Nash: The Biography.* New York: Da Capo Press.

Bruce Eder

Photo from Crosby, Stills & Nash's first album cover, 1969. (PRNewsFoto/Morrison Hotel Gallery)

Crossovers

The term *crossover* is used to describe a song, performer, or band that has moved from one musical genre to a different musical genre. The term is commonly used in the music industry to indicate a move from one market to another, or from one (usually) minor chart to a mainstream chart. Crossovers are different than combining genres to create a new genre; instead, they involve moving across genres. If the performer or band is popular, a crossover can be a way to introduce fans to a different genre.

Crossover can be conceptualized three different ways. A musician or band that combines two or more different musical genres in a composition or song can be called a crossover artist, with the music that mixes two stylistic genres a *stylistic crossover*. One well-known trend involves the use of high art musical forms either through quotation, allusion, or imitation by musicians in the genre of rock music. In the late 1960s and early 1970s the progressive rock bands Yes (*Close to the Edge*); Genesis (*Selling England by the Pound*); Emerson, Lake, and Palmer; Moody Blues (*Days of Future Passed*); and Deep Purple (*Concerto for Group and Orchestra*) borrowed and imitated classical and baroque musical forms in their songs and albums. Some rock bands flirted with classical crossover when they began to write songs for orchestral instruments, such as Electric Light Orchestra, which included violins and cellos in its lineup. Others wrote for symphonies; Procol Harem's self-titled album with the Edmonton Symphony Orchestra went gold in the United States in 1972. If the stylistic crossover involves one genre that is considered outside Western musical markets, the crossover is often called fusion, as in Celtic fusion, jazz fusion, and world fusion.

The term *crossover marketing* describes artists or albums being marketed to a new and usually wider demographic in order to increase sales. *Early Music* recordings prior to 1985 were marketed to scholars and aficionados of medieval and Renaissance music and emphasized historical accuracy and archival work. After 1985 some of these same recordings were re-released with new marketing strategies aimed at new age and adult contemporary markets. Cover art and imagery was updated from the requisite manuscript image to scenes of nature or symbols of spirituality in order to sell to these new audiences. The recordings *Chant, Quietude,* and *Chill to the Chant* are examples of record companies capitalizing on this new market, releasing new and re-releasing old Gregorian chant recordings to target

Charts

A chart is a list of songs ranked by record sales and radio airplay, published according to genre. In 1940 the leading trade magazine, *Billboard*, began to publish charts in three categories: pop, rhythm and blues (first called race music, then sepia), and country and western (first called hillbilly). *Billboard* remains the most visible chart in the music industry and now publishes weekly charts in more than twenty genres, from adult contemporary, to dance, to R&B, to country.

these new audiences. Classical music recordings have witnessed similar marketing shifts designed to broaden the market to those not usually on the receiving end of the musical genre, and to encourage those who consume the music to buy yet another recording of a well-known concerto or string quartet. While there may be subtle changes in the musical content, there need not be, as in the case of the 1990s Angel re-releases of Gregorian chant performed and recorded by the Benedictine Monks of Santo Domingo de Silos in the 1970s.

When music of one genre is received and consumed by an audience for another genre with no change to the musical content, it is called *crossover reception.* Although such crossover often involves crossover marketing, the latter is not necessary for the crossover to occur. The 1991 recording of Henryk Górecki's "Symphony of Sorrowful Songs" (Symphony no. 3, op. 36) performed by the London Sinfonietta, conducted by David Zinman, with Dawn Upshaw as soloist, crossed over from the *UK Music Week*'s classical charts to the pop charts, climbing to number six. It reached number one on the U.S. *Billboard* classical charts for 38 weeks, remaining on charts for 138 weeks. In a market in which five thousand copies sold per year is considered normal for a classical recording, Górecki's symphony has gone platinum, with over one million in sales. Other examples are Samuel Barber's "Adagio for Strings" and Pachelbel's "Canon in D."

Some records incorporate all three aspects of crossover. *Vision,* featuring the music of Hildegard von Bingen, is set to synthesized, ambient pop music by the American Richard Souther and marketed to an adult contemporary and new age audience. Similarly, the hugely successful *Officium* and *Mysterium*, settings of medieval sacred music performed by the Hilliard Ensemble (well known for its performances of early music and contemporary composer Arvo Pärt), are layered with free jazz improvisations by Norwegian saxophonist Jan Gabarek. These crossovers thus achieve crossover reception by reaching a new, broader audience; crossover marketing by targeting the adult contemporary audience; and stylistic crossover because two stylistically and socially distinct genres are combined.

An artist's or song's crossover success is often determined by other components of the media industry. The film industry's use of music, and in particular, the sales of sound tracks, has resulted in crossover success for various artists and songs. Bill Haley and the Comets' "Rock Around the Clock" received belated success through its use in the 1955 film *Blackboard Jungle.* Baroque and Renaissance music performed by Jordi Savall was catapulted to fame by the film *Tous les Matins du Monde,* which featured Savall on viol. Likewise, Samuel Barber's "Adagio for Strings," which featured in the film *Platoon,* drew a wider audience to the music and was subsequently used in David Lynch's *The Elephant Man,* as well as in Michael Moore's documentary *Sicko,* spurring on electronic dance remixes, notably by William Orbit and Ferry Corsten. Witness also the success of bluegrass music after its inclusion in the Coen brothers film *O Brother, Where Art Thou?* and a revival of sacred harp and shape note music as a result of the film *Cold Mountain.*

Similarly, the crossover success of particular artists or songs can be spurred on by the advertising industry. The Flower Duet, "Sous le dome épais" from Léo Delibes' *Lakmé*, used by British Airways (among others), and "O Fortuna," from Carl Orff's *Carmina Burana*, used by Molson beer, Carlton, and Old Spice fragrances, saw spikes in sales after being used in commercials.

Earliest Crossovers

The earliest market crossovers occurred in the 1950s and typically involved movement from the R&B charts to the pop charts. Crossover played a central role in the birth of rock 'n' roll, because many rock songs had their first success on the R&B charts and typically moved onto the pop charts when they were covered by white performers. Written and first performed by Big Joe Turner, the rock 'n' roll hit "Shake, Rattle and Roll" only had mainstream success when it was covered by Bill Haley and the Comets. Shortly thereafter Haley, originally a country artist, adopted black R&B musical forms in the hugely successful "Rock Around the Clock," the first rock 'n' roll hit to top the charts for eight straight weeks. However, African American acts who were successful on the R&B charts also crossed over to pop charts, for example, the Dominoes with "Sixty Minute Man." In 1955 Fats Domino's "Ain't That a Shame" moved from the R&B to pop charts, taking position

Tracking Sales

Nielsen SoundScan is the official means of recording sales purchases at cash registers across the United States, Canada, and the United Kingdom and provides the sales data for *Billboard* music charts. Prior to SoundScan's development in 1991, *Billboard* relied on sales data reported by store employees or owners. With the advent of the new system, purchases could be tracked at the point of sale, with the Universal Product Code (UPC) or barcode being automatically recorded and compiled as SoundScan data. These data are made available not only to *Billboard*, but also to other subscribers, including record companies, publishing companies, media and marketing agents, managers, and music retailers.

number ten, following Pat Boone's version, which sat at number one. Without making any change to his musical style, Domino continued to top the pop charts for the next eight years, with "Blueberry Hill," "Blue Monday," and "I'm Walkin'," among other hits, opening the mainstream chart door to other artists whose music was typically classified as R&B, like Little Richard and Chuck Berry. Artists and their songs could also be on two or more charts simultaneously, as was Elvis Presley's release of "Hound Dog/Don't Be Cruel," which reached number one on the pop charts, the R&B charts, and the country and Western charts in 1956.

Rock-Reggae

In some cases crossover artists seek out the cultural capital of certain marginalized or minor forms of music. Rock and punk bands from the 1970s, eager to show an allegiance to the political, ideological, and racial values of reggae, introduced reggae beats and riffs into their songs. The song "Rudie Can't Fall," by the punk band The Clash, is one of many examples on their *Sandinista* album. Blondie's "The Tide Is High," Eric Clapton's cover of Bob Marley's "I Shot the Sheriff," and even Paul Simon's "Mother and Child Reunion" are all early examples of rock-reggae crossover.

Rock-Rap

Particularly because of the different racial identities and generic boundaries of rock and rap, stylistic crossover of the two genres would appear to be impossible. But when the first big rap-rock crossover, Run-D.M.C./Aerosmith's "Walk This Way," was released, it quickly rose to number four on the *Billboard* Hot 100. Rather than simply recording over the song, Run-D.M.C. invited Aerosmith to re-record it with them. (Aerosmith's 1975 hit of the same name was the background track.) The collaboration revitalized Aerosmith's career and put rap on the mainstream charts for the first time. Part of the reason for the hit's success was the MTV video, which featured the two groups recording in separate studios before Tyler is shown crashing through the wall that separates them. This kind of rap and rock crossover soon became a genre of its own and is epitomized on the sound track for the 1993 film *Judgement Night,* in which every song is a collaboration between a rock and hip-hop artist, such as Teenage Fanclub and De La Soul. Another example of rock-rap crossover, the success of which was bolstered by the sound track for the 1998 remake of *Godzilla,* is "Come with Me," which features Puff Daddy rapping over the Led Zeppelin song "Kashmir." A music video that features a large orchestra playing a rising harmonic riff from "Kashmir" against Puff Daddy's rapping and Jimmy Page's playing was largely responsible for the song's success.

Country Crossover

In the country genre, the first musicians to have substantial crossover success were Dolly Parton and Kenny Rogers, who were on pop and country charts simultaneously. The success of country music, and the extent to which it was listened to by markets outside "country," was revealed when *Billboard* magazine began to use Soundscan to record purchases at the tills and to use these statistics as indicators of popularity. If Garth Brooks's "Ropin' the Wind" topped the pop and country charts in 1991, other country acts soon followed: Shania Twain with her album *Come on Over* and the Dixie Chicks with their songs "Wide Open Spaces," "Take Me Away," and their 2007 release *Taking the Long Way.*

LeAnn Rimes's hit song "How Do I Live" has been the biggest crossover hit to date, spending sixty-nine weeks on the Hot 100 chart and going triple platinum, while Taylor Swift's "You Belong with Me" and "Teardrops on My Guitar" are close competitors. With combined album sales, numerous awards, and chart success, Swift is the most successful country artist to cross over to pop music and songwriting in history.

Classical Crossover and "Popera"

Classical crossover refers both to musicians who are classically trained but who have pursued popular forms of music, and to classical music or opera marketed to a popular audience ("Popera"). The success of classical crossover is often attributed to The Three Tenors

Crossover Hits

LeAnn Rimes's hit song "How Do I Live" was a major crossover hit, spending sixty-nine weeks on the Hot 100 chart and going triple platinum, while Taylor Swift's "You Belong with Me" and "Teardrops on My Guitar" are close competitors. With combined album sales, numerous awards, and chart success, Swift is the most successful country artist to cross over to pop music and songwriting in history.

concerts and albums. Conceived by Italian producer Mario Dradi as a fund-raiser for Carreras's foundation, The Three Tenors (Plácido Domingo, José Carreras, and Luciano Pavarotti) sang on the eve of the 1990 Fédération Internationale de Football Association (FIFA) World Cup in Rome, as well as for subsequent FIFA celebrations in 1994, 1998, and 2002. Their concert recording from 1994 spent thirty-three weeks on Billboard's Top 200 Album Chart. Namely because of the success of The Three Tenors, Calaf's aria "Nessun Dorma" ("None Shall Sleep"), from the last act of Puccini's opera *Turandot*, sung at the 1990 World Cup, reached number two on the UK singles charts and has been linked to sports events, in particular soccer, ever since. A recent example of a singer expanding her repertoire to perform popular music, folk, or jazz is Renée Fleming, who has not only released a jazz album but has also covered popular songs by Leonard Cohen, Jefferson Airplane, Arcade Fire, and Death Cab for Cutie, and has sung on the *Lord of the Rings* film sound track. The classically trained mezzo-soprano Anne Sofie von Otter has collaborated with Elvis Costello and put out an album of pop and rock songs, as well as an album of Abba hits. Other singers who have performed "Popera" are Andrea Bocelli, Josh Groban, Sarah Brightman, and Charlotte Church.

Yet another well-known classical crossover artist is cellist Yo-Yo Ma, whose career began in the classical genre, but who recently has ventured into American bluegrass, Argentinian tangos, and traditional Chinese music (as on the sound track for the film *Crouching Tiger, Hidden Dragon*). He has also released an album of film music by the Italian Ennio Morricone and has performed with both Sting and Bobby McFerrin. These daring steps by Yo-Yo Ma have encouraged numerous contemporary string players, who no longer feel compelled to play one particular repertoire. Recent examples include Vanessa-Mae, many of whose albums have spent weeks on the UK album charts; Catya Maré; and Lucia Micarelli, among many others.

Kronos Quartet, one of the premiere crossover quartets, was first known for a devotion to contemporary music. Their crossover albums include *Pieces of Africa* (1992), a collection of contemporary concert composers from various countries in Africa, and *Early Music* (1997), which adds medieval and Renaissance music to their playlists, as if showing up the similarities between them and some of the newer pieces they do. They have also added arrangements of rock songs (e.g., Jimi Hendrix's "Purple Haze" and Sigur Ros's "Dream of Angels") to their repertoire.

Responses to classical crossover have often been negative. Classical music fans and critics often see the crossover as a sell-out and a watering down of the artistic form to pander to the masses, which indicates audiences and critics' feelings of ownership and elitism around the genre. (This happens outside classical music as well; Bob Dylan's famous tour on which he played electric guitar for the second half of his "folk" set is a case in point.) When the crossover is marketing and sales driven, audience and reviewers' responses are similarly negative, a sign that the belief that musicians are more authentic when they are not associated with capital lives on.

Because musical genres and markets are often bound by race, gender, and identity, responses to crossover often point to racial biases, gender stereotypes, issues surrounding authenticity, and feelings of entitlement. On the positive side, others point to the broader exposure crossover music enables and the freedom to combine various stylistic genres as the artist sees fit.

With changes in the music industry afoot, the downturn in record sales; decline of traditional radio formats; and combination of new digital access to music via downloading, iTunes, and iPods, it seems fair to suggest that with the continued fragmentation of charts, crossover artists and stylistic crossover will continue to flourish, though whether the word *crossover* continues to be used remains to be seen.

See also: Aerosmith; Art Music; Berry, Chuck; Brooks, Garth; Country Music; Dixie Chicks; Dylan, Bob; Domino, Fats; Film Music; Folk Music; Fusion; Jazz; Jefferson Airplane; Hendrix, Jimi; Little Richard; Ma, Yo-Yo; Music Magazines and Journalism; Music Television; Parton, Dolly; Pop Music; Presley, Elvis; Personal Music Devices; Punk Rock; R&B; Rock 'n' Roll (Rock); Rogers, Kenny; Simon, Paul

Further Reading

Brackett, David. 2009. *The Pop, Rock, and Soul Reader: Histories and Debates.* New York: Oxford University Press.

Garofalo, Reebee. 2011. *Rockin' Out: Popular Music in the USA.* New York: Prentice Hall.

Lipsitz, George. 2007. *Footsteps in the Dark: The Hidden Histories of Popular Music.* Minneapolis: University of Minnesota Press.

Shuker, Roy. 2002. *Popular Music: The Key Concepts.* London: Routledge.

Taylor, Timothy. 1997. *Global Pop, World Music, World Markets.* London: Routledge.

Kirsten Yri

Crow, Sheryl (1962–)

Sheryl Crow is an American singer/songwriter who for nearly two decades has won audiences and awards with roots rock music and lyrics that range from the personal to the political. Although she has enjoyed international success, she is a peculiarly American singer whose music is a paradoxical blend of restlessness and hunger for home, qualities central to the American character.

Born in Kennett, Missouri, on February 12, 1962, Crow grew up in a musical home. By the time she was ten, she was playing contemporary pop music by ear. In high school, her models were Eric Clapton (1945–), Bob Dylan (1941–), and Mick Jagger (1943–). She played in a cover band while she attended the University of Missouri. Graduating with a degree in classical music, she taught music at an elementary school and continued to play in a band. When she earned more than twice her teacher's salary for a McDonald's commercial, she began thinking of a move to Los Angeles. Her fiancé, a devout Christian, pressured her to choose between rock music and marriage, and she chose the music and headed for the West Coast.

She had been in Los Angeles less than a year when she was hired as a backup singer for Michael Jackson (1958–2009). Later, as a session vocalist, she performed with Sting (1951–), Rod Stewart (1945–), and Don Henley (1947–), among others, and had her songs recorded by headliners, including Eric Clapton. A demo led to a contract with A & M and eventually to her debut album, *Tuesday Night Music Club* (1993), which in turn led to a string of singles with a theme of restlessness, including "Leaving Las Vegas" and "All I Wanna Do." Crow's long apprenticeship had ended, and her dream of being one of the stars in the pages of *Rolling Stone* was becoming a reality.

Sheryl Crow at the 44th Annual Country Music Association Awards in Nashville, November 8, 2010. (S. Bukley/Dreamstime.com)

Some of the luster of the album's platinum sales was lost when its success led to a public break from friends who claimed Crow owed more credit to them than she was admitting. Her self-titled second album, released in 1996, put to rest any suspicions that Crow was dependent upon collaborators. The album outsold her debut album and produced three hits: "If It Makes You Happy," "Everyday Is a Winding Road," and "A Change Would Do You Good." Her next two albums also went platinum, and on the strength of three albums, Crow was considered a major artist in mainstream rock.

Her fourth album, *Wildflower* (2005), was certified platinum, but it received mixed reviews. Some critics heard greater maturity and intimacy and others declared the wild missing from Crow's musical flowers. The next two years brought changes and challenges to Crow's life and to her music. In 2006, she and her fiancé, cyclist Lance Armstrong (1971–), announced their split, and Crow was diagnosed with breast cancer; in 2007, she moved to a Tennessee farm and adopted a baby boy. *Detours* (2008), her most overtly political album, combined her environmentalist concerns, government failure after Katrina, and a call for tolerance with deeply personal songs including a letter to her mother and a lullaby for her son. *100 Miles from Memphis* (2010) brought Crow home metaphorically to her Missouri hometown, which is about two hours from Memphis, literally to her farm where the music was conceived, and musically as a nod to the soul music sound track of her youth.

See also: Dylan, Bob; Environmental Activism in Music; Jackson, Michael; Music Teachers; Rock 'n' Roll (Rock); Rock 'n' Roll (Rock), Women In

Official Web Site: http://www.sherylcrow.com

Further Reading

O'Dair, Barbara. 1997. *Trouble Girls: The Rolling Stone Book of Women in Rock.* New York: Random House.

Pareles, Jon. 1995. "She's Talkin' 'Bout Our Generations." *The New York Times,* March 12. http://www.nytimes.com/1995/03/12/arts/pop-view-she-s-talkin-bout-our-generations.html

Sheryl Crow. 2010. Accessed July 10, 2011. http://www.sherylcrow.com/.

Wylene Rholetter

Cult Films and Music

The label "cult film" has been applied to a wide-ranging and eclectic group of films that can be drawn from almost any genre, any time period and any national cinema. It is no wonder then that music in cult film is equally diverse. It can be diegetic and self-reflexive as in the madcap musical, employed extra-diegetically to set the mood and tone in examples of fantasy and science fiction, or in keeping with a so-bad-its-good aesthetic simply borrowed ad hoc from a music library. The concept of cult film came to wide recognition with the phenomenon of midnight movie screenings in the 1970s, and the key films showed at these screenings are indicative of the ways in which music is an integral part of the cult film experience.

Perhaps the most recognized cult film of all time, *The Rocky Horror Picture Show* (1975) is also the archetypal cult musical. Transferred to screen from Richard O'Brian's stage musical, the songs, which structure and relay the plot, are quirky, amusing and catchy. The lyrics of the opening number *Science Fiction, Double Feature* immediately signal that the film is self-reflexive and based on the notion of the cult film itself, particularly science fiction/horror B-movies and all the formulaic genre tropes and clichés that entails. Throughout the film the musical numbers foreground the kitsch aesthetics, camp performances and subversive glam rock styling. These numbers invite the audience to sing-a-long, dance-a-long, and act-a-long with the on-screen performers, sometimes literally. The audience response is participatory, an essential element of what J. P. Telotte (1991, 7) describes as the supertext of the cult film. In the most iconic number of the film, *The Time Warp,* the Criminologist, acting as both narrator and dance instructor, provides an illustrated example of the dance steps required, overtly encouraging participation. To be part of a cult film audience is, as Telotte argues, an experience, one which here involves dressing up as the characters, employing props, yelling lines of audience dialogue back at the screen, and most importantly singing and dancing along with the on-screen action. The sing-a-long phenomenon is now more widespread with organized events around screenings of *The Sound of Music* (1965), *Grease* (1978) and *Hairspray* (2007), for example. Although paradoxically this means that the experience itself is much less cultish (audiences are far more mainstream), the enjoyment of the musical numbers does encourage the participation and repeat viewing that are signifiers of cult status.

Scene from the 1975 movie *The Rocky Horror Picture Show.* Pictured are Tim Curry as transvestite Frank N. Furter (center); Little Nell as Columbia (left); Patricia Quinn, as Magenta; and Richard O'Brien as Riff Raff (right). (AP Photo)

Music is similarly an essential part of the cult film experience in genres other than the musical. The extra-diegetic music can add to the cult appeal of many different types of cult films. Examples include both artistic and creative uses of what is often unexpected or heavily foregrounded music, as well as music that contributes to a trash aesthetic by being inappropriate or "tacked on." The cult film can certainly exploit music to create mood and emotion with the best of mainstream cinema, but it may do it in ways that subvert expectation and run against the grain of accepted convention. In David Lynch's *Eraserhead* (1977)—another of the cult midnight movies of the 1970s—electronic sounds and music add to the dystopic, industrial gothic landscape that the alienated protagonist, Henry, inhabits. Paul Stump (1997, 80) calls Lynch and sound effects supervisor Alan Splett's work on *Eraserhead* an "extraordinary sonic collaboration," going on to point out that *Eraserhead,* alongside Ridley Scott and Vangelis's aural textures in *Blade Runner* (1982), demonstrates "how music can be more than just audio-emotional condiment to spice up whatever was on the screen at any given moment." Atonal music and sound effects are used to add textural qualities to the grim setting of the film. Even the diegetic sounds have a musical quality: electric lamps spark and crack, elevators hum and clunk, a wet sock sizzles as it dries on the radiator, chickens squelch alarmingly as they ooze blood. Small sounds, the rustle of a paper bag and the turning of a key in a lock or the creaking of the wooden doors on a cuckoo clock that drowns out the cuckoo, are exaggerated, too loud, and they dominate the scene creating a surreal aural experience seems as much to be diegetic music as it is background sound. The landscape of industrial noise combines with the musical score to create an ambient electronic sound track that is counterpointed by the Wurlitzer music. This creates a sensation of dissonance and strangeness that again becomes part of the cult film experience. When Henry encounters (or perhaps imagines) the hamster-cheeked woman in the radiator, the falsetto singing is accompanied by a noise like wind (or perhaps machinery) as much as by the organ music, and the sound of the wind grows to completely dominate the sound track. This song, *In Heaven,* is one of the most recognized musical pieces in *Eraserhead* and it has gained cult status of its own, having been widely covered by alternative bands such as Pixies, The Danse Society, Bauhaus, Miranda Sex Garden and Devo.

Like Lynch, several key cult filmmakers write their own musical score. This may be due to the fact that many cult films are low-budget, independent productions, but nevertheless this adds to both the cult appeal of the films and the filmmaker's status as cult auteur. With *El Topo* (1970)—widely cited as the first film on the midnight movie circuit, Alejandro Jodorowsky wrote the music as well as scripting, directing, designing and appearing in the film. As David Church (2007) writes, Jodorowsky's films "present strange and magical visions that are not easily categorized or understood, [they are] filled with violently surreal images and a hybrid blend of mysticism and religious provocation." The music evokes the western genre, juxtaposing bittersweet, rhythmical and even martial qualities that suggest both the spiritual journey and the violent action set in the epic desert landscape, yet paradoxically can be discordant and almost jarring as in the theme for *The Pig's Monastery* or carnivalesque and upbeat as in that for *The Holy Beggars.* Again, the music for *El Topo* has achieved cult recognition in its own right, the sound track having been commercially unavailable for many years.

At the other extreme, far from being integral to the filmmaking process, the music for Ed Wood's *Plan 9 From Outer Space* (1958)—which achieved cult status as the worst movie ever made—appears (like much of the film itself) to have been thrown together from whatever was on hand at the time. The incidental music has been subject to considerable rumor and speculation in its own right. Paul Mandell (1996) points out that this was because a cue sheet was never filed with the American Society of Composers, Authors and Publishers or Broadcast Music, Inc. (which deals with licensing rights). The sleeve notes on a bootleg LP of the sound track (falsely accredited to Ed Wood himself) attribute the "wonderful score" to music supervisor Gordon Zahler, whilst Rudolph Grey's Ed Wood biography *Nightmare of Ecstasy* claims the main theme was from the Russian composer Alexander Mosolov's "Iron Foundry." Mandell, pointing out that both these claims are false, identifies the music as having been put together by Gordon Zahler from the Impress Mood Music Library and the Video Moods Music Library. Zahler was "a bottom-rung music packager" who took music (illegally) from acetates of old movies and turned it into a rental library, and who "like Ed Wood, [...] was never known to have played with a full deck." Although Mandell argues that "credit should be given to [Zahler] for keenly deciding which cues would best enhance Wood's tacky continuity," the music for *Plan 9* is patchy, sometimes loops repetitively and is not always in keeping with the visuals. Nevertheless, this simply adds to Wood's seemingly incompetent direction and perfectly complements the bizarre continuity editing, tacky sets, clumsy dialogue and inept acting of the film.

In other examples of cult film music, the use of unconventional or unusual instruments subverts expectations and creates distinctive sounds. The science fiction/horror films of the 1950s, for example, frequently employ the theremin (an electronic instrument with no keys or strings which is "played" via movements of the hands in the vicinity of metal antennae) and the novachord (an early example of the polyphonic synthesizer). These can be heard on *The Day The Earth Stood Still* (1951) and *The Thing (From Another World)* (1951), for example. Peter Hutchings (2008, 143) points out that the theremin is used to suggest mental imbalance, as well as creating sensations of alienness and eeriness. For Tim Burton's biopic *Ed Wood* (1994), film score composer Howard Shore used both the theremin and the ondes martenot—an instrument that achieves a similar sound to the theremin by making oscillations in vacuum tubes, despite Wood never having the instrument in *Plan 9* or any other of his films. On the *Ed Wood* DVD extras Shore attributes his choice of the theremin to the fact he thought it "was something Ed would have used if he'd had the budget to have found somebody to play it."

As with the theremin, underground and obscure music of all kinds has an obvious affinity with cult film. It is only to be expected then that cult auteurs undertake artistic collaborations with alternative genre musicians, as cult Italian horror and giallo filmmaker Dario Argento has with prog rock band Goblin. Writing on *Suspiria* (1977), Linda Schulte-Sasse (2002) states that: "[T]he sound track, which precedes the first image, effects a sensuous immersion, a sense of compulsion as opposed to control, drive as opposed to desire." Goblin's score works as sound effect as much as incidental music. It imbues each scene with a sense of terror and paranoia, employing whispers, susurrations, screeches, screams, thunderous crashes, scratching noises and low hums, and also often sharply contrasting with moments of silence. The music seems to come from nowhere, but also matches the action, suggesting that there is some nameless horror hiding beneath the surface. Schulte-Sasse adds that: "Sound is in perfect synch with visuals, but renders unstable the boundary between conventional, non-diegetic 'mood' music and diegetic sound within the film proper." Argento also worked with other prog rock musicians, with Keith Emerson on *Inferno* (1980) and Brian Eno on *Opera* (1987). This forged something of a link between the cult horror film and the rock music genre that has been continued in films such as *House of a 1000 Corpses* (2003) which Rob Zombie (of metal band White Zombie) wrote and directed as well as creating the music for.

Of course, alongside rock musicals like *The Rocky Horror Picture Show,* bands and musicians with cult followings have themselves made films that have achieved cult status. *Forbidden Zone* (1982)—which audaciously describes itself as "the ultimate cult movie experience"—is a vehicle for The Mystic Knights of the Oingo Boingo, an avant-garde musical theatre troupe. Directed by Oingo Boingo founder Richard Elfman, the film was based around the band's stage performances and, adding to its cult appeal, it is the first film score written by Elfman's younger brother, Danny. *Forbidden Zone* possesses many of the traits of the cult film: it is shot in black and white; is set in a bizarre alternate universe; consists of a mix of live action, crudely painted sets and naïve-style animation; features bizarre make-up and costumes, including drag, partial nudity and—rather shockingly—blackface; and it features many cult stars amongst its cast. The latter include Hervé Villechaize from the television series *Fantasy Island,* Susan Tyrrell who also appeared in other cult films such as John Water's *Cry Baby* (1990), and Viva, one of Andy Warhol's superstars, who had appeared in several of the artist's films from the 1960s. The music itself is an eclectic mix of jazz, rumba, and Danny Elfman's own distinctive style. The musical numbers include the famous Cab Calloway song *Minnie the Moocher,* reworked as *Squeezit the Moocher* and performed by Danny Elfman in the role of Satan, and Marie-Pascale Elfman overtly lip-syncing to Josephine Baker's "La Petit Tonkinoise." *Forbidden Zone* was re-released in 2008 in a digitally colorized version, ultimately resulting in a screening in 2010 at the Museum of Modern Art in New York—taking the raw, subversive, trash aesthetic of cult film into the heartland of high art.

Aside from the midnight movie and underground forms of cult cinema, mainstream and independent films provide interesting examples. Music is often an integral part of the spectacle in science fiction and action-adventure films, teen movies, blaxploitation cinema and gross-out comedies draw on pop and rock genres to create a subcultural milieu, and music is used in classic cinema to evoke particular moods. Some musical themes have become instantly recognizable, entering the lexicon of the cult film and being as quotable as lines of dialogue. Even a few bars or a musical cue are often sufficient. Examples such as the shark theme in *Jaws* (1975), the Imperial March from *Star Wars* (1977), Bernard Herrmann's music for the shower scene in *Psycho* (1960) and John Carpenter's sound track for *Halloween* (1978) have achieved cult status in their own right. All of these examples are, as Jack Sullivan (2006, 243) says of Herrmann's *Psycho* theme, "inseparably linked with the film." They are also all extremely affective, working to create heightened states of fear and anticipation through dissonance and insistent beats. In a somewhat different way, Anton Kara's zither music for *The Third Man* (1949) creates an ambiguous mood, it's pacing—which Rob White describes as jaunty—belies the "darker things underneath its good cheer" (2003, 8). Mood is less significant in the teen comedy and other films than reflecting the cultural moment of youth and urban subcultures. The sound tracks for *Fast Times At Ridgemont High* (1982) and *Ferris Bueller's Day Off* (1986), for example, are dominated by chart hits from Led Zeppelin to Tom Petty and The Beatles to Sigue Sigue Sputnik, respectively, whilst the less comic but assuredly cult *Donnie Darko* (2001) made a cult hit of "Mad World" for Gary Jules. These examples—as well as the way John Landis uses rock 'n' roll to provide a narrative commentary in *Animal House* (1978) or Quentin Tarantino's contrapuntal use of Stealers Wheel in *Reservoir Dogs* (1992)—employ popular music from the 1950s onwards as a thematic device to contexualise the depictions of youth and other subcultures on screen. This is at its most overt in Blaxploitation films such as *Shaft,* where Isaac Hayes's funk track encapsulates the hip, urban masculinity of "the private dick who's a sex machine to all the chicks".

So films can become cults purely by dint of their music. The music in cult films can achieve cult status of its own; it can add to the immersive or participatory experience of watching a cult film; it can be distracting or subversive or disputed. Music in cult films can certainly be described as diverse. But one thing it never is, is predictable.

See also: Electronic Applications and Music; Elfman, Danny; Funk and Postpsychedelic Funk

Further Reading

Church, David. 2007. "Great Directors: Alejandro Todorowsky." *Senses of Cinema* 42, accessed January 19, 2011, http://www.sensesofcinema.com/2007/great-directors/jodorowsky/.

Hutchings, Peter. 2004. *The Horror Film.* Harlow: Pearson Longman.

Mandell, Paul. 1996. "Forty-Year Mystery Solved: The Music Behind *Plan 9 From Outer Space.*" *Film Score Monthly,* accessed February 12, 2011, http://sammel-surium.heimat.eu/soundtracks/P9FSM.html.

Schulte-Sasse, Linda. 2002. "The 'mother' of all horror movies: Dario Argento's *Suspiria* (1977)." *Kinoeye* 2:11, accessed December 16, 2010, http://www.kinoeye.org/02/11/schultesasse11.php.

Stump, Paul. 1997. *Digital Gothic: A Critical Discography of Tangerine Dream.* Wembley: SAF Publishing.

Sullivan, Jack. 2006. *Hitchcock's Music.* New Haven: Yale University Press.

Telotte, J. P. 1991. *The Cult Film Experience: Beyond All Reason.* Austin: University of Texas Press.

White, Rob. 2003. *The Third Man.* London: BFI Publishing.

Brigid Cherry

Index